Linux+ 2005 In Depth

Jason W. Eckert

M. John Schitka

THOMSON

COURSE TECHNOLOGY

Professional ■ Trade ■ Reference

Important: Thomson Course Technology PTR cannot provide software support. Please contact the appropriate software manufacturer's technical support line or Web site for assistance.

Thomson Course Technology PTR and the author have attempted throughout this book to distinguish proprietary trademarks from descriptive terms by following the capitalization style used by the manufacturer.

Information contained in this book has been obtained by Thomson Course Technology PTR from sources believed to be reliable. However, because of the possibility of human or mechanical error by our sources, Thomson Course Technology PTR, or others, the Publisher does not guarantee the accuracy, adequacy, or completeness of any information and is not responsible for any errors or omissions or the results obtained from use of such information. Readers should be particularly aware of the fact that the Internet is an ever-changing entity. Some facts may have changed since this book went to press.

Educational facilities, companies, and organizations interested in multiple copies or licensing of this book should contact the publisher for quantity discount information. Training manuals, CD-ROMs, and portions of this book are also available individually or can be tailored for specific needs.

ISBN-10: 1-59200-728-7
ISBN-13: 978-1-59200-728-8

Library of Congress Catalog Card Number: 2004116287

Printed in the United States of America

06 07 08 09 TW 10 9 8 7 6 5 4 3 2

Publisher and GM of Course Technology PTR:
Stacy L. Hiquet

Managing Editor:
William Pitkin III

Product Manager:
Manya Chylinski

Developmental Editor:
Dave George

Production Editors:
Elena Montillo,
Megan Belanger,
Elizabeth Furbish

Senior Manufacturing Coordinator:
Laura Burns

Technical Editor:
Burt LaFountain

Senior Marketing Manager:
Sarah O'Donnell

Marketing Managers:
Heather Hurley and
Kristin Eisenzopf

Marketing Coordinator:
Jordan Casey

Manager of Editorial Services:
Heather Talbot

Cover Design:
Mike Tanamachi

Compositor:
William Hartman

Indexer:
Sharon Shock

THOMSON

COURSE TECHNOLOGY ™

Professional ■ Trade ■ Reference

Thomson Course Technology PTR, a division of Thomson Course Technology
25 Thomson Place ■ Boston, MA 02210 ■ http://www.courseptr.com

Acknowledgments

First, we wish to thank the staff at Course Technology for an overall enjoyable experience writing a book on Linux that takes a fundamentally different approach than traditional books. More specifically, we wish to thank our Project Manager, Manya Chylinski, for her coordination and insight, as well as our Developmental Editor, Dave George, and Production Editor, Elena Montillo, for the long hours they spent pulling everything together to transform the text into its current state. As well, we wish to thank Moirag Haddad at Digital Content Factory for her advice and guidance, and Frank Gerencser, of t riOS College for freeing us up to write this book and his continuous encouragement for writing books to augment teaching.

Jason W. Eckert: I must take this time to thank my co-author, M. John Schitka for the hard work, long hours, and dedication he spent on this book. As well, I thank Starbucks Coffee for keeping me on schedule, and most importantly, my daughter Mackenzie for providing me with many of the examples used in this book as well as teaching me that having fun playing basketball is more important than writing a book.

M. John Schitka: First I want to thank my mentor and co-author Jason W. Eckert for his insight, patience, and wisdom during the long hours and late nights that went into the creation of this book. More importantly I must thank my family, my wife Jill, and children Kyra, Luke, and Noah for their support, tolerance, and patience during the time it took to write this book. Hopefully readers will find it enlightening and of benefit in their educational journey.

Finally, we wish to acknowledge the encouragement of our colleagues Mitch Mijailovic and Tonio Mladineo; if it were not for them, I doubt we would love the Linux operating system as much as we do today.

Readers are encouraged to e-mail comments, questions, and suggestions regarding *Linux+ 2005 In Depth* to the authors:

Jason W. Eckert: jasonec@trios.com

Contents at a Glance

Contents

Introduction

"...In a future that includes competition from open source, we can expect that the eventual destiny of any software technology will be to either die or become part of the open infrastructure itself." Eric S. Raymond, The Cathedral and the Bazaar

As Eric S. Raymond reminds us, Open Source Software will continue to shape the dynamics of the computer software industry for the next long while, just as it has done for the last decade. Created and perpetuated by hackers, Open Source Software refers to software in which the source code is freely available to anyone who wishes to improve it (usually through collaboration). And, of course, at the heart of Open Source Software lies Linux—an operating system whose rapid growth has shocked the world by demonstrating the nature and power of the Open Source model.

However, as Linux continues to grow, so must the number of Linux-educated users, administrators, developers, and advocates. Thus, we find ourselves in a time when Linux education is of great importance to the Information Technology industry. Key to demonstrating ability with Linux is the certification process. *Linux+ 2005 In Depth* uses carefully constructed examples, questions, and practical exercises to prepare readers with the necessary information to obtain the sought-after Linux+ certification from the Computing Technology Industry Association, or CompTIA. The Linux+ certification may also be used to fulfill the UNIX module of the cSAGE certification, which is geared toward junior-level system engineers. Once candidates pass the Linux+ exam, they are required only to pass the cSAGE core exam to earn the cSAGE Certification designation. Whatever your ultimate goal, you can be assured that reading this book in combination with study, creativity, and practice, will make the Open Source world come alive for you as it has for many others.

The Intended Audience

Simply put, this book is intended for those who wish to learn the Linux operating system and pass the Linux+ certification exam from CompTIA. It does not assume any prior knowledge of Linux or of computer hardware. Also, the topics introduced in this book, and covered in the certification exam, are geared towards systems administration, yet are also well suited for those who will use or develop programs for Linux systems.

Chapter 1, "Introduction to Linux" introduces operating systems as well as the features, benefits, and uses of the Linux operating system. As well, this chapter discusses the history and development of Linux and Open Source Software.

Chapter 2, "Preparing for Linux Installation" introduces the various hardware components inside a computer, as well as methods that can be used to collect hardware and software information prior to installing the Linux operating system.

Chapter 3, "Linux Installation and Usage" walks through a typical Linux installation given the hardware and software information collected in the previous chapter. As well, this chapter describes how to interact with a Linux system via a terminal and enter basic commands into a Linux shell such as those used to obtain help and properly shutdown the system.

Chapter 4, "Exploring Linux Filesystems" outlines the Linux filesystem structure, and the types of files that can be found within it. As well, this chapter discusses commands that can be used to view and edit the content of those files.

Chapter 5, "Linux Filesystem Management" covers those commands which can be used to locate and manage files and directories on a Linux filesystem. Furthermore, this chapter outlines the different methods used to link files as well as how to interpret and set file and directory permissions.

Chapter 6, "Linux Filesystem Administration" discusses how to create, mount, and manage filesystems in Linux. This chapter also discusses the various filesystems available for Linux systems and the device files that are used to refer to the devices which may contain these filesystems.

Chapter 7, "Advanced Installation" introduces advanced hardware concepts and configurations that may prove useful when installing Linux. As well, this chapter discusses different methods that may be used to install Linux as well as common problems that may occur during installation, and their resolutions.

Chapter 8, "Working with the BASH Shell" covers the major features of the BASH shell including redirection, piping, variables, aliases, and environment files. Also, this chapter details the syntax of basic shell scripts.

Chapter 9, "System Initialization and X Windows" covers the different bootloaders that may be used to start the Linux kernel and dual-boot the Linux operating system with other operating systems such as Windows. This chapter also discusses how daemons are started during system initialization as well as how to start and stop them afterwards. Finally, this chapter discusses the structure of Linux Graphical User Interfaces as well as their configuration and management.

Chapter 10, "Managing Linux Processes" covers the different types of processes, as well as how to view their attributes, change their priority, and kill them. Furthermore, this chapter discusses how to schedule processes to occur in the future using various utilities.

Chapter 11, "Common Administrative Tasks" details three important areas of system administration: printer administration, log file administration, and user administration.

Chapter 12, "Compression, System Backup, and Software Installation" describes utilities that are commonly used to compress or back up files on a Linux filesystem. As well, this chapter discusses how to install software from source code as well as using the Red Hat Package Manager (RPM).

Chapter 13, "Troubleshooting and Performance" discusses the system maintenance cycle as well as good troubleshooting procedures for solving hardware and software problems. Also, this chapter outlines utilities that can be used to monitor and pinpoint the cause of performance problems, as well as how to patch and recompile the kernel to fix software, hardware, and performance problems.

Chapter 14, "Network Configuration" introduces networks, network utilities, and the TCP/IP protocol, as well as how to configure the TCP/IP protocol on a NIC or PPP interface. In addition, this chapter details the configuration of name resolution.

Chapter 15, "Configuring Network Services and Security" introduces commonly configured Linux network services and their configuration, as well as firewall and routing services. In addition, this chapter details the concepts and tools that may be used to secure a Linux computer locally and from across a network.

Additional information is also contained in the appendices at the rear of the book. **Appendix A** discusses the certification process with emphasis on the Linux+ certification and how the objective list for the Linux+ certification matches each chapter in the textbook. **Appendix B** is a copy of the GNU Public License. **Appendix C** explains how to find Linux resources on the Internet and lists some common resources by category. **Appendix D** contains the answers to the Review Questions at the end of each chapter.

Features

To ensure a successful learning experience, this book includes the following pedagogical features:

◆ **Chapter Objectives**: Each chapter in this book begins with a detailed list of the concepts to be mastered within that chapter. This list provides you with a quick reference to the contents of that chapter, as well as a useful study aid.

◆ **Screenshots, Illustrations, and Tables**: Wherever applicable, screenshots and illustrations are used to aid you in the visualization of common installation, administration and management steps, theories, and concepts. In addition, many tables provide command options that may be used in combination with the specific command being discussed.

◆ **End-of-Chapter Material**: The end of each chapter includes the following features to reinforce the material covered in the chapter:

  ◆ Chapter Summary: Gives a brief but complete summary of the chapter

  ◆ Key Terms List: Lists all new terms and their definitions

  ◆ Review Questions: Test your knowledge of the most important concepts covered in the chapter

Text and Graphic Conventions

Wherever appropriate, additional information and exercises have been added to this book to help you better understand what is being discussed in the chapter. Icons throughout the text alert you to additional materials. The icons used in this textbook are as follows:

TIP

Tips are included from the authors' experiences that provide additional real-world insights into the topic being discussed.

NOTE

Notes are used to present additional helpful material related to the subject being described.

Chapter 1

Introduction to Linux

After completing this chapter, you will be able to:

◆ Understand the purpose of an operating system

◆ Outline the key features of the Linux operating system

◆ Describe the origins of the Linux operating system

◆ Identify the characteristics of various Linux distributions and where to find them

◆ Explain the common uses of Linux in industry today

inux technical expertise has quickly become significant in the computer workplace as more and more companies have switched to using Linux to meet their computing needs. Thus, it is important today to understand how Linux can be used, what benefits Linux offers to a company, and how Linux has developed and continues to develop. In the first half of this chapter, you learn about operating system terminology and features of the Linux operating system, as well as the history and development of Linux. Later in this chapter, you learn about the various types of Linux and situations in which Linux is used.

Operating Systems

Every computer has two fundamental types of components: hardware and software. **Hardware** consists of the physical components inside a computer and are electrical in nature; they contain a series of circuits that are used to manipulate the flow of information. A computer can have many different pieces of hardware in it, including the following:

◆ A processor, which computes information (also known as the central processing unit or CPU)

◆ Physical memory, which stores information needed by the processor (also known as random access memory or RAM)

◆ Hard disk drives, which store most of the information that you use

◆ Floppy disk drives, which store information on floppy disks

◆ CD-ROM drives, which read information from CD-ROMs

◆ Sound cards, which provide sound to external speakers

◆ Video cards, which display results to the computer monitor

◆ Circuit boards, which hold and provide electrical connections between various hardware components (also known as mainboards or motherboards)

Software, on the other hand, refers to the sets of instructions or **programs** that understand how to use the hardware of the computer in a meaningful way; they allow different hardware to interact with, as well as manipulate data (or files) commonly used with programs. When a bank teller types information into the computer behind the counter at a bank, for example, that bank teller is using a program that understands what to do with your bank records. Programs and data are usually stored on hardware media, such as CD-ROMs, hard disks, or floppy disks, although they can also be stored on other media or even embedded in computer chips. These programs are loaded into various parts of your computer hardware (such as your computer's memory and processor) when you first turn your computer on, and when you start additional software, such as word processors or **Internet** browsers. After a program is executed on your computer's hardware, that program is referred to as a **process**. Thus, the difference between a program and a process is small. A program is a file stored on your computer, whereas a process is that file in action, performing a certain task.

Two different types of programs are executed on a computer: **applications**, which include those programs designed for a specific use and with which you commonly interact, such as word processors, computer games, graphical manipulation programs, and computer system utilities, and **operating system (OS)** software, which consists of a series of software components used to control the hardware of your computer. Without an operating system, you would not be able to use your computer. Turning on a computer loads the operating system into computer hardware, which loads and centrally controls all other application software in the background. Applications then take the information that users send them and relay that information to the operating system. The operating system then uses the computer hardware to carry out the requests. The relationship between users, application software, operating system software, and computer hardware is illustrated in Figure 1-1.

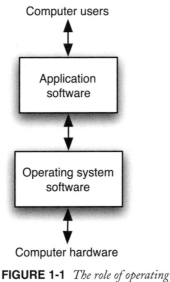

FIGURE 1-1 *The role of operating system software*

The operating system carries out many different tasks by interacting with many different types of computer hardware. For the operating system to accomplish this, it must contain the appropriate **device driver** software for every hardware device in your computer. Each device driver tells the operating system how to use that specific device. The operating system also provides a **user interface**, which is an application program that accepts user input indicating what is to be done, forwards this input to the operating system for completion, and, after it is completed, gives the results back to the user. The user interface can be a command-line prompt where the user must type a command to tell the operating system what to do, or it can be a **graphical user interface (GUI)**, which consists of a series of visual depictions of tasks known as icons, that the user can use to control the operating system, as shown in Figure 1-2.

FIGURE 1-2 *A Linux graphical user interface*

Finally, operating systems offer **system services**, which are applications that handle system-related tasks, such as printing, scheduling programs, and network access. These system services determine most of the functionality that is seen in an operating system. Different operating systems offer different system services, and many operating systems allow users to customize the services they offer.

The Linux Operating System

Linux (pronounced "Lih-nucks") is an operating system that is used today to run a variety of applications on a variety of different hardware. Similar to other operating systems, the Linux operating system loads into computer memory when you first power on your computer and initializes all of the hardware components. Next, it loads the programs required to give you an interface from which you can enter commands that tell the operating system and other applications to load to perform specific tasks. In the usual way, the operating system then uses the computer hardware to perform the tasks required by the applications.

Linux has the ability to manage thousands of tasks at the same time, including allowing multiple users to access the system simultaneously. Hence, Linux is referred to as a **multiuser** and **multitasking** operating system.

Versions of the Linux Operating System

The core component of the Linux operating system is called the Linux **kernel**. The Linux kernel and supporting function libraries are written almost entirely in the C programming language, which is one of the most common languages that software developers use when creating programs.

Although a variety of different software can be used to modify the appearance of Linux, the underlying kernel is common to all Linux. The Linux kernel is developed continuously, and, thus, it is important to understand the different version numbers of the Linux kernel to decide which kernel version is appropriate for certain needs. Because the Linux kernel is directly responsible for controlling the hardware (via device drivers) in your computer, upgrading the Linux kernel might be necessary to take advantage of new technologies such as IEEE 1394 (FireWire), or to fix problems (also known as bugs) the present kernel has with existing hardware. Consequently, a good understanding of what hardware features your system needs to use is important in deciding which kernel to use.

> **NOTE**
>
> A complete list of kernels, kernel versions, and a list of their improvements can be found on the Internet at *http://www.kernel.org*.

In some cases, a kernel module or a kernel patch can be used to provide or fix hardware supported by the kernel. Kernel modules and kernel patches are discussed later in this book.

Identifying Kernel Versions

Linux kernel versions are made up of the following three components:

- ◆ Major number
- ◆ Minor number
- ◆ Revision number

Let's look at a sample Linux kernel version, 2.5.9. In this example, the **major number** is the number 2, which indicates the major revision to the Linux kernel. The **minor number**, represented by the number 5, indicates the minor revision and stability of the Linux kernel. If the minor number is odd, it is referred to as a developmental kernel, whereas if the minor number is even, it is referred to as a production kernel. **Developmental kernels** are not fully tested and imply instability; they are tested for vulnerabilities by people who develop Linux software. **Production kernels** are developmental kernels that have been thoroughly tested by several Linux developers and are declared to be stable. In the previous example, the kernel has a major number of 2 and a minor number of 5. Because the minor number is odd, it indicates that this is a developmental kernel. This kernel will eventually be improved by Linux developers, tested, and declared stable. When this happens, the version of this kernel will change to 2.6 (indicating a production kernel).

Linux kernel changes occur frequently. Those changes that are very minor are represented by a revision number indicating the most current changes to the version of the particular kernel that is being released. For example, a 2.6.12 kernel has a major number of 2, a minor number of 6, and a revision number of 12. This kernel is the 12th release of the 2.6 kernel. Some kernels might have over 100 different revisions as a result of developers making constant improvements to the kernel code.

> **TIP**
>
> When choosing a kernel for a mission-critical computer such as an e-mail server, ensure that the minor number is even. This reduces the chance that you will encounter a bug in the kernel and, hence, saves you the time needed to change kernels.

Table 1-1 shows the latest revisions of each major and minor kernel released since the initial release of Linux.

Table 1-1 Latest revisions of common Linux kernels

Kernel Version	Date Released	Type
0.01	September 1991	First Linux kernel
0.12	January 1992	Production (stable)
0.95	March 1992	Developmental
0.98.6	December 1992	Production (stable)
0.99.15	March 1994	Developmental
1.0.8	April 1994	Production (stable)
1.1.95	March 1995	Developmental
1.2.12	July 1995	Production (stable)
1.3.100	May 1996	Developmental
2.0.36	November 1998	Production (stable)
2.1.132	December 1998	Developmental

Table 1-1 Latest revisions of common Linux kernels (Continued)

Kernel Version	Date Released	Type
2.2.26	February 2004 (latest release; was developed concurrently with newer kernels)	Production (stable)
2.3.99	May 2000	Developmental
2.4.17	December 2001	Production (stable)
2.5.75	July 2003	Developmental
2.6.7	June 2004	Production (stable)

Licensing Linux

The method of Linux licensing is one of the major reasons companies choose Linux as their operating system. As an operating system, Linux is unique compared to most other operating systems because it is freely developed and continuously improved by a large community of software developers. For this reason, it is referred to as **Open Source Software (OSS)**. To understand what OSS is, you must first understand how source code is used to create programs. **Source code** refers to the list of instructions that a software developer writes to make up a program; an example of source code is depicted in Figure 1-3.

```
#define MODULE
#include <linux/module.h>
int init_module(void){
        printk("My module has been activated.\n");
        return 0;
}
void cleanup_module(void){
        printk("My module has been deactivated.");
}
```

FIGURE 1-3 *Source code*

After the instructions are finished, the source code is compiled into a format (called machine language) that only your computer's processor can understand and execute. To edit an existing program, you must edit the source code and then recompile it.

The format and structure of source code follows certain rules defined by the **programming language** in which it was written. Many different programming languages are available that you can use to write source code for Linux. After being compiled into machine language, all programs look the same to the computer operating system, regardless of the programming language from which they were created. As a result, software developers choose a programming language to create source code based on ease of use, functionality, and comfort level.

The concept of Open Source Software enables software developers to read the source code of other people's software, modify that source code to make the program better, and redistribute that source code to other developers who might improve it further. Also, software made in this fashion must be distributed free of charge, regardless of the number of modifications made to it. People who develop Open Source Software commonly use the Internet to share their source code, manage software projects, and submit comments and fixes for bugs (flaws). In this way, the Internet acts as the glue that binds OSS developers together.

 NOTE

The complete open source definition can be found on the Internet at
http://www.opensource.org.

Some implications of Open Source Software are as follows:

◆ Software is developed very rapidly through widespread collaboration.
◆ Software bugs (errors) are noted and promptly fixed.
◆ Software features evolve very quickly based on users' needs.
◆ The perceived value of the software increases because it is based on usefulness and not on price.

It is not difficult to understand why sharing ideas and source code is beneficial to software development because sharing is beneficial to projects of any kind; however, the business model is very different. Open Source Software uses a nontraditional business model and, as a result, many find it difficult to understand how a product that is distributed freely can generate revenue. After all, without revenue any company will go out of business.

OSS products were never intended to generate revenue directly; they were designed only with the betterment of software in mind. Software creation is an art, not a specific procedure. Programs made to perform the same task might be created in several different ways; whereas one software developer might create a program that measures widgets using four pages of source code, another developer might create a program that does the same task in one page of source code. Because of this, software development has the potential to be haphazard if poorly managed. Open Source Software eliminates many of the problems associated with traditional software development. Pooling the talent of many individual software developers improves the quality and direction that software creation takes through the free sharing of ideas. No single corporate purpose or deadline exists. Also, while Open Source Software developers contribute their strengths to a project, they learn new techniques from other developers at the same time.

Because the selling of software for profit discourages the free sharing of source code, Open Source Software generates revenue indirectly. Companies usually make money by selling computer hardware that runs Open Source Software, by selling customer support for Open Source Software, or by creating closed source software programs that run on open source products such as Linux.

The features of Open Source Software might be beneficial, but legal licenses must exist to keep OSS definitions from changing. Before learning about some of the common licenses available, examine Table 1-2, which defines some general terms used to describe the types of software that exist.

Table 1-2 Software types

Type	Description
Open Source	Software in which the source code and software can be obtained free of charge and can be modified
Closed Source	Software in which the source code is not available; although this type of software might be distributed free of charge, it is usually quite costly
Freeware	Closed source software that is given out free of charge
Shareware	Closed source software that is initially given out free of charge, but that requires payment after a certain period of use

Types of Open Source Licenses

Linux adheres to the **GNU Public License (GPL),** which was developed by the **Free Software Foundation (FSF).** The GPL stipulates that the source code of any software published under its license must be freely available. If someone modifies that source code, that person must also redistribute that source code freely, thereby keeping the source code free forever.

NOTE

GNU stands for "GNUs Not UNIX."

The GPL is freely available on the Internet at *http://www.gnu.org* and in Appendix B, "GNU Public License," of this book.

Another type of open source license is the **artistic license,** which ensures that the source code of the program is freely available, yet allows the original author of the source code some control over the changes made to it. Thus, if one developer obtains and improves the source code of a program, the original author has the right to reject those improvements. As a result of this restriction, artistic licenses are rarely used because many developers do not want to work on potentially futile projects.

In addition to the two different open source licenses mentioned, many types of open source licenses are available that differ only slightly from one another. Those licenses must adhere to the open source definition but might contain extra conditions that the open source definition does not.

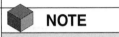

> **NOTE**
>
> A list of approved open source licenses can be found on the Internet at _http://www.opensource.org_.

Types of Closed Source Licenses

Closed source software can be distributed for free or for a cost; either way, the source code for the software is unavailable from the original developers. The majority of closed source software is sold commercially and bears the label of its manufacturer. Each of these software packages can contain a separate license that restricts free distribution of the program and its source code in many different ways.

> **NOTE**
>
> Examples of closed source software are software created by companies such as Microsoft, Novell, or Electronic Arts.

Another type of closed source software is **freeware,** in which the software program is distributed free of charge, yet the source code is unavailable. Freeware might also contain licenses that restrict the distribution of source code. Another approach to this style of closed source licensing is **shareware,** which is distributed free of charge, yet after a certain number of hours of usage or to gain certain features of the program, payment is required. Although both freeware and shareware do not commonly distribute their source code under an open source license, some people incorrectly refer to freeware as OSS, assuming that the source code is free as well.

Linux Advantages

Many operating systems are in use today; the main ones include Linux, Microsoft Windows, Novell NetWare, UNIX, and Mac OS. Notably, Linux is the fastest growing operating system released to date. Though Linux was only created in 1991, the number of Linux users estimated by Red Hat in 1998 was 7.5 million, and the number of Linux users estimated by the Linux Counter Organization in 2003 was 18 million. Many large companies, including IBM, Hewlett-Packard, Intel, and Dell, have announced support for Linux and OSS. In the year 2000, IBM announced that they would spend one billion dollars on Linux and Linux development alone.

There are a multitude of reasons why so many people have begun using Linux. The following advantages are examined in the sections that follow:

♦ Risk reduction

♦ Meeting business needs

♦ Stability and security

♦ Flexibility for different hardware platforms

♦ Ease of customization

♦ Ease of obtaining support

♦ Cost reduction

Risk Reduction

Companies invest in software to perform mission-critical tasks, such as database tracking, Internet business (e-commerce), and data manipulation. However, changes in customer needs and market competition can cause the software a company uses to change frequently. This can be very costly and time-consuming, but is a risk that companies must take. Imagine that a fictitious company, ABC Inc., buys a piece of software from a fictitious software vendor, ACME Inc., to integrate their sales and accounting information with customers via the Internet. What would happen if ACME goes out of business or stops supporting the software due to lack of sales? In either case, ABC would be using a product that has no software support, and any problems that ABC has with the software after that time would go unsolved and could result in lost revenue. In addition, all closed source software is eventually retired some time after it is purchased, forcing companies to buy new software every so often to obtain new features and maintain software support.

Instead, if ABC chooses to use an OSS product and the original developers become unavailable to maintain it, then ABC is free to take the source code, add features to it, and maintain it themselves provided the source code is redistributed free of charge. Also, most OSS does not retire after a short period of time because collaborative open source development results in constant software improvement geared to the needs of the users.

Meeting Business Needs

Recall that Linux is merely one product of open source development. Many thousands of OSS programs are in existence and new ones are created daily by software developers worldwide. Most open source Internet tools have been developed for quite some time now, and the focus in the Linux community in the past few years has been on developing application software for Linux, such as databases and office productivity suites. Almost all of this software is open source and freely available, compared to other operating systems, in which most software is closed source and costly.

OSS is easy to locate as several Web sites on the Internet allow Linux developers space to host their software for others to download; SourceForge at *http://www.sourceforge.net*, FreshMeat at *http://www.freshmeat.net*, and Ibiblio at *http://www.ibiblio.org* are some of the most common. New software is published to these sites daily; SourceForge alone hosts over 80,000 different software developments. Some common software available for Linux includes, but is not limited to the following list:

◆ Scientific and engineering software

◆ Software emulators

◆ Web servers, Web browsers, and e-commerce suites

◆ Desktop productivity software (for example, word processors, presentation software, spreadsheets)

◆ Graphics manipulation software

◆ Database software

◆ Security software

In addition to this, companies that run the UNIX operating system might find it easy to migrate to Linux. For those companies, Linux supports most UNIX commands and standards, which makes transitioning to Linux very easy because the company likely would not need to purchase additional software or retrain staff. For example, suppose a company that tests scientific products has spent much time and energy developing custom software that ran on the UNIX operating system. If this company transitions to another operating system, staff would need to be retrained or hired and much of the custom software would need to be rewritten and retested, which could result in a loss of customer confidence. If, however, that company transitions to Linux, staff would require little retraining, and little of the custom software would need to be rewritten and retested, hence saving money and minimizing impact on consumer confidence.

For companies that need to train staff on Linux usage and administration, several educational resources and certification exams exist for various Linux skill levels. Certification benefits and the CompTIA Linux+ certification are discussed in Appendix A, "Certification," of this book.

In addition, for companies that require a certain development environment or need to support previous custom software developed in the past, Linux provides support for most programming languages.

Stability and Security

OSS is developed by those people who have a use for it. This collaboration between several developers with a common need speeds up software creation, and when bugs in the software are found by these users, bug fixes are created very quickly. Often, the users who identify the bugs can fix the problem because they have the source code, or they can provide detailed descriptions of their problems so that other developers can fix them.

By contrast, customers using closed source operating systems must rely on the operating system vendor to fix any bugs. Users of closed source operating systems must report the bug to the manufacturer and wait for the manufacturer to develop, test, and release a solution to the problem known as a **hot fix**. This process might take weeks or even months to occur. For most companies and individuals, this process is slow and costly. The thorough and collaborative open source approach to testing software and fixing software bugs increases the stability of Linux; it is not uncommon to find a Linux system that has been running continuously for months or even years without being turned off.

Security is also a vital concern for many companies and individuals. Linux source code is freely available and publicly scrutinized. Like bugs, security loopholes are quickly identified and fixed, usually by several different developers. In contrast, the source code for closed source operating systems is not released to the public for scrutiny, which means customers must rely on the vendor of that closed source operating system to provide security. As a result, security breaches might go unnoticed if discovered by the wrong person. This situation is demonstrated by the number of computer viruses (destructive programs that exploit security loopholes) that can affect a closed source operating system, such as Windows, as compared to the number of viruses that can affect Linux. As of June 2004, Linux had under 100 known viruses, whereas Windows had more than 70,000 known viruses.

> **NOTE**
>
> A list of recent computer viruses can be found on the Internet at *http://www.viruslist.com*.

Flexibility for Different Hardware Platforms

Another important feature of Linux is that it can run on a variety of different computer **hardware platforms** frequently found in different companies. Although Linux is most commonly installed on the Intel x86 platform, Linux can also be installed on other types of hardware, such as the Alpha. This means that companies can run Linux on very large and expensive hardware for big tasks such as graphics rendering or chemical molecular modeling, as well as on older hardware such as an old Sun SPARC computer to extend its lifetime in a company. Few other operating systems run on more than two different hardware platforms, making Linux the ideal choice for companies that use a variety of different or specialized hardware.

Following is a partial list of hardware platforms on which Linux can run:

- Intel
- Itanium
- Mainframe (S/390)
- Cirrus Logic ARM
- Alpha
- MIPS
- M68K
- PA-RISC
- SPARC
- Ultra-SPARC
- PowerPC (Macintosh)

In addition to the platforms in the preceding list, Linux can be customized to work on most hardware, including embedded devices such as watches or microwaves. This embedded operating system technology will become more important in the future as the need increases for new functionality in present-day products. Many high-tech companies rely on embedded operating system technology to drive their systems, such as the NASA space shuttles. Currently, over 100 different companies embed Linux in their products.

> **NOTE**
>
> A list of embedded Linux vendors can be found on the Internet at *http://www.embedded-linux.org.*

Ease of Customization

Being able to control the inner workings of the Linux operating system is another attractive feature of Linux, particularly for companies that need Linux to perform specialized functions. If you desire to use Linux as an Internet Web server, you can simply recompile the Linux kernel to include only the support needed to be an Internet Web server. This results in a much smaller and faster kernel.

> **NOTE**
>
> A small kernel performs faster than a large kernel because there is less code for the processor in the computer to analyze. Generally, you should take out any unnecessary support in the kernel to improve performance.

Today, customizing and recompiling the Linux kernel is a well-documented and easy process; however, it is not the only way to customize Linux. Only software packages necessary to perform certain tasks need to be installed; thus, each Linux system can have a unique configuration and set of applications available to the user. Linux also supports the Shell and PERL programming languages, which can be utilized to automate tasks or create custom tasks, that are then invoked as needed.

Consider a company that needs an application which copies a database file from one computer to another computer, yet also requires that the database file is manipulated in a specific way, tested by another program for duplicate records, summarized, and then finally printed as a report. To this company, it might seem like a task that would require expensive software; however, in Linux, you can simply write a short PERL script that uses common Linux commands and programs together to achieve this task in only a few minutes. This type of customization is invaluable to companies because it allows them to combine several existing applications to perform a certain task, which might be specific only to that company and, hence, not previously developed by another free software developer. Most Linux configurations present hundreds of small utilities, which combined with Shell or PERL programming, can quickly and easily make new programs that meet many business needs.

Ease of Obtaining Support

For those who are new to Linux, the Internet offers a world of Linux documentation. **Frequently asked questions (FAQs)** and easy-to-read instructions known as **HOWTO** documents are arranged by topic and are available to anyone. HOWTO documents are maintained by their authors, yet centrally collected by the **Linux Documentation Project (LDP)**, which has over 250 Web sites worldwide that allow you to search or download HOWTO documents.

A search of the word HOWTO on a typical Internet **search engine** such as *http://www.google.com* displays thousands of results, or you can download the worldwide collection of HOWTO documents at *http://www.tldp.org*.

In addition, several Internet newsgroups allow Linux users to post messages and reply to previously posted messages. If someone has a specific problem with Linux, that person can simply post her problem on an Internet newsgroup and receive help from those who know the solution to the problem. Linux newsgroups are posted to often; thus, you can usually expect a solution to a problem within hours. A list of common Linux newsgroups can be found on the Internet at *http://groups.google.com*.

Appendix C, "Finding Linux Resources on the Internet," describes how to navigate Internet resources and lists some common resources useful throughout this book.

Although online support is the most common method of getting help, other methods are available. Most Linux distributions provide professional telephone support services for a modest fee, and many organizations exist to give free support to those who ask. The most common of these groups are referred to as **Linux User Groups (LUGs)**, and most large cities across the globe have at least one. LUGs are groups of Linux users who meet regularly to discuss Linux-related issues and problems. An average LUG meeting consists of several new Linux users (also known as Linux newbies), administrators, developers, and experts (also known as Linux GURUs). LUG meetings are a place to solve problems, as well as learn about the local Linux community. Most LUGs host Internet Web sites that contain a multitude of Linux resources, including summaries of past meetings and discussions. One common activity seen at a LUG meeting is referred to as an Installfest; several members bring in their computer equipment to install Linux and other Linux-related software. This approach to transferring knowledge is very valuable to LUG members because concepts can be demonstrated and the solutions to problems can be modeled by more experienced Linux users.

> **NOTE**
>
> To find a list of available LUGs in your region, search for the words LUG *<cityname>* on an Internet search engine such as *http://www.google.com*. When searching for a LUG, also keep in mind that LUGs might go by several different names; for example, the LUG in Hamilton, Ontario, Canada is known as HLUG (Hamilton Linux Users Group).

Cost Reduction

Linux is less expensive than other operating systems such as Windows because there is no cost associated with acquiring the software. In addition, a wealth of OSS can run on a variety of different hardware platforms running Linux, and a large community of developers are available who diagnose and fix bugs in a short period of time for free. However, although Linux and the Linux source code are distributed freely, implementing Linux is not cost free. Costs include purchasing the computer hardware necessary for the computers hosting Linux, hiring people to install and maintain Linux, and training users of Linux software.

The largest costs that companies face with Linux are those for the people involved in maintaining the Linux system. When using a closed source operating system, however, this administrative cost is also necessary, alongside the costs of the hardware, operating system, additional software, and fixing bugs. The overall cost of using a particular operating system is known as the **total cost of ownership (TCO)**. Table 1-3 shows an example of the factors involved in calculating the TCO for operating systems.

Table 1-3 Calculating the total cost of ownership

Operating System	Linux	Closed Source Operating System
Operating System Cost	$0	Greater than $0
Cost of Administration	Low: Stability is high and bugs are fixed quickly by open source developers.	Moderate/High: Bug fixes are created by the vendor of the operating system, which could result in costly downtime.
Cost of Additional Software	Low/None: Most software available for Linux is also open source.	High: Most software available for closed source operating systems is also closed source.
Cost of Software Upgrades	Low/None	Moderate/High: Closed source software is eventually retired and companies must buy upgrades or new products to gain functionality and stay competitive.

The History of Linux

Linux is based on the UNIX operating system developed by Ken Thompson and Dennis Ritchie of AT&T Bell Laboratories in 1969 and was developed through the efforts of many people as a result of the "hacker culture" that formed in the 1980s. Therefore, to understand how and why Linux emerged on the operating system market, you must first understand UNIX and the hacker culture. Figure 1-4 illustrates a timeline representing the history of the UNIX and Linux operating systems.

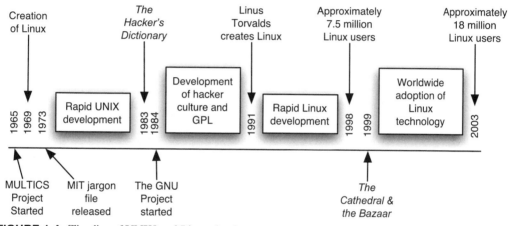

FIGURE 1-4 *Timeline of UNIX and Linux development*

UNIX

The UNIX operating system has roots running back to 1965 when the Massachusetts Institute of Technology (MIT), General Electric, and Bell Labs began development of an operating system called **Multiplexed Information and Computing Service (MULTICS)**. MULTICS was a test project intended to reveal better ways of developing time-sharing operating systems, in which the operating system regulates the amount of time each process has to use the processor; however, the project was abandoned in 1969.

Ken Thompson, who had worked on the MULTICS operating system, continued to experiment with operating system development after the project was abandoned and developed an operating system called **UNIX** in 1969 that ran on the DEC (Digital Equipment Corporation) PDP-7 computer. Shortly thereafter, Dennis Ritchie invented the C programming language that was used on Ken Thompson's UNIX operating system. The C programming language was a revolutionary language. Most programs at the time needed to be written specifically for the hardware of the computer, which involved referencing volumes of information regarding the hardware to write a simple program. However, the C programming language was much easier to use to write programs, and it was possible to run a program on several different machines without having to rewrite the code. The UNIX operating system was rewritten in the C programming language and by the late 1970s, the UNIX operating system ran on different hardware platforms, something that the computing world had never seen until that time. Hence, people called UNIX a portable operating system.

Unfortunately, the company Ken Thompson and Dennis Ritchie worked for (AT&T Bell Laboratories) was restricted by a federal court order from marketing UNIX, and the solution AT&T put into action involved selling off the UNIX source code to several different companies and encouraging standards between them. Each of these companies developed their own flavor of UNIX, yet adhered to standards agreed upon by all. AT&T also gave away free copies of the UNIX source code to certain universities to promote widespread development of UNIX; the University of California at Berkeley **BSD (Berkeley Software Distribution)** UNIX is one result of this. It entered the computing scene in the early 1980s. In 1982, one of the companies that AT&T sold UNIX source code to (Sun Microsystems) marketed UNIX on relatively cheaper hardware and sold thousands of computers that ran UNIX to various companies and universities.

Throughout the 1980s, UNIX found its place primarily in large corporations that had enough money to purchase the expensive computing equipment needed to run UNIX (usually a DEC PDP-11, VAX, or Sun Microsystems computer). A typical UNIX system in the 1980s could cost over $100,000, yet performed thousands of tasks for client computers or "dumb terminals." Today, UNIX still functions in that environment; most large companies employ different flavors of UNIX for their heavy-duty, mission-critical tasks, such as e-commerce and database hosting. Some common flavors of UNIX today include Sun Microsystems' **Solaris** UNIX, Hewlett-Packard's **HP-UX**, and IBM's **AIX** UNIX.

The Hacker Culture

The term **hacker** refers to someone with the intent to expand his knowledge of computing through experimentation. This should not be confused with the term **cracker**, which specifies someone who illegally uses computers for personal benefit or to cause damage.

Most hackers in the early days of UNIX came primarily from engineering or scientific backgrounds because those were the fields in which most UNIX development occurred. Fundamental to hacking was the idea of sharing knowledge. A famous hacker, Richard Stallman, promoted the free sharing of ideas while he worked at the Artificial Intelligence lab at MIT. He believed that free sharing of all knowledge in the computing industry would promote development. In the mid 1980s, Richard formed the Free Software Foundation (FSF) to encourage free software development. This movement was quickly accepted by the academic community in universities around the world and many university students and other hackers participated in making free software, most of which ran on UNIX. As a result, the hacker culture was commonly identified alongside the UNIX operating system.

Unfortunately, UNIX was not free software, and by the mid 1980s some of the collaboration seen earlier by different UNIX vendors diminished and UNIX development fragmented into different streams. As a result, UNIX did not represent the ideals of the FSF, and so Richard Stallman founded the **GNU Project** in 1984 to promote free development for a free operating system that was not UNIX.

> **NOTE**
>
> A description of the FSF and GNU can be found on the Internet at
> *http://www.gnu.org.*

This development eventually led to the publication of the GNU Public License (GPL), which legalized free distribution of source code and encouraged collaborative development. Any software published under this license must be freely available with its source code; any modifications made to the source code must then be redistributed free as well, keeping the software development free forever.

As more and more hackers worked together developing software, a hacker culture developed with its own implied rules and conventions. Most developers worked together without ever meeting each other; they communicated primarily via newsgroups and e-mail. As well, *The Hacker's Dictionary* was published in 1983 by MIT and detailed terminology collected since the mid 1970s regarding computing and computing culture. The FSF, GNU, GPL, and *The Hacker's Dictionary* were all tangible parts of the hacker culture, yet no tangible definition of this culture existed until the hacker Eric S. Raymond published his book *The Cathedral and the Bazaar* in 1999. In this book, Raymond describes several aspects of the hacker culture:

◆ Software users are treated as codevelopers.

◆ Software is developed primarily for peer recognition and not for money.

◆ The original author of a piece of software is regarded as the owner of that software and coordinates the cooperative software development.

◆ The use of a particular piece of software determines its value, not its cost.

◆ Attacking the author of source code is never done. Instead, bug fixes are either made or recommended.

◆ Developers must understand the implied rules of the hacker culture before being accepted into it.

This hacker culture proved to be very productive, and several thousand free tools and applications were made in the 1980s, including the famous Emacs editor, which is a common tool used in Linux today. During this time period, many programming function libraries and UNIX-like commands also appeared as a result of the work on the GNU Project. Hackers became accustomed to working together via newsgroup and e-mail correspondence. In short, this hacker culture, which supported free sharing of source code and collaborative development, set the stage for Linux.

Linux

Although Richard Stallman started the GNU Project to make a free operating system, the GNU operating system never took off. Much of the experience gained by hackers developing the GNU Project was later pooled into Linux. A Finnish student named **Linus Torvalds** first developed Linux in 1991 when he was experimenting with improving **MINIX** (Mini-UNIX, a small educational version of UNIX developed by Andrew Tannenbaum) for the Intel x86 platform. The Intel x86 platform was fast becoming standard in homes and businesses across the world, and was a good choice for any free development at the time. The key feature of the Linux operating system that attracted the development efforts of the hacker culture was the fact that Linus had published Linux under the GNU Public License.

Since 1991, when the source code for Linux was released, the number of software developers dedicated to improving Linux increased each year. The Linux kernel was developed collaboratively and was centrally managed; however, many Linux add-on packages were developed freely worldwide by those members of the hacker culture who were interested in their release. Linux was a convenient focal point for free software developers to concentrate on. During the early and mid 1990s, Linux development was radical; hackers used this time to experiment with a development project of this size. Also during this time, several **distributions** of Linux appeared. A distribution of Linux used the commonly developed Linux operating system kernel and libraries, yet was packaged with add-on software specific to a certain use.

Many distributions of Linux were formed, such as **Red Hat**, **Mandrake**, and **SuSE**, yet this branding of Linux did not imply the fragmentation that UNIX experienced in the late 1980s. All distributions of Linux shared a common kernel and utilities; the fact that they contained different add-on packages simply made them look different on the surface. Linux still derived its usefulness from collaborative development, and in 1998, the term Open Source Software (OSS) development was put into place for this type of collaborative software development. OSS was created and advocated by the hacker culture, and by 1998, there were many thousands of OSS developers worldwide. Many small companies that offered Linux solutions for business were formed, people invested in these companies, and many were released publicly on the stock market. Unfortunately, this trend was short-lived and by the year 2000, most of these companies vanished. At the same time, the OSS movement caught the attention and support of many large companies (such as IBM, Compaq, Dell, and Hewlett-Packard), and there was a shift in Linux development to support the larger computing environments and embedded Linux.

It is important to note that Linux is simply a by-product of OSS development. Recall that the OSS developers are still members of the hacker culture and, as such, are intrinsically motivated to develop software that has an important use. Thus, OSS development has changed over time; in the 1980s, the hacker culture concentrated on developing Internet and programming tools, whereas in the 1990s, the hacker culture focused on Linux operating system development. Since the year 2000, there has been great interest in developing application programs for use on the Linux operating system. Graphics programs, games, and custom business tools are only some of the popular developments that OSS developers have released in the past couple of years. Because Linux is currently very well developed, more application development can be expected from the OSS community in the next decade.

Linux Distributions

It is time-consuming and inefficient to obtain Linux by first downloading and installing the Linux kernel and then adding desired OSS packages afterward. As a rule, a user downloads a distribution of Linux containing the Linux kernel, common function libraries, and a series of OSS packages.

NOTE

Remember that although different Linux distributions appear different on the surface, they run the same kernel and contain many of the same packages.

Despite the fact that varied distributions of Linux are essentially the same under the surface, they do have important differences. Different distributions might support different hardware platforms. Also, Linux distributions ship with predefined sets of software; some Linux distributions ship with a large number of server-related tools, such as Web servers and database servers, whereas others ship with a large number of workstation and development software applications. Still others might ship with a complete set of open source tools from which a user can customize her Linux system; the user simply chooses a subset of these open source tools to install, such as a database server, to perform specific functions.

Linux distributions that ship with many specialized tools might not contain a graphical user interface (GUI); an example of this is a Linux distribution that fits on a floppy and can be used as a **router**. Most distributions, however, do ship with a GUI that can be further customized to suit the needs of the user. The core component of the GUI in Linux is referred to as **X Windows** and can be obtained from the Internet at *http://www.XFree86.org*. Several Window Managers and desktop environments are available, which together affect the look and feel of this GUI, and these components can differ from distribution to distribution. X Windows in combination with a Window Manager and desktop environment is referred to as a **GUI environment**. Two competing GUI environments are available in Linux: the **GNU Network Object Model Environment (GNOME)** and the **K Desktop Environment (KDE)**. Both these GUI environments are more or less comparable in functionality, though users might have a personal preference for one desktop over the other. This is often the case when a company wants to do a great deal of software development in the GUI environment; the GNOME desktop written in the C programming language uses the widely available gtk toolkit, whereas the KDE desktop written in the C++ programming language uses the qt toolkit. Which language and toolkit best fits the need will be the one preferred at that time. Most common Linux distributions ship with both GNOME and KDE GUI environments, whereas others offer support for both so that either GUI environment can be easily downloaded and installed. A comparison of these two GUI environments can be seen in Figures 1-5 and 1-6.

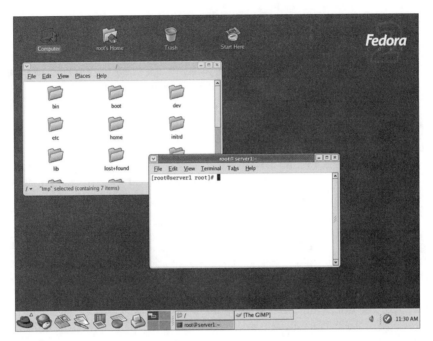

FIGURE 1-5 *The GNOME desktop*

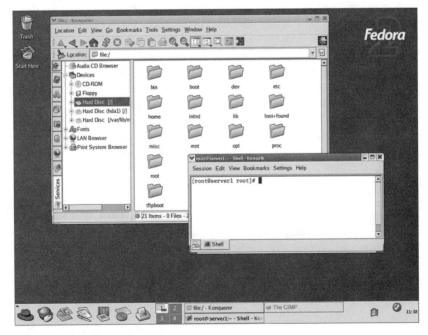

FIGURE 1-6 *The KDE desktop*

Another difference between Linux distributions is language support. Certain distributions are available with more support for certain languages than others. Two examples are SuSE Linux, which has increased support for the German language, and TurboLinux, which has increased support for Japanese and Chinese. As a result, these two distributions of Linux are most popular in countries with populations who primarily speak those languages. Many Linux distributions are specialized for different languages, and most Linux documentation, such as HOWTO documents, is available in many different languages.

Although these differences between Linux distributions can help narrow the choice of Linux distributions to install, one of the most profound reasons companies choose one distribution over another is support for package managers. A **package manager** is a software system that installs and maintains software. It keeps track of installed software, requires a standard format and documentation, and can manage and remove software from a system by recording all relevant software information in a central software database on your computer.

> **NOTE**
>
> A package manager in Linux is similar to the Add/Remove Programs applet in the Windows Control Panel.

The most widely supported package manager is the Red Hat Package Manager (RPM). Most Linux software is available in RPM format and the Red Hat Package Manager is standard on many Linux distributions. The Debian Package Manager offers the same advantages as the Red Hat Package Manager, yet few distributions offer it. In addition to obtaining software in package manager format, you can also download software in tarball format. A **tarball** is merely a compressed archive of files, like WinZip or RAR, which usually contain scripts that install the software contents to the correct location on the system. Unfortunately, tarballs do not update a central software database and, as a result, are very difficult to manage, upgrade, or remove from the system. Traditionally, most Linux software was available in tarball format, but more and more people are using package managers to install software.

> **NOTE**
>
> A complete listing of Linux distributions can be found on the Internet at *http://www.linux.org* and this list can be searched by hardware platform, software category, or language.

Anyone can create a Linux distribution by packaging Open Source Software with the Linux kernel, and as a result, over 250 publicly registered Linux distributions exist. Many of these are small, specialized distributions designed to fulfill certain functions, but some are mainstream

Linux distributions commonly used in most situations. Each distribution usually has an associated Web site from which the distribution can be downloaded for free. In addition, most Linux distributions can be obtained from several different Web sites such as *http://www.linuxiso.org*. Many distributions of Linux are also available on CD-ROM for a small fee from various computer stores and Web sites; however, downloading from the Internet is the most common method of obtaining Linux.

Table 1-4 briefly lists some mainstream Linux distributions, their features, and where to find them on the Internet.

Table 1-4 Common Linux distributions

Distribution	Features	Platforms	Location
Red Hat Linux	The most common Linux distribution used today with tools useful in any Linux environment. Two distributions of Red Hat are available: the Enterprise distribution and the Fedora distribution. Both editions ship with GNOME, KDE, and RPM.	X86 Itanium AMD64 Alpha SPARC PPC Mainframe M68K MIPS Embedded	*http://www.redhat.com*
SuSE Linux	The most common Linux distribution in Europe and the second most common Linux distribution in North America, SuSE offers software packages for almost any business needs. It ships with GNOME, KDE, and RPM.	x86 Itanium AMD64 Alpha PPC SPARC Mainframe Embedded	*http://www.suse.com*
Slackware Linux	A distribution with many features similar to UNIX, it is commonly used in multiprocessor environments due to its enhanced multiprocessor support. It ships with GNOME and KDE.	x86 Alpha SPARC	*http://www.slackware.com*

Table 1-4 Common Linux distributions (Continued)

Distribution	Features	Platforms	Location
Debian Linux	A distribution that offers the largest number of packages of all Linux, it contains software packages for any use and ships with GNOME, KDE, the Debian Package Manager, and RPM.	x86 Itanium AMD64 Alpha SPARC ARM M68K PPC	*http://www.debian.org*
TurboLinux	The most common distribution of Linux in Asia, it is famous for its clustering abilities. It ships with GNOME, KDE, and RPM.	x86 Itanium Alpha Mainframe	*http://www.turbolinux.com*
Mandrake Linux	A user-oriented distribution very similar to Red Hat with enhancements for ease of use. It ships with GNOME, KDE, and RPM.	x86 Itanium AMD64 PPC	*http://www.mandrakelinux.com*

Common Uses of Linux

As discussed earlier, an important feature of Linux is its versatility. Linux can provide services meeting the needs of differing companies in a variety of situations. Furthermore, configuring these services is straightforward given the wide range of documentation freely available on the Internet; simply choose the services that are required and then customize Linux to provide those services. These services can be used on the local computer **workstation**, or they can be configured to allow other computers to connect to it across a network. Services that are used on the local computer are referred to as **workstation services**, whereas services that are made available for other computers across a network are known as **server services**.

NOTE

A computer that hosts a server service is commonly referred to as a **server**.

Although thousands of different server and workstation services are available that you can use to customize Linux, some configurations of Linux that are commonly used today include the following:

◆ Internet servers
◆ File and print servers
◆ Application servers
◆ Supercomputers
◆ Scientific workstations
◆ Office workstations

Internet Servers

Linux hosts a wide range of Internet services, and it was from these services that Linux gained much popularity in the 1990s. All of these services are available free of charge and like all Open Source Software undergo constant improvement, which makes Linux an attractive choice when planning for the use of Internet services in a company. Companies that use services on a computer to serve client computers are said to have an Internet server. Linux provides hundreds of network services that provide the framework for an Internet server; the most common of these services include the following:

◆ Mail services
◆ Routing
◆ FTP services
◆ Firewalls and proxy services
◆ Web services
◆ News services
◆ DNS services

Many of these applications are discussed in more detail later in this book.

Mail Services

In the 1980s and early 1990s, e-mail (or electronic mail) was a service that was found primarily in universities. Today, almost every Internet user has an e-mail account and uses e-mail on a regular basis. E-mail addresses are easy to acquire and can be obtained free of charge.

NOTE

E-mail addresses can be acquired from several different Web sites; one such well-known Web site is *http://www.hotmail.com*.

E-mail is distributed via a network of e-mail servers, also known as **Mail Transfer Agents (MTAs)**. Many MTAs are freely available for Linux, including sendmail, postfix, smail, and qmail. Before the user can access the e-mail, it must be downloaded from a MTA; the service that provides this is known as a **Mail Delivery Agent (MDA)**. Linux also provides several of these services; procmail and fetchmail are two of the most common. Finally, e-mail must be viewed using a program known as a **Mail User Agent (MUA)**. Common MUAs available for Linux include mutt, pine, printmail, elm, mail, Netscape, and Eudora.

Routing

Routing is a core service that is necessary for the Internet to function. The Internet is merely a large network of interconnected networks; in other words, it connects company networks, home networks, and institutional networks together so that they can communicate to each other. A router is a computer or special hardware device that provides this interconnection; it contains information regarding the structure of the Internet and sends information from one network to another. Companies can use routers to connect their internal networks to the Internet as well as to connect their networks together inside the company. Linux is a good choice for this as it provides support for routing, and is easily customizable; many Linux distributions, which can fit on a single floppy disk, provide routing capabilities.

FTP Services

The most common and efficient method for transferring files over the Internet is by using the File Transfer Protocol (FTP). In addition, FTP is commonplace when transferring files on an internal company network because it is very quick and robust. A user simply starts the FTP service on her computer (now known as an FTP server) and allows users to connect; users on other computers then connect to this server using an FTP client program and download any desired files. Most FTP servers available on the Internet allow any user to connect and are, hence, called anonymous FTP servers. Furthermore, most operating systems such as Linux, UNIX, Microsoft Windows, and Macintosh are distributed with an FTP client program, making it easy for users to connect to these FTP servers.

> **NOTE**
>
> Although several FTP service software programs are available for Linux, the most commonly used is the Washington University FTP Server (wu-ftp), which can be downloaded from the Internet at *http://www.wu-ftpd.org*.

Firewalls and Proxy Services

The term "firewall" originates in the automobile industry; a firewall protects the passengers in a car if a fire breaks out in the engine compartment. Just as an automobile firewall protects passengers, a computer firewall protects companies from outside intruders on the Internet.

Most firewalls are computers, which are placed between the company network and the company's connection to the Internet; all traffic must then pass through this firewall, allowing the company to control traffic at this firewall, based on a complex set of rules. Linux has firewall support built directly into the kernel and utilities, such as ipchains and netfilter/iptables, which ship with most distributions, and can be used to configure the rules necessary to make a system a firewall.

> **NOTE**
>
> You can find out more about using netfilter/iptables to configure Linux firewalls on the Internet at *http://www.netfilter.org/*.

Because firewalls are usually located between a company's internal network and the Internet, they often provide other services that allow computers inside the company easy access to the Internet. The most common of these services are known as proxy services; a proxy server requests Internet resources, such as Web sites and FTP sites, on behalf of the computer inside the company. In other words, a workstation computer inside the company simply sends a request to the proxy server connected to the Internet, and the proxy server obtains and returns the requested information to the workstation computer. In addition to this, one proxy server can allow thousands of company workstation computers access to the Internet simultaneously without lengthy configuration of the workstation computers; proxy servers keep track of the information passed to each client by maintaining a Network Address Translation (NAT) table. Although ipchains and netfilter/iptables can both perform some proxy server functions, the most common proxy server used on Linux is Squid, which also retains a copy of any requested Internet resources (a process known as caching) such that it can respond quicker to future requests for the same resources.

> **NOTE**
>
> To obtain or find information regarding the Squid proxy server on the Internet, visit *http://www.squid-cache.org*.

Web Services

Although many Internet tools and services are available, the most popular is the Internet browser, which can connect client computers to servers worldwide hosting information of many types: text, pictures, music, binary data, video, and much more. The community of servers that hosts this information is known as the World Wide Web (WWW), and a server hosting information is known as a Web server. On a basic level, a Web server is just a server using Hypertext Transfer Protocol (HTTP) to provide information to requesting Web browsers running on client computers; however, Web servers can also process programs known as Common Gateway Interface (CGI) scripts and provide secure connections such as Secure Sockets Layer (SSL). A CGI is a program that runs on the Web server and enables connection to a resource running on another server on the network not connected to the Internet such as a database. This is very useful as not all information provided over the Internet needs to reside on Web servers. CGIs can be written in several programming languages, including C and C++, making them readily compatible with Linux. SSL is a secure method of communicating with a Web server in which the information passing between the client computer and the Web server is encrypted to keep it secure. This form of transmission is widely used any time confidentiality is required, such as in Internet banking or e-commerce to get a client's credit card information; it is indicated by a change in the browser's address bar from http:// to https://.

NOTE

To better understand how SSL works, obtain an e-mail address from *http://www.hotmail.com/* and note the change in the browser's address bar immediately after providing your user name and password when you log in to check your e-mail account.

Many open source Web server software packages are available for Linux. The most widely used is the Apache Web Server, comprising more than 64% of all Web servers in the world during 2003.

NOTE

For more information about the Apache Web Server on the Internet, visit *http://www.apache.org*.

News Services

Web servers host valuable information, but most do not provide any means for users to communicate with each other. This functionality is provided by a news server, which allows users to post messages in forums called **newsgroups** and allows other users to read and reply to those messages. Newsgroups are sometimes referred to as computer bulletin boards and are similar to bulletin boards seen around a school campus and in other public places; persons having, or requiring information or services post a notice advertising this, which others see and to which they respond. Newsgroup forums are grouped according to topic, and posting to a newsgroup is often a very quick way to find the solution to a problem because people who read the posting are likely to have had the same problem and found the solution. In addition, newsgroup forums can be moderated, in which a person or group responsible for the forum edits messages before they are posted to ensure they fit the forum's theme. This ensures proper newsgroup etiquette, which dictates that before posting a question you search previous postings to ensure that the question has not already been asked and answered and that only messages relevant to the newsgroups topic are posted. Many OSS developers use newsgroups to exchange information and coordinate software creation. As with e-mails, a special program called a newsreader is necessary to access newsgroups and read postings hosted on news servers. Common Linux newsreaders include Gnews, Knews, Gnus, Netscape, and pine. The most popular open source news server software available for Linux is called InterNetworkNews (INN); it is shipped with most common Linux distributions and is maintained by an open source organization called the Internet Systems Consortium, which continually develops and improves several open source Internet technologies.

> **NOTE**
>
> To obtain a newsreader for Linux from the Internet, visit *http://linux.tucows.com/news_default.html*.
>
> For more information from the Internet on how to subscribe to newsgroups, visit *http://groups.google.com/*.
>
> To obtain a copy of INN for Linux from the Internet, visit the Internet Systems Consortium at *http://www.isc.org/products/INN/*.

DNS Services

Computers communicating on a network need to be uniquely identified. This is accomplished by assigning each computer a number called an **Internet Protocol (IP) address** to allow them to identify and reference each other. An IP address is a long string of numbers, which are meaningless to users and very hard to remember; to make them easier to remember, IP addresses are masked by strings of user-friendly names such as *www.linux.org*, referred to as **fully qualified domain names (FQDNs)**. When using an Internet Web browser, such as Internet Explorer or Netscape Navigator, to request information from a Web server, the address typed into the address bar of the browser (for example, *http://www.linux.org*) is converted to an IP address before it is sent onto the Internet. To translate computer names such as *www.linux.org* to IP addresses, a server hosting the Domain Naming Service (DNS) is contacted. The DNS server, which has been supplied with the proper FQDN to IP mappings, then returns the correct IP address for the requested server and the Internet Web browser, and then uses this IP address to connect to the target Web site. For companies wanting to create a DNS server, Linux is an inexpensive solution as many distributions of Linux ship with a Domain Name Service known as BIND (Berkeley Internet Name Daemon).

> **NOTE**
>
> Each computer participating on the Internet must have an IP address.
>
> Names for computers such as *www.linux.org* are also known as fully qualified domain names (FQDNs).
>
> You can find the latest version of BIND on the Internet at the Internet Systems Consortium Web site, *http://www.isc.org*.

File and Print Servers

Networks were created to share resources, primarily printers and information. In business, it is not cost-effective to purchase and install a printer on the computer of every user who needs to print. It is far easier and cheaper to install one central printer on a server and let multiple users print to it across the computer network. Often, information must also be commonly available to users to allow them to collaborate on projects or perform their daily jobs. Duplicating data on every user machine would consume too much hard drive space, and coordinating changes to this data would be nearly impossible. By employing the use of a network, this information can be made available to all who need it and can be easily kept up-to-date. Another benefit to this central storage of information is that a user can access data regardless of the computer that he logs in to. Central storage also allows a company to safeguard its information by using devices to back up or make copies of stored data on a regular basis in the event a computer failure occurs. Most companies perform backups of data at least every week to ensure that if data is lost on the central server, it can be restored from a back-up copy quickly.

Linux is well suited to the task of centrally sharing resources. It is inherently a fast, light operating system and a distribution suited to the task can be installed on the central server. Linux is not only able to share information with other Linux and UNIX machines using services such as Network File System (NFS), but is also able to share resources with computers running other operating systems, such as Microsoft Windows, Apple Macintosh, or IBM OS/2. Client computers are able to access a shared resource on a server running Linux provided that server has the appropriate service available. The most common service used to allow clients to connect to shared information and printers on a Linux server is Samba, which makes a Linux server appear as a Windows server to Windows clients.

> **NOTE**
>
> Samba can be found on the Internet at *http://www.samba.org*.

Application Servers

An application server is one running a program that acts as an intermediary between a client computer and information, normally stored in a database.

A **database** is simply an organized collection of data that is arranged into tables of related information. The client requests some data to be changed or displayed, and the application server interacts with the database to manipulate and retrieve the required information. This is often described as a front-end/back-end relationship. The front end runs on the client computer and is the interface the user sees and interacts with to request data. The front end takes this request, formulates it such that the server can understand it, and passes the request along to the back-end application running on the server. This back-end application then interacts with the database and returns the results to the front-end application on the client computer, which then puts it into a user-friendly format and displays it to the user. With the rapid development of the Internet in the 1990s, many companies are centralizing their key software elements on Internet application servers, which can serve client computers worldwide; this approach saves both time and money when changes need to be made to the software. It also means only one central database needs to be maintained. **Database Management Systems (DBMS)** are a collection of programs and tools designed to allow for the creation, modification, manipulation, maintenance, and access of information from databases.

Several free open source DBMS programs and tools facilitate creation, management of, and retrieval of data from a database, as well as interaction with a variety of closed source databases, including those from Microsoft and Oracle.

> **NOTE**
>
> For a list of open source DBMS software available for Linux on the Internet, visit *http://scilinux.sourceforge.net/database.html*.

The most popular and widely used database software available for Linux today is MySQL (My Structured Query Language). Powerful, fast, and light, it can interact with other databases such as Oracle, and be integrated with most Web servers via CGI scripts for use as an application server on the Internet. Most other open source technology has support for MySQL.

> **NOTE**
>
> To learn more about MySQL on the Internet, visit *http://www.mysql.com*.

Application servers need not only be used for interaction with databases, but can provide management functionality as well, allowing access and administration from anywhere in the world via the Internet. Management interfaces have taken advantage of the comprehensive development surrounding client Web browsers and Internet technologies and now offer a full range of computer management capabilities from the comfortable and standard interface of the client Web browser. One common open source management interface for Linux is Webmin, which is a customizable application server that gives users the ability to manage almost all services available in Linux from anywhere on the Internet.

NOTE

Webmin can be found on the Internet at *http://www.webmin.com*.

Supercomputers

Many companies and institutions use computers to perform extraordinarily large calculations that would be unsuitable for most computers. To satisfy these tasks, companies either buy computers having multiple processors or use specialized services to combine several smaller computers together allowing them to function as one large supercomputer. Combining several smaller computers together is called **clustering**. Companies and individuals requiring this type of computing are called the supercomputing community, and this community is growing quickly today as technology advances in new directions.

Although it might seem logical to purchase computers that have a large number of processors, the performance of a computer relative to the number of processors decreases as you add processors to a computer. In other words, a computer with 64 processors does not handle 64 times as much work as one processor because of physical limitations within the computer hardware itself; a computer with 64 processors might only perform 50 times as much work as a single processor. The ability for a computer to increase workload as the number of processors increases is known as **scalability**, and most computers, regardless of the operating system used, do not scale well when there are more than 32 processors. As a result of this limitation, many people in the supercomputing community **cluster** several smaller computers together to work as one large computer. This approach results in much better scalability; 64 computers with one processor each working toward a common goal can handle close to 64 times as much as a single processor.

Most of the supercomputing community has focused on Linux when developing clustering technology; the most common method of Linux clustering is known as **Beowulf clustering**, which is easy to configure and well documented. Although there are many different ways to implement a Beowulf cluster, the most common method is to have one master computer send instructions to several slave computers, which compute parts of the calculation concurrently and send their results back to the master computer. This type of supercomputing breaks tasks down into smaller units of execution and executes them in parallel on many machines at once; thus, it is commonly referred to as parallel supercomputing and many free programs are available that are written to run on parallelized computers. Beowulf parallel supercomputer technology has been aggressively developed since the mid 1990s and has been tested in various environments; currently, thousands of Beowulf clusters exist worldwide in various institutions, companies, and universities.

NOTE

You can find more information about Beowulf clusters on the Internet at *http://www.beowulf.org.*

Scientific/Engineering Workstation

Many of the developers from Richard Stallman's Free Software Foundation came from the scientific and engineering community, which needed to develop many programs to run analyses. In the 1980s and early 1990s, this scientific and engineering community largely developed software for the UNIX operating system that was common in universities around the world; however, today, this community is focusing on developing software for Linux. Any software previously made for UNIX can be ported to Linux easily. Scientists and engineers often use parallel supercomputers to compute large tasks, and OSS developers, with a background in scientific computing, have done much of the development on Beowulf technology. One example of this is SHARCnet (Shared Hierarchical Academic Research Computing Network) in Ontario, Canada, in which several universities have developed and tested supercomputing technology and parallel programs for use in the scientific and engineering fields.

NOTE

You can find more information about SHARCnet on the Internet at *http://www.sharcnet.ca.*

Often, the programs that are required by the scientific and engineering community must be custom developed to suit the needs of the people involved; however, many OSS programs which you can use or modify, are freely available in many different scientific and engineering fields, including, but not limited to the following list:

◆ Physics, Astrophysics, and Biophysics

◆ Fluid Dynamics and Geophysics

◆ Biocomputation

◆ Materials and Polymer Chemistry

◆ General Mathematics and Optimization

◆ Data Mining

◆ Number Theory

◆ Computer/Linear/Array Algebra

◆ Mathematical Visualization and Modeling

◆ Statistics and Regression Analysis

- Data Plotting and Processing
- Computer Graphics Generation
- Computer Modeling
- Paleontology
- Molecular Modeling
- Electrical Engineering
- Artificial Intelligence
- Geographic Modeling and Earth Sciences
- Oceanography

Office Workstation

Server services for Linux have been the primary focus of OSS development for Linux in the 1990s, but recently this focus has been expanded to many other types of software, including workstation software designed to be of benefit to end users in the office and home environments. By definition, a workstation is a single-user computer, more powerful than a typical home system; however, people commonly call any single-user computer that is not a server a workstation. It is where users work and interact, running programs and connecting to servers. Today, you can find many different OSS packages that allow the ability to create, organize, and manipulate office documents and graphic art, including but not limited to the following list:

- Text editors (such as Nedit)
- Word processors (such as Abiword)
- Graphic editing software (such as Gimp)
- Desktop publishing software (such as Lyx)
- Financial software (such as Gnucash)
- Office productivity suites (such as StarOffice)

Chapter Summary

- Linux is an operating system whose kernel and many additional software packages are freely developed and improved upon by a large community of software developers in collaboration. It is based on the UNIX operating system and has roots in the hacker culture perpetuated by the Free Software Foundation.
- Because Linux is published under the GNU Public License, it is referred to as Open Source Software. Most additional software that is run on Linux is also Open Source Software.
- Companies find Linux a stable, low-risk, and flexible alternative to other operating systems, which can be installed on several different hardware platforms to meet business needs and results in a lower TCO.

◆ Linux is available in different distributions, all of which have a common kernel, but are packaged with different OSS applications.

◆ A wide variety of documentation and resources for Linux exists in the form of Internet Web sites, HOWTOs, FAQs, newsgroups, and LUGs.

◆ Linux is an extremely versatile operating system that can provide a wide range of workstation and server services to meet most computing needs of companies and individuals.

Key Terms

AIX – A version of UNIX developed by IBM.

application — The software that runs on an operating system and provides the user with specific functionality (such as word processing or financial calculation).

artistic license — An open source license that allows source code to be distributed freely, but changed at the discretion of the original author.

Beowulf clustering — A popular and widespread method of clustering computers together to perform useful tasks using Linux.

BSD (Berkeley Software Distribution) — A version of UNIX developed out of the original UNIX source code and given free to the University of California at Berkeley by AT&T.

closed source software — The software whose source code is not freely available from the original author; Windows 98, for example.

cluster — A grouping of several smaller computers that function as one large supercomputer.

clustering — The act of making a cluster; *see also* Cluster.

cracker — A person who uses computer software maliciously for personal profit.

database — An organized set of data.

Database Management System (DBMS) — The software that manages databases.

developmental kernel — A Linux kernel whose minor number is odd and has been recently developed, yet not thoroughly tested.

device driver — A piece of software, which contains instructions that the kernel of an operating system uses to control and interact with a specific type of computer hardware.

distribution — A complete set of operating system software, including the Linux kernel, supporting function libraries, and a variety of OSS packages that can be downloaded from the Internet free of charge. These OSS packages are what differentiate the various distributions of Linux.

Free Software Foundation (FSF) — An organization started by Richard Stallman, which promotes and encourages the collaboration of software developers worldwide to allow the free sharing of source code and software programs.

freeware — The computer software programs distributed and made available at no cost to the user by the developer.

frequently asked questions (FAQs) — An area on a Web site where answers to commonly posed questions can be found.

fully qualified domain name (FQDN) — A string of words identifying a server on the Internet.

GNU — An acronym, which stands for "GNU's Not Unix."

GNU Network Object Model Environment (GNOME) — One of the two competing graphical user interface (GUI) environments for Linux.

GNU Project — A free operating system project started by Richard Stallman.

GNU Public License (GPL) — A software license, ensuring that the source code for any Open Source Software will remain freely available to anyone who wants to examine, build on, or improve upon it.

graphical user interface (GUI) — The component of an operating system that provides a user-friendly interface comprising graphics or icons to represent desired tasks. Users can point and click to execute a command rather than having to know and use proper command-line syntax.

GUI environment — A GUI core component such as X Windows, combined with a Window Manager and desktop environment that provides the look and feel of the GUI. Although functionality might be similar among GUI environments, users might prefer one environment to another due to its ease of use.

hacker — A person who explores computer science to gain knowledge. Not to be confused with cracker.

hardware — The tangible parts of a computer, such as the network boards, video card, hard disk drives, printers, and keyboards.

hardware platform — A particular configuration and grouping of computer hardware, normally centered on and determined by processor type and architecture.

hot fix — A solution for a software bug made by a closed source vendor.

HOWTO — A task-specific instruction guide to performing any of a wide variety of tasks; freely available from the Linux Documentation Project at *http://www.linuxdoc.org*.

HP-UX — A version of UNIX developed by Hewlett-Packard.

Internet — A large network of interconnected networks connecting company networks, home computers, and institutional networks together so that they can communicate with each other.

Internet Protocol (IP) address — A unique string of numbers assigned to a computer to uniquely identify it on the Internet.

kernel — The central, core program of the operating system. The shared commonality of the kernel is what defines Linux; the differing OSS applications that can interact with the common kernel are what differentiates Linux distributions.

Kommon Desktop Environment (KDE) — One of the two competing graphical user interfaces (GUI) available for Linux.

Linus Torvalds — A Finnish graduate student who coded and created the first version of Linux and subsequently distributed it under the GNU Public License.

Linux — A software operating system originated by Linus Torvalds. The common core, or kernel, continues to evolve and be revised. Differing Open Source Software bundled with the Linux kernel is what defines the wide variety of distributions now available.

Linux Documentation Project (LDP) — A large collection of Linux resources, information, and help files, supplied free of charge and maintained by the Linux community.

Linux User Group (LUG) — The open forums of Linux users who discuss and assist each other in using and modifying the Linux operating system and the Open Source Software run on it. There are LUGs worldwide.

Mail Delivery Agent (MDA) — The service that downloads e-mail from a mail transfer agent.

Mail Transfer Agent (MTA) — An e-mail server.

Mail User Agent (MUA) — A program that allows e-mail to be read by a user.

major number — The number preceding the first dot in the number used to identify a Linux kernel version. It is used to denote a major change or modification.

Mandrake — A popular distribution of Linux in North America, distributed and supported by MandrakeSoft.

MINIX — Mini-UNIX created by Andrew Tannenbaum. Instructions on how to code the kernel for this version of the Unix operating system were publicly available. Using this as a starting point, Linus Torvalds improved this version of UNIX for the Intel platform and created the first version of Linux.

minor number — The number following the first dot in the number used to identify a Linux kernel version denoting a minor modification. If odd, it is a version under development and not yet fully tested. *See also* Developmental kernel and Production kernel.

Multiplexed Information and Computing Service (MULTICS) — A prototype time-sharing operating system that was developed in the late 1960s by AT&T Bell Laboratories.

multitasking — A type of operating system that has the capability to manage multiple tasks simultaneously.

multiuser — A type of operating system that has the capability to provide access to multiple users simultaneously.

newsgroup — An Internet protocol service accessed via an application program called a newsreader. This service allows access to postings (e-mails in a central place accessible by all newsgroup users) normally organized along specific themes. Users with questions on specific topics can post messages, which can be answered by other users.

Open Source Software (OSS) — The programs distributed and licensed so that the source code making up the program is freely available to anyone who wants to examine, utilize, or improve upon it.

operating system (OS) — The software used to control and directly interact with the computer hardware components.

package manager — The software used to install, maintain, and remove other software programs by storing all relevant software information in a central software database on the computer.

process — A program loaded into memory and running on the processor performing a specific task.

production kernel — A Linux kernel whose minor number (the number after the dot in the version number) is even and deemed stable for use through widespread testing.

program — The sets of instructions that know how to interact with the operating system and computer hardware to perform specific tasks; stored as a file on some media (for example, a hard disk drive).

programming language — The syntax used for developing a program. Different programming languages use different syntax.

Red Hat — One of the most popular and prevalent distributions of Linux in North America, distributed and supported by Red Hat Inc.

revision number — The number after the second dot in the version number of a Linux kernel that identifies the certain release number of a kernel.

router — A computer running routing software, or a special function hardware device, providing interconnection between networks; it contains information regarding the structure of the networks and sends information from one component network to another.

scalability — The capability of computers to increase workload as the number of processors increases.

search engine — An Internet Web site such as *http://www.google.com* where you simply enter a phrase representing your search item and you receive a list of Web sites, that contain relevant material.

server — A computer configured to allow other computers to connect to it from across a network.

server services — The services that are made available for other computers across a network.

shareware — The programs developed and provided at minimal cost to the end user. These programs are initially free but require payment after a period of time or usage.

software — The programs stored on a storage device in a computer that provide a certain function when executed.

Solaris — A version of UNIX developed by Sun Microsystems from AT&T source code.

source code — The sets of organized instructions on how to function and perform tasks that define or constitute a program.

SuSE — One of the most popular and prevalent distributions of Linux in Europe.

system service — The additional functionality provided by a program that has been incorporated into and started as part of the operating system.

tarball — A compressed archive of files that contains scripts that install Linux software to the correct locations on a computer system.

total cost of ownership (TCO) — The full sum of all accumulated costs, over and above the simple purchase price of utilizing a product. It includes such sundries as training, maintenance, additional hardware, and downtime.

UNIX — The first true multitasking, multiuser operating system developed by Ken Thompson and Dennis Ritchie, and from which Linux was originated.

user interface —The interface the user sees and uses to interact with the operating system and application programs.

workstation — A computer used to connect to services on a server.

workstation services — The services that are used to access shared resources on a network server.

X Windows — The core component of the GUI in Linux.

Review Questions

1. A _____ consists of a series of visual depictions of tasks known as icons, which the user can use to control the operating system.
    a. command prompt
    b. graphical user interface
    c. Windows interface
    d. visual user interface

2. _____ is distributed free of charge, yet after a certain number of hours of usage or to gain certain features of the program, payment is required.

   a. Shareware

   b. Freeware

   c. Artistic license software

   d. GPL license software

3. Linux documentation is provided in the form of easy-to-read instructions known as _____ documents, which are arranged by topic and are available to anyone.

   a. Installfest

   b. LUG

   c. HOWTO

   d. MANUAL

4. The UNIX operating system was rewritten in the _____ programming language.

   a. BSD

   b. DEC

   c. C

   d. Solaris

5. The core component of the GUI in Linux is referred to as _____ and can be obtained from the Internet.

   a. X Windows

   b. Linux X

   c. Visual Linux

   d. Solaris

6. True or false? A program is a file stored on your computer, whereas a process is that file in action, performing a certain task.

7. True or false? The Linux kernel is no longer under development.

8. True or false? When dealing with Linux version numbers, if the minor number is even, it is referred to as a developmental kernel, and if the minor number is odd, it is referred to as a production kernel.

9. True or false? Companies that run the UNIX operating system might find it difficult to migrate to Linux.

10. True or false? A Finnish student named Linus Torvalds first developed Linux in 1991.

11. The format and structure of source code follows certain rules defined by the _____ in which it was written.

12. A(n) _____ license ensures that the source code of the program is freely available, yet allows the original author of the source code some control over the changes made to it

13. A(n) _____ is a software system that installs and maintains software.

14. Services that are used on the local computer are referred to as _____ services.

15. The most common method of Linux clustering is known as _____ clustering, which is easy to configure and well documented.

Chapter 2

Preparing for Linux Installation

After completing this chapter, you will be able to:

◆ Describe common types of hardware and their features

◆ Obtain the hardware and software information necessary to install Linux

A computer is composed of hardware, which is simply a collection of switches and circuits that require operating system software to function in a meaningful way. This chapter introduces you to the hardware and software terminology necessary to install a Linux system and discusses how to obtain this information from several sources.

Understanding Hardware

Fundamental to the installation of Linux is an understanding of the computer's various hardware components. This allows the user the ability to verify that any hardware detected automatically during installation was detected correctly and that the hardware meets any installation requirements. The hardware components necessary to understand prior to installing Linux include the following:

- ◆ Central processing units (CPUs)
- ◆ Physical memory
- ◆ Disk drives
- ◆ Mainboards and peripheral components
- ◆ Video adapter cards
- ◆ Keyboards and mice

Central Processing Units (CPUs)

The core component of any computer is the **central processing unit (CPU)**, also known as the microprocessor or processor; it is where the vast majority of all calculations and processing of information takes place. Processors are integrated circuit boards consisting of millions of transistors forming electrical pathways through which electricity is channeled. They consist of two main components: the **Arithmetic Logic Unit (ALU)** and the **Control Unit (CU)**. The ALU is where all the mathematical calculations and logic-based operations are executed. The CU is where instruction code or commands are loaded and carried out, and often sends information to the Arithmetic Logic Unit for execution.

Processors can have their integral electronics arranged in different ways; this is referred to as the processor's **architecture** or platform. Recall from Chapter 1, "Introduction to Linux," that the Linux operating system is available for many different platforms, including SPARC (Scalable Processor Architecture), Alpha, and Intel. These different arrangements of electrical circuits can have a specific effect on the processor's speed of executing certain types of instructions. Hence, processors are categorized based on the types of instructions they execute. The two main categories of processor architectures are **Complex Instruction Set Computers (CISC)** processors and **Reduced Instruction Set Computers (RISC)** processors. CISC processors normally execute more complex individual commands than RISC processors; however, because complex commands take longer to execute on a processor, RISC processors tend to be faster than CISC processors. The discussion is limited to the Intel processor architecture throughout the remainder of this book because Intel is the most common CISC processor available in homes and businesses around the world.

> **NOTE**
>
> The new Itanium processor from Intel is a RISC processor that has some CISC features. Because it differs in design from most RISC processors, its architecture is often called the **Explicitly Parallel Instruction Computing (EPIC)** architecture.

The speed at which a processor can execute commands is related to an internal time cycle referred to as **clock speed**. Similar to the way a quartz watch keeps time, the processor has a crystal that oscillates at a determinable frequency when current is passed though it. This is the drumbeat to which the processor keeps time and by which all actions are measured. The clock speed is measured in MegaHertz (MHz), or millions of cycles per second; a processor running at 200MHz has a clock speed or oscillation frequency of 200 million cycles per second. A processor might require one cycle to complete a command or might be **superscalar**, that is, able to complete more than one command in any given cycle. In either case, the faster the clock speed of the processor, the greater the number of commands it can execute in a given span of time.

> **NOTE**
>
> The clock speed of the processor in a computer is separate from and does not need to match the clock speed of other hardware components in the computer; in most cases, the clock speed of the processor is the fastest of any hardware component inside the computer.

Clock speed alone is not the sole determination of the speed at which a processor can work. The amount of information a processor can work with or process at any given time, measured in binary digits **(bits)**, is also a major factor.

Hence, processors are also classified by how much information they can work with at a given time; the more information that can be moved or worked on at once, the faster data can be manipulated. A computer able to process 16 bits of information at a time is over twice as fast as one that can process 8 bits of information at a time; an 8-bit processor running at 800MHz is comparable to a 16-bit processor running at 350MHz. Processors today typically work with 32 or 64 bits of information at a time; most Intel processors available today, such as the Pentium Processor series, are 32-bit processors and are much less expensive than their 64-bit counterparts, such as the Intel Itanium, SPARC, and Alpha processors.

In addition to the number of bits a processor can handle at one time, a computer's cache size and location also affect a processor's ability to calculate larger volumes of data. A **cache** is a temporary store of information; processors can use cache to store recently used instruction sets or information for future use. The more information a processor can store on its local circuit board in a processor cache, the faster it can execute repetitive or frequently used instruction sets. A cache stored in the processor itself is referred to as **Level 1 (L1) cache**. Not all processors have Level 1 caches, and if they do, they are not necessarily the same size. In place of, or in addition to, Level 1 cache, processors can utilize **Level 2 (L2) cache**, which is information stored for retrieval in a separate computer chip that is connected to the processor via a high-speed link. Although not as fast as Level 1 cache, Level 2 cache is a much less expensive alternative and is more common. Newer processors usually incorporate Level 2 cache into the processor itself; in this case, another cache called **Level 3 (L3) cache** is added on a separate computer chip connected to the processor. Level 3 cache functions similarly to the Level 2 cache found in older computers.

In a situation that requires more processing ability than can be provided by a single processor, you might choose to add more than one processor to the system. Multiple processors can then work together to distribute the load and perform the same tasks faster; however, multiprocessor support must be incorporated into the Linux kernel during installation. The most common kernel configuration for using multiple processors is called **symmetric multiprocessing (SMP)** and allows the same operating system and memory use of both processors simultaneously for any task. Another configuration called **asymmetric multiprocessing (ASMP)** refers to a system in which each processor is given a certain role or set of tasks to complete independently of the other processors.

Physical Memory

Physical memory is a storage area for information that is directly wired through circuit boards to the processor. Physical memory is divided into two major categories: **random access memory (RAM)** and **read-only memory (ROM)**. Both RAM and ROM are stored on computer chips and allow access to information; however, RAM requires a constant supply of electricity to maintain stored information, whereas ROM is static in nature and is able to store information even when there is no power to the system. Following this, RAM is referred to as **volatile** memory because its contents are lost when you turn the computer off, whereas ROM is labeled as nonvolatile memory.

RAM

As discussed in Chapter 1, software programs are files that contain instructions to be executed by the processor and are loaded into RAM physical memory upon execution; the processor can then work with the instructions in memory. The amount of RAM is directly related to computer performance because greater amounts of RAM memory allow more programs to run simultaneously on the system. Different programs require different amounts of memory to execute properly; thus, software programs, including operating systems, specify a minimum amount of RAM in their documentation. A Linux machine running the GNOME desktop GUI environment requires more memory than a Linux machine that does not use any GUI environments.

RAM is classified into two major types: dynamic RAM (DRAM) and static RAM (SRAM). **Dynamic RAM (DRAM)** is the cheaper of the two types and, thus, is the most common. It has a slower access speed compared to SRAM and the information store it holds must be refreshed thousands of times per second, necessitating a continuous, uninterrupted flow of electricity. If the flow of electricity to the DRAM chip is disrupted even for the briefest of moments, the information store is lost. DRAM is the type of physical memory commonly referred to simply as computer memory and is seen as an array of integrated circuits (chips) arranged on a small board called a stick, which in turn is connected into the computer's main circuit board via slots. The number of transistors making up the chips on a stick of DRAM determines the amount of information that can be stored measured in megabytes (MB).

Two different sticks of DRAM can have the same physical dimensions, but could hold vastly different amounts of information. Three main types of DRAM sticks are available: **single inline memory modules (SIMM), dual inline memory modules (DIMM)**, and **small outline dual inline memory modules (SODIMM)**. SIMMs are the older of the two and connect their arrays of integrated circuits to the motherboard via a connection having connectors (pins) normally along only one edge; SIMMs are no longer produced and are not commonly seen today. DIMMS are widely used today and connect their arrays of integrated circuits to the motherboard via a connection having connectors (pins) along both edges; having more connections, DIMMs are able to store more information and transfer it more rapidly than SIMMs. SODIMMs are a physically smaller DIMM that is used in portable notebook computers and Macintosh systems.

As technology changes, so does the nature of DRAM and the speed at which it works. Three recent DIMM technologies include **Synchronous Dynamic Random Access Memory (SDRAM), Double Data Rate Synchronous Dynamic Random Access Memory (DDR SDRAM)**, and **Rambus Dynamic Random Access Memory (RDRAM)**. SDRAM uses the standard DIMM connector on the motherboard and transfers data to and from the store on the memory module in bursts and at a higher speed than traditional DRAM. DDR SDRAM is an enhanced SDRAM that is used on newer computers to increase speed. RDRAM is a proprietary product that uses a RIMM connection, which is a DIMM with different pin settings, and runs at a very high clock speed, thus transferring data at a rapid rate. RIMM is not an acronym, but a trademarked word of the Rambus Corporation.

The second major type of RAM, **static RAM (SRAM)**, is more expensive to produce and allows faster access time to stored information because the information store does not need constant refreshing and can go for short periods without a flow of electricity. Nonetheless, this interruption in electrical flow must be brief, and the information store is lost when the computer is powered down. SRAM is the type of physical memory used for Level 2 processor caches and any memory chips attached directly to the main circuit boards of the computer.

ROM

Read-only memory (ROM) is physical memory that can be read but not written to, and is stored in a permanent, nonvolatile manner on integrated circuits (computer chips) inside the computer. Unlike RAM, this memory store is not reliant on the flow of electricity and remains intact for an indefinite period on the computer in the absence of power. Due to this property, ROM is often used to store the initial programs used to initialize hardware components when starting a computer; and is known as **BIOS (Basic Input/Output System) ROM**. Although true ROMs are still in use, the fact that the information store in a ROM computer chip is immutable leads to variants that are maintained in the absence of electrical flow, but can be altered if need be. These ROM variants include the following:

◆ **Programmable read-only memory (PROM)**, which consists of a blank ROM computer chip that can be written to once and never rewritten again.

◆ **Erasable programmable read-only memory (EPROM)**, in which the information contents can be erased and rewritten repeatedly. The contents of EPROM must be erased and rewritten as a whole; individual parts cannot be singly modified. An example of EPROM memory is the **complementary metal oxide semiconductor (CMOS)** computer chip in a computer, which stores the configuration information used by the BIOS ROM when the system is first powered on.

◆ **Electronically erasable programmable read-only memory (EEPROM)** maintains an information store that can not only be erased and rewritten as a whole, but can also be modified singly, leaving other portions intact. This ability to store information statically in the absence of electricity yet modify it if needed is why EEPROM chips are popular in many peripheral computer components.

NOTE

The type of memory used to store photographs in digital cameras is a type of EEP-ROM memory.

Disk Drives

Most information in a computer is maintained using media that is nonvolatile and does not consist of integrated circuits; the most common media of this type used today include **hard disks**, which are stored in **hard disk drives** (also referred to as hard drives or HDDs), **compact disc read-only memory (CD-ROM)** discs, which are inserted into CD-ROM disc drives, and **floppy disks**, which are inserted into floppy disk drives. **Disk drive** devices do not transfer data as quickly as RAM or ROM, but can store vast amounts of modifiable information in a cost-effective manner on the disks they contain for later use. When information is needed by the processor, it is transferred from the disk drive to RAM, such as when the operating system starts during system startup or when application programs are executed on a running system.

Hard Disk Drives

Traditionally, most information was stored on magnetic tape by magnetic tape devices; this use of a magnetic medium was quickly transferred to the floppy drives and hard disk drives used today. The process works similarly to the way audio and video tapes are recorded and played back. A surface is covered with a ferrous material, and the constituent particles of this ferrous material can be rearranged by electromagnetic heads to record data and can then be read by detecting the pattern of arrangement using the same equipment. Unlike magnetic tape devices, which must fast-forward or rewind magnetic tape to read or write data, HDDs read and write information to and from ferrous material coating rigid metal platters by spinning these platters rapidly under articulated arms holding electromagnetic heads. HDDs are not directly wired to the processor, but must pass through a hard disk controller card that controls the flow of information to and from the HDD. These controller cards come in two general types: **Integrated Drive Electronics (IDE)** and **Small Computer Systems Interface (SCSI)**. Hard drives that connect to these controllers must be of the same type; you must use IDE hard disks with an IDE controller card and use SCSI hard disks with a SCSI controller card.

IDE controllers, also known as **Advanced Technology Attachment (ATA)** controllers, are usually circuit boards found on the bottom of an IDE hard drive and connect to the mainboard via a ribbon cable. Most mainboards contain two slots for IDE ribbon cables (a primary controller slot and a secondary controller slot), and each IDE ribbon cable can have up to two IDE hard drives attached to it; thus, most computers are limited to four IDE hard drives. Because each IDE ribbon cable can have two IDE hard drives attached to it, there must be a method that can uniquely identify each IDE hard drive. This method involves setting jumper switches on the physical IDE hard drive so that one IDE hard drive is called "master" and one IDE hard drive is called "slave" on the same ribbon cable. Hence, the master hard drive connected to the primary IDE controller slot might be called a "primary master IDE HDD." Table 2-1 lists the four possible IDE hard drive configurations and their Linux names.

Table 2-1 IDE HDD configurations

Description	Linux Name
Primary Master IDE HDD	hda
Primary Slave IDE HDD	hdb
Secondary Master IDE HDD	hdc
Secondary Slave IDE HDD	hdd

Unlike IDE, SCSI controllers are physically separate from the HDD and are usually attached to the mainboard via slots on the mainboard itself. SCSI hard drives are able to transfer data at much faster rates than IDE hard drives, and the SCSI controller card can interact with more than one HDD at a time. However, IDE hard drives and controllers are less expensive to manufacture than their SCSI counterparts and, thus, are the most common hard drive technology in homes and small- to medium-sized business. For the purposes of this chapter, the discussion is limited to IDE hard disks.

Hard drives manufactured today can store over 160GB of data, and are often divided up into small, more manageable sections called **partitions**. Each partition must then be prepared to store files. To do this, you must format each partition with a **filesystem** that specifies how data should reside on the hard disk itself.

> **NOTE**
>
> In the Windows operating system, each drive letter (for example, C:, D:, E:) can correspond to a separate filesystem that resides on a partition on the hard drive.

There are limits to the number and type of partitions into which a HDD can be divided. Hard disk drives can contain a maximum of four major partitions (called **primary partitions**). To overcome this limitation, you can optionally label one of these primary partitions as "extended"; this **extended partition** can then contain an unlimited number of smaller partitions called **logical drives**. Each logical drive within the extended partition and all other primary partitions can contain a filesystem and be used to store data. The table of all partition information for a certain hard disk is stored in the first readable sector outside all partitions called the **Master Boot Record (MBR)**. Recall that a primary master IDE HDD is referred to as hda in Linux; the first primary partition on this drive is labeled hda1, the second hda2, and so on. Because there are only four primary partitions allowed on a hard disk, logical drives inside the extended partition are labeled hda5, hda6, and so on. An example of this partition strategy is listed in Table 2-2.

Table 2-2 Example partitioning scheme for a primary master IDE HDD

Description	Linux Name	Windows Name
First primary partition on the primary master HDD	hda1	C:
Second primary partition on the primary master HDD	hda2	D:
Third primary partition on the primary master HDD	hda3	E:
Fourth primary partition on the primary master HDD (EXTENDED)	hda4	F:

Table 2-2 Example partitioning scheme for a primary master IDE HDD (Contunied)

Description	Linux Name	Windows Name
First logical drive in the extended partition on the primary master HDD	hda5	G:
Second logical drive in the extended partition on the primary master HDD	hda6	H:
Third logical drive in the extended partition on the primary master HDD	hda7	I:

Other Information Storage Devices

In addition to HDDs, other information stores are available, including floppy disks, Zip disks, DVDs and CD-ROMs. These are often referred to as **removable media** because the medium used to store the information is not fixed in the computer as with a HDD, but removable and transferable between computers.

Floppy disks store information electromagnetically like hard disks and are traditionally the most common removable medium; it is referred to as floppy because the medium covered with ferrous material used to store information is flexible (or floppy) in contrast to the rigid metal platters used in HDDs. Floppy drives, also referred to as 3½-inch floppy drives in reference to the size of the removable storage unit, can hold much less data than HDDs (only 1.44MB) and have much slower data transfer rates.

Zip disks are an evolution of floppy disks and although they look physically similar, they differ from regular floppies in that they can hold considerably more information (up to 750MB). These sophisticated floppy disks cannot use regular 3½-inch floppy disk drive units; they need to be used with special Zip drives, yet are commonly used to transport large files or make back-up copies of important information in many homes and small offices.

DVDs and CD-ROMs differ from all other disk media mentioned because they do not use ferrous material and electromagnetic heads to store and retrieve data, but instead use lasers to read reflected light pulses. A pitted layer of reflective material, normally aluminum, is sandwiched between layers of clear plastic and laser pulses are bounced off it. The pits in the surface deflect the laser pulses hitting them and the resulting pattern of disruption in reflection of laser pulses is read as stored information. This technology gives DVDs and CD-ROMs some advantages over other removable storage devices, including greater data transfer speed, larger storage capacity, and more resistance to data loss. This makes them very useful in storing large amounts of data, and as a result are the choice medium for distributing software such as the Linux operating system.

DVD and CD-ROM drives are rated by the speed at which they can read data from the CD-ROM disc compared to the speed of a regular audio compact disc (CD); typical CD-ROMs at the time of this writing can read data over 50 times (50X) the speed of an audio CD, and typical DVDs can read data over 16 times (16X) the speed of an audio CD. Most DVD and CD-ROM drives are connected to the main circuit boards in a computer via an Advanced Technology Attachment Packet Interface (ATAPI) that allows them to act like an IDE HDD. Typically, one of the four possible IDE devices in a computer is a DVD or CD-ROM drive and this drive must be configured using jumper switches on the DVD or CD-ROM drive itself in the same fashion as IDE hard disk drives.

NOTE

Although the data transfer rate of a DVD or CD-ROM drive is faster than that of a floppy or Zip drive, it is still slower than that of a HDD. If a DVD or CD-ROM drive is placed on the same IDE channel as a HDD, it impacts and slows down the effective data transfer rate of the HDD; because of this, it is wise to place DVD and CD-ROM drives on an IDE controller separate from any IDE HDDs.

Many DVD and CD-ROM drives at the time of this writing can also write information to DVD and CD-ROM discs respectively. These devices are called DVD-rewritable (DVD-RW) and compact disc-rewritable (CD-RW) drives.

Flash memory drives are a recent media type that use EEPROM chips to store information. They typically store more information than floppy disks and Zip disks, and some flash memory drives can store more information than a CD-ROM. In addition, flash memory drives can be plugged into the computer while the computer is on and can be removed in the same way; as a result, flash memory drives are quickly becoming a common medium for users who need to transfer files between computers.

Mainboards and Peripheral Components

Programs are loaded into physical memory and executed by the processor; however, some device must exist, that provides the interconnect between these hardware devices. This interconnect (also called a **bus**) is provided by a circuit board called the **mainboard** or **motherboard**. The bus serves to connect common hardware components, such as the processor, physical memory, and disk drives, but also connects **peripheral components**, such as video cards, sound cards, and **network interface cards (NICs)**. Peripheral components commonly connect to the rest of the system by means of an Input-Output bus (also known as an I/O bus or expansion bus) that is represented by different slots or ports on the mainboard itself; the three most common slots for peripheral devices include the following:

◆ ISA
◆ PCI
◆ AGP

Industry Standard Architecture (ISA) slots only allow peripheral components an interconnect that transfers information at a speed of 8MHz and are much less common than other slots because they are used to connect older components. **Peripheral Component Interconnect (PCI)** is a much newer bus connection that was introduced in 1995 and is the most common type of slot found in computers today; it can transfer information at a speed of 33MHz and can use **direct memory access (DMA)**. DMA allows a peripheral the ability to bypass the CPU and talk directly with other peripheral components to enhance performance; you can configure eight DMA channels to allow this ability. **Accelerated Graphics Port (AGP)** is designed for video card peripherals and allows a transfer speed of over 66MHz. It was not designed to replace PCI, but to enhance video card operations and allow for faster access to system memory for graphical functions. Figure 2-1 shows a mainboard with these slots.

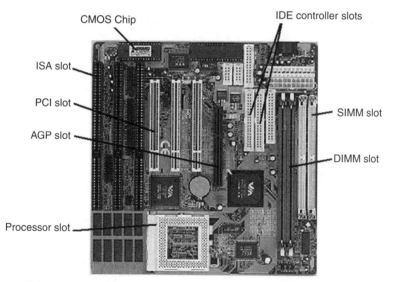

FIGURE 2-1 *Mainboard components*

Other peripherals might not have slots for peripherals on the mainboard; instead, they might connect via a cable to a port on the edge of the mainboard that is visible from the exterior of the computer (and, hence, difficult to see in Figure 2-1). These ports include the following:

◆ PS/2

◆ COM (Serial)

◆ LPT

◆ USB

◆ IEEE 1394 (FireWire)

◆ PCMCIA

PS/2 ports are small, round connectors with six pins that typically connect keyboards and mice to the computer. Some computers might instead use a larger five-pin port to connect the keyboard; this port is called an AT port and was used prior to PS/2 ports.

COM ports (also called **serial ports**) are rectangular nine-pin connectors that can be used to connect a variety of different peripherals to the mainboard, including mice, serial printers, scanners, and digital cameras. Today, COM ports are used far less than in the past because their transfer speed is quite slow; as a result, of the four COM ports commonly used (COM1, COM2, COM3, and COM4), today only ports for COM1 and COM2 are on most mainboards.

In the past, printers have commonly used a rectangular 25-pin **LPT port** (also called a **parallel port**) for connection to the mainboard. Although there are two commonly used LPT ports (LPT1 and LPT2), most computers typically only have LPT1 available on their mainboards.

Most peripheral components, such as keyboards, mice, printers, digital cameras, flash memory drives, and scanners, now connect to the mainboard by means of a **universal serial bus (USB)** port rather than a serial or parallel port. USB version 2 allows a transfer speed of up to 480MB per second (most USB supports up to 12MB per second), and can be used with a device called a USB hub to allow up to 127 different devices to connect to one USB port on the mainboard. Most computers come with two USB ports on the mainboard, and almost all USB devices can be attached to the computer for the operating system to detect and use while the computer is powered on. This feature is called hot-swapping and any device that can be attached to the mainboard of a running computer is referred to as a **hot-swappable** device.

Another hot-swappable variant of USB is **IEEE 1394 (FireWire)**, which was developed by Apple Computer Inc., in 1995. FireWire version 2 supports a transfer speed of up to 800MB per second. As a result of supporting such high transfer speeds, FireWire is commonly used to connect SCSI hard disks, scanners, flash memory drives, digital cameras, and CD-RW drives to the computer.

When considering laptop portable computers, a large number of connectors or ports might increase the physical size of the computer and decrease its portability. For these computers, **Personal Computer Memory Card International Association (PCMCIA)** ports allow a small card to be inserted into the computer (usually less than 10.5mm thick) with the electronics necessary to provide a certain function. PCMCIA slots do not require much electricity, are hot-swappable, and are commonly used for network interface cards, modems, and expansion memory. Another feature of laptop portable computers is **Advanced Power Management (APM)**, which shuts off power to components such as PCMCIA devices if they are not being used to save electricity.

You can connect peripheral components to a computer via slots or ports on the mainboard in a wide variety of ways; however, each peripheral device must be maintained separately from other devices on the system so that information does not cross paths when calculated by the CPU. This separation is obtained by two features of each peripheral component: the **IRQ (Interrupt Request)** and the **Input/Output (I/O) address**. The IRQ specifies a unique channel to the CPU itself and these channels are labeled using the numbers 0 to 15. If two devices try to use the same IRQ, a conflict occurs and neither device works; however, some devices can share IRQs if they are configured to do so. Each device must also have a small working area of RAM where the CPU can pass information to and receive information from the device; this working area is known as the I/O address and must be unique for each device. I/O addresses are written in hexadecimal notation and indicate the range of memory used; an example of an I/O address is 0x300-31F.

On older equipment (usually ISA), you had to manually configure the IRQ and I/O address; however, most peripherals today are **Plug-and-Play (PnP)** and can automatically assign the correct IRQ, I/O address, and DMA channel (if used) without any user intervention. For Plug-and-Play to work properly, the BIOS and operating system must support Plug-and-Play configurations. Today, Plug-and-Play support is standard on most computers and operating systems such as Linux.

Video Adapter Cards and Monitors

Video adapter cards (commonly referred to as video cards) are one of the most vital peripheral components in a computer because they provide a graphical display for the user when connected to a monitor device. Video cards typically plug into a slot on the motherboard (for example, ISA, PCI, AGP) but can also be part of the motherboard itself; these are called integrated video cards and are common today because they are less expensive to produce.

Every display is made up of tiny dots or pixels; the more pixels that can be displayed, the sharper the image. Typical systems today display a minimum of 800 pixels horizontally and 600 pixels vertically; this is called the **resolution** of the screen and can be simplified to 800 × 600 in our example. Each pixel can also represent a color. The total set of colors that you can display on the screen is referred to as the **color depth** and most systems today display a color depth of at least 16 million colors (also called 24-bit color depth).

Both the color depth and resolution depend on how much RAM is on the video card. Most video cards today come with 16MB of RAM on the card itself, which is enough to support most resolutions, but some video cards are configured to borrow RAM from the system mainboard. Table 2-3 lists the maximum resolutions and color depth available with certain amounts of RAM.

Table 2-3 Memory requirements for screen resolutions and color depths

Video RAM	Resolution	Color Depth
1MB	1024 × 768	256 colors (8-bit color)
	800 × 600	65,536 colors (16-bit color)
2MB	1024 × 768	65,536 colors (16-bit color)
	800 × 600	16 million colors (24-bit color)
4MB	1024 × 768	16 million colors (24-bit color)

The screen image is refreshed several times per second to allow for changes or animation on the screen; a higher **refresh rate** reduces the chances of images flickering on the screen. It is important to note that a refresh rate that is set too high can damage the monitor itself; it is important to ensure that the monitor can support the refresh rate configured on the video card. Two types of refresh rates are available: **HSync (horizontal refresh)** and **VSync (vertical refresh)**, which are measured in Hertz (Hz).

Keyboards and Mice

Video cards and monitors provide a method of viewing output, but there must be some means of providing user input and direction; keyboards and mice are devices that provide this ability. Keyboards are one of the oldest and most common input devices, and consist of a normal typewriter key set combined with special function keys allowing input to be sent to the computer. The number of additional function keys varies, giving keyboards anywhere from 84 to over 104 different keys in total. Most keyboards follow the standard QWERTY typewriter layout, but others offer a different key arrangement called Dvorak. Still others offer a split set key arrangement, one set for each hand, and are termed ergonomic keyboards. Regardless of layout or number of keys, keyboards connect to the motherboard in a variety of ways:

◆ A large circular AT five-pin connector

◆ A small circular PS/2 six-pin connector

◆ A USB connection

◆ A wireless infrared or radio connection

A relatively newer device used with most computer systems is the computer mouse developed by Douglas C. Engelbart in the 1960s. Slow to gain popularity, mice are as common today as keyboards, and in many cases, they offer a faster and more versatile interface, which has led to the phrase "point and click." Without a mouse, you would need to communicate to a computer via a keyboard device only; you could only submit tasks for the computer to perform by typing commands into a command-line interface. Mice allow versatility when using programs that are graphical in nature; moving a mouse across a desk surface moves a cursor on the video screen in a similar path, and pressing one of the buttons displays action choices or executes tasks. Mice can connect to the motherboard in a variety of ways:

◆ A serial port

◆ A small PS/2 six-pin connector

◆ A USB connection

◆ A wireless infrared or radio connection

Gathering Preinstallation Information

All operating systems require a certain minimum set of computer hardware requirements to function properly because an operating system is merely a series of software programs that interact with and control the computer hardware. Although most up-to-date hardware is sufficient to run the Linux operating system, it is nonetheless important to ensure that a computer meets the minimum hardware requirements before performing an installation.

These minimum installation requirements can be obtained from several sources. If the operating system was obtained on CD-ROM, a printed manual or file on the CD-ROM might specify these requirements, but you can also find the minimum hardware requirements for most operating systems on the vendor's Web site. For the Red Hat Linux Fedora operating system, you can find the minimum hardware requirements at *http://www.redhat.com* or in Table 2-4.

Table 2-4 Red Hat Fedora hardware requirements

Central Processing Unit (CPU)	Minimum: Pentium Class Recommended: Pentium II – 400MHz
Physical Memory Random Access Memory (RAM)	Minimum for text-mode: 128MB Minimum for graphical: 256MB Recommended for graphical: 512MB
Disk Space Free (Hard Disk Drive)	Minimum: 900MB free space Recommended: 3.4GB free space Full installation: 7.5GB free space *Additional free space is required for any file storage or the installation of other software programs.
Additional Drives	CD-ROM drive 3.5-inch floppy disk drive
Peripheral Devices	All peripheral devices (for example, video cards, sound cards, network cards) must be Red Hat-compliant.

Furthermore, each operating system supports only particular types of hardware components. Although some operating systems such as Linux support a wider variety of hardware components than other operating systems, each individual hardware component in your computer should be checked against the **Hardware Compatibility List (HCL)** readily found on the vendor's Web site.

> ### NOTE
>
> For Red Hat Linux, the HCL can be found on the Internet at *http://www.redhat.com*.

In addition to identifying hardware components to ensure that they are supported by the Linux operating system and meet minimum requirements, you should also identify the software components that will be used in the Linux operating system. These components include the computer's host name, Internet or network configuration parameters, and the software packages that need to be installed to satisfy a certain use. Each of these are discussed in Chapter 3.

Because there are many pieces of hardware and software information to document, it is good form to complete a preinstallation checklist that contains all important installation information. At minimum, a preinstallation checklist should look something like Table 2-5.

Table 2-5 Sample preinstallation checklist

CPU (Type and MHz)	Intel Pentium III 800Mhz
RAM (MB)	256MB
Keyboard model and layout	101-key keyboard connected to PS/2 port
Mouse model and device	Two-button Microsoft Intellimouse connected to COM 1 port
Hard disk type (Primary Master, and so on)	Primary Master
Hard disk size (MB)	40GB
Host name	localhost.localdomain
Network Card Internet Protocol Configuration (IP address, Netmask, Gateway, DNS servers, DHCP)	DHCP: not used IP address: 192.168.6.188 Netmask: 255.255.255.0 Gateway: 192.168.6.1 DNS servers: 200.10.2.1, 200.10.82.79
Packages to install	GNOME desktop Samba Squid Apache GIMP Emacs
Video card make and model	ATI Rage 128
Video card RAM (MB)	16MB
Monitor make and model	Samsung Syncmaster 551s
Monitor VSync and HSync Ranges	HSync: 30–55KHz VSync: 50–120Hz

Gathering Hardware Information

You can use several tools and resources to fill in the hardware information sections of the pre-installation checklist. The computer manuals that are shipped with the computer system are one such resource; most computer manuals have the specifications of each computer component listed in a table at the rear of the book or inside the front cover. Also, you might already have the Windows operating system installed on the computer prior to installing Linux; in this case, you can use common Windows utilities to view hardware information. The most comprehensive of these utilities is the System Information tool, shown in Figure 2-2.

The Windows Device Manager (in the System Applet of the Windows Control Panel) is another utility that can display most of the required hardware information, as shown in Figure 2-3.

 NOTE

To access the Windows System Information tool, simply navigate to the Start menu, All Programs, Accessories, System Tools, System Information.

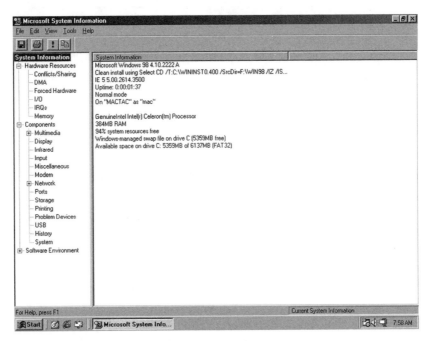

FIGURE 2-2 *The Windows System Information tool*

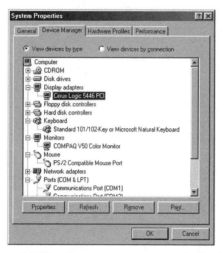

FIGURE 2-3 *The Windows Device Manager*

> **NOTE**
>
> To access the Windows 95/98/Me Device Manager, simply navigate to the Start menu, Settings, Control Panel, System, Device Manager. To access the Windows 2000/XP/2003 Device Manager, simply navigate to the Start menu, Control Panel, System, Hardware, Device Manager.

Another Windows utility useful for gaining hardware information regarding your video card and monitor is the Display applet of the Windows Control Panel, as shown in Figure 2-4.

> **NOTE**
>
> To access the Windows Display applet information regarding your video card and monitor, simply navigate to the Start menu, Control Panel, Display, Settings, Advanced.

Although system manuals and the Windows Control Panel can be used to find information about your computer, recall that each computer stores configuration information in a CMOS chip on the computer mainboard. This information in the CMOS chip is read by the BIOS ROM chip when the computer is first turned on to initialize peripherals and perform a **power-on self test (POST)**. The POST displays output similar to Figure 2-5 when you first power on the computer.

FIGURE 2-4 *The Windows Display applet*

```
Award Modular BIOS v4.51PG, AN Energy Star Ally
Copyright © 1984-98, Award Software, Inc.

ASUS P2L-B ACPI BIOS Revision 1008

Award Plug and Play BIOS Extension v1.0A
Initializing Plug and Play Cards!
Card-01: D-Link DE-220P PnP ISA Card
Card-01: Creative SB AWE64 PnP

PNP Init Completed

Detecting HDD Primary Master    ... QUANTUM FIREBALL CX6.4A
Detecting HDD Primary Slave     ... None
Detecting HDD Secondary Master  ... ATAPI CDROM
Detecting HDD Secondary Slave   ... None


Press DEL to enter SETUP
01/28/99-i440LX-<P2L-B7>
```

FIGURE 2-5 *System POST*

After the POST has completed, the BIOS looks for an operating system on a floppy, CD-ROM, or hard disk. Most settings used by the BIOS are configurable as they are stored on the CMOS chip, and after the POST has completed, most BIOSs allow you to choose these settings by pressing the Delete key, as shown in Figure 2-5. If you enter the BIOS setup utility, a screen similar to Figure 2-6 appears where you can configure devices and observe hardware settings.

NOTE

The system BIOS setup utility looks very different from manufacturer to manufacturer; however, each utility roughly contains the same general types of information and configurations.

```
                    ROM PCI/ISA BIOS (<P2L-B>)
                       CMOS SETUP UTILITY
                     AWARD SOFTWARE, INC.

     STANDARD CMOS SETUP            SUPERVISOR PASSWORD

     BIOS FEATURES SETUP           USER PASSWORD

     CHIPSET FEATURES SETUP        IDE HDD AUTO DETECTION

     POWER MANAGEMENT SETUP        SAVE & EXIT SETUP

     PNP AND PCI SETUP             EXIT WITHOUT SAVING

     LOAD BIOS DEFAULTS

     LOAD SETUP DEFAULTS

     Esc : Quit
     F10 : Save & Exit Setup
```

FIGURE 2-6 *BIOS setup utility*

Gathering Software Information

Although hardware information is valuable to obtain prior to installing Linux, the Linux installation program also asks for several software settings, such as the time zone and language support. Most of these software settings need not be documented prior to installation as they can be added during installation at the discretion of the user. Some settings, however, should be researched before starting the installation; these settings include the system network configuration and the package selections.

If you are installing a Linux system to use or provide network services, the installation program prompts for the necessary values to complete the configuration of the NIC in the computer. These values are usually assigned by the network administrator or Internet service provider (ISP) for the company. A summary of these settings is described in the following list:

◆ **Host name**—The name of the computer that is registered in the Domain Name Service (DNS) so that others can connect to it by name.

◆ **IP address**—The unique number assigned to the computer that allows it to participate on an Internet Protocol (IP) network such as the Internet.

◆ **Netmask**—Also known as the network mask or subnet mask, it specifies which portion of the IP address identifies which logical network the computer is on.

◆ **Gateway**—Also known as the default gateway or gateway of last resort, it specifies the address of a computer that accepts information from the local computer and sends it to other computers if the local computer cannot.

◆ **DNS servers**—These servers resolve **fully qualified domain names (FQDNs)** such as *www.linux.org* to IP addresses so that users can connect to those addresses across the Internet. You can list more than one DNS server; the local computer then tries the second server in the list if the first one is unavailable, and so on.

You can configure the previous settings manually during the installation program or have the settings automatically configured, provided a **Dynamic Host Configuration Protocol (DHCP) server** exists on the network. If you select the option to use DHCP during installation, the Linux computer attempts to obtain these settings from a DHCP server on the network. You can also choose to configure the aforementioned network settings later, after the installation has completed.

By far, the most important software information required before installation comes from the software packages needed to customize the Linux system to perform certain tasks. Because these software packages require disk space, you should keep available disk space in mind when choosing software packages. Because you have the option to choose from hundreds of individual packages during installation, you can only estimate the disk space needed for common Linux uses. Typically, a Red Hat Linux installation requires anywhere from 600MB of hard disk space for software during basic installation to over 6GB for software during a full installation. As a general rule of thumb, you should have at least twice the amount of hard disk space to allow for user files and future software installation. Because a full installation places over 6GB of data on the hard disk, you should have at least 12GB of hard disk space available for a full installation of Linux. Most administrators do not perform a full installation; instead, they only install the software packages that are required for the computer to function. During the installation program, sets of packages grouped by function are displayed; however, you might choose to customize this list and select only the individual packages needed. Table 2-6 lists common packages and their descriptions, which are valuable when choosing to customize packages.

Table 2-6 Common Linux packages

Package	Description
X-Windows	The core component of the graphical user interface (GUI) in Linux, which is required by the KDE and GNOME GUI environments
GNOME Desktop	A GUI environment available for Linux
KDE Desktop	A GUI environment available for Linux
Samba (SMB) Server	A program that allows easy integration of Linux and Windows for file and printer sharing
NIS (Network Information Services) Server	A program that centralizes and coordinates the changing of configuration files across Linux computers
NFS (Network File System) Server	A program that allows Linux systems to share files across a network
GIMP (GNU Image Manipulation Program)	A Graphical manipulation program
BIND/DNS Server	A program that contains a table mapping IP addresses to FQDNs for use by client computers on the Internet

Table 2-6 Common Linux packages (Continued)

Package	Description
Apache Server	The most common Web server available for Linux
MySQL Server	A database management system
Postgres SQL Server	A database management system
TeX	A program that processes text for desktop publishing.
Emacs	A common text editor
Squid Proxy Server	A program that allows several computers access to the Internet via one Internet connection
Mozilla	A common Internet Web browser
FTP Server (wu-ftpd)	A program that allows quick transfer of files across the Internet, independently of the operating system
InterNetworkNews (INN) Server	A program that hosts and manages newsgroup postings
Netfilter/iptables/ipchains	A program that allows Linux to function as a network firewall server

Chapter Summary

◆ Understanding the various hardware components of a computer before a Linux installation allows you to make the appropriate choices during installation and verify that the Linux installation was successful.

◆ CPUs process most instructions in a computer and come in two different architectures: RISC and CISC.

◆ Computer memory can be volatile (RAM) or nonvolatile (ROM).

◆ Most information is stored on hard disks, floppy disks, and CD-ROMs in a non-volatile manner. Two main types of hard disks exist: SCSI and IDE.

◆ Peripheral components, such as video adapter cards, sound cards, mice, keyboards, and NICs, attach to the mainboard via an expansion slot or port.

◆ Common expansion slots include ISA, PCI, and AGP.

◆ Common ports include PS/2, serial, parallel, USB, FireWire, and PCMCIA.

◆ All peripheral components must have a unique IRQ and I/O address to communicate with the processor. They can optionally use DMA to bypass certain processor operations.

◆ Hardware information can be gathered from computer manuals, the system BIOS, or other operating systems such as Windows.

◆ Most software information can be specified at the time of installation; however, the network configuration and package selection should be carefully planned before installation.

Key Terms

Accelerated Graphics Port (AGP) — A motherboard connection slot designed for video card peripherals allowing data transfer speeds of over 66MHz.

Advanced Power Management (APM) — A BIOS feature that shuts off power to peripheral devices that are not being used to save electricity; commonly used on laptop computers.

Advanced Technology Attachment (ATA) — *See also* Integrated Drive Electronics.

architecture — The design and layout of a CPU; also called a computer platform.

Arithmetic Logic Unit (ALU) — The section of the CPU in which all the mathematical calculations and logic-based operations are executed.

asymmetric multiprocessing — A system containing more than one processor in which each processor is given a certain role or set of tasks to complete independently of the other processors.

BIOS (Basic Input/Output System) ROM — The computer chips on a computer mainboard that contain the programs used to initialize hardware components at boot time.

bit — The smallest unit of information that a computer can compute.

bus — A term that represents the pathway information takes from one hardware device to another via a mainboard.

cache — A temporary store of information used by the processor.

central processing unit (CPU) — An integrated circuit board used to perform the majority of all calculations on a computer system; also known as a processor or microprocessor.

clock speed — The speed at which a processor (or any other hardware device) can execute commands related to an internal time cycle.

color depth — The total set of colors that can be displayed on a computer video screen.

COM ports — The rectangular, nine-pin connectors that can be used to connect a variety of different peripherals to the mainboard, including mice, serial printers, scanners, and digital cameras; also called serial ports.

compact disc-read only memory (CD-ROM) — The physically durable, removable storage media, which is resistant to data corruption and is used in CD-ROM drives and CD-RW drives.

complementary metal oxide semiconductor (CMOS) — A computer chip used to store the configurable information used by the BIOS ROM.

Complex Instruction Set Computers (CISC) — The processors that execute complex instructions on each time cycle.

Control Unit (CU) — The area in a processor where instruction code or commands are loaded and carried out.

direct memory access (DMA) — A capability provided by some bus architectures that allows peripheral devices the ability to bypass the CPU and talk directly with other peripheral components to enhance performance.

disk drive — A device that contains either a hard disk, floppy disk, CD-ROM, CD-RW, or Zip disk.

DNS servers — The servers that resolve fully qualified domain names (FQDNs) such as *www.linux.org* to IP addresses so that users can connect to them across the Internet.

Double Data Rate Synchronous Dynamic Random Access Memory (DDR SDRAM) — A form of SDRAM that can transfer information at higher speeds than traditional SDRAM.

dual inline memory modules (DIMM) — A newer connection slot having connectors (pins) along both edges allowing the array of integrated circuits comprising a stick of RAM to connect to the motherboard.

Dynamic Host Configuration Protocol (DHCP) server — A server on the network that hands out Internet Protocol (IP) configuration to computers that request it.

dynamic RAM (DRAM) — A type of RAM that needs to refresh its store of information thousands of times per second and is available as a SIMM or DIMM stick.

electronically erasable programmable read-only memory (EEPROM) — A type of ROM whose information store can not only be erased and rewritten as a whole, but can also be modified singly, leaving other portions intact.

erasable programmable read-only memory (EPROM) — A type of ROM whose information store can be erased and rewritten, but only as a whole.

Explicitly Parallel Instruction Computing (EPIC) — The RISC architecture used to describe the Itanium processor.

extended partition — A partition on a HDD that can be further subdivided into components called logical drives.

filesystem — The way in which a HDD partition is formatted to allow data to reside on the physical media; common Linux filesystems include ext2, ext3, REISERFS, and VFAT.

FireWire (IEEE 1394) — A mainboard connection technology that was developed by Apple Computer Inc., in 1995 and supports data transfer speeds of up to 800MB per second.

flash memory drive — A storage medium that uses EEPROM chips to store data.

floppy disks — A removable storage media consisting of a flexible medium coated with a ferrous material that are read by floppy disk drives.

fully qualified domain names (FQDN) — The user-friendly names used to identify machines on networks and on the Internet.

gateway — Also known as default gateway or gateway of last resort, the address of a computer that accepts information from the local computer and sends it to other computers if the local computer cannot.

hard disk drive (HDD) — A device used to write and read data to and from a hard disk.

hard disks — The nonremovable media consisting of a rigid disk coated with a ferrous material and used in hard disk drives (HDD).

Hardware Compatibility List (HCL) — A list of hardware components that have been tested and deemed compatible with a given operating system.

host name — A user-friendly name used to uniquely identify a computer on a network. This name is usually a FQDN.

hot-swappable — The ability to add or remove hardware to or from a computer while the computer and operating system are functional.

HSync (horizontal refresh) — The rate at which horizontal elements of the video screen image are refreshed, allowing for changes or animation on the screen; HSync is measured in Hertz (Hz).

Industry Standard Architecture (ISA) — An older motherboard connection slot designed to allow peripheral components an interconnect, and which transfers information at a speed of 8MHz.

Integrated Drive Electronics (IDE) — Also known as ATA, it consists of controllers that control the flow of information to and from up to four hard disks connected to the mainboard via a ribbon cable.

Internet Protocol (IP) address — The unique number that each computer participating on the Internet must have.

Interrupt Request (IRQ) — A unique channel from a device to the CPU.

I/O (Input/Output) address — The small working area of RAM where the CPU can pass information to and receive information from a device.

Level 1 (L1) cache — The cache memory stored in the processor itself.

Level 2 (L2) cache — The cache memory stored in a computer chip on the motherboard for use by the processor or within the processor itself.

Level 3 (L3) cache — The cache memory stored in a computer chip on the motherboard for use by the processor.

logical drives — The smaller partitions contained within an extended partition on a HDD.

LPT port — A rectangular, 25-pin connection to the mainboard used to connect peripheral devices such as printers; also called parallel ports.

mainboard — A circuit board that connects all other hardware components together via slots or ports on the circuit board; also called a motherboard.

Master Boot Record (MBR) — The area of a hard disk outside a partition that stores partition information and boot loaders.

motherboard — *See also* mainboard.

netmask — Also known as the network mask or subnet mask, it specifies which portion of the IP address identifies the logical network the computer is on.

network interface card (NIC) — A hardware device used to connect a computer to a network of other computers and communicate or exchange information on it.

parallel port — *See also* LPT port.

partitions — A small section of an entire hard drive created to make the hard drive easier to use. Partitions can be primary or extended.

peripheral component — The components that attach to the mainboard of a computer and provide a specific function, such as a video card, mouse, or keyboard.

Peripheral Component Interconnect (PCI) — The most common motherboard connection slot found in computers today, which can transfer information at a speed of 33MHz and use DMA.

Personal Computer Memory Card International Association (PCMCIA) — A mainboard connection technology that allows a small card to be inserted with the electronics necessary to provide a certain function.

physical memory — A storage area for information that is directly wired through circuit boards to the processor.

Plug-and-Play (PnP) — A technology that allows peripheral devices to automatically receive the correct IRQ, I/O address, and DMA settings without any user intervention.

power-on self test (POST) — The initialization of hardware components by the ROM BIOS when the computer is first powered on.

primary partitions — The separate divisions into which a HDD can be divided (up to four are allowed per HDD).

programmable read-only memory (PROM) — A blank ROM computer chip that can be written to once and never rewritten again.

PS/2 ports — The small, round mainboard connectors developed by IBM with six pins that typically connect keyboards and mice to the computer.

Rambus Dynamic Random Access Memory (RDRAM) — A proprietary type of RAM developed by the Rambus Corporation.

random access memory (RAM) — A computer chip able to store information that is then lost when there is no power to the system.

read-only memory (ROM) — A computer chip able to store information in a static, permanent manner, even when there is no power to the system.

Reduced Instruction Set Computers (RISC) processors — The relatively fast processors that understand small instruction sets.

refresh rate — The rate at which information displayed on a video screen is refreshed; it is measured in Hertz (Hz).

removable media — The information storage media that can be removed from a computer allowing transfer of data between machines.

resolution — The total number of pixels that can be displayed on a computer video screen horizontally and vertically.

serial port — *See also* COM port.

single inline memory modules (SIMM) — An older type of memory stick that connects to the mainboard using connectors along only one edge.

Small Computer Systems Interface (SCSI) — A technology that consists of controllers that can connect several SCSI HDDs to the mainboard and control the flow of data to and from the SCSI HDDs.

small outline dual inline memory modules (SODIMM) — A DIMM module that is physically smaller than traditional DIMM modules and used in notebook and Macintosh computers.

static RAM (SRAM) — An expensive type of RAM commonly used in computer chips on the mainboard and which has a fast access speed.

superscalar — The ability for a computer processor to complete more than one command in a single cycle.

symmetric multiprocessing (SMP) — A system containing more than one processor in which each processor shares tasks and memory space.

Synchronous Dynamic Random Access Memory (SDRAM) — A form of RAM that uses the standard DIMM connector and transfers data at a very fast rate.

universal serial bus (USB) — A mainboard connection technology that allows data transfer speeds of up to 480MB per second and is used for many peripheral components, such as mice, printers, and scanners.

video adapter card — A peripheral component used to display graphical images to a computer monitor.

volatile — A term used to describe information storage devices that store information only when there is electrical flow. Conversely, nonvolatile information storage devices store information even when there is no electrical flow.

VSync (vertical refresh) — The rate at which vertical elements of the video screen image are refreshed measured in Hertz (Hz).

Zip disk — A removable information storage unit similar to a floppy disk that can store much more information than floppy disks and which is used in Zip drives.

Review Questions

1. What is the core component of any computer?
   a. Bits
   b. Clock speed
   c. Arithmetic Logic Unit
   d. Central Processing Unit

2. _____ maintains an information store that can be erased and rewritten as a whole, and can also be modified singly, leaving other portions intact.
   a. Electronically erasable programmable read-only memory (EEPROM)
   b. Erasable programmable read-only memory (EPROM)
   c. Programmable read-only memory (PROM)
   d. BIOS (Basic Input/Output System) ROM

3. What is the most common type of slot found in computers today?
   a. Accelerated Graphics Port (AGP)
   b. Industry Standard Architecture (ISA)
   c. Peripheral Component Interconnect (PCI)
   d. Direct Memory Access (DMA)

4. Video refresh rates are measured in _____
   a. Kilobytes
   b. Megabytes
   c. Hertz
   d. Amps

5. When configuring a NIC, the _____ is name of the computer that is registered in the Domain Name Service (DNS) so that others can connect to it by name.

   a. Netmask

   b. Gateway

   c. IP address

   d. Host name

6. True or false? Dynamic RAM is more expensive than static RAM.

7. True or false? Flash memory drives typically store more information than floppy and Zip drives.

8. True or false? Video cards typically plug into a slot on the motherboard, but can also be part of the motherboard itself.

9. True or false? It is good form to complete a preinstallation checklist that contains all important installation information.

10. True or false? The System BIOS setup utility is the same no matter what manufacturer made the computer.

11. In a(n) _____ cache, information is stored for retrieval in a separate computer chip that is connected to the processor via a high-speed link.

12. HDDs read and write information to and from ferrous material coating rigid metal platters by spinning these platters rapidly under _____ arms holding electromagnetic heads.

13. Hard drives manufactured today can store over 160GB of data, and are often divided up into small, more manageable sections called _____.

14. _____ peripherals can automatically assign the correct IRQ, I/O address, and DMA channel (if used) without any user intervention.

15. Because a full installation of Linux places over 6GB of data on the hard disk, you should have at least _____ GB of hard disk space available for a full installation.

Chapter 3

Linux Installation and Usage

After completing this chapter, you will be able to:

◆ Install Red Hat Fedora Linux using good practices

◆ Outline the structure of the Linux interface

◆ Enter basic shell commands and find command documentation

◆ Properly shut down the Linux operating system

This chapter explores the steps involved during a Red Hat Fedora Linux installation using the hardware and software information that you obtained in Chapter 2, "Preparing for Linux Installation." The latter half of the chapter presents an overview of the various components that you will use when interacting with the operating system, as well as how to enter basic shell commands, obtain help, and properly shut down the Linux system.

Installing Linux

Although the installation of Linux requires careful planning in addition to the gathering of hardware and software information, it also requires the selection of an installation method and the configuration of various parts of the Linux operating system via an installation program.

Installation Methods

Before performing a Linux installation, you must choose the source of the Linux packages and the installation program itself. Although using CD-ROMs or DVD-ROMs that contain the appropriate packages is the most common method of installation, many different methods of installation are available to those installing Linux, including the following:

◆ Installation from an FTP server across the network

◆ Installation from an HTTP Web server across the network

◆ Installation from an NFS server across the network

◆ Installation from an SMB server across the network

◆ Installation from a Virtual Network Computing (VNC) server across the network

◆ Installation from packages located on the hard disk

The CD-ROM installation method is discussed in this chapter; other methods are discussed in Chapter 7, "Advanced Installation." To install from a CD-ROM, you simply place the Linux CD-ROM in the CD-ROM drive and turn on the computer. Most computers automatically search for a startup program on the CD-ROM immediately after being turned on, which can then be used to start the installation of Linux.

NOTE

Turning on a computer to load an operating system is commonly referred to as booting a computer. Because the Linux installation program on Linux CD-ROMs can be loaded when you first turn on the computer, they are referred to as bootable CD-ROMs.

Performing the Installation

Installing the Linux operating system involves interacting with an installation program, which prompts the user for information regarding the nature of the Linux system being installed. This installation program also allows a user the ability to identify or change hardware components that are detected automatically by the installation program. More specifically, the installation procedure for Red Hat Fedora Linux involves the following stages:

◆ Starting the installation

◆ Choosing the language, keyboard, mouse, and monitor

◆ Specifying the installation type

◆ Partitioning the hard disk

◆ Configuring the boot loader

◆ Configuring the network and firewall

◆ Choosing a system language and time zone

◆ Creating the root user

◆ Selecting packages

◆ Installing packages

◆ Completing the firstboot wizard

Starting the Installation

As mentioned earlier, to perform a CD-ROM-based installation of Red Hat Fedora Linux, you simply place the first Red Hat Fedora Linux CD-ROM in the CD-ROM drive and turn the computer on. Following this, an initial welcome screen appears that indicates that the installation program has loaded, as shown in Figure 3-1.

Pressing the Enter key at this screen performs a default graphical installation that automatically detects hardware and suits most hardware configurations that are present on the HCL. This is the method that is discussed in this chapter. However, you can also pass information to the installation program to alter the type of installation.

By far, the largest problem during installation is initiating a graphical installation; certain LCD monitors and video cards that are not on the HCL might result in a black or distorted screen during the default graphical installation. If this is the case, simply restart the installation and type linux nofb and press Enter at the boot: prompt to disable **framebuffer** support for a graphical installation. Framebuffers are abstract representations of video adapter card hardware that programs can use instead of directly communicating with the video adapter card hardware. If disabling framebuffer support does not allow a graphical install, you can restart the installation and choose to perform a text-based install by typing linux text and pressing Enter at the boot: prompt.

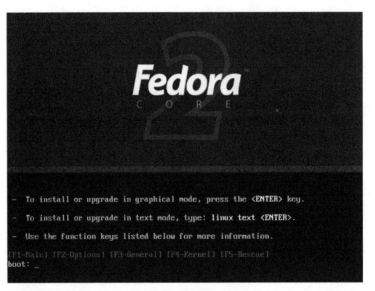

FIGURE 3-1 *Beginning a Red Hat installation*

> ### 🔲 NOTE
>
> Although most people prefer to perform a graphical install for ease of use, a text-based installation is faster because the graphical user interface need not be loaded. Text-based installations are the default for hard disk and network installations discussed in Chapter 7.

You can also specify options that prevent hardware detection, check media for errors, provide repair utilities, load additional device drivers, test memory, or load updated software. These options can be seen if you press F2 at the initial welcome screen, as shown in Figure 3-2.

Regardless of the installation options you choose, after you press Enter at the boot: prompt, you are asked to check the media used for errors prior to the installation, as shown in Figure 3-3. Although it is an optional installation step, it is good practice to test CD-ROM media that have not been used to install Linux in the past to ensure that media errors will not cause the installation to abort later on.

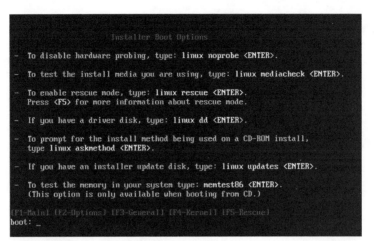

FIGURE 3-2 *Viewing installation options*

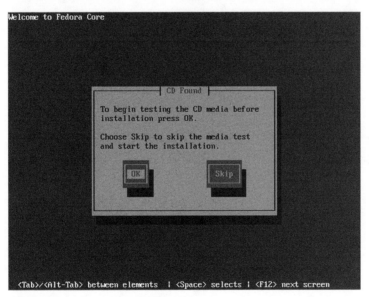

FIGURE 3-3 *Testing CD-ROM media*

Choosing the Language, Keyboard, Mouse, and Monitor

After the media have been tested, a graphical installation starts and you are presented with a graphical welcome screen. Following this screen, you are prompted to answer a series of questions to complete the installation. The first screen allows you to choose the installation language, as shown in Figure 3-4.

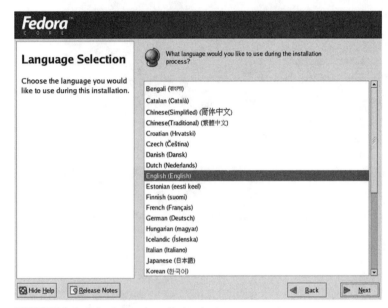

FIGURE 3-4 *Selecting an installation language*

TIP

On the left-hand side of most Red Hat installation screens is a description of the current screen and common selections.

After the language selection screen, you are asked to choose the keyboard, as shown in Figure 3-5. The default model and layout of your keyboard are automatically detected, and as a result they are seldom changed. It is good practice, however, to verify that the information on the screen is correct before continuing. When in doubt, choose a U.S. English layout because they are likely to work in most situations. If the specific make and model of your mouse is not automatically detected, the installation program prompts you for the information, as shown in Figure 3-6. To accommodate programs that can make use of the third mouse button, ensure that Emulate 3 Buttons is checked if the mouse currently does not have a third mouse button. This option, if selected, simulates a third mouse button by pressing both mouse buttons simultaneously.

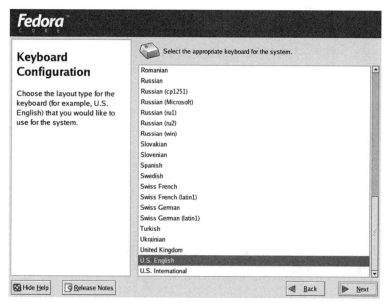

FIGURE 3-5 *Verifying keyboard configuration*

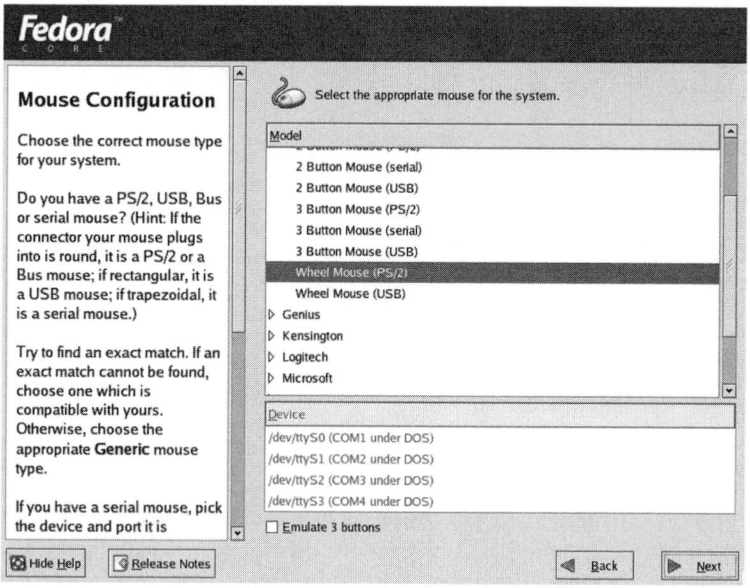

FIGURE 3-6 *Selecting a mouse type*

After you choose your keyboard and mouse, the installation program prompts you to select your monitor, as shown in Figure 3-7. Most monitors available today are automatically detected; you might simply need to verify the correct model and horizontal and vertical sync ranges detected before continuing. However, if the monitor is not automatically detected, you should try to locate it on the list of monitor models or use a generic model with the correct horizontal and vertical sync ranges.

CAUTION

If your monitor is automatically detected, you are not prompted to configure its settings.

It is very important to select the correct monitor settings because incorrect settings can cause damage to the monitor.

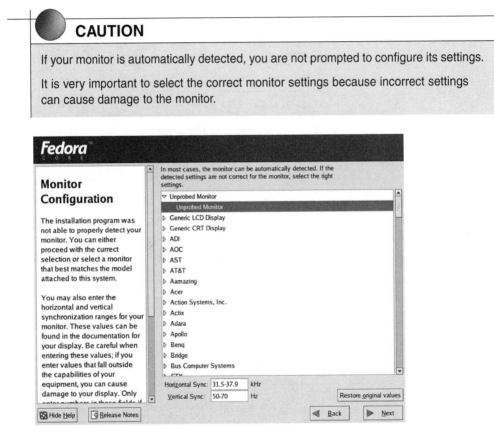

FIGURE 3-7 *Verifying monitor configuration*

Specifying the Installation Type

Next, the installation attempts to detect any previous installations of Red Hat Linux on your hard disks. If a previous version of Red Hat is detected by the installation, you are prompted to either upgrade the previous installation of Red Hat Linux that exists on the hard drive or perform a fresh installation. Typically, you only perform an upgrade if there are data and configurations on the previous installation of Red Hat Linux that are difficult to re-create or back up. If you choose a fresh installation or do not have a previous version of Red Hat installed, you are presented with four general installation types that allow you to simplify package selection, as shown in Figure 3-8.

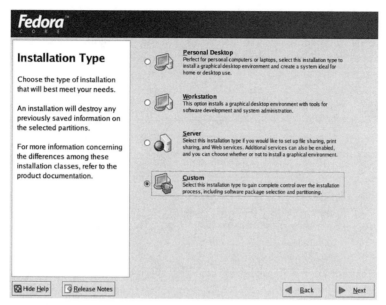

FIGURE 3-8 *Choosing an installation type*

If you choose to perform a Personal Desktop installation, a set of packages suitable for home or portable use is installed by default, including a GUI environment and common applications. Choosing Workstation installs the same applications as Personal Desktop, as well as administrative and network tools. A Server installation contains few workstation packages, but several server services. Although these selections might simplify the selection of packages, it is commonplace to choose Custom, which allows you complete control over the remainder of the installation and the ability to select only the packages needed to suit your computing needs.

NOTE

Although the user chooses an installation type here defining a general set of packages, a detailed package selection is entered later during the installation process.

TIP

It is important to consider available hard disk space when planning installation type. A Custom installation can place nearly 7GB of data on the hard disk. If you are installing a large number of packages, ensure that you have enough free space on the hard disk for user data, log files that will be generated in the future, and working space for the packages installed.

Hard Disk Partitioning

The next screen displayed after you choose the installation type allows you to choose your partitioning strategy. Recall that partitioning divides a hard disk into adjacent sections, each of which can contain a separate filesystem used to store data. Each of these filesystems can then be accessed by Linux if they are attached (or mounted) to a certain directory. When data is stored in that particular directory, it is physically stored on the respective filesystem on the hard drive. The Red Hat installation program can automatically create partitions based on common configurations; however, it is generally good practice to manually partition to suit the needs of the specific Linux system.

At minimum, Linux typically requires only two partitions to be created: a partition that is mounted to the root directory in Linux (/) and that can contain all of the files used by the operating system, applications, and users, and a partition used for **virtual memory** (also known as **swap memory**). Virtual memory consists of an area on the hard disk that can be used to store information that would normally reside in physical memory (RAM) if the physical memory is being used excessively. When programs are executed that require a great deal of resources on the computer, information is continuously swapped from physical memory to virtual memory on the hard disk, and vice versa. Traditionally, Linux swap partitions were made to be at least the size of the physical RAM in the computer; however, Linux kernels of version 2.4 or later require much more space. In general, the swap partition for 2.4 kernels should be at least twice the size of the physical RAM but can be much larger if the Linux system is intended to run large applications. Many users make the swap partition three times the size of physical RAM to avoid any problems after installation. A swap partition does not contain a filesystem and is never mounted to a directory, because the Linux operating system that is ultimately responsible for swapping information.

Although you might choose to create only root and swap partitions, extra partitions make Linux more robust against filesystem errors. For example, if the filesystem on one partition encounters an error, only data on one part of the system is affected and not the entire system (other filesystems). Because there are some common directories in Linux that are used vigorously and as a result are more prone to failure, it is good practice to mount these directories to their own filesystem. Table 3-1 lists directories that are commonly mounted to separate partitions, as well as lists their recommended sizes.

Each of these filesystems might be of different types. The most common types used today are the **ext2**, **ext3**, **VFAT**, and **REISER** filesystems, although Linux can support upward of 50 different filesystems. Each filesystem essentially performs the same function, which is to store files on a partition; however, each filesystem offers different features and is specialized for different uses. The ext2 filesystem is the traditional filesystem still used on most Linux computers, and the Virtual File Allocation Table (VFAT) filesystem is compatible with the FAT filesystem in Windows. The ext3 and REISER filesystems, however, are much more robust than the ext2 and VFAT filesystems, as they perform a function called **journaling**. A journaling filesystem is one that keeps track of the information written to the hard drive in a journal. If you copy a file on the hard drive from one directory to another, that file must pass into physical memory and then be written to the new location on the hard disk. If the power to the computer is turned off during this process, information might not be transmitted as expected and data might be lost or corrupted. With a journaling filesystem, each step required to copy the file to the new location is first written to a journal, so that the system can retrace the steps the system took prior to a power outage and complete the file copy. Both of these filesystems also host a variety of additional improvements compared to ext2 and VFAT, including faster data transfer and indexing, and as a result are common choices for Linux servers today.

Table 3-1 Common Linux filesystems and sizes

Directory	Description	Recommended Size
/	Contains all directories not present on other filesystems	Depends on the size and number of other filesystems present, but is typically 4GB or more
/boot	Contains the Linux kernel and boot files	50MB
/home	Default location for user home directories	200MB per user
/usr	System commands and utilities	Depends on the packages installed—typically 3GB
/usr/local	Location for most additional programs	Depends on the packages installed—typically 4GB
/opt	An alternate location for additional programs	Depends on the packages installed—typically 4GB
/var	Contains log files and spools	2GB
/tmp	Holds temporary files created by programs	500MB

After the number and types of filesystems required for the installation have been determined, you might choose to allow the Red Hat Linux installation program to automatically partition based on the total amount of hard disk space on your system, or you might choose to manually partition using the Disk Druid graphical partitioning tool, as shown in Figure 3-9.

Disk Druid is an easy-to-use graphical partitioning program; you can delete existing partitions, create and edit new ones, or even create a **redundant array of inexpensive disks (RAID)** volume to prevent data loss if any hard disks break down. RAID is discussed in Chapter 7.

Figure 3-10 shows Disk Druid after two partitions were created for the / filesystem (ext3) and swap. Your disk might look different than the one depicted in Figure 3-10 depending on disk size and number of partitions established. If Windows was first installed, that partition must be removed before new partitions can be added. New partitions can only be allocated from free space. To add additional partitions and filesystems, simply select the New button in Disk Druid and supply the appropriate information, as shown in Figure 3-11.

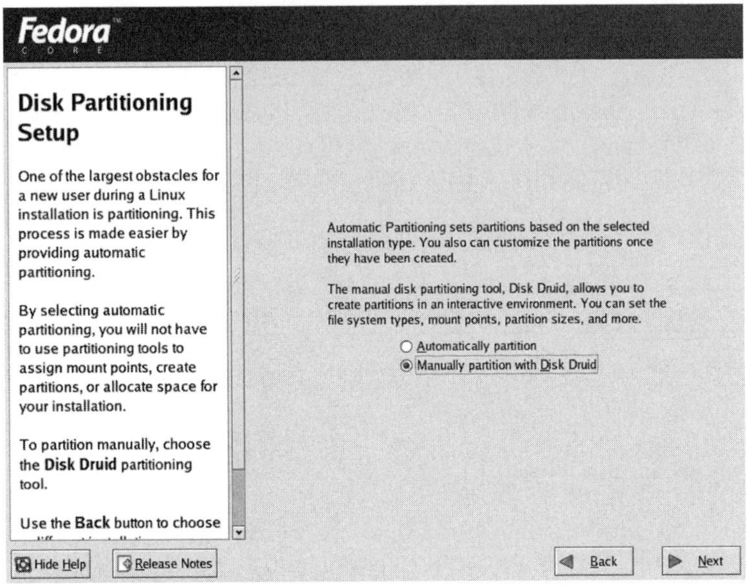

FIGURE 3-9 *Choosing a disk partitioning method*

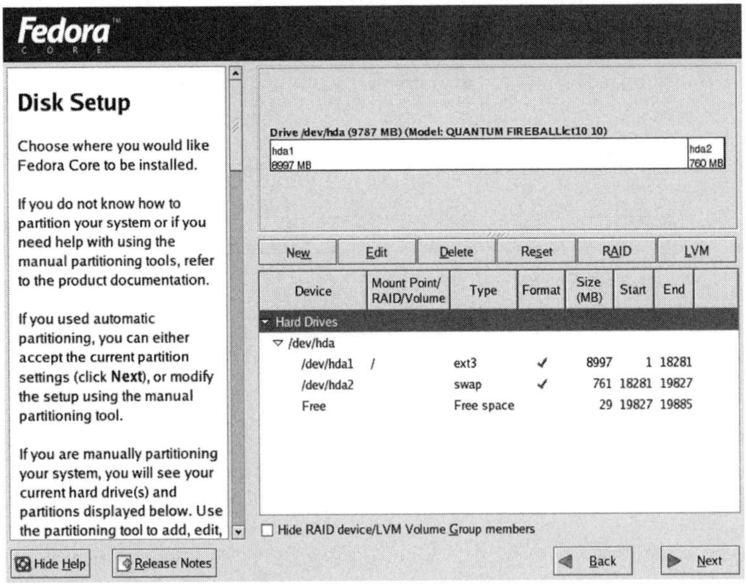

FIGURE 3-10 *The Disk Druid partitioning utility*

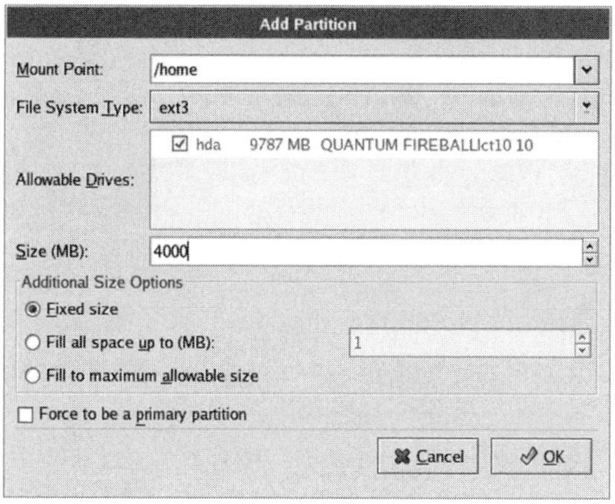

FIGURE 3-11 *Creating a new partition*

Configuring the Boot Loader

After partitions and filesystems have been specified during the installation program, you are prompted to configure the boot loader, as shown in Figure 3-12. A **boot loader** is a program started by the BIOS ROM after POST, which loads the Linux kernel into memory from a hard disk partition inside the computer, yet can also be used to boot (start) other operating systems such as Windows if they exist on the hard drive. The boot loader that you can configure during Red Hat Fedora Linux installation is **GRand Unified Bootloader (GRUB)**. Boot loaders are discussed in Chapter 8, "Working with the BASH Shell."

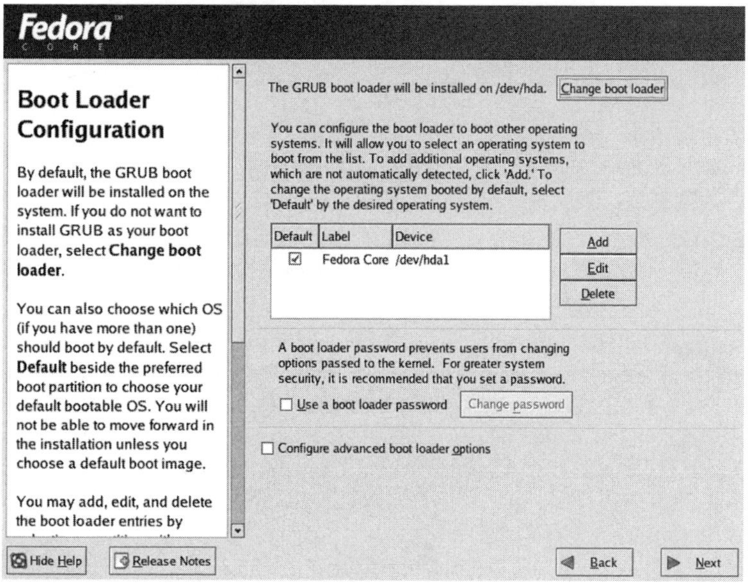

FIGURE 3-12 *Configuring a boot loader*

Red Hat Linux automatically detects Windows operating systems that reside on the hard disk and sets the boot loader to display a screen that allows you to choose the operating system to boot upon system startup; this process is called **dual booting**. If you click the Change boot loader button, as shown in Figure 3-12, you can elect to install GRUB or no boot loader at all. This is often done if you already have Windows NT, Windows 2000, Windows XP, or Windows Server 2003 installed on your hard disk and want to use the Windows boot loader to dual boot both operating systems. In addition, you can select which operating system is the default operating system to boot if none is chosen within a certain period of time at system startup, and whether passwords will be used to prevent unauthorized users from booting the operating system.

If you select the Configure advanced boot loader options check box in Figure 3-12, you can specify additional boot loader configuration, as shown in Figure 3-13.

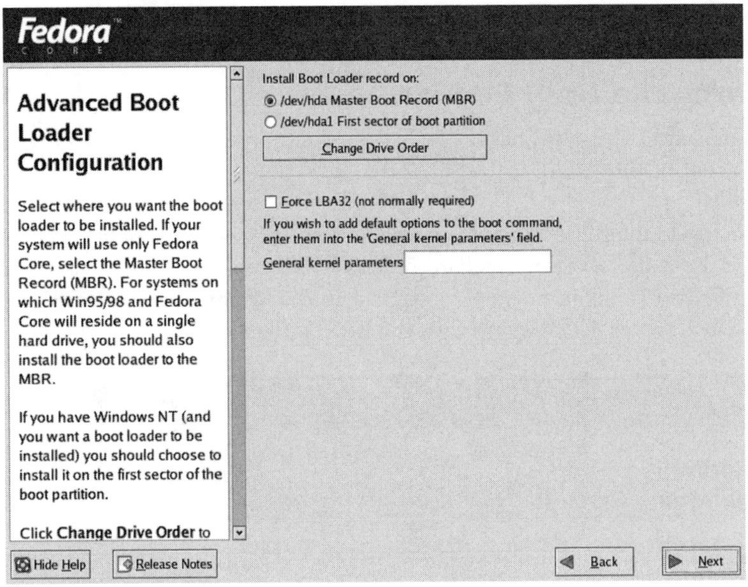

FIGURE 3-13 *Configuring advanced boot loader options*

The most common place for the boot loader to reside is on the Master Boot Record (MBR); however, you can also place it on the first hard disk sector of the / or /boot filesystem partition if you want to use a boot loader from another operating system to boot Linux. In addition to this, you can pass certain information (called **kernel parameters**) to the Linux operating system kernel via the boot loader, or you can force the use of a certain parameter called **large block addressing 32 bit (LBA32)**. LBA32 is only required if the / or /boot partition starts after the 1024th cylinder of the hard disk (after the first 8GB) and the system BIOS does not advertise this information to the boot loader.

Configuring the Network and Firewall

If the network interface card (NIC) is detected by the Red Hat installer, you see a network configuration screen similar to the one shown in Figure 3-14, which allows you to configure whether the NIC will be activated at boot time and what configuration information it will use (manually defined or via DHCP). If you are configuring IP manually, you need to enter the IP address and Netmask (or subnet mask) by clicking the Edit button shown in Figure 3-14. If you do not use DHCP, you should also set the host name, gateway (or default gateway), and primary DNS at minimum to gain Internet access. The secondary and tertiary DNS addresses are for backup purposes in the event the primary DNS is unavailable.

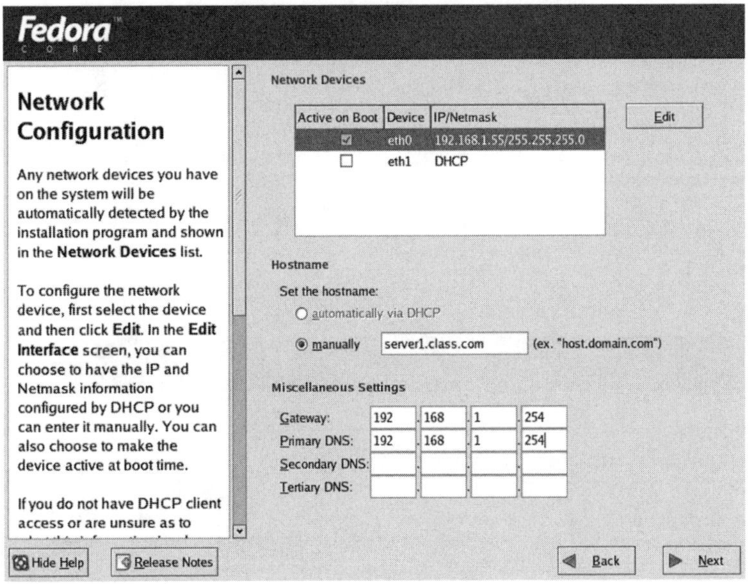

FIGURE 3-14 *Specifying a network configuration*

After the NIC has been configured, you are prompted to choose which network traffic to allow into the Linux system (called a firewall), as shown in Figure 3-15. By choosing the Enable firewall option, your Linux system prevents most traffic from entering your computer, yet allows your computer to access other network services; as a result, it is good form to use a firewall on public networks such as the Internet. In addition, you can choose to customize which traffic is allowed through your firewall.

Choosing a System Language and Time Zone

Earlier during the installation, you were prompted to choose a language for the installation process itself; however, Linux allows the support of multiple languages after installation. Thus, you must choose the language(s) which will be supported by the Linux operating system, as shown in Figure 3-16. You must also choose the appropriate time zone for your region, as depicted in Figure 3-17.

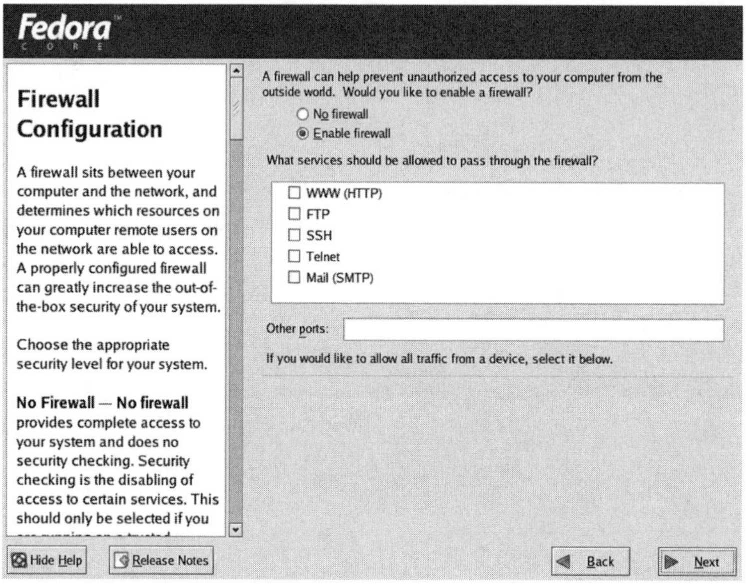

FIGURE 3-15 *Configuring a firewall*

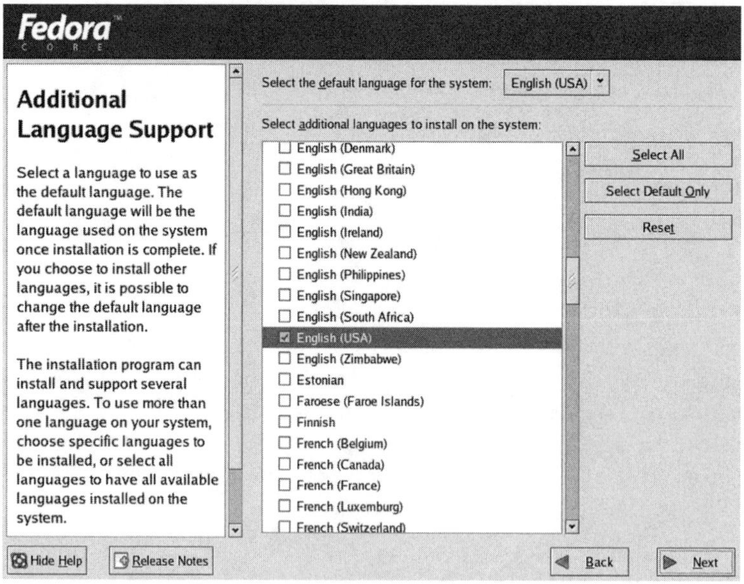

FIGURE 3-16 *Selecting additional language support*

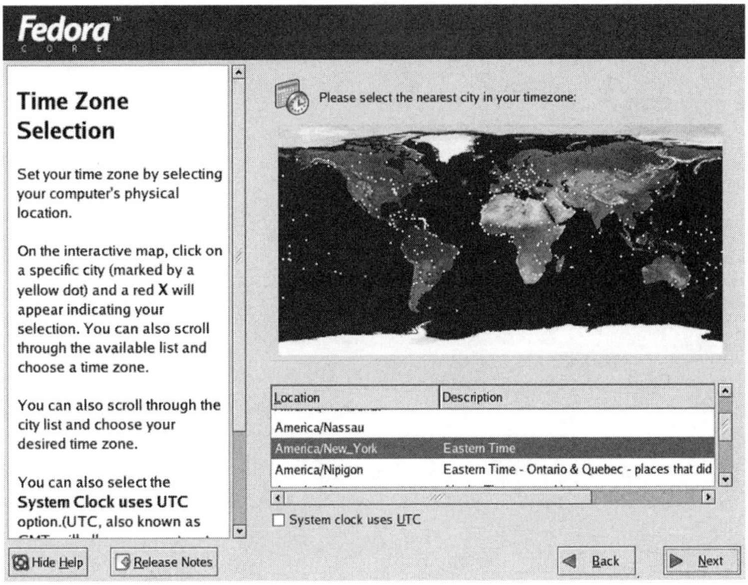

FIGURE 3-17 *Choosing a time zone*

Creating the Root User

All Linux systems require secure access, which means that each user must log in with a valid user name and password before gaining access to a user interface. This process is called **authentication**. During installation, two user accounts should be configured: the administrator account (root), which has full rights to the system, and at least one regular user account. To accomplish this, you specify a password that is at least six characters long for the root user account, as shown in Figure 3-18, and then add another user account to the system on the first boot after installation (discussed later in this chapter).

Selecting Packages

Next, the Red Hat installer provides a list of packages based on the installation type chosen earlier in Figure 3-8. You can choose the general packages required for certain functionality, as shown in Figure 3-19, or you can choose to refine the list of packages by clicking the Details link beside the appropriate package group.

Installing Packages

After the packages have been selected, the Red Hat installation program prompts you to start the file copy process, where the packages selected for installation are copied to filesystems created on the hard disk, as shown in Figure 3-20.

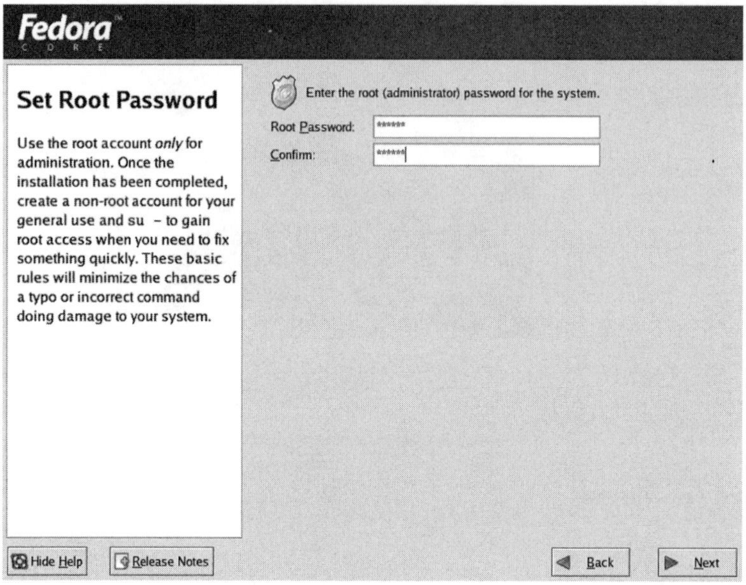

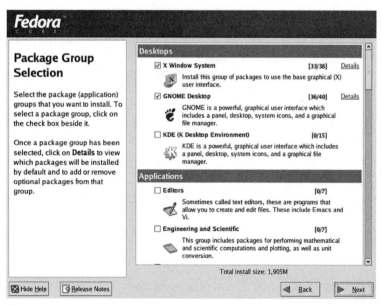

FIGURE 3-18 *Setting a root password*

FIGURE 3-19 *Selecting packages*

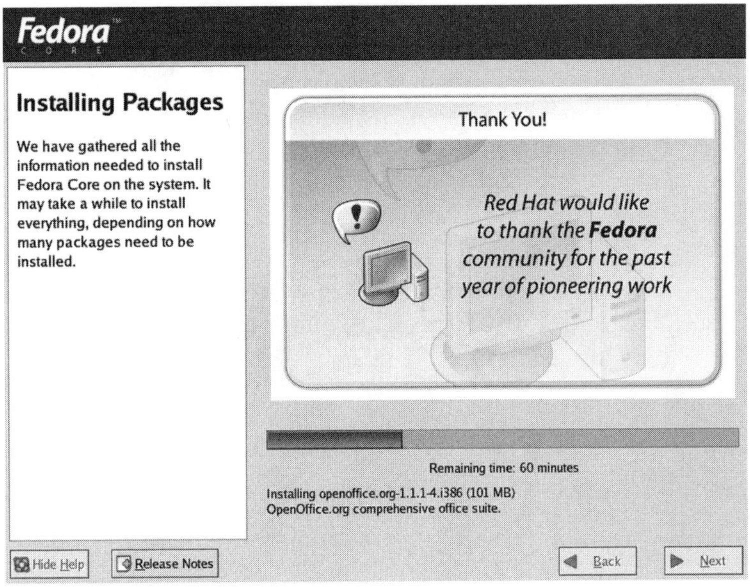

FIGURE 3-20 *Package installation*

After the package installation is finished, the Red Hat installation program displays a Congratulations screen, ejects the CD-ROM from the CD-ROM drive, and prompts you to reboot the system.

Completing the Firstboot Wizard

On the first boot after installation, an interactive utility (called the **firstboot wizard**) appears before the login prompt, as shown in Figure 3-21. After this utility has been completed, it no longer appears when the computer is booted.

If you click the Next button shown in Figure 3-21, you are required to accept a license agreement. Following this, you are prompted to set the date and time or choose to receive time from a reliable time server on the Internet using Network Time Protocol, as shown in Figure 3-22.

Next, you are prompted to choose the default resolution and color depth that will be displayed when the GUI environment is loaded, as shown in Figure 3-23. Following this, you are prompted to create a regular user account, as shown in Figure 3-24. For daily user tasks, you should avoid logging in as the root user to minimize the chance that you will inadvertently change system configuration settings.

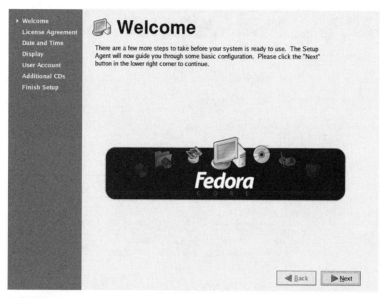

FIGURE 3-21 *The firstboot wizard*

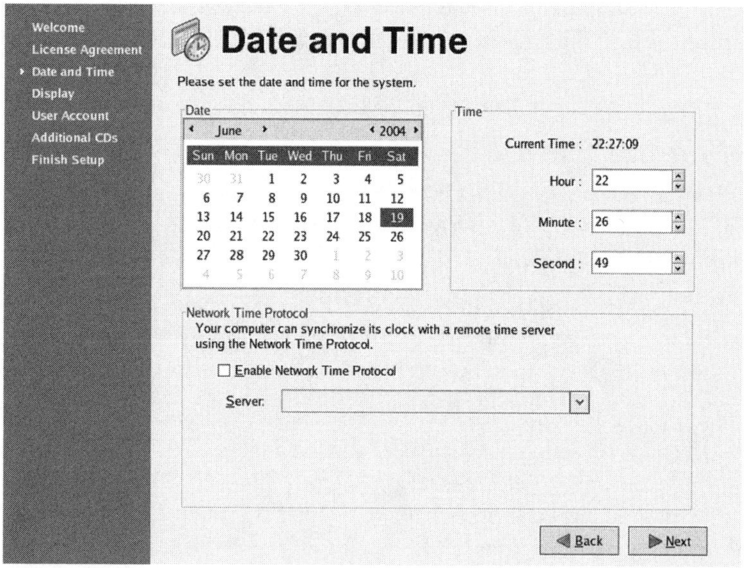

FIGURE 3-22 *Setting the date and time*

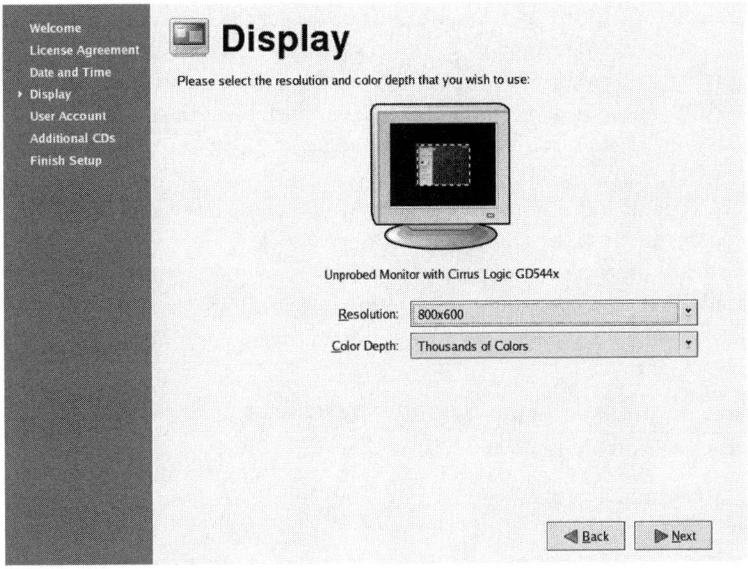

FIGURE 3-23 *Configuring screen resolution and color depth*

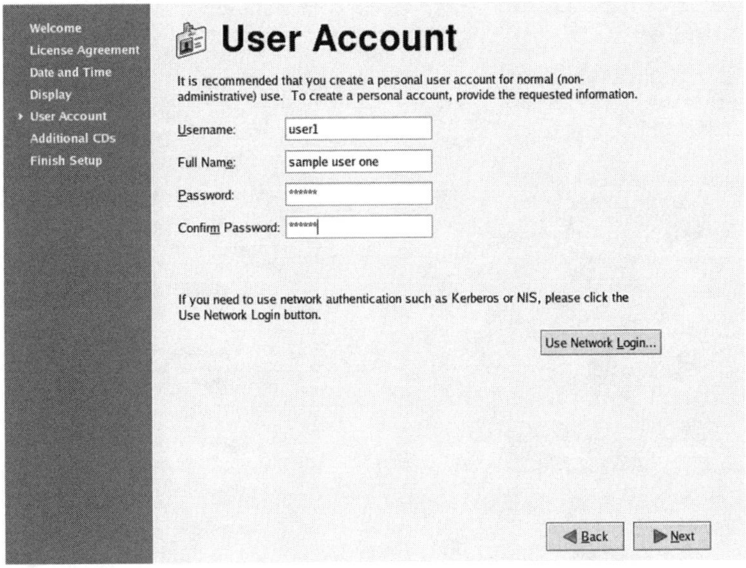

FIGURE 3-24 *Creating a regular user account*

Linux users are authenticated by a password database on the local computer by default. This password database uses MD5 shadow passwords, also by default. Shadow passwords are passwords that are simply stored in a separate database from the user account information for better security. MD5 (Message Digest 5) passwords support a length of up to 256 characters and are encrypted using an MD5 hash algorithm for added security. You can also choose to authenticate some or all users based on a database that resides on another server on the network. NIS shares password databases among Linux systems, whereas LDAP (Lightweight Directory Access Protocol), Kerberos, SMB (Server Message Blocks), and Winbind represent types of authentication and user information services that might be present on other servers on the network. In addition, you can store user information on DNS servers in your network using the Hesiod protocol. The detailed configurations of Hesiod and network authentication are beyond the scope of this book.

To configure authentication options, click the Use Network Login button shown in Figure 3-24 and specify the appropriate parameters, as shown in Figures 3-25 and 3-26.

After a user account and authentication have been configured, the installation program asks whether you want to install additional software. It then prompts you to finish the firstboot wizard and continue to load the remainder of the operating system to use the Linux system for the first time.

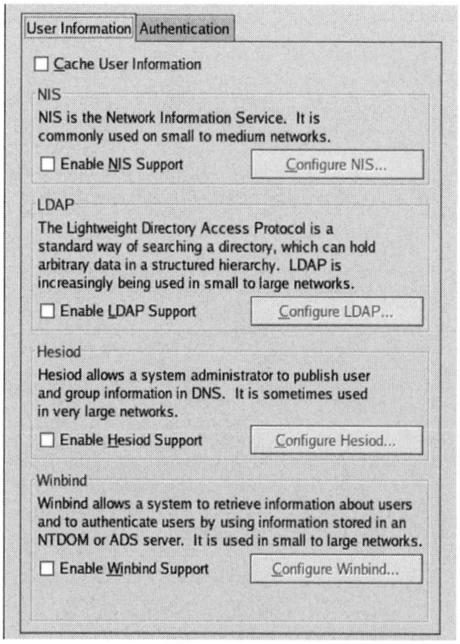

FIGURE 3-25 *Configuring user information*

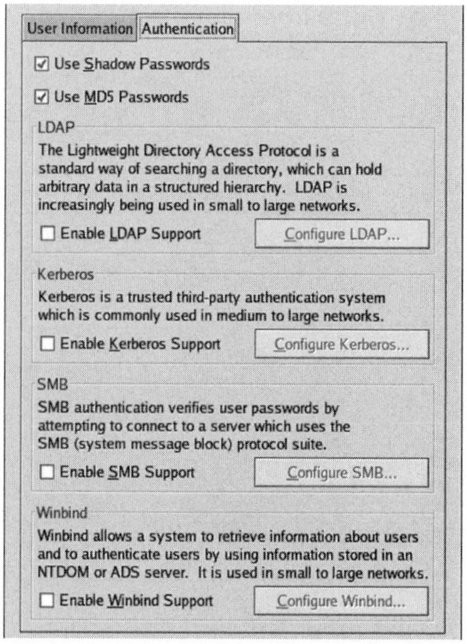

FIGURE 3-26 *Configuring authentication*

> ### NOTE
>
> Depending on your peripheral devices, you might receive additional screens during the installation. For example, if your sound card was detected, you might be prompted to configure sound.

Basic Linux Usage

After the Linux operating system has been installed, you must log in to the system with a valid user name and password and interact with the user interface to perform useful tasks. To do this, it is essential to understand the different types of user interfaces that exist, as well as basic tasks, such as command execution, obtaining online help, and shutting down the Linux system.

Shells, Terminals, and the Kernel

Recall that an operating system is merely a collection of software that allows you to use your computer hardware in a meaningful fashion. Every operating system has a core component, which loads all other components and serves to centrally control the activities of the computer. This component is known as the kernel, and in Linux is simply a file usually called "vmlinuz", which is located on the hard drive and loaded when you first turn your computer on.

When a user interacts with her computer, she is interacting with the kernel of the computer's operating system. However, this interaction cannot happen directly; it must have a channel through which it can access the kernel and a user interface that passes user input to the kernel for processing. The channel that allows a certain user to log in is called a **terminal**, and there can be many terminals in Linux that allow you to log in to the computer locally or across a network. After a user logs in to a terminal, she receives a user interface called a **shell,** which then accepts input from the user and passes this input to the kernel for processing. The shell that is used by default in Linux is the **BASH shell (Bourne Again Shell)**, which is an improved version of the Bourne shell from AT&T and the shell that is used throughout this book. The whole process looks similar to Figure 3-27.

As mentioned earlier, Linux is a multiuser and multitasking operating system, and as such can allow for thousands of terminals. Each terminal could represent a separate logged-in user that has its own shell. The four different "channels" shown in Figure 3-27 could be different users logged in to the same Linux computer. Two users could be logged in locally to the server (seated at the server itself) and the other two could be logged in across a network, such as the Internet.

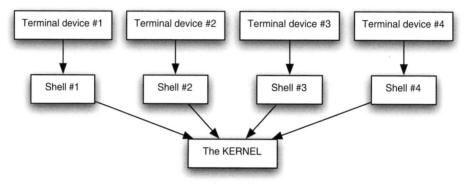

FIGURE 3-27 *Shells, terminals, and the kernel*

By default, when you log in to a terminal, you receive a command-line shell (BASH shell), which prompts you to type in commands to tell the Linux kernel what to do. However, in this computing age, most people prefer to use a graphical interface in which they can use a computer mouse to navigate and start tasks. In this case, you can simply choose to start a graphical user interface (GUI) environment on top of your BASH shell after you are logged in to a command-line terminal, or you can switch to a graphical terminal, which allows users to log in and immediately receive a GUI environment. A typical command-line terminal login prompt looks like the following:

```
Fedora Core release 2 (Tettnang)
Kernel 2.6.5-1.358 on an i686


server1 login:
```

A typical graphical terminal login for Red Hat Linux (called the gdm or GNOME Display Manager) is depicted in Figure 3-28.

To access a terminal device at the local server, you can press a combination of keys such as Ctrl+Alt+F1 to change to a separate terminal. If you are logging in across the network, you can use a variety of programs that connect to a terminal on the Linux computer. A list of local Linux terminals, and their names and types, is shown in Table 3-2.

After you are logged in to a command-line terminal, you receive a prompt where you can enter commands. If you log in as the root user (administrator), a # prompt is used:

```
Fedora Core release 2 (Tettnang)
Kernel 2.6.5-1.358 on an i686


server1 login: root
Password:
Last login: Mon Mar 8 09:45:42 on tty2
[root@server1 root]#_
```

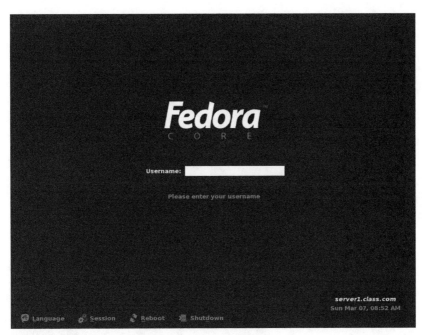

FIGURE 3-28 *The gdm (GNOME Display Manager)*

Table 3-2 Common Linux terminals

Terminal Name	Key Combination	Login Type
tty1	Ctrl+Alt+F1	command-line
tty2	Ctrl+Alt+F2	command-line
tty3	Ctrl+Alt+F3	command-line
tty4	Ctrl+Alt+F4	command-line
tty5	Ctrl+Alt+F5	command-line
tty6	Ctrl+Alt+F6	command-line
tty7 (:0)	Ctrl+Alt+F7	graphical

However, if you log in as a regular user to a command-line terminal (for example, user1), a $ prompt is used:

```
Fedora Core release 2 (Tettnang)
Kernel 2.6.5-1.358 on an i686

server1 login: user1
Password:
Last login: Mon Mar 8 09:45:42 on tty2
[user1@server1 user1]$_
```

When you log in to a graphical terminal, the GUI environment of your choice is started; the default GUI environment in Red Hat Linux is GNOME. After the GUI environment starts, you can access a command-line Terminal window by navigating to the Red Hat menu, System Tools, Terminal, as shown in Figure 3-29.

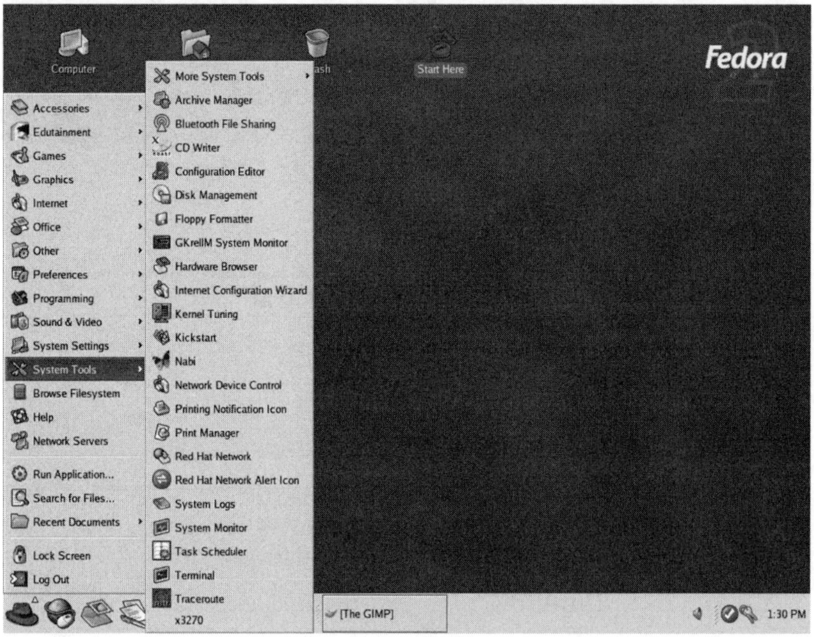

FIGURE 3-29 *Accessing a command-line terminal in a GUI environment*

Basic Shell Commands

When using a command-line terminal, the shell ultimately interprets all information the user enters onto the command line. This information includes the command itself, as well as options and arguments. **Commands** indicate the name of the program to execute and are case sensitive. **Options** are specific letters that start with a dash "-" and appear after the command name to alter the way the command works. Options are specific to the command in question; the persons who developed the command determined which options to allow for that command.

> **NOTE**
>
> Some options start with two dashes "--"; these options are referred to as POSIX options and are usually composed of a whole word, not just a letter.

Arguments also appear after the command name, yet do not start with a dash. They specify the command's working parameters, which are not predetermined by the person who developed the command. Suppose, for example, that you want to list all of the files in the /etc/ntp directory on the hard drive. You could use the ls command with the -a option (which tells the ls command to list all files) and the /etc/ntp argument (which tells ls to look in the /etc/ntp directory), as shown in the following example:

```
[root@server1 root]# ls -a /etc/ntp
. .. keys ntpservers step-tickers
[root@server1 root]#_
```

After you type the command and press Enter in the preceding output, the ls command shows us that there are three files in the /etc/ntp directory and returns your command prompt such that you can enter another command.

> **NOTE**
>
> Commands, options, and arguments are case sensitive; an uppercase letter (A), for instance, is treated differently than a lowercase letter (a).

> **TIP**
>
> Always put a space between the command name, options, and arguments; otherwise, the shell does not understand that they are separate and your command might not work as expected.

Although you can pass options and arguments to commands, not all commands need to have arguments or options supplied on the command line to work properly. The date command is one example that simply prints the current date and time:

```
[root@server1 root]# date
Tue Mar 29 08:58:36 EST 2005
[root@server1 root]#_
```

Table 3-3 lists some common commands that you can use without specifying any options or arguments.

Table 3-3 Some common Linux commands

Command	Description
clear	Clears the terminal screen
reset	Resets your terminal to use default terminal settings
finger	Displays information on system users
who	Displays currently logged-in users
w	Displays currently logged-in users and their tasks
whoami	Displays your login name
id	Displays the numbers associated with your user account name and group names; these are commonly referred to as User IDs (UIDs) and Group IDs (GIDs)
date	Displays the current date and time
cal	Displays the calendar for the current month
exit	Exits out of your current shell

If the output of a certain command is too large to fit on the terminal screen, simply use the Shift and Page Up keys simultaneously to view previous screens of information. Also, Shift and Page Down can be used to navigate in the opposite direction when pressed simultaneously.

You can recall commands previously entered in the BASH shell using the keyboard cursor keys (the up, down, right, and left arrow keys). Thus, if you want to enter the same command again, simply cycle through the list of available commands with the keyboard cursor keys and press Enter to reexecute that command.

Shell Metacharacters

Another important feature of the shell includes shell **metacharacters**, which are keyboard characters that have special meaning. One of the most commonly used metacharacters is the $ character, which tells the shell that the following text refers to a variable. A variable is simply a piece of information that is stored in memory; variable names are typically uppercase words and most variables are set by the Linux system automatically when you log in. An example of how you might use the $ metacharacter to refer to a variable is by using the echo command (which prints text to the terminal screen):

```
[root@server1 root]# echo Hi There!
Hi There!
[root@server1 root]# echo My shell is $SHELL
My Shell is /bin/bash
[root@server1 root]#_
```

Notice from the preceding output that $SHELL was translated into its appropriate value from memory (/bin/bash, the BASH shell). The shell recognized SHELL as a variable because it was prefixed by the $ metacharacter. A list of common BASH shell metacharacters that are discussed throughout this book are listed in Table 3-4.

Table 3-4 Common BASH shell metacharacters

Metacharacter(s)	Description
$	Shell variable
~	Special home directory variable
&	Background command execution
;	Command termination
< << > >>	Input/Output redirection
|	Command piping
* ? [ ]	Shell wildcards
' " \	Metacharacter quotes
`	Command substitution
( ) { }	Command grouping

It is good practice to avoid metacharacters when typing commands unless you need to take advantage of their special functionality, as the shell readily interprets them, which might lead to unexpected results.

> **NOTE**
>
> If you accidentally use one of these characters and your shell does not return you to the normal prompt, simply press the Ctrl and c keys in combination and your current command is canceled.

There are some circumstances in which you might need to use a metacharacter in a command and prevent the shell from interpreting its special meaning. To do this, simply enclose the metacharacters in single quotation marks ' '. Single quotation marks protect those metacharacters from being interpreted specially by the shell (that is, a $ is interpreted as a $ character and not a variable identifier). You can also use double quotation marks " " to perform the same task; however, double quotation marks do not protect $, \, and ` characters. If only one character needs to be protected from shell interpretation, you can precede that character by a \ rather than enclosing it within quotation marks. An example of this type of quoting is:

```
[root@server1 root]# echo My Shell is $SHELL
My Shell is /bin/bash
[root@server1 root]# echo 'My Shell is $SHELL'
My Shell is $SHELL
[root@server1 root]# echo "My Shell is $SHELL"
My Shell is /bin/bash
[root@server1 root]# echo My Shell is \$SHELL
My Shell is $SHELL
[root@server1 root]#_
```

As shown in Table 3-4, not all quote characters protect characters from the shell. The back quote characters ` ` can be used to perform command substitution; anything between back quotes is treated as another command by the shell and its output is substituted in place of the back quotes. Take the expression `date` as an example:

```
[root@server1 root]# echo Today is `date`
Today is Tue Mar 29 09:28:11 EST 2005
[root@server1 root]#_
```

Getting Command Help

Most distributions of Linux contain more than 1000 different Linux commands in most configurations, and, thus, it is impractical to memorize the syntax and use of each command. Fortunately, Linux stores documentation for each command in central locations so that it can be accessed easily. The most common form of documentation for Linux commands is **manual pages** (commonly referred to as man pages). Simply type the man command followed by a command name, and extensive information about that Linux command is displayed page-by-page on the terminal screen. This information includes a description of the command and its syntax, as well as available options, related files, and commands. For example, to receive information on the format and usage of the whoami command, you can use the following command:

```
[root@server1 root]# man whoami
```

The manual page is then displayed page-by-page on the terminal screen. You can use the cursor (arrow) keys on the keyboard to scroll though the information or press q to quit. The manual page for whoami is similar to the following:

```
WHOAMI(1)                    User Commands                    WHOAMI(1)


NAME
       whoami - print effective userid

SYNOPSIS
       whoami [OPTION]...

DESCRIPTION
       Print  the user name associated with the current effective
       user id. Same as id -un.

       --help   display this help and exit

       --version
         output version information and exit

AUTHOR
    Written by Richard Mlynarik.

REPORTING BUGS
       Report bugs to <bug-coreutils@gnu.org>.

COPYRIGHT
       Copyright © 2004 Free Software Foundation, Inc.
       This is free software; see the source for  copying  condi_
       tions. There is NO warranty; not even for MERCHANTABILITY
       or FITNESS FOR A PARTICULAR PURPOSE.
```

```
SEE ALSO
       The full documentation for whoami is maintained as a  Tex_
       info manual. If the info and who programs are properly
       installed at your site, the command

              info coreutils whoami

       should give you access to the complete manual.

whoami 5.2.1                  May 2004                    WHOAMI(1)
[root@server1 root]#_
```

Notice that the whoami command is displayed as WHOAMI(1) at the top of the preceding manual page output. The (1) denotes a section of the manual pages; section (1) means that whoami is a command that can be executed by any user. All manual pages contain certain section numbers that describe the category of the command in the manual page database; you can find a list of the different manual page section numbers in Table 3-5.

Table 3-5 Manual page section numbers

Manual Page Section	Description
1	Commands that any user can execute
2	Linux system calls
3	Library routines
4	Special device files
5	File formats
6	Games
7	Macro packages
8	Commands that only the root user can execute
9	Linux kernel routines
n	New commands not categorized yet

Sometimes, there is more than one command, library routine, or file that has the same name. If you run the man command with that name as an argument, Linux returns the manual page with the lowest section number. For example, if there is a file called whoami as well as a command named whoami and you type man whoami, the manual page for the whoami command (section 1 of the manual pages) is displayed. To display the manual page for the whoami file format instead, you simply type man 5 whoami to display the whoami file format (section 5 of the manual pages).

Recall that many commands are available to the Linux user; thus, it might be cumbersome to find the command that you need to perform a certain task without using a Linux command dictionary. Fortunately, you have the ability to search the manual pages by keyword. To find all of the commands that have the word "usb" in their name or description, type the following:

```
[root@server1 root] # man -k usb
```

This command produces the following output:

```
energizerups         (8)  - Driver for Energizer (Megatec protocol over USB To RS232
                            Interface (V1.0) BaudRate 2400bps) UPS equipment
fxload               (8)  - Firmware download to EZ-USB devices
lsusb                (8)  - list all USB devices
sane-canon630u       (5)  - SANE backend for the Canon 630u USB flatbed scanner
sane-find-scanner    (1)  - find SCSI and USB scanners and their device files
sane-gt68xx          (5)  - SANE backend for GT-68XX based USB flatbed scanners
sane-ma1509          (5)  - SANE backend for Mustek BearPaw 1200F USB scanner
sane-mustek_usb      (5)  - SANE backend for Mustek USB flatbed scanners
sane-plustek         (5)  - SANE backend for Plustek parallel port and LM983[1/2/3] based
                            USB flatbed scanners
sane-sm3600          (5)  - SANE backend for Microtek scanners with MO11 USB chip
sane-usb             (5)  - USB configuration tips for SANE
usbmodules           (8)  - List kernel driver modules available for a
plugged in USB device
[root@server1 root]#_
```

After you find the command needed, you can simply run the man command on that command without the -k option to find out detailed information about the command.

🔷 NOTE

You can also use the apropos usb command to perform the same function as the man -k usb command. Both commands yield the exact same output on the terminal screen.

If you do not see any output from the man -k or apropos commands following a Linux installation, you might need to run the makewhatis command to index the manual page database.

Another utility, originally intended to replace the man command in Linux, is the GNU **info pages**. You can access this utility by typing the info command followed by the name of the command in question. The info command returns an easy-to-read description of each command and also contains links to other information pages (called hyperlinks). Today, however, both the info pages and the manual pages are used to find documentation because manual pages have been utilized in Linux since its conception, and for over two decades in the UNIX operating system. An example of using the info utility to find information about the whoami command follows:

```
[root@server1 root]# info whoami
```

The info page is then displayed interactively:

```
File: coreutils.info, Node: whoami invocation, Next: groups invocation, Prev: logname
invocation, Up: User information


`whoami': Print effective user id
==================================


`whoami' prints the user name associated with the current effective
user id. It is equivalent to the command `id -un'.

   The only options are `--help' and `--version'. *Note Common options::.

   An exit status of zero indicates success, and a nonzero value indicates failure.

Welcome to Info version 4.6. Type ? for help, m for menu item.
[root@server1 root]#_
```

> **NOTE**
>
> While in the info utility, press the ? key or Ctrl+h key combination to display a help screen that describes the usage of info. As with the man command, you can use the q key to quit.

Some commands do not have manual pages or info pages. These commands are usually functions that are built into the BASH shell itself. To find help on these commands, you must use the help command as follows:

```
[root@server1 root]# help echo
echo: echo [-neE] [arg ...]
    Output the ARGs. If -n is specified, the trailing newline is
    suppressed. If the -e option is given, interpretation of the
```

following backslash-escaped characters is turned on:
```
\a    alert (bell)
\b    backspace
\c    suppress trailing newline
\E    escape character
\f    form feed
\n    new line
\r    carriage return
\t    horizontal tab
\v    vertical tab
\\    backslash
\num  the character whose ASCII code is NUM (octal).
```

You can explicitly turn off the interpretation of the above characters with the -E option.
```
[root@server1 root]#_
```

Shutting Down the Linux System

Because the operating system handles writing data from computer memory to the disk drives in a computer, simply turning off the power to the computer might result in damaged user and system files. Thus, it is important to prepare the operating system for shutdown before turning off the power to the hardware components of the computer. To do this, you can issue the shutdown command, which can halt or reboot (restart) your computer after a certain period of time. To halt your system in 15 minutes, for example, you could type:

```
[root@server1 root] # shutdown -h +15
```

This produces output similar to the following:

```
Broadcast message from root (tty2) (Tue Mar 29 04:08:18 2005):

The system is going DOWN for system halt in 15 minutes!
```

Notice from the preceding output that you do not receive the command prompt back again after the shutdown command has started. Thus, to stop the shutdown, simply press the Ctrl and c keys in combination to cancel the command. Alternatively, you can log in to another terminal and issue the command shutdown -c to cancel the shutdown.

To halt your system now, you could type:

```
[root@server1 root] # shutdown -h now
```

This command produces output similar to the following:

```
Broadcast message from root (tty2) (Tue Mar 29 04:08:18 2005):

The system is going DOWN for system halt NOW!
```

Other examples of the shutdown command and their descriptions are shown in Table 3-6.

Table 3-6 Commands to halt and reboot the Linux operating system

Command	Description
shutdown -h +4	Halts your system in four minutes
shutdown -r +4	`Reboots your system in four minutes
shutdown -h now	Halts your system immediately
shutdown -r now	Reboots your system immediately
shutdown -c	Cancels a scheduled shutdown
halt	Halts your system immediately
reboot	Reboots your system immediately

Chapter Summary

◆ Most software information can be specified at the time of installation; however, the network configuration and package selection should be carefully planned before installation.

◆ Although many methods are available for installation of Linux, a CD-ROM-based installation is the easiest, most common method and seldom requires the creation of an installation boot disk.

◆ A typical Linux installation prompts the user for information such as language, boot loader, hard disk partitions, network configuration, firewall configuration, time zone, user accounts, authentication, and package selection.

◆ Users must log in to a terminal and receive a shell before they are able to interact with the Linux system and kernel. One user can log in several different times simultaneously to several different terminals locally or across a network.

◆ Regardless of the type of terminal that you use (graphical or command-line), you are able to enter commands, options, and arguments at a shell prompt to perform system tasks, obtain command help, or shut down the Linux system. The shell is case sensitive and understands a variety of special characters called shell metacharacters, which should be protected if their special meaning is not required.

Key Terms

arguments — The text that appears after a command name, does not start with a dash "-" character, and specifies information the command requires to work properly.

authentication — The process whereby each user must log in with a valid user name and password before gaining access to the user interface of a system.

BASH shell — The Bourne Again Shell; it is the default command-line interface in Linux.

boot loader — A small program started by BIOS ROM, which executes the Linux kernel in memory.

command — A program that exists on the hard drive and is executed when typed on the command line.

Disk Druid — An easy-to-use graphic program used to partition or modify the partitions on an HDD.

dual booting — The process of installing more than one operating system on a computer. The user can then choose the operating system to load at system startup.

ext2 — A nonjournaling Linux filesystem.

ext3 — A journaling Linux filesystem.

firstboot wizard — A configuration utility that is run at system startup immediately following a Red Hat Fedora Linux installation.

framebuffer — An abstract representation of video hardware used by programs such that they do not need to communicate directly with the video hardware.

GRand Unified Bootloader (GRUB) — A common boot loader used in Linux.

info pages — A set of local, easy-to-read command syntax documentation available by typing the `info` command-line utility.

journaling — A filesystem function that keeps track of the information that needs to be written to the hard drive in a journal; common Linux journaling filesystems include ext3 and REISER.

kernel parameters — The specific pieces of information that can be passed to the Linux kernel to alter how it works.

large block addressing 32-bit (LBA32) — A parameter that can be specified that enables large block addressing in a boot loader; it is required only if a large hard disk that is not fully supported by the system BIOS is used.

manual pages — The most common set of local command syntax documentation, available by typing the `man` command-line utility. Also known as man pages.

metacharacters — The key combinations that have special meaning in the Linux operating system.

options — The specific letters that start with a dash "-" or two and appear after the command name to alter the way the command works.

redundant array of inexpensive disks (RAID) — A type of storage that can be used to combine hard disks together for fault tolerance.

REISER — A journaling filesystem used in Linux.

shell — A user interface that accepts input from the user and passes the input to the kernel for processing.

swap memory — *See also* Virtual memory.

terminal — The channel that allows a certain user to log in and communicate with the kernel via a user interface.

VFAT (Virtual File Allocation Table) — A nonjournaling filesystem that might be used in Linux.

virtual memory — An area on a hard disk (swap partition) that can be used to store information that normally resides in physical memory (RAM), if the physical memory is being used excessively.

Review Questions

1. What is the first screen during the graphical portion of the installation of Linux?
   a. Configuring the mouse
   b. Choosing the keyboard
   c. Choosing the installation language
   d. Specifying the installation type

2. _____ consists of an area on the hard disk for storing information that would normally reside in physical memory (RAM) if the physical memory is being used excessively.
   a. Virtual memory
   b. Memory partition
   c. Physical RAM
   d. The Linux kernel

3. What is the recommended size for the default location for user home directories (per user)?
   a. 50 MB
   b. 100 MB
   c. 200 MB
   d. 400 MB

4. The _____ command displays information on system users.
   a. clear
   b. finger
   c. who
   d. whoami

5. Which of the following commands reboots the system immediately?
   a. shutdown –r now
   b. shutdown –r +4
   c. shutdown –h +4
   d. shutdown –h now

6. True or false? Installing the Linux operating system involves interacting with an installation program, which prompts the user for information regarding the nature of the Linux system being installed.

7. True or false? If a previous version of Red Hat is detected by the installation, you are required to upgrade the previous installation of Red Hat Linux that exists on the hard drive.

8. True or false? During installation, only one user account should be configured: the administrator account (root), which has full rights to the system.

9. True or false? In a shell, commands are case sensitive.

10. True or false? All commands must have either a manual or info page.

11. _____ are abstract representations of video adapter card hardware that programs can use instead of directly communicating with the video adapter card hardware.

12. A(n) _____ installation contains few workstation packages, but several server services.

13. _____ booting refers to the Boot Loader allowing the user to choose between Linux and another operating system, such as Windows.

14. After a user logs in to a terminal, she receives a user interface called a(n) _____, which then accepts input from the user and passes this input to the kernel for processing.

15. The most common form of documentation for Linux commands are _____ pages.

Chapter 4

Exploring Linux Filesystems

After completing this chapter, you will be able to:

◆ Understand and navigate the Linux directory structure using relative and absolute pathnames

◆ Describe the various types of Linux files

◆ View filenames and file types

◆ Use shell wildcards to specify multiple filenames

◆ Display the contents of text files and binary files

◆ Search text files for regular expressions using `grep`

◆ Identify common text editors used today

◆ Use the vi editor to manipulate text files

An understanding of the structure and commands surrounding the Linux filesystem is essential for effectively using Linux to manipulate data. In the first part of this chapter, you explore the Linux filesystem hierarchy by changing your position in the filesystem tree and listing filenames of various types. Next, you examine the shell wildcard metacharacters used to specify multiple filenames as well as view the contents of files using standard Linux commands. You then learn about the regular expression metacharacters used when searching for text within files, and are introduced to the vi text editor and its equivalents.

The Linux Directory Structure

Fundamental to using the Linux operating system is an understanding of how Linux stores files on the hard drive. Typical Linux systems could have thousands of data and program files on the hard drive; thus, a structure that organizes those files is necessary to make it easier to find and manipulate data and run programs. Recall from the previous chapter that Linux uses a logical directory tree to organize files into different directories (also known as folders). When a user stores files in a certain **directory**, they are physically stored in the filesystem of a certain partition on a hard disk inside the computer. Most people are familiar with the Windows operating system directory tree structure as depicted in Figure 4-1; each filesystem on a hard drive partition is referred to by a drive letter (such as C: or D:) and has a root directory (indicated by the \ character) containing subdirectories that together form a hierarchical tree.

It is important to describe directories in the directory tree properly; the **absolute pathname** to a file or directory is the full pathname of a certain file or directory starting from the root directory. From Figure 4-1, the absolute pathname for the color directory is C:\windows\color and the absolute pathname for the sue directory is D:\home\sue. In other words, we refer to C:\windows\color as the color directory below the windows directory below the root of C drive. Similarly, we refer to D:\home\sue as the sue directory below the home directory below the root of D drive.

Linux uses a similar directory structure; however, there are no drive letters. There is a single root (referred to using the / character), and different filesystems on hard drive partitions are mounted to different directories on this directory tree such that filesystems are transparent to the user. An example of a sample Linux directory tree equivalent to the Windows sample directory tree shown in Figure 4-1 is depicted in Figure 4-2.

From Figure 4-2, the absolute pathname for the color directory is /windows/color and the absolute pathname for the sue directory is /home/sue. In other words, we refer to the /windows/color directory as the color directory below the windows directory below the root of the system (the / character). Similarly, we refer to the /home/sue directory as the sue directory below the home directory below the root of the system.

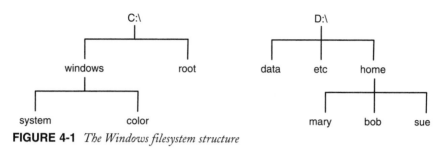

FIGURE 4-1 *The Windows filesystem structure*

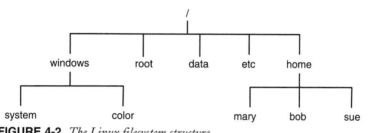

FIGURE 4-2 *The Linux filesystem structure*

Changing Directories

When a user logs in to his Linux system, he is placed in his **home directory**, which is a place unique to each user to store his personal files. Regular users usually have a home directory named after their user account under the /home directory as in /home/sue. The root user, however, has a home directory called root under the root directory of the system (/root), as shown in Figure 4-2. You can confirm the system directory that you are currently in by observing the name at the end of the shell prompt or by typing the **pwd (print working directory) command** at a command-line prompt and pressing Enter. If you are logged in as the root user, the following output is displayed on the terminal screen:

```
[root@server1 root]# pwd
/root
[root@server1 root]#_
```

However, if you are logged in as the user sue, you see the following output:

```
[sue@server1 sue]$ pwd
/home/sue
[sue@server1 sue]$_
```

To change directories, you can issue the **cd (change directory) command** with an argument specifying the destination directory. If you do not specify a destination directory, the cd command simply returns you to your home directory:

```
[root@server1 root]# cd /home/mary
[root@server1 mary]# pwd
/home/mary
```

```
[root@server1 mary]# cd /etc
[root@server1 etc]# pwd
/etc
[root@server1 etc]# cd
[root@server1 root]# pwd
/root
[root@server1 root]#_
```

The ~ **metacharacter** can also be used to refer to the current user's home directory. Or, you can also use the ~ metacharacter to specify another user's home directory by appending a user name at the end of the ~ metacharacter:

```
[root@server1 root]# cd ~mary
[root@server1 mary]# pwd
/home/mary
[root@server1 mary]# cd ~
[root@server1 root]# pwd
/root
[root@server1 root]#_
```

In many of the examples discussed earlier, the argument specified after the cd command is an absolute pathname to a directory, meaning that the system has all the information it needs to find the destination directory because the pathname starts from the root (/) of the system. However, in most Linux commands, you can also use a relative pathname in place of an absolute pathname to reduce typing. A **relative pathname** is the pathname of a target file or directory relative to your current directory in the tree. To specify a directory underneath your current directory, simply refer to that directory by name (do not start the pathname with a / character). To refer to a directory one step closer to the root of the tree (also known as a parent directory), simply use two dots (..). An example of using relative pathnames to move around the directory tree is shown next:

```
[root@server1 root]# cd /home/mary
[root@server1 mary]# pwd
/home/mary
[root@server1 mary]# cd ..
[root@server1 home]# pwd
/home
[root@server1 home]# cd mary
[root@server1 mary]# pwd
/home/mary
[root@server1 mary]#_
```

In the preceding example, we used ".." to move up one parent directory and then used the word "mary" to specify the mary **subdirectory** relative to our current location in the tree; however, you can also move more than one level up or down the directory tree:

```
[root@server1 root]# cd /home/mary
[root@server1 mary]# pwd
/home/mary
[root@server1 mary]# cd ../..
[root@server1 /]# pwd
/
[root@server1 /]# cd home/mary
[root@server1 mary]# pwd
/home/mary
[root@server1 mary]#_
```

> **NOTE**
>
> You can also use one dot (.) to refer to the current directory. Although this is not useful when using the cd command, you do use one dot later in this book.

Although absolute pathnames are straightforward to use as arguments to commands when specifying the location of a certain file or directory, relative pathnames can save you a great deal of typing and reduce the potential for error if your current directory is far away from the root directory. Suppose, for example, that the current directory is /home/sue/projects/acme/plans and you need to change this to the /home/sue/projects/acme directory. Using an absolute pathname, you would type cd /home/sue/projects/acme; however, using a relative pathname, you only need to type cd .. to perform the same task because the /home/sue/projects/acme directory is one parent directory above the current location in the directory tree.

An alternative method for saving time when typing pathnames as arguments to commands is to use the **Tab-completion feature** of the BASH shell. To do this, type enough unique letters of a directory and press the Tab key to allow the BASH shell to find the intended file or directory being specified and fill in the appropriate information. If there is more than one possible match, the Tab-completion feature alerts you with a beep; pressing the Tab key again after this beep presents you with a list of possible files or directories.

Observe the directory structure in Figure 4-2. To use the Tab-completion feature to change the current directory to /home/sue, you simply type cd /h and then press the Tab key. This changes the previous characters on the terminal screen to display cd /home/ (the BASH shell was able to fill in the appropriate information because the /home directory is the only directory underneath the / directory that starts with the letter "h"). Then, you could add an s character to the command such that the command line displays cd /home/s, and press the Tab key once again to allow the shell to fill in the remaining letters. This results in the command cd /home/sue/ being displayed on the terminal screen (the sue directory is the only directory that begins with the s character underneath the /home directory). At this point, you can press Enter to execute the command and change the current directory to /home/sue.

NOTE

The Tab-completion feature of the BASH shell can also be used to specify the path-name to files and executable programs as well as directories.

Viewing Files and Directories

After a directory structure exists to organize files into an easy-to-use format, you can list directory contents to locate the file you need to execute, view, or edit. Before doing this, you should understand the various types of files and filenames that can be listed, as well as the different commands used to select filenames for viewing.

File Types

Fundamental to viewing files and directories is a solid understanding of the various types of files present on most Linux systems. Several different types of files can exist on a Linux system; the most common include the following:

- ◆ Text files
- ◆ Binary data files
- ◆ Executable program files
- ◆ Directory files
- ◆ Linked files
- ◆ Special device files
- ◆ Named pipes and sockets

Most files on a Linux system that contain configuration information are **text files**. Programs are also files that exist on the hard drive before they are executed in memory to become processes, and are usually associated with several supporting **binary data files** that store information such as common functions and graphics. In addition, directories themselves are just special files that serve as placeholders to organize other files. When you create a directory, a file is placed on the hard drive to represent that directory.

Linked files are files that have an association with one another; they can represent the same data or they can point to another file (also known as a shortcut file). **Special device files** are less common than the other file types that have been mentioned, yet they are important for systems administrators because they represent different devices on the system, such as hard disks and serial ports. These device files are used in conjunction with commands that manipulate devices on the system; special device files are typically found only in the /dev directory and are discussed in later chapters of this book. As with special device files, **named pipe files** are uncommon and used primarily by administrators. Named pipes identify a channel that passes information from one process in memory to another, and in some cases can be mediated by files on the hard drive. Writes to the file are processed while another process reads from it to achieve this passing of information. Another variant of a named pipe file is a **socket file**, which allows a process on another computer to write to a file on the local computer while another process reads from that file.

Filenames

Files are recognized by their **filenames**, which can include up to 255 characters, yet are rarely longer than 20 characters on most Linux systems. Filenames are typically composed of alphanumeric characters, the underscore (_) character, the dash (-) character, and the period (.) character.

NOTE

It is important to avoid using the shell metacharacters discussed in the previous chapter when naming files. Using a filename that contains a shell metacharacter as an argument to a Linux command might produce unexpected results.

Filenames that start with a period (.) are referred to as hidden files, and require a special command to be seen. This command is discussed later in this chapter.

Although filenames used by the Windows operating system typically end with a period and three characters that describe the file type, as in document.txt (text) and server.exe (**executable program**), most files on the hard drive of a Linux system do not follow this pattern. However, some files on the Linux filesystem do contain characters at the end of the filename that indicate the file type. These characters are commonly referred to as **filename extensions**; Table 4-1 lists common examples of filename extensions and their associated file types.

Table 4-1 Common filename extensions

Metacharacter	Description
.c	C programming language source code files
.cc, .cpp	C++ programming language source code files
.html, .htm	HTML (Hypertext Markup Language) files
.ps	Files formatted for printing with postscript
.txt	Text files
.tar	Archived files (contain other files within)

Table 4-1 Common filename extensions (Continued)

Metacharacter	Description
.gz, .bz2, .Z	Compressed files
.tar.gz, .tgz, .tar.bz2, .tar.Z	Compressed archived files
.conf, .cfg	Configuration files (contain text)
.so	Shared object (programming library) files
.o	Compiled object files
.pl	PERL (Practical Extraction and Report Language) programs
.tcl	Tcl (Tool Command Language) programs
.jpg, .jpeg, .png, .tiff, .xpm, .gif	Binary files that contain graphical images
.sh	Shell scripts (contain text that is executed by the shell)

Listing Files

Linux hosts a variety of commands, which can be used to display files and their types in various directories on hard drive partitions. By far, the most common method for displaying files is to use the **ls command**. Following is an example of a file listing in the root user's home directory:

```
[root@server1 root]# pwd
/root
[root@server1 root]# ls
current   myprogram  project   project12  project2  project4
Desktop   myscript   project1  project13  project3  project5
[root@server1 root]#_
```

> ### ■ NOTE
>
> The files listed previously and discussed throughout this chapter are for example purposes only.

The ls command displays all the files in the current directory in columnar format; however, you can also pass an argument to the ls command indicating the directory to be listed if the current directory listing is not required. In the following example, the files are listed underneath the /home/bob directory without changing the current directory.

```
[root@server1 root]# pwd
/root
[root@server1 root]# ls /home/bob
assignment1    file1    letter    letter2    project1
[root@server1 root]#_
```

◤ TIP

When running the `ls` command, notice that files of different types are often represented as different colors; however, the specific colors used to represent files of certain types might vary from terminal to terminal and distribution to distribution. As a result, do not use color alone to determine the file type.

◼ NOTE

Windows uses the `dir` command to list files and directories; to simplify the learning of Linux for Windows users, there is a `dir` command in Linux, which is simply a pointer or shortcut to the `ls` command.

Recall from the previous chapter that you can use switches to alter the behavior of commands. To view a list of files and their type, use the `-F` switch to the `ls` command:

```
[root@server1 root]# pwd
/root
[root@server1 root]# ls -F
current@  myprogram*  project    project12  project2   project4
Desktop/  myscript*   project1   project13  project3   project5
[root@server1 root]#_
```

The `ls -F` command appends a special character at the end of each filename displayed to indicate the type of file. In the preceding output, note that the filenames current, Desktop, myprogram, and myscript have special characters appended to their names. The @ symbol indicates a linked file, the * symbol indicates an executable file, the / indicates a subdirectory, the = character indicates a socket, and the | character indicates a named pipe. All other file types do not have a special character appended to them and could be text files, binary data files, or special device files.

> **NOTE**
>
> It is common convention to name directories starting with an uppercase letter, such as the D in the Desktop directory shown in the preceding output. This ensures that directories are listed at the beginning of the 1s command output and allows you to quickly determine which names refer to directories when running the 1s command without any options that specify file type.

Although the 1s -F command is a quick way of getting file type information in an easy-to-read format, at times you need to obtain more detailed information about each file. The 1s -1 command can be used to provide a long listing for each file in a certain directory.

```
[root@server1 root]# pwd
/root
[root@server1 root]# ls -l
total 548
lrwxrwxrwx   1 root   root        9 Apr  7 09:56 current -> project12
drwx------   3 root   root     4096 Mar 29 10:01 Desktop
-rwxr-xr-x   1 root   root   519964 Apr  7 09:59 myprogram
-rwxr-xr-x   1 root   root       20 Apr  7 09:58 myscript
-rw-r--r--   1 root   root       71 Apr  7 09:58 project
-rw-r--r--   1 root   root       71 Apr  7 09:59 project1
-rw-r--r--   1 root   root       71 Apr  7 09:59 project12
-rw-r--r--   1 root   root        0 Apr  7 09:56 project13
-rw-r--r--   1 root   root       71 Apr  7 09:59 project2
-rw-r--r--   1 root   root       90 Apr  7 10:01 project3
-rw-r--r--   1 root   root       99 Apr  7 10:01 project4
-rw-r--r--   1 root   root      108 Apr  7 10:01 project5
[root@server1 root]#_
```

Each file listed in the preceding example has eight components of information listed in columns from left to right:

1. A file type character
   - The d character represents a directory.
   - The l character represents a symbolically linked file (discussed in Chapter 5, "Linux Filesystem Management").
   - The b or c characters represent special device files (discussed in Chapter 6).
   - The n character represents a named pipe.
   - The s character represents a socket.
   - The – character represents all other file types (text files, binary data files).

2. A list of permissions on the file (also called the mode of the file)

3. A hard link count (discussed in Chapter 5)

4. The owner of the file (discussed in Chapter 5)

5. The group owner of the file (discussed in Chapter 5)

6. The file size

7. The most recent modification time of the file

8. The filename (some files are shortcuts or pointers to other files and indicated with an arrow -> as with the file called "current" in the preceding output; these are known as symbolic links and are discussed in Chapter 5)

For the file named project in the previous example, you can see that this file is a regular file because the long listing of it begins with a – character, the permissions on the file are rw-r--r-- , the hard link count is 1, the owner of the file is the root user, the group owner of the file is the root group, the size of the file is 71 bytes, and the file was modified last on April 7th at 9:58 AM.

> **NOTE**
>
> On most Linux systems, a shortcut to the ls command can be used to display the same columns of information as the ls -l command. Some users prefer to use this shortcut, commonly known as an alias, which is invoked when a user types ll at a command prompt. This is known as the **ll command**.

The ls -F and ls -l commands are valuable to a user who wants to display file types; however, neither of these commands can display all file types using special characters. To display the file type of any file, you can use the **file command**; simply give the file command an argument specifying what file to analyze. You can also pass multiple files as arguments or use the * metacharacter to refer to all files in the current directory. An example of using the file command in the root user's home directory is:

```
[root@server1 root]# pwd
/root
[root@server1 root]# ls
current  myprogram  project   project12  project2  project4
Desktop  myscript   project1  project13  project3  project5
[root@server1 root]# file Desktop
Desktop:   directory
[root@server1 root]# file project Desktop
project:   ASCII text
Desktop:   directory
[root@server1 root]# file *
Desktop:   directory
```

```
current:   symbolic link to project12
myprogram: ELF 32-bit LSB executable, Intel 80386, version 1, dynamically linked (uses
 shared libs), stripped
myscript:  Bourne-Again shell script text executable
project:   ASCII text
project1:  ASCII text
project12: ASCII text
project13: empty
project2:  ASCII text
project3:  ASCII text
project4:  ASCII text
project5:  ASCII text
[root@server1 root]#_
```

As shown in the preceding example, the `file` command can also identify the differences
between types of executable files. The myscript file is a text file that contains executable commands (also known as a shell script), whereas the myprogram file is a 32-bit executable compiled program. The `file` command also identifies empty files such as project13 in the previous
example.

Some filenames inside each user's home directory represent important configuration files or
program directories. Because these files are rarely edited by the user and can clutter up the listing of files, they are normally hidden from view when using the `ls` and `file` commands.
Recall that filenames for hidden files start with a period character (.). To view them, simply
pass the `-a` option to the `ls` command. Some hidden files that are commonly seen in the root
user's home directory are shown next:

```
[root@server1 root]# ls
current  myprogram  project   project12  project2  project4
Desktop  myscript   project1  project13  project3  project5
[root@server1 root]# ls -a
.                         .gimp-1.2         project
..                        .gnome            project1
.bash_history             .gnome-desktop    project12
.bash_logout              .gnome_private    project13
.bash_profile             .gtkrc            project2
.bashrc                   .ICEauthority     project3
.cshrc                    .kde              project4
current                   .mcop             project5
.DCOPserver_server1_0     .MCOP-random-seed .sane
Desktop                   .mcoprc           .sawfish
.first_start_kde          .mozilla          .tcshrc
.galeon                   myprogram         .Xauthority
.gconf                    myscript          .Xresources
.gconfd                   .nautilus         .xsession-errors
[root@server1 root]#_
```

As discussed earlier, the (.) character refers to the current working directory and the (..) character refers to the parent directory relative to your current location in the directory tree. Each of these pointers is seen as a special (or fictitious) file when using the ls -a command, as each starts with a period.

You can also specify several options simultaneously for most commands on the command line and receive the combined functionality of all the options. For example, to view all hidden files and their file types, you could type:

```
[root@server1 root]# ls -aF
./                      .gimp-1.2/         project
../                     .gnome/            project1
.bash_history           .gnome-desktop/    project12
.bash_logout            .gnome_private/    project13
.bash_profile           .gtkrc             project2
.bashrc                 .ICEauthority      project3
.cshrc                  .kde/              project4
current@                .mcop/             project5
.DCOPserver_server1_0@  .MCOP-random-seed  .sane/
Desktop/                .mcoprc            .sawfish/
.first_start_kde        .mozilla/          .tcshrc
.galeon/                myprogram*         .Xauthority
.gconf/                 myscript           .Xresources
.gconfd/                .nautilus/         .xsession-errors
[root@server1 root]#_
```

The aforementioned options to the ls command (-l, -F, -a) are the most common options you would use when navigating the Linux directory tree; however, many options are available in the ls command that alter the listing of files on the filesystem. Table 4-2 depicts the most common of these options and their descriptions.

Table 4-2 Common options to the ls command

Option	Description
-a, --all	Lists all filenames
-A, --almost-all	Lists most filenames (excludes the . and .. special files)
-C	Lists filenames in column format
--color=n	Lists filenames without color
-d, --directory	Lists directory names instead of their contents
-f	Lists all filenames without sorting
-F, --classify	Lists filenames classified by file type
--full-time	Lists filenames in long format and displays the full modification time

Table 4-2 Common options to the ls command (Continued)

Option	Description
-l	Lists filenames in long format
-lh, -l --human-readable	Lists filenames in long format with human-readable (easy-to-read) file sizes
-lG, -l --no-group, -o	Lists filenames in long format but omits the group information
-r, --reverse	Lists filenames reverse sorted
-R, --recursive	Lists filenames in the specified directory and all subdirectories
-s	Lists filenames and their associated size in kilobytes (KB)
-S	Lists filenames sorted by file size
-t	Lists filenames sorted by modification time
-U	Lists filenames without sorting
-x	Lists filenames in rows rather than in columns

Wildcard Metacharacters

In the previous section, you saw that the * metacharacter was used to indicate or "match" all the files in the current directory much like a wildcard matches certain cards in a card game. As a result, the * metacharacter is called a **wildcard metacharacter**. These characters can simplify commands that specify more than one filename on the command line, as you saw with the file command earlier. These wildcard metacharacters are interpreted by the shell and can be used with most common Linux filesystem commands, including a few that have already been mentioned (ls, file, and cd). These metacharacters match certain portions of filenames, or the entire filename itself. Table 4-2 displays a list of wildcard metacharacters and their descriptions.

Table 4-3 Wildcard metacharacters

Metacharacter	Description
*	Matches 0 or more characters in a filename
?	Matches 1 character in a filename
[aegh]	Matches 1 character in a filename—provided this character is either an a, e, g, or h
[a-e]	Matches 1 character in a filename—provided this character is either an a, b, c, d, or e
[!a-e]	Matches 1 character in a filename—provided this character is NOT an a, b, c, d, or e

Wildcards can be demonstrated using the ls command. Examples of using wildcard metacharacters to narrow down the listing produced by the ls command are shown next.

```
[root@server1 root]# ls
current  myprogram  project   project12  project2  project4
Desktop  myscript   project1  project13  project3  project5
[root@server1 root]# ls project*
project  project1  project12  project13  project2  project3  project4  project5
[root@server1 root]# ls project?
project1  project2  project3  project4  project5
[root@server1 root]# ls project??
project12  project13
[root@server1 root]# ls project[135]
project1  project3  project5
[root@server1 root]# ls project[!135]
project2  project4
```

Displaying the Contents of Text Files

So far, this chapter has discussed commands that can be used to navigate the Linux directory structure and view filenames and file types; it is usual now to display the contents of these files. By far, the most common file type that users display is text files. These files are usually small and contain configuration information or instructions that the shell interprets (called a shell script), but can also contain other forms of text, as in e-mail letters. To view an entire text file on the terminal screen (also referred to as **concatenation**), you can use the **cat command**. The following is an example of using the cat command to display the contents of an e-mail message (in the fictitious file project4):

```
[root@server1 root]# ls
current  myprogram  project   project12  project2  project4
Desktop  myscript   project1  project13  project3  project5
[root@server1 root]# cat project4
Hi there, I hope this day finds you well.

Unfortunately we were not able to make it to your dining
room this year while vacationing in Algonquin Park - I
especially wished to see the model of the Highland Inn
and the train station in the dining room.

I have been reading on the history of Algonquin Park but
no where could I find a description of where the Highland
Inn was originally located on Cache lake.
```

```
If it is no trouble, could you kindly let me know such that
I need not wait until next year when I visit your lodge?

Regards,
Mackenzie Elizabeth
[root@server1 root]#_
```

You can also use the cat command to display the line number of each line in the file in addition to the contents by passing the -n option to the cat command. In the following example, the number of lines in the project4 file are displayed:

```
[root@server1 root]# cat -n project4
    1  Hi there, I hope this day finds you well.
    2
    3  Unfortunately we were not able to make it to your dining
    4  room this year while vacationing in Algonquin Park - I
    5  especially wished to see the model of the Highland Inn
    6  and the train station in the dining room.
    7
    8  I have been reading on the history of Algonquin Park but
    9  no where could I find a description of where the Highland
   10  Inn was originally located on Cache lake.
   11
   12  If it is no trouble, could you kindly let me know such that
   13  I need not wait until next year when I visit your lodge?
   14
   15  Regards,
   16  Mackenzie Elizabeth
[root@server1 root]#_
```

In some cases, you might want to display the contents of a certain text file in reverse order, which is useful when displaying files that have text appended to them continuously by system services. These files, also known as **log files**, contain the most recent entries at the bottom of the file. To display a file in reverse order, use the **tac command** (tac is cat spelled backwards), as shown next with the file project4:

```
[root@server1 root]# tac project4
Mackenzie Elizabeth
Regards,

I need not wait until next year when I visit your lodge?
If it is no trouble, could you kindly let me know such that

Inn was originally located on Cache lake.
no where could I find a description of where the Highland
I have been reading on the history of Algonquin Park but
```

```
and the train station in the dining room.
especially wished to see the model of the Highland Inn
room this year while vacationing in Algonquin Park - I
Unfortunately we were not able to make it to your dining

Hi there, I hope this day finds you well.
[root@server1 root]#_
```

If the file displayed is very large and you only want to view the first few lines of it, you can use the **head command**. The head command displays the first 10 lines (including blank lines) of a text file to the terminal screen, but can also take a numeric option specifying a different number of lines to display. The following shows an example of using the head command to view the top of the project4 file:

```
[root@server1 root]# head project4
Hi there, I hope this day finds you well.

Unfortunately we were not able to make it to your dining
room this year while vacationing in Algonquin Park - I
especially wished to see the model of the Highland Inn
and the train station in the dining room.

I have been reading on the history of Algonquin Park but
no where could I find a description of where the Highland
Inn was originally located on Cache lake.
[root@server1 root]# head -3 project4
Hi there, I hope this day finds you well.

Unfortunately we were not able to make it to your dining
[root@server1 root]#_
```

Just as the head command displays the beginning of text files, the **tail command** can be used to display the end of text files. By default, the tail command displays the final 10 lines of a file, but can also take a numeric option specifying the number of lines to display to the terminal screen, as shown in the following example with the project4 file:

```
[root@server1 root]# tail project4

I have been reading on the history of Algonquin Park but
no where could I find a description of where the Highland
Inn was originally located on Cache lake.

If it is no trouble, could you kindly let me know such that
I need not wait until next year when I visit your lodge?
```

```
Regards,
Mackenzie Elizabeth
[root@server1 root]# tail -2 project4
Regards,
Mackenzie Elizabeth
[root@server1 root]#_
```

The `tail` command also accepts another option specifying the line number at which to start when displaying text to the terminal screen. For example, to display the end of a text file starting from line 10 and continuing until the end of the file, simply use the +10 option to the `tail` command, as shown next:

```
[root@server1 root]# tail +10 project4
Inn was originally located on Cache lake.

If it is no trouble, could you kindly let me know such that
I need not wait until next year when I visit your lodge?

Regards,
Mackenzie Elizabeth
[root@server1 root]#_
```

Although some text files can be displayed completely on the terminal screen, you might encounter text files that are too large to be displayed. In this case, the `cat` command displays the entire file contents in order to the terminal screen and the top of the file is not displayed because there is not enough screen area to do so. Thus, it is useful to display text files in a page-by-page fashion by using either the `more` or `less` commands.

The **more command** gets its name from the `pg` command once used on UNIX systems. The `pg` command displayed a text file page-by-page on the terminal screen starting at the beginning of the file; pressing the spacebar or Enter key displays the next page and so on. The `more` command does more than `pg` did, because it displays the next complete page of a text file if you press the spacebar, but displays only the next line of a text file if you press Enter. In that way, you can browse the contents of a text file page-by-page or line-by-line. The fictitious file project5 is an excerpt from Shakespeare's tragedy *Macbeth* and is too large to be displayed fully on the terminal screen using the `cat` command. Using the `more` command to view its contents results in the following output:

```
[root@server1 root]# more project5
Go bid thy mistress, when my drink is ready,
She strike upon the bell. Get thee to bed.
Is this a dagger which I see before me,
The handle toward my hand? Come, let me clutch thee.
I have thee not, and yet I see thee still.
Art thou not, fatal vision, sensible
To feeling as to sight? or art thou but
```

```
A dagger of the mind, a false creation,
Proceeding from the heat-oppressed brain?
I see thee yet, in form as palpable
As this which now I draw.
Thou marshall'st me the way that I was going;
And such an instrument I was to use.
Mine eyes are made the fools o' the other senses,
Or else worth all the rest; I see thee still,
And on thy blade and dudgeon gouts of blood,
Which was not so before. There's no such thing:
It is the bloody business which informs
Thus to mine eyes. Now o'er the one halfworld
Nature seems dead, and wicked dreams abuse
The curtain'd sleep; witchcraft celebrates
Pale Hecate's offerings, and wither'd murder,
Alarum'd by his sentinel, the wolf,
--More--(71%)
```

Note from the preceding output that the more command displays the first page without returning you to the shell prompt. Instead, the more command displays a prompt at the bottom of the terminal screen that indicates how much of the file is displayed on the screen as a percentage of the total file size. In the preceding example, 71% of the project5 file is displayed. At this prompt, you can press the spacebar to advance one whole page, or the Enter key to advance to the next line. In addition, the more command allows other user interaction at this prompt. Pressing the h character at the prompt displays a help screen as shown in the following output, and pressing the q character quits the more command completely without viewing the remainder of the file.

```
--More--(71%)
Most commands optionally preceded by integer argument k. Defaults in brackets. Star (*)
indicates argument becomes new default.
-------------------------------------------------------------------------
<space>                 Display next k lines of text [current screen size]
z                       Display next k lines of text [current screen size]*
<return>                Display next k lines of text [1]*
d or ctrl-D             Scroll k lines [current scroll size, initially 11]*
q or Q or <interrupt>   Exit from more
s                       Skip forward k lines of text [1]
f                       Skip forward k screenfuls of text [1]
b or ctrl-B             Skip backward k screenfuls of text [1]
'                       Go to place where previous search started
=                       Display current line number
/<regular expression>   Search for kth occurrence of regular expression[1]
n                       Search for kth occurrence of last r.e [1]
```

```
!<cmd> or :!<cmd>      Execute <cmd> in a subshell
v                      Start up /usr/bin/vi at current line
ctrl-L                 Redraw screen
:n                     Go to kth next file [1]
:p                     Go to kth previous file [1]
:f                     Display current file name and line number
.                Repeat previous command
-------------------------------------------------------------------
--More--(71%)
```

Just as the more command was named as a result of allowing more user functionality, the **less command** is named similarly, as it can do more than the more command (remember that "less is more", more or less). Like the more command, the less command can browse the contents of a text file, page-by-page by pressing the spacebar and line-by-line by pressing the Enter key; however, you can also use the cursor keys on the keyboard to scroll up and down the contents of the file. The output of the less command when used to view the project5 file is as follows:

```
[root@server1 root]# less project5
Go bid thy mistress, when my drink is ready,
She strike upon the bell. Get thee to bed.
Is this a dagger which I see before me,
The handle toward my hand? Come, let me clutch thee.
I have thee not, and yet I see thee still.
Art thou not, fatal vision, sensible
To feeling as to sight? or art thou but
A dagger of the mind, a false creation,
Proceeding from the heat-oppressed brain?
I see thee yet, in form as palpable
As this which now I draw.
Thou marshall'st me the way that I was going;
And such an instrument I was to use.
Mine eyes are made the fools o' the other senses,
Or else worth all the rest; I see thee still,
And on thy blade and dudgeon gouts of blood,
Which was not so before. There's no such thing:
It is the bloody business which informs
Thus to mine eyes. Now o'er the one halfworld
Nature seems dead, and wicked dreams abuse
The curtain'd sleep; witchcraft celebrates
Pale Hecate's offerings, and wither'd murder,
Alarum'd by his sentinel, the wolf,
Whose howl's his watch, thus with his stealthy pace.
project5
```

Like the more command, the less command displays a prompt at the bottom of the file using the : character or the filename of the file being viewed (project5 in our example), yet the less command contains more keyboard shortcuts for searching out text within files. At the prompt, you can press the h key to obtain a help screen or the q key to quit. The first help screen for the less command is shown next:

```
                SUMMARY OF LESS COMMANDS

  Commands marked with * may be preceded by a number, N.
  Notes in parentheses indicate the behavior if N is given.


h  H                  Display this help.
q  :q  Q  :Q  ZZ      Exit.
---------------------------------------------------------------


               MOVING


e  ^E  j  ^N  CR   *  Forward  one line   (or N lines).
y  ^Y  k  ^K  ^P   *  Backward one line   (or N lines).
f  ^F  ^V  SPACE   *  Forward  one window (or N lines).
b  ^B  ESC-v       *  Backward one window (or N lines).
z                  *  Forward  one window (and set window to N).
w                  *  Backward one window (and set window to N).
ESC-SPACE          *  Forward  one window, but don't stop at end-of-file
d  ^D              *  Forward  one half-window(and set half-window to N)
u  ^U              *  Backward one half-window(and set half-window to N)
ESC-(  RightArrow  *  Left  8 character positions (or N positions).
ESC-)  LeftArrow   *  Right 8 character positions (or N positions).
F                     Forward forever; like "tail -f".


HELP -- Press RETURN for more, or q when done
```

The more and less commands can also be used in conjunction with the output of commands if that output is too large to fit on the terminal screen. To do this, simply use the | metacharacter after the command, followed by either the more or less command, as follows:

```
[root@server1 root]# cd /etc
[root@server1 etc]# ls -l | more
total 3688
-rw-r--r--   1 root    root      15276 Mar 22 12:20 a2ps.cfg
-rw-r--r--   1 root    root       2562 Mar 22 12:20 a2ps-site.cfg
drwxr-xr-x   4 root    root       4096 Jun 11 08:45 acpi
-rw-r--r--   1 root    root         46 Jun 16 16:42 adjtime
drwxr-xr-x   2 root    root       4096 Jun 11 08:47 aep
-rw-r--r--   1 root    root        688 Feb 17 00:35 aep.conf
```

```
-rw-r--r--    1 root    root        703 Feb 17 00:35 aeplog.conf
drwxr-xr-x    4 root    root       4096 Jun 11 08:47 alchemist
-rw-r--r--    1 root    root       1419 Jan 26 10:14 aliases
-rw-r-----    1 root    smmsp     12288 Jun 17 13:17 aliases.db
drwxr-xr-x    2 root    root       4096 Jun 11 11:11 alternatives
drwxr-xr-x    3 amanda  disk       4096 Jun 11 10:16 amanda
-rw-r--r--    1 amanda  disk          0 Mar 22 12:28 amandates
-rw-------    1 root    root        688 Mar  4 22:34 amd.conf
-rw-r-----    1 root    root        105 Mar  4 22:34 amd.net
-rw-r--r--    1 root    root        317 Feb 15 14:33 anacrontab
-rw-r--r--    1 root    root        331 May  5 08:07 ant.conf
-rw-r--r--    1 root    root       6200 Jun 16 16:42 asound.state
drwxr-xr-x    3 root    root       4096 Jun 11 10:37 atalk
-rw-------    1 root    root          1 May  5 13:39 at.deny
-rw-r--r--    1 root    root        325 Apr 14 13:39 auto.master
-rw-r--r--    1 root    root        581 Apr 14 13:39 auto.misc
--More--
```

In the preceding example, the output of the `ls -l` command was redirected to the `more` command, which displays the first page of output on the terminal. You can then advance through the output page-by-page or line-by-line. This type of redirection is discussed in Chapter 8, "Working with the BASH Shell."

Displaying the Contents of Binary Files

It is important to employ text file commands, such as `cat`, `tac`, `head`, `tail`, `more`, and `less`, only on files that contain text; otherwise, you might find yourself with random output on the terminal screen or even a dysfunctional terminal. To view the contents of binary files, you typically use the program that was used to create the file; however, some commands can be used to safely display the contents of most binary files. The **strings command** searches for text characters in a binary file and outputs them to the screen. In many cases, these text characters might indicate what the binary file is used for. For example, to find the text characters inside the /bin/echo binary executable program page-by-page, you could use the following command:

```
[root@server1 root]# strings /bin/echo | more
/lib/ld-linux.so.2
PTRh|
<nt7<e
|[^_]
[^_]
[^_]
Try `%s --help' for more information.
Usage: %s [OPTION]... [STRING]...
```

```
Echo the STRING(s) to standard output.
  -n              do not output the trailing newline
  -e              enable interpretation of the backslash-escaped characters
                     listed below
  -E              disable interpretation of those sequences in STRINGs
      --help      display this help and exit
      --version   output version information and exit
Without -E, the following sequences are recognized and interpolated:
  \NNN   the character whose ASCII code is NNN (octal)
  \\     backslash
  \a     alert (BEL)
  \b     backspace
  \c     suppress trailing newline
  \f     form feed
  \n     new line
--More--
```

Although this output might not be easy to read, it does contain portions of text that can point a user in the right direction to find out more about the /bin/echo command. Another command that is safe to use on binary files and text files is the **od command**, which displays the contents of the file in octal format (numeric base 8 format). An example of using the od command to display the first five lines of the file project4 is shown in the following example:

```
[root@server1 root]# od project4 | head -5
0000000 064510 072040 062550 062562 020054 020111 067550 062560
0000020 072040 064550 020163 060544 020171 064546 062156 020163
0000040 067571 020165 062567 066154 006456 006412 052412 063156
0000060 071157 072564 060556 062564 074554 073440 020145 062567
0000100 062562 067040 072157 060440 066142 020145 067564 066440
[root@server1 root]#_
```

> **NOTE**
>
> You can use the -x option to the od command to display a file in hexadecimal format (numeric base 16 format).

Searching for Text Within Files

Recall that Linux was modeled after the UNIX operating system. The UNIX operating system is often referred to as the "grandfather" of all operating systems because it is over 30 years old and has formed the basis for most advances in computing technology. The major use of the UNIX operating system in the past 30 years involved simplifying business and scientific management through database applications. As a result, many commands (referred to as **text tools**) were developed for the UNIX operating system that could search for and manipulate text, such as database information, in many different and advantageous ways. A set of text wildcards was also developed to ease the searching of specific text information. These text wildcards are called **regular expressions (regexp)** and are recognized by several text tools and programming languages including, but not limited to, the following:

◆ grep
◆ awk
◆ sed
◆ vi
◆ Emacs
◆ ex
◆ ed
◆ C++
◆ PERL
◆ Tcl

Because Linux is a close relative of the UNIX operating system, these text tools and regular expressions are available to Linux as well. By combining text tools together (as you shall see later), a typical Linux system can search for and manipulate data in almost every way possible. As a result, regular expressions and the text tools that use them are commonly used in business today.

Regular Expressions

As mentioned earlier, regular expressions (also referred to by the word "regexp") allow you to specify a certain pattern of text within a text document. They work similarly to wildcard metacharacters in that they are used to match characters, yet they have many differences:

◆ Wildcard metacharacters are interpreted by the shell, whereas regular expressions are interpreted by a text tool program.
◆ Wildcard metacharacters match characters in filenames (or directory names) on a Linux filesystem, whereas regular expressions match characters *within* text files on a Linux filesystem.
◆ Wildcard metacharacters typically have different definitions than regular expression metacharacters.
◆ More regular expression metacharacters are available than wildcard metacharacters.

In addition, regular expression metacharacters are divided into two different categories: common regular expressions and extended regular expressions. Common regular expressions are available to most text tools; however, extended regular expressions are less common and available in only certain text tools. Table 4-4 shows definitions and examples of some common and extended regular expressions.

Table 4-4 Regular expressions

Regular Expression	Description	Example	Type
*	Matches 0 or more occurrences of the previous character	letter* matches lette, letter, letterr, letterrrr, letterrrrr, and so on	Common
?	Matches 0 or 1 occurrences of the previous character	letter? matches lette, letter	Extended
+	Matches 1 or more occurrences of the previous character	letter+ matches letter, letterr, letterrrr, letterrrrr, and so on	Extended
. (period)	Matches 1 character of any type	letter. matches lettera, letterb, letterc, letter1, letter2, letter3, and so on	Common
[...]	Matches one character from the range specified within the braces	letter[1238] matches letter1, letter2, letter3, letter8 letter[a-c] matches lettera, letterb, and letterc	Common
[^...]	Matches one character NOT from the range specified within the braces	letter[^1238] matches letter4, letter5, letter6, lettera , letterb, and so on (any character except 1, 2, 3, or 8)	Common
{ }	Matches a specific number or range of the previous character	letter{3} matches letterrr, whereas letter{2,4} matches letterr, letterrr, and letterrrr	Extended
^	Matches the following characters if they are the first characters on the line	^letter matches letter if letter is the first set of characters in the line	Common
$	Matches the previous letter characters if they are the last characters on the line	$ matches letter if letter is the last set of characters in the line	Common
(...|...)	Matches either of two sets of characters	(mother|father) matches the word "mother" or "father"	Extended

The grep Command

The most common text tool that allows you the ability to search for information using regular expressions is the grep command. The **grep (global regular expression print) command** is used to display lines in a text file that match a certain common regular expression. To display lines of text that match extended regular expressions, you must use the **egrep command** (or the -E option to the grep command). In addition, the **fgrep command** (or the -F option to the grep command) does not interpret any regular expressions and consequently returns results much faster. Take, for example, the project4 file shown earlier:

```
[root@server1 root]# cat project4
Hi there, I hope this day finds you well.

Unfortunately we were not able to make it to your dining
room this year while vacationing in Algonquin Park - I
especially wished to see the model of the Highland Inn
and the train station in the dining room.

I have been reading on the history of Algonquin Park but
no where could I find a description of where the Highland
Inn was originally located on Cache lake.

If it is no trouble, could you kindly let me know such that
I need not wait until next year when I visit your lodge?

Regards,
Mackenzie Elizabeth
[root@server1 root]#_
```

The grep command requires two arguments at minimum, the first argument specifies which text to search for, and the remaining arguments specify the files to search inside. If a pattern of text is matched, the grep command displays the entire line on the terminal screen. For example, to list only those lines in the file project4 that contain the words "Algonquin Park," enter the following command:

```
[root@server1 root]# grep "Algonquin Park" project4
room this year while vacationing in Algonquin Park - I
I have been reading on the history of Algonquin Park but
[root@server1 root]#_
```

To return the lines that do not contain the text "Algonquin Park," you can use the -v option of the grep command to reverse the meaning of the previous command:

```
[root@server1 root]# grep -v "Algonquin Park" project4
Hi there, I hope this day finds you well.
```

```
Unfortunately we were not able to make it to your dining
especially wished to see the model of the Highland Inn
and the train station in the dining room.

no where could I find a description of where the Highland
Inn was originally located on Cache lake.

If it is no trouble, could you kindly let me know such that
I need not wait until next year when I visit your lodge?

Regards,
Mackenzie Elizabeth
[root@server1 root]#_
```

Keep in mind that the text being searched is case sensitive; to perform a case-insensitive search, use the -i option to the grep command:

```
[root@server1 root]# grep "algonquin park" project4
[root@server1 root]#_
[root@server1 root]# grep -i "algonquin park" project4
room this year while vacationing in Algonquin Park - I
I have been reading on the history of Algonquin Park but
[root@server1 root]#_
```

Another important note to keep in mind regarding text tools such as grep is that they match only patterns of text; they are unable to discern words or phrases unless they are specified. For example, if you want to search for the lines that contain the word "we," you can use the following grep command:

```
[root@server1 root]# grep "we" project4
Hi there, I hope this day finds you well.
Unfortunately we were not able to make it to your dining
[root@server1 root]#_
```

However, notice from the preceding output that the first line displayed does not contain the word "we"; the word "well" contains the text pattern "we" and is displayed as a result. To display only lines that contain the word "we," you can type the following to match the letters "we" surrounded by space characters:

```
[root@server1 root]# grep " we " project4
Unfortunately we were not able to make it to your dining
[root@server1 root]#_
```

All of the previous grep examples did not use regular expression metacharacters to search for text in the project4 file. Some examples of using regular expressions (see Table 4-4) when searching this file are shown throughout the remainder of this section.

To view lines that contain the word "toe" or "the" or "tie," you can enter the following command:

```
[root@server1 root]# grep " t.e " project4
especially wished to see the model of the Highland Inn
and the train station in the dining room.
I have been reading on the history of Algonquin Park but
no where could I find a description of where the Highland
[root@server1 root]#_
```

To view lines that start with the word "I," you can enter the following command:

```
[root@server1 root]# grep "^I " project4
I have been reading on the history of Algonquin Park but
I need not wait until next year when I visit your lodge?
[root@server1 root]#_
```

To view lines that contain the text "lodge" or "lake," you need to use an extended regular expression and the egrep command, as follows:

```
[root@server1 root]# egrep "(lodge|lake)" project4
Inn was originally located on Cache lake.
I need not wait until next year when I visit your lodge?
[root@server1 root]#_
```

Editing Text Files

Recall that text files are the most common type of file that Linux users and administrators will modify. Most system configuration is stored in text files, as well as common information such as e-mail and program source code. Consequently, many text editors are packaged with most Linux distributions and many more are available for Linux systems via the Internet. Text editors come in two varieties: editors that can be used on the command line, including vi (vim), mcedit, and Emacs, and editors that must be used in a GUI environment, including xemacs, nedit, gedit, and kedit.

The vi Editor

The **vi editor** (pronounced "vee eye") is one of the oldest and most popular visual text editors available for UNIX operating systems; its Linux equivalent (known as vim—vi improved) is standard on almost every Linux distribution as a result. Although the vi editor is not the easiest of the editors to use when editing text files, it has the advantage of portability. A Red Hat Linux user who is proficient in using the vi editor will find editing files on all other UNIX and Linux systems easy because the interface and features of the vi editor are nearly identical across Linux and UNIX systems. In addition, the vi editor supports regular expressions and can perform over 1000 different functions for the user.

To open an existing text file for editing, you can type vi filename (or vim filename) where *filename* specifies the file to be edited. To open a new file for editing, simply type vi or vim at the command line:

```
[root@server1 root]# vi
```

The vi editor then runs interactively and replaces the command-line interface with the following output:

```
~
~
~
~
~
~                      VIM - Vi IMproved
~
~                       version 6.2.457
~                    by Bram Moolenaar et al.
~           Vim is open source and freely distributable
~
~                   Sponsor Vim development!
~       type  :help sponsor<Enter>    for information
~
~       type  :q<Enter>               to exit
~       type  :help<Enter>  or  <F1>  for on-line help
~       type  :help version6<Enter>   for version info
~
~
~
~
~
~
~           0,0-1     All
```

The tilde ~ characters shown along the left indicate the end of the file; they are pushed further down the screen as you enter text. The vi editor is called a bimodal editor because it functions in one of two modes: **command mode** and **insert mode**. When a user first opens the vi editor, she is placed in command mode and can use the keys on the keyboard to perform useful functions, such as deleting text, copying text, saving changes to a file, and exiting the vi editor. To insert text into the document, you must enter insert mode by typing one of the characters listed in Table 4-5. One such method to enter insert mode is to type the i key on the keyboard while in command mode; the vi editor then displays --INSERT-- at the bottom of the screen and allows the user to enter a sentence such as the following:

```
This is a sample sentence.
~
~
~
~
~
~
~
~
~
~
-- INSERT --
```

When in insert mode, you can use the keyboard to type text as required but when finished you must press the Esc key to return to command mode to perform other functions via keys on the keyboard. Table 4-6 provides a list of keys useful in command mode and their associated functions. After you are in command mode, to save the text in a file called samplefile in the current directory, you need to press the : character (by pressing the Shift and ; keys simultaneously) to reach a : prompt where you can enter a command to save the contents of the current document to a file, as shown in the following example and in Table 4-7.

```
This is a sample sentence.
~
~
~
~
~
~
~
~
~
:w samplefile
```

As shown in Table 4-7, you can quit the vi editor by pressing the : character and entering **q!**, which then returns the user to the shell prompt:

```
This is a sample sentence.
~
~
~
~
~
~
~
~
~
:q!
[root@server1 root]# _
```

Table 4-5 Common keyboard keys used to change to and from insert mode

Key	Description
i	Changes to insert mode and places the cursor before the current character for entering text
a	Changes to insert mode and places the cursor after the current character for entering text
o	Changes to insert mode and opens a new line underneath the current line for entering text
I	Changes to insert mode and places the cursor at the beginning of the current line for entering text
A	Changes to insert mode and places the cursor at the end of the current line for entering text
O	Changes to insert mode and opens a new line above the current line for entering text
Esc	Changes back to command mode while in insert mode

Table 4-6 Key combinations commonly used in command mode

Key	Description
w, W, e, E	Moves the cursor forward one word to the beginning of the next word, respectively.
b, B	Moves the cursor backward one word
53G	Moves the cursor to line 53
G	Moves the cursor to the last line in the document
0, ^	Moves the cursor to the beginning of the line
$	Moves the cursor to the end of the line
x	Deletes the character the cursor is on
3x	Deletes three characters starting from the character the cursor is on
dw	Deletes one word starting from the character the cursor is on
d3w, 3dw	Deletes three words starting from the character the cursor is on
dd	Deletes one whole line starting from the line the cursor is on
d3d, 3dd	Deletes three whole lines starting from the line the cursor is on
d$	Deletes from cursor character to the end of the current line
d^, d0	Deletes from cursor character to the beginning of the current line
yw	Copies one word (starting from the character the cursor is on) into a temporary buffer in memory for later use

Table 4-6 Key combinations commonly used in command mode (Continued)

Key	Description
y3w, 3yw	Copies three words (starting from the character the cursor is on) into a temporary buffer in memory for later use
yy	Copies the current line into a temporary buffer in memory for later use
y3y, 3yy	Copies three lines (starting from the current line) into a temporary buffer in memory for later use
y$	Copies the current line from the cursor to the end of the line into a temporary buffer in memory for later use
y^, y0	Copies the current line from the cursor to the beginning of the line into a temporary buffer in memory for later use
p	Pastes the contents of the temporary memory buffer underneath the current line
P	Pastes the contents of the temporary memory buffer above the current line
J	Joins the line underneath the current line to the current line
Ctrl+g	Displays current line statistics
u	Undoes the last function (undo)
.	Repeats the last function (repeat)
/pattern	Searches for the first occurrence of pattern in the forward direction
?pattern	Searches for the first occurrence of pattern in the reverse direction
n	Repeats the previous search in the forward direction
N	Repeats the previous search in the reverse direction

Table 4-7 Key combinations commonly used at the command mode : prompt

Function	Description
:q	Quits from the vi editor if no changes were made
:q!	Quits from the vi editor and does not save any changes
:wq	Saves any changes to the file and quits from the vi editor
:w filename	Saves the current document to a file called filename
:!date	Executes the date command using a BASH shell

Table 4-7 Key combinations commonly used at the command mode (Continued)

Function	Description
:r !date	Reads the output of the date command into the document under the current line
:r filename	Reads the contents of the text file called filename into the document under the current line
:set all	Displays all vi environment settings
:set	Sets a vi environment setting to a certain value
:s/the/THE/g	Searches for the regular expression "the" and replaces each occurrence globally throughout the current line with the word "THE"
:1,$ s/the/THE/g	Searches for the regular expression "the" and replaces each occurrence globally from line 1 to the end of the document with the word "THE"

The vi editor also offers some advanced features to Linux users, as depicted in Table 4-7. Examples of some of these features are discussed next, using the project4 file shown earlier in this chapter. To edit the project4 file, simply type vi project4 and view the following screen:

```
Hi there, I hope this day finds you well.

Unfortunately we were not able to make it to your dining
room this year while vacationing in Algonquin Park - I
especially wished to see the model of the Highland Inn
and the train station in the dining room.

I have been reading on the history of Algonquin Park but
no where could I find a description of where the Highland
Inn was originally located on Cache lake.

If it is no trouble, could you kindly let me know such that
I need not wait until next year when I visit your lodge?

Regards,
Mackenzie Elizabeth
~
~
~
~
~
~
~
"project4" 17L, 583C
```

Note that the name of the file as well as the number of lines and characters in total are displayed at the bottom of the screen (project4 has 17 lines and 583 characters in this example). To insert the current date and time at the bottom of the file, you can simply move the cursor to the final line in the file and type the following at the : prompt while in command mode:

```
Hi there, I hope this day finds you well.

Unfortunately we were not able to make it to your dining
room this year while vacationing in Algonquin Park - I
especially wished to see the model of the Highland Inn
and the train station in the dining room.

I have been reading on the history of Algonquin Park but
no where could I find a description of where the Highland
Inn was originally located on Cache lake.

If it is no trouble, could you kindly let me know such that
I need not wait until next year when I visit your lodge?

Regards,
Mackenzie Elizabeth
~
~
~
~
~
~
~
~
:r !date
```

When you press Enter, the output of the date command is inserted below the current line:

```
Hi there, I hope this day finds you well.

Unfortunately we were not able to make it to your dining
room this year while vacationing in Algonquin Park - I
especially wished to see the model of the Highland Inn
and the train station in the dining room.

I have been reading on the history of Algonquin Park but
no where could I find a description of where the Highland
Inn was originally located on Cache lake.
```

```
If it is no trouble, could you kindly let me know such that
I need not wait until next year when I visit your lodge?

Regards,
Mackenzie Elizabeth
Sat Apr 30 18:33:10 EDT 2005
~
~
~
~
~
~
```

To change all occurrences of the word "Algonquin" to "ALGONQUIN," you can simply type the following at the : prompt while in command mode:

```
Hi there, I hope this day finds you well.

Unfortunately we were not able to make it to your dining
room this year while vacationing in Algonquin Park - I
especially wished to see the model of the Highland Inn
and the train station in the dining room.

I have been reading on the history of Algonquin Park but
no where could I find a description of where the Highland
Inn was originally located on Cache lake.

If it is no trouble, could you kindly let me know such that
I need not wait until next year when I visit your lodge?

Regards,
Mackenzie Elizabeth
Sat Apr 30 18:33:10 EDT 2005


~
~
~
~
~
~
:1,$ s/Algonquin/ALGONQUIN/g
```

The output changes to the following:

```
Hi there, I hope this day finds you well.

Unfortunately we were not able to make it to your dining
room this year while vacationing in ALGONQUIN Park - I
especially wished to see the model of the Highland Inn
and the train station in the dining room.

I have been reading on the history of ALGONQUIN Park but
no where could I find a description of where the Highland
Inn was originally located on Cache lake.

If it is no trouble, could you kindly let me know such that
I need not wait until next year when I visit your lodge?

Regards,
Mackenzie Elizabeth
Sat Apr 30 18:33:10 EDT 2005


~
~
~
~
~
~
~
```

Another attractive feature of the vi editor is its ability to customize the user environment through settings that can be altered at the : prompt while in command mode. Simply type set all at this prompt to observe the list of available settings and their current values:

```
:set all
--- Options ---
  aleph=224           fileencoding=        menuitems=25          swapsync=fsync
noarabic              fileformat=unix      modeline              switchbuf=
  arabicshape         filetype=            modelines=5           syntax=
noallowrevins       nofkmap                modifiable            tabstop=8
noaltkeymap           foldclose=           modified              tagbsearch
  ambiwidth=single    foldcolumn=0         more                  taglength=0
noautoindent          foldenable           mouse=                tagrelative
noautoread            foldexpr=0           mousemodel=extend     tagstack
noautowrite           foldignore=#         mousetime=500         term=xterm
noautowriteall        foldlevel=0          nonumber              notermbidi
  background=light    foldlevelstart=-1  nopaste                 termencoding=
  backspace=2         foldmethod=manual  pastetoggle=            noterse
```

```
nobackup                foldminlines=1      patchexpr=              textauto
   backupcopy=auto      foldnestmax=20      patchmode=            notextmode
   backupext=~          formatoptions=tcq nopreserveindent          textwidth=0
   backupskip=/tmp/*    formatprg=          previewheight=12        thesaurus=
nobinary                nogdefault         nopreviewwindow        notildeop
nobomb                  helpheight=20       printdevice=            timeout
   bufhidden=           helplang=en         printencoding=          timeoutlen=1000
   buflisted          nohidden             printfont=courier notitle
   buftype=             history=50          printoptions=           titlelen=85
-- More --
```

Note from the preceding output that most settings are set to either on or off; those that are turned off are prefixed with a "no." In the preceding example, line numbering is turned off (nonumber in the preceding output); however, you can turn it on by typing set number at the : prompt while in command mode. This results in the following output in vi:

```
 1 Hi there, I hope this day finds you well.
 2
 3 Unfortunately we were not able to make it to your dining
 4 room this year while vacationing in ALGONQUIN Park - I
 5 especially wished to see the model of the Highland Inn
 6 and the train station in the dining room.
 7
 8 I have been reading on the history of ALGONQUIN Park but
 9 no where could I find a description of where the Highland
10 Inn was originally located on Cache lake.
11
12 If it is no trouble, could you kindly let me know such that
13 I need not wait until next year when I visit your lodge?
14
15 Regards,
16 Mackenzie Elizabeth
17 Sat Apr 30 18:33:10 EDT 2005
18
~
~
~
~
~
~

:set number
```

Conversely, to turn line numbering off, you could simply type set nonumber at the : prompt while in command mode.

Other Common Text Editors

Although the vi editor is the most common text editor used on Linux and UNIX systems, other text editors that are easier to use exist.

The **mcedit editor (Midnight Commander Editor)** is an easy-to-use text editor that contains support for regular expressions and the ability to use the mouse for highlighting text. To edit the project4 file using the mcedit editor, simply type mcedit project4 at a command prompt and the following is displayed on the terminal screen:

```
project4          [----]  0 L:[  1+ 0   1/ 18] *(0   / 583b)
Hi there, I hope this day finds you well.


Unfortunately we were not able to make it to your dining
room this year while vacationing in Algonquin Park - I
especially wished to see the model of the Highland Inn
and the train station in the dining room.

I have been reading on the history of Algonquin Park but
no where could I find a description of where the Highland
Inn was originally located on Cache lake.

If it is no trouble, could you kindly let me know such that
I need not wait until next year when I visit your lodge?

Regards,
Mackenzie Elizabeth


1Help   2Save  3Mark  4Replac  5Copy  6Move  7Search  8Delete  9PullDn  10Quit
```

Note that you can access much of the functionality of mcedit by using the function keys on the keyboard as described at the bottom of the screen (F1 = Help, F2 = Save, and so on).

Although mcedit is a simple and straightforward text editor to use, it lacks the functionality seen in the vi editor. An alternative to the vi editor that offers an equal set of functionality is the GNU **Emacs (Editor MACroS) editor**. To open the project4 file in the Emacs editor, simply type emacs project4 and the following is displayed on the terminal screen:

```
File  Edit  Options  Buffers  Tools  Help
Hi there, I hope this day finds you well.

Unfortunately we were not able to make it to your dining
room this year while vacationing in Algonquin Park - I
especially wished to see the model of the Highland Inn
and the train station in the dining room.
```

```
I have been reading on the history of Algonquin Park but
no where could I find a description of where the Highland
Inn was originally located on Cache lake.

If it is no trouble, could you kindly let me know such that
I need not wait until next year when I visit your lodge?

Regards,
Mackenzie Elizabeth


-uu:---F1  project4   (Fundamental)--L1--All----------------------------
For information abou the GNU Project and its goals, type C-h C-p.
```

The Emacs editor uses the Ctrl key in combination with certain letters to perform special functions, can be used with the LISP (LISt Processing) artificial intelligence programming language, and supports hundreds of keyboard functions such as the vi editor. Table 4-8 shows a list of some common keyboard functions used in the Emacs editor.

Table 4-8 Keyboard functions commonly used in the GNU Emacs editor

Key	Description
Ctrl+a	Moves the cursor to the beginning of the line
Ctrl+e	Moves the cursor to the end of the line
Ctrl+h	Displays Emacs documentation
Ctrl+d	Deletes the current character
Ctrl+k	Deletes from the cursor position to the end of the line
Esc+d	Deletes the current word
Ctrl+x + Ctrl+c	Exits the Emacs editor
Ctrl+x + Ctrl+s	Saves the current document
Ctrl+x + Ctrl+w	Saves the current document as a new filename
Ctrl+x + u	Undoes the last change

Unfortunately, the Emacs editor is not an easy-to-use editor because the user must memorize several key combinations to work effectively or use advanced features; a version of Emacs that runs in the KDE or GNOME GUI environments is called the **xemacs editor** and is much easier to use because the key combinations are replaced by graphical icons for many features. To open the project4 file with the xemacs editor, simply open a command-line terminal in either the KDE or GNOME desktop, and type xemacs project4, as shown in Figure 4-3.

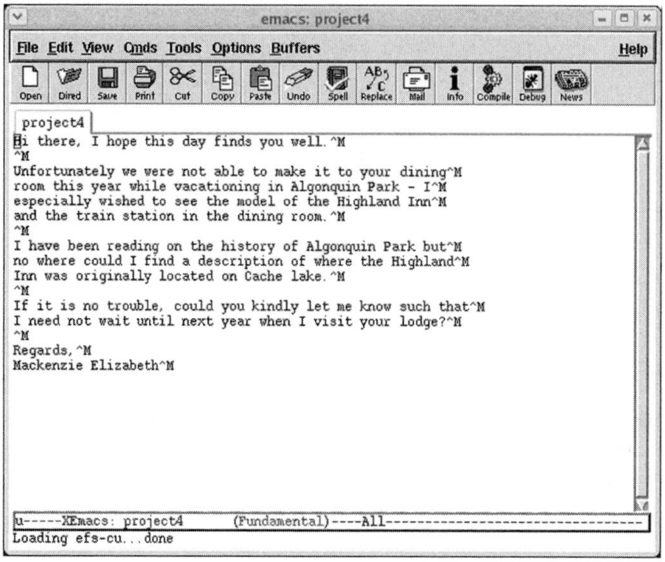

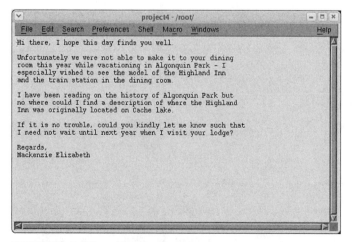

FIGURE 4-3 *The xemacs text editor*

Although the xemacs editor might not be available in every distribution that contains a GUI environment, there is an easy-to-use graphical editor derived from UNIX systems that is common on most Linux distributions: the **nedit editor**. An example of the display seen when you type nedit project4 on a command-line terminal in a GUI environment is shown in Figure 4-4.

FIGURE 4-4 *The nedit text editor*

As well, the GNOME and KDE GUI environments are now distributed with their own text editors (**gedit editor** and **kedit editor**), which are similar to nedit yet offer more functionality. Examples of the displays seen when a user types `gedit project4` and `kedit project4` on a command-line terminal in a GUI environment are shown in Figures 4-5 and 4-6, respectively.

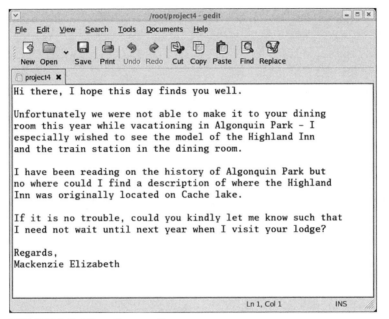

FIGURE 4-5 *The gedit text editor*

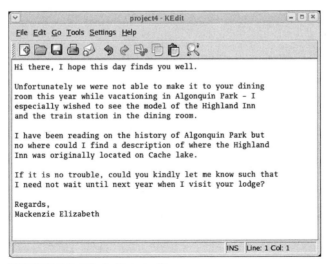

FIGURE 4-6 *The kedit text editor*

Chapter Summary

◆ The Linux filesystem is arranged hierarchically using a series of directories to store files, and the location of these directories and files can be described using absolute or relative pathnames.

◆ Many types of files can exist on the Linux filesystem, such as text files, binary data, executable programs, directories, linked files, and special device files.

◆ The ls command can be used to view filenames and offers a wide range of options to modify this view.

◆ Wildcard metacharacters can be used to simplify the selection of several files when using common Linux file commands.

◆ Text files are the most common file type whose contents can be viewed by several utilities, such as head, tail, cat, tac, more, and less.

◆ Regular expression metacharacters can be used to specify certain patterns of text when used with certain programming languages and text tool utilities such as grep.

◆ Although many command-line and graphical text editors exist, vi (vim) is a powerful, bimodal text editor that is standard on most UNIX and Linux systems.

Key Terms

~ metacharacter — A metacharacter used to represent a user's home directory.

absolute pathname — The full pathname to a certain file or directory starting from the root directory.

binary data file — A file that contains machine language (binary 1s and 0s) and stores information (such as common functions and graphics) used by binary compiled programs.

cat command — A Linux command used to display (or concatenate) the entire contents of a text file to the screen.

cd (change directory) command — A Linux command used to change the current directory in the directory tree.

command mode — One of the two input modes in vi; it allows a user to perform any available text editing task that is not related to inserting text into the document.

concatenation — The joining of text together to make one larger whole. In Linux, words and strings of text are joined together to form a displayed file.

directory — A special file on the filesystem used to organize other files into a logical tree structure.

egrep command — A variant of the grep command used to search files for patterns using extended regular expressions.

Emacs (Editor MACroS) editor — A popular and widespread text editor more conducive to word processing than vi; developed by Richard Stallman.

executable program — A file that can be executed by the Linux operating system to run in memory as a process and perform a useful function.

fgrep command — A variant of the grep command that does not allow the use of regular expressions.

file command — A Linux command that displays the file type of a specified filename.

filename — The user-friendly identifier given to a file.

filename extension — A series of identifiers following a dot (.) at the end of a filename used to denote the type of the file; the filename extention .txt denotes a text file.

gedit editor — A text editor for the GNOME desktop.

grep (Global Regular Expression Print) command — A Linux command that searches files for patterns of characters using regular expression metacharacters.

head command — A Linux command that displays the first set of lines of a text file; by default, the head command displays the first 10 lines.

home directory — A directory on the filesystem set aside for users to store personal files and information.

insert mode — One of the two input modes in vi; it allows the user the ability to insert text into the document but does not allow any other functionality.

kedit editor — A text editor for the KDE desktop.

less command — A Linux command used to display a text file page-by-page on the terminal screen; users can then use the cursor keys to navigate the file.

linked file — The files that represent the same data as other files.

ll command — An alias for the ls -l command; it gives a long file listing.

log file — A file that contains past system events.

ls command — A Linux command used to list the files in a given directory.

mcedit editor (Midnight Commander Editor) — A user-friendly terminal text editor that supports regular expressions and the computer mouse.

more command — A Linux command used to display a text file page-by-page and line-by-line on the terminal screen.

named pipe file — A temporary connection that sends information from one command or process in memory to another; it can also be represented by a file on the filesystem.

nedit editor — A commonly used graphical text editor available in most Linux distributions.

od command — A Linux command used to display the contents of a file in octal format.

pwd (print working directory) command — A Linux command used to display the current directory in the directory tree.

regular expressions (regexp) — The special metacharacters used to match patterns of text within text files; they are commonly used by many text tool commands such as grep.

relative pathname — The pathname of a target directory relative to your current directory in the tree.

socket file — A named pipe connecting processes on two different computers; it can also be represented by a file on the filesystem.

special device file — A file used to identify hardware devices such as hard disks and serial ports.

strings command — A Linux command used to search for and display text characters in a binary file.

subdirectory — A directory that resides within another directory in the directory tree.

Tab-completion feature — A feature of the BASH shell that fills in the remaining characters of a unique filename or directory name when the user presses the Tab key.

tac command — A Linux command that displays a file to the screen beginning with the last line of the file and ending with the first line of the file.

tail command — A Linux command used to display the last set number of lines of text in a file; by default, the tail command displays the last 10 lines of the file.

text file — A file that stores information in a readable text format.

text tools — The programs that allow for the creation, modification, and searching of text files.

vi editor — A powerful command-line text editor available on most UNIX and Linux systems.

wildcard metacharacters — The metacharacters used to match certain characters in a file or directory name; they are often used to specify multiple files.

xemacs editor — A graphical version of the Emacs text editor.

Review Questions

1. Which Linux command is used to display the current directory?

   a. cd

   b. pwd

   c. ~

   d. dir

2. Which file name extension is used for compiled object files?

    a. .o

    b. .so

    c. .Z

    d. .sh

3. Which flag to the ls command is used to list all files?

    a. -a

    b. -A

    c. -F

    d. −r

4. Which vi command changes to insert mode and places the cursor before the current character for entering text?

    a. a

    b. A

    c. i

    d. I

5. Which Emacs command displays documentation?

    a. Ctrl+a

    b. Ctrl+d

    c. Ctrl+e

    d. Ctrl+h

6. True or false? Most files on a Linux system that contain configuration information are text files.

7. True or false? To view the contents of binary files, you typically use the program that was used to create the file.

8. True or false? Wildcard metacharacters are interpreted by a text tool program, whereas regular expressions are interpreted by the shell.

9. True or false? Although the vi editor is very easy to use, it is not portable.

10. True or false? The mcedit editor (Midnight Commander Editor) is an easy-to-use text editor that contains support for regular expressions and the ability to use the mouse for highlighting text.

11. The _____ feature of the BASH shell allows you to enter the beginning characters of a directory name, and press the tab key to allow the shell to complete the name.

12. _____ files have an association with one another; they can represent the same data or they can point to another file.

13. The _____ command can be used to provide a long listing for each file in a certain directory.

14. The _____ command displays the first 10 lines (including blank lines) of a text file to the terminal screen, but can also take a numeric option specifying a different number of lines to display.

15. The most common text tool that allows you the ability to search for information using regular expressions is the _____ command.

Chapter 5

Linux Filesystem Management

After completing this chapter, you will be able to:

◆ Explain the function of the Filesystem Hierarchy Standard

◆ Use standard Linux commands to manage files and directories

◆ Find files and directories on the filesystem

◆ Understand and create linked files

◆ Modify file and directory ownership

◆ Define and change Linux file and directory permissions

◆ Identify the default permissions created on files and directories

◆ Apply special file and directory permissions

In the previous chapter, you learned about navigating the Linux filesystem, as well as viewing and editing files. This chapter focuses on the organization of files on the Linux filesystem, as well as their linking and security. First, you explore standard Linux directories using the Filesystem Hierarchy Standard. Next, you explore common commands used to manage files and directories, followed by a discussion on finding files and directories. Finally, you learn about describing file and directory linking and common and special permissions available for files and directories.

The Filesystem Hierarchy Standard

Many thousands of files are on a typical Linux system, which are logically organized into directories in the Linux directory tree. This complexity also allows different Linux distributions to place files in different locations. As a result, a great deal of time can be spent searching for a common configuration file on a foreign Linux system. To solve this problem, the **Filesystem Hierarchy Standard (FHS)** was created.

FHS defines a standard set of directories for use by all Linux and UNIX systems, as well as the file and subdirectory contents of each directory. This ensures that, because the filename and location follow a standard convention, a Red Hat Linux user will find the correct configuration file on a SuSE Linux or Hewlett-Packard UNIX computer with little difficulty. The FHS also gives Linux software developers the ability to locate files on a Linux system regardless of the distribution, allowing them to create software that is not distribution-specific.

A comprehensive understanding of the standard types of directories found on Linux systems is valuable when locating and managing files and directories; some standard UNIX and Linux directories defined by FHS and their descriptions are found in Table 5-1. These directories are discussed throughout this chapter and the following chapters.

NOTE

To read the complete Filesystem Hierarchy Standard definition, visit the Internet at *http://www.pathname.com/fhs/*.

Table 5-1 Linux directories defined by the Filesystem Hierarchy Standard

Directory	Description
/bin	Contains binary commands for use by all users
/boot	Contains the Linux kernel and files used by the boot loader
/dev	Contains device files
/etc	Contains system-specific configuration files
/home	Is the default location for user home directories
/lib	Contains shared program libraries (used by the commands in /bin and /sbin) as well as kernel modules
/mnt	Is the empty directory used for accessing (mounting) disks, such as floppy disks and CD-ROMs
/opt	Stores additional software programs
/proc	Contains process and kernel information
/root	Is the root user's home directory
/sbin	Contains system binary commands (used for administration)
/tmp	Holds temporary files created by programs
/usr	Contains most system commands and utilities—contains the following directories: /usr/bin—User binary commands /usr/games—Educational programs and games /usr/include—C program header files /usr/lib—Libraries /usr/local—Local programs /usr/sbin—System binary commands /usr/share—Files that are architecture independent /usr/src—Source code /usr/X11R6—The X Window system
/usr/local	Is the location for most additional programs
/var	Contains log files and spools

Managing Files and Directories

As mentioned earlier, using a Linux system involves navigating several directories and manipulating the files inside them. Thus, an efficient Linux user must understand how to create directories as needed, copy or move files from one directory to another, and delete files and directories. These tasks are commonly referred to as file management tasks.

Following is an example of a directory listing while the user is logged in as the root user:

```
[root@server1 root]# pwd
/root
[root@server1 root]# ls -F
current@  myprogram*  project    project12  project2  project4
Desktop/  myscript    project1   project13  project3  project5 [root@server1 root]#_
```

As shown in the preceding output, only one directory (Desktop), two executable files (myprogram and myscript), and several project-related files (project*) exist. Although this directory structure is not cluttered and appears in an easy-to-read format on the terminal screen, typical home directories on a Linux system contain many more files; a typical Linux user might have over 100 files in his home directory. As a result, it is good practice to organize these files into subdirectories based on file purpose. Because several project files are in the root user's home directory in the preceding output, you could create a subdirectory called proj_files to contain the project-related files and decrease the size of the directory listing. To do this, you use the **mkdir (make directory) command**, which takes arguments specifying the absolute or relative pathnames of the directories to create. To create a proj_files directory underneath the current directory, you can use the mkdir command with a relative pathname:

```
[root@server1 root]# mkdir proj_files
[root@server1 root]# ls -F
current@  myprogram*  project    project12  project2  project4  proj_files/
Desktop/  myscript*   project1   project13  project3  project5
[root@server1 root]#_
```

Now, you can move the project files into the proj_files subdirectory by using the **mv (move) command**. The mv command requires two arguments at minimum: the **source file/directory** and the **target file/directory**. If several files are to be moved, simply specify several source arguments; the last argument then becomes the target directory. Both the source(s) and destination can be absolute or relative pathnames, and the source can contain wildcards if several files are to be moved. For example, to move all of the project files to the proj_files directory, you could type mv with the source argument project* (to match all files starting with the letters "project") and the target argument proj_files (relative pathname to the destination directory), as shown in the following output:

```
[root@server1 root]# mv project* proj_files
[root@server1 root]# ls -F
current@  Desktop/  myprogram*  myscript*  proj_files/
[root@server1 root]# ls -F proj_files
```

```
project  project1  project12  project13  project2  project3  project4  project5
[root@server1 root]#_
```

In the preceding output, the current directory listing does not show the project files anymore, yet the listing of the proj_files subdirectory indicates that they were moved successfully.

> ### NOTE
>
> If the target is the name of a directory, the mv command moves those files to that directory. If the target is a filename of an existing file in a certain directory and there is one source file, the mv command overwrites the target with the source. If the target is a filename of a nonexistent file in a certain directory, the mv command creates a new file with that filename in the target directory and moves the source file to that file.

Another important use of the mv command is to rename files, which is simply moving a file to the same directory but with a different filename. To rename the myscript file from earlier examples to myscript2, you can use the following mv command:

```
[root@server1 root]# ls -F
current@ Desktop/ myprogram* myscript* proj_files/
[root@server1 root]# mv myscript myscript2
[root@server1 root]# ls -F
current@ Desktop/ myprogram* myscript2* proj_files/
[root@server1 root]#_
```

Similarly, the mv command can rename directories. If the source is the name of an existing directory, it is renamed to whatever directory name is specified as the target.

The mv command works similarly to a "cut and paste" operation in which the file is copied to a new directory and deleted from the source directory. There might be times, however, when the file in the source directory should be maintained; this is referred to as copying a file and can be accomplished using the **cp (copy) command**. Much like the mv command, the cp command takes two arguments at minimum. The first argument specifies the source file/directory to be copied and the second argument specifies the target file/directory. If several files need to be copied to a destination directory, simply specify several source arguments and the final argument on the command line becomes the target directory. Each argument can be an absolute or relative pathname and can contain wildcards or the special metacharacters "." (specifies the current directory) and ".." (specifies the parent directory). For example, to make a copy of the file /etc/hosts in the current directory (/root), you can specify the absolute pathname to the /etc/hosts file (/etc/hosts) and the relative pathname indicating the current directory(.):

```
[root@server1 root]# cp /etc/hosts .
[root@server1 root]# ls -F
current@ Desktop/ hosts myprogram* myscript2* proj_files/
[root@server1 root]#_
```

You can also make copies of files in the same directory. To make a copy of the hosts file called hosts2 in the current directory, type the following command:

```
[root@server1 root]# cp hosts hosts2
[root@server1 root]# ls -F
current@ Desktop/ hosts hosts2 myprogram* myscript2* proj_files/ [root@server1 root]#_
```

One notable difference between the mv and cp commands, aside from their purpose, is that they work on directories differently. The mv command simply renames a directory, whereas the cp command creates a whole new copy of the directory and its contents. To copy a directory full of files in Linux, you must tell the cp command that the copy will be **recursive** (involve files and subdirectories too) by using the -r option. The following example demonstrates copying the proj_files directory and all of its contents to the /home/user1 directory without and with the -r option:

```
[root@server1 root]# ls -F
current@ Desktop/ hosts myprogram* myscript2* proj_files/
[root@server1 root]# ls -F /home/user1
Desktop/
[root@server1 root]# cp proj_files /home/user1
cp: omitting directory `proj_files'
[root@server1 root]# ls -F /home/user1
Desktop/
[root@server1 root]# cp -r proj_files /home/user1
[root@server1 root]# ls -F /home/user1
Desktop/  proj_files/
[root@server1 root]#_
```

When copying or moving files, if the target is a file that exists, the mv and cp commands warn the user that the target file will be overwritten and ask whether to continue. This is not a feature of the command as normally invoked, but is a feature of the default configuration in Red Hat Linux because the BASH shell in Red Hat Linux contains aliases to the cp and mv commands.

NOTE

Aliases are special variables in memory that point to commands; they are fully discussed in Chapter 8, "Working with the BASH Shell."

When you type mv, you are really running the mv command with the -i option, which interactively prompts the user to choose whether to overwrite the existing file if the target file already exists when the command is executed; this is called **interactive mode**. Similarly, when you type the cp command, the cp -i command is run to perform the same function. To see the aliases present in your current shell, simply type alias, as shown in the following output:

```
[root@server1 root]# alias
alias cp='cp -i'
alias l.='ls -d .* --color=tty'
alias ll='ls -l --color=tty'
alias ls='ls --color=tty'
alias mc='. /usr/share/mc/bin/mc-wrapper.sh
alias mv='mv -i'
alias rm='rm -i'
alias vi='vim'
alias which='alias | /usr/bin/which --tty-only --read-alias --show-dot --show-tilde'
[root@server1 root]#_
```

If you want to override this interactive option, use the -f (force) option to override the choice, as shown in the following example in which the root user tries to rename the hosts file to the hosts2 file that already exists without and with the -f option to the mv command:

```
[root@server1 root]# ls -F
current@ Desktop/ hosts  hosts2  myprogram*  myscript2*  proj_files/ [root@server1
    root]# mv hosts hosts2
mv: overwrite `hosts2'? n
[root@server1 root]# mv -f hosts hosts2
[root@server1 root]# ls -F
current@ Desktop/ hosts2  myprogram*  myscript2*  proj_files/ [root@server1 root]#_
```

Creating directories, copying, and moving files are file management tasks that preserve or create data on the hard disk. To remove files or directories, you must use either the rm command or the rmdir command.

The **rm (remove) command** takes a list of arguments specifying the absolute or relative pathnames of files to remove. As with most commands, wildcards can be used to simplify specifying multiple files to remove. After a file has been removed from the filesystem, it cannot be recovered. As a result, the rm command is aliased in Red Hat Linux to the rm command with the -i option, which interactively prompts the user to choose whether to continue with the deletion. Like the cp and mv commands, the rm command also accepts the -f option to override this choice and immediately delete the file. An example demonstrating the use of the rm and rm -f commands to remove the current and hosts2 files is shown in the following example:

```
[root@server1 root]# ls -F
current@ Desktop/ hosts2  myprogram*  myscript2*  proj_files/
[root@server1 root]# rm current
rm: remove `current'? y
```

```
[root@server1 root]# rm -f hosts2
[root@server1 root]# ls -F
Desktop/  myprogram*  myscript2*  proj_files/
[root@server1 root]# _
```

To remove a directory, you can use the rmdir command; however, the **rmdir (remove directory) command** only removes a directory if it contains no files. To remove a directory and the files inside, you must use the rm command and specify that a directory full of files should be removed. Recall from earlier that you need to use the recursive option (-r) with the cp command to copy directories; to remove a directory full of files, you can also use a recursive option (−r) with the rm command. If, for example, the root user wants to remove the proj_files subdirectory and all of the files within it without being prompted to confirm each file deletion, the command she must use is rm -rf proj_files as shown in the following example:

```
[root@server1 root]# ls -F
Desktop/  myprogram*  myscript2*  proj_files/
[root@server1 root]# rmdir proj_files
rmdir: `proj_files': Directory not empty
[root@server1 root]# rm -rf proj_files
[root@server1 root]# ls -F
Desktop/  myprogram*  myscript2*
[root@server1 root]# _
```

TIP

In most commands, such as rm and cp, both the -r and the -R options have the same meaning (recursive).

NOTE

The -r option to the rm command is dangerous if you are not certain which files exist in the directory to be deleted recursively. As a result, the -r option to the rm command is commonly referred to as the -résumé option; if you use it incorrectly, you might need to prepare your résumé.

It is important to note that the aforementioned file management commands are commonly used by Linux users, developers, and administrators alike. Table 5-2 shows a summary of these common file management commands.

Table 5-2 Common Linux file management commands

Command	Description
mkdir	Creates directories
rmdir	Removes empty directories
mv	Moves/renames files and directories
cp	Copies files and directories full of files (with the −r option)
alias	Displays BASH shell aliases
rm	Removes files and directories full of files (with the −r option)

Finding Files

Before using the file management commands mentioned in the preceding section, you must know the locations of the files involved. The fastest method to search for files in the Linux directory tree is to use the **locate command**, which is a shortcut to the slocate (or secure locate) command. For example, to view all of the files underneath the root directory that have the word "inittab" as, or part of, the filename, you can simply type locate inittab at a command prompt, which produces the following output:

```
[root@server1 root]# locate inittab
/usr/share/terminfo/a/ansi+inittabs
/usr/share/vim/vim62/syntax/inittab.vim
/usr/share/man/ja/man5/inittab.5.gz
/usr/share/man/pl/man5/inittab.5.gz
/usr/share/man/it/man5/inittab.5.gz
/usr/share/man/man5/inittab.5.gz
/usr/share/man/fr/man5/inittab.5.gz
/usr/share/man/ko/man5/inittab.5.gz
/etc/inittab
[root@server1 root]# _
```

Quite often, the locate command returns too much information to display on the screen, as it searches all files on the filesystem. Often, you can use the more (or less) command to pause the output, as in locate inittab | more, or else you must ensure that the word being searched is very specific. The locate command looks in a premade database that contains a list of all the files on the system. This database is indexed much like a textbook for fast searching, yet can become outdated as files are added and removed from the system, which happens on a regular basis. As a result, the database used for the locate command (/var/lib/slocate/slocate.db) is updated each day automatically and can be updated manually by running either the updatedb or slocate -u commands at a command prompt.

A slower, yet more versatile method for locating files on the filesystem is to use the **find command**. The `find` command does not use a premade index of files, but instead searches the directory tree recursively starting from a certain directory for files that meet a certain criteria. The format of the `find` command is as follows:

```
find <start directory> -criteria <what to find>
```

For example, to find any files named "inittab" underneath the /etc directory, you can use the command `find /etc -name inittab` and receive the following output:

```
[root@server1 root]# find /etc -name inittab
/etc/inittab
[root@server1 root]# _
```

You can also use wildcard metacharacters with the `find` command; however, these wildcards must be protected from shell interpretation, as they must only be interpreted by the `find` command. To do this, ensure that any wildcard metacharacters are enclosed within quote characters. An example of using the `find` command with wildcard metacharacters to find all files that start with the letters "host" underneath the /etc directory is shown in the following output:

```
[root@server1 root]# find /etc -name "host*"
/etc/hosts.deny
/etc/hosts.canna
/etc/logd/scripts/shared/hostlist
/etc/ups/hosts.conf
/etc/hosts.allow
/etc/host.conf
/etc/hosts
[root@server1 root]# _
```

Although searching by name is the most common criteria used with the `find` command, many other criteria can be used with the `find` command as well. To find all files starting from the /var directory that have a size greater than 4096K (Kilobytes), you can use the following command:

```
[root@server1 root]# find /var -size +4096k
/var/log/lastlog
/var/lib/rpm/Packages
/var/lib/rpm/Filemd5s
/var/lib/rpm/Basenames
/var/lib/canna/dic/canna/zipcode.ctd
/var/lib/imap/db/_db.004
/var/lib/slocate/slocate.db
[root@server1 root]# _
```

As well, if you want to find all the directories only underneath the /mnt directory, you can type the following command:

```
[root@server1 dev]# find /mnt -type d
/mnt
/mnt/floppy
/mnt/cdrom
[root@server1 root]# _
```

Table 5-3 provides a list of some common criteria used with the `find` command.

Table 5-3 Common criteria used with the `find` command

Criteria	Description
-amin -x	Searches for files that were accessed less than x minutes ago
-amin +x	Searches for files that were accessed more than x minutes ago
-atime -x	Searches for files that were accessed less than x days ago
-atime +x	Searches for files that were accessed more than x days ago
-empty	Searches for empty files or directories
-fstype x	Searches for files if they are on a certain filesystem x (where n could be ext2, ext3, and so on)
-group x	Searches for files that are owned by a certain group or GID (x)
-inum x	Searches for files that have an inode number of x
-mmin -x	Searches for files that were modified less than x minutes ago
-mmin +x	Searches for files that were modified more than x minutes ago
-mtime -x	Searches for files that were modified less than x days ago
-mtime +x	Searches for files that were modified more than x days ago
-name x	Searches for a certain filename x (x can contain wildcards)
-regexp x	Searches for certain filenames using regular expressions instead of wildcard metacharacters
-size -x	Searches for files with a size less than x
-size x	Searches for files with a size of x
-size +x	Searches for files with a size greater than x

Table 5-3 **Common criteria used with the find command (Continued)**

Criteria	Description
-type x	Searches for files of type x where x is: ◆ b for block files ◆ c for character files ◆ d for directory files ◆ p for named pipes ◆ f for regular files ◆ l for symbolic links (shortcuts) ◆ s for sockets
-user x	Searches for files owned by a certain user or UID (x)

Although the find command can be used to search for files based on many criteria, it might take several minutes to complete the search if the number of directories and files being searched is large. To reduce the time needed to search, narrow down the directories searched by specifying a subdirectory when possible. It takes less time to search the /usr/local/bin directory and its subdirectories, compared to searching the /usr directory and all of its subdirectories. As well, if the filename that you are searching for is an executable file, that file can likely be found in less time using the **which command**. The which command only searches directories that are listed in a special variable called the **PATH variable** in the current BASH shell. Before exploring the which command, you must understand the usage of PATH.

Executable files can be stored in directories scattered around the directory tree. Recall from FHS that most executable files are stored in directories named bin or sbin, yet there are over 20 bin and sbin directories scattered around the directory tree after a typical Red Hat Linux installation. To ensure that users do not need to specify the full pathname to commands such as ls (which is the executable file /bin/ls), there exists a special variable called PATH that is placed into memory each time a user logs in to the Linux system. Recall that you can see the contents of a certain variable in memory by using the $ metacharacter with the echo command:

```
[root@server1 root]# echo $PATH
/usr/kerberos/sbin:/usr/kerberos/bin:/usr/local/sbin:/usr/local/bin:/sbin:/bin:/usr/sbin:
/usr/bin:/usr/X11R6/bin:/root/bin
[root@server1 root]# _
```

The PATH variable lists directories that are searched for executable files if a relative or absolute pathname was not specified when executing a command on the command line. In the preceding output, when a user types the ls command on the command line and presses Enter, the system recognizes that the command was not an absolute pathname (for example, /bin/ls) or relative pathname (for example, ../../bin/ls) and then proceeds to look for the ls executable file in the /usr/kerberos/sbin directory, then the /usr/kerberos/bin directory, then the /usr/local/sbin directory, and so on. If all the directories in the PATH variable are searched and no `ls` command is found, the shell gives an error message to the user stating that the command was not found. In the preceding output, the /bin directory is in the PATH variable and, thus, the `ls` command is found and executed, but not until the previous directories in the PATH variable are searched first.

To search the directories in the PATH variable for the file called "grep," you could use the word "grep" as an argument for the `which` command and receive the following output:

```
[root@server1 sbin]# which grep
/bin/grep
[root@server1 root]# _
```

If the file being searched does not exist in the PATH variable directories, the `which` command lets you know in which directories it was not found, as shown in the following output:

```
[root@server1 sbin]# which grepper
/usr/bin/which: no grepper in (/usr/kerberos/sbin:/usr/kerberos/bin:/us
r/local/sbin:/usr/local/bin:/sbin:/bin:/usr/sbin:/usr/bin:/usr/X11R6/bin:/root/bin)
[root@server1 root]# _
```

Linking Files

Recall that files can be linked to one another. This linking can happen in one of two ways: One file might simply be a pointer or shortcut to another file (known as a **symbolic link** or symlink), or two files might share the same data (known as a **hard link**).

To better understand how files are linked, you must understand how files are stored on a filesystem. On a structural level, a filesystem has three main sections:

◆ The superblock
◆ The inode table
◆ Data blocks

The **superblock** is the section that contains information about the filesystem in general, such as the number of inodes and data blocks, as well as how much data a data block stores in Kilobytes. The **inode table** consists of several **inodes** (information nodes); each inode describes one file or directory on the filesystem, and contains a unique inode number for identification. More importantly, the inode stores information such as the file size, data block locations, last date modified, permissions, and ownership. When a file is deleted, only its inode (which serves as a pointer to the actual data) is deleted. The data that makes up the contents of the file as well as the filename are stored in **data blocks**, which are referenced by the inode. In filesystem-neutral terminology, blocks are known as allocation units because they are the unit by which disk space is allocated for storage.

> ### NOTE
>
> Each file and directory must have an inode. All files except for special device files also have data blocks associated with the inode. Special device files are discussed in Chapter 6, "Linux Filesystem Administration."
>
> Directories are simply files that are used to organize other files; they too have an inode and data blocks, but their data blocks contain a list of filenames that are located within the directory.

Hard-linked files are direct copies of one another, as they share the same inode and inode number. All hard linked files have the same size, and when one file is modified, the other hard linked files are updated as well. This relationship between hard linked files can be seen in Figure 5-1. You can hard-link a file an unlimited number of times; however, the hard linked files must reside on the same filesystem. This is because inode numbers are unique only on the same filesystem and hard links are recognized by ignoring this rule.

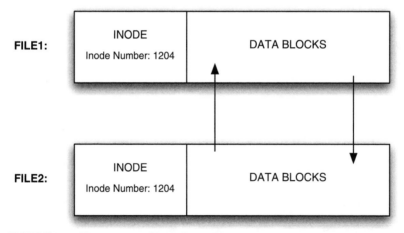

FIGURE 5-1 *The structure of hard-linked files*

To create a hard link, you must use the **ln (link) command** and specify two arguments: the existing file to hard link and the target file that will be created as a hard link to the existing file. Each argument can be the absolute or relative pathname to a file. Take, for example, the following contents of the root user's home directory:

```
[root@server1 root]# ls -l
total 520
drwx------    3 root      root         4096 Apr  8 07:12 Desktop
-rwxr-xr-x    1 root      root       519964 Apr  7 09:59 file1
-rwxr-xr-x    1 root      root         1244 Apr 27 18:17 file3 [root@server1 root]# _
```

If you want to make a hard link to file1 called file2, as in Figure 5-1, you can issue the command `ln file1 file2` at the command prompt; a file called file2 is created and hard-linked to file1. To view the hard-linked filenames after creation, you can use the `ls -l` command:

```
[root@server1 root]# ln file1 file2
[root@server1 root]# ls -l
total 1032
drwx------   3 root    root       4096 Apr  8 07:12 Desktop
-rwxr-xr-x   2 root    root     519964 Apr  7 09:59 file1
-rwxr-xr-x   2 root    root     519964 Apr  7 09:59 file2
-rwxr-xr-x   1 root    root       1244 Apr 27 18:17 file3 [root@server1 root]# _
```

Notice from the preceding long listing that file1 and file2 share the same inode, as they have the same size, permissions, ownership, modification date, and so on. Also note that the link count (the number after the permission set) for file1 has increased from the number one to the number two in the preceding output. A link count of one indicates that only one inode is shared by the file. A file that is hard-linked to another file shares two inodes and, thus, has a link count of two. Similarly, a file that is hard-linked to three other files shares four inodes and, thus, has a link count of four.

Although hard links share the same inode, deleting a hard linked file does not delete all the other hard linked files. Removing a hard link can be achieved by removing one of the files, which then lowers the link count.

To view the inode number of hard-linked files to verify that they are identical, you can use the `-i` option to the `ls` command in addition to any other options. The inode number is placed on the left of the directory listing on each line, as shown in the following output:

```
[root@server1 root]# ls -li
total 1032
37595 drwx------   3 root    root       4096 Apr  8 07:12 Desktop
 1204 -rwxr-xr-x   2 root    root     519964 Apr  7 09:59 file1
 1204 -rwxr-xr-x   2 root    root     519964 Apr  7 09:59 file2
17440 -rwxr-xr-x   1 root    root       1244 Apr 27 18:17 file3 [root@server1 root]# _
```

> **NOTE**
>
> Directory files are not normally hard-linked, as the result would consist of two directories that contain the same contents. However, the root user has the ability to hard-link directories in some cases, using the `-F` or `-d` option to the `ln` command. Only directories that have files regularly added and need to maintain identical file contents are typically hard-linked.

Symbolic links (shown in Figure 5-2) are different than hard links because they do not share the same inode and inode number with their target file; one is merely a pointer to the other and, thus, both files have different sizes. The data blocks in a symbolically linked file contain only the pathname to the target file. When a user edits a symbolically linked file, he is actually editing the target file. Thus, if the target file is deleted, the symbolic link serves no function, as it points to a nonexistent file.

> **NOTE**
>
> Symbolic links are sometimes referred to as "soft links" or "symlinks."

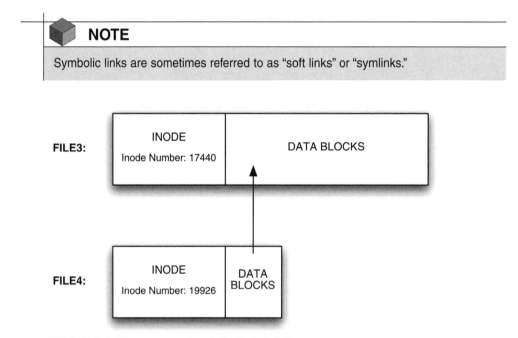

FIGURE 5-2 *The structure of symbolically linked files*

To create a symbolic link, you use the -s option to the ln command. To create a symbolic link to file3 called file4, as in Figure 5-2, you can type ln -s file3 file4 at the command prompt. As with hard links, the arguments specified can be absolute or relative pathnames. To view the symbolically linked filenames after creation, you can use the ls -l command, as shown in the following example:

```
[root@server1 root]# ln -s file3 file4
[root@server1 root]# ls -l
total 1032
drwx------    3 root     root        4096 Apr  8 07:12 Desktop
-rwxr-xr-x    2 root     root      519964 Apr  7 09:59 file1
-rwxr-xr-x    2 root     root      519964 Apr  7 09:59 file2
-rwxr-xr-x    1 root     root        1244 Apr 27 18:17 file3
lrwxrwxrwx    1 root     root           5 Apr 27 19:05 file4 -> file3 [root@server1 root]# _
```

Notice from the preceding output that file4 does not share the same inode, because the permissions, size, and modification date are different from file3. In addition, symbolic links are easier to identify than hard links; the file type character (before the permissions) is l, which indicates a symbolic link, and the filename points to the target using an arrow. The ls -F command also indicates symbolic links by appending an @ symbol, as shown in the following output:

```
[root@server1 root]# ls -F
Desktop/  file1*  file2*  file3*  file4@
[root@server1 root]# _
```

Another difference between hard links and symbolic links is that symbolic links need not reside on the same filesystem as their target. Instead, they point to the target filename and do not require the same inode, as shown in the following output:

```
[root@server1 root]# ls -li
total 1032
37595 drwx------   3 root    root     4096 Apr  8 07:12 Desktop
 1204 -rwxr-xr-x   2 root    root   519964 Apr  7 09:59 file1
 1204 -rwxr-xr-x   2 root    root   519964 Apr  7 09:59 file2
17440 -rwxr-xr-x   1 root    root     1244 Apr 27 18:17 file3
19926 lrwxrwxrwx   1 root    root        5 Apr 27 19:05 file4 -> file3
[root@server1 root]# _
```

NOTE

Unlike hard links, symbolic links are commonly made to directories to simplify navigating the filesystem tree. Also, symbolic links made to directories are typically used to maintain compatibility with other UNIX and Linux systems. On Red Hat Fedora Linux, the /etc/init.d directory is symbolically linked to the /etc/rc.d/init.d directory and the /usr/tmp directory is symbolically linked to the /var/tmp directory for this reason.

File and Directory Permissions

Recall that all users must successfully log in with a user name and password to gain access to a Linux system. After logging in, users are identified by their user name and group memberships; all access to resources depends on whether their user name and group memberships have the required **permission**. Thus, a firm understanding of ownership and permissions is necessary to operate a Linux system in a secure manner and to prevent unauthorized users access to sensitive files, directories, and commands.

File and Directory Ownership

When a user creates a file or directory, that user's name and **primary group** becomes the owner and group owner of the file, respectively. This affects the permission structure, as you see in the next section; however, it also determines who has the ability to modify file and directory permissions and ownership. The owner of the file or directory and the root user are the only two users on a Linux system who can modify permissions on a file or directory or change its ownership.

To view your current user name, you can use the whoami command. To view your group memberships and primary group, you can use the groups command. An example of these two commands when logged in as the root user is shown in the following output:

```
[root@server1 root]# whoami
root
[root@server1 root]# groups
root bin daemon sys adm disk wheel
[root@server1 root]# _
```

Notice from the preceding output that the root user is a member of seven groups, yet the root user's primary group is also called "root," as it is the first group mentioned in the output of the group's command. If this user creates a file, the owner is "root" and the group owner is also "root." To quickly create an empty file, you can use the **touch command**:

```
[root@server1 root]# touch file1
[root@server1 root]# ls -l
total 4
drwx------    3 root      root        4096 Apr  8 07:12 Desktop
-rw-r--r--    1 root      root           0 Apr 29 15:40 file1 [root@server1 root]# _
```

Notice from the preceding output that the owner of file1 is "root" and the group owner is the root group. To change the ownership of a file or directory, you can use the **chown (change owner) command**, which takes two arguments at minimum: the new owner and the files or directories to change. Both arguments can be absolute or relative pathnames, and you can also change permissions recursively throughout the directory tree using the -R option to the chown command. To change the ownership of file1 to the user user1 and the ownership of the directory Desktop and all of its contents to user1 as well, you can enter the following commands:

```
[root@server1 root]# chown user1 file1
[root@server1 root]# chown -R user1 Desktop
[root@server1 root]# ls -l
total 4
drwx------    3 user1     root        4096 Apr  8 07:12 Desktop
-rw-r--r--    1 user1     root           0 Apr 29 15:40 file1
[root@server1 root]# ls -l Desktop
total 16
-rw-------    1 user1     root         163 Mar 29 09:58 Floppy
```

```
-rw-r--r--    1 user1    root    3578 Mar 29 09:58 Home
-rw-r--r--    1 user1    root    1791 Mar 29 09:58 Start Here
drwx------    2 user1    root    4096 Mar 29 09:58 Trash
[root@server1 root]# _
```

Recall that the owner of a file or directory and the root user have the ability to change ownership of a particular file or directory. If a regular user changes the ownership of a file or directory that he owns, that user cannot gain the ownership back. Instead, the new owner of that file or directory must change it to the original user. However, the previous examples involve the root user, who always has the ability to regain the ownership:

```
[root@server1 root]# chown root file1
[root@server1 root]# chown -R root Desktop
[root@server1 root]# ls -l
total 4
drwx------    3 root    root    4096 Apr  8 07:12 Desktop
-rw-r--r--    1 root    root       0 Apr 29 15:40 file1 [root@server1 root]# ls -l
Desktop
total 16
-rw-------    1 root    root     163 Mar 29 09:58 Floppy
-rw-r--r--    1 root    root    3578 Mar 29 09:58 Home
-rw-r--r--    1 root    root    1791 Mar 29 09:58 Start Here
drwx------    2 root    root    4096 Mar 29 09:58 Trash
[root@server1 root]# _
```

Just as the chown (change owner) command can be used to change the owner of a file or directory, you can use the **chgrp (change group) command** to change the group owner of a file or directory. The chgrp command takes two arguments at minimum: the new group owner and the files or directories to change. As with the chown command, the chgrp command also accepts the -R option to change group ownership recursively throughout the directory tree. To change the group owner of file1 and the Desktop directory recursively throughout the directory tree, you can execute the following commands:

```
[root@server1 root]# chgrp sys file1
[root@server1 root]# chgrp -R sys Desktop
[root@server1 root]# ls -l
total 4
drwx------    3 root    sys     4096 Apr  8 07:12 Desktop
-rw-r--r--    1 root    sys        0 Apr 29 15:40 file1
[root@server1 root]# ls -l Desktop
total 16
-rw-------    1 root    sys      163 Mar 29 09:58 Floppy
-rw-r--r--    1 root    sys     3578 Mar 29 09:58 Home
-rw-r--r--    1 root    sys     1791 Mar 29 09:58 Start Here
drwx------    2 root    sys     4096 Mar 29 09:58 Trash
[root@server1 root]# _
```

> **NOTE**
>
> Regular users can change the group of a file or directory only to a group of which they are a member.

Normally, you change both the ownership and group ownership on a file when that file needs to be maintained by someone else. As a result, you can change both the owner and the group owner at the same time using the chown command. To change the owner to user1 and the group owner to root for file1 and the directory Desktop recursively, you can enter the following commands:

```
[root@server1 root]# chown user1.root file1
[root@server1 root]# chown -R user1.root Desktop
[root@server1 root]# ls -l
total 4
drwx------    3 user1    root     4096 Apr  8 07:12 Desktop
-rw-r--r--    1 user1    root        0 Apr 29 15:40 file1
[root@server1 root]# ls -l Desktop
total 16
-rw-------    1 user1    root      163 Mar 29 09:58 Floppy
-rw-r--r--    1 user1    root     3578 Mar 29 09:58 Home
-rw-r--r--    1 user1    root     1791 Mar 29 09:58 Start Here
drwx------    2 user1    root     4096 Mar 29 09:58 Trash
[root@server1 root]# _
```

Note that there must be no spaces before and after the . character in the chown commands shown in the preceding output.

> **NOTE**
>
> You can also use the : character instead of the . character in the chown command to change both the owner and group ownership (for example, chown -R user1:root Desktop).

Most files that reside in a user's home directory should be owned by that user for good security; some files in a user's home directory (especially the hidden files and directories) require this to function properly. To change the ownership back to the root user for file1 and the Desktop directory to avoid future problems, you can type the following:

```
[root@server1 root]# chown root.root file1
[root@server1 root]# chown -R root.root Desktop
[root@server1 root]# ls -l
total 4
```

```
drwx------      3 root      root      4096 Apr  8 07:12 Desktop
-rw-r--r--      1 root      root         0 Apr 29 15:40 file1 [root@server1 root]# ls -l
Desktop
total 16
-rw-------      1 root      root       163 Mar 29 09:58 Floppy
-rw-r--r--      1 root      root      3578 Mar 29 09:58 Home
-rw-r--r--      1 root      root      1791 Mar 29 09:58 Start Here
drwx------      2 root      root      4096 Mar 29 09:58 Trash
[root@server1 root]# _
```

Managing File and Directory Permissions

Every file and directory file on a Linux filesystem contains information regarding permissions in its inode. The section of the inode that stores permissions is called the **mode** of the file and is divided into three sections based on the user(s) who receive the permissions to that file or directory:

◆ User (owner) permissions
◆ Group (group owner) permissions
◆ Other (everyone on the Linux system) permissions

Furthermore, you can assign three regular permissions to each of these user(s):

◆ Read
◆ Write
◆ Execute

Interpreting the Mode

Recall that the three sections of the mode and the permissions that you can assign to each section are viewed when you perform an ls -l command; a detailed depiction of this is shown in Figure 5-3. It is important to note that the root user supersedes all file and directory permissions; in other words, the root user has all permissions to every file and directory regardless of what the mode of the file or directory indicates.

Consider the root user's home directory listing shown in the following example:

```
[root@server1 root]# ls -l
total 28
drwx------      3 root      root      4096 Apr  8 07:12 Desktop
-r---w---x      1 root      root       282 Apr 29 22:06 file1
-------rwx      1 root      root       282 Apr 29 22:06 file2
-rwxrwxrwx      1 root      root       282 Apr 29 22:06 file3
----------      1 root      root       282 Apr 29 22:06 file4
-rw-r--r--      1 root      root       282 Apr 29 22:06 file5
-rw-r--r--      1 user1     sys        282 Apr 29 22:06 file6 [root@server1 root]# _
```

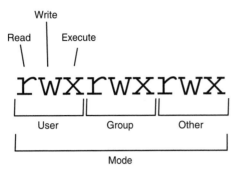

FIGURE 5-3 *The structure of a mode*

Note from the preceding output that all permissions (as shown in Figure 5-3) need not be on a file or directory; if the permission is unavailable, a dash character (-) replaces its position in the mode. Be certain not to confuse the character to the left of the mode (which determines the file type) with the mode, as it is unrelated to the permissions on the file or directory. From the preceding output, the Desktop directory gives the **user** or **owner** of the directory (the root user) read, write, and execute permission, yet members of the **group** (the root group) do not receive any permissions to the directory. Note that **other** (everyone on the system) does not receive permissions to this directory either.

Permissions are additive; the root user is also a member of the root group and is always a part of the other category, thus the root user receives the permissions that are available to all three categories of users. In the preceding example, this means that the root user has read, write, and execute permission to the Desktop directory.

Along the same lines, the file called file1 in the preceding output gives the user or owner of the file (the root user) read permission, and gives members of the group (the root group) write permission, and finally gives other (everyone on the system) execute permission. Because permissions are additive and the root user is matched by all three categories of users, the root user shall receive read, write, and execute to file1.

Because permissions are additive in Linux, the other category seldom contains entries on sensitive files as it applies to all users. Although file2 in our example does not give the user or group any permissions, all users receive read, write, and execute permission via the other category. Thus, file2 should not contain sensitive data because all users have full access to it. For the same reason, it is bad form to assign all permissions to a file that contains sensitive data, as shown with file3 in the preceding example.

On the contrary, it is also possible to have a file that has no permissions assigned to it, as shown in the preceding file4. In this case, the only user who has permissions to the file is the root user. Also remember that the owner of the file can change these permissions if needed.

The permission structure that you choose for a file or directory might result in too few or too many permissions. You can follow some general guidelines to avoid these situations. The owner of a file or directory is typically the person who maintains it; members of the group are typically users in the same company department and must have limited access to the file or directory. As a result, most files and directories that you find on a Linux filesystem have more permissions assigned to the user of the file/directory than to the group of the file/directory, and the other category has either the same permissions or less than the group of the file/directory, depending on how private that file or directory is. The file file5 in the previous output depicts this common permission structure. In addition, files in a user's home directory are typically owned by that user; however, you might occasionally find files that are not. For these files, their permission definition changes, as shown in the previous file6. The user or owner of file6 is user1, who has read and write permissions to the file. The group owner of file6 is the sys group; thus, any members of the sys group have read permission to the file. Finally, everyone on the system receives read permission to the file via the other category. Regardless of the mode, the root user receives all permissions to this file.

Interpreting Permissions

After you understand how to identify the permissions that are applied to user, group, and other on a certain file or directory, you can then interpret the function of those permissions. Permissions for files are interpreted differently than those for directories. Also, if a user has a certain permission on a directory, that user does not have the same permission for all files or subdirectories within that directory; file and directory permissions are treated separately by the Linux system. Table 5-4 shows a summary of the different permissions and their definitions.

Table 5-4 Linux permissions

Permission	Definition for Files	Definition for Directories
Read	Allows a user to open and read the contents of a file	Allows a user to list the contents of the directory (if he has also been given execute permission)
Write	Allows a user to open, read, and edit the contents of a file	Allows a user the ability to add or remove files to and from the directory (if he has also been given execute permission)
Execute	Allows a user the ability to execute the file in memory (if it is a program file) and shell scripts	Allows a user the ability to enter the directory and work with directory contents

The implications of the permission definitions described in Table 5-4 are important to understand. If a user has the read permission to a text file, that user can use, among others, the `cat`, `more`, `head`, `tail`, `less`, `strings`, and `od` commands to view its contents. That same user can also open that file with a text editor such as vi; however, the user does not have the ability to save any changes to the document unless that user has the write permission to the file as well.

Recall from earlier that some text files contain instructions for the shell to execute and are called shell scripts. Shell scripts are executed in much the same way that binary compiled programs are; the user who executes the shell script must then have execute permission to that file to execute it as a program.

TIP

It is important to avoid giving execute permission to files that are not programs or shell scripts. This ensures that these files will not be executed accidentally, causing the shell to interpret the contents.

Remember that directories are simply special files that have an inode and a data section, yet the contents of the data section is a list of that directory's contents. If you want to read that list, using the ls command for example, then you require the read permission to the directory. To modify that list, by adding or removing files, you require the write permission to the directory. Thus, if you want to create a new file in a directory with a text editor such as vi, you must have the write permission to that directory. Similarly, when a source file is copied to a target directory with the cp command, a new file is created in the target directory and you must have the write permission to the target directory for the copy to be successful. Conversely, to delete a certain file, you must have the write permission to the directory that contains that file. It is also important to note that a user who has the write permission to a directory has the ability to delete all files and subdirectories within it.

The execute permission on a directory is sometimes referred to as the search permission, and works similarly to a light switch. When a light switch is turned on, you can navigate a room and use the objects within it. However, when a light switch is turned off, you cannot see the objects in the room, nor can you walk around and view them. A user who does not have the execute permission to a directory is prevented from listing the directory's contents, adding and removing files, and working with files and subdirectories inside that directory, regardless of what permissions the user has to them. In short, a quick way to deny a user from accessing a directory and all of its contents in Linux is to take away the execute permission on that directory. Because the execute permission on a directory is crucial for user access, it is commonly given to all users via the other category, unless the directory must be private.

Changing Permissions

To change the permissions for a certain file or directory, you can use the **chmod (change mode) command**. The chmod command takes two arguments at minimum; the first argument specifies the criteria used to change the permissions (Table 5-5) and the remaining arguments indicate the filenames to change.

Table 5-5 Criteria used within the chmod command

Category	Operation	Permission
u (user)	+ (adds a permission)	r (read)
g (group)	- (removes a permission)	w (write)
o (other)	= (makes a permission equal to)	x (execute)
a (all categories)		

Take, for example, the directory list used earlier:

```
[root@server1 root]# ls -l
total 28
drwx------    3 root     root         4096 Apr  8 07:12 Desktop
-r---w---x    1 root     root          282 Apr 29 22:06 file1
-------rwx    1 root     root          282 Apr 29 22:06 file2
-rwxrwxrwx    1 root     root          282 Apr 29 22:06 file3
----------    1 root     root          282 Apr 29 22:06 file4
-rw-r--r--    1 root     root          282 Apr 29 22:06 file5
-rw-r--r--    1 user1    sys           282 Apr 29 22:06 file6 [root@server1 root]# _
```

To change the mode of file1 to rw-r--r--, you must add the write permission to the user of the file, add the read permission and take away the write permission for the group of the file, and add the read permission and take away the execute permission for other.

From the information listed in Table 5-5, you can use the following command:

```
[root@server1 root]# chmod u+w,g+r-w,o+r-x file1
[root@server1 root]# ls -l
total 28
drwx------    3 root     root         4096 Apr  8 07:12 Desktop
-rw-r--r--    1 root     root          282 Apr 29 22:06 file1
----r--rwx    1 root     root          282 Apr 29 22:06 file2
-rwxrwxrwx    1 root     root          282 Apr 29 22:06 file3
----------    1 root     root          282 Apr 29 22:06 file4
-rw-r--r--    1 root     root          282 Apr 29 22:06 file5
-rw-r--r--    1 user1    sys           282 Apr 29 22:06 file6 [root@server1 root]# _
```

NOTE

You should ensure that there are no spaces between any criteria used in the chmod command because all criteria make up the first argument only.

You can also use the = criteria from Table 5-5 to specify the exact permissions to change. To change the mode on file2 in the preceding output to the same as file1 (rw-r--r--), you can use the following chmod command:

```
[root@server1 root]# chmod u=rw,g=r,o=r file2
[root@server1 root]# ls -l
total 28
drwx------    3 root    root       4096 Apr  8 07:12 Desktop
-rw-r--r--    1 root    root        282 Apr 29 22:06 file1
-rw-r--r--    1 root    root        282 Apr 29 22:06 file2
-rwxrwxrwx    1 root    root        282 Apr 29 22:06 file3
----------    1 root    root        282 Apr 29 22:06 file4
-rw-r--r--    1 root    root        282 Apr 29 22:06 file5
-rw-r--r--    1 user1   sys         282 Apr 29 22:06 file6 [root@server1 root]# _
```

If the permissions to be changed are identical for the user, group, and other categories, you can use the "a" character to refer to all categories as shown in Table 5-5 and in the following example when adding the execute permission to user, group, and other for file1:

```
[root@server1 root]# chmod a+x file1
[root@server1 root]# ls -l
total 28
drwx------    3 root    root       4096 Apr  8 07:12 Desktop
-rwxr-xr-x    1 root    root        282 Apr 29 22:06 file1
-rw-r--r--    1 root    root        282 Apr 29 22:06 file2
-rwxrwxrwx    1 root    root        282 Apr 29 22:06 file3
----------    1 root    root        282 Apr 29 22:06 file4
-rw-r--r--    1 root    root        282 Apr 29 22:06 file5
-rw-r--r--    1 user1   sys         282 Apr 29 22:06 file6 [root@server1 root]# _
```

However, if there is no character specifying the category of user to affect, all users are assumed, as shown in the following example when adding the execute permission to user, group, and other for file2:

```
[root@server1 root]# chmod +x file2
[root@server1 root]# ls -l
total 28
drwx------    3 root    root       4096 Apr  8 07:12 Desktop
-rwxr-xr-x    1 root    root        282 Apr 29 22:06 file1
-rwxr-xr-x    1 root    root        282 Apr 29 22:06 file2
-rwxrwxrwx    1 root    root        282 Apr 29 22:06 file3
----------    1 root    root        282 Apr 29 22:06 file4
-rw-r--r--    1 root    root        282 Apr 29 22:06 file5
-rw-r--r--    1 user1   sys         282 Apr 29 22:06 file6
[root@server1 root]# _
```

All of the aforementioned `chmod` examples use the symbols listed in Table 5-5 as the criteria used to change the permissions on a file or directory. You might instead choose to use numeric criteria with the `chmod` command to change permissions. All permissions are stored in the inode of a file or directory as binary powers of two:

◆ read = 2^2 = 4
◆ write = 2^1 = 2
◆ execute = 2^0 = 1

Thus, the mode of a file or directory can be represented using the numbers 421421421 instead of rwxrwxrwx. Because permissions are grouped into the categories user, group, and other, you can then simplify this further by using only three numbers, one for each category that represents the sum of the permissions, as depicted in Figure 5-4.

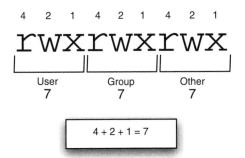

FIGURE 5-4 *Numeric representation of the mode*

Similarly, to represent the mode rw-r--r--, you can use the numbers 644 because user has read and write (4+2=6), group has read (4), and other has read (4). The mode rwxr-x--- can also be represented by 750 because user has read, write, and execute (4+2+1=7), group has read and execute (4+1=5), and other has nothing (0). Table 5-6 provides a list of the different permissions and their corresponding numbers.

To change the mode of the file1 file used earlier to r-xr-----, you can use the command `chmod 540 file1`, as shown in the following example:

```
[root@server1 root]# chmod 540 file1
[root@server1 root]# ls -l
total 28
drwx------    3 root     root         4096 Apr  8 07:12 Desktop
-r-xr-----    1 root     root          282 Apr 29 22:06 file1
-rwxr-xr-x    1 root     root          282 Apr 29 22:06 file2
-rwxrwxrwx    1 root     root          282 Apr 29 22:06 file3
----------    1 root     root          282 Apr 29 22:06 file4
-rw-r--r--    1 root     root          282 Apr 29 22:06 file5
-rw-r--r--    1 user1    sys           282 Apr 29 22:06 file6
[root@server1 root]# _
```

Table 5-6 Numeric representations of the permissions in a mode

Mode (one section only)	Corresponding Number
rwx	4 + 2 + 1 = **7**
rw-	4 + 2 = **6**
r-x	4 + 1 = **5**
r--	4
-wx	2 + 1 = **3**
-w-	**2**
--x	1
---	**0**

Similarly, to change the mode of all files in the directory that start with the word "file" to 644 (which is common permissions for files), you can use the following command:

```
[root@server1 root]# chmod 644 file*
[root@server1 root]# ls -l
total 28
drwx------  3 root     root         4096 Apr  8 07:12 Desktop
-rw-r--r--  1 root     root          282 Apr 29 22:06 file1
-rw-r--r--  1 root     root          282 Apr 29 22:06 file2
-rw-r--r--  1 root     root          282 Apr 29 22:06 file3
-rw-r--r--  1 root     root          282 Apr 29 22:06 file4
-rw-r--r--  1 root     root          282 Apr 29 22:06 file5
-rw-r--r--  1 user1    sys           282 Apr 29 22:06 file6
[root@server1 root]# _
```

Like the chown and chgrp commands, the chmod command can also be used to change the permission on a directory and all of its contents recursively by using the -R option, as shown in the following example when changing the mode of the Desktop directory:

```
[root@server1 root]# chmod -R 755 Desktop
[root@server1 root]# ls -l
total 28
drwxr-xr-x  3 root     root         4096 Apr  8 07:12 Desktop
-rw-r--r--  1 root     root          282 Apr 29 22:06 file1
-rw-r--r--  1 root     root          282 Apr 29 22:06 file2
-rw-r--r--  1 root     root          282 Apr 29 22:06 file3
-rw-r--r--  1 root     root          282 Apr 29 22:06 file4
-rw-r--r--  1 root     root          282 Apr 29 22:06 file5
-rw-r--r--  1 user1    sys           282 Apr 29 22:06 file6
```

```
[root@server1 root]# ls -l Desktop
total 16
-rwxr-xr-x    1 root      root        163 Mar 29 09:58 Floppy
-rw-r-xr-x    1 root      root       3578 Mar 29 09:58 Home
-rw-r-xr-x    1 root      root       1791 Mar 29 09:58 Start Here
drwxr-xr-x    2 root      root       4096 Mar 29 09:58 Trash
[root@server1 root]# _
```

Default Permissions

Recall that permissions provide security for files and directories by allowing only certain users access, and that there are common guidelines for setting permissions on files and directories, so that permissions are not too strict or too permissive. Also important to maintaining security are the permissions that are given to new files and directories after they are created. New files are given rw-rw-rw- by the system when they are created (because execute should not be given unless necessary), and new directories are given rwxrwxrwx by the system when they are created. These default permissions are too permissive for most files, as they allow other full access to directories and nearly full access to files. Hence, a special variable on the system called the **umask** (user mask) takes away permissions on new files and directories immediately after they are created. The most common umask that you will find is 022, which specifies that nothing (0) is taken away from the user, write permission (2) is taken away from members of the group, and write permission (2) is taken away from other on new files and directories when they are first created and given permissions by the system.

NOTE

Keep in mind that the umask applies only to newly created files and directories; it is never used to modify the permissions of existing files and directories. You must use the chmod command to modify existing permissions.

An example of how a umask of 022 can be used to alter the permissions of a new file or directory after creation is shown in Figure 5-5.

To verify the umask used, you can use the **umask command** and note the final three digits in the output. To ensure that the umask functions as shown in Figure 5-5, simply create a new file using the touch command and a new directory using the mkdir command, as shown in the following output:

```
[root@server1 root]# ls -l
total 28
drwx------    3 root      root       4096 Apr  8 07:12 Desktop
[root@server1 root]# umask
0022
```

```
[root@server1 root]# mkdir dir1
[root@server1 root]# touch file1
[root@server1 root]# ls -l
total 8
drwx------   3 root    root    4096 Apr  8 07:12 Desktop
drwxr-xr-x   2 root    root    4096 May  3 21:39 dir1
-rw-r--r--   1 root    root       0 May  3 21:40 file1 [root@server1 root]# _
```

Because the umask is a variable stored in memory, it can be changed. To change the current umask, you can specify the new umask as an argument to the umask command. Suppose, for example, you want to change the umask to 007; the resulting permissions on new files and directories is calculated in Figure 5-6.

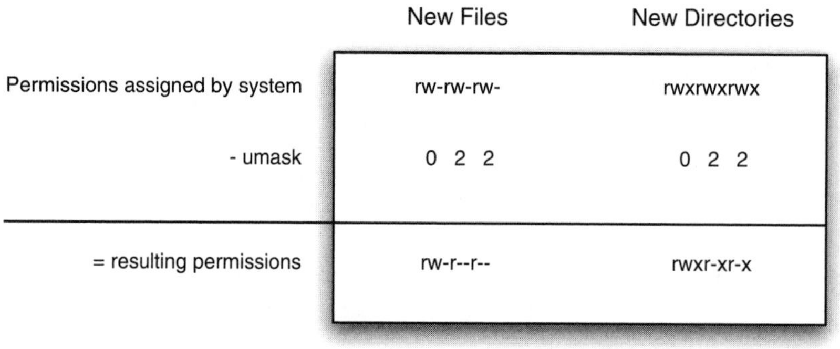

	New Files	New Directories
Permissions assigned by system	rw-rw-rw-	rwxrwxrwx
- umask	0 2 2	0 2 2
= resulting permissions	rw-r--r--	rwxr-xr-x

FIGURE 5-5 *Performing a umask 022 calculation*

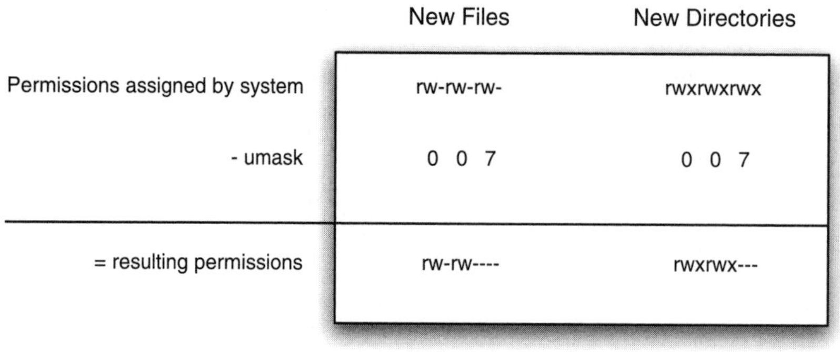

	New Files	New Directories
Permissions assigned by system	rw-rw-rw-	rwxrwxrwx
- umask	0 0 7	0 0 7
= resulting permissions	rw-rw----	rwxrwx---

FIGURE 5-6 *Performing a umask 007 calculation*

To change the umask to 007 and view its effect, you can type the following commands on the command line:

```
[root@server1 root]# ls -l
total 8
drwx------   3 root     root       4096 Apr  8 07:12 Desktop
drwxr-xr-x   2 root     root       4096 May  3 21:39 dir1
-rw-r--r--   1 root     root          0 May  3 21:40 file1 [root@server1 root]# umask
007
[root@server1 root]# umask
0007
[root@server1 root]# mkdir dir2
[root@server1 root]# touch file2
[root@server1 root]# ls -l
total 12
drwx------   3 root     root       4096 Apr  8 07:12 Desktop
drwxr-xr-x   2 root     root       4096 May  3 21:39 dir1
drwxrwx---   2 root     root       4096 May  3 21:41 dir2
-rw-r--r--   1 root     root          0 May  3 21:40 file1
-rw-rw----   1 root     root          0 May  3 21:41 file2 [root@server1 root]# _
```

Special Permissions

Read, write, and execute are the regular file permissions that you would use to assign security to files; however, you can optionally use three more special permissions on files and directories:

◆ SUID (Set User ID)
◆ SGID (Set Group ID)
◆ Sticky bit

Defining Special Permissions

The SUID has no special function when set on a directory; however, if the SUID is set on a file and that file is executed, the person who executed the file temporarily becomes the owner of the file while it is executing. Many commands on a typical Linux system have this special permission set; the ping command (/bin/ping) that is used to test network connectivity is one such file. Because this file is owned by the root user, when a regular user executes the ping command, that user temporarily becomes the root user while the ping command is executing in memory. This ensures that any user can test network connectivity as the person who has all rights to do so on the system. Furthermore, the SUID can only be applied to binary compiled programs. The Linux kernel does not let you apply the SUID to a shell script because shell scripts are easy to edit and, thus, pose a security hazard to the system.

Contrary to the SUID, the SGID has a function when applied to both files and directories. Just as the SUID allows regular users to execute a binary compiled program and become the owner of the file for the duration of execution, the SGID allows regular users to execute a binary compiled program and become a member of the group that is attached to the file. Thus, if a file is owned by the group "sys" and also has the SGID permission, any user who executes that file will be a member of the group "sys" during execution. If a command or file requires the user executing it to have the same permissions applied to the sys group, setting the SGID on the file simplifies assigning rights to the file for user execution.

The SGID also has a special function when placed on a directory. When a user creates a file, recall that that user's name and primary group become the owner and group owner of the file, respectively. However, if a user creates a file in a directory that has the SGID permission set, that user's name becomes the owner of the file and the directory's group becomes the group owner of the file.

Finally, the sticky bit was used on files in the past to lock them in memory; however, today the sticky bit performs a useful function only on directories. Recall from earlier that the write permission applied to a directory allows you the ability to add and remove any file to or from that directory. Thus, if you have the write permission to a certain directory but no permission to files within it, you could delete all of those files. Consider a company that requires a common directory that gives all employees the ability to add files; this directory must give everyone the write permission.

Unfortunately, the write permission also gives all employees the ability to delete all files and directories within, including the ones that others have added to the directory. If the sticky bit is applied to this common directory in addition to the write permission, employees can add files to the directory but only delete those files that they have added and not others.

NOTE

Note that all special permissions also require the execute permission to work properly; the SUID and SGID work on executable files, and the SGID and sticky bit work on directories (which must have execute permission for access).

Setting Special Permissions

The mode of a file that is displayed using the ls -l command does not have a section for special permissions. However, because special permissions require execute, they mask the execute permission when displayed using the ls -l command, as shown in Figure 5-7.

The system allows you to set special permissions even if the file or directory does not have execute permission. However, the special permissions will not perform their function. If the special permissions are set on a file or directory without execute permissions, then the ineffective special permissions are capitalized as seen in Figure 5-8.

To set the special permissions, you can visualize them to the left of the mode, as shown in Figure 5-9.

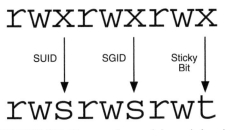

FIGURE 5-7 *Representing special permissions in the mode*

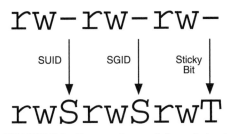

FIGURE 5-8 *Representing special permission in the absence of the execute permission*

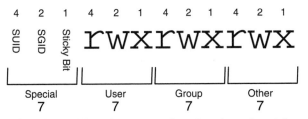

FIGURE 5-9 *Numeric representation of regular and special permissions*

Thus, to set all of the special permissions on a certain file or directory, you can use the command `chmod 7777 name`, as indicated from Figure 5-9. However, the SUID and SGID bits are typically set on files. To change the permissions on the file1 file used earlier such that other has the ability to view and execute the file as the owner and a member of the group, you can use the command `chmod 6755 file1`, as shown in the following example:

```
[root@server1 root]# ls -l
total 12
drwx------    3 root     root         4096 Apr  8 07:12 Desktop
drwxr-xr-x    2 root     root         4096 May  3 21:39 dir1
```

```
drwx------     2 root      root        4096 May  3 21:41 dir2
-rw-r--r--     1 root      root           0 May  3 21:40 file1
-rw-------     1 root      root           0 May  3 21:41 file2
[root@server1 root]# chmod 6755 file1
[root@server1 root]# ls -l
total 12
drwx------     3 root      root        4096 Apr  8 07:12 Desktop
drwxr-xr-x     2 root      root        4096 May  3 21:39 dir1
drwx------     2 root      root        4096 May  3 21:41 dir2
-rwsr-sr-x     1 root      root           0 May  3 21:40 file1
-rw-------     1 root      root           0 May  3 21:41 file2 [root@server1 root]# _
```

Similarly, to set the sticky bit permission on the directory dir1 used earlier, you can use the command chmod 1777 dir1, which allows all users (including other) to add files to the dir1 directory. This is because you gave the write permission; however users can only delete the files that they own in dir1 because you set the sticky bit. This is shown in the following example:

```
[root@server1 root]# ls -l
total 12
drwx------     3 root      root        4096 Apr  8 07:12 Desktop
drwxr-xr-x     2 root      root        4096 May  3 21:39 dir1
drwx------     2 root      root        4096 May  3 21:41 dir2
-rwsr-sr-x     1 root      root           0 May  3 21:40 file1
-rw-------     1 root      root           0 May  3 21:41 file2
[root@server1 root]# chmod 1777 dir1
[root@server1 root]# ls -l
total 12
drwx------     3 root      root        4096 Apr  8 07:12 Desktop
drwxrwxrwt     2 root      root        4096 May  3 21:39 dir1
drwx------     2 root      root        4096 May  3 21:41 dir2
-rwsr-sr-x     1 root      root           0 May  3 21:40 file1
-rw-------     1 root      root           0 May  3 21:41 file2
[root@server1 root]# _
```

Also, remember that assigning special permissions without execute renders those permissions useless. If you forget to give execute permission to either user, group, or other and the long listing covers the execute permission with a special permission. In that case, the special permission is capitalized as shown in the following example when dir2 is not given execute underneath the position in the mode that indicates the sticky bit (t):

```
[root@server1 root]# ls -l
total 12
drwx------     3 root      root        4096 Apr  8 07:12 Desktop
drwxrwxrwt     2 root      root        4096 May  3 21:39 dir1
drwx------     2 root      root        4096 May  3 21:41 dir2
```

```
-rwsr-sr-x    1 root    root         0 May  3 21:40 file1
-rw-------    1 root    root         0 May  3 21:41 file2
[root@server1 root]# chmod 1770 dir2
[root@server1 root]# ls -l
total 12
drwx------    3 root    root      4096 Apr  8 07:12 Desktop
drwxrwxrwt    2 root    root      4096 May  3 21:39 dir1
drwxrwx--T    2 root    root      4096 May  3 21:41 dir2
-rwsr-sr-x    1 root    root         0 May  3 21:40 file1
-rw-------    1 root    root         0 May  3 21:41 file2 [root@server1 root]# _
```

Chapter Summary

◆ The Linux directory tree obeys the Filesystem Hierarchy Standard, which allows Linux users and developers the ability to locate system files in standard directories.

◆ Many file management commands exist to create, change the location of, or remove files and directories. The most common of these include cp, mv, rm, rmdir, and mkdir.

◆ You can find files on the filesystem using a preindexed database (the locate command) or by the searching directories listed in the PATH variable (the which command). However, the most versatile command used to find files is the find command, which searches for files based on a wide range of criteria.

◆ Files can be created as a pointer to another file or as a linked duplicate of another file. These are called symbolic and hard links, respectively.

◆ Each file and directory has an owner and a group owner. The owner of the file or directory has the ability to change permissions and give ownership to others.

◆ Permissions can be set on the user or owner of a file, members of the group of the file, as well as everyone on the system (other).

◆ There are three regular file and directory permissions (read, write, execute) and three special file and directory permissions (SUID, SGID, sticky bit). The definitions of these permissions are separate between files and directories.

◆ Permissions can be changed using the chmod command by specifying symbols or numbers to represent the changed permissions.

◆ To ensure security, new files and directories receive default permissions from the system less the value of the umask variable.

◆ The root user has all permissions to all files and directories on the Linux filesystem. Similarly, the root user can change the ownership of any file or directory on the Linux filesystem.

Key Terms

/bin directory — The directory that contains binary commands for use by all users.

/boot directory — The directory that contains the Linux kernel and files used by the boot loader data block.

/dev directory — The directory that contains device files.

/etc directory — The directory that contains system-specific configuration files.

/home directory — The default location for user home directories.

/lib directory — The directory that contains shared program libraries (used by the commands in /bin and /sbin) as well as kernel modules.

/mnt directory — An empty directory used for accessing (mounting) disks, such as floppy disks and CD-ROMs.

/opt directory — The directory that stores additional software programs.

/proc directory — The directory that contains process and kernel information.

/root directory — The root user's home directory.

/sbin directory — The directory that contains system binary commands (used for administration).

/tmp directory — The directory that holds temporary files created by programs.

/usr directory — The directory that contains most system commands and utilities.

/usr/local directory — The location for most additional programs.

/var directory — The directory that contains log files and spools.

chgrp (change group) command — The command used to change the group owner of a file or directory.

chmod (change mode) command — The command used to change the mode (permissions) of a file or directory.

chown (change owner) command — The command used to change the owner and group owner of a file or directory.

cp (copy) command — The command used to create copies of files and directories.

data blocks — A filesystem allocation unit in which the data that makes up the contents of the file as well as the filename are stored.

Filesystem Hierarchy Standard (FHS) — A standard outlining the location of set files and directories on a Linux system.

find command — The command used to find files on the filesystem using various criteria.

group — When used in the mode of a certain file or directory, the collection of users who have ownership of that file or directory.

hard link — A file joined to other files on the same filesystem that shares the same inode.

inode — The portion of a file that stores information on the file's attributes, access permissions, location, ownership, and file type.

inode table — The collection of inodes for all files and directories on a filesystem.

interactive mode — The mode that file management commands use when a file can be overwritten; the system interacts with a user asking for the user to confirm the action.

ln (link) command — The command used to create hard and symbolic links.

locate command — The command used to locate files from a file database.

mkdir (make directory) command — The command used to create directories.

mode — The part of the inode that stores information on access permissions.

mv (move) command — The command used to move/rename files and directories.

other — When used in the mode of a certain file or directory, it refers to all users on the Linux system.

owner — The user whose name appears in a long listing of a file or directory and who has the ability to change permissions on that file or directory.

PATH variable — A variable that stores a list of directories that will be searched in order when commands are executed without an absolute or relative pathname.

permissions — A list that identifies who can access a file or folder, and their level of access.

primary group — The default group to which a user belongs.

recursive — A term referring to itself and its own contents; a recursive search includes all subdirectories in a directory and their contents.

rm (remove) command — The command used to remove files and directories.

rmdir (remove directory) command — The command used to remove empty directories.

source file/directory — The portion of a command that refers to the file or directory from which information is taken.

superblock — The portion of a filesystem that stores critical information, such as the inode table and block size.

symbolic link — A pointer to another file on the same or another filesystem; commonly referred to as a shortcut.

target file/directory — The portion of a command that refers to the file or directory to which information is directed.

touch command — The command used to create new files. It was originally used to update the time stamp on a file.

umask — A special variable used to alter the permissions on all new files and directories by taking select default file and directory permissions away.

umask command — The command used to view and change the umask variable.

user — When used in the mode of a certain file or directory, the owner of that file or directory.

which command — The command used to locate files that exist within directories listed in the PATH variable.

Review Questions

1. Which directory in the Filesystem Hierarchy stores additional software programs?
    a. /var
    b. /sbin
    c. /lib
    d. /opt

2. What command would you use to search for empty files or directories?
    a. find –inum 0
    b. find –size -1
    c. find -empty
    d. find -x

3. At a minimum, what arguments are required by the chgrp command?
    a. new group owner and the files or directories to change
    b. user name, new group owner, and files or directories to change
    c. old group owner, new group owner
    d. files and directories to change

4. What permission must a user have for a directory in order to list its contents?
    a. Read
    b. Write
    c. Execute
    d. List

5. To set all of the special permissions on a certain file or directory, you can use the command chmod _____ name.
   a. 0007
   b. 0077
   c. 0777
   d. 7777

6. True or false? The rmdir command is used to remove directories that contain files.

7. True or false? The `locate` command often returns too much information to display on the screen, as it searches all files on the filesystem.

8. True or false? Directories are files used to organize other files.

9. True or false? A file must have at least one permission assigned to it.

10. True or false? It is important to avoid giving execute permission to files that are not programs or shell scripts.

11. The _____ command is used to rename directories.

12. In a(n) _____ link, two files share the same data.

13. When a user creates a file or directory, that user's name and _____ group becomes the owner and group owner of the file, respectively.

14. The section of the inode that stores permissions is called the _____ of the file and is divided into three sections based on the user(s) who receive the permissions to that file or directory.

15. A special variable on the system called the _____ takes away permissions on new files and directories immediately after they are created.

Chapter 6

Linux Filesystem Administration

After completing this chapter, you will be able to:

◆ Identify the structure and types of device files in the /dev directory

◆ Understand common filesystem types and their features

◆ Mount and unmount floppy disks to and from the Linux directory tree

◆ Mount and unmount CD-ROMs to and from the Linux directory tree

◆ Create hard disk partitions

◆ Mount and unmount hard disk partitions to and from the Linux directory tree

◆ Monitor free space on mounted filesystems

◆ Check filesystems for errors

◆ Use hard disk quotas to limit user space usage

Navigating the Linux directory tree and manipulating files are common tasks that are performed on a daily basis by all users. However, administrators must provide this directory tree for users, as well as manage and fix the disk devices that support it. In this chapter, you learn about the various device files that represent disk devices and the different filesystems that can be placed on those devices. Next, you learn how to create and manage filesystems on floppy disks and CD-ROMs, followed by a discussion of hard disk partitioning and filesystem management. Finally, this chapter concludes with a discussion of disk usage, filesystem errors, and restricting the ability for users to store files.

The /dev Directory

Fundamental to administering the disks used to store information is an understanding of how these disks are specified by the Linux operating system. Most devices on a Linux system (such as disks, terminals, and serial ports) are represented by a file on the hard disk called a **device file**. There is one file per device and these files are typically found in the **/dev directory**. This allows you to specify devices on the system by using the pathname to the file that represents it in the /dev directory. To specify the first floppy disk in the Linux system, you can type the pathname /dev/fd0 (floppy disk 0) in the appropriate section of a command. In addition, to represent the second floppy disk in the Linux system, you can specify the pathname to the file /dev/fd1 (floppy disk 1).

Furthermore, each device file specifies how data should be transferred to and from the device. You have two methods for transferring data to and from a device. The first method involves transferring information character-by-character to and from the device. Devices that transfer data in this fashion are referred to as **character devices**. The second method transfers chunks or blocks of information at a time by using physical memory to buffer the transfer. Devices that use this method of transfer are called **block devices**, and can transfer information much faster than character devices. Device files that represent disks, such as floppy disks, CD-ROMs, and hard disks, are typically block device files because a fast data transfer rate is preferred. Tape drives and most other devices, however, are typically represented by character device files.

To see whether a particular device transfers data character-by-character or block-by-block, recall that the ls -l command displays a c or b character in the type column indicating the type of device file. To view the type of the file /dev/fd0, you can use the following command:

```
[root@server1 root]# ls -l /dev/fd0
brw-rw----    1 root     floppy     2,   0 Feb 23 16:02 /dev/fd0
[root@server1 root]#_
```

From the leftmost character in the preceding output, you can see that the /dev/fd0 file is a block device file. Table 6-1 provides a list of some common device files and their types.

Table 6-1 Common device files

Device File	Description	Block or Character
/dev/fd0	First floppy disk on the system	Block
/dev/fd1	Second floppy disk on the system	Block
/dev/hda1	First primary partition on the first IDE hard disk drive (primary master)	Block
/dev/hdb1	First primary partition on the second IDE hard disk drive (primary slave)	Block
/dev/hdc1	First primary partition on the third IDE hard disk drive (secondary master)	Block
/dev/hdd1	First primary partition on the fourth IDE hard disk drive (secondary slave)	Block
/dev/sda1	First primary partition on the first SCSI hard disk drive	Block
/dev/sdb1	First primary partition on the second SCSI hard disk drive	Block
/dev/tty1	First local terminal on the system (Ctrl+Alt+F1)	Character
/dev/tty2	Second local terminal on the system (Ctrl+Alt+F2)	Character
/dev/ttyS0	First serial port on the system (COM1)	Character
/dev/ttyS1	Second serial port on the system (COM2)	Character
/dev/psaux	PS/2 mouse port	Character
/dev/lp0	First parallel port on the system (LPT1)	Character
/dev/null	Device file that represents nothing; any data sent to this device is discarded	Character
/dev/st0	First SCSI tape device in the system	Character
/dev/usb/*	USB device files	Character

After a typical Red Hat Fedora Linux installation, over 18,000 different device files are in the /dev directory; most of these device files represent devices that might not exist on the particular Linux system and, hence, are never used. Providing this large number of redundant device files on a Linux system does not require much disk space because all device files consist of inodes and no data blocks; as a result, the entire contents of the /dev directory is usually less than 700 Kilobytes in size, which could easily fit on a floppy disk. When using the ls -l command to view device files, the portion of the listing describing the file size in Kilobytes is replaced by two numbers: the major number and the minor number. The **major number** of a device file points to the device driver for the device in the Linux kernel; several different devices can share the same major number if they are of the same general type (that is, two different floppy disk drives might share the same major number). The **minor number** indicates the particular device itself; the first floppy disk drive in the computer will have a different minor number than the second floppy disk drive in the computer. In the following output, you see that both /dev/fd0 and /dev/fd1 share the same major number of 2, yet the minor number for /dev/fd0 is 0 and the minor number for /dev/fd1 is 1, which differentiates them from one another.

```
[root@server1 root]# ls -l /dev/fd0 /dev/fd1
brw-rw----   1 root      floppy    2,   0 Feb 23 16:02 /dev/fd0
brw-rw----   1 root      floppy    2,   1 Feb 23 16:02 /dev/fd1
[root@server1 root]#_
```

Together, the device file type (block or character), the major number (device driver), and the minor number (specific device) make up the unique characteristics of each device file. To create a device file, you simply need to know these three pieces of information.

If a device file becomes corrupted, it is usually listed as a regular file instead of a block or character special file. Recall from Chapter 5, "Linux Filesystem Management," that the find /dev -type f command can be used to search for regular files underneath the /dev directory to identify whether corruption has taken place. If you find a corrupted device file, or accidentally delete a device file, the **mknod command** can be used to re-create the device file if you know the type, major, and minor numbers. An example of re-creating the /dev/fd0 block device file used earlier with a major number of 2 and a minor number of 0 is shown in the following example:

```
[root@server1 root]# ls -l /dev/fd0
brw-rw----   1 root      floppy    2,   0 Feb 23 16:02 /dev/fd0
[root@server1 root]# rm -f /dev/fd0
[root@server1 root]# ls -l /dev/fd0
[root@server1 root]# mknod /dev/fd0 b 2 0
[root@server1 root]# ls -l /dev/fd0
brw-r--r--   1 root      root      2,   0 May  8 13:26 /dev/fd0
[root@server1 root]#_
```

However, if you do not know the type, major, or minor number of the device, you can use the **/dev/MAKEDEV** program to re-create the device based on the common name:

```
[root@server1 root]# ls -l /dev/fd0
brw-r--r--   1 root     root      2,   0 May  8 13:26 /dev/fd0
[root@server1 root]# rm -f /dev/fd0
[root@server1 root]# ls -l /dev/fd0
[root@server1 root]# /dev/MAKEDEV fd0
[root@server1 root]# ls -l /dev/fd0
brw-rw----   1 root     floppy    2,   0 May  8 13:30 /dev/fd0
[root@server1 root]#_
```

Recall from earlier that most device files present in the /dev directory are never used. To see a list of devices that are currently used on the system and their major numbers, you can view the contents of the **/proc/devices** file, as shown next:

```
[root@server1 root]# cat /proc/devices
Character devices:
  1 mem
  4 tty
  4 ttyS
  5 /dev/tty
  5 /dev/console
  5 /dev/ptmx
  6 lp
  7 vcs
 10 misc
 13 input
 14 sound
 21 sg
 29 fb
 36 netlink
128 ptm
136 pts
162 raw
180 usb
216 rfcomm

Block devices:
  1 ramdisk
  2 fd
  3 ide0
  9 md
 22 ide1
253 device-mapper
254 mdp
[root@server1 root]#_
```

Filesystems

Recall from Chapter 2, "Preparing for Linux Installation," that files must be stored on the hard disk in a defined format called a **filesystem**, so that the operating system can work with them. The type of filesystem used determines how files are managed on the physical hard disk. Each filesystem can have different methods for storing files and features that make the filesystem robust against errors. Although many different types of filesystems are available, all filesystems share three common components as discussed in Chapter 5: the superblock, the inode table, and the data blocks. On a structural level, these three components work together to organize files and allow rapid access to and retrieval of data. All storage media, such as floppy disks, hard disks, and CD-ROMs, need to be formatted with a filesystem before they can be used.

> **NOTE**
>
> Creating a filesystem on a device is commonly referred to as **formatting**.

Filesystem Types

As mentioned, many filesystems are available for use in the Linux operating system. Each has its own strengths and weaknesses, thus some are better suited to some tasks and not as well-suited to others. One benefit of Linux is that you need not use only one type of filesystem on the system; you can use several different devices formatted with different filesystems under the same directory tree. In addition, files and directories appear the same throughout the directory tree regardless of whether there is one filesystem or twenty different filesystems in use by the Linux system. Table 6-2 lists some common filesystems available for use in Linux. For a full listing of filesystem types and their features, you can refer to the Filesystem HOWTO on the Internet at _http://www.tldp.org/HOWTO/Filesystems-HOWTO.html_.

Table 6-2 Common Linux filesystems

Filesystem	Description
bfs	Boot File System—A small, bootable filesystem used to hold the files necessary for system startup; it is commonly used on UNIX systems.
cdfs	Compact Disc filesystem—A filesystem used to view all tracks and data on a CD-ROM as normal files.
ext2	Second extended filesystem—The traditional filesystem used on Linux, it supports access control lists (individual user permissions). In addition, it retains its name from being the new version of the original extended filesystem, based on the Minix filesystem.

Table 6-2 Common Linux filesystems (Continued)

Filesystem	Description
ext3	Third extended filesystem – A variation on ext2 that allows for journaling and, thus, has a faster startup and recovery time.
hfs	Hierarchical File System—A filesystem native to Apple Macintosh computers.
hpfs	High Performance File System—An IBM proprietary OS/2 filesystem that provides long filename support and is optimized to manipulate data on large disk volumes.
iso9660	The CD-ROM filesystem—A filesystem that originated from the International Standards Organization recommendation 9660 and is used to access data stored on CD-ROMs.
minix	The MINIX filesystem—The filesystem used by Linus Torvalds in the early days of Linux development.
msdos	The DOS FAT filesystem.
ntfs	New Technology File System—A Microsoft proprietary filesystem developed for its NT 4.0 and Windows 2000 operating systems; currently available as a read-only filesystem under Linux.
reiserfs	The REISERFS filesystem—A journalizing filesystem similar to ext3 more suited for use with databases.
udf	The Universal Disk Format filesystem—A filesystem used by software programs that write to a CD-R, CD-RW, or DVD.
vfat	The DOS FAT filesystem with long filename support.
vxfs	The Veritas filesystem—A journalizing filesystem that offers large file support and supports access control lists (individual user permissions) and is commonly used by major versions of UNIX.

Mounting

The term **mounting** originated in the 1960s when information was stored on large tape reels that had to be mounted on computers to make the data available. Today, mounting still refers to making data available. More specifically, it refers to the process whereby a device is made accessible to users via the logical directory tree. This device is attached to a certain directory on the directory tree called a **mount point**. Users can then create files and subdirectories in this mount point directory, which are then stored on the filesystem that was mounted to that particular directory.

Remember that directories are merely files that do not contain data; instead, they contain a list of files and subdirectories organized within them. Thus, it is easy for the Linux system to cover up directories to prevent user access to that data. This is essentially what happens when a device is mounted to a certain directory; the mount point directory is temporarily covered up by that device while the device remains mounted. Any file contents that were present in the mount point directory prior to mounting are not lost; when the device is unmounted, the mount point directory is uncovered, and the previous file contents are revealed. Suppose, for example, that you mount a floppy device that contains a filesystem to the /mnt directory. The /mnt directory is a directory that contains two subdirectories and is a commonly used and convenient mount point for mounting removable media devices. Before mounting, the directory structure would resemble that depicted in Figure 6-1. After the floppy is mounted to the /mnt directory, the contents of the /mnt directory would be covered up by the floppy filesystem, as illustrated in Figure 6-2.

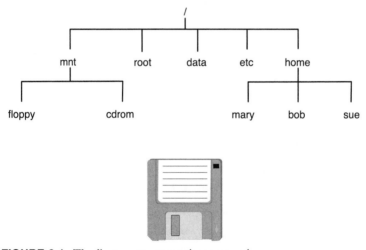

FIGURE 6-1 *The directory structure prior to mounting*

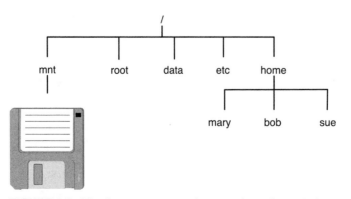

FIGURE 6-2 *The directory structure after mounting a floppy device*

If a user then stores a file in the /mnt directory, as shown in Figure 6-2, that file will be stored on the floppy disk device. Similarly, if a user creates a subdirectory under the /mnt directory depicted in Figure 6-2, that subdirectory will be made on the floppy disk.

It is important to note that any existing directory can be used as a mount point. If a user mounts a floppy device to the /bin directory, all files in the /bin directory are covered up for the duration that floppy disk is mounted, including the command used to unmount the floppy. Thus, it is safe practice to create empty directories used specifically for mounting devices to avoid making existing files inaccessible to users.

When the Linux system is first turned on, a filesystem present on the hard drive is mounted to the / directory. This is referred to as the **root filesystem** and contains most of the operating system files. Other filesystems present on hard disks inside the computer can also be mounted to various mount point directories underneath the / directory at boot time, as well as via entries in the **/etc/fstab** (filesystem table) file discussed in the following sections.

The **mount command** is used to mount devices to mount point directories and the **umount command** is used to unmount devices from mount point directories; both of these commands are discussed throughout the remainder of this chapter.

Working with Floppy Disks

When transferring small amounts of information from computer to computer, it is commonplace to use floppy disk removable media to store the files. However, floppy disks must be prepared before they are used in Linux.

Recall that each disk device must be formatted with a filesystem prior to being used to store files. To do this, you can use the **mkfs (make filesystem) command** and specify the filesystem type using the -t switch and the device file representing the floppy disk device. To format the floppy disk inside the first floppy disk drive in the computer with the ext2 filesystem, place a floppy disk in the floppy disk drive and type the following command:

```
[root@server1 root]# mkfs -t ext2 /dev/fd0
mke2fs 1.35 (28-Feb-2004)
Filesystem label=
OS type: Linux
Block size=1024 (log=0)
Fragment size=1024 (log=0)
184 inodes, 1440 blocks
72 blocks (5.00%) reserved for the super user
First data block=1
1 block group
8192 blocks per group, 8192 fragments per group
184 inodes per group
```

```
Writing inode tables: done
Writing superblocks and filesystem accounting information: done

This filesystem will be automatically checked every 28 mounts or
180 days, whichever comes first. Use tune2fs -c or -i to override.
[root@server1 root]#_
```

Alternatively, you can specify a different filesystem after the -t option, such as the DOS FAT filesystem. This results in a different output from the mkfs command, as shown in the following example:

```
[root@server1 root]# mkfs -t msdos /dev/fd0
mkfs.msdos 2.8 (28 Feb 2001)
[root@server1 root]#_
```

If you do not specify the filesystem using the mkfs command, the default filesystem assumed is the ext2 filesystem, as shown in the following example:

```
[root@server1 root]# mkfs /dev/fd0
mke2fs 1.35 (28-Feb-2004)
Filesystem label=
OS type: Linux
Block size=1024 (log=0)
Fragment size=1024 (log=0)
184 inodes, 1440 blocks
72 blocks (5.00%) reserved for the super user
First data block=1
1 block group
8192 blocks per group, 8192 fragments per group
184 inodes per group

Writing inode tables: done
Writing superblocks and filesystem accounting information: done

This filesystem will be automatically checked every 26 mounts or
180 days, whichever comes first. Use tune2fs -c or -i to override.
[root@server1 root]#_
```

Although the most common command to create filesystems is the mkfs command, other variants and shortcuts to the mkfs command exist. For example, to create an ext2 filesystem, you could type mke2fs /dev/fd0 on the command line. Other alternatives to the mkfs command are listed in Table 6-3.

Table 6-3 Commands used to create filesystems

Command	Description
mkfs	Used to create filesystems of most types
mkfs.msdos, mkdosfs, mkfs.vfat	Used to create a DOS FAT filesystem
mkfs.ext2, mke2fs	Used to create an ext2 filesystem
mkfs.ext3, mke2fs –j	Used to create an ext3 filesystem (j = journalizing)
mkisofs	Used to create a CD-ROM filesystem
mkfs.reiserfs, mkreiserfs	Used to create a REISERFS filesystem

After a floppy disk has been formatted with a filesystem, it must be mounted on the directory tree before it can be used. A list of currently mounted filesystems can be obtained by using the mount command with no options or arguments, which reads the information listed in the **/etc/mtab** (mount table) file, as shown in the following output:

```
[root@server1 root]# mount
/dev/hda1 on / type ext3 (rw)
none on /proc type proc (rw)
none on /sys type sysfs (rw)
none on /dev/pts type devpts (rw,gid=5,mode=620)
usbdevfs on /proc/bus/usb type usbdevfs (rw)
none on /dev/shm type tmpfs (rw)
[root@server1 root]# cat /etc/mtab
/dev/hda1 / ext3 rw 0 0
none /proc proc rw 0 0
none /sys sysfs rw 0 0
none /dev/pts devpts rw,gid=5,mode=620 0 0
usbdevfs /proc/bus/usb usbdevfs rw 0 0
none /dev/shm tmpfs rw 0 0
[root@server1 root]#_
```

From the preceding output, you can see that the device /dev/hda1 is mounted on the / directory and contains an ext3 filesystem. The other filesystems listed are special filesystems that are used by the system and are discussed later in this book.

To mount a device on the directory tree, you can use the mount command with options and arguments to specify the filesystem type, the device to mount, and the directory on which to mount the device (mount point). It is important to ensure that no user is currently using the mount point directory; otherwise, the system gives you an error message and the disk is not mounted. To check whether the /mnt/floppy directory is being used by any users, you can use the **fuser command** with the -u option, as shown in the following output:

```
[root@server1 root]# fuser -u /mnt/floppy
[root@server1 root]#_
```

The preceding output indicates the /mnt/floppy directory is not being used by any user processes. To mount the first floppy device formatted with the ext2 filesystem to the /mnt/floppy directory, simply type the following command:

```
[root@server1 root]# mount -t ext2  /dev/fd0  /mnt/floppy
[root@server1 root]# mount
/dev/hda1 on / type ext3 (rw)
none on /proc type proc (rw)
none on /sys type sysfs (rw)
none on /dev/pts type devpts (rw,gid=5,mode=620)
usbdevfs on /proc/bus/usb type usbdevfs (rw)
none on /dev/shm type tmpfs (rw)
/dev/fd0 on /mnt/floppy type ext2 (rw)
[root@server1 root]#_
```

Notice that /dev/fd0 appears mounted to the /mnt/floppy directory in the preceding output of the mount command. To access and store files on the floppy device, you can now treat the /mnt/floppy directory as the root of the floppy disk. When an ext2 filesystem is created on a disk device, one directory, called lost+found, is created by default. The default directory is used by the fsck command discussed later in this chapter. To explore the recently mounted floppy filesystem, you can use the following commands:

```
[root@server1 root]# cd /mnt/floppy
[root@server1 floppy]# pwd
/mnt/floppy
[root@server1 floppy]# ls -F
lost+found/
[root@server1 floppy]#_
```

To copy files to the floppy device, simply specify the /mnt/floppy directory as the target for the cp command, as shown next:

```
[root@server1 floppy]# cd /etc
[root@server1 etc]# cat hosts
# Do not remove the following line, or various programs
# that require network functionality will fail.
127.0.0.1              server1.class.com server1
[root@server1 etc]# cp hosts /mnt/floppy
[root@server1 etc]# cd /mnt/floppy
[root@server1 floppy]# ls -F
```

```
hosts   lost+found/
[root@server1 floppy]# cat hosts
# Do not remove the following line, or various programs
# that require network functionality will fail.
127.0.0.1               server1.class.com server1
[root@server1 floppy]#_
```

Similarly, you can also create subdirectories underneath the floppy device to store files; these subdirectories are referenced underneath the mount point directory. To make a directory called workfiles on the floppy mounted in the previous example and copy the /etc/inittab file to it, you can use the following commands:

```
[root@server1 floppy]# pwd
/mnt/floppy
[root@server1 floppy]# ls -F
hosts   lost+found/
[root@server1 floppy]# mkdir workfiles
[root@server1 floppy]# ls -F
hosts   lost+found/   workfiles/
[root@server1 floppy]# cd workfiles
[root@server1 workfiles]# pwd
/mnt/floppy/workfiles
[root@server1 workfiles]# cp /etc/inittab .
[root@server1 workfiles]# ls -F
inittab
[root@server1 workfiles]#_
```

Even though you can eject the floppy disk from the floppy disk drive without permission from the system, doing so is likely to cause error messages to appear on the terminal screen. Before a floppy is ejected, it must be properly unmounted using the umount command. The umount command can take the name of the device to unmount or the mount point directory as an argument. Similar to mounting a floppy disk, unmounting a floppy disk also requires that the mount point directory has no users using it. If you try to unmount the floppy disk mounted to the /mnt/floppy directory while it is being used, you receive an error message similar to the one in the following example:

```
[root@server1 floppy]# pwd
/mnt/floppy
[root@server1 floppy]# umount /mnt/floppy
umount: /mnt/floppy: device is busy
[root@server1 floppy]# fuser -u /mnt/floppy
/mnt/floppy:         17368c(root)
[root@server1 floppy]# cd /root
[root@server1 root]# umount /mnt/floppy
[root@server1 root]# mount
```

```
/dev/hdc1 on / type ext3 (rw)
none on /proc type proc (rw)
none on /sys type sysfs (rw)
none on /dev/pts type devpts (rw,gid=5,mode=620)
usbdevfs on /proc/bus/usb type usbdevfs (rw)
none on /dev/shm type tmpfs (rw)
[root@server1 root]#_
```

Notice from the preceding output that you were still using the /mnt/floppy directory because it was the current working directory. The fuser command also indicated that the root user had a process using the directory. After the current working directory was changed, the umount command was able to unmount the floppy from the /mnt/floppy directory, and the output of the mount command indicated that the floppy disk was no longer mounted.

Recall that mounting simply attaches a disk device to the Linux directory tree so that you can treat the device like a directory full of files and subdirectories. A device can be mounted to any existing directory. However, if the directory contains files, those files are inaccessible until the device is unmounted. Suppose, for example, that you create a directory called /flopper for mounting floppy disks and a file inside called samplefile, as shown in the following output:

```
[root@server1 root]# mkdir /flopper
[root@server1 root]# touch /flopper/samplefile
[root@server1 root]# ls -F /flopper
samplefile
[root@server1 root]#_
```

If the floppy disk used earlier is mounted to the /flopper directory, a user who uses the /flopper directory will be using the floppy disk; however, when nothing is mounted to the /flopper directory, the previous contents are available for use:

```
[root@server1 root]# mount -t ext2 /dev/fd0 /flopper
[root@server1 root]# mount
/dev/hda1 on / type ext3 (rw)
none on /proc type proc (rw)
none on /sys type sysfs (rw)
none on /dev/pts type devpts (rw,gid=5,mode=620)
usbdevfs on /proc/bus/usb type usbdevfs (rw)
none on /dev/shm type tmpfs (rw)
/dev/fd0 on /flopper type ext2 (rw)
[root@server1 root]# ls -F /flopper
hosts  lost+found/  workfiles/
[root@server1 root]# umount /flopper
[root@server1 root]# ls -F /flopper
samplefile
[root@server1 root]#_
```

The `mount` command used in the preceding output specifies the filesystem type, the device to mount, and the mount point directory. To save time typing on the command line, you can alternatively specify one argument and allow the system to look up the remaining information in the /etc/fstab (filesystem table) file. The /etc/fstab file has a dual purpose; it is used to mount devices at boot time and is consulted when a user does not specify enough arguments on the command line when using the `mount` command.

There are six fields present in the /etc/fstab file:

```
<device to mount>   <mount point>   <type>   <mount options>   <dump#>   <fsck#>
```

The device to mount can be the path to a device file or the label that describes the volume to mount. The mount point specifies where to mount the device. The type can be a specific value (such as ext3) or can be automatically detected. The mount options are additional options that the `mount` command accepts when mounting the volume (such as read only, or "ro"). Any filesystems with the mount option "noauto" are not automatically mounted at boot time; a complete list of options that the `mount` command accepts can be found by viewing the manual page for the `mount` command.

The dump# is used by the `dump` command discussed later in Chapter 12 of this book when backing up filesystems; a 1 in this field indicates that the filesystem should be backed up, whereas a 0 indicates that no backup is necessary. The fsck# is used by the `fsck` command discussed later in this chapter when checking filesystems at boot time for errors; any filesystems with a 1 in this field are checked first before any filesystems with a number 2, and filesystems with a number 0 are not checked.

NOTE

To mount all filesystems in the /etc/fstab file that are intended to mount at boot time, you can simply type the `mount -a` command.

The following output displays the contents of the /etc/fstab file:

```
[root@server1 root]# cat /etc/fstab
LABEL=/        /            ext3     defaults                       1 1
none           /dev/pts     devpts   gid=5,mode=620                 0 0
none           /dev/shm     tmpfs    defaults                       0 0
none           /proc        proc     defaults                       0 0
none           /sys         sysfs    defaults                       0 0
/dev/hda2      swap         swap     defaults                       0 0
/dev/cdrom     /mnt/cdrom   udf,iso9660 noauto,owner,kudzu,ro 0 0
/dev/fd0       /mnt/floppy  auto     noauto,owner,kudzu       0 0
[root@server1 root]# _
```

Thus, to mount the first floppy device (/dev/fd0) to the /mnt/floppy directory and automatically detect the type of filesystem on the device, simply specify enough information for the mount command to find the appropriate line in the /etc/fstab file:

```
[root@server1 root]# mount /dev/fd0
[root@server1 root]# mount
/dev/hda1 on / type ext3 (rw)
none on /proc type proc (rw)
none on /sys type sysfs (rw)
none on /dev/pts type devpts (rw,gid=5,mode=620)
usbdevfs on /proc/bus/usb type usbdevfs (rw)
none on /dev/shm type tmpfs (rw)
/dev/fd0 on /mnt/floppy type ext2 (rw,nosuid,nodev)
[root@server1 root]# umount /dev/fd0
[root@server1 root]#_
```

The mount command in the preceding output succeeded because there existed a line in /etc/fstab that described the mounting of the /dev/fd0 device.

Alternatively, you could specify the mount point as an argument to the mount command to mount the same device via the correct entry in /etc/fstab:

```
[root@server1 root]# mount /mnt/floppy
[root@server1 root]# mount
/dev/hda1 on / type ext3 (rw)
none on /proc type proc (rw)
none on /sys type sysfs (rw)
none on /dev/pts type devpts (rw,gid=5,mode=620)
usbdevfs on /proc/bus/usb type usbdevfs (rw)
none on /dev/shm type tmpfs (rw)
/dev/fd0 on /mnt/floppy type ext2 (rw,nosuid,nodev)
[root@server1 root]# umount /mnt/floppy
[root@server1 root]#_
```

Table 6-4 lists commands that are useful when mounting and unmounting floppy disks.

Although the commands listed in Table 6-4 allow a user complete control over the mounting process, floppy disks are typically mounted automatically to the /mnt/floppy directory when you access the floppy disk using a GUI environment. From the GNOME desktop, simply double-click the Computer icon and then double-click the Floppy icon, as shown in Figure 6-3. From the KDE desktop, you can double-click the Start Here icon, select Devices, and double-click the Floppy icon, as shown in Figure 6-4.

Mounting a floppy in the GUI environment places an icon representing the floppy on the desktop. You can then double-click the floppy icon to open a listing of the files on the floppy, or right-click the floppy icon to obtain a menu from which you can unmount the floppy by selecting Unmount Volume.

Table 6-4 Useful commands when mounting and unmounting filesystems

Command	Description
mount	Displays mounted filesystems
mount −t <type> <device> <mount point> directory	Mounts a <device> of a certain <type> to a <mount point>
fuser −u <directory>	Displays the users using a particular directory
umount <mount point> *or* umount <device>	Unmounts a <device> from its <mount point> directory

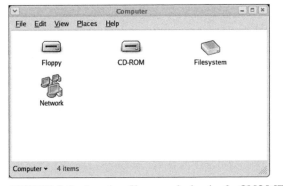

FIGURE 6-3 *Accessing filesystem devices in the GNOME desktop*

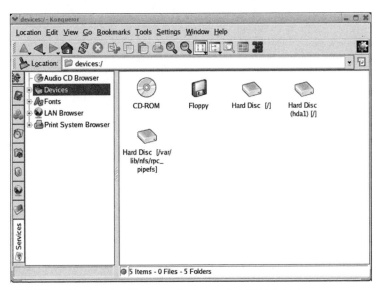

FIGURE 6-4 *Accessing filesystem devices in the KDE desktop*

Working with CD-ROMs

Most software that is not downloaded from the Internet is packaged on CD-ROM discs because they have a much larger storage capacity than floppy disks; one CD-ROM disc can store more than 500 times the data a floppy disk can store. Like floppies, CD-ROMs can be mounted with the mount command and unmounted with the umount command, as shown in Table 6-4; however, the device file used with these commands is different. Most Linux systems have an ATAPI-compliant IDE CD-ROM drive that attaches to the mainboard via an IDE ribbon cable. These CD-ROMs act as a normal IDE hard disk, and must be configured in one of the four configurations discussed in Chapter 2. These configurations and their associated device file are shown in the following list:

- Primary master (/dev/hda)
- Primary slave (/dev/hdb)
- Secondary master (/dev/hdc)
- Secondary slave (/dev/hdd)

Thus, you can specify your CD-ROM device file if the configuration is known. At installation, however, Red Hat Fedora Linux creates a symbolic link called /dev/cdrom to the appropriate device; if a system's CD-ROM is configured as a secondary slave, a long listing of /dev/cdrom shows the following:

```
[root@server1 root]# ls -l /dev/cdrom
lrwxrwxrwx   1 root   root    8 Jun 11 11:19 /dev/cdrom -> /dev/hdd
[root@server1 root]#_
```

Similarly, if the Linux system has a SCSI CD-ROM device, the long listing points to the appropriate SCSI device, as shown next:

```
[root@server1 root]# ls -l /dev/cdrom
lrwxrwxrwx   1 root   root    8 Jun 11 11:19 /dev/cdrom -> /dev/sdb
[root@server1 root]#_
```

In addition, CD-ROMs typically use the iso9660 filesystem type and are not writable; thus, to mount a CD-ROM to the /mnt/cdrom directory, you should use the filesystem type of iso9660 and add the -r (read-only) option to the mount command. To mount a sample CD-ROM to /mnt/cdrom and view its contents, you could use the following commands:

```
[root@server1 root]# mount -r -t iso9660 /dev/cdrom /mnt/cdrom
[root@server1 root]# mount
/dev/hda1 on / type ext3 (rw)
none on /proc type proc (rw)
none on /sys type sysfs (rw)
none on /dev/pts type devpts (rw,gid=5,mode=620)
usbdevfs on /proc/bus/usb type usbdevfs (rw)
none on /dev/shm type tmpfs (rw)
```

```
/dev/cdrom on /mnt/cdrom type iso9660 (ro)
[root@server1 root]# ls -l /mnt/cdrom
autorun.inf*   install*   graphics/   jungle/   jungle.txt*   joystick/
[root@server1 root]# umount /mnt/cdrom
[root@server1 root]#_
```

As with floppies, you can specify only a single argument to the mount command to mount a CD-ROM via an entry in the /etc/fstab file, and use the umount command to unmount the CD-ROM from the directory tree. Also remember that the mount point directory must not be in use to successfully mount or unmount CD-ROM discs; the fuser command can be used to verify this.

Unlike floppy disks, CD-ROMs cannot be ejected from the CD-ROM drive until the CD-ROM is properly unmounted, because the mount command locks the CD-ROM device as a precaution. When you insert a CD-ROM into your CD-ROM drive while in a GUI environment, it is automatically mounted to the /mnt/cdrom directory. Alternatively, you can also access the CD-ROM icon in a GUI environment to mount a CD-ROM that was not mounted automatically, as shown earlier in Figures 6-3 and 6-4.

After a CD-ROM has been mounted in a GUI environment, an icon is placed on the desktop that can be used to access the contents of the CD-ROM. Similar to floppy disks, you can right-click the CD-ROM icon on the desktop and choose Eject to unmount and eject the CD-ROM.

Working with Hard Disks

Hard disk drives come in two flavors, IDE and SCSI. IDE hard disk drives attach to the mainboard with an IDE cable and must be configured in one of four configurations, each of which has a different device file:

- ◆ Primary master (/dev/hda)
- ◆ Primary slave (/dev/hdb)
- ◆ Secondary master (/dev/hdc)
- ◆ Secondary slave (/dev/hdd)

SCSI hard disk drives typically have faster data transfer speeds, and usually connect to the mainboard via a controller card inserted into an expansion slot. Not only do SCSI drives offer faster access speed, but depending on the type, there might be 15 or more SCSI hard disks attached to a single controller. As a result of these benefits, SCSI hard disks are well suited to Linux servers that require a great deal of storage space for programs and user files. However, SCSI hard disks have different device files associated with them:

- ◆ First SCSI hard disk drive (/dev/sda)
- ◆ Second SCSI hard disk drive (/dev/sdb)

- Third SCSI hard disk drive (/dev/sdc)
- Fourth SCSI hard disk drive (/dev/sdd)
- Fifth SCSI hard disk drive (/dev/sde)
- Sixth SCSI hard disk drive (/dev/sdf)
- And so on

Hard Disk Partitioning

Recall that hard disks have the largest storage capacity of any device that you use to store information on a regular basis. This also poses some problems; as the size of a disk increases, organization becomes more difficult and the chance of error increases. To solve these problems, one typically divides a hard disk into smaller, more usable sections called **partitions**. Each partition can contain a separate filesystem and can be mounted to different mount point directories. Recall from Chapter 2 that Linux requires two partitions at minimum: a partition that is mounted to the root directory (the root partition) and a partition used to hold virtual memory (the swap partition). The swap partition does not require a filesystem, because it is written to and maintained by the operating system alone. It is good practice, however, to use more than just two partitions on a Linux system. This division can be useful to:

- Segregate different types of data—for example, home directory data is stored on a separate partition mounted to /home.
- Allow for the use of more than one type of filesystem on one hard disk drive—for example, some filesystems are tuned for database use.
- Reduce the chance that filesystem corruption will render a system unusable; if the partition that is mounted to the /home directory becomes corrupted, it does not affect the system because operating system files are stored on a separate partition mounted to the / directory.
- Speed up access to stored data by keeping filesystems as small as possible.

Segregation of data into physically separate areas of the hard disk drive can be exceptionally useful from an organizational standpoint. Keeping different types of data on different partitions gives you the ability to manipulate one type of data without affecting the rest of the system. This also reduces the likelihood that filesystem corruption will affect all files in the directory tree. Access speed is improved because a smaller area needs to be searched by the magnetic heads in a hard disk drive to locate data. This process is similar to searching for a penny in a 20,000-square-foot warehouse. It takes much less time to find the penny if that warehouse is divided into four separate departments of 5,000 square feet each, and you know which department the penny is located in. Searching and maneuvering is much quicker and easier in a smaller defined space than in a larger one.

On a physical level, hard disks are circular metal platters that spin at a fast speed. Data is read off these disks in concentric circles called **tracks**; each track is divided into **sectors** of information, and sectors are combined into more usable **blocks** of data, as shown in Figure 6-5. Most

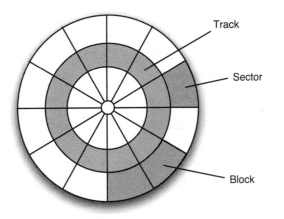

FIGURE 6-5 *The physical areas of a hard disk*

hard disk drives have several platters inside them, organized on top of each other such that they can be written to simultaneously to speed up data transfer. A series consisting of the same concentric track on all of the metal platters inside a hard disk drive is known as a **cylinder**.

Partition definitions are stored in the first readable sector of the hard disk known as the Master Boot Record (MBR) or master boot block (MBB). If this area of the hard disk becomes corrupted, the entire contents of the hard disk might be lost.

NOTE

It is common for Linux servers to have several hard disks. In these situations, it is also common to configure one partition on each hard disk and mount each partition to different directories on the directory tree. Thus, if one partition fails, an entire hard disk can be replaced with a new one and the data retrieved from a back-up source.

Recall from Chapter 2 that hard disks can contain up to four primary partitions; to overcome this limitation, you can use an extended partition in place of one of these primary partitions. An extended partition can then contain many more subpartitions called logical drives. Because it is these partitions that you place a filesystem on, there exist device files that refer to the various types of partitions that you can have on a hard disk. These device files start with the name of the hard disk (/dev/hda, /dev/hdb, /dev/sda, /dev/sdb, and so on) and append a number indicating the partition on that hard disk. The first primary partition is given the number 1, the second primary partition is given the number 2, the third primary partition is given the number 3, and the fourth primary partition is given the number 4. If any one of these primary partitions is labeled as an extended partition, the logical drives within are named starting with number 5. Table 6-5 lists some common hard disk partition names.

Table 6-5 Common hard disk partition device files for /dev/hda and /dev/sda

Partition	IDE Device Name (Assuming /dev/hda)	SCSI Device Name (Assuming /dev/sda)
1st primary partition	/dev/hda1	/dev/sda1
2nd primary partition	/dev/hda2	/dev/sda2
3rd primary partition	/dev/hda3	/dev/sda3
4th primary partition	/dev/hda4	/dev/sda4
1st logical drive in the extended partition	/dev/hda5	/dev/sda5
2nd logical drive in the extended partition	/dev/hda6	/dev/sda6
3rd logical drive in the extended partition	/dev/hda7	/dev/sda7
4th logical drive in the extended partition	/dev/hda8	/dev/sda8
5th logical drive in the extended partition	/dev/hda9	/dev/sda9
nth logical drive in the extended partition	/dev/hda**n**	/dev/sda**n**

Note from Table 6-5 that any one of the primary partitions can be labeled as an extended partition. Also, for different disk drives than those listed in Table 6-5 (for example, /dev/hdc), the partition numbers remain the same (for example, /dev/hdc1, /dev/hdc2, and so on).

Hard disk partitions can be created specific to a certain filesystem. To create a partition that will later be formatted with an ext2 or ext3 filesystem, you should create a Linux partition (also known as type 83). Similarly, you should create a Linux swap partition (also known as type 82) if that partition is intended for use as virtual memory. This explicit choice of partition type allows for partitions that better suit the needs of a filesystem.

A typical Linux hard disk structure for the primary master IDE hard disk (/dev/hda) can contain a partition for the / filesystem (/dev/hda1) and an extended partition (/dev/hda2) that further contains a swap partition (/dev/hda5) and some free space, as shown in Figure 6-6.

A more complicated Linux hard disk structure for the primary master IDE hard disk might involve preserving the Windows operating system partition, allowing a user to boot into and use the Linux operating system or boot into and use the Windows operating system. This is known as dual booting and is discussed in the next chapter.

In Figure 6-7, the Windows partition was created as a primary partition (/dev/hda1) and the Linux partitions are contained within the extended partition (/dev/hda2). Figure 6-7 also creates a separate filesystem for users' home directories mounted to /home (/dev/hda6).

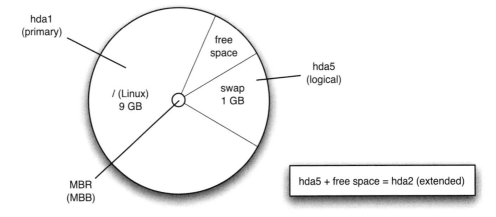

FIGURE 6-6 *A sample Linux partitioning strategy*

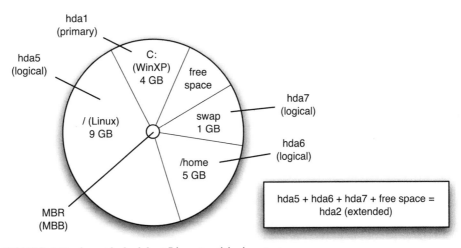

FIGURE 6-7 *A sample dual-boot Linux partitioning strategy*

Working with Hard Disk Partitions

Recall that the creation of partitions can be accomplished at installation using the Disk Druid utility. Disk Druid is an easy-to-use partitioning tool specifically designed for installation only. To create partitions after installation, you can use the **fdisk command**. To use the fdisk command, simply specify the hard disk to partition as an argument. An example of using fdisk with the secondary master IDE hard disk (/dev/hdc) is shown in the following output:

```
[root@server1 root]# fdisk /dev/hdc


The number of cylinders for this disk is set to 2491.
There is nothing wrong with that, but this is larger than 1024,
```

and could in certain setups cause problems with:
1) software that runs at boot time (e.g., old versions of LILO)
2) booting and partitioning software from other OSs
   (e.g., DOS FDISK, OS/2 FDISK)

Command (m for help):_

Note from the preceding output that the fdisk command displays a prompt for the user to accept fdisk commands; a list of possible fdisk commands can be seen if the user presses the m key at this prompt, as shown in the following example:

```
Command (m for help): m
Command action
   a   toggle a bootable flag
   b   edit bsd disklabel
   c   toggle the dos compatibility flag
   d   delete a partition
   l   list known partition types
   m   print this menu
   n   add a new partition
   o   create a new empty DOS partition table
   p   print the partition table
   q   quit without saving changes
   s   create a new empty Sun disklabel
   t   change a partition's system id
   u   change display/entry units
   v   verify the partition table
   w   write table to disk and exit
   x   extra functionality (experts only)

Command (m for help):_
```

To print a list of the partitions currently set on /dev/hdc, you could press the p key at the fdisk prompt:

```
Command (m for help): p

Disk /dev/hdc: 20.4 GB, 20490559488 bytes
255 heads, 63 sectors/track, 2491 cylinders
Units = cylinders of 16065 * 512 = 8225280 bytes

   Device Boot    Start     End   Blocks   Id  System
/dev/hdc1   *         1     510  4096543+  83  Linux
/dev/hdc2           511     561   409657+  82  Linux swap
/dev/hdc3           562    1247  5510295   83  Linux

Command (m for help):_
```

Notice that the device names appear on the left side of the preceding output, including the partition that is booted to (/dev/hdc1), the start and end location of partitions on the physical hard disk (start and end cylinders), the number of total blocks for storing information in the partition, as well as the partition type and description (83 is a Linux partition, 82 is a Linux swap partition). A Linux partition can contain a Linux filesystem, such as ext2 or ext3.

To remove the /dev/hdc3 partition and all the data contained on the filesystem within, you could use the d key noted earlier:

```
Command (m for help): d
Partition number (1-4): 3


Command (m for help): p


Disk /dev/hdc: 20.4 GB, 20490559488 bytes
255 heads, 63 sectors/track, 2491 cylinders
Units = cylinders of 16065 * 512 = 8225280 bytes


   Device Boot    Start      End    Blocks   Id  System
/dev/hdc1    *        1      510   4096543+  83  Linux
/dev/hdc2            511      561    409657+  82  Linux swap

Command (m for help):_
```

To create an extended partition using the fourth primary partition (/dev/hdc4) with two logical drives (/dev/hdc5 and /dev/hdc6), you could use the n key noted earlier and specify the partition to create, the starting cylinder on the hard disk, and the size in blocks (+1000M makes a 1000MB partition):

```
Command (m for help): n
Command action
   e   extended
   p   primary partition (1-4)
e
Partition number (1-4): 4
First cylinder (562-2491, default 562): 562
Last cylinder or +size or +sizeM or +sizeK (562-2491, default 2491): 1247


Command (m for help): p


Disk /dev/hdc: 20.4 GB, 20490559488 bytes
255 heads, 63 sectors/track, 2491 cylinders
Units = cylinders of 16065 * 512 = 8225280 bytes


   Device Boot    Start      End    Blocks   Id  System
/dev/hdc1    *        1      510   4096543+  83  Linux
```

```
/dev/hdc2              511        561    409657+   82  Linux swap
/dev/hdc4              562       1247   5510295     5  Extended

Command (m for help): n
Command action
   l   logical (5 or over)
   p   primary partition (1-4)
l
First cylinder (562-1247, default 562): 562
Last cylinder or +size or +sizeM or +sizeK (562-1247, default 1247): +1000M

Command (m for help): p

Disk /dev/hdc: 20.4 GB, 20490559488 bytes
255 heads, 63 sectors/track, 2491 cylinders
Units = cylinders of 16065 * 512 = 8225280 bytes

   Device Boot    Start      End    Blocks    Id  System
/dev/hdc1    *         1      510   4096543+   83  Linux
/dev/hdc2              511     561    409657+   82  Linux swap
/dev/hdc4              562    1247   5510295     5  Extended
/dev/hdc5              562     689   1028128+   83  Linux

Command (m for help): n
Command action
   l   logical (5 or over)
   p   primary partition (1-4)
l
First cylinder (690-1247, default 690): 690
Last cylinder or +size or +sizeM or +sizeK (690-1247, default 1247): +2000M

Command (m for help): p

Disk /dev/hdc: 20.4 GB, 20490559488 bytes
255 heads, 63 sectors/track, 2491 cylinders
Units = cylinders of 16065 * 512 = 8225280 bytes

   Device Boot    Start      End    Blocks    Id  System
/dev/hdc1    *         1      510   4096543+   83  Linux
/dev/hdc2              511     561    409657+   82  Linux swap
/dev/hdc4              562    1247   5510295     5  Extended
/dev/hdc5              562     689   1028128+   83  Linux
/dev/hdc6              690     944   2048256    83  Linux

Command (m for help):_
```

Notice from preceding output that the default type for new partitions created with fdisk is 83 (Linux); to change this, you can type the t key at the fdisk prompt. To change the /dev/hdc6 partition to type 82 (Linux swap), you can do the following at the fdisk prompt:

```
Command (m for help): t
Partition number (1-6): 6
Hex code (type L to list codes): L
```

```
 0  Empty           1c  Hidden W95 FAT3 70  DiskSecure Mult bb  Boot Wizard hid
 1  FAT12           1e  Hidden W95 FAT1 75  PC/IX           be  Solaris boot
 2  XENIX root      24  NEC DOS         80  Old Minix       c1  DRDOS/sec (FAT-
 3  XENIX usr       39  Plan 9          81  Minix / old Lin c4  DRDOS/sec (FAT-
 4  FAT16 <32M      3c  PartitionMagic  82  Linux swap      c6  DRDOS/sec (FAT-
 5  Extended        40  Venix 80286     83  Linux           c7  Syrinx
 6  FAT16           41  PPC PReP Boot   84  OS/2 hidden C:  da  Non-FS data
 7  HPFS/NTFS       42  SFS             85  Linux extended  db  CP/M / CTOS / .
 8  AIX             4d  QNX4.x          86  NTFS volume set de  Dell Utility
 9  AIX bootable    4e  QNX4.x 2nd part 87  NTFS volume set df  BootIt
 a  OS/2 Boot Manag 4f  QNX4.x 3rd part 8e  Linux LVM       e1  DOS access
 b  W95 FAT32       50  OnTrack DM      93  Amoeba          e3  DOS R/O
 c  W95 FAT32 (LBA) 51  OnTrack DM6 Aux 94  Amoeba BBT      e4  SpeedStor
 e  W95 FAT16 (LBA) 52  CP/M            9f  BSD/OS          eb  BeOS fs
 f  W95 Ext'd (LBA) 53  OnTrack DM6 Aux a0  IBM Thinkpad hi ee  EFI GPT
10  OPUS            54  OnTrackDM6      a5  FreeBSD         ef  EFI (FAT-12/16/
11  Hidden FAT12    55  EZ-Drive        a6  OpenBSD         f0  Linux/PA-RISC b
12  Compaq diagnost 56  Golden Bow      a7  NeXTSTEP        f1  SpeedStor
14  Hidden FAT16 <3 5c  Priam Edisk     a8  Darwin UFS      f4  SpeedStor
16  Hidden FAT16    61  SpeedStor       a9  NetBSD          f2  DOS secondary
17  Hidden HPFS/NTF 63  GNU HURD or Sys ab  Darwin boot     fd  Linux raid auto
18  AST SmartSleep  64  Novell Netware  b7  BSDI fs         fe  LANstep
1b  Hidden W95 FAT3 65  Novell Netware  b8  BSDI swap       ff  BBT
```

```
Hex code (type L to list codes): 82
Changed system type of partition 6 to 82 (Linux swap)
```

```
Command (m for help): p
```

```
Disk /dev/hdc: 20.4 GB, 20490559488 bytes
255 heads, 63 sectors/track, 2491 cylinders
Units = cylinders of 16065 * 512 = 8225280 bytes
```

```
   Device Boot    Start      End    Blocks   Id  System
/dev/hdc1    *        1      510   4096543+  83  Linux
/dev/hdc2           511      561    409657+  82  Linux swap
```

```
/dev/hdc4        562    1247   5510295   5  Extended
/dev/hdc5        562     689   1028128+ 83  Linux
/dev/hdc6        690     944   2048256  82  Linux swap

Command (m for help):_
```

Finally, to save partition changes to the hard disk and attempt to reload the new partition information back into memory, simply use the w key at the fdisk prompt:

```
Command (m for help): w
The partition table has been altered!

Calling ioctl() to re-read partition table.
WARNING: Re-reading the partition table failed with error 16: Device or resource busy.
The kernel still uses the old table
The new table will be used at the next reboot.
Syncing disks.
[root@server1 root]#_
```

If the fdisk command indicates that the new partition information must be reloaded manually (as in the preceding example), simply reboot your machine. For this reason, it is good form to always reboot your machine after running fdisk.

After the machine has rebooted, you can then use the mkfs, mount, and umount commands discussed earlier specifying the partition device file as an argument. To create an ext2 filesystem on the /dev/hdc5 partition created earlier, you can use the following command:

```
[root@server1 root]# mkfs -t ext2 /dev/hdc5
mke2fs 1.35 (28-Feb-2004)
Filesystem label=
OS type: Linux
Block size=4096 (log=2)
Fragment size=4096 (log=2)
128768 inodes, 257032 blocks
12851 blocks (5.00%) reserved for the super user
First data block=0
8 block groups
32768 blocks per group, 32768 fragments per group
16096 inodes per group
Superblock backups stored on blocks:
        32768, 98304, 163840, 229376

Writing inode tables: done
Writing superblocks and filesystem accounting information: done
```

```
This filesystem will be automatically checked every 36 mounts or
180 days, whichever comes first. Use tune2fs -c or -i to override.
[root@server1 root]#_
```

Following this, you can choose to convert this filesystem to ext3 by using the **tune2fs command** to create a journal file on the filesystem:

```
[root@server1 root]# tune2fs -j /dev/hdc5
tune2fs 1.35 (28-Feb-2004)
Creating journal inode: done
This filesystem will be automatically checked every 36 mounts or
180 days, whichever comes first. Use tune2fs -c or -i to override.
[root@server1 root]#_
```

Alternatively, you could have used the mke2fs -j /dev/hdc5 or mkfs.ext3 /dev/hdc5 commands to create an ext3 filesystem. To mount this ext3 filesystem to a new mount point directory called /data and view the contents, you can use the following commands:

```
[root@server1 root]# mkdir /data
[root@server1 root]# mount -t ext3 /dev/hdc5 /data
[root@server1 root]# mount
/dev/hdc1 on / type ext3 (rw)
none on /proc type proc (rw)
none on /sys type sysfs (rw)
none on /dev/pts type devpts (rw,gid=5,mode=620)
usbdevfs on /proc/bus/usb type usbdevfs (rw)
none on /dev/shm type tmpfs (rw)
/dev/hdc5 on /data type ext3 (rw)
[root@server1 root]# ls -F /data
lost+found/
[root@server1 root]#_
```

To allow the system to mount this filesystem automatically at every boot, simply edit the /etc/fstab file such that it has the following entry for /dev/hdc5:

```
[root@server1 root]# cat /etc/fstab
LABEL=/          /            ext3      defaults               1 1
none             /dev/pts     devpts    gid=5,mode=620         0 0
none             /dev/shm     tmpfs     defaults               0 0
none             /proc        proc      defaults               0 0
none             /sys         sysfs     defaults               0 0
/dev/hda2        swap         swap      defaults               0 0
/dev/cdrom       /mnt/cdrom   udf,iso9660 noauto,owner,kudzu,ro 0 0
/dev/fd0         /mnt/floppy  auto      noauto,owner,kudzu     0 0
/dev/hdc5        /data        ext3      defaults               0 0
[root@server1 root]#_
```

Monitoring Filesystems

After filesystems are created on disk devices and those disk devices are mounted to the directory tree, they should be checked periodically for errors, disk space usage, and inode usage. This minimizes the problems that can occur as a result of a damaged filesystem and reduces the likelihood that a file cannot be saved due to insufficient disk space.

Disk Usage

Several filesystems can be mounted to the directory tree. As mentioned earlier, the more filesystems that are used, the less likely a corrupted filesystem will interfere with normal system operations. Conversely, more filesystems typically results in less hard disk space per filesystem and might result in system errors if certain filesystems fill up with data. Many users create filesystems for the /, /usr, and /var directories during installation. The /usr directory contains most utilities and installed programs on a Linux system, and should have enough space for future software installations. The /var directory grows in size continuously as it stores log files. Old log files should be removed periodically to leave room for new ones. The / filesystem is the most vital of these, and should always contain a great deal of free space used as working space for the operating system. As a result, the / filesystem should be monitored frequently. If free space on the / filesystem falls below 10%, the system might suffer from poorer performance or cease to operate.

The easiest method for monitoring free space by mounted filesystems is to use the **df (disk free space) command**, as shown in the following output:

```
[root@server1 root]# df
Filesystem           1k-blocks      Used Available Use% Mounted on
/dev/hdc1              4032092   2848744    978524  75% /
none                   192232         0    192232   0% /dev/shm
[root@server1 root]#_
```

From the preceding output, the only filesystem used is the / filesystem; the /usr and /var directories are simply directories on the / filesystem, which increases the importance of monitoring the / filesystem. Because the / filesystem is 75% used in the preceding output, there is no immediate concern. However, log files and software installed in the future will increase this number and might warrant the purchase of an additional hard disk for data to reside on.

Alternatively, you can view the output of the df command in a more user-friendly (or human-readable) format by using the -h option, which prints sizes in the most convenient format (G = gigabyte, M = megabyte), as shown next:

```
[root@server1 root]# df -h
Filesystem           Size  Used Avail Use% Mounted on
/dev/hdc1            3.8G  2.8G  955M  75% /
none                 188M     0  187M   0% /dev/shm
[root@server1 root]#_
```

It is important to remember that the df command only views mounted filesystems; thus, to get disk free space statistics for a floppy filesystem, you should mount it prior to viewing the output of the df command:

```
[root@server1 root]# mount /dev/fd0
[root@server1 root]# df
Filesystem           1k-blocks     Used Available Use% Mounted on
/dev/hdc1             4032092    2848756    978512  75% /
none                  192232          0    192232   0% /dev/shm
/dev/fd0                1412         17      1323   2% /mnt/floppy
[root@server1 root]# umount /dev/fd0
[root@server1 root]# df
Filesystem           1k-blocks     Used Available Use% Mounted on
/dev/hdc1             4032092    2848756    978512  75% /
none                  192232          0    192232   0% /dev/shm
[root@server1 root]#_
```

If a filesystem is approaching full capacity, it might be useful to examine which directories on that filesystem are taking up the most disk space such that you can remove or move files from that directory to another filesystem that has sufficient space. To view the size of a directory and its contents in Kilobytes, you can use the **du (directory usage) command**. If the directory is large, you should use either the more or less command to view the output page-by-page, as shown with the following /usr directory:

```
[root@server1 root]# du /usr |more
4        /usr/local/share/man/man5
4        /usr/local/share/man/man2
4        /usr/local/share/man/man6
4        /usr/local/share/man/man9
4        /usr/local/share/man/mann
4        /usr/local/share/man/man8
4        /usr/local/share/man/man4
4        /usr/local/share/man/man7
4        /usr/local/share/man/man3
4        /usr/local/share/man/man1
44       /usr/local/share/man
4        /usr/local/share/info
52       /usr/local/share
4        /usr/local/src
4        /usr/local/bin
4        /usr/local/etc
4        /usr/local/include
4        /usr/local/libexec
4        /usr/local/sbin
```

```
4        /usr/local/games
4        /usr/local/lib
88       /usr/local
32       /usr/share/idl/bonobo-activation-2.0
--More--
```

To view only a summary of the total size of a directory, simply use the -s switch to the du command, as shown in the following example with the /usr directory:

```
[root@server1 root]# du -s /usr
2633772 /usr
[root@server1 root]# _
```

As with the df command, the du command also accepts the -h option to make the view more human readable; the following indicates that the total size of the /usr directory is 2.6 Gigabytes:

```
[root@server1 root]# du -hs /usr
2.6G    /usr
[root@server1 root]# _
```

Recall that every filesystem has an inode table that contains the inodes for the files and directories on the filesystem; this inode table is made during filesystem creation and is usually proportionate to the size of the filesystem. Each file and directory uses one inode; thus, a filesystem with several small files might use up all of the inodes in the inode table and prevent new files from being created on the filesystem. To view the total number of inodes and free inodes for an ext2 or ext3 filesystem, you can use the dumpe2fs command with the -h switch, as shown in the following output:

```
[root@server1 root]# df
Filesystem       1k-blocks      Used Available Use% Mounted on
/dev/hdc1         4032092    2848756    978512   75% /
none               192232          0    192232    0% /dev/shm
[root@server1 root]# dumpe2fs -h /dev/hda1
dumpe2fs 1.35 (28-Feb-2004)
Filesystem volume name:   /
Last mounted on:          <not available>
Filesystem UUID:          419890df-6ee5-47b1-a891-a84462652e45
Filesystem magic number:  0xEF53
Filesystem revision #:    1 (dynamic)
Filesystem features:      has_journal dir_index filetype needs_recovery sparse_super
Default mount options:    (none)
Filesystem state:         clean
Errors behavior:          Continue
Filesystem OS type:       Linux
Inode count:              1151904
```

```
Block count:                 2303311
Reserved block count:        115165
Free blocks:                 644098
Free inodes:                 796808
First block:                 0
Block size:                  4096
Fragment size:               4096
Blocks per group:            32768
Fragments per group:         32768
Inodes per group:            16224
Inode blocks per group:      507
Filesystem created:          Sun Jun 20 04:07:03 2004
Last mount time:             Mon Jul 12 11:49:22 2004
Last write time:             Mon Jul 12 11:49:22 2004
Mount count:                 5
Maximum mount count:         -1
Last checked:                Sun Jun 20 04:07:03 2004
Check interval:              0 (<none>)
Reserved blocks uid:         0 (user root)
Reserved blocks gid:         0 (group root)
First inode:                 11
Inode size:                  128
Journal inode:               8
First orphan inode:          309037
Default directory hash:      tea
Directory Hash Seed:         d972eedf-28f8-4cac-9417-039a32206be0
Journal backup:              inode blocks
[root@server1 root]# _
```

In the preceding output, you can see that there are 1151904 inodes in the inode table and that 796808 of them are free to use when creating new files and directories.

Checking Filesystems for Errors

Filesystems themselves can accumulate errors over time. These errors are often referred to as **filesystem corruption** and are common on most filesystems. Those filesystems that are accessed frequently are more prone to corruption than those that are not. As a result, such filesystems should be checked regularly for errors. The most common filesystem corruption occurs because a system was not shut down properly using the shutdown, halt, or reboot commands. Data is stored in memory for a short period of time before it is written to a file on the hard disk. This process of saving data to the hard disk is called **syncing**. If the computer's power is turned off, data in memory might not be synced properly to the hard disk and corruption might occur. Filesystem corruption can also occur if the hard disks are used frequently for time-intensive tasks such as database access. As the usage of any system increases, so does the possibility for operating system errors when writing to the hard disks. Along the same lines, the physical hard disks themselves are mechanical in nature and can wear during time. Some areas of the disk might become unusable if they cannot hold a magnetic charge; these areas are known as **bad blocks**. When the operating system finds a bad block, it puts a reference to that bad block in the bad blocks table on the filesystem. Any entries in the bad blocks table are not used for any future disk storage.

To check a filesystem for errors, you can use the **fsck (filesystem check) command**, which can check filesystems of many different types. The fsck command takes an option specifying the filesystem type and an argument specifying the device to check; if the filesystem type is not specified, the ext2 filesystem is assumed. It is also important to note that the filesystem being checked must be unmounted beforehand for the fsck command to work properly, as shown next:

```
[root@server1 root]# fsck -t ext2 /dev/fd0
Parallelizing fsck version 1.23 (15-Aug-2001)
fsck 1.35 (28-Feb-2004)
e2fsck 1.35 (28-Feb-2004)
/dev/fd0 is mounted.

WARNING!!!  Running e2fsck on a mounted filesystem may cause
SEVERE filesystem damage.

Do you really want to continue (y/n)? n

check aborted.
[root@server1 root]# umount /dev/fd0
[root@server1 root]# fsck -t ext2 /dev/fd0
fsck 1.35 (28-Feb-2004)
e2fsck 1.35 (28-Feb-2004)
/dev/fd0: clean, 14/184 files, 45/1440 blocks
[root@server1 root]# _
```

NOTE

Because the / filesystem cannot be unmounted, you should only run the fsck command on the / filesystem in single-user mode, which is discussed later in Chapter 8, "Working with the Bash Shell."

Notice from the preceding output that the `fsck` command does not give lengthy output on the terminal screen when checking the filesystem; this is because the `fsck` command only performs a quick check for errors unless the `-f` option is used to perform a full check, as shown in the following example:

```
[root@server1 root]# fsck -f -t ext2 /dev/fd0
fsck 1.35 (28-Feb-2004)
e2fsck 1.35 (28-Feb-2004)
Pass 1: Checking inodes, blocks, and sizes
Pass 2: Checking directory structure
Pass 3: Checking directory connectivity
Pass 4: Checking reference counts
Pass 5: Checking group summary information
/dev/fd0: 14/184 files (0.0% non-contiguous), 45/1440 blocks [root@server1 root]# _
```

Table 6-6 displays a list of common options used with the `fsck` command.

Table 6-6 Common options to the `fsck` command

Option	Description
-f	Performs a full filesystem check
-a	Allows fsck to automatically repair any errors
-A	Checks all filesystems in /etc/fstab that have a 1 or 2 in the sixth field
-Cf	Performs a full filesystem check and displays a progress line
-AR	Checks all filesystems in /etc/fstab that have a 1 or 2 in the sixth field but skips the / filesystem
-V	Displays verbose output

If the `fsck` command finds a corrupted file, it displays a message to the user asking whether to fix the error; to avoid these messages, you may use the `-a` option listed in Table 6-6 to specify that the `fsck` command should automatically repair any corruption. If there are files that the `fsck` command cannot repair, it places them in the lost+found directory on that filesystem and renames the file to the inode number.

To view the contents of the lost+found directory, simply mount the device and view the contents of the lost+found directory immediately underneath the mount point. Because it is difficult to identify lost files by their inode number, most users delete the contents of this directory periodically. Recall that the lost+found directory is automatically created when an ext2 or ext3 filesystem is created by the `mkfs` command.

Just as you can use the mke2fs command to make an ext2 filesystem, you can use the e2fsck command to check an ext2 or ext3 filesystem. Similarly, the reiserfsck command can check a reiserfs filesystem. These commands accept more options and can check a filesytem more thoroughly than fsck. For example, by using the -c option to the e2fsck command, you can check for bad blocks on the hard disk and add them to a bad block table on the filesystem so that they are not used in the future, as shown in the following example:

```
[root@server1 root]# e2fsck -c /dev/fd0
e2fsck 1.35 (28-Feb-2004)
Checking for bad blocks (read-only test): done
Pass 1: Checking inodes, blocks, and sizes
Pass 2: Checking directory structure
Pass 3: Checking directory connectivity
Pass 4: Checking reference counts
Pass 5: Checking group summary information

/dev/fd0: ***** FILE SYSTEM WAS MODIFIED *****
/dev/fd0: 14/184 files (0.0% non-contiguous), 45/1440 blocks [root@server1 root]# _
```

> **NOTE**
>
> The badblocks command can be used to perform the same function as the e2fsck command with the -c option.

Recall from earlier that the fsck command is run at boot time when filesystems are mounted from entries in the /etc/fstab file. Any entries in /etc/fstab that have a 1 in the sixth field are checked first, followed by entries that have a 2 in the sixth field. However, typically every 20–40 times an ext2 or ext3 filesystem is mounted (or every 180 days alternatively), a full filesystem check is forced. This might delay booting for several minutes or even hours depending on the size of the filesystems being checked. To change this interval, you can use the -i option to the tune2fs command, as shown next:

```
[root@server1 root]# tune2fs -i 0 /dev/fd0
tune2fs 1.35 (28-Feb-2004)
Setting interval between check 0 seconds
[root@server1 root]# _
```

The tune2fs command can be used to change or "tune" filesystem parameters after a filesystem has been created. Changing the interval between checks to 0 seconds, as shown in the preceding example, disables filesystem checks.

Hard Disk Quotas

If there are several users on a Linux system, there must be enough hard disk space to support the files that each user is expected to store on the hard disk. However, if hard disk space is limited or company policy limits disk usage, you should impose limits on filesystem usage. These restrictions are called **hard disk quotas**, and can be applied to users or groups of users. Furthermore, **quotas** can restrict how many files and directories a user can create (that is, restrict the number of inodes created) on a particular filesystem, or the total size of all files that a user can own on a filesystem. Two types of quota limits are available: soft limits and hard limits. **Soft limits** allow the user to extend them for a certain period of time (seven days by default), whereas **hard limits** are rigid and prevent the user from going past them. Quotas are typically enabled at boot time if there are quota entries in /etc/fstab, but can also be turned on and off afterward by using the **quotaon** and **quotaoff** commands, respectively.

To set up quotas for the / filesystem and restrict the user user1, you can carry out the following steps:

1. Edit the /etc/fstab file to add the usrquota and grpquota mount options for the / filesystem. The resulting /etc/fstab file should look like the following:

```
[root@server1 root]# cat /etc/fstab
LABEL=/          /              ext3     defaults,usrquota,grpquota  1 1
none             /dev/pts       devpts   gid=5,mode=620              0 0
none             /proc          proc     defaults                    0 0
none             /sys           sysfs    defaults                    0 0
none             /dev/shm       tmpfs    defaults                    0 0
/dev/hdc2        swap           swap     defaults                    0 0
/dev/cdrom       /mnt/cdrom     iso9660  noauto,owner,kudzu,ro       0 0
/dev/fd0         /mnt/floppy    auto     noauto,owner,kudzu          0 0
[root@server1 root]# _
```

2. Remount the root filesystem as read-write to update the system with the new options from /etc/fstab. The command to do this is:

```
[root@server1 root]# mount / -o remount,rw
[root@server1 root]# _
```

3. Create two files in the root of the filesystem called aquota.user and aquota.group. For the / filesystem, you should create the files /aquota.user and /aquota.group. Following this, run the quotacheck -mavug command, which looks on the system for file ownership and updates the quota database for all filesystems with quota options listed in /etc/fstab (-a), giving verbose output (-v) for all users and groups (-u and -g) even if

the filesystem is used by other processes (-m). This places information in the
aquota.user and aquota.group files.

```
[root@server1 root]# touch /aquota.user
[root@server1 root]# touch /aquota.group
[root@server1 root]# quotacheck -mavug
quotacheck: Scanning /dev/hdc1 [/] done
quotacheck: Checked 22249 directories and 337809 files
[root@server1 root]# _
```

4. Turn quotas on for the / filesystem using quotaon / command:

```
[root@server1 root]# quotaon /
[root@server1 root]# _
```

Alternatively, you can use the quotaoff / command to turn them off.

5. Edit the quotas for certain users by using the **edquota command** as follows: edquota
-u <username>. This brings up the vi editor and allows you to set soft and hard quotas for the number of blocks a user can own on the filesystem (typically, 1 block = 1
Kilobyte) and the total number of inodes (files and directories) that a user can own on
the filesystem. A soft limit and hard limit of zero (0) indicates that there is no limit.
To set a hard limit of 20Mb (=20480Kb) and 1000 inodes, as well as a soft limit of
18Mb (=18432Kb) and 900 inodes, you can do the following:

```
[root@server1 root]# edquota -u user1
Disk quotas for user user1 (uid 500):
```

Filesystem	blocks	soft	hard	inodes	soft	hard
/dev/hda1	1188	0	0	326	0	0

```
  ~
  ~
  ~
  ~
"/tmp//EdP.aclpslv" 3L, 216C
```

Next place the appropriate values in the columns provided, and then save and quit the
vi editor:

```
Disk quotas for user user1 (uid 500):
```

Filesystem	blocks	soft	hard	inodes	soft	hard
/dev/hda1	1188	18432	20480	326	900	1000

```
  ~
  ~
```

```
    ~

    ~

    :wq
    "/tmp/EdP.aclpslv" 3L, 216C written
    [root@server1 root]# _
```

6. Edit the time limit for which users can go beyond soft quotas by using the edquota
    -u -t command. The default time limit for soft quotas is seven days, but can be
    changed as follows:

```
    [root@server1 root]# edquota -u -t
    Grace period before enforcing soft limits for users:
    Time units may be: days, hours, minutes, or seconds
       Filesystem              Block grace period      Inode grace period
       /dev/hda1                     7days                  7days
       ~

       ~

       ~


    "/tmp//EdP.alvzfSy" 4L, 233C
```

7. Ensure that quotas were updated properly by gathering a report for quotas by user on
    the / filesystem using the **repquota command**, as shown in the following output.

```
    [root@server1 root]# repquota /
    *** Report for user quotas on device /dev/hdc1
    Block grace time: 7days; Inode grace time: 7days
                            Block limits              File limits
    User            used    soft    hard  grace    used  soft  hard  grace
    ----------------------------------------------------------------------
    root       -- 6420573     0       0          376520    0     0
    bin        --   14912     0       0              47    0     0
    daemon     --      16     0       0               5    0     0
    lp         --       8     0       0               2    0     0
    news       --    4396     0       0             228    0     0
    uucp       --    9612     0       0              23    0     0
    games      --       0     0       0              65    0     0
    rpm        --  101056     0       0             120    0     0
    vcsa       --       8     0       0             143    0     0
    rpcuser    --      32     0       0               8    0     0
```

pcap	--	256	0	0	14	0	0
smmsp	--	12	0	0	3	0	0
apache	--	48	0	0	12	0	0
squid	--	16	0	0	4	0	0
webalizer	--	24	0	0	6	0	0
xfs	--	8	0	0	3	0	0
named	--	36	0	0	9	0	0
ntp	--	12	0	0	3	0	0
gdm	--	28	0	0	1	0	0
pvm	--	8	0	0	2	0	0
wnn	--	4184	0	0	44	0	0
postfix	--	88	0	0	22	0	0
mailman	--	4	0	0	2	0	0
amanda	--	1108	0	0	74	0	0
netdump	--	32	0	0	9	0	0
quagga	--	32	0	0	8	0	0
radvd	--	8	0	0	2	0	0
radiusd	--	24	0	0	9	0	0
ldap	--	8	0	0	2	0	0
mysql	--	16	0	0	5	0	0
postgres	--	5352	0	0	279	0	0
fax	--	60	0	0	5	0	0
nut	--	28	0	0	5	0	0
privoxy	--	624	0	0	48	0	0
tomcat	--	24	0	0	6	0	0
cyrus	--	16808	0	0	34	0	0
exim	--	40	0	0	10	0	0
user1	--	1188	18432	20480	326	900	1000

```
[root@server1 root]# _
```

Note that most users in the preceding output are system users and do not have quotas applied to them. These users are discussed in Chapter 10, "Managing Linux Processes."

The aforementioned commands must be performed by the root user; however, regular users can view their own quota using the **quota command**. The root user can also use the quota command but can also use it to view quotas of other users:

```
[root@server1 root]# quota
Disk quotas for user root (uid 0): none
[root@server1 root]# quota -u user1
Disk quotas for user user1 (uid 500):
Filesystem blocks  quota  limit grace files  quota  limit grace
/dev/hdc1    1188  18432  20480        326    900   1000
[root@server1 root]# _
```

Chapter Summary

◆ Disk devices are represented by device files that reside in the /dev directory. These device files specify the type of data transfer, the major number of the device driver in the Linux kernel, and the minor number of the specific device.

◆ Each disk device must contain a filesystem, which is then mounted to the Linux directory tree for usage using the mount command. The filesystem can later be unmounted using the umount command. The directory used to mount the device must not be in use by any logged-in users for mounting and unmounting to take place.

◆ Hard disks must be partitioned into distinct sections before filesystems are created on those partitions. The fdisk command can be used to partition a hard disk.

◆ Many different filesystems are available to Linux; each filesystem is specialized for a certain purpose and several different filesystems can be mounted to different mount points on the directory tree. You can create a filesystem on a device using the mkfs command and its variants.

◆ It is important to monitor disk usage using the df, du, and dumpe2fs commands to avoid running out of storage space. Similarly, it is important to check disks for errors using the fsck command and its variants.

◆ If hard disk space is limited, you can use hard disk quotas to limit the space that each user has on filesystems.

Key Terms

/dev directory — The directory off the root where device files are typically stored.

/dev/MAKEDEV — The command used to re-create a device file if one or more of the following pieces of device information is unknown: major number, minor number, or type (character or block).

/etc/fstab — A file used to specify which filesystems to mount automatically at boot time and queried by the mount command if an insufficient number of arguments are specified.

/etc/mtab — A file that stores a list of currently mounted filesystems.

/proc/devices — A file that contains currently used device information.

bad blocks — The areas of a storage medium unable to store data properly.

block — The unit of data commonly used by filesystem commands; a block can contain several sectors.

block devices — The storage devices that transfer data to and from the system in chunks of many data bits by caching the information in RAM; they are represented by block device files.

character devices — The storage devices that transfer data to and from the system one data bit at a time; they are represented by character device files.

cylinder — A series of tracks on a hard disk that are written to simultaneously by the magnetic heads in a hard disk drive.

device file — A file used by Linux commands that represents a specific device on the system; these files do not have a data section and use major and minor numbers to reference the proper driver and specific device on the system, respectively.

df (disk free space) command — A command that displays disk free space by filesystem.

du (directory usage) command — A command that displays directory usage.

edquota command — A command used to specify quota limits for users and groups.

fdisk command — A command used to create, delete, and manipulate partitions on hard disks.

filesystem — The organization imposed on a physical storage medium that is used to manage the storage and retrieval of data.

filesystem corruption — The errors in a filesystem structure that prevent the retrieval of stored data.

formatting — The process in which a filesystem is placed on a disk device.

fsck (filesystem check) command — A command used to check the integrity of a filesystem and repair damaged files.

fuser command — A command used to identify any users or processes using a particular file or directory.

hard disk quotas — The limits on the number of files, or total storage space on a hard disk drive, available to a user.

hard limit — A limit imposed that cannot be exceeded.

major number — The number used by the kernel to identify which device driver to call to interact properly with a given category of hardware; hard disk drives, CD-ROMs, and video cards are all categories of hardware; similar devices share a common major number.

minor number — The number used by the kernel to identify which specific hardware device, within a given category, to use a driver to communicate with; *see also* Major number.

mkfs (make filesystem) command — A command used to format or create filesystems.

mknod command — A command used to re-create a device file, provided the major number, minor number, and type (character or bock) are known.

mount command — A command used to mount filesystems on devices to mount point directories.

mount point — The directory in a file structure to which something is mounted.

mounting — A process used to associate a device with a directory in the logical directory tree such that users can store data on that device.

partition — A physical division of a hard disk drive.

quota command — A command used to view disk quotas imposed on a user.

quotaoff command — A command used to deactivate disk quotas.

quotaon command — A command used to activate disk quotas.

quotas — The limits that can be imposed on users and groups for filesystem usage.

repquota command — A command used to produce a report on quotas for a particular filesystem.

root filesystem — The filesystem that contains most files that make up the operating system; it should have enough free space to prevent errors and slow performance.

sector — The smallest unit of data storage on a hard disk; sectors are arranged into concentric circles called tracks and can be grouped into blocks for use by the system.

soft limit — A limit imposed that can be exceeded for a certain period of time.

syncing — The process of writing data to the hard disk drive that was stored in RAM.

track — The area on a hard disk that forms a concentric circle of sectors.

tune2fs command — A command used to modify ext2 and ext3 filesystem parameters.

umount command — A command used to break the association between a device and a directory in the logical directory tree.

Review Questions

1. What is the traditional filesystem used on Linux?

   a. bfs

   b. ext2

   c. ext3

   d. hpfs

2. If a CD-ROM drive is configured as a secondary slave, what is the name of the associated device file?

   a. /dev/hda

   b. /dev/hdb

   c. /dev/hdc

   d. /dev/hdd

3. In a hard drive, data is read from disks in concentric circles called _____.

   a. tracks

   b. sectors

   c. cylinders

   d. blocks

4. To view the size of a directory and its contents in Kilobytes, you can use the _____ command.

   a. pwd

   b. fdisk

   c. fsck

   d. du

5. Using the _____ flag of the fsck command performs a full filesystem check and displays a progress line.

   a. -AR

   b. -Cf

   c. -a

   d. -A

6. True or false? The type of filesystem used determines how files are managed on the physical hard disk.

7. True or false? Subdirectories cannot be created on a mounted floppy drive.

8. True or false? All the partitions on a hard drive share a single filesystem.

9. True or false? After filesystems are created on disk devices and those disk devices are mounted to the directory tree, there is no need for any further maintenance.

10. True or false? Quotas can restrict how many files and directories a user can create.

11. Most devices on a Linux system (such as disks, terminals, and serial ports) are represented by a file on the hard disk called a(n) _____ file.

12. When the Linux system is first turned on, a filesystem present on the hard drive is mounted to the / directory. This is referred to as the _____ filesystem and contains most of the operating system files.

13. Hard disk drives come in two flavors, IDE and _____.

14. To create partitions after installation, you can use the _____ command.

15. The process of saving data from memory to the hard disk is called _____.

Chapter 7

Advanced Installation

After completing this chapter, you will be able to:

◆ Describe the types and structure of SCSI devices

◆ Identify default IRQs, I/O addresses, and DMAs

◆ Explain how Plug-and-Play can be used to assign configuration to peripheral devices

◆ Explain how APM and ACPI can be used to control power to peripheral devices

◆ Outline the steps used to install Linux from source files on a DVD, hard disk, or network server

◆ Understand methods used to automate the Linux installation

◆ Install Red Hat Fedora Linux using a kickstart file

◆ Troubleshoot the installation process

A Linux installation is a large and complicated task; it requires a great deal of hardware and software knowledge. In Chapter 3, "Linux Installation and Usage," you examined the installation process using common hardware components and practices. This chapter examines hardware further and emphasizes hardware that is less common and more difficult to configure. In addition, you explore various methods for installing Linux and common installation problems.

Advanced Hardware Configuration

Some of the hardware peripherals your system utilizes might require specialized setup and configuration. Chapter 2, "Preparing for Linux Installation," emphasized the IDE hard disk drive configuration, as it is the most common configuration found in home and office computers as of this writing. Chapter 2 also introduced the configuration of peripheral components using IRQs, I/O addresses, and DMAs. This section explores the configuration of SCSI hard disks, RAID, and common peripheral configurations seen in most computers.

SCSI Hard Disk Drive Configuration

The Small Computer System Interface (SCSI) was designed as a way to connect multiple peripherals to the system in a scalable, high-speed manner. Recall that a SCSI device is not usually connected directly to the mainboard, but rather to a controller card, which, in turn, connects all devices attached to it to the mainboard. Disk devices attach to the SCSI controller card via one cable with several connectors for the devices to plug in to. Information is then sent from device to device along this cable in a daisy-chain fashion. To prevent signals from bouncing back and forth on the cable, each end of the cable must be terminated with a device that stops signals from being perpetuated. This device is called a **terminator**. Typically, one terminator is on the controller card itself, as shown in the top half of Figure 7-1. Some systems that have several hard drives attached to one controller, however, typically place the controller in the middle of the daisy chain, as shown in the bottom half of Figure 7-1.

SCSI disk drives must be configured such that each hard disk drive can be uniquely identified by the system; this is accomplished by assigning a unique ID number known as a **SCSI ID** or **target ID** to each device. Most SCSI controllers today support up to 15 devices and identify these devices with the numbers 0–15 (one number must be reserved for the controller card itself). This SCSI ID also gives priority to the device. The highest priority device is given the number 7, followed by 6, 5, 4, 3, 2, 1, 0, 15, 14, 13, 12, 11, 10, 9, and 8.

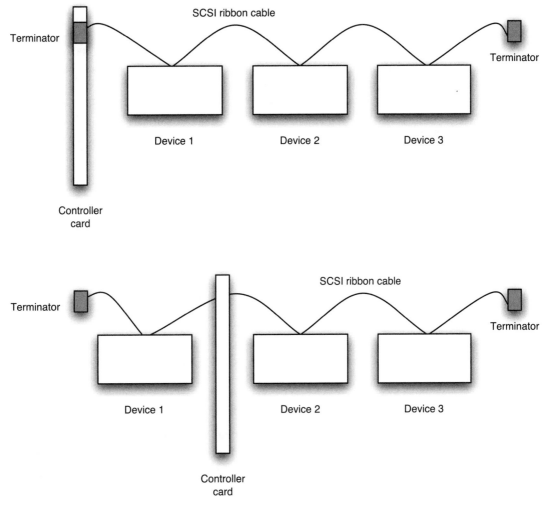

FIGURE 7-1 *Connecting SCSI devices*

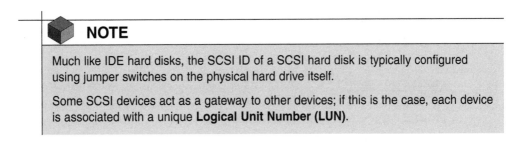

NOTE

Much like IDE hard disks, the SCSI ID of a SCSI hard disk is typically configured using jumper switches on the physical hard drive itself.

Some SCSI devices act as a gateway to other devices; if this is the case, each device is associated with a unique **Logical Unit Number (LUN)**.

SCSI technology has evolved over time; it was initially adopted as an industry-defined standard in 1986. At that time, SCSI used an 8-bit-wide data path on a controller card that held up to seven devices and had a data transfer speed of 5MB per second. This was commonly referred to as SCSI-1 (SCSI Standard 1). By 1994, it had evolved to a standard that used a 16-bit-wide data path on a controller card that could hold up to 15 devices and had a transfer speed of 20MB per second. This advent was referred to as SCSI-2 (SCSI Standard 2). SCSI-3 was introduced a short time later and provided speeds of over 160MB per second. Newer technology, such as FireWire (IEEE 1394), can transfer data to and from SCSI devices at speeds over 800MB per second. Table 7-1 describes various SCSI technologies.

Table 7-1 Common SCSI standards

SCSI Type	Speed (MB/s)	Bus Width (bits)	Connector	Number of Devices Supported
SCSI-1 (narrow, slow)	5	8	50-pin Centronics or 50-pin LPT (Line Port Terminal) type	7
SCSI-2 (Fast)	10	8	50-pin LPT type	7
SCSI-2 (Wide)	20	16	68-pin LPT type	15
SCSI-3		16	68-pin LPT type	15
(Ultra)	40			
(Ultra2 Wide)	80			
(Ultra3 Wide)	160			

You can identify the type of SCSI device by observing the connector. To identify a SCSI-1 50-pin Centronic or LPT connector, you can compare them to Figures 7-2 and 7-3, respectively.

SCSI-2 devices initially used a 50-pin LPT connector, as shown in Figure 7-3. However, later versions of SCSI-2 and SCSI-3 used a 68-pin LPT connector, as depicted in Figure 7-4.

50-pin Centronic connector used with older 8-bit-wide data path devices. Normally held in place via spring clips.

FIGURE 7-2 *A 50-pin Centronics SCSI connector*

50-pin LPT connector used for 8-bit-wide data paths.

FIGURE 7-3 *A 50-pin LPT SCSI connector*

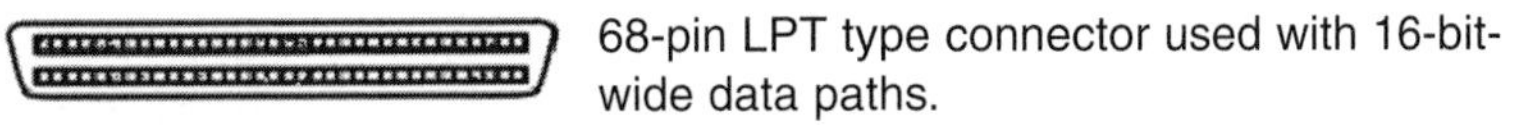

68-pin LPT type connector used with 16-bit-wide data paths.

FIGURE 7-4 *A 68-pin LPT SCSI connector*

Mainboard Flow Control: IRQs, DMAs, and I/O Addresses

Recall from the preceding section that multiple SCSI devices attached to a single controller card need to be uniquely identified and their requests for service prioritized. The same is true of multiple devices attached to the mainboard via expansion slots. Recall that the unique identifier used with peripheral components is the **Interrupt Request (IRQ)**.

The processor of a computer executes processes in physical memory for devices. Its time and capacity must be shared among all devices in the computer, which can be accomplished in one of two ways: polling or interruption. In **polling**, the processor polls system devices to see if there are tasks to be run. Not all devices have processes to run and, thus, the processor wastes time and resources polling them. There is also no efficient way of prioritizing tasks using processor polling. The second method is a more effective way to share processor time; the processor is interrupted by devices only when resources are needed. IRQs are so named because they are used to identify devices and give priorities that are considered when a device needs to access the processor. If two devices require access to the processor at the same time, the one with the lowest IRQ (highest priority) is given access first.

Initially, eight IRQs were created to identify and prioritize devices attached to the original ISA slots that used an 8-bit wide data path and were numbered 0 through 7. The highest priority was given the lowest number, thus a device with an IRQ of 0 had a higher priority than a device assigned an IRQ of 4. With the evolution of the 16-bit wide ISA expansion slot came the need for eight more IRQs, numerically identified as 8 through 15. Unlike SCSI, however, these additional IRQs were not appended to the priority list, but rather squeezed into the middle of the priority sequence between IRQ 2 and IRQ 3. This means that IRQs do not follow a straightforward priority order; although IRQ 10 has higher priority than IRQ 13, IRQ 10 also has a higher priority than IRQ 4. The IRQ priority scheme is illustrated in Figure 7-5.

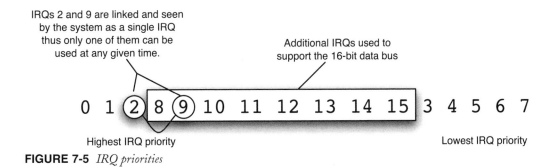

FIGURE 7-5 *IRQ priorities*

One consequence of adding the eight additional IRQs is that IRQ 2 and IRQ 9 are linked such that they are seen by the system as a single IRQ; only one or the other can be used at any given time. This also means that though numbered 0 through 15, only 15 IRQs are available on the system.

Although IRQs are used to identify and assign priority sequence to devices, not all 15 IRQs are available, because the system reserves some for certain devices. Before utilizing an IRQ and assigning it to a device, it is important to ensure that the IRQ is free to use. Assigning the same IRQ to two devices causes system problems, and either device might not function properly. Table 7-2 outlines common IRQ assignments used on systems today.

Table 7-2 Default IRQ assignments

IRQ	Description
0	System timer
1	Keyboard
2	Linked to IRQ 9—available if 9 not used
3	COM2, COM4
4	COM1, COM3
5	Available (usually for sound card or LPT2)
6	Floppy disk controller
7	Parallel port (LPT1)
8	Real-time clock
9	Linked to IRQ2—available if 2 not used
10	Available
11	Available
12	Available
13	Math coprocessor
14	Primary IDE hard disk drive controller
15	Secondary IDE hard disk drive controller

In addition to identification and priority control, each peripheral device needs its own working space in physical memory where it can communicate with other devices. This working space is identified by a hexadecimal number range representing a certain area of RAM and is referred to as an **Input/Output (I/O) address**. Many I/O addresses are commonly reserved for certain devices on a system, as listed in Table 7-3. As with IRQs, it is important to ensure that the I/O address of a device has not been assigned to another device, because neither device will function properly.

Table 7-3 Default I/O address assignments

I/O Address	Device
3F8-3FF	COM1
2F8-2FF	COM2
3E8-3EF	COM3
2E8-2EF	COM4
378-37F	LPT1
278-27F	LPT2
000-01F	DMA controller
020-03F	Primary interrupt controller
040-05F	Timer
060-06F	Keyboard
070-07F	Real-time clock
0A0-0BF	Secondary interrupt controller
0F0-1F7	Math coprocessor
1F0-1F7	Hard disk
3D0-3DF	VGA
3F0-3F7	Floppy disk controller

NOTE

At minimum, each device must have a unique IRQ and I/O address.

Direct memory access (DMA) improves efficiency and performance on the system by allowing a device direct access to physical memory via one of a limited number of unique channels. Normally, only the processor is allowed direct access to physical memory and devices must pass all calls to it through the processor. If a device makes great use of physical memory, such as a sound card, the constant load on the processor can impact system performance. Granting such devices direct access to physical memory improves overall system performance; sound cards, network cards, and SCSI disk controllers benefit greatly from DMA channels, because they read and write a great deal of data to physical memory.

Again, there is a development history with DMA channels. Eight-bit data buses used four DMA channels; this number was expanded to eight channels with the introduction of the 16-bit data bus. The fourth DMA channel is unavailable due to the expansion. As with IRQs and I/O addresses, only one device at a time can use a DMA channel, and so DMA assignments should be unique. Table 7-4 details the default DMA channel assignments.

Table 7-4 Default DMA assignments

DMA	Device	Data Path Width
0	Available	8 bits
1	Available	8 bits
2	Floppy disk drive controller	8 bits
3	Available	8 bits
4	Unavailable, used by DMA itself	16 bits
5	Available	16 bits
6	Available	16 bits
7	Available	16 bits

Plug-and-Play

Assigning each device a unique IRQ and I/O address is a time-consuming and error-prone task to perform manually; for this reason, **Plug-and-Play (PnP)** technology has been introduced. A Plug-and-Play BIOS automatically assigns the necessary configuration information (IRQs, I/O addresses, and DMAs) to devices and avoids conflicts. For Plug-and-Play to work properly, the device and operating system must support it as well as the computer BIOS.

Plug-and-Play assigns configuration information in a set manner described as follows:

1. A table is generated that contains all IRQs, I/O addresses, and DMA channels that are available by default and not used by the system.

2. The system probes all devices connected to it to see if they are PnP capable.

3. The system then retrieves a table it stored on a **complementary metal-oxide semi-conductor (CMOS)** memory chip prior to shutdown. This table contains the devices connected to the system during the last boot and the IRQ, I/O address, and DMA assignments made. If the list has not changed, the boot process skips the following steps (4–7); if a change is detected, the system continues to Step 4.

4. The system marks any assignments made to non-PnP devices as unavailable in the table created in Step 1.

5. The system checks the BIOS settings to see if any IRQ, I/O address, or DMA settings have been marked as reserved or unavailable and then marks them as unavailable in the table created in Step 1.

6. The BIOS then assigns any PnP-capable devices with the necessary configuration information known available from the table updated in Steps 4 and 5.

7. The table of currently connected devices and their settings is stored for use in Step 3 on future startups.

APM and ACPI

Hard disks and peripheral components use a great deal of electricity when they are not in use. As a result, hardware manufacturers have released two standards that can be used to shut off power to certain components when they are not being used: **Advanced Power Management (APM)** and **Advanced Configuration and Power Interface (ACPI)**.

APM is the older of the two standards and, as discussed in Chapter 2, is primarily used to shut off power to peripheral components on portable laptop computers. Unfortunately, APM is supported only by the BIOS of the computer and must be configured through the system BIOS setup utility invoked on system startup.

ACPI was initially developed in 1996 by Compaq, Intel, Microsoft, Phoenix, and Toshiba, and was designed to replace APM because it allows users to configure power options from within the operating system rather than from the BIOS setup utility. In addition, ACPI can be used to provide information such as CPU temperature and portable laptop computer battery level to users of the operating system. With ACPI, you can specify settings that tell your operating system to shut down power to the entire computer temporarily (called standby mode) or certain sets of peripheral components after a certain period of time (called sleep states).

NOTE

APM and ACPI are mutually exclusive; you cannot enable both features on the same computer. Most portable laptop computer manufacturers have switched to ACPI on computers manufactured in 2002 and later.

Normally, ACPI support is detected and enabled during a Red Hat Fedora installation. If, however, ACPI was not enabled during the installation, simply add the string "apm=off acpi=on" to the end of the kernel line in the /boot/grub/grub.conf file if your boot loader is **Grand Unified Bootloader (GRUB)** or the line append "apm=off acpi=on" to the /etc/lilo.conf file if your boot loader is **LInux LOader (LILO)**. Boot loaders are further discussed in Chapter 9, "System Initialization and X Windows."

After ACPI has been enabled, it is configured with default options supported by your hardware. You can also download and use certain applications or applets to view or configure its settings; one example is heatload, which can monitor CPU temperature. Another example is the Linux ACPI Client, which is a command-line utility that you can download to view ACPI settings, as shown in the following example:

```
[root@server1 root]# acpi -V
Battery 1: discharging, 91%, 02:39:07 remaining
Thermal 1: ok, 44.1 degrees C
AC Adapter 1: off-line
[root@server1 root]#_
```

> **NOTE**
>
> Although ACPI is supported by nearly all mainboards and operating systems as of this writing, it is still a work in progress; you should always ensure that your system has the most recent ACPI Linux kernel patch from *http://acpi.sourceforge.net*. Patching the Linux kernel is discussed in Chapter 13, "Troubleshooting and Performance."

RAID Configuration

Recall that you typically create several partitions during installation to decrease the likelihood that the failure of a filesystem on one partition will affect the rest of the system. These partitions should be spread across several different hard disks to minimize the impact of a hard disk failure; if one hard disk fails, the data on the other hard disks is unaffected.

If a hard disk failure occurs, you must power down the computer, replace the failed hard disk drive, power on the computer, and restore the data that was originally on the hard disk drive from a back-up source such as a tape device. The whole process can take several hours. For systems that must experience little or no downtime, such as a database server, there exist hard disk configurations that reduce the time it takes to recover from a hard disk failure. These configurations are called **fault tolerant** and are typically implemented by a **Redundant Array of Independent Disks (RAID)**. RAID configurations can be handled by software running on an operating system (software-based RAID), but are more commonly handled by the hardware contained within a SCSI hard disk controller (hardware-based RAID). To configure hardware-based RAID, you must enter the setup utility for your specific SCSI hard disk controller.

However, you can configure software-based RAID during installation by selecting the RAID button on the Disk Setup screen shown earlier in Figure 3-10.

Currently, seven basic RAID configurations are available, labeled level 0 through 6. RAID level 0 refers to RAID configurations that are not fault tolerant. One type of RAID level 0 is referred to as **spanning**, and consists of two hard disks that are seen as one large volume. Thus, if you had two 2GB hard disks, you could create one 4GB partition. Another type of RAID level 0 is called **disk striping**. If three hard disks are in this RAID configuration, a file that is saved to the hard disk is divided into three sections and each section is written to the hard disk concurrently; this allows the file to be saved in one-third the amount of time. This same file can be read in one-third the amount of time for the same reason. Unfortunately, if a hard disk fails in a RAID level 0 configuration, all data is lost.

RAID level 1 is often referred to as **disk mirroring**, and provides fault tolerance in the case of a hard disk failure. In this RAID configuration, the same data is written to two separate hard disks at the same time. This results in two hard disks that have identical information. If one fails, another copy can replace the failed hard disk in a short period of time. The only drawback to RAID level 1 is the cost, because you need to purchase twice the hard disk space needed for a given computer.

RAID level 2 is no longer used and was a variant of RAID 0 that allowed for error and integrity checking on hard disk drives. Modern hard disk drives do this intrinsically.

RAID level 3 is disk striping with a parity bit, or marker, which indicates what data is where. It requires a minimum of three hard disk drives to function, and one of these hard disks is used to store the parity information. Should one of the hard disks containing data fail, you can replace the hard disk drive and regenerate the data using the parity information stored on the parity disk. If the parity disk fails, the system must be restored from a back-up device.

RAID level 4 is only a slight variant on RAID level 3. RAID level 4 offers greater access speed than RAID level 3, because it can store data in blocks and, thus, does not need to access all disks in the array at once to read data.

RAID level 5 replaces RAID levels 3 and 4, and is the most common RAID configuration as of this writing. It is commonly referred to as **disk striping with parity**. As with RAID levels 3 and 4, it requires a minimum of three hard disk drives for implementation; however, the parity information is not stored on a separate drive, but is intermixed with data on the drives the set comprises. This offers better performance and fault tolerance; if any drive in the RAID configuration fails, the information on the other drives can be used to regenerate the lost information after the failed hard disk has been replaced. If two hard disks fail, the system must be restored from a back-up device. An example of how a RAID level 5 configuration can be restored using parity information is shown in Figure 7-6. The parity bits shown in Figure 7-6 are a sum of the information on the other two disks (22 + 12 = 34). If the third hard disk fails, the information can be regenerated because only one element is missing from each equation:

$$22 + 12 = 34$$
$$68 - 65 = 3$$
$$13 - 9 = 4$$

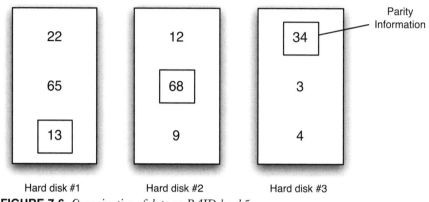

FIGURE 7-6 *Organization of data on RAID level 5*

RAID level 6 is basically the same as RAID level 5, but adds a second set of parity bits for added fault tolerance and allows up to two simultaneous hard disk drive failures while remaining fault tolerant.

> ### NOTE
> RAID levels are often combined; RAID level 15 refers to a Stripe Set with Parity (RAID level 5) that is mirrored (RAID level 1) to another Stripe Set with Parity.

Installation Methods

Modern computers contain a CD-ROM/CD-RW or DVD/DVD-RW device that can be used to start a CD-ROM-based installation such as the one discussed in Chapter 3. You can obtain the four Red Hat Fedora Core 2 CD-ROMs easily by downloading the **International Standards Organization (ISO) images** from one of several Web sites. You can then use these images in conjunction with a writable CD-R/CD-RW drive to create the installation CD-ROMs and boot your computer using the first CD-ROM to start the Linux installation.

> ### NOTE
> To obtain the ISO images from the Internet for a Red Hat Fedora Linux installation, visit *http://fedora.redhat.com* or *http://www.linuxiso.org*.
>
> To write information to a CD-ROM (a process called **burning**) using an ISO image, you must use a burning program that supports your CD-R/CD-RW device; examples of common burning programs include X-CD-Roast and Nero.

Although a CD-ROM-based installation is the most common installation method for Linux computers at the time of this writing, other methods can be used to install Linux. For example, you can install Linux from a DVD, from ISO image files on a hard disk, or from source files on a network server using the NFS, FTP, or HTTP protocol.

DVD Installation

In the past, Linux distributions typically fit on one or two CD-ROMs. However, many more recent distributions require several CD-ROMs to hold all the packages that are available for the distribution. As a result, you can choose to download a single DVD ISO image that contains all of the packages for your Linux distribution, rather than several CD-ROM ISO images. These DVD ISO images are typically available from the same Web sites that host the CD-ROM ISO images for your Linux distribution.

You can then use this DVD ISO image with a writable DVD-R/DVD-RW device to create the installation DVD, and, much like starting a CD-ROM image, boot your computer using it to start the Linux installation.

Hard Disk Installation

Not everyone installs Linux from CD-ROM or DVD. If you have downloaded the Red Hat Fedora Linux ISO installation images from the Internet, you can install Linux directly from the downloaded ISO images on the hard disk, provided that you have free space outside the partition that contains the ISO images for the Linux operating system.

> ### 🔲 NOTE
>
> After the ISO images have been copied to the hard disk on a partition that is formatted with either the FAT, ext2, or ext3 filesystem, you can start an installation and specify the target image. Because starting an installation by booting from the first Red Hat Fedora Linux installation CD-ROM assumes the source of files is the CD-ROM, you should create an installation startup CD-ROM or bootable USB flash memory drive (if your computer supports booting from a USB flash memory drive) to start the installation.
>
> To create an installation startup CD-ROM, simply navigate to the images directory on the first Red Hat Fedora installation CD-ROM. This directory contains a boot.iso ISO image file that can be used to create an installation startup CD-ROM using a CD-R/CD-RW device and a burning program. If you want to create a bootable USB flash memory drive, you can use the bootdisk.img file in the images directory. To image the bootdisk.img file to the USB flash memory drive, you can use the dd command in Linux. Simply mount the first Red Hat Fedora CD-ROM and use the dd command to copy the image to the USB flash memory drive. (Most USB flash memory drives are

> recognized as the first partition on the first SCSI hard disk for ease of mounting.) If
> your Red Hat Fedora CD-ROM is mounted to /mnt/cdrom, the command to image the
> bootdisk.img file to the USB flash memory drive is `dd if=/mnt/cdrom/images/boot-
> disk.img of=/dev/sda1`.

Next, you boot from either the installation startup CD-ROM or the USB flash memory drive.
When presented with the screen shown in Figure 7-7, press Enter. Without a Red Hat Fedora
Linux installation CD-ROM in the CD-ROM drive of the computer, a text-based installa-
tion begins and asks you for the language and keyboard information shown in Figures 7-8 and
Figure 7-9, respectively. Next, the installation program prompts you for the installation source
files for Red Hat Fedora Linux, as shown in Figure 7-10.

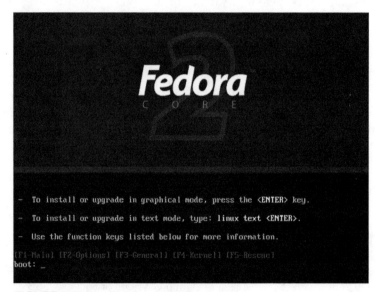

FIGURE 7-7 *Installation welcome screen*

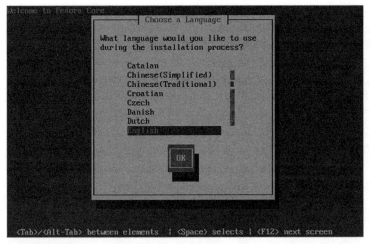

FIGURE 7-8 *Language selection screen*

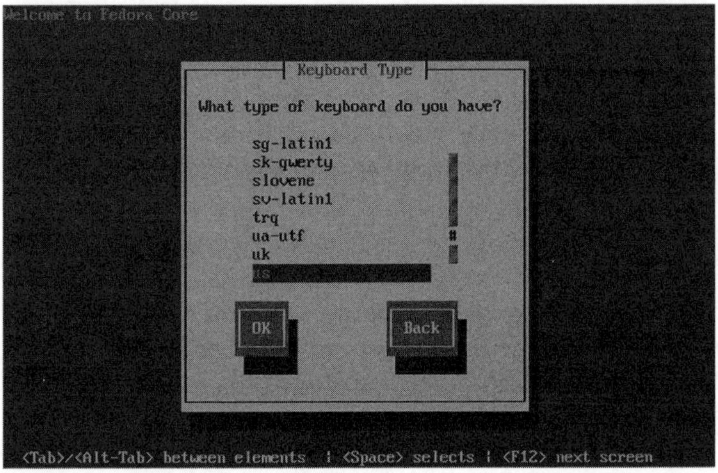

FIGURE 7-9 *Keyboard selection screen*

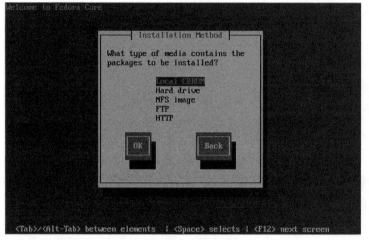

FIGURE 7-10 *Selecting an installation method*

After choosing to install from the hard disk in Figure 7-10, the installation prompts you for the partition and directory that contain the ISO images of the Red Hat Linux installation media, as shown in Figure 7-11. After the correct information has been specified, a graphical installation is run and you are required to specify the information needed to complete the installation.

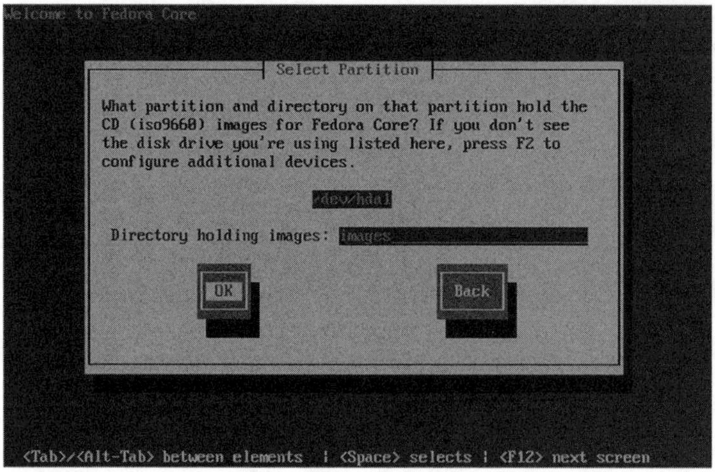

FIGURE 7-11 *Specifying source file location for a hard disk–based installation*

Network-Based Installations

Although less common than CD-ROM, DVD, or hard disk installations, you can also choose to use installation media that is stored on another machine and is accessible across a network via a network interface card (NIC) in the computer. For this method of installation, you must create an installation startup CD-ROM or bootable USB flash memory drive as described in the previous section; they contain common NIC drivers and programs that allow you to connect to a server with the appropriate installation files via one of the following protocols:

- **Network File System (NFS)**
- **File Transfer Protocol (FTP)**
- **Hypertext Transfer Protocol (HTTP)**

> ### NOTE
>
> The configuration of NFS, FTP, and HTTP is discussed in Chapter 15, "Linux Networking."
>
> Linux can also be installed across the network from a Windows server hosting the installation files. This method uses the Server Message Block (SMB) protocol and must be set up manually in Red Hat Linux; as a result, it is not discussed here.

After the installation startup CD-ROM or bootable USB flash memory drive has been imaged, you can simply boot the client computer using it and choose the appropriate options in Figures 7-7, 7-8, and 7-9, shown previously.

Next, you are prompted to choose either a NFS, FTP, or HTTP installation, as shown earlier in Figure 7-10. Regardless of the installation type chosen, you are then prompted to configure the network settings, as shown in Figure 7-12. The values for the IP address and subnet mask are typically assigned by the Internet service provider (ISP) or the network administrator, so that the computer using the IP address can communicate with the correct set of machines on the network. You can, however, choose to receive the configuration from a DHCP or BOOTP server on the network automatically. The default gateway and the primary DNS name server are optional if configuring manually, but should be used if the values are known.

If you chose an NFS installation in Figure 7-10, the installation prompts for the DNS name or IP address of the NFS server on the network and the directory on the NFS server that contains the installation files, as shown in Figure 7-13.

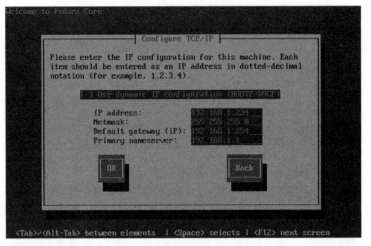

FIGURE 7-12 *Configuring local network settings*

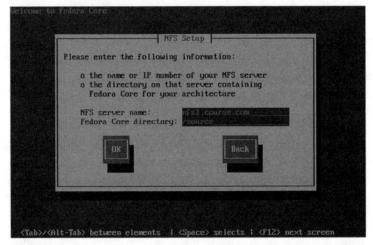

FIGURE 7-13 *Specifying source file location for an NFS-based installation*

Alternatively, if you chose to perform an FTP installation, you are prompted to enter the type of FTP installation (anonymous or user login) as well as the DNS name or IP address of the FTP server, as shown in Figure 7-14.

Like an FTP installation, an HTTP installation requires the DNS name or IP address of the Web server, as well as the name of the directory underneath the Web server content directory that contains installation source files, as shown in Figure 7-15.

Unless you chose an NFS installation, a graphical installation starts after the source files have been located and you are prompted for the information necessary to complete the process.

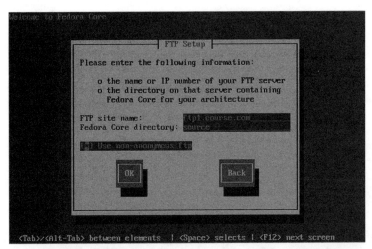

FIGURE 7-14 *Specifying source file location for an FTP-based installation*

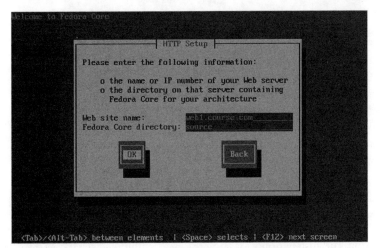

FIGURE 7-15 *Specifying source file location for an HTTP-based installation*

Automating Linux Installations

Some organizations deploy several Linux servers and workstations that require the same configuration. For these organizations, it is time-consuming to answer all of the installation questions on a computer-by-computer basis. Instead, these organizations often use **disk imaging software** to duplicate the hard disk contents from one computer to the next, or use an automated installation script to automate each installation.

Many disk imaging programs such as Symantec Ghost shown in Figure 7-16 are currently available. These programs are typically loaded from a boot floppy disk and copy whole partitions or hard disks to other hard disks in the same computer or across the network. The main limitation of disk imaging programs is that the hardware in all computers that need to be imaged must be nearly identical. After the disk imaging is complete and you boot your freshly imaged computer, the Linux operating system loads using the device drivers that were in the original computer.

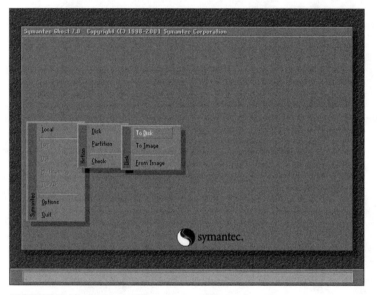

FIGURE 7-16 *Symantec Ghost*

Some Linux distributions such as Red Hat Fedora provide an installation program that accepts a script file that specifies the choices that you would normally choose when you install the operating system. In Red Hat, this script is called the **kickstart file**. After a normal Red Hat Fedora Linux installation, the installation program creates a sample kickstart file (/root/anaconda-ks.cfg) that contains the choices you made during the installation program. Alternatively, you can navigate to the Red Hat button, System Tools, Kickstart to open the **Kickstart Configurator** and configure a new kickstart file, as shown in Figure 7-17.

To save the settings you choose in the Kickstart Configurator to a kickstart file, simply choose Save File from the File menu in Figure 7-17. Normally, kickstart files are text files and can be edited with a text editor; a sample kickstart file is shown in the following output:

```
[root@server1 root]# cat ks.cfg
#Generated by Kickstart Configurator
#platform=x86, AMD64, or Intel EM64T
#System language
lang en_US
```

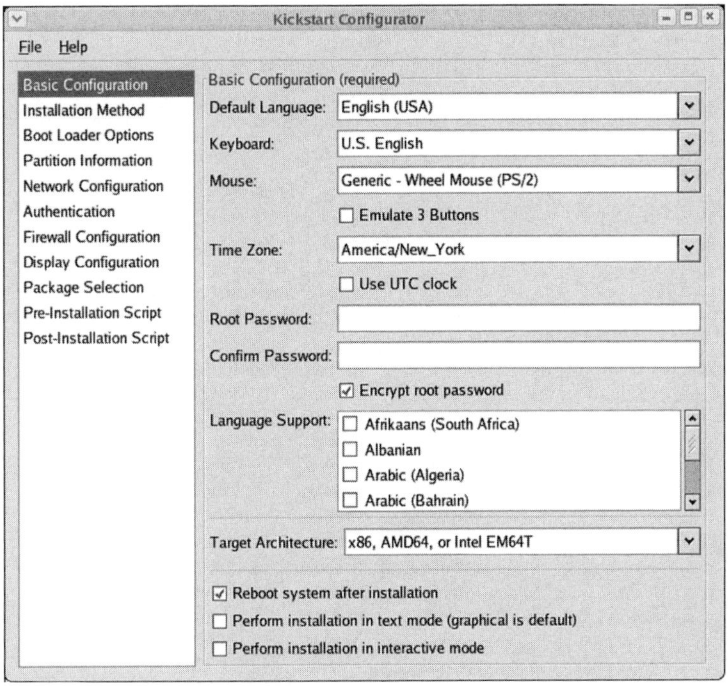

FIGURE 7-17 *The Kickstart Configurator*

```
#Language modules to install
langsupport en_US
#System keyboard
keyboard us
#System mouse
mouse msintelli
#System timezone
timezone America/Toronto
#Root password
rootpw --iscrypted $1$fDvvuliu$oWVUitAzGLsyXzzMS3Wt31
#Install OS instead of upgrade
install
#Use CDROM installation media
cdrom
#System bootloader configuration
bootloader --location=mbr
#Clear the Master Boot Record
zerombr yes
#Partition clearing information
clearpart --all --initlabel
```

```
#Disk partitioning information
part / --fstype ext3 --size 9000
part swap --size 600
#System authorization infomation
auth  --useshadow  --enablemd5
#Network information
network --bootproto=static --ip=192.168.1.88 --netmask=255.255.255.0
   --gateway=192.168.1.254 --nameserver=192.168.1.254 --device=eth0
#Firewall configuration
firewall --disabled
#XWindows configuration information
xconfig --depth=16 --resolution=1024x768 --defaultdesktop=GNOME --startxonboot
#Package install information
%packages --resolvedeps
@ everything
[root@server1 root]# _
```

> ### NOTE
>
> Any line in a kickstart file that starts with a # symbol is a comment line and is ignored by the installation program.
>
> To use the kickstart file shown previously, simply format a floppy disk with the ext2 filesystem and copy the ks.cfg file to it. When you start the installation by booting the computer from an installation CD-ROM, DVD, installation startup CD-ROM, or bootable USB flash memory drive, you receive an initial Red Hat Fedora welcome screen and boot: prompt, as shown earlier in Figure 7-7. Instead of pressing Enter at this prompt, type the command `linux ks=floppy:/ks.cfg` and press Enter. This forces the installation program to look for configuration information in the ks.cfg file on the floppy.
>
> The firstboot wizard is not run following a kickstart installation.

Troubleshooting Installation

Computers today typically have different hardware BIOS configurations, and installing on different computers is almost never the same. As a result, you might encounter problems while installing Linux on one computer but not another. These problems are almost entirely related to hardware support or configuration, and are typically fixed with a change to the hardware configuration of the system. Furthermore, you can divide these problems into three categories based on when they occur:

◆ Problems starting the installation
◆ Problems during installation
◆ Problems after installation

Problems Starting the Installation

You will typically start a Linux installation by booting from a CD-ROM, DVD, installation startup CD-ROM, or bootable USB flash memory drive. For this to occur, you must ensure that the boot order located in the BIOS is set to look for an operating system on the CD-ROM, DVD, or USB flash memory drive before it looks to the hard disk. The BIOS on different computers can be radically different; some BIOSes have sections labeled First Boot Device, Second Boot Device, and Third Boot Device, whereas others have a section labeled Boot Order. To ensure that you are changing the correct setting, consult the user's manual for your mainboard.

Recall that BIOS settings are stored in a CMOS memory chip on the computer, which is given a continuous supply of power via a small lithium battery attached to the mainboard. If this battery dies, any changes to the BIOS settings are lost and default values are loaded. When this occurs, the system warns the user upon system startup with a message similar to "BIOS Error – Defaults Loaded – Press F1 to continue." In this case, the battery needs to be replaced before the boot order is changed; otherwise, the setting is lost when the computer is powered off.

While checking the BIOS for the boot order, it is good practice to also check the BIOS for any reserved peripheral configuration (IRQ, I/O addresses, DMA). Recall that most devices on systems today are Plug-and-Play and receive their configuration from the BIOS of the system. Some older ISA devices must have this information statically configured; thus, the possibility exists that Plug-and-Play will assign a configuration that is already in use by an older ISA device. If there are ISA devices in the computer that are statically configured in this manner, you must ensure that their configuration is reserved in the BIOS such that it is not available to be assigned by Plug-and-Play.

Problems During Installation

After the installation program has loaded, you are prompted for the method of installation. For those who install Linux graphically, the installation program must first detect the video card and mouse in the computer and load the appropriate drivers into memory. If, after the initial welcome screen (Figure 7-7), the graphical installation screens do not appear or appear as scrambled lines across the computer screen, the video card is not likely supported by the mode and resolution of the graphical installation. To solve this, you should restart the installation and at the initial welcome screen, type either `linux nofb` and press Enter to start the installation without framebuffer support, or type `linux lowres` and press Enter to start the installation with a resolution of 640×480.

If the graphical installation starts successfully but the mouse does not work, an alternative is to start a text-based installation. Simply restart the installation and type `linux text` and press Enter at the initial welcome screen.

On some older systems, the installation might freeze randomly during the installation; this is a result of improper device communication. To fix this, simply restart the computer and disable Plug-and-Play support in the BIOS of the computer prior to installation. After the installation has completed, Plug-and-Play support can be enabled again in the BIOS.

Sometimes, an installation ends abnormally and the screen displays a "fatal signal 11" error message. This indicates an error known as a segmentation fault; it indicates that a program accessed a certain area of RAM that was not assigned. Although this might be a problem with software, during installation it is likely a hardware problem. Unfortunately, this hardware problem could be almost anywhere in the computer, but is likely an error with the RAM itself. Often, this error can be fixed by turning off the CPU cache memory or increasing the number of wait states in the BIOS. If the memory is too slow for the mainboard (for example, the memory is 70ns RAM and the mainboard requires 60ns RAM), the RAM in the computer should be replaced. Some BIOSes allow the user to change the voltage for the RAM and CPU; incorrect values can cause a "fatal signal 11" error as well. Other causes include bad memory chips, an AMD K6 processor, laptop power management conflicts, and overclocked CPUs.

> ### 🧊 NOTE
>
> An **overclocked** CPU is a CPU that has a speed greater than the speed that was originally intended for the processor. Although this might lead to increased performance, it also produces more heat on the processor and can result in intermittent computer crashes.
>
> If the installation fails with an error other than fatal signal 11, you should consult the support documentation for your distribution of Linux or newsgroups on the Internet. Also, certain hardware, such as Winmodems, is not compatable with Linux; ensure that all hardware is listed on the Hardware Compatibility List for your Linux distribution prior to installation.

Some installations fail to place a boot loader on the hard disk properly; this is often the case with large hard disk drives that have over 1024 cylinders. To avoid this problem, ensure that the / partition starts before the 1024th cylinder (usually the 8GB mark on most hard disks) or create a partition for the /boot directory that starts before the 1024th cylinder.

Problems after Installation

Although a Red Hat Linux installation might finish successfully, you might still have problems if the installation program did not detect the hardware in the computer properly or certain programs failed to be installed. As a result, it is good form to check the **installation log files** after installation as well as verify settings on the system after installation to ensure that all hardware was detected with the correct values.

Two installation log files are created by the Red Hat installation program: /root/install.log, which contains a list of packages that were installed as well as a list of those that were not installed, and /root/install.log.syslog, which lists all of the system events that occurred during the installation, such as the creation of user and group accounts.

To verify hardware settings, you can examine the content of the /proc directory or boot-up log files. The /proc directory is mounted to a special filesystem contained within RAM that lists system information made available by the Linux kernel; because this is an administrative filesystem, all files within are readable only by the root user. A listing of the /proc directory shows the following file and subdirectory contents:

```
[root@server1 root]# ls -F /proc
1/      2091/   2381/   3505/   3576/   acpi/       ide/        pci
10/     2110/   2382/   3507/   4/      asound/     interrupts  scsi/
114/    2119/   2383/   3509/   4063/   bluetooth/  iomem       self@
153/    2131/   2384/   3511/   4064/   buddyinfo   ioports     slabinfo
1651/   2141/   2385/   3513/   4065/   bus/        irq/        stat
1655/   2156/   3/      3515/   4089/   cmdline     kcore       swaps
16725/  2186/   311/    3516/   4093/   cpuinfo     kmsg        sys/
1676/   2187/   3117/   3519/   4509/   crypto      loadavg     sysrq-trigger
1696/   2198/   3142/   3542/   5/      devices     locks       sysvipc/
1724/   2211/   3270/   3544/   6/      diskstats   mdstat      tty/
1768/   2223/   3333/   3546/   7/      dma         meminfo     uptime
1774/   2259/   3343/   3548/   8/      dri/        misc        version
1781/   2278/   3346/   3555/   8605/   driver/     modules     vmstat
1840/   2297/   3348/   3563/   8668/   execdomains mounts@
1850/   2313/   3350/   3566/   8684/   fb          mtrr
2/      2379/   3352/   3568/   8687/   filesystems net/
2076/   2380/   3359/   3570/   9/      fs/         partitions
[root@server1 root]# _
```

The subdirectories that start with a number in the preceding output are used to display process information; other directories can contain kernel parameters. The files listed in the preceding output are text representations of various parts of the Linux system; they are updated regularly by the Linux kernel and can be viewed using standard text commands, such as cat or more.

To view the information that Linux has detected regarding the CPU in the computer, simply view the contents of the cpuinfo file in the /proc directory:

```
[root@server1 root]# cat /proc/cpuinfo
processor       : 0
vendor_id       : GenuineIntel
cpu family      : 6
model           : 8
model name      : Pentium III (Coppermine)
stepping        : 10
cpu MHz         : 800.049
cache size      : 256 KB
fdiv_bug        : no
hlt_bug         : no
f00f_bug        : no
coma_bug        : no
fpu             : yes
fpu_exception   : yes
cpuid level     : 2
wp              : yes
flags           : fpu vme de pse tsc msr pae mce cx8 mtrr pge mca cmov pat pse36 mmx fxsr
                  sse
bogomips        : 1585.15
[root@server1 root]# _
```

The preceding output indicates that there is only one processor that runs at 800MHz (approximately) and has 256KB of processor cache. If, for example, the computer in actuality has two processors instead of one, Linux has failed to detect the second processor. In this case, you might need to change a setting in BIOS or research a solution to the problem on the mainboard or processor manufacturer's Web site.

It is also important to ensure that Linux has detected the correct amount of RAM in the system after installation. To do this, you can view the contents of the /proc/meminfo file, as shown in the following output:

```
[root@server1 root]# cat /proc/meminfo
MemTotal:        257108 kB
MemFree:          10116 kB
Buffers:          24668 kB
Cached:           54032 kB
SwapCached:        2876 kB
Active:          164472 kB
Inactive:         27132 kB
HighTotal:            0 kB
HighFree:             0 kB
```

```
LowTotal:        257108 kB
LowFree:          10116 kB
SwapTotal:       525160 kB
SwapFree:        513032 kB
Dirty:                4 kB
Writeback:            0 kB
Mapped:          153736 kB
Slab:             40856 kB
Committed_AS:    279444 kB
PageTables:        2708 kB
VmallocTotal:   3874808 kB
VmallocUsed:      37772 kB
VmallocChunk:   3836956 kB
HugePages_Total:      0
HugePages_Free:       0
Hugepagesize:      4096 kB
[root@server1 root]# _
```

In the preceding output, the total amount of memory (MemTotal) is 257108KB or 256MB. If this value is incorrect because the computer has 512MB of RAM, you can specify the correct values to the kernel by adding "mem=512M" to the kernel line in the /boot/grub/grub.conf file if your boot loader is GRUB or by adding the line append "mem=512M" to the /etc/lilo.conf file if your boot loader is LILO.

Likewise, to ensure that the IRQs, DMAs, and I/O ports are recognized at the correct values, you could view the dma, interrupts, and ioports files in the /proc directory as shown in the following examples:

```
[root@server1 root]# cat /proc/dma
 4: cascade
[root@server1 root]# cat /proc/interrupts
          CPU0
  0:   10934177       XT-PIC  timer
  1:      23045       XT-PIC  i8042
  2:          0       XT-PIC  cascade
  5:          0       XT-PIC  Ensoniq AudioPCI
  8:          1       XT-PIC  rtc
  9:          0       XT-PIC  uhci_hcd, uhci_hcd
 10:     232095       XT-PIC  eth0
 11:     926055       XT-PIC  acpi, r128@PCI:1:0:0
 12:     445114       XT-PIC  i8042
 14:     153741       XT-PIC  ide0
 15:     110933       XT-PIC  ide1
NMI:          0
ERR:          0
```

```
[root@server1 root]# cat /proc/ioports
0000-001f : dma1
0020-0021 : pic1
0040-005f : timer
0060-006f : keyboard
0070-0077 : rtc
0080-008f : dma page reg
00a0-00a1 : pic2
00c0-00df : dma2
00f0-00ff : fpu
0170-0177 : ide1
01f0-01f7 : ide0
02f8-02ff : serial
0376-0376 : ide1
0378-037a : parport0
037b-037f : parport0
03c0-03df : vga+
03f6-03f6 : ide0
03f8-03ff : serial
0cf8-0cff : PCI conf1
5000-500f : 0000:00:07.4
6000-607f : 0000:00:07.4
9000-9fff : PCI Bus #01
  9000-90ff : 0000:01:00.0
a000-a00f : 0000:00:07.1
  a000-a007 : ide0
  a008-a00f : ide1
a400-a41f : 0000:00:07.2
  a400-a41f : uhci_hcd
[root@server1 root]# _
```

Like memory, if the values are incorrect for any of the hardware devices listed in the preceding output, you could add the correct parameters to the /etc/grub/grub.conf file (if GRUB is your boot loader) or /etc/lilo.conf (if LILO is your boot loader). This sends the correct device information to the Linux kernel during system startup.

Several devices require that their driver be inserted into the Linux kernel as a module. Sound cards, network interface cards, and USB devices typically have modules inserted into the kernel. To see a list of modules currently inserted into the Linux kernel, simply view the /proc/modules file as shown in the following output:

```
[root@server1 root]# cat /proc/modules
snd_mixer_oss 13824 2 - Live 0x14cf2000
snd_ens1371 17120 3 - Live 0x14cd7000
```

```
snd_rawmidi 17184 1 snd_ens1371, Live 0x14cd1000
snd_seq_device 6152 1 snd_rawmidi, Live 0x14c4e000
snd_pcm 68872 1 snd_ens1371, Live 0x14ce0000
snd_page_alloc 7940 1 snd_pcm, Live 0x1286b000
snd_timer 17156 1 snd_pcm, Live 0x14c90000
snd_ac97_codec 50436 1 snd_ens1371, Live 0x14cb1000
snd 38372 9
snd_mixer_oss,snd_ens1371,snd_rawmidi,snd_seq_device,snd_pcm,snd_timer,snd_ac97_codec,
    Live 0x14cbf000
gameport 3328 1 snd_ens1371, Live 0x1286e000
soundcore 6112 3 snd, Live 0x128be000
parport_pc 19392 1 - Live 0x14c8a000
lp 8236 0 - Live 0x14c46000
parport 29640 2 parport_pc,lp, Live 0x14c81000
autofs4 10624 0 - Live 0x128ba000
rfcomm 27164 0 - Live 0x14c79000
l2cap 16004 5 rfcomm, Live 0x1285c000
bluetooth 33636 4 rfcomm,l2cap, Live 0x128a5000
sunrpc 101064 1 - Live 0x14c97000
3c59x 30376 0 - Live 0x14c3d000
floppy 47440 0 - Live 0x14c6c000
sg 27552 0 - Live 0x14c35000
scsi_mod 91344 1 sg, Live 0x14c54000
microcode 4768 0 - Live 0x12868000
dm_mod 33184 0 - Live 0x128b0000
uhci_hcd 23708 0 - Live 0x1289e000
button 4504 0 - Live 0x12865000
battery 6924 0 - Live 0x12857000
asus_acpi 8472 0 - Live 0x12861000
ac 3340 0 - Live 0x1285a000
r128 72368 2 - Live 0x1288b000
ipv6 184288 8 - Live 0x128c1000
ext3 102376 1 - Live 0x12871000
jbd 40216 1 ext3, Live 0x12847000
[root@server1 root]# _
```

From the preceding output, the module for the 3COM 590c NIC card (3c59x) as well as the sound support module (soundcore) are inserted into the kernel. If a module that represents the driver for a particular hardware device is not in the kernel, you might need to add the module manually, as discussed later in Chapter 14.

Many more files are in the /proc directory than those discussed earlier that can be useful when examining a system after installation. Table 7-5 describes these files.

Table 7-5 Files commonly found in the /proc directory

Filename	Description
apm	Contains information about Advanced Power Management
cmdline	Contains the current location of the Linux kernel
cpuinfo	Contains information regarding the processors in the computer
devices	Contains a list of the character and block devices that are currently in use by the Linux kernel
execdomains	Contains a list of execution domains for processes on the system; execution domains allow a process to execute in a specific manner
fb	Contains a list of framebuffer devices in use on the Linux system; typically, these include video adapter card devices
filesystems	Contains a list of filesystems supported by the Linux kernel
interrupts	Contains a list of IRQs in use on the system
iomem	Contains a list of memory addresses currently used
ioports	Contains a list of memory address ranges reserved for device use
isapnp	Contains a list of Plug-and-Play devices in ISA slots on the Linux system
kcore	Represents the physical memory inside the computer; this file should not be viewed
kmsg	Is a temporary storage location for messages from the kernel
loadavg	Contains statistics on the performance of the processor
locks	Contains a list of files currently locked by the kernel
mdstat	Contains the configuration of multiple-disk RAID hardware
meminfo	Contains information regarding physical and virtual memory on the Linux system
misc	Contains a list of miscellaneous devices (major number = 10)
modules	Contains a list of currently loaded modules in the Linux kernel
mounts	Contains a list of currently mounted filesystems
partitions	Contains information regarding partition tables loaded in memory on the system
pci	Contains a list of the PCI devices on the system and their configurations
swaps	Contains information on virtual memory utilization
scsi	Contains information on SCSI devices on the Linux system
version	Contain the version information for the Linux kernel and libraries

Hardware is detected by the Linux kernel at system startup. However, this information is displayed too quickly to read. In addition, the software programs loaded during system startup are hidden by default during the graphical boot process; you must use your mouse to click Show Details during the graphical boot process to see them. Like the hardware information, program information is also displayed too fast to read. Fortunately, the system logs all information regarding hardware detection and the startup of system processes in log files that can be viewed at a later time.

To view the hardware detected during boot time, you can use the dmesg command shown in the following output. This information is also stored in the /var/log/dmesg log file:

```
[root@server1 root]# dmesg | tail
Bluetooth: RFCOMM socket layer initialized
Bluetooth: RFCOMM TTY layer initialized
parport0: PC-style at 0x378 [PCSPP,TRISTATE,EPP]
parport0: Printer, Brother HL-1440 series
parport_pc: Via 686A parallel port: io=0x378
lp0: using parport0 (polling).
lp0: console ready
agpgart: Found an AGP 2.0 compliant device at 0000:00:00.0.
agpgart: Putting AGP V2 device at 0000:00:00.0 into 1x mode
agpgart: Putting AGP V2 device at 0000:01:00.0 into 1x mode
[root@server1 root]# _
```

You can also view the system processes that started successfully or unsuccessfully during boot time by viewing the contents of the /var/log/boot.log or /var/log/messages log files. The boot.log file contains only service startup information, whereas messages contains boot information as well as other messages from the system after boot time. A sample boot.log is shown in the following output:

```
[root@server1 root]# tail /var/log/boot.log
Jul 16 08:38:33 server1 privoxy: privoxy startup succeeded
Jul 16 08:38:34 server1 gpm: gpm startup succeeded
Jul 16 08:38:35 server1 IIim: htt startup succeeded
Jul 16 08:38:36 server1 canna:  succeeded
Jul 16 08:38:36 server1 crond: crond startup succeeded
Jul 16 08:38:38 server1 xfs: xfs startup succeeded
Jul 16 08:38:38 server1 anacron: anacron startup succeeded
Jul 16 08:38:38 server1 atd: atd startup succeeded
Jul 16 08:38:38 server1 readahead: Starting background readahead:
Jul 16 08:38:39 server1 rc: Starting readahead:  succeeded
[root@server1 root]# _
```

> **NOTE**
>
> Both boot.log and messages can become very large in size over time. As a result, the system archives old copies of these log files in the /var/log directory and appends a number to them to indicate how recent the archive is. For example, to view the most recent archive of /var/log/boot.log, you could view the /var/log/boot.log.1 file. Similarly, you could view /var/log/boot.log.2 to view the second most recent archive of /var/log/boot.log.

Chapter Summary

◆ Many different SCSI standards have been developed since 1986. SCSI hard disk drives are uniquely identified by a SCSI ID and attach to a controller via a terminated cable.

◆ Each peripheral device must be configured with an IRQ and I/O address prior to use, and can optionally use a DMA channel. This configuration can be given to devices automatically if they are Plug-and-Play compliant.

◆ Portable laptop computers typically use APM or ACPI to shut down power to peripheral devices when not in use to save battery power.

◆ Computers that require fault tolerance typically employ SCSI hard disks configured using RAID.

◆ Although Linux is typically installed from CD-ROM media, it can also be installed using files located on DVD, hard disks, and NFS, FTP, and HTTP servers. You need to create an installation startup CD-ROM or bootable USB flash memory drive to perform these types of installation.

◆ You can use disk imaging software or a kickstart file to simplify the installation of Linux on several computers.

◆ Unsupported video cards, overclocked CPUs, PnP support, and improper RAM settings can cause an installation to fail.

◆ The /proc directory contains information regarding detected hardware on the system and is useful when verifying whether an installation was successful.

Key Terms

/proc/cpuinfo — The directory that contains information on current CPU setup on the system.

/proc/dma — The directory that contains information on current direct memory access assignments on the system.

/proc/interrupts — The directory that contains information on current Interrupt Request assignments on the system.

/proc/ioports — The directory that contains information on current Input/Output address assignments on the system.

/proc/meminfo — The directory that contains information on the current memory usage situation, both physical and virtual, on the system.

/proc/modules — The directory that contains information on what modules are currently incorporated into the kernel.

Advanced Configuration and Power Interface (ACPI) — A standard that allows an operating system the ability to control when power is supplied to peripheral components.

Advanced Power Management (APM) — A standard that allows a computer BIOS the ability to control when power is supplied to peripheral components.

burning — The process of writing information to a CD-R, CD-RW, DVD-R, or DVD-RW.

complementary metal-oxide semiconductor (CMOS) — A memory store on the mainboard used to store configuration information for use during the boot process; not a true ROM chip, it requires a low level flow of electricity from an onboard battery to maintain the memory store.

direct memory access (DMA) — A channel that allows a hardware device direct access to physical memory.

disk imaging software — The software that is used to make identical copies of hard drives or hard drive partitions.

disk mirroring — A RAID configuration, also known as RAID 1, that consists of two identical hard disks, which are written to in parallel with the same information to ensure fault tolerance.

disk striping — A RAID configuration, a type of RAID 0, which is used to write separate information to different hard disks to speed up access time.

disk striping with parity — A RAID configuration, also known as RAID 5, that is used to write separate information to hard disks to speed up access time, and also contains parity information to ensure fault tolerance.

fault tolerant — A device that exhibits a minimum of downtime in the event of a failure.

File Transfer Protocol (FTP) — The most common protocol used to transfer files across the Internet.

Grand Unified Bootloader (GRUB) — A program used to boot the Linux operating system.

Hypertext Transfer Protocol (HTTP) — The underlying protocol used to transfer information over the Internet.

Input/Output (I/O) address — An address in physical memory that is used by a particular hardware device.

installation log files — The files created at installation to record actions that occurred or failed during the installation process.

Interrupt Request (IRQ) — A method of sharing processor time used by the processor to prioritize simultaneous requests for service from peripheral devices.

International Standards Organization (ISO) images — The large, single files that are exact copies of the information contained on a CD-ROM or DVD.

Kickstart Configurator — A graphical utility that can be used to create a kickstart file.

kickstart file — A file that can be specified at the beginning of a Red Hat Fedora Linux installation to automate the installation process.

LInux LOader (LILO) — A program used to boot the Linux operating system.

Logical Unit Number (LUN) — A unique identifier for each device attached to any given node in a SCSI chain.

Network File System (NFS) — A distributed filesystem developed by Sun Microsystems that allows computers of differing types to access files shared on the network.

overclocked — A CPU that runs at a higher clock speed than it has been rated for.

Plug-and-Play (PnP) — The process of automatically allowing devices to be assigned required IRQ, I/O address, and DMA information by the system BIOS.

polling — The act of querying devices to see if they have services that need to be run.

Redundant Array of Independent Disks (RAID) — The process of combining the storage space of several hard disk drives into one larger, logical storage unit.

SCSI ID — A number that uniquely identifies and prioritizes devices attached to a SCSI controller.

spanning — A type of RAID level 0 that allows two or more devices to be represented as a single large volume.

target ID — *See also* SCSI ID.

terminator — A device used to terminate an electrical conduction medium to absorb the transmitted signal and prevent signal bounce.

Review Questions

1. What is the default IRQ assignment for the system timer?

   a. 0

   b. 3

   c. 5

   d. 15

2. How many basic RAID configurations are currently available?

   a. 5

   b. 6

   c. 7

   d. 9

3. What is the most commonly used Linux installation method?

   a. DVD based

   b. ISO image based

   c. CD-ROM based

   d. Source files over a network

4. On some older systems, the installation might freeze randomly during the installation; this is a result of _____.

   a. a segmentation fault

   b. unsupported sound drivers

   c. an incompatible video card

   d. improper device communication

5. In the /proc directory, which file contains a list of Plug-and-Play devices in ISA slots on the Linux system?

   a. execdomains

   b. ioports

   c. isapnp

   d. pci

6. True or false? A SCSI device is usually connected to the mainboard.

7. True or false? Sound cards, network cards, and SCSI disk controllers benefit greatly from DMA channels as they read and write a great deal of data to physical memory.

8. True or false? The main limitation of disk imaging programs is that the hardware in all computers that need to be imaged must be nearly identical.

9. True or false? You can ensure that Linux has detected the correct amount of RAM in the system after installation by viewing the contents of the /proc/raminfo file.

10. True or false? The boot.log file contains system startup information and messages related to the system after boot time.

11. The unique identifier used with peripheral components is the _____.

12. RAID level 1 is often referred to as disk _____, and provides fault tolerance in the case of a hard disk failure.

13. Linux can be installed across the network from a Windows server hosting the installation files. This method uses the _____ protocol.

14. BIOS settings are stored in a(n) _____ memory chip on the computer, which is given a continuous supply of power via a small lithium battery attached to the mainboard.

15. Two installation log files are created by the Red Hat installation program: /root/install.log, which contains a list of packages that were installed as well as a list of those that were not installed, and /root/ _____, which lists all of the system events that occurred during the installation.

Chapter 8

Working with the BASH Shell

After completing this chapter, you will be able to:

◆ Redirect the input and output of a command

◆ Identify and manipulate common shell environment variables

◆ Create and export new shell variables

◆ Edit environment files to create variables upon shell startup

◆ Describe the purpose and nature of shell scripts

◆ Create and execute basic shell scripts

◆ Effectively use common decision constructs in shell scripts

A solid understanding of shell features is vital to both administrators and users, as they interact with the shell on a daily basis. The first part of this chapter describes how the shell can manipulate command input and output using redirection and pipe shell metacharacters. Next, you explore the different types of variables present in a BASH shell after login as well as their purpose and usage. Finally, this chapter ends with an introduction to creating and executing BASH shell scripts.

Command Input and Output

The BASH shell is responsible for providing a user interface and interpreting commands entered on the command line. In addition to this, the BASH shell can manipulate command input and output, provided the user specifies certain shell metacharacters on the command line alongside the command. Command input and output are represented by labels known as **file descriptors**. Three file descriptors are available to each command that can be manipulated by the BASH shell:

◆ Standard Input (stdin)
◆ Standard Output (stdout)
◆ Standard Error (stderr)

Standard Input (stdin) refers to the information that is processed by the command during execution, and is often in the form of user input typed on the keyboard. **Standard Output (stdout)** refers to the normal output of a command, whereas **Standard Error (stderr)** refers to any error messages generated by the command. Both Standard Output and Standard Error are displayed on the terminal screen by default. All three components are depicted in Figure 8-1.

Figure 8-1 also shows that each file descriptor is represented by a number; stdin is represented by the number 0, stdout is represented by the number 1, and stderr is represented by the number 2.

Although all three components are available to any command, not all commands use every component. The file /etc/hosts /etc/h command used in Figure 8-1 gives Standard Output (the listing of the /etc/hosts file) and Standard Error (an error message indicating that the /etc/h file does not exist) to the terminal screen, as shown in the following output:

```
[root@server1 root]# ls /etc/hosts /etc/h
ls: /etc/h: No such file or directory
/etc/hosts
[root@server1 root]# _
```

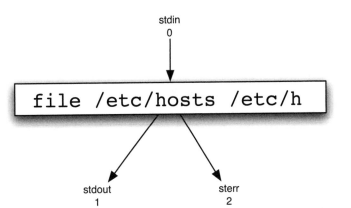

FIGURE 8-1 *The three common file descriptors*

Redirection

You can use the BASH shell to redirect Standard Output and Standard Error from the terminal screen to a file on the filesystem using the > shell metacharacter followed by the absolute or relative pathname of the file. To redirect only the Standard Output to a file called goodoutput for the command used in Figure 8-1, you simply append the number of the file descriptor (1) followed by the **redirection** symbol > and the file to redirect the Standard Output to (goodoutput) as shown in the following output:

```
[root@server1 root]# ls /etc/hosts /etc/h  1>goodoutput
ls: /etc/h: No such file or directory
[root@server1 root]# _
```

■ NOTE

You can include a space character after the > metacharacter, but it is not necessary.

Notice from the preceding output that the Standard Error is still displayed to the terminal screen as it was not redirected to a file. The listing of /etc/hosts was not displayed, as it was redirected to a file called goodoutput in the current directory. If the goodoutput file did not exist prior to running the command in the preceding output, it is created automatically. However, if the goodoutput file did exist prior to the redirection, the BASH shell clears its contents before executing the command. To see that the Standard Output was redirected to the goodoutput file, you can run the following commands:

```
[root@server1 root]# ls -F
Desktop/   goodoutput
```

```
[root@server1 root]# cat goodoutput
/etc/hosts
[root@server1 root]# _
```

Similarly, you can redirect the Standard Error of a command to a file; simply specify file descriptor number 2, as shown in the following output:

```
[root@server1 root]# ls /etc/hosts /etc/h  2>badoutput
/etc/hosts
[root@server1 root]# cat badoutput
ls: /etc/h: No such file or directory
[root@server1 root]# _
```

In the preceding output, only the Standard Error was redirected to a file called badoutput; thus, the Standard Output (a listing of /etc/hosts) was displayed on the terminal screen.

Because redirecting the Standard Output to a file for later use is more common than redirecting the Standard Error to a file, the BASH shell assumes Standard Output in the absence of a numeric file descriptor:

```
[root@server1 root]# ls /etc/hosts /etc/h  >goodoutput
ls: /etc/h: No such file or directory
[root@server1 root]# cat goodoutput
/etc/hosts
[root@server1 root]# _
```

In addition, you can redirect both Standard Output and Standard Error to separate files at the same time, as shown in the following output:

```
[root@server1 root]# ls /etc/hosts /etc/h  >goodoutput  2>badoutput
[root@server1 root]# cat goodoutput
/etc/hosts
[root@server1 root]# cat badoutput
ls: /etc/h: No such file or directory
[root@server1 root]# _
```

> ### NOTE
>
> The order of redirection on the command line does not matter; the command `ls /etc/hosts /etc/h >goodoutput 2>badoutput` is the same as `ls /etc/hosts /etc/h 2>badoutput >goodoutput`.

It is important to use separate filenames to hold the contents of Standard Output and Standard Error; using the same filename for both results in a loss of data because the system attempts to write both contents to the file at the same time:

```
[root@server1 root]# ls /etc/hosts /etc/h  >goodoutput  2>goodoutput
[root@server1 root]# cat goodoutput
/etc/hosts
: No such file or directory
[root@server1 root]# _
```

To redirect both Standard Output and Standard Error to the same file without any loss of data, you must use special notation. To specify that Standard Output be sent to the file good-output and Standard Error be sent to the same place as Standard Output, you can do the following:

```
[root@server1 root]# ls /etc/hosts /etc/h  >goodoutput  2>&1
[root@server1 root]# cat goodoutput
ls: /etc/h: No such file or directory
/etc/hosts
[root@server1 root]# _
```

Alternatively, you can specify that the Standard Error be sent to the file badoutput and Standard Output be sent to the same place as Standard Error:

```
[root@server1 root]# ls /etc/hosts /etc/h  2>badoutput  >&2
[root@server1 root]# cat badoutput
ls: /etc/h: No such file or directory
/etc/hosts
[root@server1 root]# _
```

In all of the examples used earlier, the contents of the files used to store the output from commands were cleared prior to use by the BASH shell. Another example of this is shown in the following output when redirecting the Standard Output of the date command to the file date-output:

```
[root@server1 root]# date >dateoutput
[root@server1 root]# cat dateoutput
Wed May 25 10:55:18 EDT 2005
[root@server1 root]# date >dateoutput
[root@server1 root]# cat dateoutput
Wed May 25 10:55:30 EDT 2005
[root@server1 root]# _
```

To prevent the file from being cleared by the BASH shell and append output to the existing output, you can specify two > metacharacters alongside the file descriptor, as shown in the following output:

```
[root@server1 root]# date >dateoutput
[root@server1 root]# cat dateoutput
Wed May 25 10:58:17 EDT 2005
[root@server1 root]# date >>dateoutput
```

```
[root@server1 root]# cat dateoutput
Wed May 25 10:58:17 EDT 2005
Wed May 25 10:59:26 EDT 2005
[root@server1 root]# _
```

You can also redirect a file to the Standard Input of a command using the < metacharacter. Because there is only one file descriptor for input, there is no need to specify the number 0 before the < metacharacter to indicate Standard Input, as shown next:

```
[root@server1 root]# cat </etc/hosts
# Do not remove the following line, or various programs
# that require network functionality will fail.
127.0.0.1    server1 localhost.localdomain localhost
[root@server1 root]# _
```

In the preceding output, the BASH shell located and sent the /etc/hosts file to the cat command as Standard Input. Because the cat command normally takes the filename to be displayed as an argument on the command line (for example, cat /etc/hosts), there is no need to use Standard Input redirection with the cat command as used in the previous example; however, some commands on the Linux system only accept files when they are passed by the shell through Standard Input. The **tr command** is one such command that can be used to replace characters in a file sent via Standard Input. To translate all of the lowercase l characters in the /etc/hosts file to uppercase L characters, you can run the following command:

```
[root@server1 root]# tr l L </etc/hosts
# Do not remove the foLLowing Line, or various programs
# that require network functionaLity wiLL faiL.
127.0.0.1       server1 LocaLhost.LocaLdomain LocaLhost
[root@server1 root]# _
```

The preceding command does not modify the /etc/hosts file; it simply takes a copy of the /etc/hosts file, manipulates it, and then sends the Standard Output to the terminal screen. To save a copy of the Standard Output for later use, you can use both Standard Input and Standard Output redirection together:

```
[root@server1 root]# tr l L </etc/hosts >newhosts
[root@server1 root]# cat newhosts
# Do not remove the foLLowing Line, or various programs
# that require network functionaLity wiLL faiL.
127.0.0.1       server1 LocaLhost.LocaLdomain LocaLhost
[root@server1 root]# _
```

As with redirecting Standard Output and Standard Error in the same command, you should use different filenames when redirecting Standard Input and Standard Output. However, this is because the BASH shell clears a file that already exists before performing the redirection. An example of this is shown in the following output:

```
[root@server1 root]# sort <newhosts >newhosts
[root@server1 root]# cat newhosts
[root@server1 root]# _
```

The newhosts file has no contents when displayed in the preceding output. Because the BASH shell saw that output redirection was indicated on the command line, it cleared the contents of the file newhosts, then sorted the blank file and saved the output (nothing in our example) into the file newhosts. Because of this feature of shell redirection, Linux administrators commonly use the command >filename at the command prompt to clear the contents of a file.

NOTE

The contents of log files are typically cleared periodically using the command >/path/to/logfile.

Table 8-1 summarizes the different types of redirection shown in this section.

Table 8-1 Common redirection examples

Command	Description
command 1>file command >file	The Standard Output of the command is sent to a file instead of to the terminal screen.
command 2>file	The Standard Error of the command is sent to a file instead of to the terminal screen.
command 1>fileA 2>fileB command >fileA 2>fileB	The Standard Output of the command is sent to fileA instead of to the terminal screen, and the Standard Error of the command is sent to fileB instead of to the terminal screen.
command 1>file 2>&1 command >file 2>&1 command 1>&2 2>file command >&2 2>file	Both the Standard Output and the Standard Error are sent to the same file instead of to the terminal screen.
command 1>>file command >>file	The Standard Output of the command is appended to a file instead of being sent to the terminal screen.
command 2>>file	The Standard Error of the command is appended to a file instead of being sent to the terminal screen.
command 0<file command <file	The Standard Input of a command is taken from a file.

Pipes

Note from Table 8-1 that redirection only occurs from a command to a file and vice versa. You can also send the Standard Output of one command to another command as Standard Input. To do this, you must use the pipe | shell metacharacter and specify commands on either side. The shell then sends the Standard Output of the command on the left to the command on the right, which then interprets the information as Standard Input. This process is depicted in Figure 8-2.

> **NOTE**
>
> The whole command that includes the pipe | metacharacter is commonly referred to as a **pipe**.

> **TIP**
>
> The pipe symbol can be created on most keyboards by pressing Shift+\.

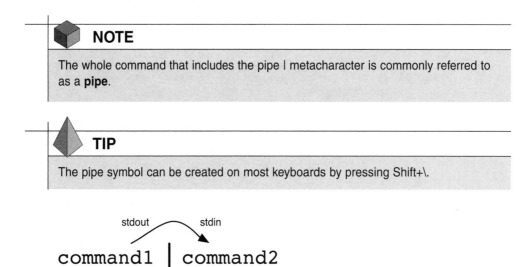

FIGURE 8-2 *Piping information from one command to another*

For example, the Standard Output of the ls -l /etc command is too large to fit on one terminal screen. To send the Standard Output of this command to the less command, which views Standard Input page-by-page, you could use the following command:

```
[root@server1 root]# ls -l /etc | less
total 3564
-rw-r--r--  1 root    root     15276 Mar 22 12:20 a2ps.cfg
-rw-r--r--  1 root    root      2562 Mar 22 12:20 a2ps-site.cfg
drwxr-xr-x  4 root    root      4096 Jun 11 08:45 acpi
-rw-r--r--  1 root    root        46 Jul 16 15:34 adjtime
drwxr-xr-x  2 root    root      4096 Jun 11 08:47 aep
-rw-r--r--  1 root    root       688 Feb 17 00:35 aep.conf
-rw-r--r--  1 root    root       703 Feb 17 00:35 aeplog.conf
drwxr-xr-x  4 root    root      4096 Jun 11 08:47 alchemist
-rw-r--r--  1 root    root      1419 Jan 26 10:14 aliases
-rw-r-----  1 root    smmsp    12288 Jul 19 13:19 aliases.db
drwxr-xr-x  2 root    root      4096 Jun 11 11:11 alternatives
```

```
drwxr-xr-x   3 amanda   disk     4096 Jun 11 10:16 amanda
-rw-r--r--   1 amanda   disk        0 Mar 22 12:28 amandates
-rw-------   1 root     root      688 Mar  4 22:34 amd.conf
-rw-r-----   1 root     root      105 Mar  4 22:34 amd.net
-rw-r--r--   1 root     root      317 Feb 15 14:33 anacrontab
-rw-r--r--   1 root     root      331 May  5 08:07 ant.conf
-rw-r--r--   1 root     root     6203 Jul 16 15:34 asound.state
drwxr-xr-x   3 root     root     4096 Jun 11 10:37 atalk
-rw-------   1 root     root        1 May  5 13:39 at.deny
-rw-r--r--   1 root     root      325 Apr 14 13:39 auto.master
-rw-r--r--   1 root     root      581 Apr 14 13:39 auto.misc
:
```

> **NOTE**
>
> You need not have spaces around the | metacharacher; the command ls -l
> /etc|less and ls -l /etc | less are equivalent.

A common use of piping is to reduce the amount of information displayed on the terminal screen from commands that display too much information. Take the following output from the mount command:

```
[root@server1 root]# mount
/dev/hdc2 on / type ext3 (rw)
none on /proc type proc (rw)
none on /sys type sysfs (rw)
/dev/hdc1 on /boot type ext3 (rw)
none on /dev/pts type devpts (rw,gid=5,mode=620)
none on /dev/shm type tmpfs (rw)
none on /proc/sys/fs/binfmt_misc type binfmt_misc (rw)
[root@server1 root]# _
```

To view only those lines that contain the information regarding filesystems mounted from the secondary master IDE hard disk (/dev/hdc), you could send the Standard Output of the mount command to the grep command as Standard Input, as shown in the following output:

```
[root@server1 root]# mount | grep /dev/hdc
/dev/hdc2 on / type ext3 (rw)
/dev/hdc1 on /boot type ext3 (rw)
[root@server1 root]# _
```

The grep command in the preceding output receives the full output from the mount command and then displays only those lines that have /dev/hdc in them. The grep command normally takes two arguments; the first specifies the text to search for and the second specifies the filename(s) to search within. The grep command used in the preceding output requires no second argument because the material to search comes from Standard Input (the mount command) instead of from a file.

Furthermore, you can use more than one pipe | metacharacter on the command line to pipe information from one command to another command in much the same fashion as an assembly line in a factory. A manufacturing factory usually contains several departments, of which each performs a specialized task very well. For example, one department might assemble the product, another might paint the product, and yet another might package the product. Every product must pass through each department to be complete.

Similarly, Linux has several commands that can manipulate data in some manner. The piping of each of these commands can be compared to the flow of a manufacturing factory; information is manipulated by one command and then that manipulated information is sent to another command, which manipulates it further. After being manipulated by several commands in this fashion, the information is in a form that the user desires. This process is depicted in Figure 8-3.

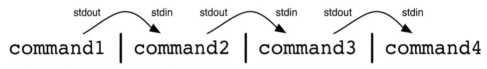

FIGURE 8-3 *Piping several commands*

Any command that can take from Standard Input and give to Standard Output is called a **filter command**. It is important to note that commands such as ls and mount are not filter commands because they do not accept Standard Input from other commands, but instead find information from the system and display it to the user. As a result, these commands must be at the beginning of a pipe. Other commands such as the vi editor are interactive and as such cannot exist within a pipe because they cannot take from Standard Input and give to Standard Output.

Several hundred filter commands are available to Linux users; Table 8-2 lists some common ones useful throughout this book.

Table 8-2 Common filter commands

Command	Description
sort	Sorts lines in a file alphanumerically
sort −r	Reverse sorts lines in a file alphanumerically
wc	Counts the number of lines, words, and characters in a file
wc −l	Counts the number of lines in a file
wc −w	Counts the number of words in a file
wc −c	Counts the number of characters in a file

Table 8-2 Common filter commands (Continued)

Command	Description
pr	Formats a file for printing (has several options available); it places a date and page number at the top of each page
pr –d	Formats a file double-spaced
tr	Replaces characters in the text of a file
grep	Displays lines in a file that match a regular expression
nl	Numbers line in a file
awk	Can be used to extract, manipulate, and format text using pattern-action statements
sed	Can be used to manipulate text using search-and-replace expressions

Take, for example, the prologue from Shakespeare's *Romeo and Juliet*:

```
[root@server1 root]# cat prologue
Two households, both alike in dignity,
In fair Verona, where we lay our scene,
From ancient grudge break to new mutiny,
Where civil blood makes civil hands unclean.
From forth the fatal loins of these two foes
A pair of star-cross'd lovers take their life;
Whole misadventured piteous overthrows
Do with their death bury their parents' strife.
The fearful passage of their death-mark'd love,
And the continuance of their parents' rage,
Which, but their children's end, nought could remove,
Is now the two hours' traffic of our stage;
The which if you with patient ears attend,
What here shall miss, our toil shall strive to mend.
[root@server1 root]# _
```

If you want to replace all lowercase a characters with uppercase A characters in the preceding file, sort the contents by the first character on each line, double-space the output, and view the results page-by-page, you can use the following pipe:

```
[root@server1 root]# cat prologue | tr a A | sort | pr -d | less
```

```
2002-05-30 09:32                                      Page 1


And the continuAnce of their pArents' rAge,


A pAir of stAr-cross'd lovers tAke their life;
```

Do with their deAth bury their pArents' strife.

From Ancient grudge breAk to new mutiny,

From forth the fAtAl loins of these two foes

In fAir VeronA, where we lAy our scene,

Is now the two hours' trAffic of our stAge;

The feArful pAssAge of their deAth-mArk'd love,

The which if you with pAtient eArs Attend,

Two households, both Alike in dignity,
:

The command used in the preceding example displays the final Standard Output to the terminal screen via the less command. In many cases, you might want to display the results of the pipe as well as have a saved copy in a file on the hard disk. As a result, there exists a **tee command**, which is a filter command that takes information from Standard Input and sends that information to a file, as well as to Standard Output.

To save a copy of the manipulated prologue before displaying it to the terminal screen with the less command, you can use the following command:

```
[root@server1 root]# cat prologue | tr a A | sort | pr -d | tee newfile | less
```

2002-05-30 09:32   Page 1

And the continuAnce of their pArents' rAge,

A pAir of stAr-cross'd lovers tAke their life;

Do with their deAth bury their pArents' strife.

From Ancient grudge breAk to new mutiny,

From forth the fAtAl loins of these two foes

In fAir VeronA, where we lAy our scene,

Is now the two hours' trAffic of our stAge;

The feArful pAssAge of their deAth-mArk'd love,

```
The which if you with pAtient eArs Attend,

Two households, both Alike in dignity,
:q
[root@server1 root]# _
[root@server1 root]# cat newfile

2002-05-30 09:58                                    Page 1

And the continuAnce of their pArents' rAge,

A pAir of stAr-cross'd lovers tAke their life;

Do with their deAth bury their pArents' strife.

From Ancient grudge breAk to new mutiny,

From forth the fAtAl loins of these two foes

In fAir VeronA, where we lAy our scene,

Is now the two hours' trAffic of our stAge;

The feArful pAssAge of their deAth-mArk'd love,

The which if you with pAtient eArs Attend,

Two households, both Alike in dignity,

WhAt here shAll miss, our toil shAll strive to mend.

Where civil blood mAkes civil hAnds uncleAn.

Which, but their children's end, nought could remove,

Whole misAdventured piteous overthrows

[root@server1 root]# _
```

In addition, you can combine redirection and piping together; however, input redirection must occur at the beginning of the pipe and output redirection must occur at the end of the pipe. An example of this is shown in the following output, which replaces all lowercase a characters with uppercase A characters in the prologue file used in the previous example, then sorts the file, numbers each line, and saves the output to a file called newprologue instead of sending the output to the terminal screen.

```
[root@server1 root]# tr a A <prologue | sort | nl >newprologue
[root@server1 root]# cat newprologue
     1  And the continuAnce of their pArents' rAge,
     2  A pAir of stAr-cross'd lovers tAke their life;
     3  Do with their deAth bury their pArents' strife.
     4  From Ancient grudge breAk to new mutiny,
     5  From forth the fAtAl loins of these two foes
     6  In fAir VeronA, where we lAy our scene,
     7  Is now the two hours' trAffic of our stAge;
     8  The feArful pAssAge of their deAth-mArk'd love,
     9  The which if you with pAtient eArs Attend,
    10  Two households, both Alike in dignity,
    11  WhAt here shAll miss, our toil shAll strive to mend.
    12  Where civil blood mAkes civil hAnds uncleAn.
    13  Which, but their children's end, nought could remove,
    14  Whole misAdventured piteous overthrows
[root@server1 root]# _
```

Many Linux commands can be used to provide large amounts of useful text information. As a result, Linux administrators often use the sed and awk filter commands in conjunction with pipes to manipulate text information obtained from these commands.

The sed command is typically used to search for a certain string of text, and replaces that text string with another text string using the syntax s/search/replace/. For example, the following output demonstrates how sed can be used to search for the string "the" and replace it with the string "THE" in the prologue file used earlier:

```
[root@server1 root]# cat prologue | sed s/the/THE/
Two households, both alike in dignity,
In fair Verona, where we lay our scene,
From ancient grudge break to new mutiny,
Where civil blood makes civil hands unclean.
From forth THE fatal loins of these two foes
A pair of star-cross'd lovers take THEir life;
Whole misadventured piteous overthrows
Do with THEir death bury their parents' strife.
The fearful passage of THEir death-mark'd love,
And THE continuance of their parents' rage,
Which, but THEir children's end, nought could remove,
Is now THE two hours' traffic of our stage;
The which if you with patient ears attend,
What here shall miss, our toil shall strive to mend.
[root@server1 root]# _
```

Notice from the preceding output that sed only searched for and replaced the first occurrence of the string "the" in each line. To have sed globally replace all occurrences of the string "the" in each line, simply append a g to the search-and-replace expression:

```
[root@server1 root]# cat prologue | sed s/the/THE/g
Two households, both alike in dignity,
In fair Verona, where we lay our scene,
From ancient grudge break to new mutiny,
Where civil blood makes civil hands unclean.
From forth THE fatal loins of THEse two foes
A pair of star-cross'd lovers take THEir life;
Whole misadventured piteous overthrows
Do with THEir death bury THEir parents' strife.
The fearful passage of THEir death-mark'd love,
And THE continuance of THEir parents' rage,
Which, but THEir children's end, nought could remove,
Is now THE two hours' traffic of our stage;
The which if you with patient ears attend,
What here shall miss, our toil shall strive to mend.
[root@server1 root]# _
```

You can also tell sed the specific lines to search by prefixing the search-and-replace expression. For example, to force sed to replace the string "the" with "THE" globally on lines that contain the string "love," you can use the following command:

```
[root@server1 root]# cat prologue | sed /love/s/the/THE/g
Two households, both alike in dignity,
In fair Verona, where we lay our scene,
From ancient grudge break to new mutiny,
Where civil blood makes civil hands unclean.
From forth the fatal loins of these two foes
A pair of star-cross'd lovers take THEir life;
Whole misadventured piteous overthrows
Do with their death bury their parents' strife.
The fearful passage of THEir death-mark'd love,
And the continuance of their parents' rage,
Which, but their children's end, nought could remove,
Is now the two hours' traffic of our stage;
The which if you with patient ears attend,
What here shall miss, our toil shall strive to mend.
[root@server1 root]# _
```

You can also force sed to perform a search-and-replace on certain lines only. To replace the string "the" with "THE" globally on lines 5 to 8 only, you can use the following command:

```
[root@server1 root]# cat prologue | sed 5,8s/the/THE/g
Two households, both alike in dignity,
In fair Verona, where we lay our scene,
From ancient grudge break to new mutiny,
Where civil blood makes civil hands unclean.
From forth THE fatal loins of THEse two foes
A pair of star-cross'd lovers take THEir life;
Whole misadventured piteous overthrows
Do with THEir death bury THEir parents' strife.
The fearful passage of their death-mark'd love,
And the continuance of their parents' rage,
Which, but their children's end, nought could remove,
Is now the two hours' traffic of our stage;
The which if you with patient ears attend,
What here shall miss, our toil shall strive to mend.
[root@server1 root]# _
```

You can also use sed to remove unwanted lines of text. To delete all the lines that contain the word "the," you can use the following command:

```
[root@server1 root]# cat prologue | sed /the/d
Two households, both alike in dignity,
In fair Verona, where we lay our scene,
From ancient grudge break to new mutiny,
Where civil blood makes civil hands unclean.
Whole misadventured piteous overthrows
The which if you with patient ears attend,
What here shall miss, our toil shall strive to mend.
[root@server1 root]# _
```

Like sed, the awk command searches for patterns of text and performs some action on the text found. However, the awk command treats each line of text as a record in a database, and each word in a line as a database field. For example, the line "Hello, how are you?" has four fields: "Hello," "how," "are," and "you?". These fields can be referenced in the awk command using $1, $2, $3, and $4. For example, to display only the first and fourth words only on lines of the prologue file that contains the word "the," you can use the following command:

```
[root@server1 root]# cat prologue | awk '/the/ {print $1, $4}'
From fatal
A star-cross'd
Do death
The of
```

```
And of
Which, children's
Is two
[root@server1 root]# _
```

By default, the awk command uses space or tab characters as delimiters for each field in a line. Most configuration files on Linux systems, however, are delimited using colon (:) characters. To change the delimiter that awk uses, you can specify the -F option to the command. For example, the following example lists the last 10 lines of the colon-delimited file /etc/passwd, and views only the 6th and 7th fields for lines that contain the word "bob" in the last 10 lines of the file:

```
[root@server1 root]# tail /etc/passwd
ldap:x:55:55:LDAP User:/var/lib/ldap:/bin/false
mysql:x:27:27:MySQL Server:/var/lib/mysql:/bin/bash
postgres:x:26:26:PostgreSQL Server:/var/lib/pgsql:/bin/bash
fax:x:78:78:mgetty fax spool user:/var/spool/fax:/sbin/nologin
nut:x:57:57:Network UPS Tools:/var/lib/ups:/bin/false
privoxy:x:73:73::/etc/privoxy:/sbin/nologin
tomcat:x:53:53:Tomcat server:/var/lib/tomcat:/sbin/nologin
cyrus:x:76:12:Cyrus IMAP Server:/var/lib/imap:/bin/bash
exim:x:93:93::/var/spool/exim:/sbin/nologin
bob:x:500:500::/home/bob:/bin/bash
[root@server1 root]# tail /etc/passwd | awk -F: '/bob/ {print $6, $7}'
/home/bob /bin/bash
[root@server1 root]# _
```

> **NOTE**
>
> Both awk and sed allow you to specify regular expressions in the search pattern.

Shell Variables

A BASH shell has several **variables** in memory at any one time. Recall that a variable is simply a reserved portion of memory containing information that might be accessed. Most variables in the shell are referred to as **environment variables** because they are typically set by the system and contain information that the system and programs access regularly. Users can also create their own custom variables. These variables are called **user-defined variables**. In addition to these two types of variables, special variables are available that are useful when executing commands and creating new files and directories.

Environment Variables

Many environment variables are set by default in the BASH shell. To see a list of these variables and their current values, you can use the **set command**, as shown in the following output:

```
[root@server1 root]# set
BASH=/bin/bash
BASH_ENV=/root/.bashrc
BASH_VERSINFO=([0]="2" [1]="05b" [2]="0" [3]="1" [4]="release" [5]="i386-redhat-linux-
gnu")
BASH_VERSION='2.05b.0(1)-release'
COLORS=/etc/DIR_COLORS.xterm
COLORTERM=gnome-terminal
COLUMNS=80
DESKTOP_SESSION=default
DESKTOP_STARTUP_ID=
DIRSTACK=()
DISPLAY=:0.0
EUID=0
GDMSESSION=default
GNOME_DESKTOP_SESSION_ID=Default
GNOME_KEYRING_SOCKET=/tmp/keyring-1rv68W/socket
GROUPS=()
GTK_RC_FILES=/etc/gtk/gtkrc:/root/.gtkrc-1.2-gnome2
G_BROKEN_FILENAMES=1
HISTFILE=/root/.bash_history
HISTFILESIZE=1000
HISTSIZE=1000
HOME=/root
HOSTNAME=server1
HOSTTYPE=i386
IFS=$' \t\n'
INPUTRC=/etc/inputrc
KDEDIR=/usr
LANG=en_US.UTF-8
LESSOPEN='|/usr/bin/lesspipe.sh %s'
LINES=24
LOGNAME=root
LS_COLORS='no=00:fi=00:di=00;34:ln=00;36:pi=40;33:so=00;35:bd=40;33;01:cd=40;33;01:or=01;
05;37;41:mi=01;05;37;41:ex=00;32:*.cmd=00;32:*.exe=00;32:*.com=00;32:*.btm=00;32:*.bat=00
;32:*.sh=00;32:*.csh=00;32:*.tar=00;31:*.tgz=00;31:*.arj=00;31:*.taz=00;31:*.lzh=00;31:*.
zip=00;31:*.z=00;31:*.Z=00;31:*.gz=00;31:*.bz2=00;31:*.bz=00;31:*.tz=00;31:*.rpm=00;31:*.
cpio=00;31:*.jpg=00;35:*.gif=00;35:*.bmp=00;35:*.xbm=00;35:*.xpm=00;35:*.png=00;35:*.tif=
00;35:'
```

```
MACHTYPE=i386-redhat-linux-gnu
MAIL=/var/spool/mail/root
MAILCHECK=60
OPTERR=1
OPTIND=1
OSTYPE=linux-gnu
PATH=/usr/kerberos/sbin:/usr/kerberos/bin:/usr/local/sbin:/usr/local/bin:/sbin:/bin:/usr/
sbin:/usr/bin:/usr/X11R6/bin:/usr/java/j2sdk1.4.2_04/bin:/:/root/bin
PIPESTATUS=([0]="0")
PPID=3177
PROMPT_COMMAND='echo -ne "\033]0;${USER}@${HOSTNAME%%.*}:${PWD/#$HOME/~}\007"'
PS1='[\u@\h \W]\$ '
PS2='> '
PS4='+ '
PWD=/root
QTDIR=/usr/lib/qt-3.3
SESSION_MANAGER=local/server1:/tmp/.ICE-unix/2868
SHELL=/bin/bash
SHELLOPTS=braceexpand:emacs:hashall:histexpand:history:interactive-comments:monitor
SHLVL=2
SSH_AGENT_PID=2931
SSH_ASKPASS=/usr/libexec/openssh/gnome-ssh-askpass
SSH_AUTH_SOCK=/tmp/ssh-DuFw2868/agent.2868
SUPPORTED=en_US.UTF-8:en_US:en
TERM=xterm
UID=0
USER=root
USERNAME=root
WINDOWID=41943116
XAUTHORITY=/root/.Xauthority
_=set
[root@server1 root]# _
```

Some environment variables shown in the preceding output are used by programs that require information about the system; the OSTYPE (Operating System TYPE) and SHELL (Pathname to shell) variables are examples from the preceding output. Other variables are used to set the user's working environment; the most common of these include the following:

◆ PS1—The default shell prompt

◆ HOME—The absolute pathname to the user's home directory

◆ PWD—The present working directory in the directory tree

◆ PATH—A list of directories to search for executable programs

The PS1 variable represents the BASH shell prompt. To view the contents of this variable only, you can use the **echo command** and specify the variable name prefixed by the $ shell metacharacter, as shown in the following output:

```
[root@server1 root]# echo $PS1
[\u@\h \W]\$
[root@server1 root]# _
```

Note that a special notation is used to define the prompt in the preceding output: \u indicates the user name, \h indicates the host name, and \W indicates the name of the current directory. A list of BASH notation can be found by navigating the manual page for the BASH shell.

To change the value of a variable, you simply need to specify the variable name followed immediately by an equal sign (=) and the new value. The following output demonstrates how you can change the value of the PS1 variable. The new prompt takes effect immediately and allows the user to type commands.

```
[root@server1 root]# PS1="This is the new prompt: #"
This is the new prompt: # _
This is the new prompt: # date
Fri May 27 10:15:56 EDT 2005
This is the new prompt: # _
This is the new prompt: # who
root      pts/0    May 30 09:58 (3.0.0.2)
This is the new prompt: # _
This is the new prompt: # PS1="[\u@\h \W]#"
[root@server1 root]# _
```

The HOME variable is used by programs that require the pathname to the current user's home directory to store or search for files, and, therefore, it should not be changed. If the root user logs in to the system, the HOME variable is set to /root; alternatively, the HOME variable is set to /home/user1 if the user named user1 logs in to the system. Recall that the tilde ~ metacharacter represents the current user's home directory; this metacharacter is a pointer to the HOME variable as shown next:

```
[root@server1 root]# echo $HOME
/root
[root@server1 root]# echo ~
/root
[root@server1 root]# HOME=/etc
[root@server1 root]# echo $HOME
/etc
[root@server1 root]# echo ~
/etc
[root@server1 root]# _
```

Like the HOME variable, the PWD (Print Working Directory) variable is vital to the user's environment and should not be changed. PWD stores the current user's location in the directory tree. It is affected by the cd command and used by other commands such as pwd when the current directory needs to be identified. The following output demonstrates how this variable works:

```
[root@server1 root]# pwd
/root
[root@server1 root]# echo $PWD
/root
[root@server1 root]# cd /etc
[root@server1 etc]# pwd
/etc
[root@server1 root]# echo $PWD
/etc
[root@server1 root]# _
```

The PATH variable is one of the most important variables in the BASH shell, as it allows users to execute commands by typing the command name alone. Recall that most commands are represented by an executable file on the hard drive typically organized into directories named bin or sbin throughout the Linux directory tree. To execute the ls command, you could either type the absolute or relative pathname to the file (that is, /bin/ls or ../../bin/ls), or simply type the letters "ls" and allow the system to search the directories listed in the PATH variable for a command named ls. Sample contents of the PATH variable are shown in the following output:

```
[root@server1 root]# echo $PATH
/usr/kerberos/sbin:/usr/kerberos/bin:/usr/local/sbin:/usr/local/bin:
/sbin:/bin:/usr/sbin:/usr/bin:/usr/X11R6/bin:/root/bin
[root@server1 root]# _
```

From the preceding output, if the user simply types the command ls at the command prompt and presses Enter, the shell notices that there is no / character in the pathname and proceeds to search for the file ls in the /usr/kerberos/sbin directory, then the /usr/kerberos/bin directory, the /usr/local/sbin directory, the /usr/local/bin directory, the /sbin directory, and then the /bin directory before finding the ls executable file. If no ls file is found in any directory in the PATH variable, the shell returns an error message as shown next with a misspelled command:

```
[root@server1 root]# lss
bash: lss: command not found
[root@server1 root]# _
```

Thus, if a command is located within a directory that is listed in the PATH variable, you can simply type the name of the command on the command line to execute it, as the shell will be able to find the appropriate executable file on the filesystem. All of the commands used in this book up until this section have been located in directories listed in the PATH variable. However, if the executable file is not in a directory listed in the PATH variable, the user must specify either the absolute or relative pathname to the executable file. An example of this is shown next using the myprogram file in the /root directory (a directory that is not listed in the PATH variable):

```
[root@server1 root]# pwd
/root
[root@server1 root]# ls -F
Desktop/  myprogram*
[root@server1 root]# myprogram
bash: myprogram: command not found
[root@server1 root]# /root/myprogram
This is a sample program.
[root@server1 root]# ./myprogram
This is a sample program.
[root@server1 root]# cp myprogram /bin
[root@server1 root]# myprogram
This is a sample program.
[root@server1 root]# _
```

After the myprogram executable file was copied to the /bin directory in the preceding output, the user was able to execute it by simply typing its name because the /bin directory is listed in the PATH variable.

Table 8-3 provides a list of environment variables used in most BASH shells.

Table 8-3 Common BASH environment variables

Variable	Description
BASH	The full path to the BASH shell
BASH_VERSION	The version of the current BASH shell
DISPLAY	The variable used to redirect the output of X Windows to another computer or device
ENV	The location of the BASH run-time configuration file (usually ~/.bashrc)
EUID	The effective UID (User ID) of the current user
HISTFILE	The filename used to store previously entered commands in the BASH shell (usually ~/.bash_history)
HISTFILESIZE	The number of previously entered commands that can be stored in the HISTFILE upon logout for use during the next login; it is typically 1000 commands

Table 8-3 Common BASH environment variables (Continued)

Variable	Description
HISTSIZE	The number of previously entered commands that will be stored in memory during the current login session; it is typically 1000 commands
HOME	The absolute pathname of the current user's home directory
HOSTNAME	The host name of the Linux system
LOGNAME	The user name of the current user used when logging in to the shell
MAIL	The location of the mailbox file (where e-mail is stored)
OLDPWD	The most recent previous working directory
OSTYPE	The current operating system
PATH	The directories to search for executable program files in the absence of an absolute or relative pathname containing a / character
PS1	The current shell prompt
PWD	The current working directory
RANDOM	The variable that creates a random number when accessed
SHELL	The absolute pathname of the current shell
TERM	The variable used to determine the terminal settings; it is typically set to "linux" or "xterm" on newer Linux systems and "console" on older Linux systems
TERMCAP	The variable used to determine the terminal settings on older systems that use a TERMCAP database (/etc/termcap)

User-Defined Variables

You can set your own variables using the same method discussed earlier to change the contents of existing environment variables. To do so, you simply specify the name of the variable (known as the **variable identifier**) immediately followed by the equal sign (=) and the new contents. When creating new variables, it is important to note the following features of variable identifiers:

◆ They can contain alphanumeric characters (0–9, A–Z, a–z), the dash (-) character, or the underscore (_) character.

◆ They must not start with a number.

◆ They are typically capitalized to follow convention (for example, HOME, PATH, and so on).

To create a variable called MYVAR with the contents "This is a sample variable" and display its contents, you can use the following commands:

```
[root@server1 root]# MYVAR="This is a sample variable"
[root@server1 root]# echo $MYVAR
This is a sample variable
[root@server1 root]# _
```

The preceding command created a variable that is available to the current shell. Most commands that are run by the shell are run in a separate **subshell**, which is created by the current shell. Any variables created in the current shell are not available to those subshells and the commands running within them. Thus, if a user creates a variable to be used within a certain program such as a database editor, that variable should be exported to all subshells using the **export command** to ensure that all programs started by the current shell have the ability to access the variable.

Recall from earlier that all environment variables in the BASH shell can be listed using the set command; user-defined variables are also indicated in this list. Similarly, to see a list of all exported environment and user-defined variables in the shell, you can use the **env command**. Because the outputs of set and env are typically large, you would commonly redirect the Standard Output of these commands to the grep command to display certain lines only.

To see the difference between the set and env commands as well as export the MYVAR variable created earlier, you can perform the following commands:

```
[root@server1 root]# set | grep MYVAR
MYVAR=$'This is a sample variable.'
[root@server1 root]# env | grep MYVAR
[root@server1 root]# _
[root@server1 root]# export MYVAR
[root@server1 root]# env | grep MYVAR
MYVAR=This is a sample variable.
[root@server1 root]# _
```

Not all environment variables are exported; the PS1 variable is an example of a variable that does not need to be available to subshells and is not exported as a result. However, it is good form to export user-defined variables because they will likely be used by processes that run in subshells. As a result, to create and export a user-defined variable called MYVAR2, you can use the export command alone, as shown in the following output:

```
[root@server1 root]# export MYVAR2="This is another sample variable"
[root@server1 root]# set | grep MYVAR2
MYVAR2=$'This is another sample variable.'
_=MYVAR2
[root@server1 root]# env | grep MYVAR2
MYVAR2=This is another sample variable.
[root@server1 root]# _
```

Other Variables

Other variables are not displayed by the set or env commands; these variables perform specialized functions in the shell.

The UMASK variable used earlier in this textbook is an example of a special variable that performs a special function in the BASH shell and must be set by the umask command. Also recall that when you type the cp command, you are actually running an alias to the cp -i command. Aliases are shortcuts to commands stored in special variables that can be created and viewed using the **alias command**. To create an alias to the command mount -t ext2 /dev/fd0 /mnt/floppy called mf and view it, you can use the following commands:

```
[root@server1 root]# alias mf="mount -t ext2 /dev/fd0 /mnt/floppy"
[root@server1 root]# alias
alias cp='cp -i'
alias l.='ls -d .* --color=tty'
alias ll='ls -l --color=tty'
alias ls='ls --color=tty'
alias mc='. /usr/share/mc/bin/mc-wrapper.sh'
alias mf='mount -t ext2 /dev/fd0 /mnt/floppy'
alias mv='mv -i'
alias rm='rm -ic'
alias vi='vim'
alias which='alias | /usr/bin/which --tty-only --read-alias --show-dot --show-tilde'
[root@server1 root]# _
```

Now, you simply need to run the mf command to mount a floppy device that contains an ext2 filesystem to the /mnt/floppy directory, as shown in the following output:

```
[root@server1 root]# mf
[root@server1 root]# mount
/dev/hdc2 on / type ext3 (rw)
none on /proc type proc (rw)
none on /sys type sysfs (rw)
/dev/hdc1 on /boot type ext3 (rw)
none on /dev/pts type devpts (rw,gid=5,mode=620)
none on /dev/shm type tmpfs (rw)
none on /proc/sys/fs/binfmt_misc type binfmt_misc (rw)
/dev/fd0 on /mnt/floppy type ext2 (rw)
[root@server1 root]# _
```

You can also create aliases to multiple commands, provided they are separated by the ; metacharacter introduced in Chapter 2, "Preparing for Linux Installation." To create and test an alias called dw that runs the date command followed by the who command, you can do the following:

```
[root@server1 root]# alias dw="date;who"
[root@server1 root]# alias
alias cp='cp -i'
alias dw='date;who'
alias l.='ls -d .* --color=tty'
alias ll='ls -l --color=tty'
alias ls='ls --color=tty'
alias mc='. /usr/share/mc/bin/mc-wrapper.sh'
alias mf='mount -t ext2 /dev/fd0 /mnt/floppy'
alias mv='mv -i'
alias rm='rm -i'
alias vi='vim'
alias which='alias | /usr/bin/which --tty-only --read-alias --show-dot --show-tilde'
[root@server1 root]# dw
Sun Jun  5 10:25:45 EDT 2005
root     pts/0    Jun  1 08:44 (3.0.0.2)
root     pts/1    Jun  1 11:54 (:0)
[root@server1 root]# _
```

NOTE

It is important to use unique alias names because the shell searches for them before it searches for executable files; if you create an alias called who, that alias would be used instead of the who command on the filesystem.

Environment Files

Recall that variables are stored in memory. When a user exits the BASH shell, all variables stored in memory are destroyed along with the shell itself. To ensure that variables are accessible to a shell at all times, you must place variables in a file that is executed each time a user logs in and starts a BASH shell. These files are called **environment files**. Some common BASH shell environment files and the order in which they are executed are listed next:

1. /etc/profile
2. ~/.bash_profile
3. ~/.bash_login
4. ~/.profile

The /etc/profile file is always executed immediately after login for all users on the system and sets most environment variables, such as HOME and PATH. After /etc/profile finishes executing, the home directory of the user is searched for the hidden environment files .bash_profile, .bash_login, and .profile. If these files exist, the first one found is executed; as a result, only one of these files is typically used. These hidden environment files allow a user to set customized variables independent of BASH shells used by other users on the system; any values assigned to variables in these files override those set in /etc/profile due to the order of execution.

To add a variable to any of these files, you simply add a line that has the same format as the command used on the command line. To add the MYVAR2 variable used previously to the .bash_profile file, simply edit the file using a text editor such as vi and add the line export MYVAR2="This is another sample variable" to the file.

Variables are not the only type of information that can be entered into an environment file; any command that can be executed on the command line can also be placed inside any environment file. If you want to set the UMASK to 077, display the date after each login, and create an alias, you can add the following lines to one of the hidden environment files in your home directory:

```
umask 077
date
alias dw="date;who"
```

A special environment file also exists that is always executed before the other hidden environment files are searched and when a user starts any new BASH shell after login; this file is located in the current user's home directory and called .bashrc (BASH run-time configuration).

Also, you might want to execute cleanup tasks upon exiting the shell; to do this, simply add those cleanup commands to the .bash_logout file in your home directory.

Shell Scripts

In the previous section, you learned that the BASH shell can execute commands that exist within environment files. The BASH shell also has the ability to execute other text files containing commands and special constructs. These files are referred to as **shell scripts** and are typically used to create custom programs that perform administrative tasks on Linux systems. Any command that can be entered on the command line in Linux can be entered into a shell script because it is a BASH shell that interprets the contents of the shell script itself. The most basic shell script is one that contains a list of commands, one per line, for the shell to execute in order, as shown next in the text file called myscript:

```
[root@server1 root]# cat myscript
#!/bin/bash
#this is a comment
date
who
ls -F /
[root@server1 root]# _
```

The first line in the preceding shell script (#!/bin/bash) is called a **hashpling**; it specifies the pathname to the shell that interprets the contents of the shell script. Different shells can use different constructs in their shell scripts; thus, it is important to identify which shell was used to create a particular shell script. The hashpling allows a user who uses the C shell the ability to use a BASH shell when executing the myscript shell script shown previously. The second line of the shell script is referred to as a comment because it begins with a # character and is ignored by the shell; the only exception to this is the hashpling on the first line of a shell script. The remainder of the shell script shown in the preceding output consists of three commands that will be executed by the shell in order: date, who, and ls.

If you have read permission to a shell script, you can execute the shell script by starting another BASH shell and specifying the shell script as an argument. To execute the myscript shell script shown earlier, you can use the following command:

```
[root@server1 root]# bash myscript
Sat Jun  4 08:46:43 EDT 2005
root    pts/0    Jun  1 08:44 (3.0.0.2)
bin/   etc/    lib/         mnt/    root/    sys/         udev/
boot/  home/   lost+found/  opt/    sbin/    tftpboot/    usr/
dev/   initrd/ misc/        proc/   selinux/ tmp/         var/
[root@server1 root]# _
```

Alternatively, if you have read and execute permission to a shell script, you can execute the shell script like any other executable program on the system, as shown next using the myscript shell script:

```
[root@server1 root]# chmod a+x myscript
[root@server1 root]# ./myscript
Sat Jun  4 08:48:56 EDT 2005
root    pts/0    Jun  1 08:44 (3.0.0.2)
bin/   etc/    lib/         mnt/    root/    sys/         udev/
boot/  home/   lost+found/  opt/    sbin/    tftpboot/    usr/
dev/   initrd/ misc/        proc/   selinux/ tmp/         var/
[root@server1 root]# _
```

The preceding output is difficult to read because the output from each command is not separated by blank lines or identified by a label. Utilizing the echo command results in a more user-friendly myscript, as shown next:

```
[root@server1 root]# cat myscript
#!/bin/bash
echo "Today's date is:"
date
echo ""
echo "The people logged into the system include:"
who
echo ""
```

```
echo "The contents of the / directory are:"
ls -F /
[root@server1 root]# ./myscript
Today's date is:
Sat Jun  4 08:48:56 EDT 2005

The people logged into the system include:
root     pts/0    Jun  1 08:44 (3.0.0.2)

The contents of the / directory are:
bin/    etc/    lib/        mnt/    root/    sys/        udev/
boot/   home/   lost+found/ opt/    sbin/    tftpboot/   usr/
dev/    initrd/ misc/       proc/   selinux/ tmp/        var/
[root@server1 root]# _
```

Escape Sequences

In the previous example, you used the echo command to manipulate data that appeared on the screen. The echo command also supports several special notations called **escape sequences** that you can use to further manipulate the way text is displayed to the terminal screen, provided the -e option is specified to the echo command. Table 8-4 provides a list of these echo escape sequences.

Table 8-4 Common echo escape sequences

Escape Sequence	Description
\???	Inserts an ASCII character represented by a three-digit octal number (???)
\\	Backslash
\a	ASCII beep
\b	Backspace
\c	Prevents a new line following the command
\f	Form feed
\n	Starts a new line
\r	Carriage return
\t	Horizontal tab
\v	Vertical tab

The escape sequences listed in Table 8-4 can be used to further manipulate the output of the myscript shell script used earlier, as shown in the following example:

```
[root@server1 root]# cat myscript
#!/bin/bash
echo -e "Today's date is: \c"
date
echo -e "\nThe people logged into the system include:"
who
echo -e "\nThe contents of the / directory are:"
ls -F /
[root@server1 root]# ./myscript
Today's date is: Sat Jun  4 08:48:56 EDT 2005

The people logged into the system include:
root     pts/0    Jun 1 08:44 (3.0.0.2)

The contents of the / directory are:
bin/    etc/      lib/        mnt/     root/     sys/        udev/
boot/   home/     lost+found/ opt/     sbin/     tftpboot/   usr/
dev/    initrd/   misc/       proc/    selinux/  tmp/        var/
[root@server1 root]# _
```

Notice from preceding output that the \c escape sequence prevented the newline character at the end of the output "Today's date is:" when myscript was executed. Similarly, newline characters (\n) were inserted prior to displaying "The people logged into the system include:" and "The contents of the / directory are:" to create blank lines between command outputs. This eliminated the need for using the echo "" command shown earlier.

Reading Standard Input

At times, a shell script might need input from the user executing the program; this input can then be stored in a variable for later use. The **read command** takes user input from Standard Input and places it in a variable specified by an argument to the read command. After the input has been read into a variable, the contents of that variable can then be used, as shown in the following shell script:

```
[root@server1 root]# cat newscript
#!/bin/bash
echo -e "What is your name? -->\c"
read USERNAME
echo "Hello $USERNAME"
[root@server1 root]# chmod a+x newscript
[root@server1 root]# ./newscript
```

```
What is your name? --> Fred
Hello Fred
[root@server1 root]# _
```

Note from the preceding output that the echo command used to pose a question to the user ends with - - > to simulate an arrow prompt on the screen and the \c escape sequence to place the cursor after the arrow prompt; this is common among Linux administrators when writing shell scripts.

Decision Constructs

Decision constructs are the most common type of construct used in shell scripts; they alter the flow of a program based on whether a command in the program completed successfully or based on a decision that the user makes given a question posed by the program. This is reflected in Figures 8-4 and 8-5.

FIGURE 8-4 *A sample decision construct*

FIGURE 8-5 *A sample decision construct*

The if Construct

The most common type of decision construct is known as the if construct; the syntax of the if construct is shown next:

> **if** *this is true*
>
> **then**
>> *do these commands*
>
> **elif** *this is true*
>
> **then**
>> *do these commands*
>
> **else**
>> *do these commands*
>
> **fi**

Some common rules govern if constructs:

1. elif (else if) and else statements are optional.
2. You can have an unlimited number of elif statements.
3. The *do these commands* section can consist of multiple commands, one per line.
4. The *do these commands* section is typically indented from the left-hand side of the text file for readability, but does not need to be.
5. The end of the statement must be a backward "if" (fi).
6. The *this is true* part of the if syntax shown earlier can be a command or a test statement:
   - Commands return true if they perform their function properly.
   - Test statements are enclosed within square brackets [ ] or prefixed by the word "test" and used to test certain conditions on the system.

An example of using a basic if construct to ensure that the /etc/hosts file is only copied to the /etc/sample directory if that directory could be created successfully is shown in the following output:

```
[root@server1 root]# cat testmkdir
#!/bin/bash
if mkdir /etc/sample
then
    cp /etc/hosts /etc/sample
    echo "The hosts file was successfully copied to /etc/sample"
else
    echo "The /etc/sample directory could not be created."
fi
```

```
[root@server1 root]# chmod a+x testmkdir
[root@server1 root]# ./testmkdir
The hosts file was successfully copied to /etc/sample
[root@server1 root]# _
```

In the preceding output, the mkdir /etc/sample command is always run; if it runs successfully, the shell script proceeds to the cp /etc/hosts /etc/sample and echo "The hosts file was successfully copied to /etc/sample" commands. If the mkdir /etc/sample command was unsuccessful, the shell script skips ahead and executes the echo "The /etc/sample directory could not be created." command. If there were more lines of text following the fi in the preceding shell script, they are executed after the if construct regardless of its outcome.

Often, it is useful to use the if construct to alter the flow of the program given input from the user. Recall the myscript shell script used earlier:

```
[root@server1 root]# cat myscript
#!/bin/bash
echo -e "Today's date is: \c"
date
echo -e "\nThe people logged into the system include:"
who
echo -e "\nThe contents of the / directory are:"
ls -F /
[root@server1 root]# _
```

To ask the user whether to display the contents of the / directory, you could use the following if construct in the myscript file:

```
[root@server1 root]# cat myscript
#!/bin/bash
echo -e "Today's date is: \c"
date
echo -e "\nThe people logged into the system include:"
who
echo -e "\nWould you like to see the contents of /?(y/n)-->\c"
read ANSWER
if [ $ANSWER = "y" ]
then
    echo -e "\nThe contents of the / directory are:"
    ls -F /
fi
[root@server1 root]# ./myscript
Today's date is: Sat Jun  4 09:13:31 EDT 2005

The people logged into the system include:
root      pts/0    Jun  1 08:44 (3.0.0.2)
```

```
Would you like to see the contents of /?(y/n)--> y

The contents of the / directory are:
bin/   etc/   lib/         mnt/   root/     sys/        udev/
boot/  home/  lost+found/  opt/   sbin/     tftpboot/   usr/
dev/   initrd/ misc/       proc/  selinux/  tmp/        var/
[root@server1 root]# _
```

Notice from the preceding output that the test statement [$ANSWER = "y"] is used to test whether the contents of the ANSWER variable are equal to the letter "y." Any other character in this variable causes this **test statement** to return false and the directory listing is then skipped altogether. The type of comparison used previously is called a string comparison because two values are compared for strings of characters; it is indicated by the operator of the test statement, which is the equal sign (=) in this example. Table 8-5 shows a list of common operators used in test statements and their definitions.

> **NOTE**
>
> The test statement [$ANSWER = "y"] is equivalent to the test statement test $ANSWER = "y".
>
> It is important to ensure that there is a space character after the beginning square bracket and before the ending square bracket; otherwise, the test statement produces an error.

Table 8-5 Common test statements

Test Statement	Returns true if:
[A = B]	String A is equal to String B.
[A != B]	String A is not equal to String B.
[A -eq B]	A is numerically equal to B.
[A -ne B]	A is numerically not equal to B.
[A –lt B]	A is numerically less than B.
[A –gt B]	A is numerically greater than B.
[A –le B]	A is numerically less than or equal to B.
[A –ge B]	A is numerically greater than or equal to B.
[-r A]	A is a file/directory that exists and is readable (r permission).
[-w A]	A is a file/directory that exists and is writable (w permission).

Table 8-5 Common test statements (Continued)

Test Statement	Returns true if:
[-x A]	A is a file/directory that exists and is executable (x permission).
[-f A]	A is a file that exists.
[-d A]	A is a directory that exists.

You can also combine any test statement together with another test statement using the special comparison operators −o (OR) and -a (AND) or reverse the meaning of a test statement with the ! (NOT) operator; examples of using these operators in test statements are listed in Table 8-6.

 NOTE

There can be several −o, -a, and ! operators in one test statement.

Table 8-6 Special operators in test statements

Test Statement	Returns true if:
[A = B −o C = D]	String A is equal to String B OR String C is equal to String D.
[A = B −a C = D]	String A is equal to String B AND String C is equal to String D.
[! A = B]	String A is NOT equal to String B.

Considering the myscript shell script, you can proceed with the directory listing if the user enters "y" or "Y" in the following example:

```
[root@server1 root]# cat myscript
#!/bin/bash
echo -e "Today's date is: \c"
date
echo -e "\nThe people logged into the system include:"
who
echo -e "\nWould you like to see the contents of /?(y/n)-->\c"
read ANSWER
if [ $ANSWER = "y" -o $ANSWER = "Y" ]
then
     echo -e "\nThe contents of the / directory are:"
     ls -F /
fi
```

```
[root@server1 root]# ./myscript
Today's date is: Sat Jun  4 09:13:31 EDT 2005

The people logged into the system include:
root     pts/0    Jun  1 08:44 (3.0.0.2)

Would you like to see the contents of /?(y/n)--> Y

The contents of the / directory are:
bin/   etc/    lib/          mnt/    root/    sys/        udev/
boot/  home/   lost+found/   opt/    sbin/    tftpboot/   usr/
dev/   initrd/ misc/         proc/   selinux/ tmp/        var/
[root@server1 root]# _
```

The case Construct

The if construct used earlier is well suited for a limited number of choices. But consider the
myscript example used earlier, this time with several elif statements to perform different
tasks based on the user input:

```
[root@server1 root]# cat myscript
#!/bin/bash
echo -e "What would you like to see?
Todays date (d)
Currently logged in users (u)
The contents of the / directory (r)

Enter your choice(d/u/r)-->\c"
read ANSWER
if [ $ANSWER = "d" -o $ANSWER = "D" ]
then
     echo -e "Today's date is: \c"
     date
elif [ $ANSWER = "u" -o $ANSWER = "U" ]
then
     echo -e "\nThe people logged into the system include:"
     who
elif [ $ANSWER = "r" -o $ANSWER = "R" ]
then
     echo -e "\nThe contents of the / directory are:"
     ls -F /
fi
[root@server1 root]# _
```

```
[root@server1 root]# ./myscript
What would you like to see?
Todays date (d)
Currently logged in users (u)
The contents of the / directory (r)

Enter your choice(d/u/r)--> d
Today's date is: Sat Jun  4 11:10:03 EDT 2005
[root@server1 root]# _
```

The preceding shell script becomes increasingly difficult to read as the number of choices available increases. Thus, when presenting several choices, it is commonplace to use a `case` construct. The syntax of the `case` construct is shown next:

```
case variable in
     pattern1  )  do this
                        ;;
     pattern2  )  do this
                        ;;
     pattern3  )  do this
                        ;;
esac
```

The `case` statement compares the value of a variable with several different patterns of text or numbers. If there is a match, the commands to the right of the pattern are executed (*do this* in the preceding syntax). As with the `if` construct, the `case` construct must be ended by a backward "case" (esac).

An example that simplifies the previous myscript example by using the `case` construct is shown in the following output:

```
[root@server1 root]# cat myscript
#!/bin/bash
echo -e "What would you like to see?
Todays date (d)
Currently logged in users (u)
The contents of the / directory (r)

Enter your choice(d/u/r)-->\c"
read ANSWER

case $ANSWER in
   d | D ) echo -e "\nToday's date is: \c"
        date
           ;;
```

```
            u | U ) echo -e "\nThe people logged into the system include:"
                   who
                   ;;
            r | R ) echo -e "\nThe contents of the / directory are:"
                   ls -F /
                   ;;
               *) echo -e "Invalid choice! \a"
                   ;;
esac
[root@server1 root]# ./myscript
What would you like to see?
Todays date (d)
Currently logged in users (u)
The contents of the / directory (r)

Enter your choice(d/u/r)--> d
Today's date is: Sat Jun  4 11:33:23 EDT 2005
[root@server1 root]# _
```

The preceding example prompts the user with a menu and allows the user to select an item that is then placed into the ANSWER variable. If the ANSWER variable is equal to the letter "d" or "D," the date command is executed; however, if the ANSWER variable is equal to the letter "u" or "U," the who command is executed, and if the ANSWER variable is equal to the letter "r" or "R," the ls command is executed. If the ANSWER variable contains something other than the aforementioned letters, the * wildcard metacharacter matches it and prints an error message to the screen. As with if constructs, any statements present in the shell script following the case construct are executed after the case construct.

The && and || Constructs

Although the if and case constructs are versatile, there are some shortcut constructs that take less time when only one decision needs to be made during the execution of a program; these constructs are && and ||. The syntax of these constructs is listed next:

```
command  &&  command
```

```
command  ||  command
```

For the preceding && syntax, the command on the right of the && construct is only executed if the command on the left of the && construct completed successfully. The opposite is true for the || syntax; the command on the right of the || construct is only executed if the command on the left of the || construct did not complete successfully.

Consider the testmkdir example used earlier:

```
[root@server1 root]# cat testmkdir
#!/bin/bash
if mkdir /etc/sample
then
    cp /etc/hosts /etc/sample
    echo "The hosts file was successfully copied to /etc/sample"
else
    echo "The /etc/sample directory could not be created."
fi
[root@server1 root]# _
```

You can consider rewriting the preceding shell script utilizing the && construct as follows:

```
[root@server1 root]# cat testmkdir
#!/bin/bash
mkdir /etc/sample && cp /etc/hosts /etc/sample
[root@server1 root]# _
```

The preceding shell script creates the directory /etc/sample and only copies the /etc/hosts file to it if the mkdir /etc/sample command was successful. You can instead use the || construct to generate error messages if one of the commands fails to execute properly:

```
[root@server1 root]# cat testmkdir
#!/bin/bash
mkdir /etc/sample || echo "Could not create /etc/sample"
cp /etc/hosts /etc/sample || echo "Could not copy /etc/hosts"
[root@server1 root]# _
```

Chapter Summary

- Three components are available to commands: Standard Input, Standard Output, and Standard Error. Not all commands use every component.
- Standard Input is typically user input taken from the keyboard, whereas Standard Output and Standard Error are sent to the terminal screen by default.
- You can redirect the Standard Output and Standard Error of a command to a file using redirection symbols. Similarly, you can use redirection symbols to redirect a file to the Standard Input of a command.
- To redirect the Standard Output from one command to the Standard Input of another, you must use the pipe symbol.
- Most variables available to the BASH shell are environment variables that are loaded into memory after login from environment files.

◆ You can create your own variables in the BASH shell and export them such that they are available to programs started by the shell. These variables can also be placed in environment files such that they are loaded into memory on every shell login.

◆ The UMASK variable and command aliases are special variables that must be set using a certain command.

◆ Shell scripts can be used to execute several Linux commands.

◆ Decision constructs can be used within shell scripts to execute certain Linux commands based on user input or the results of a certain command.

Key Terms

| — A shell metacharacter used to pipe Standard Output from one command to the Standard Input of another command.

< — A shell metacharacter used to obtain Standard Input from a file.

> — A shell metacharacter used to redirect Standard Output and Standard Error to a file.

alias command — A command used to create special variables that are shortcuts to longer command strings.

awk command — A filter command used to search for and display text.

decision construct — A special construct used in a shell script to alter the flow of the program based on the outcome of a command or contents of a variable. Common decision constructs include if, case, &&, and ||.

echo command — A command used to display or echo output to the terminal screen. It might utilize escape sequences.

env command — A command used to display a list of exported variables present in the current shell, except special variables.

environment files — The files used immediately after login to execute commands; they are typically used to load variables into memory.

environment variables — The variables that store information commonly accessed by the system or programs executing on the system—together these variables form the user environment.

escape sequences — The character sequences that have special meaning inside the echo command. They are prefixed by the \ character.

export command — A command used to send variables to subshells.

file descriptors — The numeric labels used to define command input and command output.

filter command — A command that can take from Standard Input and send to Standard Output. In other words, a filter is a command that can exist in the middle of a pipe.

grep (Global Regular Expression Print) command — A program used to search one or more text files for a desired string of characters.

hashpling — The first line in a shell script, which defines the shell that will be used to interpret the commands in the script file.

pipe — A string of commands connected by | metacharacters.

read command — A command used to read Standard Input from a user into a variable.

redirection — The process of changing the default locations of Standard Input, Standard Output, and Standard Error.

sed command — A filter command used to search for and manipulate text.

set command — A command used to view all variables in the shell, except special variables.

shell scripts — The text files that contain a list of commands or constructs for the shell to execute in order.

sort command — A command used to sort lines in a file.

Standard Error (stderr) — A file descriptor that represents any error messages generated by a command.

Standard Input (stdin) — A file descriptor that represents information input to a command during execution.

Standard Output (stdout) — A file descriptor that represents the desired output from a command.

subshell — A shell started by the current shell.

tee command — A command used to take from Standard Input and send to both Standard Output and a specified file.

test statement — A statement used to test a certain condition and generate a True/False value.

tr command — A command used to transform or change characters received from Standard Input.

user-defined variables — The variables that are created by the user and are not used by the system. These variables are typically exported to subshells.

variable — An area of memory used to store information. Variables are created from entries in environment files when the shell is first created after login, and are destroyed when the shell is destroyed upon logout.

variable identifier — The name of a variable.

Review Questions

1. What symbol is used to redirect to standard output in the BASH shell?

    a. #

    b. ?

    c. >

    d. ~

2. What is the pipe shell metacharacter?

    a. |

    b. >

    c. &

    d. @

3. Most variables in the shell are referred to as _____ variables because they are typically set by the system and contain information that the system and programs access regularly.

    a. shell

    b. environment

    c. system

    d. user-defined

4. The _____ variable is one of the most important variables in the BASH shell, as it allows users to execute commands by typing the command name alone.

    a. BIN

    b. HOME

    c. PWD

    d. PATH

5. The _____ statement compares the value of a variable with several different patterns of text or numbers.

    a. &&

    b. case

    c. ||

    d. if

6. True or false? Input redirection must occur at the beginning of the pipe and output redirection must occur at the end of the pipe.

7. True or false? The `sed` command can only be used to perform a global search and replace.

8. True or false? The `awk` command treats each line of text as a record in a database, and each word in a line as a database field.

9. True or false? To change the value of a variable, you specify the variable name followed immediately by the new value.

10. True or false? You can not create aliases to multiple commands.

11. Command input and output are represented by labels known as file _____.

12. The _____ filter command numbers line in a file.

13. To display a user's working directory the command echo _____ would be used.

14. Most commands that are run by the shell are run in a separate _____, which is created by the current shell.

15. To see a list of all exported environment and user-defined variables in the shell, you can use the _____ command.

Chapter 9

System Initialization and X Windows

After completing this chapter, you will be able to:

◆ Summarize the major steps necessary to boot a Linux system

◆ Configure the LILO and GRUB boot loaders

◆ Dual boot Linux with the Windows operating system using LILO, GRUB, and NTLOADER

◆ Understand how the init daemon initializes the system at boot time into different runlevels

◆ Configure the system to start daemons upon system startup

◆ Explain the purpose of the major Linux GUI components: X Windows, Window Manager, and desktop environment

◆ List common Window Managers and desktop environments used in Linux

◆ Configure X Windows settings using various Linux utilities

Earlier in this book, you installed the GRUB boot loader for the Linux kernel during the Red Hat Fedora installation program. In this chapter, you investigate the boot process in greater detail. You explore the different types and configurations of boot loaders, as well as the process of dual booting the Linux operating system with the Windows operating system. Later in this chapter, you learn the procedure used to start daemons after the kernel has loaded and how to manipulate this procedure to start and stop new daemons. Finally, you examine the various components the Linux GUI comprises, and how to configure the Linux GUI using common Linux utilities.

The Boot Process

When a computer first initializes, the BIOS on the mainboard performs a **Power On Self Test (POST)**. Following the POST, the BIOS checks its configuration in the CMOS chip on the mainboard for boot devices to search for and operating systems to execute. Typically, computers first check for an operating system on floppy disk and on CD-ROM devices present in the computer and contain a disk. This ensures that installation of an operating system from CD-ROM or floppy disk can occur at boot time. After these two devices are checked for an operating system, the computer usually checks the **Master Boot Record (MBR)** on the first hard disk inside the computer.

> **NOTE**
>
> Recall that you can alter the order in which boot devices are checked in the computer BIOS.

The MBR might have a **boot loader** on it that can then locate and execute the kernel of the operating system. Alternatively, the Master Boot Record might contain a pointer to a partition on the system that contains a boot loader on the first sector; the partition to which the Master Boot Record points is referred to as the **active partition**. There can be only one active partition per hard disk.

Regardless of whether the boot loader is loaded from the Master Boot Record or the first sector of the active partition, the remainder of the boot process is the same. The boot loader then executes the Linux kernel from the partition that contains it.

> **NOTE**
>
> The Linux kernel is stored in the **/boot** directory and is named **vmlinuz-<kernel version>**.

After the Linux kernel is loaded into memory, the boot loader is no longer active; instead, the Linux kernel continues to initialize the system by loading daemons into memory. A **daemon** is simply a system process that performs useful tasks, such as printing, scheduling, and operating system maintenance. The first daemon process on the system is called the **initialize (init) daemon**; it is responsible for loading all other daemons on the system required to bring the system to a usable state in which users can log in and interact with services. The whole process is depicted in Figure 9-1.

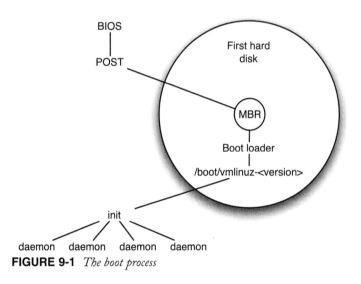

FIGURE 9-1 *The boot process*

Boot Loaders

As discussed in the previous section, the primary function of boot loaders during the boot process is to load the Linux kernel into memory. However, boot loaders can perform other functions as well, including passing information to the kernel during system startup and booting other operating systems that are present on the hard disk. Using one boot loader to boot one of several operating systems is known as dual booting; the boot loader simply loads a different operating system kernel based on user input.

Although you can use many different boot loaders to boot Linux, the two most common boot loaders used on Linux systems today are LILO and GRUB.

> **NOTE**
>
> Only one operating system can be active at any one time.

LILO

Linux Loader (LILO) is the traditional Linux boot loader. Although it can reside on the first sector of an active Linux partition, it is typically located on the Master Boot Record of the hard disk. When the computer completes the POST and locates the LILO boot loader, a LILO boot: prompt appears. You can then press the Tab key to see a list of operating systems that you can boot. Following this, you can enter the name of an operating system and press Enter, press Enter to boot the default operating system (usually Linux), or wait five seconds for the system to boot the default operating system automatically.

After the operating system is fully loaded, you can configure the LILO boot loader by editing the **/etc/lilo.conf** file; an example of this file is shown next:

```
[root@server1 root]# cat /etc/lilo.conf
prompt
timeout=50
default=linux
boot=/dev/hda
map=/boot/map
install=/boot/boot.b
lba32

image=/boot/vmlinuz-2.6.5-1.358
        label=linux
        initrd=/boot/initrd-2.6.5-1.358.img
        read-only
        append="rhgb quiet root=/dev/hda1"
[root@server1 root]# _
```

The preceding /etc/lilo.conf file indicates that LILO boots the linux kernel /boot/vmlinuz-2.6.5-1.358 provided the user chooses the operating system name linux (label=linux). Furthermore, the system continues to boot the default operating system (default=linux) if the user does not enter any input for five seconds (timeout=50). And furthermore, the LILO boot loader tells the Linux kernel to use a Red Hat Graphical Boot after it has loaded (rhgb), suppress detailed kernel messages (quiet), and mount the root filesystem on /dev/hda1 (root=/dev/hda1).

> **NOTE**
>
> You can also use `root=LABEL=/` instead of `root=/dev/hda1` in the preceding example to force LILO to read the appropriate entry from the /etc/fstab file for the root filesystem.

Table 9-1 lists some keywords commonly used in /etc/lilo.conf and their definitions.

Table 9-1 Common /etc/lilo.conf keywords

Keyword	Description
image=	Specifies the absolute pathname to the Linux kernel.
root=	Specifies the device and partition that contains the Linux root filesystem.
prompt	Displays a LILO boot prompt provided there is no message= keyword specified.
message=	Specifies the absolute pathname to the file that contains a graphical LILO screen that can be used instead of a prompt. You can press Ctrl+x at this graphical screen to switch to the LILO boot: prompt.
timeout=	Specifies the number of $1/10^{th}$ seconds to wait for user input before loading the default operating system kernel.
default=	Specifies the label for the default operating system kernel.
label=	Specifies the friendly name given to an operating system kernel.
boot=	Specifies where LILO should be installed. If the device specified is a partition on a hard disk, LILO is installed at the beginning of the partition. If the device specified is a disk, LILO is installed to the MBR on that device.
linear	Specifies that LILO uses linear sector addressing.
read-only	Initially mounts the Linux root filesystem as read-only to reduce any errors with running fsck during system startup.
initrd=	Specifies the pathname to a ramdisk image used to load modules into memory needed for the Linux kernel at boot time.
password=	Specifies a password required to boot the Linux kernel.
append=	Specifies parameters that are passed to the Linux kernel when loaded.
map=	Specifies the file that contains the exact location of the Linux kernel on the hard disk.
install=	Specifies the file that contains the physical layout of the disk drive.
lba32	Specifies large block addressing (32-bit) for hard drives that have more than 1024 cylinders.

> **NOTE**
>
> Lines can be commented out of /etc/lilo.conf by preceding those lines with a # symbol.

The `append=` keyword in /etc/lilo.conf is useful for passing information to the Linux kernel manually at boot time if the kernel does not detect the correct system information. Recall that the system exports detected hardware information to the /proc directory; viewing the contents of files in the /proc directory indicates whether hardware was detected correctly by the Linux kernel. If the Linux kernel does not recognize all the physical memory in the /proc/meminfo file, you can simply add the line `append="mem=xxxM"` to /etc/lilo.conf, where *xxx* is the correct amount of memory in Megabytes. In addition, if the hard disk used is not detected properly by the system, you can send the correct cylinders, heads, and sectors for the hard disk to the kernel at boot time; to do this, you add the line `append="hd=C,H,S"` to /etc/lilo.conf, where C=cylinders, H=heads, and S=sectors.

> **NOTE**
>
> Almost any hardware information can be passed to the kernel via the `append=` keyword. The format of the information depends on the type of hardware involved.

If you change the /etc/lilo.conf file, LILO must be reinstalled using the new information in /etc/lilo.conf for those changes to take effect. To do this, you can simply use the **lilo command**:

```
[root@server1 root]# lilo
Added linux *
[root@server1 root]# _
```

> **NOTE**
>
> To uninstall LILO from an active partition or the MBR, you can use the `lilo -U` command.

Although LILO is a robust boot loader, it might encounter errors and fail to load properly; if this occurs, you are given an error code that indicates the nature of the problem. Table 9-2 lists common LILO error messages and possible solutions.

Table 9-2 LILO error messages

Error Message	Description
L	The first part of the LILO boot loader failed to load, usually as a result of incorrect hard disk parameters. Simply rebooting the machine sometimes fixes this problem; however, you might also need to add the word "linear" to /etc/lilo.conf.
LI	The second part of the LILO boot loader failed to load or the /boot/boot.b file is missing. Adding the word "linear" to /etc/lilo.conf might fix the problem.
LIL, LIL-, LIL?	LILO has loaded properly but cannot find certain files required to operate, such as the /boot/map and /boot/boot.b files. Adding the word "linear" to /etc/lilo.conf might fix the problem.

> **NOTE**
>
> A LILO version available for Intel Pentium and Itanium computers that use Extensible Firmware Interface (EFI) is **ELILO**, which can be downloaded at *http://sourceforge.net/projects/elilo/.*

GRUB

GRand Unified Boot loader (GRUB) resembles common UNIX boot loaders and is more recent than the LILO boot loader. The first major part of the GRUB boot loader (called Stage1) typically resides on the Master Boot Record; the remaining parts of the boot loader (called Stage1.5 and Stage2) reside in the /boot/grub directory. GRUB Stage1 simply points to GRUB Stage1.5, which loads filesystem support and proceeds to load GRUB Stage2. GRUB Stage2 performs the actual boot loader functions and displays a graphical boot loader screen similar to that shown in Figure 9-2.

Much like LILO, the configuration of GRUB is accomplished by editing a configuration file; however, GRUB does not need to be reinstalled after editing this configuration file as LILO does because the configuration file (**/boot/grub/grub.conf**) is read directly by the Stage2 boot loader. An example /boot/grub/grub.conf file is shown next:

```
[root@server1 root]# cat /boot/grub/grub.conf
# grub.conf generated by anaconda
#
# Note that you do not have to rerun grub after making changes to this # file
```

```
# NOTICE:   You have a /boot partition.  This means that
#           all kernel and initrd paths are relative to /, eg.
#           root (hd0,0)
#           kernel /vmlinuz-version ro root=/dev/hda1
#           initrd /initrd-version.img
#boot=/dev/hda
default=0
timeout=10
splashimage=(hd0,0)/boot/grub/splash.xpm.gz
password --md5 $1$•~A_tÕ.R$W.uLzTHpvhCchfSOiTTSOO
title Fedora Core (2.6.5-1.358)
        root (hd0,0)
        kernel /boot/vmlinuz-2.6.5-1.358 ro root=/dev/hda1 rhgb quiet
        initrd /boot/initrd-2.6.5-1.358.img
[root@server1 root]# _
```

> **NOTE**
>
> Alternatively, you can view and edit the /etc/grub.conf file, which is simply a symbolic link to /boot/grub/grub.conf.

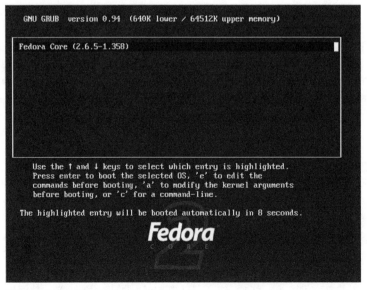

FIGURE 9-2 *GRUB boot loader screen*

To understand the entries in the /boot/grub/grub.conf file, you must first understand how GRUB refers to partitions on hard disks. Hard disks and partitions on those hard disks are identified by numbers in the following format: (hd<drive#>,<partition#>). Thus, the (hd0,0) notation in the preceding /boot/grub/grub.conf file refers to the first hard disk on the system (regardless of whether it is SCSI or IDE) and the first partition on that hard disk, respectively. Similarly, the second partition on the first hard disk is referred to as (hd0,1), and the fourth partition on the third hard disk is referred to as (hd2,3).

In addition, GRUB calls the partition that contains Stage2 of the GRUB boot loader the **GRUB root partition**. Normally, the GRUB root partition is the filesystem that contains the /boot directory and should not be confused with the Linux root filesystem. If your system has a separate partition mounted to /boot, GRUB refers to the file /boot/grub/grub.conf as /grub/grub.conf. If your system does not have a separate filesystem for the /boot directory, this file is simply referred to as /boot/grub/grub.conf in GRUB.

Thus, the example /boot/grub/grub.conf file shown earlier displays a graphical boot screen (splashimage=(hd0,0)/boot/grub/splash.xpm.gz) and boots the default operating system kernel on the first hard drive (default=0) in 10 seconds (timeout=10). The default operating system kernel is located on the GRUB root filesystem (root (hd0,0)) and is called /boot/vmlinuz-2.6.5-1.358.

The kernel then mounts the root filesystem on /dev/hda1 initially as read-only to avoid problems with the fsck command and uses a ramdisk image to load modules needed at boot time (initrd /boot/initrd-2.6.5-1.358.img).

NOTE

To pass information to the kernel from the GRUB boot loader, simply add the appropriate keywords to the kernel line in /boot/grub/grub.conf. Alternatively, you can also add a line that uses the append= keyword using the same syntax as the append= keyword in /etc/lilo.conf.

Normally, GRUB allows users to manipulate the boot loader during system startup; to prevent this, you can optionally password protect GRUB modifications during boot time. The line password --md5 1•~A_tÕ.R$W.uLzTHpvhCchfS0iTTS00 in the preceding /boot/grub/grub.conf file prompts a user for a password if the user wants to modify the boot loader during system startup. Furthermore, the password specified in this file is encrypted to prevent users from viewing the password when viewing the file.

> **NOTE**
>
> To create an encrypted password for use in /boot/grub/grub.conf, you can use the
> **grub-md5-crypt command**.

If passwords are enabled, you need to press p at the first graphical GRUB screen similar to
Figure 9-2 if you want to manipulate the boot process. After the password is accepted, you can
press e to edit the configuration used from /boot/grub/grub.conf, as shown in Figure 9-3, or
press c to obtain a grub> prompt.

If you choose to open a grub> prompt, you can enter a variety of commands to view system
hardware configuration, find and display files, alter the configuration of GRUB, or boot an
operating system kernel. To view all available commands when at the grub> prompt, simply
type help at this screen, as shown in Figure 9-4.

The grub prompt can also be used to boot the system in the same manner as seen in
/boot/grub/grub.conf; to boot the Linux operating system used in the previous examples, you
would simply type the kernel and initrd lines from /boot/grub/grub.conf at the grub> prompt
(pressing Enter after each line), followed by the word "boot," and press Enter again to continue the boot process.

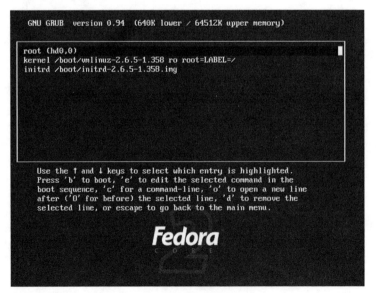

FIGURE 9-3 *Configuring the GRUB boot loader screen*

```
   GNU GRUB  version 0.94  (640K lower / 64512K upper memory)

[ Minimal BASH-like line editing is supported.  For the first word, TAB
  lists possible command completions.  Anywhere else TAB lists the possible
  completions of a device/filename.  ESC at any time exits.]

grub> help
background RRGGBB                          blocklist FILE
boot                                       cat FILE
chainloader [--force] FILE                 clear
color NORMAL [HIGHLIGHT]                    configfile FILE
displayapm                                 displaymem
find FILENAME                              foreground RRGGBB
geometry DRIVE [CYLINDER HEAD SECTOR [     halt [--no-apm]
help [--all] [PATTERN ...]                 hide PARTITION
initrd FILE [ARG ...]                      kernel [--no-mem-option] [--type=TYPE]
makeactive                                 map TO_DRIVE FROM_DRIVE
md5crypt                                   module FILE [ARG ...]
modulenounzip FILE [ARG ...]               pager [FLAG]
partnew PART TYPE START LEN                parttype PART TYPE
reboot                                     root [DEVICE [HDBIAS]]
rootnoverify [DEVICE [HDBIAS]]             serial [--unit=UNIT] [--port=PORT] [--
setkey [TO_KEY FROM_KEY]                   setup [--prefix=DIR] [--stage2=STAGE2_
splashimage FILE                                  [--dumb] [--no-echo] [--no-ed
terminfo [--name=NAME --cursor-address               MODE
unhide PARTITION                           uppermem KBYTES
vbeprobe [MODE]

grub>
```

FIGURE 9-4 *Viewing help at the GRUB boot loader screen prompt*

Recall that you are required to choose the GRUB boot loader during installation. Regardless, you can switch from GRUB to LILO and vice versa at any time after installation. To install LILO, you must type lilo at the command prompt and the LILO boot loader is installed based on the configuration of the /etc/lilo.conf file, as shown in the previous section. However, to install the GRUB boot loader, you must use the **grub-install command**. To install GRUB Stage1 on the Master Boot Record of the first IDE hard disk, you can type the following command:

```
[root@server1 root]# grub-install /dev/hda
Installation finished. No error reported.
This is the contents of the device map /boot/grub/device.map.
Check if this is correct or not. If any of the lines is incorrect,
fix it and re-run the script `grub-install'.

# this device map was generated by anaconda
(fd0)     /dev/fd0
(hd0)     /dev/hda
[root@server1 root]# _
```

Alternatively, to install GRUB Stage1 at the beginning of the first primary partition of the same hard disk, you can type the following at the command prompt:

```
[root@server1 root]# grub-install /dev/hda1
Installation finished. No error reported.
This is the contents of the device map /boot/grub/device.map.
Check if this is correct or not. If any of the lines is incorrect,
fix it and re-run the script `grub-install'.

# this device map was generated by anaconda
(fd0)     /dev/fd0
(hd0)     /dev/hda
[root@server1 root]# _
```

Dual Booting Linux

Linux servers are usually dedicated to their role all day long. However, those who use Linux as a workstation might want to use the Linux operating system at certain times only; at other times, the same computer could be used with a different operating system. Because you can use only one operating system at a time, a mechanism must exist that allows you to choose which operating system to load at boot time; this mechanism is typically handled by the boot loader.

Using LILO or GRUB to Dual Boot Other Operating Systems

If you are using a Linux boot loader to **dual boot** another operating system in addition to Linux, it is easiest if Linux is installed after the other operating system has been installed; this allows the installation program to detect the other operating system on the disk and place the appropriate entries in the boot loader configuration file.

Take, for example, an installation of Linux that creates Linux partitions on the free space of a hard disk containing a partition (/dev/hda1) with the Windows operating system installed on it, as shown in Figure 9-5.

If the Windows partition is preserved during partitioning, the boot loader configuration options include a section that allows you to choose to dual boot Linux with the Windows operating system using GRUB, as shown in Figure 9-6.

NOTE

Although GRUB is installed during a Red Hat Fedora installation, the installation program creates an /etc/lilo.conf.anaconda file. This file can be renamed /etc/lilo.conf so you can choose to use LILO afterward without having to create an /etc/lilo.conf file from scratch.

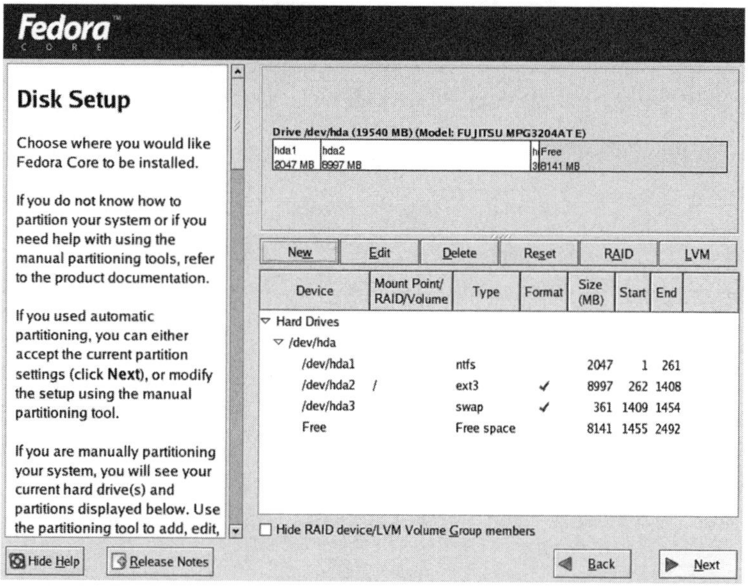

FIGURE 9-5 *Partitioning for a dual boot system*

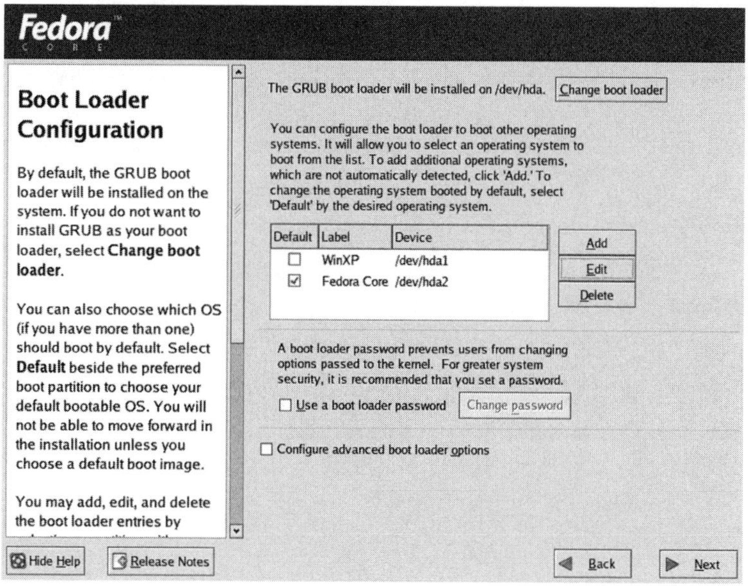

FIGURE 9-6 *Configuring GRUB for a dual boot system*

The /etc/lilo.conf.anaconda file generated by the installation program depicted in Figures 9-5 and 9-6 is shown next:

```
[root@server1 root]# cat /etc/lilo.conf.anaconda
prompt
timeout=50
default=linux
boot=/dev/hda
map=/boot/map
install=/boot/boot.b
lba32

image=/boot/vmlinuz-2.6.5-1.358
        label=linux
        initrd=/boot/initrd-2.6.5-1.358.img
        read-only
        append="rhgb quiet root=/dev/hda2"

other=/dev/hda1
        optional
        label=WinXP
[root@server1 root]# _
```

Because LILO cannot boot a Windows kernel directly, there is an `other=` keyword in the preceding /etc/lilo.conf that loads the boot loader that is present on the /dev/hda1 partition. The `optional` keyword allows this operating system to be ignored if it becomes unavailable and the `label` keyword identifies this operating system using a name that will be displayed if you press the Tab key at the `LILO` boot: prompt.

The /boot/grub/grub.conf file created by the installation program seen in Figures 9-5 and 9-6 is shown in the following output:

```
[root@server1 root]# cat /boot/grub/grub.conf
# grub.conf generated by anaconda
#
# Note that you do not have to rerun grub after making changes to this # file
# NOTICE:  You have a /boot partition.  This means that
#          all kernel and initrd paths are relative to /, eg.
#          root (hd0,0)
#          kernel /vmlinuz-version ro root=/dev/hda1
#          initrd /initrd-version.img
#boot=/dev/hda
default=0
timeout=10
splashimage=(hd0,0)/boot/grub/splash.xpm.gz
```

```
title Fedora Core (2.6.5-1.358)
       root (hd0,1)
       kernel /boot/vmlinuz-2.6.5-1.358 ro root=/dev/hda2 rhgb quiet
       initrd /boot/initrd-2.6.5-1.358.img
title WinXP
       rootnoverify (hd0,0)
       chainloader +1
[root@server1 root]# _
```

The `title` keyword in the preceding output identifies the new operating system and is displayed at the GRUB graphical screen during boot time. The `rootnoverify (hd0,0)` line indicates that the operating system lies on the first partition on the first hard disk and that it should not be automatically mounted by GRUB (because it might contain a foreign filesystem). Because GRUB cannot load a Windows kernel directly, GRUB must load the Windows boot loader from the Windows partition; this boot loader typically starts on the first block of the Windows partition. The `chainloader +1` line allows GRUB to load another boot loader starting from the first block of the partition (hd0,0).

Using FIPS

It is common to use all the space on a hard disk drive in a workstation computer for a Windows partition when installing Windows; however, this leaves no free space to install Linux. One solution to this problem is to repartition the hard disk with a smaller Windows partition and reinstall the Windows operating system on it. Linux can then be installed on the free space outside the Windows partition. Another solution is to resize the Windows partition using a utility such as **First nondestructive Interactive Partition Splitter (FIPS)**; this preserves the Windows operating system on the Windows partition, yet allows for free space to install Linux.

Prior to using FIPS, some guidelines regarding its use should be met. These limitations are:

◆ Version 2.0 of FIPS supports the FAT16 and FAT32 filesystems only. The NTFS file system is not supported by FIPS.

◆ FIPS works only with primary Windows partitions and does not resize logical drives within extended partitions.

◆ FIPS works by splitting the Windows partition into two primary partitions. The first contains the original Windows filesystem, and the second can be used for Linux or safely removed and replaced with Linux partitions during a Linux installation. Recall that there can be only four primary partitions per hard disk; ensure that there is a free primary partition for FIPS to use.

◆ There must be sufficient free space within the existing Windows partition to allow for the installation of Linux after the partition has been resized.

FIPS can be downloaded from the Internet at *http://www.igd.fhg.de/~aschaefe/fips/*. You should read the FIPS.doc file that comes with the program and meet the requirements outlined inside. A sample list of steps to follow to resize a Windows partition using FIPS is:

1. Remove any old, unwanted, unused, or unnecessary files from the Windows partition to be resized to free up the greatest amount of space for Linux.

2. Defragment the Windows partition to be resized using a defragmentation program such as DEFRAG.

3. Ensure there is sufficient free space on the Windows partition to install Linux.

4. Run programs to check the integrity of the hard disk drive and identify any bad sectors with a program such as CHKDSK or SCANDISK. Back up all data on the Windows partition in case of failure during the FIPS process.

5. Obtain or create a DOS or Windows 9x boot disk. Copy the files FIPS.exe, ERRORS.txt, and RESTORRB.exe to the boot disk.

6. Boot the system using the boot disk created in the previous step. At the DOS prompt, type "fips" to invoke the FIPS program.

7. After it has determined what free space there is, FIPS displays the suggested partition split. Adjust the partition division to the desired split of hard disk drive space. After you indicate that FIPS can split the partition, it offers to create a back-up copy of the MBR on the hard disk drive with an extension of .000. You can restore this back-up copy of the MBR using the RESTORRB.exe in the future.

8. FIPS resizes the original Windows partition to a smaller size and creates a new partition from free space previously on the original Windows partition.

9. Run SCANDISK on the original Windows partition to ensure there are no errors.

10. Run the Linux installation program; when prompted to partition, you can safely remove the second partition created by FIPS and replace it with Linux partitions.

Provided the FIPS procedure completed successfully, there is only one difference that might be present while using the Windows operating system: Drive letters assigned by the Windows operating system to drives such as CD-ROMs can be changed because there is now a different partition structure on the hard disk drive.

Using a Windows Boot Loader to Dual Boot Linux

You can choose to use a Windows boot loader to load the Linux operating system; simply specify the location of GRUB or LILO in the Windows boot loader configuration. Similar to LILO and GRUB, the **NTLOADER** boot loader that is available with Windows NT, Windows 2000, Windows XP, and Windows Server 2003 can be used to display a screen at boot time that prompts the user to choose an operating system to boot. Thus, if the operating system that is dual booted with Linux is Windows NT, Windows 2000, Windows XP, or Windows Server 2003, you can use the Windows NTLOADER boot loader to load LILO or GRUB.

You must ensure that Windows NT, Windows 2000, Windows XP, or Windows Server 2003 is installed on the system first and located on the first primary active partition of the system; the NTLOADER boot loader is placed on the MBR of the hard disk by default. Next, you can install Linux and specify that GRUB is installed on the first sector of the partition rather than on the MBR, as shown in Figure 9-7; otherwise, GRUB overwrites the NTLOADER on the MBR of the hard disk.

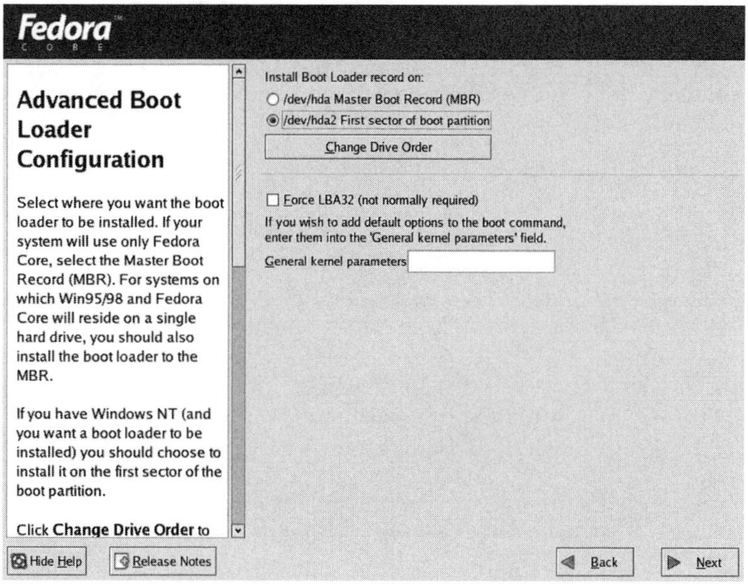

FIGURE 9-7 *Configuring GRUB to reside on a Linux partition*

After Linux has been successfully installed, boot your computer again using the first Red Hat Fedora CD-ROM. At the welcome screen, type `linux rescue` at the boot: prompt and press Enter. Following this, click OK at the Choose a Language and Keyboard Type screens, choose No at the Setup Networking screen, and choose Continue at the Rescue screen. When prompted that the root filesystem of the Linux installation on the hard disk has been mounted to /mnt/sysimage, click OK and you receive a command prompt.

Next, you create a directory to mount a floppy disk (`mkdir /mnt/floppy`), place a floppy disk formatted with the FAT filesystem in your floppy drive, and mount your floppy disk (`mount -t vfat /dev/fd0 /mnt/floppy`).

You can then create a bootable image file of GRUB. Suppose that GRUB was installed to the first sector of the / partition /dev/hda2; to create an image of the first sector of /dev/hda2 called linboot.bin on the floppy device, you can execute the following command at the command prompt:

```
[root@server1 root]# cd /mnt/floppy
[root@server1 floppy]# dd if=/dev/hda2 bs=512 count=1 of=linboot.bin
1+0 records in
1+0 records out
[root@server1 floppy]# cd
[root@server1 root]# umount /mnt/floppy
[root@server1 root]# _
```

After the image has been successfully created, you can reboot your computer by typing exit at the command prompt and boot into the Windows operating system. Copy the linboot.bin file to C:\, and configure the NTLOADER configuration file (C:\boot.ini) to include a section that can be used to boot it. A sample **boot.ini** file is shown next:

```
[boot loader]
timeout=30
default=multi(0)disk(0)rdisk(0)partition(1)\WINDOWS
[operating systems]
multi(0)disk(0)rdisk(0)partition(1)\WINDOWS="Microsoft Windows XP Professional"
/fastdetect
```

The preceding boot.ini file boots the default Windows operating system labeled "Microsoft Windows XP Professional" from the first partition (partition(1)) on the first hard disk (rdisk(0)) on the first IDE hard disk controller (multi(0)) in 30 seconds (timeout=30).

To have NTLOADER boot the Linux operating system, you must specify the path to the linboot.bin file created earlier and specify a label to be displayed at the NTLOADER boot screen:

```
[boot loader]
timeout=30
default=multi(0)disk(0)rdisk(0)partition(1)\WINDOWS
[operating systems]
multi(0)disk(0)rdisk(0)partition(1)\WINDOWS="Microsoft Windows XP
Professional" /fastdetect
C:\linboot.bin="Red Hat Fedora Core 2"
```

When the system is rebooted, the NTLOADER boot loader loads and presents a list of operating systems from which to choose, including Linux, as portrayed in Figure 9-8.

NOTE

After installation, you can install LILO to the first sector of the partition instead of GRUB if desired and re-create a linboot.bin file that can be used by NTLOADER.

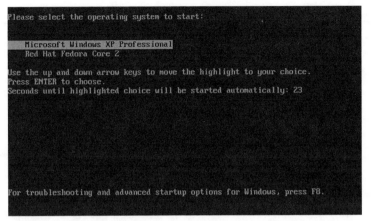

FIGURE 9-8 *NTLOADER operating system choice screen at boot time*

Linux Initialization

Recall that after a boot loader loads the Linux operating system kernel into memory, the kernel resumes control and executes the first daemon process on the system called init. The init daemon then uses its configuration file **/etc/inittab** (init table) to load other daemons on the system that provide system services and ultimately allow users to log in and use the system. Furthermore, the init daemon is responsible for unloading daemons that are loaded in memory when the system is halted or rebooted.

Runlevels

Because several daemons might need to be managed by the init daemon on a typical Linux system, the init daemon categorizes the system into runlevels. A **runlevel** defines the number and type of daemons that are loaded into memory and executed by the kernel on a particular system. At any one time, a Linux system might be in any of seven standard runlevels; these runlevels are defined in Table 9-3.

Table 9-3 Linux runlevels

Runlevel	Common Name	Description
0	Halt	A system that has no daemons active in memory and is ready to be powered off.
1, s, S, single	**Single User Mode**	A system that has only enough daemons to allow one user to log in and perform system maintenance tasks. A user is automatically logged in to the system as the root user when entering Single User Mode.

Table 9-3 Linux runlevels (Continued)

Runlevel	Common Name	Description
2	**Multiuser Mode**	A system that has most daemons started and allows multiple users the ability to log in and use system services. Most common network services other than specialized network services are available in this runlevel as well.
3	**Extended Multiuser Mode**	A system that has the same abilities as Multiuser Mode, yet with all extra networking services started (for example, SNMP, NFS).
4	Not used	Not normally used, but can be customized to suit your needs.
5	Graphical Mode	A system that has the same abilities as Extended Multiuser Mode, yet with a graphical login program called the **GNOME Display Manager (gdm)** started on tty7 that allows for graphical logins.
6	Reboot	A special runlevel used to reboot the system.

NOTE

Because the init daemon is responsible for starting and stopping daemons and, hence, changing runlevels, runlevels are often called **initstates**.

To see the current runlevel of the system and the previous runlevel (if runlevels have been changed since system startup), you can use the **runlevel command,** as shown in the following output:

```
[root@server1 root]# runlevel
N 5
[root@server1 root]# _
```

The preceding runlevel command indicates that the system is in runlevel 5 and that the most recent runlevel prior to entering this runlevel is nonexistent (N).

To change the runlevel on a running system, you simply need to specify the **init command** followed by the new runlevel; to change from runlevel 5 to runlevel 1 to perform system maintenance tasks, you can use the following commands:

```
[root@server1 root]# runlevel
N 5
[root@server1 root]# init 1
INIT: Switching to runlevel: 1
INIT: Sending processes the TERM signal
```

A list of daemons that are being stopped by the init
*daemon while the system enters single user mode.**

```
Telling INIT to go to single user mode.
INIT: Going single user
INIT: Sending processes the TERM signal
INIT Sending processes the KILL signal
sh-2.05b# _
sh-2.05b# runlevel
1 S
sh-2.05b# _
```

NOTE

The **telinit command** is a shortcut to the init command; thus, the command telinit 1 can instead be used to switch to Single User Mode.

When in Single User Mode, the runlevel command displays S (Single User Mode) for the current runlevel and 1 (Single User Mode) for the most recent runlevel; however, when the runlevel is changed back to runlevel 5, as shown in the following output, the runlevel command displays the current and most recent runlevels properly.

```
sh-2.05b# init 5
INIT: Switching to runlevel: 5
INIT: Sending processes the TERM signal
INIT: Sending processes the KILL signal
```

A list of daemons that are being started by the init
*daemon while the system enters runlevel 5.**

```
[root@server1 root]# _
[root@server1 root]# runlevel
S 5
[root@server1 root]# _
```

> **NOTE**
>
> You can also boot to a certain runlevel when the system is at the `LILO boot:` prompt; simply type the name of the Linux image followed by 1, S, s, or `single`.

The /etc/inittab file

When the init daemon needs to change the runlevel of the system by starting or stopping daemons, it consults the /etc/inittab file. This file is also consulted when bringing the system to a certain runlevel at boot time. An example of /etc/inittab is shown next:

```
[root@server1 root]# cat /etc/inittab
#
# inittab       This file describes how the INIT process should set up
#               the system in a certain run-level.
#
# Author:       Miquel van Smoorenburg, <miquels@drinkel.nl.mugnet.org>
#               Modified for RHS Linux by Marc Ewing and Donnie Barnes
#

# Default runlevel. The runlevels used by RHS are:
#   0 - halt (Do NOT set initdefault to this)
#   1 - Single user mode
#   2 - Multiuser, without NFS (The same as 3, if you do not have networking)
#   3 - Full multiuser mode
#   4 - unused
#   5 - X11
#   6 - reboot (Do NOT set initdefault to this)

id:5:initdefault:

# System initialization.
si::sysinit:/etc/rc.d/rc.sysinit

l0:0:wait:/etc/rc.d/rc 0
l1:1:wait:/etc/rc.d/rc 1
l2:2:wait:/etc/rc.d/rc 2
l3:3:wait:/etc/rc.d/rc 3
l4:4:wait:/etc/rc.d/rc 4
l5:5:wait:/etc/rc.d/rc 5
l6:6:wait:/etc/rc.d/rc 6
```

```
# Trap CTRL-ALT-DELETE
ca::ctrlaltdel:/sbin/shutdown -t3 -r now

# When our UPS tells us power has failed, assume we have a few minutes
# of power left.  Schedule a shutdown for 2 minutes from now.
# This does, of course, assume you have power installed and your
# UPS connected and working correctly.
pf::powerfail:/sbin/shutdown -f -h +2 "Power Failure; System Shutting Down"

# If power was restored before the shutdown kicked in, cancel it.
pr:12345:powerokwait:/sbin/shutdown -c "Power Restored; Shutdown Cancelled"

# Run gettys in standard runlevels
1:2345:respawn:/sbin/mingetty tty1
2:2345:respawn:/sbin/mingetty tty2
3:2345:respawn:/sbin/mingetty tty3
4:2345:respawn:/sbin/mingetty tty4
5:2345:respawn:/sbin/mingetty tty5
6:2345:respawn:/sbin/mingetty tty6

# Run xdm in runlevel 5
x:5:respawn:/etc/X11/prefdm -nodaemon
[root@server1 root]# _
```

The format of entries in the /etc/inittab file are as follows:

```
label : runlevel(s) : action : command
```

The `label` is just an identifier that allows the init daemon to examine this file in alphabetical order; the `runlevel` specifies to which runlevel the line in /etc/inittab corresponds; the command tells the init daemon what to execute when entering the runlevel; and the `action` tells the init daemon how to execute the command.

Thus, the line `id:5:initdefault:` in the /etc/inittab file tells the init daemon that runlevel 5 is the default runlevel to boot to when initializing the Linux system at system startup. In addition, the `si::sysinit:/etc/rc.d/rc.sysinit` line tells the init daemon to run the program **/etc/rc.d/rc.sysinit** before entering a runlevel at system initialization. This program initializes the hardware components of the system, sets environment variables such as PATH and HOSTNAME, checks filesystems, and performs system tasks required for daemon loading. The output from the /etc/rc.d/rc.sysinit program is displayed on the terminal screen during system startup as soon as the graphical boot starts; simply click Show Details at the graphical boot screen to see the individual actions.

Because the default runlevel is 5, only the line `l5:5:wait:/etc/rc.d/rc 5` will be executed in the next section of the /etc/inittab file seen earlier. This line executes the /etc/rc.d/rc 5 command and waits for it to finish before proceeding to the rest of the /etc/inittab file. The

/etc/rc.d/rc 5 command executes all files that start with S or K in the /etc/rc.d/rc5.d/ directory. Each file in this directory is a symbolic link to a script that starts a certain daemon, and each of these files is executed in alphabetical order; the S or the K indicates whether to Start or Kill the daemon upon entering this runlevel, respectively. Some sample contents of the /etc/rc.d/rc5.d directory are shown in the following output:

```
[root@server1 root]# ls /etc/rc.d/rc5.d
K01yum              K35cyrus-imapd   K84ospf6d           S26apmd
K05innd             K35dhcpd         K84ospfd            S28autofs
K05saslauthd        K35smb           K84ripd             S40smartd
K10dc_server        K35vncserver     K84ripngd           S44acpid
K10psacct           K36lisa          K85zebra            S54hpoj
K10radiusd          K45arpwatch      K89netplugd         S55cups
K12dc_client        K45named         K90isicom           S55sshd
K12mailman          K46radvd         K92ipvsadm          S56rawdevices
K12mysqld           K50netdump       S00microcode_ctl    S56xinetd
K15gkrellmd         K50snmpd         S01sysstat          S80sendmail
K15httpd            K50snmptrapd     S04readahead_early  S80spamassassin
K15postgresql       K50tux           S05kudzu            S84privoxy
K16rarpd            K50vsftpd        S06cpuspeed         S85gpm
K20bootparamd       K54dovecot       S08ip6tables        S87IIim
K20iscsi            K55routed        S08iptables         S90canna
K20netdump-server   K61ldap          S09isdn             S90crond
K20nfs              K65identd        S10network          S90FreeWnn
K20rstatd           K65kadmin        S12syslog           S90xfs
K20rusersd          K65kprop         S13irqbalance       S95anacron
K20rwalld           K65krb524        S13portmap          S95atd
K20rwhod            K65krb5kdc       S14nfslock          S96readahead
K20tomcat           K70aep1000       S18rpcgssd          S97messagebus
K24irda             K70bcm5820       S19rpcidmapd        S97rhnsd
K25squid            K74ntpd          S19rpcsvcgssd       S99local
K28amd              K74ups           S20random           S99mdmonitor
K34dhcrelay         K74ypserv        S24pcmcia           S99mdmpd
K34yppasswdd        K74ypxfrd        S25bluetooth
K35atalk            K84bgpd          S25netfs
[root@server1 root]# _
```

From the preceding output, you can see that the init daemon will start the cron daemon (S90crond) upon entering this runlevel and kill the ldap daemon (K61ldap) if it exists in memory upon entering this runlevel. In addition, the files in the preceding directory are executed in alphabetical order; the file K65identd is executed before the file K65kadmin.

Recall that runlevel 1 (Single User Mode) contains only enough daemons for a single user to log in and perform system tasks; if a user tells the init daemon to change to this runlevel using the init 1 command, the init daemon finds the appropriate entry in /etc/inittab (l1:1:wait:/etc/rc.d/rc 1) and proceeds to execute every file that starts with S or K in the /etc/rc.d/rc1.d directory. Because few daemons are started in Single User Mode, most files in this directory start with a K:

```
[root@server1 root]# ls /etc/rc.d/rc1.d
K01yum              K20rstatd         K50vsftpd         K84ospfd
K03messagebus       K20rusersd        K50xinetd         K84ripd
K03rhnsd            K20rwalld         K54dovecot        K84ripngd
K05anacron          K20rwhod          K55routed         K85zebra
K05atd              K20tomcat         K56acpid          K86nfslock
K05innd             K24irda           K60crond          K87irqbalance
K05saslauthd        K25squid          K61hpoj           K87portmap
K09privoxy          K25sshd           K61ldap           K88syslog
K10cups             K28amd            K65identd         K89netplugd
K10dc_server        K30sendmail       K65kadmin         K90bluetooth
K10psacct           K30spamassassin   K65kprop          K90isicom
K10radiusd          K34dhcrelay       K65krb524         K90network
K10xfs              K34yppasswdd      K65krb5kdc        K91isdn
K12canna            K35atalk          K68rpcgssd        K92ip6tables
K12dc_client        K35cyrus-imapd    K69rpcidmapd      K92iptables
K12FreeWnn          K35dhcpd          K69rpcsvcgssd     K92ipvsadm
K12mailman          K35smb            K70aep1000        K95kudzu
K12mysqld           K35vncserver      K70bcm5820        K96pcmcia
K15gkrellmd         K36lisa           K72autofs         K99mdmonitor
K15gpm              K40smartd         K74apmd           K99mdmpd
K15httpd            K44rawdevices     K74ntpd           K99microcode_ctl
K15postgresql       K45arpwatch       K74ups            K99readahead
K16rarpd            K45named          K74ypserv         K99readahead_early
K17IIim             K46radvd          K74ypxfrd         S00single
K20bootparamd       K50netdump        K75netfs          S01sysstat
K20iscsi            K50snmpd          K80random         S06cpuspeed
K20netdump-server   K50snmptrapd      K84bgpd
K20nfs              K50tux            K84ospf6d
[root@server1 root]# _
```

Most daemons that are loaded upon system startup are executed from entries in /etc/inittab that run the /etc/rc.d/rc command at system startup to load daemons from files that start with an S in the appropriate /etc/rc.d/rc*.d directory (where * refers to the default runlevel). As with the /etc/rc.d/rc.sysinit program, a message during boot time indicates whether each file in the /etc/rc.d/rc*.d directory has loaded successfully or unsuccessfully. An excerpt from this list is shown next:

```
Starting up APM daemon:                               [  OK  ]
Starting automount: No Mountpoints Defined            [  OK  ]
Starting xinetd:                                      [  OK  ]
Starting sendmail:                                    [  OK  ]
Starting console mouse services:                      [  OK  ]
```

```
Starting crond:                                        [  OK  ]
Starting xfs:                                          [  OK  ]
Starting anacron:                                      [  OK  ]
Starting atd:                                          [  OK  ]
```

However, these messages are hidden by the graphical boot screen by default; to see these messages, you must click Show Details on the graphical boot screen. To view them afterward, recall from Chapter 7, "Advanced Installation," that you can view the contents of the /var/log/boot.log and /var/log/messages log files.

The remainder of the /etc/inittab file loads optional components and allows for login programs to run on terminals. For terminal logins, the **mingetty** program is started on tty1 through tty6 and restarted (respawn) continuously to allow for login after login. In addition, gdm is started only upon entering runlevel 5 from the last entry in /etc/inittab.

After the entries in /etc/inittab have been executed, the **/etc/rc.d/rc.local** file is executed to perform tasks that must occur after system startup. The entire Linux initialization process is summarized in Figure 9-9.

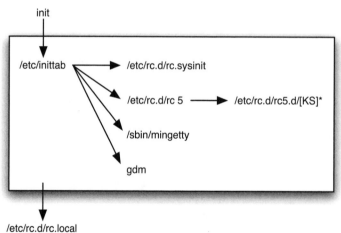

FIGURE 9-9 *The Linux initialization process*

Configuring Daemon Startup

Recall from the preceding section that most daemons are started by the init daemon from symbolic links in the the **/etc/rc.d/rc*.d** directories depending on the runlevel entered. Most of these links point to the appropriate daemon executable file in the **/etc/rc.d/init.d** directory. A partial listing of the /etc/rc.d/rc5.d directory demonstrates this:

```
[root@server1 root]# ls -l /etc/rc.d/rc5.d |head
total 0
```

```
lrwxrwxrwx  1 root root 13 Jun 11 08:46 K01yum -> ../init.d/yum
lrwxrwxrwx  1 root root 14 Jun 11 10:17 K05innd -> ../init.d/innd
lrwxrwxrwx  1 root root 19 Jun 11 08:45 K05saslauthd -> ../init.d/saslauthd
lrwxrwxrwx  1 root root 19 Jun 11 08:46 K10dc_server -> ../init.d/dc_server
lrwxrwxrwx  1 root root 16 Jun 11 08:45 K10psacct -> ../init.d/psacct
lrwxrwxrwx  1 root root 17 Jun 11 10:16 K10radiusd -> ../init.d/radiusd
lrwxrwxrwx  1 root root 19 Jun 11 08:46 K12dc_client -> ../init.d/dc_client
lrwxrwxrwx  1 root root.17 Jun 11 10:15 K12mailman -> ../init.d/mailman
lrwxrwxrwx  1 root root 16 Jun 11 10:18 K12mysqld -> ../init.d/mysqld
[root@server1 root]# _
```

In addition, most daemons accept the arguments start, stop, and restart. Thus, to manipulate daemons after system startup, you can execute them directly from the /etc/rc.d/init.d directory, as shown next with the xinetd daemon:

```
[root@server1 root]# /etc/rc.d/init.d/xinetd restart
Stopping xinetd:                                    [  OK  ]
Starting xinetd:                                    [  OK  ]
[root@server1 root]# _
```

> **NOTE**
>
> The /etc/init.d directory is symbolically linked to the /etc/rc.d/init.d directory; thus, the /etc/init.d/xinetd restart command would perform the same function as the command used in the preceding example.

Because most daemon executable files are centrally stored in the /etc/rc.d/init.d directory, if you want to add a daemon that is automatically started by the init daemon upon entering a certain runlevel at system startup, you can add the executable file for the daemon to this directory and create the appropriate links in each of the /etc/rc.d/rc*.d directories to start or kill the daemon upon entering certain runlevels.

Thus, to configure the init daemon to automatically start an executable daemon file called testdaemon when entering runlevels 2, 3, and 5 only, you can perform the following commands:

```
[root@server1 root]# cp testdaemon /etc/rc.d/init.d
[root@server1 root]# cd /etc/rc.d/init.d
[root@server1 root]# ln -s testdaemon /etc/rc.d/rc2.d/S99testdaemon
[root@server1 root]# ln -s testdaemon /etc/rc.d/rc3.d/S99testdaemon
[root@server1 root]# ln -s testdaemon /etc/rc.d/rc5.d/S99testdaemon
[root@server1 root]# _
```

Similarly, to configure the init daemon to automatically kill testdaemon when entering runlevel 0, 1, and 6, you can execute the following commands:

```
[root@server1 root]# cd /etc/rc.d/init.d
[root@server1 root]# ln -s testdaemon /etc/rc.d/rc0.d/K01testdaemon
[root@server1 root]# ln -s testdaemon /etc/rc.d/rc1.d/K01testdaemon
[root@server1 root]# ln -s testdaemon /etc/rc.d/rc6.d/K01testdaemon
[root@server1 root]# _
```

To see whether the daemon loaded successfully at boot time, simply view the contents of the /var/log/messages file after the system has fully initialized, as shown next:

```
[root@server1 root]# grep testdaemon /var/log/messages
Jun 15 12:44:34 server1 testdaemon: testdaemon startup succeeded
[root@server1 root]# _
```

For ease of administration, Red Hat Fedora places a large number of files that start with K in most /etc/rc.d/rc*.d directories even though the daemons represented by those files are not likely started. This allows a user to rename the file such that it starts with S to start the daemon upon entering that runlevel. Alternatively, you can use the **ntsysv** utility to modify the file entries in the /etc/rc.d/rc*.d directories.

If you type ntsysv --level 5 to modify the daemons that will be started in runlevel 5, the screen depicted in Figure 9-10 is displayed.

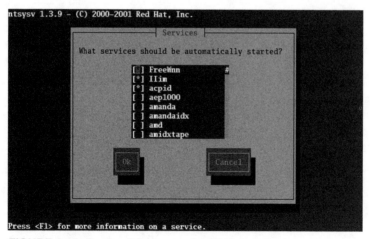

FIGURE 9-10 *Results of the ntsysv --level 5 command*

The X Windows System

Until this section, focus has been placed on performing tasks using a BASH shell command-line interface obtained after logging in to a character terminal. Although the command-line interface is the most common among administrators, graphical user interfaces (GUIs) can be used to simplify some administrative tasks. In addition, Linux users typically use graphical interfaces for running user programs; thus, it is important to possess a good understanding of the components that the Linux GUI comprises, as well as how to start, stop, and configure them.

Linux GUI Components

The Linux graphical user interface (GUI) was designed to function in the same manner regardless of the video hardware on the computer system. As a result, it is composed of many components, which work separately from the video hardware (video adapter card and monitor). These components are illustrated in Figure 9-11.

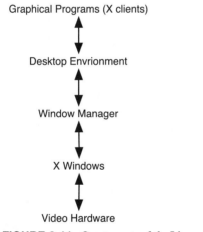

FIGURE 9-11 *Components of the Linux GUI*

A large part of a typical Linux installation comprises all of the components listed in Figure 9-11. A typical installation of Red Hat Fedora Linux usually uses 2–4GB of data on the hard disk for the GUI and related programs.

X Windows

The core component of the GUI in Linux is **X Windows**. X Windows provides the ability to draw graphical images in windows that are displayed on a terminal screen. The programs that tell X Windows how to draw the graphics and display the results are known as **X clients**. X clients need not run on the same computer as X Windows; you can use X Windows on one computer to send graphical images to an X client on an entirely different computer by changing the DISPLAY environment variable discussed in Chapter 8, "Working with the BASH

Shell." Because of this, X Windows is sometimes referred to as the server component of X Windows, or simply the **X server**.

X Windows was jointly developed by Digital Equipment Corporation (DEC) and the Massachusetts Institute of Technology (MIT) in 1984. Then, it was code-named Project Athena and was released in 1985 as X Windows in hopes that a new name would be found to replace the X. Shortly thereafter, X Windows was sought by many UNIX vendors and by 1988, MIT released version 11 release 2 of X Windows (X11R2). Since 1988, X Windows has been maintained by The Open Group, which released version 11 release 6 of X Windows (X11R6) in 1995. Since 2004, X Windows has been maintained as Open Source Software by the **X.org** Foundation.

> **NOTE**
>
> To find out more about X Windows, visit the X.org Foundation on the Internet at *http://www.x.org.*

Until recently, X Windows was governed by a separate license than the GPL, which restricted the usage of X Windows and its source code. As a result, open source developers created an open source version of X Windows in the 1990s. This freely available version of X Windows is used in many Linux distributions and is called **XFree86** because it was originally intended for the Intel x86 platform.

> **NOTE**
>
> To find out more about XFree86, visit The XFree86 Project on the Internet at *http://www.xfree86.org.*
>
> Today, Linux distributions offer either X Windows or the XFree86 implementation of X Windows because they are both Open Source Software. Red Hat Fedora Core 2 uses X Windows instead of XFree86.

Window Managers and Desktop Environments

Although X Windows performs most of the graphical functions in a GUI, there also exists a **Window Manager** that modifies the look and feel of X Windows. Thus, to change the appearance and behavior of X Windows, you can simply change the Window Manager used with X Windows. Optionally, you can use a **desktop environment** in addition to a Window Manager. Desktop environments come with a full set of GUI tools designed to be packaged together, including Web browsers, file managers, and drawing programs. Desktop environments also provide development "toolkits" that allow software to be created more rapidly in much the same way a toolkit allows a carpenter to complete a project faster. As discussed earlier in this book, the two most common desktop environments that are used on Linux are the **K Desktop Environment (KDE)** and the **GNU Object Model Environment (GNOME)**.

KDE is the traditional desktop environment used on Linux systems; it was started by Matthias Ettrich in 1996 and uses the **K Window Manager (kwin)** and the **Qt toolkit** for the C++ programming language. A typical KDE desktop screen is depicted in Figure 9-12.

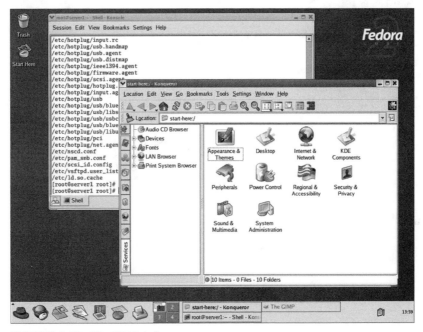

FIGURE 9-12 *The KDE desktop*

> ### NOTE
>
> To learn more about the KDE desktop, visit the Internet at *http://www.kde.org*.

The Qt toolkit was created by a company called Trolltech in Norway and, unfortunately, was not released as Open Source Software until 1998. In the mid-1990s, most open source developers preferred to develop in the C programming language instead of C++. They also did not like that the Qt toolkit source code was not freely modifiable at the time. As a result, the GNOME Desktop Environment was created in 1997. GNOME typically uses the **Metacity Window Manager** and the **GTK+ toolkit** for the C programming language. The GTK+ toolkit was originally developed for the **GNU Image Manipulation Program (GIMP)**, and like the GIMP, is open source. The GNOME desktop is the default desktop in Red Hat Fedora Linux and can be seen in Figure 9-13.

FIGURE 9-13 *The GNOME desktop*

NOTE

To learn more about the GNOME desktop, you can visit the Internet at
http://www.gnome.org.

Although less common than GNOME and KDE, the **Xfce desktop environment** (Figure 9-14) is another desktop environment that is used on many Linux systems. Xfce ships with a small set of easy-to-use tools and consumes less hardware resources than KDE or GNOME. As a result, Xfce is typically run on Linux servers that do not have many hardware resources available.

NOTE

To learn more about the Xfce desktop, you can visit the Internet at
http://www.xfce.org.

Although desktop environments are commonplace for Linux users today, you can choose to use a Window Manager only. Many different Window Managers are available for Linux, such as the **Tab Window Manager** shown in Figure 9-15. Table 9-4 lists some other common Window Managers.

FIGURE 9-14 *The Xfce desktop*

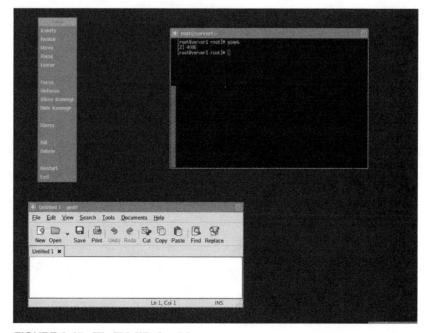

FIGURE 9-15 *The Tab Window Manager*

Table 9-4 Common Window Managers

Window Manager	Description
enlightenment	A highly configurable Window Manager that allows for multiple desktops with different settings. It is commonly used by the GNOME desktop.
fvwm	The feeble virtual Window Manager. It was based on the Tab Window Manager yet intended to use less computer memory and give the desktop a 3-D look.
kwin	The Window Manager used for the KDE desktop.
metacity	The Window Manager used for the GNOME desktop in Red Hat Fedora Core 2. It allows the user to configure custom themes that modify the look and feel of the desktop.
mwm	The motif Window Manager. It is a basic Window Manager that allows the user to configure settings using standard X utilities.
sawfish	A Window Manager commonly used for the GNOME desktop. It allows the user to configure most of its settings via tools or scripts.
twm	The Tab Window Manager. It is one of the oldest and most basic Window Managers.
wmaker	The window maker Window Manager. It provides drag-and-drop mouse movement and imitates the NeXTSTEP operating system interface made by Apple Computer, Inc.

NOTE

Window Managers and desktop environments are not a replacement for a command-line interface. As a result, several dozen terminal programs provide a command-line interface from within a Window Manager or desktop environment. These terminal programs are typically configured using settings from a termcap database (/etc/termcap) or from a terminfo database (/usr/share/terminfo/*). The default terminals in the GNOME and KDE desktops contain all the functionality needed to perform administrative and user tasks; however, other terminals such as the xterm terminal shown earlier in the Tab Window Manager (Figure 9-15) might require special configuration to display text properly on some systems.

Starting and Stopping X Windows

There must exist some method of starting X Windows, the Window Manager, and the desktop environment (if used). Recall from earlier in this chapter that runlevel 5 starts the GNOME Display Manager (gdm) to display the graphical login screen depicted in Figure 9-16.

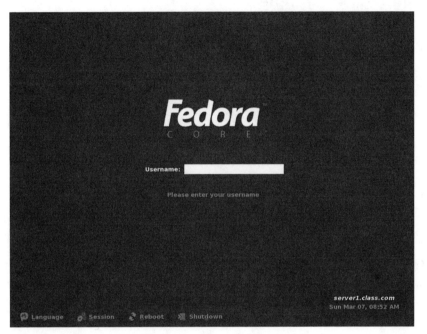

FIGURE 9-16 *The GNOME Display Manager*

This login screen allows the user to choose the desktop environment or Window Manager used from the session menu prior to logging in to the system and starting X Windows.

> ### NOTE
>
> You can configure the appearance and behavior of gdm by navigating to System Settings, Login Screen from the GNOME or KDE desktop, or by editing the /etc/X11/gdm/gdm.conf file.
>
> The gdm is a variant of the **X Display Manager (xdm)**, which displays a basic graphical login for users. In addition, other Linux distributions might use the **KDE Display Manager (kdm)** to display a KDE style graphical login for users.

If, however, you use runlevel 3 instead of runlevel 5, you can type gdm at a character terminal to start the GNOME Display Manager manually, or use the startx command to start

X Windows and the Window Manager or desktop environment specified in the .Xclients file in your home directory. If this file does not exist, the GNOME desktop environment is started by default. If this file exists, it usually points to the .Xclients-default file in your home directory, as shown in the following output:

```
[root@localhost root]# cat .Xclients
#!/bin/bash

# Created by Red Hat Desktop Switcher

if [ -e "$HOME/.Xclients-$HOSTNAME$DISPLAY" ]; then
    exec $HOME/.Xclients-$HOSTNAME$DISPLAY
else
    exec $HOME/.Xclients-default
fi
[root@localhost root]# cat .Xclients-default
# Created by Red Hat Desktop Switcher
exec gnome-session
[root@localhost root]# _
```

Notice from the preceding output that the .Xclients-default file contains a line that executes the gnome-session command that in turn starts the Metacity Window Manager and the GNOME desktop on top of X Windows. Similarly, to start other desktops or Window Managers on X Windows, you can edit the .Xclients-default file and change the word gnome-session to startkde (to start the KDE desktop), startxfce4 (to start the Xfce desktop), or /usr/X11R6/bin/twm (to start the Tab Window Manager).

The settings used in the .Xclients-default file can also be set using the graphical **Desktop Switching Tool** in the GNOME or KDE Desktop Environments; simply navigate to the Red Hat button, Preferences, More Preferences, Desktop Switching Tool. An example of this tool is depicted in Figure 9-17.

FIGURE 9-17 *The Desktop Switching Tool*

Configuring X Windows

X Windows is the component of the GUI that interfaces with the video hardware in the computer. For X Windows to perform its function, it needs information regarding the keyboard, mouse, monitor, and video adapter card. Some X Windows configuration utilities require you to specify the specific hardware information for these components, whereas other utilities automatically detect most if not all of the components. As a result, you should collect all hardware information for these devices before configuring X Windows. For the keyboard and mouse, you should note the type and model. For the video adapter card, X Windows might require the following information:

♦ The video adapter card model

♦ The amount of RAM on the video adapter card

♦ The **chipset** on the video adapter card (which might be the same as the model)

X Windows might also require the following information about the computer monitor that is attached to the video adapter card:

♦ **Maximum resolution** supported

♦ Horizontal sync (hsync) range

♦ Vertical sync (vsync) range

If your system uses the X.org implementation of X Windows, the mouse, keyboard, monitor, and video adapter card information is stored in the **/etc/X11/xorg.conf** file in text format. If your system uses the XFree86 implementation of X Windows, this information is stored in the **/etc/X11/XF86Config** file instead. You can edit these files manually or use a program to edit them indirectly.

> **NOTE**
>
> If you plan to edit X Windows configuration files manually, ensure that you read its associated manual or info page first. For Red Hat Fedora Core 2, ensure that you read the xorg.conf manual page.

Because one mistake in the /etc/X11/xorg.conf or /etc/X11/XF86Config files could prevent the GUI from running, it is good practice to use a configuration program to edit these files.

To configure the mouse in Red Hat Fedora Linux, you can use either the **mouseconfig** or **system-config-mouse** commands in either a GUI or terminal environment. In a terminal environment, these commands display a screen similar to the one depicted in Figure 9-18.

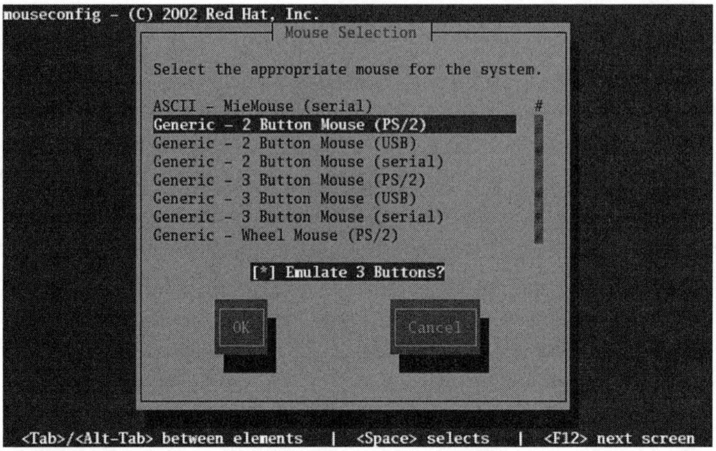

FIGURE 9-18 *Mouse configuration using mouseconfig*

After the type of mouse has been selected from the menu in Figure 9-18, you must restart X Windows for the changes to take effect. To restart X Windows, you simply need to log out of X Windows and restart it by logging in to the gdm or typing startx at the command prompt. Another method used to log out of X Windows is the Ctrl+Alt+Backspace key combination.

Similarly, to configure your keyboard, you can use the **system-config-keyboard** command from either a GUI or terminal environment and restart X Windows. In a GUI environment, this command displays a screen similar to the one depicted in Figure 9-19.

FIGURE 9-19 *Keyboard configuration using system-config-keyboard*

In addition, you can use the **system-config-display** command to configure the video adapter card and monitor information for the X.org implementation of X Windows in Red Hat Fedora Core 2. Regardless of whether this command is run from a GUI or terminal environment, it automatically detects your video and monitor hardware. It then proceeds to load a graphical environment (if one doesn't already exist) and a configuration utility that can be used to set the maximum resolution and color depth, as shown in Figure 9-20.

NOTE

Alternatively, you can navigate to the Red Hat button, System Settings, Display within the GNOME or KDE desktop to start the configuration utility shown in Figure 9-20.

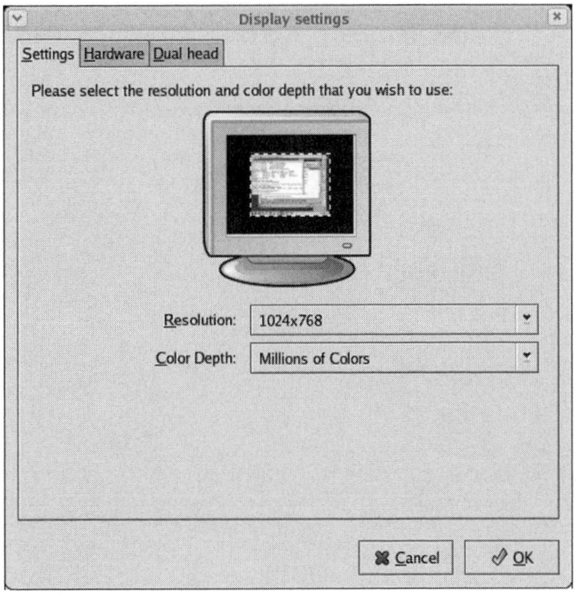

FIGURE 9-20 *Configuring resolution and color depth using system-config-display*

Although your video card and monitor are automatically detected and configured, you can alter these settings by clicking the Hardware tab of the configuration utility, as shown in Figure 9-21. In addition, if you have two video cards and two monitors, you can configure them to work as a single large display by clicking the Dual head tab, as shown in Figure 9-22.

After you click OK in the configuration utility, the previous /etc/X11/xorg.conf file is saved as /etc/X11/xorg.conf.backup and the new settings are written to /etc/X11/xorg.conf. You must then restart X Windows for the changes to take effect.

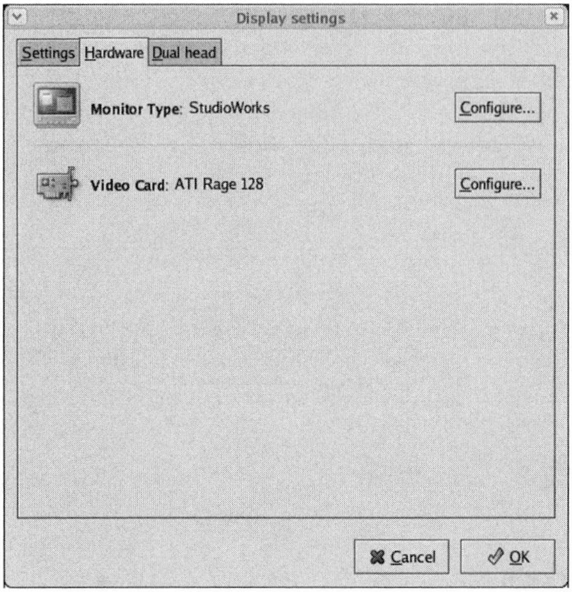

FIGURE 9-21 *Configuring video card and monitor hardware using system-config-display*

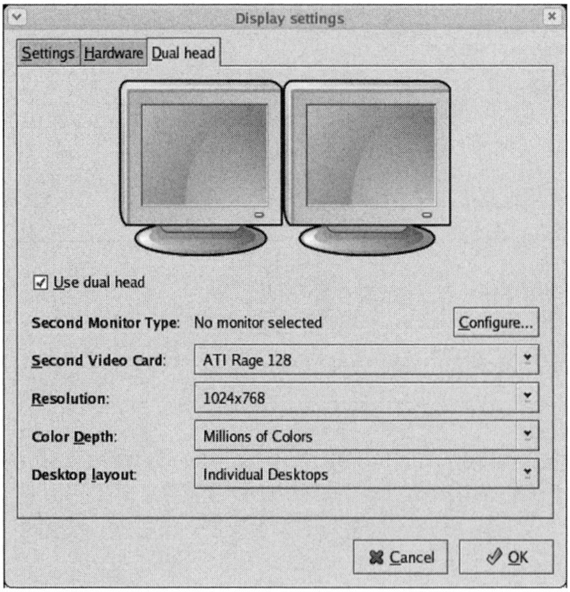

FIGURE 9-22 *Configuring more than one display using system-config-display*

After configuring X Windows, you can fine-tune the vsync and hsync of the video card using the **xvidtune** utility after X Windows has started. Simply open a BASH shell in the GUI and type xvidtune to start the utility, as shown in Figure 9-23.

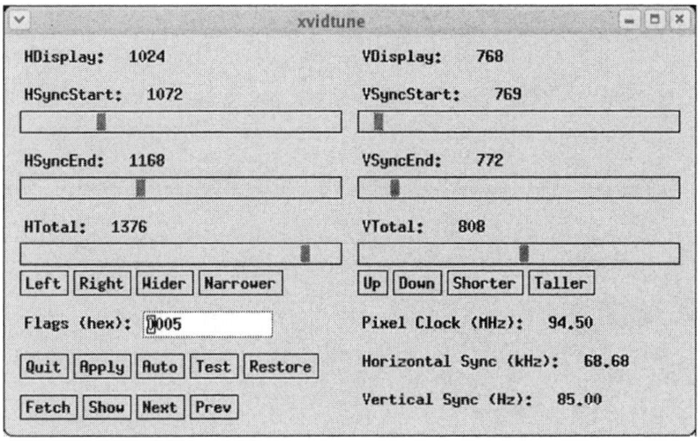

FIGURE 9-23 *The xvidtune utility*

Although most monitors today support a wide range of hsync and vsync values, choosing too high of a value for either might damage the monitor. In addition, choosing an hsync or vsync value that is too low might result in headaches over time because the human eye can see lower refresh rates.

A wide variety of X Windows configuration utilities are available in addition to those discussed in this section. These configuration utilities are listed in Table 9-5 and are available depending on the version of X.org or XFree86 as well as the distribution used.

Table 9-5 Common X Windows configuration utilities

Command	Description
Xorg -configure	When run by the root user, hardware information is automatically detected and written to an X.org configuration file called /root/xorg.conf.new. You must copy this file to the /etc/X11 directory and rename it to xorg.conf for it to be used.
XFree86 -configure	When run by the root user, hardware information is automatically detected and written to an XFree86 configuration file called /root/XF86Config.new. You must copy this file to the /etc/X11 directory and rename it to XF86Config for it to be used.
XF86Setup	A text-based XFree86 configuration utility included with older versions of XFree86.

Table 9-5 Common X Windows configuration utilities (Continued)

Command	Description
xf86config	A text-based XFree86 configuration utility included with XFree86 version 4.
xorgconfig	A text-based X.org configuration utility.
xf86cfg	A graphical XFree86 configuration utility included with XFree86 version 4.
xorgcfg	A graphical X.org configuration utility.

Chapter Summary

◆ Boot loaders are typically loaded by the system BIOS from the MBR or the first sector of the active partition of a hard disk.

◆ The boot loader is responsible for loading the Linux kernel.

◆ The LILO boot loader uses the /etc/lilo.conf configuration file, whereas the GRUB boot loader uses the /boot/grub/grub.conf configuration file.

◆ You can use the LILO or GRUB boot loader to dual boot Linux and the Windows operating system. Alternatively, the Windows NTLOADER boot loader can be used to do the same.

◆ The FIPS utility can be used to split a FAT or FAT32 partition to create enough space to install Linux.

◆ Seven standard runlevels are used to categorize a Linux system based on the number and type of daemons loaded in memory.

◆ The init daemon is responsible for loading and unloading daemons using its configuration file /etc/inittab.

◆ Daemons are typically stored in the /etc/rc.d/init.d directory and loaded at system startup from entries in the /etc/rc.d/rc*.d directories.

◆ The Linux GUI has several interchangeable components, including the X server, X clients, Window Manager, and optional desktop environment.

◆ X Windows is the core component of the Linux GUI that draws graphics to the terminal screen. It comes in one of two open source implementations: X.org and XFree86.

◆ You can start the Linux GUI from runlevel 3 by typing startx at a command prompt, or from runlevel 5 by using the gdm.

◆ Configuring X Windows requires a thorough knowledge of the video hardware used by the computer. The system-config-mouse, mouseconfig, system-config-keyboard, system-config-display, and xvidtune utilities can be used to configure the hardware settings used by X Windows.

Key Terms

/boot — The directory that contains the kernel and boot-related files.

/boot/grub/grub.conf — The GRUB configuration file.

/etc/inittab — The configuration file for the init daemon.

/etc/lilo.conf — The LILO configuration file.

/etc/rc.d/init.d — The directory in which most daemons are located.

/etc/rc.d/rc*.d — The directories used to start and kill daemons in each runlevel.

/etc/rc.d/rc.local — The final script executed during system startup.

/etc/rc.d/rc.sysinit — The first script executed during system startup.

/etc/X11/XF86Config — The configuration file used by the XFree86 implementation of X Windows.

/etc/X11/xorg.conf — The configuration file used by the X.org implementation of X Windows.

active partition — The partition searched for an operating system after the MBR.

boot loader — A program used to load an operating system.

boot.ini — The file used to configure NTLOADER.

chipset — The common set of computer chips on a peripheral component such as a video adapter card.

daemon — A Linux system process that provides a certain service.

desktop environment — The software that works with a Window Manager to provide a standard GUI environment that uses standard programs and development tools.

Desktop Switching Tool — A graphical tool that allows Red Hat Linux users to set the default desktop environment or Window Manager.

dual boot — A configuration in which two or more operating systems exist on the hard disk of a computer; a boot loader allows the user to choose which operating system to load at boot time.

ELILO — A boot loader used with computers that support Intel Extensible Firmware Interface (EFI) technology.

Extended Multiuser Mode — Also called runlevel 3; the mode that provides most daemons and a full set of networking daemons.

First nondestructive Interactive Partition Splitter (FIPS) — A program used to create a new partition out of the free space on an existing FAT16 or FAT32 partition.

GNOME Display Manager (gdm) — A graphical login program that provides a graphical login screen.

GNU Image Manipulation Program (GIMP) — An open source graphics manipulation program that uses the GTK+ toolkit.

GNU Object Model Environment (GNOME) — The default desktop environment in Red Hat Fedora Linux; it was created in 1997.

Grand Unified Bootloader (GRUB) — A common boot loader used on Linux systems.

grub-install command — The command used to install the GRUB boot loader.

grub-md5-crypt command — The command used to generate an encrypted password for use in the /etc/grub/grub.conf file.

GRUB root partition — The partition containing the second stage of the GRUB boot loader and the /boot/grub/grub.conf file.

GTK+ toolkit — A development toolkit for C programming; it is used in the GNOME desktop and the GNU Image Manipulation Program (GIMP).

init command — The command used to change the operating system from one runlevel to another.

initialize (init) daemon — The first process started by the Linux kernel; it is responsible for starting and stopping other daemons.

initstate — *See also* Runlevel.

K Desktop Environment (KDE) — A desktop environment created by Matthias Ettrich in 1996.

KDE Display Manager (kdm) — A graphical login screen for users that resembles the KDE desktop.

K Window Manager (kwin) — The Window Manager that works under the KDE Desktop Environment.

lilo command — The command used to reinstall the LILO boot loader based on the configuration information in /etc/lilo.conf.

Linux Loader (LILO) — A common boot loader used on Linux systems.

Master Boot Record (MBR) — A small area normally located on the first sector of the first hard disk drive used to define partitions and a boot loader.

maximum resolution — The best clarity of an image displayed to the screen; it is determined by the number of pixels making up the image (for example, 640×480 pixels).

Metacity Window Manager — The default Window Manager for the GNOME Desktop Environment in Red Hat Fedora Core 2.

mingetty — A program used to display a login prompt on a character-based terminal.

mouseconfig — A command used to configure a mouse for use by X Windows.

Multiuser Mode — Also called runlevel 2; the mode that provides most daemons and a partial set of networking daemons.

NTLOADER — The boot loader used to boot Windows NT, Windows 2000, and Windows XP operating system kernels.

ntsysv — A utility that can be used to alter the daemons that are started in each runlevel.

Power On Self Test (POST) — An initial series of tests run when a computer is powered on to ensure that hardware components are functional.

Qt toolkit — The software toolkit used with the K Desktop Environment.

runlevel — A term that defines a certain type and number of daemons on a Linux system.

runlevel command — The command used to display the current and most recent (previous) runlevel.

Single User Mode — Also called runlevel 1; the mode that provides a single terminal and a limited set of services.

system-config-display — A command used to configure a video adapter card and monitor for use by X Windows.

system-config-keyboard — A command used to configure a keyboard for use by X Windows.

system-config-mouse — *See also* Mouseconfig.

Tab Window Manager (twm) — One of the oldest Window Managers used on Linux systems.

telinit command — An alias to the init command.

vmlinuz-<kernel version> — The Linux kernel file.

Window Manager — The GUI component that is responsible for determining the appearance of the windows drawn on the screen by X Windows.

X client — The component of X Windows that requests graphics to be drawn from the X server and displays them on the terminal screen.

X Display Manager (xdm) —A graphical login screen.

Xfce desktop environment — A desktop environment that is commonly used by Linux systems.

XFree86 — A common implementation of X Windows used in Linux distributions.

X.org — A common implementation of X Windows used in Linux distributions.

X server — The component of X Windows that draws graphics to windows on the terminal screen.

xvidtune — A program used to fine-tune the vsync and hsync video card settings for use in X Windows.

X Windows — The component of the Linux GUI that displays graphics to windows on the terminal screen.

Review Questions

1. Which of the following happens first during computer bootup?
   a. The Linux kernel is loaded
   b. BIOS performs the POST
   c. BIOS checks its configuration in the CMOS chip on the mainboard for boot devices
   d. Computer checks the master boot record

2. What is the last stage in the boot process when using the GRand Unified Boot loader (GRUB)?
   a. 1
   b. 1.5
   c. 2
   d. 2.5

3. What is the name of the first daemon process executed on the system after a boot loader loads the Linux operating system kernel into memory?
   a. shell
   b. proc
   c. main
   d. init

4. You can use X Windows on one computer to send graphical images to an X-client on an entirely different computer by changing the _____ environment variable.
   a. DISPLAY
   b. HOST
   c. WINDOW
   d. XWINDOW

5. What is the Window Manager used for the GNOME desktop in Red Hat Fedora Core 2?

   a. sawfish

   b. kwin

   c. metacity

   d. mwm

6. True or false? The Linux boot loader is typically located on the first sector of an active Linux partition.

7. True or false? If you are using a Linux boot loader to dual boot another operating system in addition to Linux, it is easiest if Linux is installed after the other operating system has been installed.

8. True or false? Most daemons that are loaded upon system startup are executed from entries in /etc/inittab.

9. True or false? A typical installation of Red Hat Fedora Linux usually uses 1–2GB of data on the hard disk for the GUI and related programs.

10. True or false? When configuring monitor refresh rates, choosing an hsync or vsync value that is too high might result in headaches over time.

11. To uninstall LILO from an active partition or the MBR, you can use the lilo - _____ command.

12. The _____ boot loader that is available with Windows NT, Windows 2000, Windows XP, and Windows Server 2003 can be used to display a screen at boot time that prompts the user to choose an operating system to boot.

13. A(n) _____ defines the number and type of daemons that are loaded into memory and executed by the kernel on a particular system.

14. The _____ Manager modifies the look and feel of X Windows.

15. To configure the mouse in Red Hat Fedora Linux, you can use either the _____ or system-config-mouse commands in either a GUI or terminal environment.

Chapter 10

Managing Linux Processes

After completing this chapter, you will be able to:

◆ Categorize the different types of processes on a Linux system

◆ View processes using standard Linux utilities

◆ Illustrate the difference between common kill signals

◆ Describe how binary programs and shell scripts are executed

◆ Create and manipulate background processes

◆ Use standard Linux utilities to modify the priority of a process

◆ Schedule commands to execute in the future using the at daemon

◆ Schedule commands to execute repetitively using the cron daemon

A typical Linux system can run thousands of processes simultaneously, including those that you have explored in previous chapters. In this chapter, you focus on viewing and managing processes. In the first part of the chapter, you examine the different types of processes on a Linux system and how to view them and terminate them. You then discover how processes are executed on a system, run in the background, and prioritized. Finally, you are introduced to the various methods used to schedule commands to execute in the future.

Linux Processes

Throughout previous chapters of this book as well as in the workplace, the terms "program" and "process" have been and will be used interchangeably; however, there is a definite, yet fine, difference between these two terms. A **program** is an executable file on the hard disk that can be run when you execute it. A **process** refers to a program that is running in memory and on the CPU; in other words, a process is a program in action.

If you start a process while logged in to a terminal, that process runs in that terminal and is labeled a **user process**. Examples of user processes include ls, grep, find, and most other commands that you have executed throughout this book. Recall that a system process that is not associated with a terminal is called a **daemon process**; these processes are typically started on system startup, but you can also start them manually. Most daemon processes provide system services, such as printing, scheduling, and system maintenance, as well as network server services, such as Web servers, database servers, file servers, and print servers.

Every process has a unique **process ID (PID)** that allows the kernel to identify it uniquely. In addition, each process can start an unlimited number of other processes called **child processes**. Conversely, each process must have been started by an existing process called a **parent process**. As a result, each process has a **parent process ID (PPID)**, which identifies the process that started it. An example of the relationship between parent and child processes is depicted in Figure 10-1.

NOTE

PIDs are not necessarily given to new processes in sequential order; each PID is generated from free entries in a process table used by the Linux kernel.

Remember that although each process can have an unlimited number of child processes, it can only have one parent process.

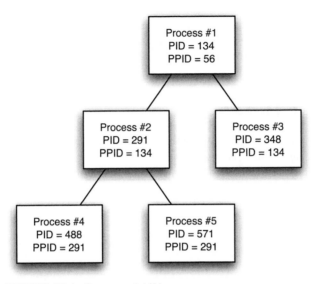

FIGURE 10-1 *Parent and child processes*

Recall that the first process started by the Linux kernel is the init daemon, which has a PID of 1 and a PPID of 0 referring to the kernel itself. The init daemon then starts most other daemons, including those that allow for user logins. After you log in to the system, the login program starts a BASH shell. The BASH shell then interprets user commands and starts all user processes. Thus, each process on the Linux system can be traced back to the init daemon by examining the series of PPIDs, as shown in Figure 10-2.

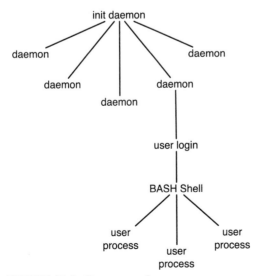

FIGURE 10-2 *Process genealogy*

NOTE

The `init` daemon is often referred to as the "grandfather of all user processes."

Viewing Processes

Although several Linux utilities can view processes, the most versatile and common is the **ps command**. Without arguments, the ps command simply displays a list of processes that are running in the current shell. An example of this, while logged in to tty2, is shown in the following output:

```
[root@server1 root]# ps
  PID TTY          TIME CMD
 3232 tty2     00:00:00 bash
 3271 tty2     00:00:00 ps
[root@server1 root]# _
```

The preceding output shows that two processes were running in the terminal tty2 when the ps command executed. The command that started each process (CMD) is listed next to the time it has taken on the CPU (TIME), its PID, and terminal (TTY). In this case, the process took less than one second to run, and so the time elapsed reads nothing. To find out more about these processes, you could instead use the -f, or full, option to the ps command, as shown next:

```
[root@server1 root]# ps -f
UID        PID  PPID  C STIME TTY          TIME CMD
root      3232  2390  0 08:45 tty2     00:00:00 -bash
root      4414  3232  0 08:54 tty2     00:00:00 ps -f
[root@server1 root]# _
```

This listing provides more information about each process. It displays the user who started the process (UID), the PPID, the time it was started (STIME), as well as the CPU utilization (C), which starts at zero and is incremented with each processor cycle that the process runs on the CPU.

The most valuable information provided by the ps -f command is each process's PPID and lineage. The bash process (PID = 3232) displays a shell prompt and interprets user input; it started the ps process (PID = 4414) because the ps process had a PPID of 3232.

Because daemon processes are not associated with a terminal, they are not displayed by the ps -f command. To display an entire list of processes across all terminals and including daemons, you can add the -e option to any ps command, as shown in the following output:

```
[root@server1 root]# ps -ef
UID        PID  PPID  C STIME TTY          TIME CMD
root         1     0  0 14:26 ?        00:00:05 init [5]
root         2     1  0 14:26 ?        00:00:00 [ksoftirqd/0]
```

```
root          3      1   0 14:26 ?        00:00:00 [events/0]
root          4      3   0 14:26 ?        00:00:00 [kblockd/0]
root          6      3   0 14:26 ?        00:00:00 [khelper]
root          5      1   0 14:26 ?        00:00:00 [khubd]
root          7      3   0 14:26 ?        00:00:00 [pdflush]
root          8      3   0 14:26 ?        00:00:00 [pdflush]
root         10      3   0 14:26 ?        00:00:00 [aio/0]
root          9      1   0 14:26 ?        00:00:00 [kswapd0]
root        114      1   0 14:27 ?        00:00:00 [kseriod]
root        153      1   0 14:27 ?        00:00:00 [kjournald]
root        347      1   0 14:27 ?        00:00:00 udevd
root       1681      1   0 14:27 ?        00:00:00 syslogd -m 0
root       1685      1   0 14:27 ?        00:00:00 klogd -x
rpc        1706      1   0 14:27 ?        00:00:00 portmap
rpcuser    1726      1   0 14:27 ?        00:00:00 rpc.statd
root       1754      1   0 14:27 ?        00:00:00 rpc.idmapd
root       1798      1   0 14:27 ?        00:00:00 hcid: processing events
root       1804      1   0 14:27 ?        00:00:00 /usr/sbin/sdpd
root       1811      1   0 14:27 ?        00:00:00 [krfcommd]
root       1870      1   0 14:27 ?        00:00:00 /usr/sbin/smartd
root       1880      1   0 14:27 ?        00:00:00 /usr/sbin/acpid
root       1915      1   0 14:28 ?        00:00:00 cupsd
root       2110      1   0 14:28 ?        00:00:00 /usr/sbin/sshd
root       2125      1   0 14:28 ?        00:00:00 xinetd -stayalive -pidfile
/var/run/xinetd.pid
root       2144      1   0 14:28 ?        00:00:00 sendmail: accepting connections
root       2165      1   0 14:28 ?        00:00:01 /usr/bin/spamd -d -c -a -m5 -H
htt        2220      1   0 14:28 ?        00:00:00 /usr/sbin/htt
htt        2221   2220   0 14:28 ?        00:00:00 htt_server -nodaemon
bin        2232      1   0 14:28 ?        00:00:00 /usr/sbin/cannaserver -syslog -u
root       2245      1   0 14:28 ?        00:00:00 crond
wnn        2257      1   0 14:28 ?        00:00:00 /usr/bin/jserver
xfs        2293      1   0 14:28 ?        00:00:01 xfs -droppriv -daemon
daemon     2312      1   0 14:28 ?        00:00:00 /usr/sbin/atd
dbus       2331      1   0 14:28 ?        00:00:00 dbus-daemon-1 --system
root       2347      1   0 14:28 ?        00:00:00 mdadm --monitor --scan
root       2389      1   0 14:28 tty1     00:00:00 /sbin/mingetty tty1
root       2390      1   0 14:28 ?        00:00:00 login -- root
root       2391      1   0 14:28 tty3     00:00:00 /sbin/mingetty tty3
root       2399      1   0 14:28 tty4     00:00:00 /sbin/mingetty tty4
root       2407      1   0 14:28 tty5     00:00:00 /sbin/mingetty tty5
root       2415      1   0 14:28 tty6     00:00:00 /sbin/mingetty tty6
root       2423      1   0 14:28 ?        00:00:00 /usr/bin/gdm-binary -nodaemon
root       2824   2423   0 14:28 ?        00:00:00 /usr/bin/gdm-binary -nodaemon
```

```
root      2839  2824  4 14:28 ?      00:00:38 /usr/X11R6/bin/X :0 -audit 0 -auth
/var/gdm/:0.Xauth -nolisten tcp vt7
root      2901  2824  0 14:28 ?      00:00:01 gnome-session
root      3193  3192  0 14:29 ?      00:00:00 gnome-pty-helper
root      3194  3192  0 14:29 pts/1 00:00:00 bash
root      3232  2390  0 14:30 tty2  00:00:00 -bash
root      3429  3194  0 14:41 tty2  00:00:00 ps -ef
[root@server1 root]# _
```

As shown in the preceding output, the init daemon (PID=1) starts most other daemons because those daemons have a PPID of 1. In addition, there is a ? in the TTY column for daemons because they do not run on a terminal.

Because the output of the ps -ef command can be several hundred lines long on a Linux server, you usually pipe its output to the less command to send the output to the terminal screen page-by-page, or to the grep command, which can be used to display lines containing only certain information. For example, to display only the BASH shells in the preceding output, you could use the following command:

```
[root@server1 root]# ps -ef | grep bash
root      3194  3192  0 14:29 pts/1  00:00:00 bash
root      3232  2390  0 14:30 tty2   00:00:00 -bash
root      3431  3194  0 14:44 tty2   00:00:00 grep bash
[root@server1 root]# _
```

Notice that the grep bash command is also displayed alongside the BASH shells in the preceding output because it was running in memory at the time the ps command was executed. This might not always be the case because the Linux kernel schedules commands to run based on a variety of different factors.

The -e and -f options are the most common options used with the ps command; however, many other options are available. The -l option to the ps command lists even more information about each process than the -f option. An example of using this option to view the processes in the terminal tty2 is shown in the following output:

```
[root@server1 root]# ps -l
F S   UID   PID  PPID  C PRI  NI ADDR SZ WCHAN  TTY         TIME CMD
4 S     0  3232  3192  0  75   0 - 1238 wait4  tty2    00:00:00 bash
4 R     0  3438  3232  0  77   0 -  744 -      tty2    00:00:00 ps
[root@server1 root]# _
```

The process flag (F) indicates particular features of the process; the flag of 4 in the preceding output indicates that the root user ran the process. The **process state** (S) column is the most valuable to systems administrators because it indicates what the process is currently doing. If a process is not being run on the processor at the current time, you see an S (sleeping) in the process state column; processes are in this state most of the time, as seen with bash in the preceding output. You will see an R in this column if the process is currently running on the processor, or a T if it has stopped or is being traced by another process. In addition to these, you might also see a Z in this column indicating a **zombie process**. When a process finishes executing, the parent process must check to see if it executed successfully and then release the child process's PID so that it can be used again. While a process is waiting for its parent process to release the PID, the process is said to be in a zombie state, because it has finished but still retains a PID. On a busy Linux server, zombie processes can accumulate and prevent new processes from being created; if this occurs, you can simply kill the parent process of the zombies, as discussed in the next section.

> **NOTE**
>
> Zombie processes are also known as defunct processes.

Process priority (PRI) is the priority used by the kernel for the process; it is measured between 0 (high priority) and 127 (low priority). The **nice value** (NI) can be used to affect the process priority indirectly; it is measured between -20 (a greater chance of a high priority) and 19 (a greater chance of a lower priority). The ADDR in the preceding output indicates the memory address of the process, whereas the WCHAN indicates what the process is waiting for while sleeping. In addition, the size of the process in memory (SZ) is also listed and measured in kilobytes; often, it is roughly equivalent to the size of the executable file on the filesystem.

Some options to the ps command are not prefixed by a dash character; these are referred to as Berkeley style options. The two most common of these are the a option, which lists all processes across terminals, and the x option, which lists processes that do not run on a terminal, as shown in the following output:

```
[root@server1 root]# ps ax
  PID TTY      STAT   TIME COMMAND
    1 ?        S      0:05 init [5]
    2 ?        SWN    0:00 [ksoftirqd/0]
    3 ?        SW<    0:00 [events/0]
    4 ?        SW<    0:00 [kblockd/0]
    6 ?        SW<    0:00 [khelper]
    5 ?        SW     0:00 [khubd]
    7 ?        SW     0:00 [pdflush]
    8 ?        SW     0:00 [pdflush]
   10 ?        SW<    0:00 [aio/0]
    9 ?        SW     0:00 [kswapd0]
  114 ?        SW     0:00 [kseriod]
  153 ?        SW     0:00 [kjournald]
  347 ?        S<     0:00 udevd
 1681 ?        S      0:00 syslogd -m 0
 1685 ?        S      0:00 klogd -x
```

```
1706 ?      S     0:00 portmap
1726 ?      S     0:00 rpc.statd
1754 ?      S     0:00 rpc.idmapd
1798 ?      S     0:00 hcid: processing events
1804 ?      S     0:00 /usr/sbin/sdpd
1811 ?      SW<   0:00 [krfcommd]
1870 ?      S     0:00 /usr/sbin/smartd
1880 ?      S     0:00 /usr/sbin/acpid
1915 ?      S     0:00 cupsd
2110 ?      S     0:00 /usr/sbin/sshd
2125 ?      S     0:00 xinetd -stayalive -pidfile /var/run/xinetd.pid
2165 ?      S     0:01 /usr/bin/spamd -d -c -a -m5 -H
2190 ?      S     0:00 gpm -m /dev/input/mice -t imps2
2220 ?      S     0:00 /usr/sbin/htt
2221 ?      S     0:00 htt_server -nodaemon
2232 ?      S     0:00 /usr/sbin/cannaserver -syslog -u bin
2245 ?      S     0:00 crond
2257 ?      S     0:00 /usr/bin/jserver
2293 ?      S     0:01 xfs -droppriv -daemon
2312 ?      S     0:00 /usr/sbin/atd
2331 ?      S     0:00 dbus-daemon-1 --system
2347 ?      S     0:00 mdadm --monitor --scan
2389 tty1   S     0:00 /sbin/mingetty tty1
2390 ?      S     0:00 login -- root
2391 tty3   S     0:00 /sbin/mingetty tty3
2399 tty4   S     0:00 /sbin/mingetty tty4
2407 tty5   S     0:00 /sbin/mingetty tty5
2415 tty6   S     0:00 /sbin/mingetty tty6
2423 ?      S     0:00 /usr/bin/gdm-binary -nodaemon
2824 ?      S     0:00 /usr/bin/gdm-binary -nodaemon
2839 ?      S     1:21 /usr/X11R6/bin/X :0 -audit 0 -auth /var/gdm/:0.Xauth -nolisten
                       tcp vt7
2901 ?      S     0:01 gnome-session
2964 ?      S     0:00 /usr/bin/ssh-agent /root/.Xclients
2978 ?      S     0:03 /usr/libexec/gconfd-2 5
2981 ?      S     0:00 /usr/bin/gnome-keyring-daemon
2985 ?      S     0:04 /usr/bin/metacity --sm-client-id=default1
3140 ?      S     0:04 gnome-panel --sm-client-id default2
3142 ?      S     0:02 nautilus --no-default-window --sm-client-id default3
3144 ?      S     0:00 magicdev --sm-client-id default4
3146 ?      S     0:00 eggcups --sm-client-id default6
3148 ?      S     0:00 pam-panel-icon --sm-client-id default0
3150 ?      RN    0:06 /usr/bin/python /usr/bin/rhn-applet-gui
3151 ?      S     0:00 /sbin/pam_timestamp_check -d root
```

```
3192 ?      S      0:07 gnome-terminal
3193 ?      S      0:00 gnome-pty-helper
3194 pts/1  S      0:00 bash
3232 tty2   S      0:00 -bash
3545 tty2   R      0:00 ps ax
[root@server1 root]# _
```

The columns just listed are equivalent to those discussed earlier; however, the process state column is identified with STAT and might contain a W to indicate that the process has no contents in memory, a < symbol to indicate a high-priority process, or an N to indicate a low-priority process.

Several dozen options to the ps command can be used to display processes and their attributes; the options listed in this section are the most common and are summarized in Table 10-1.

Table 10-1   Common options to the ps command

Option	Description
-e	Displays all processes running on terminals as well as processes that do not run on a terminal (daemons)
-f	Displays a full list of information about each process, including the UID, PID, PPID, CPU utilization, start time, terminal, processor time, and command name
-l	Displays a long list of information about each process, including the flag, state, UID, PID, PPID, CPU utilization, priority, nice value, address, size, WCHAN, terminal, and command name
a	Displays all processes running on terminals
x	Displays all processes that do not run on terminals

The ps command is not the only command that can view process information. The kernel exports all process information subdirectories under the /proc directory; each subdirectory is named the appropriate PID of the process about which it contains information, as shown in the following output:

```
[root@server1 root]# ls /proc
1      2110  2389  2994  3193  9          filesystems  mtrr
10     2125  2390  3     3194  acpi       fs           net
114    2144  2391  3140  3211  asound     ide          partitions
153    2153  2399  3142  3213  bluetooth  interrupts   pci
1681   2165  2407  3144  3216  buddyinfo  iomem        scsi
1685   2175  2415  3146  3218  bus        ioports      self
1706   2190  2423  3148  3220  cmdline    irq          slabinfo
```

```
1726  2220  2824  3150  3232  cpuinfo      kcore      stat
1754  2221  2839  3151  3427  crypto       kmsg       swaps
1798  2232  2901  3154  347   devices      loadavg    sys
1804  2245  2964  3177  3576  diskstats    locks      sysrq-trigger
1811  2257  2978  3179  4     dma          mdstat     sysvipc
1870  2293  2981  3181  5     dri          meminfo    tty
1880  2312  2983  3183  6     driver       misc       uptime
1915  2331  2985  3190  7     execdomains  modules    version
2     2347  2987  3192  8     fb           mounts     vmstat
[root@server1 root]# _
```

Thus, any program that can read from the /proc directory can display process information. The most common program used to display processes, aside from ps, is the **top command** and its variants. The top command displays an interactive screen listing processes organized by processor time. Processes that use the most processor time are listed at the top of the screen. An example of the screen that appears when you type the top command is shown next:

```
top - 15:02:31 up 35 min,  3 users,  load average: 0.11, 0.26, 0.25
Tasks:  81 total,   2 running,  79 sleeping,   0 stopped,   0 zombie
Cpu(s):  8.4% us,  3.8% sy,  0.3% ni, 82.1% id,  5.2% wa,  0.3% hi,  0.0% si
Mem:    257108k total,   248228k used,    8880k free,   17416k buffers
Swap:   525160k total,        0k used,  525160k free,   80824k cached
_
  PID USER      PR  NI  VIRT  RES  SHR S %CPU %MEM    TIME+  COMMAND
 3601 root      15   0  3216  836 1620 R  3.9  0.3  0:00.02 top
 2839 root      15   0 71928  24m  50m S  2.0  9.7  1:50.14 X
    1 root      16   0  2028  460 1316 S  0.0  0.2  0:05.45 init
    2 root      34  19     0    0    0 S  0.0  0.0  0:00.00 ksoftirqd/0
    3 root       5 -10     0    0    0 S  0.0  0.0  0:00.06 events/0
    4 root       5 -10     0    0    0 S  0.0  0.0  0:00.00 kblockd/0
    6 root       5 -10     0    0    0 S  0.0  0.0  0:00.01 khelper
    5 root      15   0     0    0    0 S  0.0  0.0  0:00.00 khubd
    7 root      16   0     0    0    0 S  0.0  0.0  0:00.01 pdflush
    8 root      15   0     0    0    0 S  0.0  0.0  0:00.03 pdflush
   10 root       7 -10     0    0    0 S  0.0  0.0  0:00.00 aio/0
    9 root      15   0     0    0    0 S  0.0  0.0  0:00.07 kswapd0
  114 root      15   0     0    0    0 S  0.0  0.0  0:00.00 kseriod
  153 root      15   0     0    0    0 S  0.0  0.0  0:00.12 kjournald
  347 root       6 -10  1736  288 1228 S  0.0  0.1  0:00.02 udevd
 1681 root      16   0  2396  624 1296 S  0.0  0.2  0:00.07 syslogd
 1685 root      16   0  3024  440 1244 S  0.0  0.2  0:00.01 klogd
 1706 rpc       16   0  1656  580 1372 S  0.0  0.2  0:00.00 portmap
 1726 rpcuser   23   0  2604  724 1380 S  0.0  0.3  0:00.00 rpc.statd
```

Note that the top command displays many of the same columns that the ps command does, yet it contains a summary paragraph at the top of the screen and a cursor between the summary paragraph and the process list. From the preceding output, you can see that the top command itself uses the most processor time, followed by X Windows (X) and the init daemon.

You might come across a process that has encountered an error during execution and continuously uses up system resources. These processes are referred to as **rogue processes**, and appear at the top of the listing produced by the top command. The top command can also be used to change the priority of processes or kill them; thus, you can stop rogue processes from the top command immediately after they are identified. Process priority and killing processes are discussed later in this chapter.

To get a full listing of the different commands that you can use while in the top utility, simply press h to get a help screen. An example of this help screen is shown next:

```
Help for Interactive Commands - procps version 3.2.0
Window 1:Def: Cumulative mode Off.  System: Delay 3.0 secs; Secure mode Off.

    Z,B       Global: 'Z' change color mappings; 'B' disable/enable bold
    l,t,m     Toggle Summaries: 'l' load avg; 't' task/cpu stats; 'm' mem info
    1,I       Toggle SMP view: '1' single/separate states; 'I' Irix/Solaris mode

    f,o     . Fields/Columns: 'f' add or remove; 'o' change display order
    F or O  . Select sort field
    <,>     . Move sort field: '<' next col left; '>' next col right
    R       . Toggle normal/reverse sort
    c,i,S   . Toggle: 'c' cmd name/line; 'i' idle tasks; 'S' cumulative time
    x,y     . Toggle highlights: 'x' sort field; 'y' running tasks
    z,b     . Toggle: 'z' color/mono; 'b' bold/reverse (only if 'x' or 'y')
    u       . Show specific user only
    n or #  . Set maximum tasks displayed

    k,r       Manipulate tasks: 'k' kill; 'r' renice
    d or s    Set update interval
    W         Write configuration file
    q         Quit
            ( commands shown with '.' require a visible task display window )
Press 'h' or '?' for help with Windows,
any other key to continue
```

Killing Processes

As indicated earlier, a large number of rogue and zombie processes use up system resources and should be sent a **kill signal** to terminate them and increase overall system performance. The most common command used to send kill signals is the **kill command**. There are 64 different kill signals that the kill command can send to a certain process, and each of them operates in a different manner. To view the different kill signal names and associated numbers, you can use the -1 option to the kill command, as shown in the following output:

```
[root@server1 root]# kill -l
 1) SIGHUP       2) SIGINT       3) SIGQUIT      4) SIGILL
 5) SIGTRAP      6) SIGABRT      7) SIGBUS       8) SIGFPE
 9) SIGKILL     10) SIGUSR1     11) SIGSEGV     12) SIGUSR2
13) SIGPIPE     14) SIGALRM     15) SIGTERM     17) SIGCHLD
18) SIGCONT     19) SIGSTOP     20) SIGTSTP     21) SIGTTIN
22) SIGTTOU     23) SIGURG      24) SIGXCPU     25) SIGXFSZ
26) SIGVTALRM   27) SIGPROF     28) SIGWINCH    29) SIGIO
30) SIGPWR      31) SIGSYS      33) SIGRTMIN    34) SIGRTMIN+1
35) SIGRTMIN+2  36) SIGRTMIN+3  37) SIGRTMIN+4  38) SIGRTMIN+5
39) SIGRTMIN+6  40) SIGRTMIN+7  41) SIGRTMIN+8  42) SIGRTMIN+9
43) SIGRTMIN+10 44) SIGRTMIN+11 45) SIGRTMIN+12 46) SIGRTMIN+13
47) SIGRTMIN+14 48) SIGRTMIN+15 49) SIGRTMAX-15 50) SIGRTMAX-14
51) SIGRTMAX-13 52) SIGRTMAX-12 53) SIGRTMAX-11 54) SIGRTMAX-10
55) SIGRTMAX-9  56) SIGRTMAX-8  57) SIGRTMAX-7  58) SIGRTMAX-6
59) SIGRTMAX-5  60) SIGRTMAX-4  61) SIGRTMAX-3  62) SIGRTMAX-2
63) SIGRTMAX-1  64) SIGRTMAX
[root@server1 root]# _
```

Most of the kill signals listed in the preceding output are not useful for systems administrators. The five most common kill signals used for administration are listed in Table 10-2.

Table 10-2 Common administrative kill signals

Name	Number	Description
SIGHUP	1	Also known as the hang-up signal, it stops a process then restarts it with the same PID. If you edit the configuration file used by a running daemon, that daemon might be sent a SIGHUP to restart the process; when the daemon starts again, it reads the new configuration file.
SIGINT	2	This signal sends an interrupt signal to a process. Although this signal is one of the weakest kill signals, it works most of the time. When you use the Ctrl+c key combination to kill a currently running process, a SIGINT is actually being sent to the process.
SIGQUIT	3	Also known as a core dump, the quit signal terminates a process by taking the process information in memory and saving it to a file called core on the hard disk in the current working directory. You can use the Ctrl+\ key combination to send a SIGQUIT to a process that is currently running.

Table 10-2 Common administrative kill signals (Continued)

Name	Number	Description
SIGTERM	15	The software termination signal is the most common kill signal used by programs to kill other processes. It is the default kill signal used by the kill command.
SIGKILL	9	Also known as the absolute kill signal, it forces the Linux kernel to stop executing the process by sending the process's resources to a special device file called /dev/null.

To send a kill signal to a process, you specify the kill signal to send as an option to the `kill` command, followed by the appropriate PID of the process. For example, to send a SIGQUIT to a process called sample, you could use the following commands to locate and terminate the process:

```
[root@server1 root]# ps -ef | grep sample
root      1199     1  0 Jun30 tty3    00:00:00 /sbin/sample
[root@server1 root]# kill -3 1199
[root@server1 root]# _
[root@server1 root]# ps -ef | grep sample
[root@server1 root]# _
```

NOTE

Alternatively, you could have used the command `kill -SIGQUIT 1199` to do the same thing as does the `kill -3 1199` command used in the preceding output.

If you do not specify the kill signal when using the `kill` command, the `kill` command uses a SIGTERM signal, because it is the default kill signal.

Some processes have the ability to ignore certain kill signals that are sent to them. This is known as **trapping** a signal. The only kill signal that cannot be trapped by any process is the SIGKILL. Thus, if a SIGINT, SIGQUIT, and SIGTERM do not terminate a stubborn process, you can use a SIGKILL to terminate it. However, you should only use SIGKILL as a last resort because it prevents a process from closing temporary files and other resources properly.

If you send a kill signal to a process that has children, that parent process terminates all of its child processes before terminating itself. Thus, to kill several related processes, you can simply send a kill signal to their parent process. In addition, to kill a zombie process, it is often necessary to send a kill signal to its parent process.

Another command that can be used to send kill signals to processes is the **killall command**. The killall command works similarly to the kill command in that it takes the kill signal as an option; however, it uses the process name to kill instead of the PID. This allows multiple processes of the same name to be killed in one command. An example of using the killall command to send a SIGQUIT to multiple sample processes is shown in the following output:

```
[root@server1 root]# ps -ef | grep sample
root      1729     1  0 Jun30 tty3     00:00:00 /sbin/sample
root     20198     1  0 Jun30 tty4     00:00:00 /sbin/sample
[root@server1 root]# killall -3 sample
[root@server1 root]# _
[root@server1 root]# ps -ef | grep sample
[root@server1 root]# _
```

> **NOTE**
>
> Alternatively, you could use the command killall -SIGQUIT sample to do the same as the kill -3 sample command used in the preceding output.
>
> As with the kill command, if you do not specify the kill signal when using the killall command, it assumes a SIGTERM signal.

In addition to the kill and killall commands, the top command can be used to kill processes. While in the top utility, simply press the k key and supply the appropriate PID and kill signal when prompted.

Process Execution

You can execute three main types of Linux commands:

- Binary programs
- Shell scripts
- Shell functions

Most commands such as ls, find, and grep are binary programs that exist on the filesystem until executed. They were written in a certain programming language and compiled into a binary format that only the computer can understand. Other commands such as cd and exit are built in to the BASH shell running in memory and they are called shell functions. Shell scripts can also contain a list of binary programs, shell functions, and special constructs for the shell to execute in order.

When executing compiled programs or shell scripts, the BASH shell that interprets the command you typed creates a new BASH shell. This process is known as **forking** and is carried out by the fork function in the BASH shell. This new subshell then executes the binary program or shell script using its exec function. After the binary program or shell script has completed, the new BASH shell uses its exit function to kill itself and return control to the original BASH shell. The original BASH shell uses its wait function to wait for the new BASH shell to carry out the aforementioned tasks before returning a prompt to the user. Figure 10-3 depicts this process when a user types the ls command at the command line.

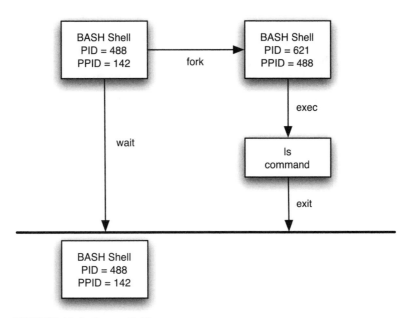

FIGURE 10-3 *Process forking*

Running Processes in the Background

As discussed in the previous section, the BASH shell forks a subshell to execute most commands on the Linux system. Unfortunately, the original BASH shell must wait for the command in the subshell to finish before displaying a shell prompt to accept new commands; commands run in this fashion are known as **foreground processes**.

Alternatively, you can omit the wait function shown in Figure 10-3 by appending an ampersand (&) character to the command. Commands run in this fashion are known as **background processes**. When a command is run in the background, the shell immediately returns the shell prompt for the user to enter another command. To run the sample command in the background, you can enter the following command:

```
[root@server1 root]# sample &
[1] 2583
[root@server1 root]# _
```

> **NOTE**
>
> Space characters between the command and the ampersand (&) are optional; the command `sample&` is equivalent to the command `sample &`, used in the preceding output.

The shell returns the PID (2583 in the preceding example) and the background job ID (1 in the preceding example) such that you can manipulate the background job after it has been run. After the process has been started, you can use the `ps` command to view the PID or the **jobs command** to view the background job ID, as shown in the following output:

```
[root@server1 root]# jobs
[1]+  Running                 sample &
[root@server1 root]# ps | grep sample
2583 tty2    00:00:00 sample
[root@server1 root]# _
```

To terminate the background process, you can send a kill signal to the PID as shown earlier in this chapter, or to the background job ID. Background job IDs must be prefixed by a % character. To send the sample background process created earlier a SIGINT signal, you could use the following `kill` command:

```
[root@server1 root]# jobs
[1]+  Running                 sample &
[root@server1 root]# kill -2 %1
[root@server1 root]# jobs
[root@server1 root]# _
```

> **NOTE**
>
> You can also use the `killall -2 sample` command or the `top` utility to terminate the sample background process used in the preceding example.

After a background process has been started, it can be moved to the foreground by using the **foreground (fg) command** followed by the background job ID. Similarly, a foreground process can be paused using the Ctrl+z key combination and sent to the background with the **background (bg) command**. The Ctrl+z key combination assigns the foreground process a background job ID that is then used as an argument to the `bg` command. To start a sample process in the background and move it to the foreground, then pause it and move it to the background again, you can use the following commands:

```
[root@server1 root]# sample &
[1] 7519
[root@server1 root]# fg %1
sample


[Ctrl]-z
[1]+  Stopped                 sample
[root@server1 root]# bg %1
[1]+ sample &
[root@server1 root]# jobs
[1]+  Running                 sample &
[root@server1 root]# _
```

When there are multiple background processes executing in the shell, the jobs command indicates the most recent one with a + symbol, and the second most recent one with a – symbol. If you place the % notation in a command without specifying the background job ID, the command operates on the most recent background process. An example of this is shown in the following output, in which four sample processes are started and sent SIGQUIT kill signals using the % notation:

```
[root@server1 root]# sample &
[1] 7605
[root@server1 root]# sample2 &
[2] 7613
[root@server1 root]# sample3 &
[3] 7621
[root@server1 root]# sample4 &
[4] 7629
[root@server1 root]# jobs
[1]   Running                 sample &
[2]   Running                 sample2 &
[3]-  Running                 sample3 &
[4]+  Running                 sample4 &
[root@server1 root]# kill -3 %
/sbin/sample4: 7629 Quit
[4]+  Exit 131                sample4
[root@server1 root]# jobs
[1]   Running                 sample &
[2]-  Running                 sample2 &
[3]+  Running                 sample3 &
[root@server1 root]# kill -3 %
/sbin/sample3: 7621 Quit
[3]+  Exit 131                sample3
```

```
[root@server1 root]# jobs
[1]-  Running                 sample &
[2]+  Running                 sample2 &
[root@server1 root]# kill -3 %
/sbin/sample2: 7613 Quit
[2]+  Exit 131                sample2
[root@server1 root]# jobs
[1]+  Running                 sample &
[root@server1 root]# kill -3 %
/sbin/sample: 7605 Quit

[1]+  Exit 131                sample
[root@server1 root]# jobs
[root@server1 root]# _
```

Process Priorities

Recall that Linux is a multitasking operating system; it can perform several different tasks at the same time. Because most computers contain only a single CPU, Linux executes small amounts of each process on the processor in series; this makes it seem to the user as if processes are executing simultaneously. The amount of time a process has to use the CPU is called a **time slice**; the more time slices a process has, the more time it has to execute on the CPU and the faster it executes. Time slices are typically measured in milliseconds; thus, several hundred processes can be executing on the processor in a single second.

The ps -1 command lists the Linux kernel priority (PRI) of a process; this value is directly related to the amount of time slices a process has on the CPU. A PRI of 0 is the most likely to get time slices on the CPU, and a PRI of 127 is the least likely to receive time slices on the CPU. An example of this command is shown next:

```
[root@server1 root]# ps -1
F S   UID   PID  PPID  C PRI  NI ADDR SZ WCHAN  TTY           TIME CMD
4 S     0  3194  3192  0  75   0 -  1238 wait4  pts/1     00:00:00 bash
4 S     0  3896  3194  0  76   0 -   953 -      pts/1     00:00:00 sleep
4 S     0  3939  3194 13  75   0 -  7015 -      pts/1     00:00:01 gedit
4 R     0  3940  3194  0  77   0 -   632 -      pts/1     00:00:00 ps
[root@server1 root]# _
```

The bash, sleep, gedit, and ps processes all have different PRI values because the kernel automatically assigns time slices based on several factors. You cannot change the PRI directly, but can influence it indirectly by assigning a certain nice value to a process. A negative nice value increases the likelihood that the process will receive more time slices, whereas a positive nice value does the opposite. The range of nice values is depicted in Figure 10-4.

−20	0	+19
Most likely to receive time slices, the PRI is closer to zero	The default nice value for new processes	Least likely to receive time slices, the PRI is closer to 127

FIGURE 10-4 *The nice value scale*

All users can be "nice" to other users of the same computer by lowering the priority of their own processes by increasing their nice value. However, only the root user has the ability to increase the priority of a process by lowering its nice value.

Processes are started with a nice value of 0 by default, as shown in the NI column of the ps -l output previously. To start a process with a nice value of +19 (low priority), you can use the **nice command** and specify the nice value using the -n option and the command to start. If the -n option is omitted, a nice value of +10 is assumed. To start the ps -l command with a nice value of +19, you can issue the following command:

```
[root@server1 root]# nice -n 19 ps -l
F S   UID   PID  PPID  C PRI  NI ADDR SZ WCHAN  TTY       TIME CMD
4 S     0  3194  3192  0  75   0 -  1238 wait4  pts/1  00:00:00 bash
4 S     0  3896  3194  0  76   0 -   953 -      pts/1  00:00:00 sleep
4 S     0  3939  3194  0  76   0 -  7015 -      pts/1  00:00:02 gedit
4 R     0  3946  3194  0  99  19 -   703 -      pts/1  00:00:00 ps
[root@server1 root]# _
```

Notice from the preceding output that NI is 19 for the ps command, as compared to 0 for the bash, sleep, and bash commands. Furthermore, the PRI of 99 for the ps command results in fewer time slices than the PRI of 76 for the sleep and gedit commands and the PRI of 75 for the bash shell.

Conversely, to increase the priority of the ps -l command, you can use the following command:

```
[root@server1 root]# nice -n -20 ps -l
F S   UID   PID  PPID  C PRI  NI ADDR SZ WCHAN  TTY       TIME CMD
4 S     0  3194  3192  0  75    0 -  1238 wait4 pts/1  00:00:00 bash
4 S     0  3896  3194  0  76    0 -   953 -     pts/1  00:00:00 sleep
4 S     0  3939  3194  0  76    0 -  7015 -     pts/1  00:00:02 gedit
4 R     0  3947  3194  0  60  -20 -   687 -     pts/1  00:00:00 ps
[root@server1 root]# _
```

Note from the preceding output that the nice value of -20 for the ps command resulted in a PRI of 60, which is more likely to receive time slices than the PRI of 76 for the sleep and gedit commands and the PRI of 75 for the bash shell.

NOTE

On some Linux systems, background processes are given a nice value of 4 by default to lower the chance they will receive time slices.

After a process has been started, you can change its priority by using the **renice command** and specifying the change to the nice value, as well as the PID of the processes to change. Suppose, for example, three sample processes are currently executing on a terminal:

```
[root@server1 root]# ps -l
F S   UID   PID  PPID  C PRI  NI ADDR   SZ WCHAN  TTY         TIME CMD
4 S     0  1229  1228  0  71   0  -     617 wait4  pts/0   00:00:00 bash
4 S     0  1990  1229  0  69   0  -     483 nanos1 pts/0   00:00:00 /bin/sample
4 S     0  2180  1229  0  70   0  -     483 nanos1 pts/0   00:00:00 /bin/sample
4 S     0  2181  1229  0  71   0  -     483 nanos1 pts/0   00:00:00 /bin/sample
4 R     0  2196  1229  0  75   0  -     768 -      pts/0   00:00:00 ps
[root@server1 root]# _
```

To lower priority of the first two sample processes by changing the nice value from 0 to +15 and view the new values, you can execute the following commands:

```
[root@server1 root]# renice +15 1990 2180
1990: old priority 0, new priority 15
2180: old priority 0, new priority 15
[root@server1 root]# ps -l
F S   UID   PID  PPID  C PRI  NI ADDR   SZ WCHAN  TTY         TIME CMD
4 S     0  1229  1228  0  71   0  -     617 wait4  pts/0   00:00:00 bash
4 S     0  1990  1229  0  73  15  -     483 nanos1 pts/0   00:00:00 /bin/sample
4 S     0  2180  1229  0  76  15  -     483 nanos1 pts/0   00:00:00 /bin/sample
4 S     0  2181  1229  0  71   0  -     483 nanos1 pts/0   00:00:00 /bin/sample
4 R     0  2196  1229  0  75   0  -     768 -      pts/0   00:00:00 ps
[root@server1 root]# _
```

NOTE

You can also use the top utility to change the nice value of a running process; simply press the r key and supply the PID and the nice value when prompted.

As with the nice command, only the root user can change the nice value to a negative value using the renice command.

The root user can use the `renice` command to change the priority of all processes that are owned by a certain user or group. To change the nice value to +15 for all processes owned by the users mary and bob, you could execute the command `renice +15 -u mary bob` at the command prompt. Similarly, to change the nice value to +15 for all processes started by members of the group sys, you could execute the command `renice +15 -g sys` at the command prompt.

Scheduling Commands

Although most processes are begun by users executing commands while logged in to a terminal, at times you might want to schedule a command to execute at some point in the future. Scheduling system maintenance commands to run during nonworking hours is good practice, as it does not disrupt normal business activities.

Two different daemons can be used to schedule commands: the **at daemon (atd)** and the **cron daemon (crond)**. The at daemon can be used to schedule a command to execute once in the future, whereas the cron daemon is used to schedule a command to execute repeatedly in the future.

Scheduling Commands with atd

To schedule a command or set of commands for execution at a later time by the at daemon, you can specify the time as an argument to the **at command**; some common time formats used with the `at` command are listed in Table 10-3.

Table 10-3 Common at commands

Command	Description
at 10:15pm	Schedules commands to run at 10:15 PM on the current date
at 10:15pm July 15	Schedules commands to run at 10:15 PM on July 15
at midnight	Schedules commands to run at midnight on the current date
at noon July 15	Schedules commands to run at noon on July 15
at teatime	Schedules commands to run at 4:00 PM on the current date
at tomorrow	Schedules commands to run the next day
at now + 5 minutes	Schedules commands to run in five minutes
at now + 10 hours	Schedules commands to run in 10 hours
at now + 4 days	Schedules commands to run in four days

Table 10-3 Common at commands (Continued)

Command	Description
at now + 2 weeks	Schedules commands to run in two weeks
at now at batch	Schedules commands to run immediately
at 9:00am 01/03/2006 at 9:00am 01032006 at 9:00am 03.01.2006	Schedules commands to run at 9:00 AM on January 3, 2006

After being invoked, the at command displays an at> prompt allowing you to type commands to be executed, one per line. After the commands have been entered, use the Crtl+d key combination to schedule the commands using atd.

> **NOTE**
>
> The at daemon uses the current shell's environment when executing scheduled commands; the shell environment and scheduled commands are stored in the **/var/spool/at** directory.
>
> If the standard output of any command scheduled using atd has not been redirected to a file, it is mailed to the user. You can check your local mail by typing mail at a command prompt. More information about the mail utility can be found in its man page or info page.

To schedule the commands date and who to run at 10:15 PM on July 15th, you can use the following commands:

```
[root@server1 root]# at 10:15pm July 15
at> date > /root/atfile
at> who >> /root/atfile
at> [Ctrl]-d
job 1 at 2004-07-26 22:15
[root@server1 root]# _
```

As shown in the preceding output, the at command returns an at job ID such that you can subsequently query or remove the scheduled command. To display a list of at Job IDs, you can specify the -l option to the at command:

```
[root@server1 root]# at -l
1       2004-07-26 22:15 a root
[root@server1 root]# _
```

> ### NOTE
>
> Alternatively, you can use the `atq` command to see scheduled at jobs; the `atq` command is simply a shortcut to the `at -l` command.
>
> When running the `at -l` command, a regular user only sees his own scheduled at jobs; however, the root user sees all scheduled at jobs.

To see the contents of the at job listed in the previous output alongside the shell environment at the time the at job was scheduled, you can use the `-c` option to the `at` command and specify the appropriate at Job ID:

```
[root@server1 root]# at -c 1
#!/bin/sh
# atrun uid=0 gid=0
# mail     root 0
umask 22
SSH_AGENT_PID=2964; export SSH_AGENT_PID
HOSTNAME=server1; export HOSTNAME
DESKTOP_STARTUP_ID=; export DESKTOP_STARTUP_ID
HISTSIZE=1000; export HISTSIZE
GTK_RC_FILES=/etc/gtk/gtkrc:/root/.gtkrc-1.2-gnome2; export GTK_RC_FILES
WINDOWID=33554952; export WINDOWID
QTDIR=/usr/lib/qt-3.3; export QTDIR
USER=root; export USER
GNOME_KEYRING_SOCKET=/tmp/keyring-1ZSvC3/socket; export GNOME_KEYRING_SOCKET
SSH_AUTH_SOCK=/tmp/ssh-sece2901/agent.2901; export SSH_AUTH_SOCK
KDEDIR=/usr; export KDEDIR
SESSION_MANAGER=local/server1:/tmp/.ICE-unix/2901; export SESSION_MANAGER
USERNAME=root; export USERNAME
PATH=/usr/kerberos/sbin:/usr/kerberos/bin:/usr/local/sbin:/usr/local/bin:/sbin:/bin:/usr/
sbin:/usr/bin:/usr/X11R6/bin:/usr/java/j2sdk1.4.2_04/bin/::/root/bin; export PATH
DESKTOP_SESSION=default; export DESKTOP_SESSION
MAIL=/var/spool/mail/root; export MAIL
PWD=/root; export PWD
INPUTRC=/etc/inputrc; export INPUTRC
LANG=en_US.UTF-8; export LANG
GDMSESSION=default; export GDMSESSION
SSH_ASKPASS=/usr/libexec/openssh/gnome-ssh-askpass; export SSH_ASKPASS
SHLVL=2; export SHLVL
HOME=/root; export HOME
GNOME_DESKTOP_SESSION_ID=Default; export GNOME_DESKTOP_SESSION_ID
BASH_ENV=/root/.bashrc; export BASH_ENV
```

```
LOGNAME=root; export LOGNAME
LESSOPEN=\|/usr/bin/lesspipe.sh\ %s; export LESSOPEN
G_BROKEN_FILENAMES=1; export G_BROKEN_FILENAMES
COLORTERM=gnome-terminal; export COLORTERM
XAUTHORITY=/root/.Xauthority; export XAUTHORITY
cd /root || {
        echo 'Execution directory inaccessible' >&2
        exit 1
}
${SHELL:-/bin/sh} << `(dd if=/dev/urandom count=200 bs=1 2>/dev/null|LC_ALL=C tr -d -c
'[:alnum:]')`

date > /root/atfile
who >> /root/atfile
[root@server1 root]# _
```

To remove the at job used in the preceding example, simply specify the -d option to the at command, followed by the appropriate at Job ID, as shown in the following output:

```
[root@server1 root]# at -d 1
[root@server1 root]# at -l
[root@server1 root]# _
```

> **NOTE**
>
> Alternatively, you can use the atrm 1 command to remove the first at job; the atrm command is simply a shortcut to the at -d command.

If there are many commands to be scheduled using the at daemon, you can choose to place these commands in a shell script and schedule the shell script to execute at a later time using the -f option to the at command. An example of scheduling a shell script called myscript using the at command is shown next:

```
[root@server1 root]# cat myscript
#this is a sample shell script
date > /root/atfile
who >> /root/atfile
[root@server1 root]# at 10:15pm July 16 -f myscript
job 2 at 2004-07-26 22:15
[root@server1 root]# _
```

If the **/etc/at.allow** and **/etc/at.deny** files do not exist, only the root user is allowed to schedule tasks using the at daemon. To give this ability to other users, simply create an /etc/at.allow file and add the names of users allowed to use the at daemon, one per line. Conversely, you can use the /etc/at.deny file to deny certain users access to the at daemon; any user not listed in this file is then allowed to use the at daemon. If both files exist, the system checks the /etc/at.allow file and does not process the entries in the /etc/at.deny file.

> ### NOTE
>
> On Red Hat Fedora Linux systems, only an /etc/at.deny file exists by default. Because this file is initially left blank, all users are allowed to use the at daemon after a Red Hat Fedora Linux installation.

Scheduling Commands with crond

The at daemon is useful for scheduling tasks that occur on a certain date in the future, yet is ill suited for scheduling repetitive tasks because each task requires its own at job ID. The cron daemon is better suited for repetitive tasks because it uses configuration files called **cron tables** to specify when a command should be executed.

Cron tables have six fields separated by space or tab characters. The first five fields specify the times to run the command and the sixth field is the absolute pathname to the command to be executed. As with the at command, you can place commands in a shell script and schedule the shell script to run repetitively; in this case, the sixth field is the absolute pathname to the shell script. Each of the fields in a cron table is depicted in Figure 10-5.

Thus, to execute the /root/myscript shell script at 5:20 PM and 5:40 PM Monday to Friday regardless of the day of the month or month of the year, you could use the cron table depicted in Figure 10-6.

1   2   3   4   5   command

```
1 = Minute past the hour (0–59)
2 = Hour (0–23)
3 = Day of month (1–31)
4 = Month of year (1–12)
5 = Day of week
      0 = Sun  (or 7 = Sun)
      1 = Mon
      2 = Tues
      3 = Wed
      4 = Thurs
      5 = Fri
      6 = Sat
```

FIGURE 10-5 *User cron table format*

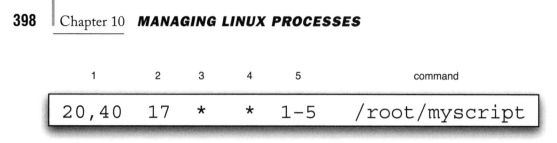

FIGURE 10-6 *Sample user cron table entry*

The first field in Figure 10-6 specifies the minute past the hour. Because the command must be run at 20 minutes and 40 minutes past the hour, this field has two values separated by a comma. The second field specifies the time in 24-hour format; 5 PM being the 17th hour. The third and fourth fields specify the day of month and month of year, respectively, to run the command, respectively. Because the command might run during any month regardless of the day of month, both fields use the * wildcard metacharacter to match all values. The final field indicates the day of the week to run the command; as with the first field, the command must be run on multiple days, but a range of days was specified (day 1 to day 5).

Two different types of cron tables are used by the cron daemon. User cron tables exist in **/var/spool/cron** and represent tasks that individual users schedule, whereas the system cron tables contain system tasks and exist in the **/etc/cron.d** directory as well as in the **/etc/crontab** file.

User Cron Tables

On a newly installed Red Hat Fedora Linux system, all users have the ability to schedule tasks using the cron daemon. However, you can create an **/etc/cron.allow** file to list users who have the ability to schedule tasks using the cron daemon. All other users are denied. Conversely, you can create an **/etc/cron.deny** file to list those users who are denied the ability to schedule tasks. Thus, any users not listed in this file are allowed to schedule tasks only. If both files exist, only the /etc/cron.allow file is processed.

To create or edit a user cron table, you can use the -e option to the **crontab command**, which opens the vi editor. You can then enter the appropriate cron table entries. Suppose, for example, that the root user executed the crontab -e command. To schedule /bin/command1 to run at 4:30 AM every Friday and /bin/command2 to run at 2:00 PM on the first day of every month, you can add the following lines while in the vi editor:

```
30 4 * * 5 /bin/command1
0 14 1 * * /bin/command2
~
~
~
~
~
~
```

```
~
~
~
~
~
~
~
~
~
~
"/tmp/crontab.4101"  2L 41C
```

When the user saves the changes and quits the vi editor, the information is stored in the file /var/spool/cron/*username* where *username* is the name of the user who executed the crontab -e command. In the preceding example, the file would be named /var/spool/cron/root.

To list your user cron table, you can use the -l option to the crontab command. The following output lists the cron table created earlier:

```
[root@server1 root]# crontab -l
# DO NOT EDIT THIS FILE - edit the master and reinstall.
# (/tmp/crontab.4101 installed on Mon Jul  26 20:31:56 2004)
# (Cron version -- $Id: crontab.c,v 2.13 1994/01/17 03:20:37 vixie Exp)
30 4 * * 5 /bin/command1
0 14 1 * * /bin/command2
[root@server1 root]# _
```

Furthermore, to remove a cron table and all scheduled jobs, you can use the -r option to the crontab command, as illustrated next:

```
[root@server1 root]# crontab -r
[root@server1 root]# crontab -l
no crontab for root
[root@server1 root]# _
```

The root user can edit, list, or remove any other user's cron table by using the -u option to the crontab command followed by the user name. For example, to edit the cron table for the user mary, the root user could use the command crontab -e -u mary at the command prompt. Similarly, to list and remove mary's cron table, the root user could execute the commands crontab -l -u mary and crontab -r -u mary, respectively.

The System Cron Table

Linux systems are typically scheduled to run many commands during nonbusiness hours. These commands might perform system maintenance, back up data, or run CPU-intensive programs. Most of these commands are scheduled by the cron daemon from entries in the system

cron table /etc/crontab, which can only be edited by the root user. A sample /etc/crontab file
is shown in the following output:

```
[root@server1 root]# cat /etc/crontab
SHELL=/bin/bash
PATH=/sbin:/bin:/usr/sbin:/usr/bin
MAILTO=root
HOME=/

# run-parts
01 * * * * root run-parts /etc/cron.hourly
02 4 * * * root run-parts /etc/cron.daily
22 4 * * 0 root run-parts /etc/cron.weekly
42 4 1 * * root run-parts /etc/cron.monthly

[root@server1 root]# _
```

The initial section of the cron table specifies the environment used while executing commands. The remainder of the file is similar to the format of a user cron table. The first five fields
specify the time to run the command, yet the sixth field specifies who to run the command as
(the root user in the preceding output). The remaining fields represent the command to run;
the run-parts command is used to execute all files in a certain directory listed as an argument.

Thus, the line:

```
01 * * * * root run-parts /etc/cron.hourly
```

in the /etc/crontab file listed earlier executes all files inside the /etc/cron.hourly directory as
the root user at one minute past the hour, every hour of every day.

Similarly, the line:

```
02 4 * * * root run-parts /etc/cron.daily
```

in the /etc/crontab file listed earlier executes all files inside the /etc/cron.daily directory as the
root user at 4:02 AM, every day.

The remaining lines of the /etc/crontab file listed earlier run any files in the /etc/cron.weekly
directory at 4:22 AM on Sundays and any files in the /etc/cron.monthly directory at 4:42 AM
on the first day of each month.

Because the /etc/crontab file organizes tasks hourly, daily, weekly, and monthly, you can simply copy a script file to the appropriate directory to schedule it using the system cron table. To
run a script called myscript on a daily basis, you can copy the file to the /etc/cron.daily directory. Alternatively, you can simply create a symbolic link in the /etc/cron.daily directory that
points to the myscript shell script.

You can also place a cron table with the same information in the /etc/cron.d directory. Any cron
tables found in this directory can have the same format as /etc/crontab and are run by the sys-

tem. This is useful if the hourly, daily, weekly, and monthly intervals are of no use for a particular task. For example, the `sa1` command is run every 10 minutes as the root user by the cron daemon from the file /etc/cron.d/sysstat, as shown next:

```
[root@server1 root]# cat /etc/cron.d/sysstat
# run system activity accounting tool every 10 minutes
*/10 * * * * root /usr/lib/sa/sa1 1 1
# generate a daily summary of process accounting at 23:53
53 23 * * * root /usr/lib/sa/sa2 -A

[root@server1 root]# _
```

Notice from the preceding output that although the second noncommented line runs at 11:53 PM using standard notation, the special notation */10 was used in the first column of the first noncommented line to indicate all minutes at 10-minute intervals. Instead, you can use 0-59/10 to specify running the `sa1` command from the 0th to 59th minute at 10-minute intervals.

Chapter Summary

- Processes are programs that are executing on the system.
- User processes are run in the same terminal as the user who executed them, whereas daemon processes are system processes that do not run on a terminal.
- Every process has a parent process associated with it and, optionally, several child processes.
- Process information is stored in the /proc filesystem; the ps and top commands can be used to view this information.
- Zombie and rogue processes that exist for long periods of time use up system resources and should be killed to improve system performance.
- You can send kill signals to a process using the kill, killall, and top commands.
- The BASH shell forks a subshell to execute most commands.
- Processes can be run in the background by appending an & to the command name; the BASH shell assigns each background process a background job ID such that it can be manipulated afterward.
- The priority of a process can be affected indirectly by altering its nice value; nice values range from -20 (high priority) to +19 (low priority). Only the root user can increase the priority of a process.
- Commands can be scheduled to run at a later time using the at and cron daemons. The at daemon schedules tasks to occur at a later time, whereas the cron daemon uses cron tables to schedule tasks to occur repetitively in the future.

Key Terms

/etc/at.allow — A file listing all users who can use the at command.

/etc/at.deny — A file listing all users who cannot access the at command.

/etc/cron.allow — A file listing all users who can use the cron command.

/etc/cron.d — A directory that contains additional system cron tables.

/etc/cron.deny — A file listing all users who cannot access the cron command.

/etc/crontab — The default system cron table.

/var/spool/at — A directory that stores the information used to schedule commands using the at daemon.

/var/spool/cron — A directory that stores user cron tables.

at command — The command used to schedule commands and tasks to run at a preset time in the future.

at daemon (atd) — The system daemon that executes tasks at a future time; it is configured with the at command.

background (bg) command — The command used to run a foreground process in the background.

background process — A process that does not require the BASH shell to wait for its termination; upon execution, the user receives the BASH shell prompt immediately.

child process — A process that was started by another process (parent process).

cron daemon (crond) — The system daemon that executes tasks repetitively in the future—it is configured using cron tables.

cron table — A file specifying tasks to be run by the cron daemon; there are user cron tables and system cron tables.

crontab command — The command used to view and edit user cron tables.

daemon process — A system process that is not associated with a terminal.

foreground (fg) command — The command used to run a background process in the foreground.

foreground process — A process for which the BASH shell that executed it must wait for its termination.

forking — The act of creating a new BASH shell child process from a parent BASH shell process.

jobs command — The command used to see the list of background processes running in the current shell.

kill command — The command used to kill or terminate a process.

kill signal — The type of signal sent to a process by the kill command; different kill signals affect processes in different ways.

killall command — The command that kills all instances of a process by command name.

nice command — The command used to change the priority of a process as it is started.

nice value — The value that indirectly represents the priority of a process; the higher the value, the lower the priority.

parent process — A process that has started other processes (child processes).

parent process ID (PPID) — The PID of the parent process that created the current process.

process — A program currently loaded into physical memory and running on the system.

process ID (PID) — A unique identifier assigned to every process as it begins.

process priority — A number assigned to a process, used to determine how many time slices on the processor that process will receive; the higher the number, the lower the priority.

process state — The current state of the process on the processor; most processes are in the sleeping or running state.

program — A structured set of commands stored in an executable file on a filesystem; it can be executed to create a process.

ps command — The command used to obtain information about processes currently running on the system.

renice command — The command used to alter the nice value of a process currently running on the system.

rogue process — A process that has become faulty in some way and continues to consume far more system resources than it should.

time slice — The amount of time a process is given on a CPU in a multiprocessing operating system.

top command — The command used to give real-time information about the most active processes on the system; it can also be used to renice or kill processes.

trapping — The process of ignoring a kill signal.

user process — A process begun by a user and which runs on a terminal.

zombie process — A process that has finished executing, but whose parent has not yet released its PID; it still retains a spot in the kernel's process table.

Review Questions

1. To display an entire list of processes across all terminals and including daemons, you can add the _____ option to any ps command.

   a. -a

   b. -e

   c. -f

   d. -o

2. What is the lowest process priority?

   a. 0

   b. 1

   c. 127

   d. 255

3. The _____ kill signal is also known as the hang-up signal; it stops a process then restarts it with the same PID.

   a. SIGHUP

   b. SIGINT

   c. SIGQUIT

   d. SIGTERM

4. What command is used to initially run a process in the background?

   a. bg

   b. jobs

   c. fg

   d. &

5. Administrators schedule processes to perform system maintenance, back up data, or run CPU-intensive programs using the _____ command.

   a. run

   b. cron

   c. crond

   d. atd

6. True or false? A process refers to a program that is running in memory and on the CPU.

7. True or false? PIDs are given to new processes in sequential order.

8. True or false? The ps command is the only command used to view process information.

9. True or false? The only kill signal that cannot be trapped by any process is the SIGKILL.

10. True or false? The at teatime command schedules commands to run at 4:00 PM on the current date.

11. Each process can start an unlimited number of other processes called _____ processes.

12. When viewing information about processes using the ps command, if a process is not being run on the processor at the current time, you see a(n) _____ in the process state column.

13. A process that has encountered an error during execution and continuously uses up system resources is called a(n) _____ process.

14. When executing compiled programs or shell scripts, the BASH shell that interprets the command you typed in creates a new BASH shell. This process is known as

    _____.

15. The amount of time a process has to use the CPU is called a time _____.

Chapter 11

Common Administrative Tasks

After completing this chapter, you will be able to:

◆ Set up, manage, and print to printers on a Linux system

◆ Understand the purpose of log files and how they are administered

◆ Create, modify, manage, and delete user and group accounts using command-line and graphical utilities

In previous chapters, you learned how to administer filesystems, X Windows, system startup, and processes. In this chapter, you examine other essential areas of Linux administration. First, you learn about the print process and how to administer and set up printers, followed by a discussion on managing log files using the System Log Daemon and the logrotate utility. Finally, you examine system databases that store user and group information, and the utilities that can be used to create, modify, and delete user and group accounts on a Linux system.

Printer Administration

Printing work files is commonly required by most users on a Linux system, and printing log files and system configuration information is good procedure in case of a system failure. Thus, a firm understanding of how to set up, manage, and print to printers is vital for those who set up and administer Linux servers.

The Common UNIX Printing System

Today, the most common printing system used on Linux computers is the **Common Unix Printing System (CUPS)**. Fundamental to using CUPS on a Linux system is an understanding of the process by which information is sent to a printer. A set of information that is sent to a printer at the same time is called a **print job**. Print jobs can consist of a file, several files, or the output of a command. To send a print job to a printer, you must first use the **lp command** and specify what to print.

Next, the **cups daemon (cupsd)** assigns the print job a unique **print job ID** and places a copy of the print job into a temporary directory on the filesystem called the **print queue**, provided the printer is **accepting** requests. If the printer is **rejecting** requests, the cups daemon prints an error message stating that the printer is not accepting print jobs.

> **NOTE**
>
> Accepting print jobs into a print queue is commonly called **spooling** or **queuing**.
>
> The print queue for a printer is typically /var/spool/cups. Regardless of how many printers you have on your Linux system, all print jobs are sent to the same directory.

After a print job is in the print queue, it is ready to be printed. If the printer is **enabled**, and ready to accept the print job, the cups daemon then sends the print job from the print queue to the printer and removes the copy of the print job in the print queue. Conversely, if the printer is **disabled**, the print job remains in the print queue.

> **NOTE**
>
> Sending print jobs from a print queue to a printer is commonly called **printing**.

An example of this process for a printer called printer1 is illustrated in Figure 11-1.

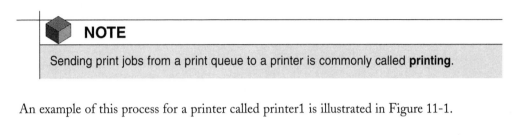

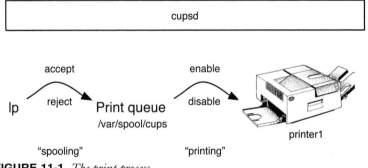

FIGURE 11-1 *The print process*

To see a list of all printers on the system and their status, you can use the -t (total) option to the **lpstat command**, as shown in the following output:

```
[root@server1 root]# lpstat -t
scheduler is running
system default destination: printer1
device for p1: parallel:/dev/lp0
p1 accepting requests since Jan 01 00:00
printer p1 is idle. enabled since Jan 01 00:00
[root@server1 root]# _
```

The preceding output indicates that there is only one printer on the system called *printer1* that prints to a printer connected to the first parallel port on the computer (/dev/lp0) and that there are no print jobs in its print queue. In addition, the cups daemon (scheduler) is running and accepting jobs into the print queue for this printer. Also, the cups daemon sends print jobs from the print queue to the printer because the printer is enabled.

You can manipulate the status of a printer using either the accept, reject, enable, or disable commands followed by the printer name. Thus, to enable spooling and disable printing for the printer *printer1*, you can use the following commands:

```
[root@server1 root]# accept printer1
[root@server1 root]# disable printer1
[root@server1 root]# lpstat -t
scheduler is running
system default destination: printer1
device for printer1: parallel:/dev/lp0
printer1 accepting requests since Jan 01 00:00
printer printer1 disabled since Jan 01 00:00 -
        Paused
[root@server1 root]# _
```

Any print jobs now sent to the printer *printer1* are sent to the print queue, but remain in the print queue until the printer is started again.

> **NOTE**
>
> If you want to enable a printer, you must specify the full path to the enable command
> (/usr/bin/enable) because there is also a BASH shell function called enable.

You can also use the -r option to the disable and reject commands to specify a reason for the action, as shown in the following output:

```
[root@server1 root]# disable -r "Changing toner cartridge" printer1
[root@server1 root]# lpstat -t
scheduler is running
system default destination: printer1
device for printer1: parallel:/dev/lp0
printer1 accepting requests since Jan 01 00:00
printer printer1 disabled since Jan 01 00:00 - Changing toner cartridge
[root@server1 root]# _
```

Managing Print Jobs

Recall that you create a print job by using the lp command. To print a copy of the /etc/inittab file to the printer *printer1* shown in earlier examples, you can use the following command, which returns a print job ID that you can use to manipulate the print job afterward:

```
[root@server1 root]# lp -d printer1 /etc/inittab
request id is printer1-1 (1 file(s))
[root@server1 root]# _
```

The lp command uses the -d option to specify the destination printer name. If this option is omitted, the lp command assumes the default printer on the system. Because *printer1* is the only printer on the system and, hence, is the default printer, the command lp /etc/inittab is equivalent to the one used in the preceding output.

> ### NOTE
>
> You can set the default printer for all users on your system by using the lpoptions -d printername command, where printername is the name of the default printer. This information is stored in the /etc/cups/lpoptions file.
>
> Each user on a Linux system can specify his own default printer by adding the line default printername to the .lpoptions file in his home directory, where printername is the name of the default printer. Alternatively, you can use the PRINTER or LPDEST variables to set the default printer. For example, to specify *printer2* as the default printer, you can add either the line export PRINTER=printer2 or the line export LPDEST=printer2 to an environment file in your home directory such as .bash_profile.

Table 11-1 lists some common options to the lp command.

Table 11-1 Common options to the lp command

Option	Description
-d *printername*	Specifies the name of printer to send the print job.
-i *print job ID*	Specifies a certain print job ID to modify.
-n *number*	Prints a certain *number* of copies.
-m	Mails you confirmation of print job completion.
-o *option*	Specifies certain printing options. Common printing options include the following: cpi = *number*—Sets the characters per inch to *number* landscape—Prints in landscape orientation number-up = *number*—Prints *number* pages on a single page, where *number* is 1, 2, or 4 sides = *string*—Sets double-sided printing, where *string* is either 'two-sided-short-edge' or 'two-sided-long-edge'
-q *priority*	Specifies a print job priority from 1 (low priority) to 100 (high priority). By default, all print jobs have a priority of 50.

You can also specify several files to be printed using a single lp command by specifying the files as arguments. In this case, only one print job is created to print all of the files. To print the files /etc/hosts and /etc/issue to the printer *printer1*, you can execute the following command:

```
[root@server1 root]# lp -d printer1 /etc/hosts /etc/issue
request id is printer1-2 (2 file(s))
[root@server1 root]# _
```

The lp command accepts information from Standard Input; thus, you can place the lp command at the end of a pipe to print information. To print a list of logged-in users, you can use the following pipe:

```
[root@server1 root]# who | lp -d printer1
request id is printer1-3 (1 file(s))
[root@server1 root]# _
```

To see a list of print jobs in the queue for *printer1*, you can use the lpstat command. Without arguments, this command displays all jobs in the print queue that you have printed:

```
[root@server1 root]# lpstat
printer1-1      root      2048   Fri 29 Jul 2005 06:18:22 PM EDT
printer1-2      root      3072   Fri 29 Jul 2005 07:05:49 PM EDT
printer1-3      root      1024   Fri 29 Jul 2005 07:06:50 PM EDT
[root@server1 root]# _
```

Table 11-2 lists other options that you can use with the lpstat command.

Table 11-2 Common options to the lpstat command

Option	Description
-a	Displays a list of printers that are accepting print jobs
-d	Displays the default destination printer
-o *printername*	Displays the print jobs in the print queue for *printername* only
-p	Displays a list of printers that are enabled
-r	Shows whether the cups daemon (scheduler) is running
-t	Shows all information about printers and their print jobs

To remove a print job that is in the print queue, you can use the **cancel command** followed by the print job IDs of the jobs to remove. To remove the print job IDs printer1-1 and printer1-2 created earlier, you can use the following command:

```
[root@server1 root]# cancel p1-1 p1-2
[root@server1 root]# lpstat
printer1-3      root        3072    Fri 30 Jul 2005 07:05:49 PM EDT
[root@server1 root]# _
```

You can instead remove all jobs started by a certain user; simply specify the -u option to the `cancel` command followed by the user name. To remove all jobs in a print queue, you can use the -a option to the `cancel` command, as shown in the following example:

```
[root@server1 root]# cancel -a
[root@server1 root]# lpstat
[root@server1 root]# _
```

Not all users might be allowed access to a certain printer. As a result, you can restrict who can print to certain printers by using the **lpadmin command**. For example, to deny all users other than root and user1 from printing to the printer1 printer created earlier, you can use the following command:

```
[root@server1 root]# lpadmin -u allow:root,user1 -u deny:all -d printer1
[root@server1 root]# _
```

The LPD Printing System

Although CUPS is the preferred printing system for Linux computers today, many older Linux computers use the traditional **Line Printer Daemon (LPD)** printing system. In this printing system, the **lpr command** is used to print documents to the print queue much like the lp command, the **lpc command** can be used to view the status of printers, the **lpq command** can be used to view print jobs in the print queue much like the lpstat command, and the **lprm command** can be used to remove print jobs much like the cancel command.

For those users who are used to using the LPD printing system, CUPS contains versions of the lpr, lpc, lpq, and cancel commands. The following output displays the status of all printers on the system, prints two copies of /etc/inittab to printer1, views the print job in the queue, and removes the print job:

```
[root@server1 root]# lpc status
printer1:
        printer is on device 'parallel' speed -1
        queuing is enabled
        printing is enabled
        no entries
        daemon present
[root@server1 root]# lpr -#2 -P printer1 /etc/inittab
[root@server1 root]# lpq
printer1 is ready and printing
Rank    Owner   Job     File(s)     Total Size
active  root    1       inittab     2048 bytes
```

```
[root@server1 root]# lprm 1
[root@server1 root]# lpq
printer1 is ready
no entries
[root@server1 root]# _
```

Configuring Printers

Recall that the core component of printing is the cups daemon (cupsd), which accepts print jobs into a queue and sends them to the printer. The file that contains settings for cupsd is **/etc/cups/cupsd.conf**, and the file that contains the configuration information for each printer installed on the system is **/etc/cups/printers.conf**. Instead of editing these files manually, it is easier to use the **Printer Configuration tool**, as shown in Figure 11-2. To access this tool, you can type system-config-printer-gui in a terminal screen in a desktop environment or navigate to the Red Hat button, System Settings, Printing.

> **NOTE**
>
> There is also a terminal version of the Printer Configuration tool; simply type system-config-printer-tui at a terminal command prompt.

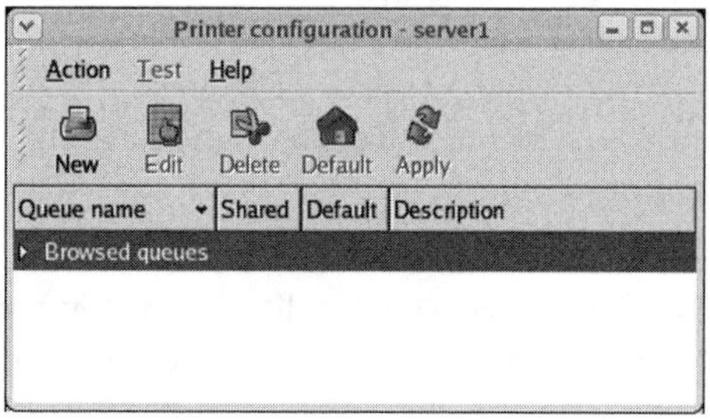

FIGURE 11-2 *The Printer Configuration tool*

The Printer Configuration tool depicted in Figure 11-2 indicates that there are no configured printers on the system. To add a printer, you can click the New button, then Forward, and specify the name and description of the print queue, as shown in Figure 11-3.

Because the print process involves sending jobs to a print queue before sending them to a printer, the Printer Configuration tool is used to configure the queue instead of the printer; the printer name is often referred to as the queue name for the same reason.

After you click Forward in Figure 11-3, you are prompted to choose the print queue type. Several different printer types might be configured. You would choose Locally-connected if the printer is attached to the local computer via a serial, parallel, or USB cable, as shown in Figure 11-4. Alternatively, you might choose to print to a printer that is connected to a remote

Linux computer across a network running CUPS or LPD, a remote Windows server, a remote NetWare server, or a network printer that uses the Hewlett-Packard JetDirect technology, as shown in Figure 11-5.

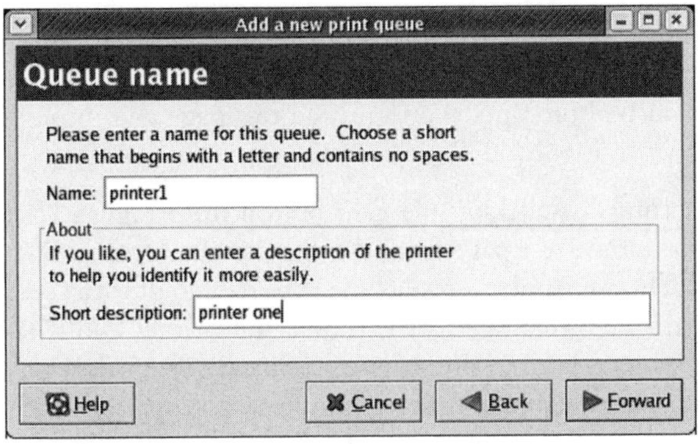

FIGURE 11-3 *Specifying the name of a new printer*

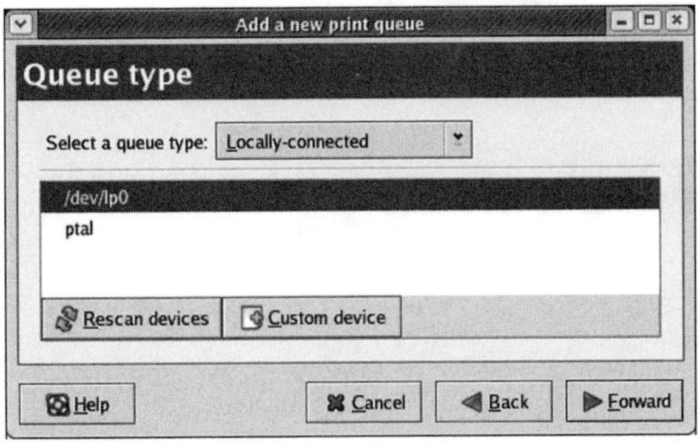

FIGURE 11-4 *Specifying the queue type for a new printer*

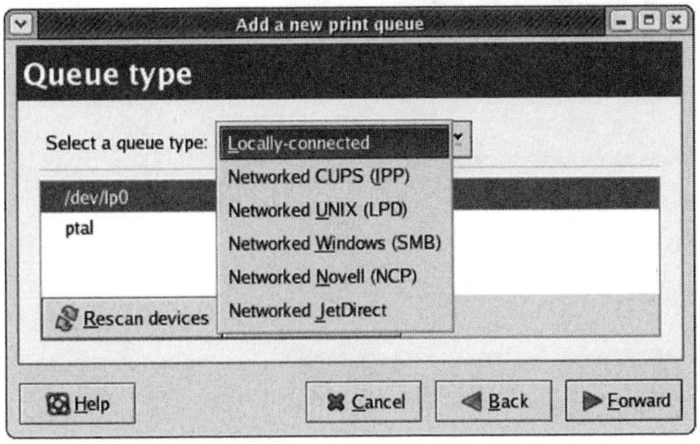

FIGURE 11-5 *Different queue types available for a new printer*

After the type of printer is chosen, you must supply the specific information about the printer. For a local printer, you must choose the port that connects to the printer, such as /dev/lp0 shown earlier Figure 11-4. For remote printers, you need to specify the name or IP address of the remote server, printer name, or printer port.

Following this, you are prompted to choose the model of your printer, as shown in Figure 11-6, and confirm the printer creation, as shown in Figure 11-7. After the printer has been created, the Printer Configuration tool prompts you to print a test page and displays a line that represents the printer, as shown in Figure 11-8.

You can modify all printer settings by clicking the Edit button from Figure 11-8, or print a test page by selecting the appropriate test page from the Test menu. After adding or modifying printer settings, you must choose Apply to restart the cups daemon for the settings to take effect. Also notice from Figure 11-8 that printer1 is the default printer and is not shared to network users. To configure printer sharing, simply choose Sharing from the Action menu in Figure 11-8, select "This queue is available to other computers," and specify which computers are allowed to print to the printer, as shown in Figure 11-9.

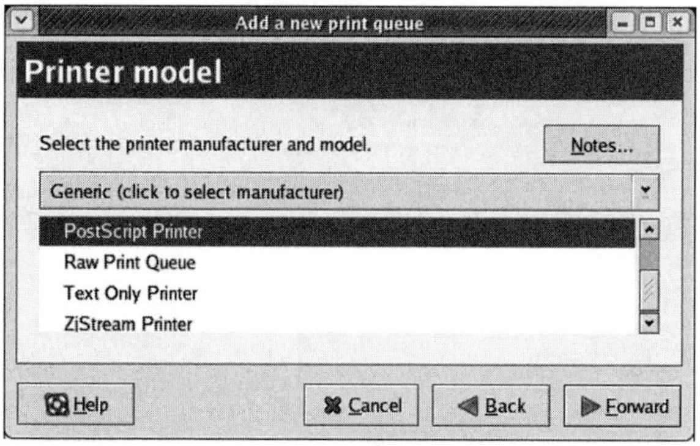

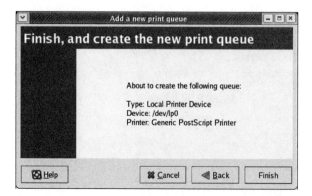

FIGURE 11-6 *Selecting the printer model for a new printer*

FIGURE 11-7 *Completing the creation of a new printer*

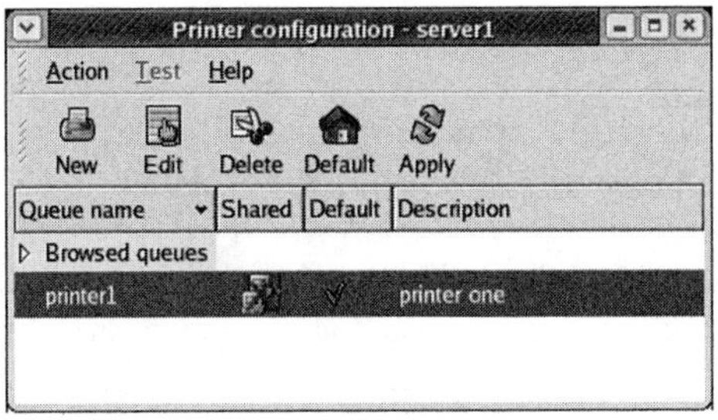

FIGURE 11-8 *Viewing a configured printer*

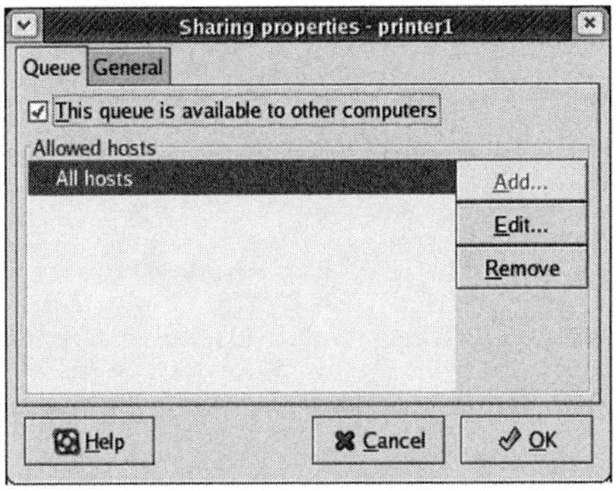

FIGURE 11-9 *Sharing a printer to network users*

If you click on the General tab in Figure 11-9, you can configure CUPS to automatically search for other shared CUPS printers and allow remote computers the ability to print to the printer using the LPD protocol, as shown in Figure 11-10.

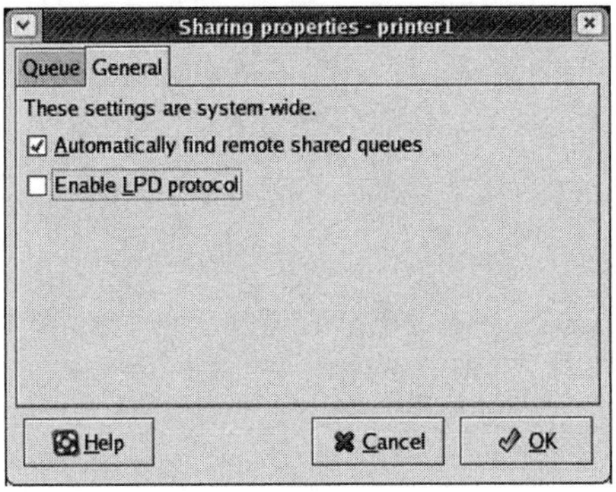

FIGURE 11-10 *Specifying shared printer options*

Log File Administration

To identify and troubleshoot problems on a Linux system, you must view the events that occur over time. Because administrators cannot observe all events that take place on a Linux system, most daemons record information and error messages to files stored on the filesystem. These files are referred to as **log files** and are typically stored in the **/var/log** directory. Many programs store their log files in subdirectories of the /var/log directory. For example, the /var/log/samba directory contains the log files created by the samba file-sharing daemons. Table 11-3 lists some common log files found in the /var/log directory and their descriptions.

Table 11-3 Common Linux log files found in /var/log

Log File	Description
boot.log	Contains information regarding daemon startup obtained during system initialization
cron	Contains information and error messages generated by the cron and at daemons
dmesg	Contains detected hardware information obtained during system startup
maillog	Contains information and error messages generated by the sendmail daemon
secure	Contains information and error messages regarding network access generated by daemons such as sshd and xinetd
wtmp	Contains a history of all login sessions
rpmpkgs	Contains a list of packages installed by the Red Hat Package Manager and related error messages
xferlog	Contains information and error messages generated by the FTP daemon
Xorg.0.log XFree86	Contains information and error messages generated by X Windows
lastlog	Contains a list of users and their last login time; must be viewed using the lastlog command
messages	Contains information regarding daemon startup obtained at system initialization as well as important system messages produced after system initialization

The System Log Daemon

The logging of most events is handled centrally in Linux via the **System Log Daemon (syslogd)**. When this daemon is loaded upon system startup, it creates a socket (/dev/log) for other system processes to write to. It then reads any information written to this socket and saves the information in the appropriate log file according to entries in the **/etc/syslog.conf** file. A sample /etc/syslog.conf file is shown in the following output:

```
[root@server1 root]# cat /etc/syslog.conf
# Log all kernel messages to the console.
# Logging much else clutters up the screen.
#kern.*                                  /dev/console

# Log anything (except mail) of level info or higher.
# Don't log private authentication messages!
*.info;mail.none;authpriv.none;cron.none    /var/log/messages

# The authpriv file has restricted access.
authpriv.*                               /var/log/secure

# Log all the mail messages in one place.
mail.*                                   /var/log/maillog


# Log cron stuff
cron.*                                   /var/log/cron

# Everybody gets emergency messages
*.emerg                                          *

# Save news errors of level crit and higher in a special file.
uucp,news.crit                           /var/log/spooler

# Save boot messages also to boot.log
local7.*                                 /var/log/boot.log

#
# INN
#
news.=crit                               /var/log/news/news.crit
news.=err                                /var/log/news/news.err
news.notice                              /var/log/news/news.notice
[root@server1 root]# _
```

Any line that starts with a # character is a comment in the /etc/syslog.conf file. All other entries have the following format:

```
facility.priority      /var/log/logfile
```

The **facility** is the area of the system to listen to, whereas the **priority** refers to the importance of the information. For example, a facility of kern and priority of warning indicates that the System Log Daemon should listen for kernel messages of priority warning and more serious. When found, the System Log Daemon places these messages in the /var/log/logfile file. The aforementioned entry would read:

```
kern.warning     /var/log/logfile
```

 NOTE

You can also send information to the syslog daemon on a remote Linux or UNIX server; simply specify the notation @servername in place of /var/log/logfile.

To only log warning messages from the kernel to /var/log/logfile, you can use the following entry instead:

```
kern.=warning     /var/log/logfile
```

Alternatively, you can log all error messages from the kernel to /var/log/logfile by using the * wildcard, as shown in the following entry:

```
kern.*     /var/log/logfile
```

In addition, you can specify multiple facilities and priorities; to log all error messages except warnings from the kernel to /var/log/logfile, you can use the following entry:

```
kern.*;kern.!=warn     /var/log/logfile
```

To log all error messages from the kernel and news daemons, you can use the following entry:

```
kern,news.*     /var/log/logfile
```

To log all warnings from all facilities except for the kernel, you can use the "none" keyword, as shown in following entry:

```
*.=warn;kern.none     /var/log/logfile
```

Table 11-4 describes the different facilities available and their descriptions.

Table 11-4 Facilities used by the System Log Daemon

Facility	Description
auth, or, security	Specifies messages from the login system, such as the login program, the getty program, and the su command
authpriv	Specifies messages from the login system when authenticating users across the network or to system databases
cron	Specifies messages from the cron and at daemons

Table 11-4 Facilities used by the System Log Daemon (Continued)

Facility	Description
daemon	Specifies messages from system daemons such as the FTP daemon
kern	Specifies messages from the Linux kernel
lpr	Specifies messages from the printing system (lpd)
mail	Specifies messages from the e-mail system (sendmail)
mark	Specifies time stamps used by syslogd; used internally only
news	Specifies messages from the Inter Network News daemon and other USENET daemons
syslog	Specifies messages from the syslog daemon
user	Specifies messages from user processes
uucp	Specifies messages from the uucp (UNIX to UNIX copy) daemon
local0-7	Specifies local messages; these are not used by default but can be defined for custom use

Table 11-5 displays the different priorities available listed in ascending order.

Table 11-5 Priorities used by the System Log Daemon

Priority	Description
debug	Indicates all information from a certain facility
info	Indicates normal information messages as a result of system operations
notice	Indicates information that should be noted for future reference, yet does not indicate a problem
warning, or, warn	Indicates messages that might be the result of an error but are not critical to system operations
error, or, err	Indicates all other error messages not described by other priorities
crit	Indicates system critical errors such as hard disk failure
alert	Indicates an error that should be rectified immediately, such as a corrupt system database
emerg, or, panic	Indicates very serious system conditions that would normally be broadcast to all users

Managing Log Files

Although log files can contain important system information, they might take up unnecessary space on the filesystem over time. Thus, it is important to clear the contents of log files over time.

> **TIP**
>
> Do not remove log files because the permissions and ownership will be removed as well.

Before clearing log files, it is good form to print them and store them in a safe place for future reference. To clear a log file, recall that you can use a > redirection symbol. The following commands display the size of the /var/log/messages log file before and after it has been printed and cleared:

```
[root@server1 root]# ls -l /var/log/messages
-rw-------   1 root     root     21705 Jul 14 10:52 /var/log/messages
[root@server1 root]# lp -d printer1 /var/log/messages
[root@server1 root]# >/var/log/messages
[root@server1 root]# ls -l /var/log/messages
-rw-------   1 root     root         0 Jul 14 10:52 /var/log/messages
[root@server1 root]# _
```

You can also schedule commands to print and clear log files on a repetitive basis using the cron daemon.

Alternatively, you can schedule the **logrotate** utility to back up and clear log files from entries stored in the **/etc/logrotate.conf** file and files stored in the /etc/logrotate.d directory. The logrotate command typically renames log files on a cyclic basis; a log file called test.log is renamed test.log.1 on the first cycle and a new test.log is created to accept system information. On the second cycle, test.log.1 is renamed test.log.2, test.log is renamed test.log.1, and a new test.log file is created to accept system information.

You can specify the number of log files that logrotate keeps. If logrotate is configured to keep only two copies of old log files, such as the files test.log.1 and test.log.2, then test.log.2 is removed on the next cycle.

An example of the /etc/logrotate.conf file is shown in the following output:

```
[root@server1 root]# cat /etc/logrotate.conf
# see "man logrotate" for details
# rotate log files weekly
weekly
```

```
# keep 4 weeks worth of backlogs
rotate 4

# create new (empty) log files after rotating old ones
create

# uncomment this if you want your log files compressed
#compress

# RPM packages drop log rotation information into this directory
include /etc/logrotate.d

# no packages own wtmp -- we'll rotate them here
/var/log/wtmp {
    monthly
    create 0664 root utmp
    rotate 1
}

# system-specific logs may be also be configured here.
[root@server1 root]# _
```

In the preceding output, any # characters indicate a comment and are ignored. The other lines indicate that log files contained in this file and all other files in the /etc/logrotate.d directory (include /etc/logrotate.d) are rotated on a weekly basis unless otherwise specified. In addition, four copies of old log files are kept (rotate 4). For the file /var/log/wtmp, this rotation occurs monthly instead of weekly, only one old log file is kept, and the new log file created has the permissions "0664"(rw-rw-r--), the owner "root," and the group "utmp."

The /etc/logrotate.conf file specifies the default parameters used by the logrotate command; however, most rotation information regarding log files is stored in the /etc/logrotate.d directory. Take the file /etc/logrotate.d/psacct as an example:

```
[root@server1 root]# cat /etc/logrotate.d/psacct
# Logrotate file for psacct RPM

/var/account/pacct {
prerotate
        /usr/sbin/accton
endscript
        compress
        notifempty
        daily
        rotate 31
        create 0600 root root
```

```
postrotate
        /usr/sbin/accton /var/account/pacct
endscript
}
```

```
[root@server1 root]# _
```

The file just shown indicates that the /var/account/pacct file should be rotated daily, new log files are owned by root and have the permissions 600 (rw-------), and log files are only rotated if they are not empty. Log files are compressed after being rotated and up to 31 copies of old log files can exist. In addition, the /usr/sbin/accton program is run before each rotation and the /usr/sbin/accton /var/account/pacct program is run after each rotation.

On most Linux systems, the logrotate utility is automatically scheduled to run daily via the file /etc/cron.daily/logrotate; however, you might choose to run it manually by typing the command logrotate /etc/logrotate.conf at a command prompt.

Over time, the logrotate command generates several copies of each log file, as shown in the following listing of the /var/log directory:

```
[root@server1 log]# ls /var/log
acpid       httpd        pgsql             secure
amanda      iptraf       ppp               secure.1
boot.log    lastlog      prelink.log       secure.2
boot.log.1  mail         privoxy           spooler
boot.log.2  maillog      quagga            spooler.1
boot.log.3  maillog.1    radius            spooler.2
canna       maillog.2    routed            squid
cron        mailman      rpmpkgs           tomcat
cron.1      messages     rpmpkgs.1         uucp
cups        messages.1   rpmpkgs.2         vbox
dmesg       messages.2   rpmpkgs.3         wtmp
exim        mysqld.log   sa                Xorg.0.log
fax         mysqld.log.1 samba             Xorg.0.log.old
gdm         news         scrollkeeper.log  Xorg.setup.log
[root@server1 root]# _
```

Given the preceding output, the most recent events are recorded in the boot.log file, followed by the boot.log.1 file, followed by the boot.log.2 file, and so on.

Administering Users and Groups

You must log in to a Linux system with a valid user name and password before a BASH shell is granted. This process is called **authentication** because the user name and password are authenticated against a system database that contains all **user account** information. Authenticated users are then granted access to files, directories, and other resources on the system based on their user account.

The system database that contains user account information typically consists of two files: **/etc/passwd** and **/etc/shadow**. Every user typically has a line that describes the user account in /etc/passwd and a line that contains the encrypted password and expiration information in /etc/shadow.

Older Linux systems stored the encrypted password in the /etc/passwd file and did not use an /etc/shadow file at all. This is considered poor security today because processes often require access to the user information in /etc/passwd. Storing the encrypted password in a separate file that cannot be accessed by processes prevents a process from obtaining all user account information. Recall that you are prompted whether to use "Shadow passwords" during installation; if this item is not selected, only the /etc/passwd file exists after installation. To convert the system so that it uses an /etc/shadow file to store the encrypted password after installation, you can run the **pwconv command**. Alternatively, the **pwunconv command** can be used to revert back to using an /etc/passwd file only.

Each line of the /etc/passwd file has the following colon-delimited format:

```
name:password:UID:GID:GECOS:homedirectory:shell
```

The name in the preceding output refers to the name of the user. If an /etc/shadow is not used, the password field contains the encrypted password for the user; otherwise, it just contains an x character as a placeholder for the password stored in /etc/shadow.

The **User Identifier (UID)** specifies the unique User ID that is assigned to each user. Typically, UIDs that are less than 100 refer to user accounts that are used by daemons when logging in to the system. The root user always has a UID of zero.

The **Group Identifier (GID)** is the primary Group ID for the user. Each user can be a member of several groups, but only one of those groups can be the primary group. The **primary group** of a user is the group that is made the group owner of any file or directory that the user creates. Similarly, when a user creates a file or directory, that user becomes the owner of that file or directory.

GECOS represents a text description of the user and is typically left blank; this information was originally used in the **General Electric Comprehensive Operating System (GECOS)**. The last two fields represent the absolute pathname to the user's home directory and the shell, respectively.

An example of an /etc/passwd file is shown next:

```
[root@server1 root]# cat /etc/passwd
root:x:0:0:root:/root:/bin/bash
bin:x:1:1:bin:/bin:/sbin/nologin
daemon:x:2:2:daemon:/sbin:/sbin/nologin
adm:x:3:4:adm:/var/adm:/sbin/nologin
lp:x:4:7:lp:/var/spool/lpd:/sbin/nologin
```

```
sync:x:5:0:sync:/sbin:/bin/sync
shutdown:x:6:0:shutdown:/sbin:/sbin/shutdown
halt:x:7:0:halt:/sbin:/sbin/halt
mail:x:8:12:mail:/var/spool/mail:/sbin/nologin
news:x:9:13:news:/etc/news:
uucp:x:10:14:uucp:/var/spool/uucp:/sbin/nologin
operator:x:11:0:operator:/root:/sbin/nologin
games:x:12:100:games:/usr/games:/sbin/nologin
gopher:x:13:30:gopher:/var/gopher:/sbin/nologin
ftp:x:14:50:FTP User:/var/ftp:/sbin/nologin
nobody:x:99:99:Nobody:/:/sbin/nologin
rpm:x:37:37::/var/lib/rpm:/sbin/nologin
vcsa:x:69:69:virtual console memory owner:/dev:/sbin/nologin
nscd:x:28:28:NSCD Daemon:/:/sbin/nologin
sshd:x:74:74:Privilege-separated SSH:/var/empty/sshd:/sbin/nologin
ident:x:98:98:pident user:/:/sbin/nologin
rpc:x:32:32:Portmapper RPC user:/:/sbin/nologin
rpcuser:x:29:29:RPC Service User:/var/lib/nfs:/sbin/nologin
nfsnobody:x:65534:65534:Anonymous NFS User:/var/lib/nfs:/sbin/nologin
pcap:x:77:77::/var/arpwatch:/sbin/nologin
mailnull:x:47:47::/var/spool/mqueue:/sbin/nologin
smmsp:x:51:51::/var/spool/mqueue:/sbin/nologin
apache:x:48:48:Apache:/var/www:/sbin/nologin
squid:x:23:23::/var/spool/squid:/sbin/nologin
webalizer:x:67:67:Webalizer:/var/www/usage:/sbin/nologin
dbus:x:81:81:System message bus:/:/sbin/nologin
xfs:x:43:43:X Font Server:/etc/X11/fs:/sbin/nologin
named:x:25:25:Named:/var/named:/sbin/nologin
ntp:x:38:38::/etc/ntp:/sbin/nologin
gdm:x:42:42::/var/gdm:/sbin/nologin
htt:x:100:101:IIIMF Htt:/usr/lib/im:/sbin/nologin
pvm:x:24:24::/usr/share/pvm3:/bin/bash
canna:x:39:39:Canna Service User:/var/lib/canna:/sbin/nologin
wnn:x:49:49:Wnn System Account:/home/wnn:/sbin/nologin
dovecot:x:97:97:dovecot:/usr/libexec/dovecot:/sbin/nologin
postfix:x:89:89::/var/spool/postfix:/sbin/nologin
mailman:x:41:41:GNU Mailing List Manager:/var/mailman:/sbin/nologin
amanda:x:33:6:Amanda user:/var/lib/amanda:/bin/bash
netdump:x:34:34:Network Crash Dump user:/var/crash:/bin/bash
quagga:x:92:92:Quagga routing suite:/var/run/quagga:/sbin/nologin
radvd:x:75:75:radvd user:/:/sbin/nologin
radiusd:x:95:95:radiusd user:/:/bin/false
ldap:x:55:55:LDAP User:/var/lib/ldap:/bin/false
mysql:x:27:27:MySQL Server:/var/lib/mysql:/bin/bash
```

```
postgres:x:26:26:PostgreSQL Server:/var/lib/pgsql:/bin/bash
fax:x:78:78:mgetty fax spool user:/var/spool/fax:/sbin/nologin
nut:x:57:57:Network UPS Tools:/var/lib/ups:/bin/false
privoxy:x:73:73::/etc/privoxy:/sbin/nologin
tomcat:x:53:53:Tomcat server:/var/lib/tomcat:/sbin/nologin
cyrus:x:76:12:Cyrus IMAP Server:/var/lib/imap:/bin/bash
exim:x:93:93::/var/spool/exim:/sbin/nologin
user1:x:500:500:sample user one:/home/user1:/bin/bash
[root@server1 root]# _
```

The root user is usually listed at the top of the /etc/passwd file as just shown, followed by user accounts used by daemons when logging in to the system, followed by regular user accounts. The final line of the preceding output indicates that the user user1 has a UID of 500, a primary GID of 500, a GECOS of "sample user one," the home directory /home/user1, and uses the BASH shell.

Like /etc/passwd, the /etc/shadow file is colon-delimited, yet has the following format:

```
name:password:lastchange:min:max:warn:disable1:disable2:
```

Although the first two fields in the /etc/shadow file are the same as those in /etc/passwd, the contents of the password field are different; the password field in the /etc/shadow file contains the encrypted password, whereas the password field in /etc/passwd contains an x character, because it is not used.

The lastchange field represents the date of the most recent password change; it is measured in the number of days since January 1, 1970. For example, the number 10957 represents January 1, 2000, because January 1, 2000, is 10957 days after January 1, 1970.

NOTE

Traditionally, a calendar date was represented by a number indicating the number of days since January 1, 1970. Many calendar dates found in configuration files follow the same convention.

To prevent unauthorized access to a Linux system, it is good form to change passwords for user accounts regularly; thus, passwords can be set to expire at certain intervals. The next three fields of the /etc/shadow file indicate information about password expiration; min represents the number of days a user must wait before she changes her password after receiving a new one, max represents the number of days a user can use the same password without changing it, and warn represents the number of days before a password expires that a user is warned to change her password.

By default on Red Hat Fedora Linux systems, min is equal to zero days, max is equal to 99999 days, and warn is equal to seven days. Thus, you can change your password immediately after receiving a new one, your password expires in 99999 days, and you are warned seven days in advance before your password needs to be changed.

When a password has expired, the user is still allowed to log in to the system for a certain period of time, after which the user is disabled from logging in. The number of days after a password expires that a user account is disabled is represented by the disable1 field in /etc/shadow. In addition, you can choose to disable a user from logging in at a certain date, such as the end of an employment contract. The disable2 field in /etc/shadow represents the number of days since January 1, 1970, that a user account will be disabled.

An example /etc/shadow file is shown next:

```
[root@server1 root]# cat /etc/shadow
root:$1$1Py5hQF6$9FX9nLNBfOkz.GmY61R.F/:12617:0:99999:7:::
bin:*:12617:0:99999:7:::
daemon:*:12617:0:99999:7:::
adm:*:12617:0:99999:7:::
lp:*:12617:0:99999:7:::
sync:*:12617:0:99999:7:::
shutdown:*:12617:0:99999:7:::
halt:*:12617:0:99999:7:::
mail:*:12617:0:99999:7:::
news:*:12617:0:99999:7:::
uucp:*:12617:0:99999:7:::
operator:*:12617:0:99999:7:::
games:*:12617:0:99999:7:::
gopher:*:12617:0:99999:7:::
ftp:*:12617:0:99999:7:::
nobody:*:12617:0:99999:7:::
rpm:!!:12617:0:99999:7:::
vcsa:!!:12617:0:99999:7:::
nscd:!!:12617:0:99999:7:::
sshd:!!:12617:0:99999:7:::
ident:!!!:12617:0:99999:7:::
rpc:!!:12617:0:99999:7:::
rpcuser:!!!:12617:0:99999:7:::
nfsnobody:!!!:12617:0:99999:7:::
pcap:!!!:12617:0:99999:7:::
mailnull:!!!:12617:0:99999:7:::
smmsp:!!!:12617:0:99999:7:::
apache:!!!:12617:0:99999:7:::
squid:!!!:12617:0:99999:7:::
webalizer:!!!:12617:0:99999:7:::
dbus:!!!:12617:0:99999:7:::
xfs:!!!:12617:0:99999:7:::
```

```
named:!!:12617:0:99999:7:::
ntp:!!:12617:0:99999:7:::
gdm:!!:12617:0:99999:7:::
htt:!!:12617:0:99999:7:::
pvm:!!:12617:0:99999:7:::
canna:!!:12617:0:99999:7:::
wnn:!!:12617:0:99999:7:::
dovecot:!!:12617:0:99999:7:::
postfix:!!:12617:0:99999:7:::
mailman:!!:12617:0:99999:7:::
amanda:!!:12617:0:99999:7:::
netdump:!!:12617:0:99999:7:::
quagga:!!:12617:0:99999:7:::
radvd:!!:12617:0:99999:7:::
radiusd:!!:12617:0:99999:7:::
ldap:!!:12617:0:99999:7:::
mysql:!!:12617:0:99999:7:::
postgres:!!:12617:0:99999:7:::
fax:!!:12617:0:99999:7:::
nut:!!:12617:0:99999:7:::
privoxy:!!:12617:0:99999:7:::
tomcat:!!:12617:0:99999:7:::
cyrus:!!:12617:0:99999:7:::
exim:!!:12617:0:99999:7:::
user1:$1$AkhHivrA$J2rMs4me5bC/YdINSsYYp/:12617:0:99999:7::: [root@server1 root]# _
```

Note from the preceding output that most user accounts used by daemons do not receive an encrypted password.

Although every user must have a primary group listed in the /etc/passwd file, each user can be a member of multiple groups. All groups and their members are listed in the **/etc/group** file. The /etc/group file has the following colon-delimited fields:

```
name:password:GID:members
```

The first field is the name of the group, followed by a group password.

NOTE

The password field usually contains an x, because group passwords are rarely used. If used, you need to specify a password to change your primary group membership using the **newgrp command** discussed later in this chapter. These passwords are set using the gpasswd command and can be stored in the /etc/gshadow file for added security. Refer to the gpasswd manual or info page for more information.

The GID represents the unique Group ID for the group and the members field indicates the list of group members. An example /etc/group file is shown next:

```
[root@server1 root]# cat /etc/group
root:x:0:root
bin:x:1:root,bin,daemon
daemon:x:2:root,bin,daemon
sys:x:3:root,bin,adm
adm:x:4:root,adm,daemon
tty:x:5:
disk:x:6:root
lp:x:7:daemon,lp
mem:x:8:
kmem:x:9:
wheel:x:10:root
mail:x:12:mail,postfix,exim
news:x:13:news
uucp:x:14:uucp,nut
man:x:15:
games:x:20:
gopher:x:30:
dip:x:40:
ftp:x:50:
lock:x:54:
nobody:x:99:
users:x:100:
rpm:x:37:
floppy:x:19:
vcsa:x:69:
utmp:x:22:
slocate:x:21:
nscd:x:28:
sshd:x:74:
ident:x:98:
rpc:x:32:
rpcuser:x:29:
nfsnobody:x:65534:
pcap:x:77:
mailnull:x:47:
smmsp:x:51:
apache:x:48:
squid:x:23:
webalizer:x:67:
dbus:x:81:
```

```
xfs:x:43:
named:x:25:
ntp:x:38:
gdm:x:42:
htt:x:101:
pvm:x:24:
canna:x:39:
wnn:x:49:
dovecot:x:97:
postdrop:x:90:
postfix:x:89:
mailman:x:41:
netdump:x:34:
quaggavt:x:102:
quagga:x:92:
radvd:x:75:
radiusd:x:95:
ldap:x:55:
mysql:x:27:
postgres:x:26:
fax:x:78:
nut:x:57:
privoxy:x:73:
tomcat:x:53:
exim:x:93:
user1:x:500:
[root@server1 root]# _
```

From the preceding output, the "bin" group has a GID of 1, and three users as members: root, bin, and daemon.

Creating User Accounts

You can create user accounts on the Linux system by using the **useradd command**, specifying the user name as an argument, as shown next:

```
[root@server1 root]# useradd bobg
[root@server1 root]# _
```

In this case, all other information such as the UID, shell, and home directory location are taken from two files that contain user account creation default values.

The first file, **/etc/login.defs**, contains parameters that set the default location for e-mail, password expiration information, minimum password length, range of UIDs and GIDs available for use, as well as specifying whether to create home directories by default.

A sample /etc/login.defs file is depicted in the following example:

```
[root@server1 root]# cat /etc/login.defs
# *REQUIRED*
# Directory where mailboxes reside, _or_ name of file, relative to the
# home directory. If you _do_ define both, MAIL_DIR takes precedence.
#   QMAIL_DIR is for Qmail
#
#QMAIL_DIR      Maildir
MAIL_DIR        /var/spool/mail
#MAIL_FILE      .mail

# Password aging controls:
#
#   PASS_MAX_DAYS   Maximum number of days a password may be used.
#   PASS_MIN_DAYS   Minimum number of days allowed between password
#                   changes.
#   PASS_MIN_LEN    Minimum acceptable password length.
#   PASS_WARN_AGE   Number of days warning given before a password
#                   expires.
#
PASS_MAX_DAYS   99999
PASS_MIN_DAYS   0
PASS_MIN_LEN    5
PASS_WARN_AGE   7

#
# Min/max values for automatic uid selection in useradd
#
UID_MIN                 500
UID_MAX                 60000

#
# Min/max values for automatic gid selection in groupadd
#
GID_MIN                 500
GID_MAX                 60000

#
# If defined, this command is run when removing a user.
# It should remove any at/cron/print jobs etc. owned by
# the user to be removed (passed as the first argument).
#
#USERDEL_CMD    /usr/sbin/userdel_local
```

```
#
# If useradd should create home directories for users by default
# on RH systems, we do. This option is ORed with the -m flag on
# useradd command line.
#
CREATE_HOME     yes

[root@server1 root]# _
```

The second file, **/etc/default/useradd**, contains information regarding the default primary group, the location of home directories, the default number of days to disable accounts with expired passwords, the date to disable user accounts, the shell used, and the skeleton directory used. The **skeleton directory** on most Linux systems is **/etc/skel** and contains files that are copied to all new users' home directories when the home directory is created. Most of these files are environment files such as .bash_profile and .bashrc.

A sample /etc/default/useradd file is shown in the following output:

```
[root@server1 root]# cat /etc/default/useradd
# useradd defaults file
GROUP=100
HOME=/home
INACTIVE=-1
EXPIRE=
SHELL=/bin/bash
SKEL=/etc/skel
[root@server1 root]# _
```

To override any of the default parameters in the /etc/login.defs and /etc/default/useradd for a user, you can specify options to the useradd command when creating user accounts. For example, to create a user named maryj with a UID of 762, you can use the -u option to the useradd command, as shown in the following example:

```
[root@server1 root]# useradd -u 762 maryj
[root@server1 root]# _
```

Table 11-6 lists some common options available to the useradd command and their descriptions.

Table 11-6 Common options to the useradd command

Option	Description
-c *"description"*	Adds a description for the user to the GECOS field of /etc/passwd.
-d *homedirectory*	Specifies the absolute pathname to the user's home directory.
-e *expirydate*	Specifies a date to disable the account from logging in.

Table 11-6 Common options to the useradd command (Continued)

Option	Description
-f *days*	Specifies the number of days until a user account with an expired password is disabled.
-g *group*	Specifies the primary group for the user account. By default in Red Hat Fedora Linux, a group is created with the same name as the user and made the primary group for that user.
-G *group1, group2,etc.*	Specifies all other group memberships for the user account.
-m	Specifies that a home directory should be created for the user account. By default in Red Hat Fedora Linux, home directories are created for all users via an entry in the /etc/login.defs file.
-k *directory*	Specifies the skeleton directory used when copying files to a new home directory.
-s *shell*	Specifies the absolute pathname to the shell used for the user account.
-u *UID*	Specifies the UID of the user account.

After a user account has been added, the password field in the /etc/shadow file contains two ! characters, indicating that no password has been set for the user account. To set the password, simply type the **passwd command**, type the name of the new user account at a command prompt, and then supply the appropriate password when prompted. An example of setting the password for the bobg user is shown in the following:

```
[root@server1 root]# passwd bobg
Changing password for user bobg.
New UNIX password:
Retype new UNIX password:
passwd: all authentication tokens updated successfully.
[root@server1 root]# _
```

> **NOTE**
>
> Without arguments, the passwd command changes the password for the current user.
>
> All user accounts must have a password set before they are used to log in to the system.
>
> The root user can set the password on any user account using the passwd command; however, regular users can change their password only using this command.

> **TIP**
>
> Passwords should be difficult to guess and contain a combination of uppercase, lowercase, and special characters to increase system security. An example of a good password to choose is C2Jr1;Pwr.

Modifying User Accounts

To modify the information regarding a user account after creation, you can edit the /etc/passwd or /etc/shadow file; however, this is not recommended practice because typographical errors in these files might prevent the system from functioning. The **usermod command** can be used to modify most information regarding user accounts. For example, to change the login name of the user bobg to barbg, you can use the -l option to the usermod command:

```
[root@server1 root]# usermod -l barbg bobg
[root@server1 root]# _
```

Table 11-7 displays a complete list of options used with the usermod command to modify user accounts.

Table 11-7 Common options to the usermod command

Option	Description
-c *"description"*	Specifies a new description for the user in the GECOS field of /etc/passwd
-d *homedirectory*	Specifies the absolute pathname to a new home directory
-e *expirydate*	Specifies a date to disable the account from logging in
-f *days*	Specifies the number of days until a user account with an expired password is disabled
-g *group*	Specifies a new primary group for the user account
-G *group1, group2, etc.*	Specifies all other group memberships for the user account
-l *name*	Specifies a new login name
-s *shell*	Specifies the absolute pathname to a new shell used for the user account
-u *UID*	Specifies a new UID for the user account

The only user account information that the usermod command cannot modify is the password expiration information stored in /etc/shadow (min, max, warn) discussed earlier. To change this information, you can use the **chage command** with the appropriate option. For example, to specify that the user bobg must wait 2 days before changing his password after receiving a new password, as well as specify that his password expires every 50 days with 7 days of warning prior to expiration, you can use the following options to the chage command:

```
[root@server1 root]# chage -m 2 -M 50 -W 7 bobg
[root@server1 root]# _
```

It might be necessary in certain situations to prevent a user from logging in temporarily; this is commonly called **locking an account**. To lock an account, you can use the command usermod -L *username* at the command prompt. This places a ! character at the beginning of the encrypted password field in the /etc/shadow file. To unlock the account, simply type usermod -U *username* at the command prompt, which removes the ! character from the password field in the /etc/shadow file.

Alternatively, you can use the passwd -l *username* command to lock a user account and the passwd -u *username* command to unlock a user account.

Yet another method commonly used to lock a user account is to change the shell specified in /etc/passwd for a user account from /bin/bash to an invalid shell such as /bin/false. Without a valid shell, a user cannot use the system. To lock a user account this way, you can edit the /etc/passwd file and make the appropriate change, use the -s option to the usermod command, or use the **chsh command**. The following example uses the chsh command to change the shell to /bin/false for the user bobg:

```
[root@server1 root]# chsh -s /bin/false bobg
Changing shell for bobg.
Warning: "/bin/false" is not listed in /etc/shells
Shell changed.
[root@server1 root]# _
```

Deleting User Accounts

To delete a user account, you can use the **userdel command** and specify the user name as an argument; this removes entries from both /etc/passwd and /etc/shadow corresponding to the user account. Furthermore, you can specify the -r option to the userdel command to remove the home directory for the user and all of its contents.

When a user account is deleted, any files that were previously owned by the user become owned by a number that represents the UID of the deleted user. Any future user account that is given the same UID then becomes the owner of those files.

Suppose, for example, that the user bobg leaves the company. To delete bobg's user account and display the ownership of his old files, you can use the following commands:

```
[root@server1 root]# userdel bobg
[root@server1 root]# ls -la /home/bobg
total 52
drwx------    4 502    502        4096 Jul 17 15:37 .
drwxr-xr-x    5 root   root       4096 Jul 17 15:37 ..
-rw-r--r--    1 502    502          24 Jul 17 15:37 .bash_logout
-rw-r--r--    1 502    502         191 Jul 17 15:37 .bash_profile
-rw-r--r--    1 502    502         124 Jul 17 15:37 .bashrc
-rw-r--r--    1 502    502        5542 Jul 17 15:37 .canna
-rw-r--r--    1 502    502         820 Jul 17 15:37 .emacs
-rw-r--r--    1 502    502         118 Jul 17 15:37 .gtkrc
-rw-r--r--    3 502    502        4096 Jul 17 15:37 .kde
drwxr-xr-x    2 502    502        4096 Jul 17 15:37 .xemacs
-rw-r--r--    1 502    502        3511 Jul 17 15:37 .zshrc
[root@server1 root]# _
```

From the preceding output, you can see that the UID of the bobg user was 502. If the user sueb was hired by the company to replace bobg, you can assign the UID of 502 to her user account so that she can own all of bobg's old files and reuse them as needed.

To create the user sueb with a UID of 502 and list the ownership of the files in bobg's home directory, you can use the following commands:

```
[root@server1 root]# useradd -u 502 sueb
[root@server1 root]# ls -la /home/bobg
total 52
drwx------    4 sueb   sueb       4096 Jul 17 15:37 .
drwxr-xr-x    5 root   root       4096 Jul 17 18:56 ..
-rw-r--r--    1 sueb   sueb         24 Jul 17 15:37 .bash_logout
-rw-r--r--    1 sueb   sueb        191 Jul 17 15:37 .bash_profile
-rw-r--r--    1 sueb   sueb        124 Jul 17 15:37 .bashrc
-rw-r--r--    1 sueb   sueb       5542 Jul 17 15:37 .canna
-rw-r--r--    1 sueb   sueb        820 Jul 17 15:37 .emacs
-rw-r--r--    1 sueb   sueb        118 Jul 17 15:37 .gtkrc
-rw-r--r--    3 sueb   sueb       4096 Jul 17 15:37 .kde
drwxr-xr-x    2 sueb   sueb       4096 Jul 17 15:37 .xemacs
-rw-r--r--    1 sueb   sueb       3511 Jul 17 15:37 .zshrc
[root@server1 root]# _
```

Managing Groups

By far, the easiest method to add groups to a system is to edit the /etc/group file using a text editor. Another method is to use the **groupadd command**. To add a group called group1 to the system and assign it a GID of 492, you can use the following command:

```
[root@server1 root]# groupadd -g 492 group1
[root@server1 root]# _
```

Then, you can use the -G option to the usermod command to add members to the group. To add the user maryj to this group and view the addition, you can use the following usermod command:

```
[root@server1 root]# usermod -G group1 maryj
[root@server1 root]# tail -1 /etc/group
group1:x:492:maryj
[root@server1 root]# _
```

There also exists a **groupmod command** that can be used to modify the group name and GID, as well as a **groupdel command**, which can be used to remove groups from the system.

To see a list of groups of which you are a member, simply run the groups command; to see the GIDs for each group, simply run the id command. The primary group is always listed first by each command. The following output shows the output of these commands when executed by the root user:

```
[root@server1 root]# groups
root bin daemon sys adm disk wheel
[root@server1 root]# id
uid=0(root) gid=0(root) groups=0(root),1(bin),2(daemon),3(sys),4(adm),6(disk),10(wheel)
[root@server1 root]# _
```

You can see from the preceding output that the primary group for the root user is the root group. This group is attached as the group owner for all files that are created by the root user, as shown in the following output:

```
[root@server1 root]# touch samplefile1
[root@server1 root]# ls -l samplefile1
-rw-r--r--    1 root      root           0 Jul 17 19:22 samplefile1 [root@server1 root]#
_
```

To change the primary group temporarily to another group that is listed in the output of the groups and id commands, you can use the newgrp command. Any new files created afterward will then have the new group owner. The following output demonstrates how changing the primary group for the root user affects file ownership:

```
[root@server1 root]# newgrp sys
[root@server1 root]# id
uid=0(root) gid=3(sys)
```

```
groups=0(root),1(bin),2(daemon),3(sys),4(adm),6(disk),10(wheel)
[root@server1 root]# touch samplefile2
[root@server1 root]# ls -l samplefile2
-rw-r--r--    1 root      sys            0 Jul 17 19:28 samplefile2 [root@server1 root]# _
```

> **NOTE**
>
> If you use group passwords as described earlier in this section, you can use the new-
> grp command to change your primary group to a group of which you are not a mem-
> ber, provided you supply the appropriate password when prompted.

Although command-line utilities are commonly used to administer users and groups, you can instead use a graphical utility to create, modify, and delete user and group accounts on the system. These utilities run the appropriate command-line utility in the background. To create and manage users and groups in Red Hat Fedora Core 2 from within a desktop environment, you navigate to the Red Hat button, System Settings, Users and Groups, as shown in Figure 11-11.

Alternatively, you can use the system-config-users command at a terminal within a desktop environment to obtain the screen in Figure 11-11.

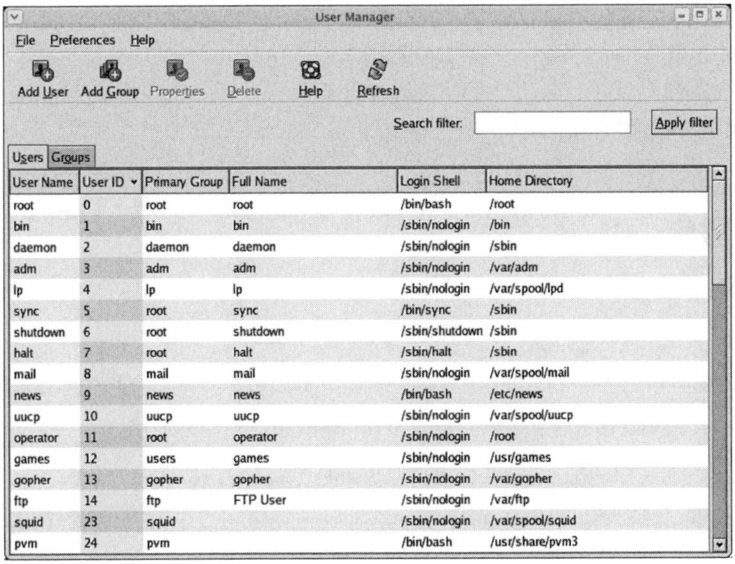

FIGURE 11-11 *Configuring users and groups within a desktop environment*

Chapter Summary

◆ Print jobs are spooled to a print queue before being printed to a printer.

◆ You can configure spooling or printing for a printer by using the accept, reject, enable, and disable commands.

◆ Print jobs are created using the lp command, can be viewed in the print queue using the lpstat command, and are removed from the print queue using the cancel command.

◆ You can create local and remote printers using the Printer Configuration tool or by modifying the /etc/cups/printers.conf file.

◆ Most log files on a Linux system are stored in the /var/log directory.

◆ System events are typically logged to files by the System Log Daemon.

◆ Log files should be cleared or rotated over time to save disk space; the logrotate utility can be used to rotate log files.

◆ User and group account information is typically stored in the /etc/passwd, /etc/shadow, and /etc/group files.

◆ You can use the useradd command to create users and the groupadd command to create groups.

◆ All users must have a valid password before logging in to a Linux system.

◆ Users can be modified with the usermod, chage, chsh, and passwd commands, and groups can be modified using the groupmod command.

◆ The userdel and groupdel commands can be used to remove users and groups from the system, respectively.

Key Terms

/etc/cups/cupsd.conf — A file that holds daemon configuration for the cups daemon.

/etc/cups/printers.conf — A file that holds printer configuration for the cups daemon.

/etc/default/useradd — A file that contains default values for user creation.

/etc/group — The file that contains group definitions and memberships.

/etc/login.defs — A file that contains default values for user creation.

/etc/logrotate.conf — The file used by the logrotate utility to specify rotation parameters for log files.

/etc/passwd — The file that contains user account information.

/etc/shadow — The file that contains the encrypted password as well as password and account expiry parameters for each user account.

/etc/skel — A directory that contains files that are copied to all new users' home directories upon creation.

/etc/syslog.conf — The file that specifies the events for which the System Log Daemon listens and the log files to which it saves the events.

/var/log — A directory that contains most log files on a Linux system.

accepting printer — A printer that accepts print jobs into the print queue.

authentication — The act of verifying a user's identity by comparing a user name and password to a system database (/etc/passwd and /etc/shadow).

cancel command — The command used to remove print jobs from the print queue in the CUPS print system.

chage command — The command used to modify password expiry information for user accounts.

chsh command — The command used to change a valid shell to an invalid shell.

Common Unix Printing System (CUPS) — The printing system commonly used on Linux computers.

cups daemon (cupsd) — The daemon responsible for printing in the CUPS printing system.

disabled printer — A printer that does not send print jobs from the print queue to a printer.

enabled printer — A printer that sends print jobs from the print queue to a printer.

facility — The area of the system from which information is gathered when logging system events.

General Electric Comprehensive Operating System (GECOS) — The field in the /etc/passwd file that contains a description of the user account.

Group Identifier (GID) — A unique number given to each group.

groupadd command — The command used to add a group to the system.

groupdel command — The command used to delete a group from the system.

groupmod command — The command used to modify the name or GID of a group on the system.

Line Printer Daemon (LPD) — A printing system typically used on legacy Linux computers.

locking an account — The act of making an account temporarily unusable by altering the password information for it stored on the system.

log file — A file containing information about the Linux system.

logrotate command — The command used to rotate log files; typically uses the configuration information stored in /etc/logrotate.conf.

lp command — The command used to create print jobs in the print queue in the CUPS printing system.

lpadmin command — The command used to perform printer administration in the CUPS printing system.

lpc command — The command used to view the status of and control printers in the LPD printing system.

lpq command — The command used to view the contents of print queues in the LPD printing system.

lpr command — The command used to create print jobs in the print queue in the LPD printing system.

lprm command — The command used to remove print jobs from the print queue in the LPD printing system.

lpstat command — The command used to view the contents of print queues and printer information in the CUPS printing system.

newgrp command — The command used to change temporarily the primary group of a user.

passwd command — The command used to modify the password associated with a user account.

primary group — The group that is specified for a user in the /etc/passwd file and that is specified as group owner for all files created by a user.

print job — The information sent to a printer for printing.

print job ID — A unique numeric identifier used to mark and distinguish each print job.

print queue — A directory on the filesystem that holds print jobs that are waiting to be printed.

Printer Configuration tool — A graphical utility used to configure printers on the system.

printing — The process by which print jobs are sent from a print queue to a printer.

priority — The importance of system information when logging system events.

pwconv command — The command used to enable the use of the /etc/shadow file.

pwunconv command — The command used to disable the use of the /etc/shadow file.

queuing — _See also_ Spooling.

rejecting printer — A printer that does not accept print jobs into the print queue.

skeleton directory — A directory that contains files that are copied to all new users' home directories upon creation; the default skeleton directory on Linux systems is /etc/skel.

spooling — The process of accepting a print job into a print queue.

System Log Daemon (syslogd) — The daemon that logs system events to various log files via information stored in /etc/syslog.conf.

user account — The information regarding a user that is stored in a system database (/etc/passwd and /etc/shadow), which can be used to log in to the system and gain access to system resources.

User Identifier (UID) — A unique number assigned to each user account.

useradd command — The command used to add a user account to the system.

userdel command — The command used to remove a user account from the system.

usermod command — The command used to modify the properties of a user account on the system.

Review Questions

1. Which flag for the lp command is used to set the print job priority?

   a. -d

   b. -m

   c. -n

   d. -q

2. The core component of printing is the _____ daemon, which accepts print jobs into a queue and sends them to the printer.

   a. cups

   b. print

   c. lpt

   d. queue

3. In what directory are most log files found?

   a. /logs

   b. /dev/logs

   c. /var/log

   d. /sys/log

4. Which file holds encrypted user passwords in modern Linux systems?

   a. /etc/passwd

   b. /etc/password

   c. /etc/auth

   d. /etc/shadow

5. Which option to the useradd command specifies the user's primary group?

   a. -g

   b. -m

   c. crond

   d. atd

6. True or false? Because the print process involves sending jobs to a print queue before sending them to a printer, the printer name is often referred to as the queue name.

7. True or false? To identify and troubleshoot problems on a Linux system, administrators typically review all events on the system.

8. True or false? It is not important to clear the contents of log files over time since Linux automatically removes log files that are over a month old.

9. True or false? Typically, UIDs that are less than 100 refer to user accounts that are used by daemons when logging in to the system.

10. True or false? When a password has expired, the user is barred from using the system immediately.

11. The most common printing system used on Linux computers is the _____ Printing System.

12. To remove a print job that is in the print queue, you can use the _____ command followed by the print job IDs of the jobs to remove.

13. The _____ facility specifies messages from the login system.

14. The process of logging into a Linux system with a user name and password is called _____.

15. To see a list of groups that you are a member of, simply run the _____ command.

Chapter 12

Compression, System Backup, and Software Installation

After completing this chapter, you will be able to:

◆ Outline the features of common compression utilities

◆ Compress and decompress files using common compression utilties

◆ Perform system backups using the `tar`, `cpio`, and `dump` commands

◆ View and extract archives using the `tar`, `cpio`, and `restore` commands

◆ Use burning software to back up files to CD-RW and DVD-RW

◆ Describe common types of Linux software

◆ Compile and install software packages from source code

◆ Use the Red Hat Package Manager to install, manage, and remove software packages

In the preceding chapter, you examined common administrative tasks that are performed on a regular basis. In this chapter, you also learn about tasks that are performed frequently, but you focus on file- and software-related administration. You begin this chapter learning about utilities commonly used to compress files on filesystems, followed by a discussion of system backup and archiving utilities. Finally, you learn about the different forms of software available for Linux systems, how to compile source code into functional programs, and the features and usage of the Red Hat Package Manager.

Compression

At times, you might want to reduce the size of a file or set of files due to limited disk space. You might also want to compress files that are sent across a computer network such as the Internet to decrease transfer time. In either case, several utilities can perform a standard set of instructions on a file to reduce its size by stripping out characters. This procedure is called **compression**, and the standard set of instructions used to compress a file is known as a **compression algorithm**. To decompress a file, you can simply run the compression algorithm in reverse.

Because compression utilities use different compression algorithms, they achieve different rates of compression for similar types of files. The rate of compression is known as a **compression ratio**; if a compression utility compresses a file to 52% of its original size, it has a compression ratio of 48%.

Many compression utilities are available to Linux users; this section examines the three most common:

- ◆ compress
- ◆ gzip
- ◆ bzip2

The compress Utility

The compress utility is one of the oldest compression utilities common to most UNIX and Linux systems. The compression algorithm that it uses is called Adaptive Lempel-Ziv coding (LZW) and it has an average compression ratio of 40–50%.

To compress a file using the compress utility, you can specify the files to compress as arguments to the **compress command**. Each file is renamed with a .Z filename extension to indicate that it is compressed. In addition, you can use the -v (verbose) option to the compress command to display the compression ratio during compression. The following output displays the filenames and size of the samplefile and samplefile2 files before and after compression:

```
[root@server1 root]# ls -l
total 28
drwx------    3 root     root          4096 Jul 21 08:15 Desktop
-rw-r--r--    1 root     root         20239 Jul 21 08:15 samplefile
-rw-rw-r--    1 root     root           574 Jul 21 08:18 samplefile2
[root@server1 root]# compress -v samplefile samplefile2
samplefile:   -- replaced with samplefile.Z Compression: 48.06%
samplefile2:  -- replaced with samplefile2.Z Compression: 26.13%
[root@server1 root]# ls -l
total 20
drwx------    3 root     root          4096 Jul 21 08:15 Desktop
-rw-rw-r--    1 root     root           424 Jul 21 08:18 samplefile2.Z
-rw-r--r--    1 root     root         10512 Jul 21 08:15 samplefile.Z
[root@server1 root]# _
```

> **NOTE**
>
> The compress utility preserves the original ownership, modification, and access time for each file that it compresses.
>
> By default, the compress utility does not compress symbolic links or very small files; to force the compress utility to compress these files, you must use the -f option. You can compress all of the files in a certain directory by using the -r option and specifying the directory name as an argument to the compress command.

After compression, the **zcat command** can be used to display the contents of a compressed file, as shown in the following output:

```
[root@server1 root]# zcat samplefile2.Z
Hi there, I hope this day finds you well.

Unfortunately we were not able to make it to your dining
room this year while vacationing in Algonquin Park - I
especially wished to see the model of the Highland Inn
and the train station in the dining room.

I have been reading on the history of Algonquin Park but
no where could I find a description of where the Highland
Inn was originally located on Cache lake.
```

```
If it is no trouble, could you kindly let me know such that
I need not wait until next year when I visit your lodge?

Regards,
Mackenzie Elizabeth


[root@server1 root]# _
```

NOTE

A **zmore command** and a **zless command** also exist, which can be used to view the contents of a compressed file page-by-page.

To decompress files that have been compressed with the compress utility, simply use the **uncompress command** followed by the names of the files to be decompressed. This restores the original filename. The following output decompresses and displays the filenames for the samplefile.Z and samplefile2.Z files created earlier:

```
[root@server1 root]# uncompress -v samplefile.Z samplefile2.Z
samplefile.Z:  -- replaced with samplefile
samplefile2.Z:  -- replaced with samplefile2
[root@server1 root]# ls -l
total 28
drwx------    3 root     root          4096 Jul 21 08:15 Desktop
-rw-r--r--    1 root     root         20239 Jul 21 08:15 samplefile
-rw-rw-r--    1 root     root           574 Jul 21 08:18 samplefile2
[root@server1 root]# _
```

NOTE

You are prompted for confirmation if any existing files will be overwritten during decompression. To prevent this confirmation, you can use the -f option to the uncompress command.

You can omit the .Z extension when using the uncompress command; the command uncompress -v samplefile samplefile2 would achieve the same results as the command shown in the preceding output.

Furthermore, the compress utility is a filter command that can take information from Standard Input and send it to Standard Output. For example, to send the output of the who command to the `compress` utility and save the compressed information to a file called file.Z, you can execute the following command:

```
[root@server1 root]# who | compress -v >file.Z
Compression: 21.35%
[root@server1 root]# _
```

Following this, you can display the contents of file.Z using the `zcat` command, or decompress it using the `uncompress` command, as shown in the following output:

```
[root@server1 root]# zcat file.Z
root     pts/1    Jul 20 19:22 (3.0.0.2)
root     tty5     Jul 15 19:03
root     pts/1    Jul 17 19:58
[root@server1 root]# uncompress -v file.Z
file.Z:  -- replaced with file
[root@server1 root]# _
```

Table 12-1 provides a summary of options commonly used with the `compress` utility.

Table 12-1 Common options used with the compress utility

Option	Description
-c	When used with the uncompress command, it displays the contents of the compress file to Standard Output (same function as the zcat command).
-f	When used with the compress command, it can be used to compress symbolic links. When used with the uncompress command, it overwrites any existing files without prompting the user.
-r	Specifies to compress or decompress all files recursively within a specified directory.
-v	Displays verbose output (compression ratio and filenames) during compression and decompression.

The gzip utility

The **GNU zip (gzip)** utility uses a Lempel-Ziv compression algorithm (LZ77) that varies slightly from the one used by the `compress` utility. Typically, this algorithm yields better compression than the one used by `compress`; the average compression ratio for `gzip` is 60–70%.

Like the `compress` utility, symbolic links are not compressed by the `gzip` utility unless the `-f` option is given, and the `-r` option can be used to compress all files in a certain directory. In addition, the ownership, modification, and access times of compressed files are preserved by default, and the `-v` option to the `gzip` command can be used to display the compression ratio and filename. However, `gzip` uses the `.gz` filename extension by default.

To compress the samplefile and samplefile2 files shown earlier and view the compression ratio, you can use the following command:

```
[root@server1 root]# gzip -v samplefile samplefile2
samplefile:             56.8% -- replaced with samplefile.gz
samplefile2:            40.7% -- replaced with samplefile2.gz
[root@server1 root]# _
```

You can also use the zcat and zmore commands to send the contents of a compressed file to Standard Output. Along the same lines, the gzip command can accept information via Standard Input. Thus, to compress the output of the date command to a file called file.gz and view its contents afterward, you can use the following commands:

```
[root@server1 root]# date | gzip -v >file.gz
- 6.8%
[root@server1 root]# zcat file.gz
Mon Jul 25 19:24:56 EDT 2005
[root@server1 root]# _
```

To decompress the file.gz file in the preceding output, you can use the -d option to the gzip command, or the **gunzip command**, as shown in the following output:

```
[root@server1 root]# gunzip -v file.gz
file.gz:                - 6.8% -- replaced with file
[root@server1 root]# _
```

Like the uncompress command, the gunzip command prompts you to overwrite existing files unless the -f option is specified. Furthermore, you can omit the .gz extension when decompressing files, as shown in the following example:

```
[root@server1 root]# ls -l
total 20
drwx------    3 root     root         4096 Jul 21 08:15 Desktop
-rw-rw-r--    1 root     root          370 Jul 21 08:18 samplefile2.gz
-rw-r--r--    1 root     root         8763 Jul 21 08:15 samplefile.gz
[root@server1 root]# gunzip -v samplefile samplefile2
samplefile.gz:          56.8% -- replaced with samplefile
samplefile2.gz:         40.7% -- replaced with samplefile2
[root@server1 root]# ls -l
total 28
drwx------    3 root     root         4096 Jul 21 08:15 Desktop
-rw-r--r--    1 root     root        20239 Jul 21 08:15 samplefile
-rw-rw-r--    1 root     root          574 Jul 21 08:18 samplefile2
[root@server1 root]# _
```

One of the largest advantages the gzip utility has over the compress utility is its ability to control the level of compression via a numeric option. The -1 option is also known as fast compression and results in a lower compression ratio. Alternatively, the -9 option is known as best compression and results in the highest compression ratio at the expense of time. If no level of compression is specified, the gzip command assumes the number 6.

The following command compresses the samplefile file shown earlier using fast compression and displays the compression ratio:

```
[root@server1 root]# gzip -v -1 samplefile
samplefile:              51.3% -- replaced with samplefile.gz
[root@server1 root]# _
```

Notice from the preceding output that samplefile was compressed with a compression ratio of 51.3%, which is much lower than the compression ratio of 56.8% obtained earlier when samplefile was compressed with the default level of 6.

NOTE

You need not specify the level of compression when decompressing files, as it is built in to the compressed file itself.

Many more options are available to the gzip utility than to the compress utility, and many of these options have a POSIX option equivalent. Table 12-2 shows a list of these options.

Table 12-2 Common options used with the gzip utility

Option	Description
-#	Specifies how thorough the compression will be, where **#** can be the number 1–9. The option -1 represents fast compression, which takes less time to compress but results in a lower compression ratio. The option -9 represents thorough compression, which takes more time but results in a higher compression ratio.
--best	Results in a higher compression ratio; same as the -9 option.
-c --stdout --to-stdout	Displays the contents of the compress file to Standard Output (same function as the zcat command) when used with the gunzip command.
-d --decompress --uncompress	Decompresses the files specified (same as the gunzip command) when used with the gzip command.
-f --force	Compresses symbolic links when used with the gzip command. When used with the gunzip command, it overwrites any existing files without prompting the user.

Table 12-2 Common options used with the gzip utility (Continued)

Option	Description
--fast	Results in a lower compression ratio; same as the -1 option.
-h --help	Displays the syntax and available options for the gzip and gunzip commands.
-l --list	Lists the compression ratio for files that have been compressed with gzip.
-n --no-name	Does not allow gzip and gunzip to preserve the original modification and access time for files.
-q --quiet	Suppresses all warning messages.
-r --recursive	Specifies to compress or decompress all files recursively within a specified directory.
-S *.suffix* --suffix *.suffix*	Specifies a file suffix other than .gz when compressing or decompressing files.
-t --test	Performs a test decompression such that a user can view any error messages before decompression, when used with the gunzip command; it does not decompress files.
-v --verbose	Displays verbose output (compression ratio and filenames) during compression and decompression.

The bzip2 utility

The **bzip2** utility differs from the compress and gzip utilities previously discussed in that it uses the Burrows-Wheeler Block Sorting Huffman Coding algorithm when compressing files. In addition, the bzip2 utility cannot be used to compress a directory full of files, the zcat and zmore commands cannot be used to view files compressed with bzip2, and the compression ratio is 50–75% on average.

Like the compress and gzip utilities, symbolic links are only compressed if the -f option is used, and the -v option can be used to display compression ratios. Also, file ownership, modification, and access time are preserved during compression.

The filename extension given to files compressed with bzip2 is .bz2. To compress the samplefile and samplefile2 files and view their compression ratio and filenames, you can use the following commands:

```
[root@server1 root]# bzip2 -v samplefile samplefile2
samplefile:  2.637:1, 3.034 bits/byte, 62.08% saved, 20239 in,7675 out.
samplefile2: 1.483:1, 5.394 bits/byte, 32.58% saved, 574 in,387 out.
[root@server1 root]# ls -l
total 16
drwx------    3 root     root         4096 Jul 21 08:15 Desktop
-rw-rw-r--    1 root     root          387 Jul 21 08:18 samplefile2.bz2
-rw-r--r--    1 root     root         7675 Jul 21 08:15 samplefile.bz2
[root@server1 root]# _
```

Because the compression algorithm is different than the one used by the `compress` and `gzip` utilities, you must use the **bzcat command** to display the contents of compressed files to Standard Output, as shown in the following example:

```
[root@server1 root]# bzcat samplefile2.bz2
Hi there, I hope this day finds you well.

Unfortunately we were not able to make it to your dining
room this year while vacationing in Algonquin Park - I
especially wished to see the model of the Highland Inn
and the train station in the dining room.

I have been reading on the history of Algonquin Park but
no where could I find a description of where the Highland
Inn was originally located on Cache lake.

If it is no trouble, could you kindly let me know such that
I need not wait until next year when I visit your lodge?

Regards,
Mackenzie Elizabeth

[root@server1 root]# _
```

NOTE

A **bzmore command** and a **bzless command** also exist, which can be used to view the contents of a bzip2-compressed file page-by-page.

To decompress files, you can use the **bunzip2 command** followed by the filename(s) to decompress; unlike compress and gzip, you must include the filename extension when decompressing files. To decompress the samplefile and samplefile2 files created earlier and view the results, you can use the following command:

```
[root@server1 root]# bunzip2 -v samplefile.bz2 samplefile2.bz2
  samplefile.bz2: done
  samplefile2.bz2: done
[root@server1 root]# _
```

The bunzip2 command prompts the user for confirmation if any files are to be overwritten, unless the -f option is specified. Table 12-3 lists other common options used with the bzip2 utility.

Table 12-3 Common options used with the bzip2 utility

Option	Description
-#	Specifies the block size used during compression; -1 indicates a block size of 100K, whereas -9 indicates a block size of 900K.
-c --stdout	Displays the contents of the compress file to Standard Output when used with the bunzip2 command.
-d --decompress	Decompresses the files specified (same as the bunzip2 command) when used with the bzip2 command.
-f --force	Compresses symbolic links when used with the bzip2 command. When used with the bunzip2 command, it overwrites any existing files without prompting the user.
-k --keep	Keeps the original file during compression; a new file is created with the extension .bz2.
-q --quiet	Suppresses all warning messages.
-s --small	Minimizes memory usage during compression.
-t --test	Performs a test decompression such that a user can view any error messages before decompression, when used with the bunzip2 command; it does not decompress files.
-v --verbose	Displays verbose output (compression ratio) during compression and decompression.

System Backup

Files and directories can be copied to an alternate location at regular intervals. These back-up copies can then be distributed to other computers or used to restore files if a system failure occurs that results in a loss of information. This entire process is known as **system backup**, and the back-up copies of files and directories are called **archives**.

Archives can be created on many different types of media such as tapes, Zip disks, floppy disks, CD-RW/DVD-RW discs, or hard disks. The most common medium used to back up data on Linux systems is tape; however, CD-RW/DVD-RW backup is fast becoming more popular than tape backup. Backing up data to CD-RW/DVD-RW requires special burning software; as a result, it is examined later in this section.

Table 12-4 shows a list of some common device files for use with different tape devices.

Table 12-4   Common tape device files

Device File	Description
/dev/st0	First SCSI tape device (rewinding)
/dev/st1	Second SCSI tape device (rewinding)
/dev/st2	Third SCSI tape device (rewinding)
/dev/nst0	First SCSI tape device (nonrewinding)
/dev/ht0	First ATAPI IDE tape device (rewinding)
/dev/nht0	First ATAPI IDE tape device (nonrewinding)
/dev/ftape	First floppy tape device

> **NOTE**
>
> The **magnetic tape (mt) command** can be used to manipulate tape devices or pre-pare a tape for system backup. For example, to rewind the first SCSI tape device on a system, you can use the command `mt -f /dev/st0 rewind`.

A typical Linux system can have hundreds of thousands of files on it, but not all of these files need be included in an archive. Temporary files in the /tmp and /var/tmp directories need not be included, nor does any cached Internet content found in the .netscape (if you use the Netscape Navigator Web browser) or .mozilla (if you use the Mozilla Web browser) directories under each user's home directory.

As a general rule of thumb, you should back up user files from home directories and any important system configuration files such as /etc/passwd. In addition to this, you might want to back up files used by system services. For example, you need to back up Web site files if the Linux computer is used as a Web server. Programs such as grep and vi need not be backed up because they can be restored from the original installation media in the event of a system failure.

After files have been selected for system backup, you can use a back-up utility to copy the files to the appropriate media. Several back-up utilities are available to Linux administrators; the most common are the following:

- tar
- cpio
- dump/restore
- burning software

The tar Utility

The **tape archive (tar)** utility is one of the oldest and most common back-up utilities; it can create an archive in a file on a filesystem or directly on a device.

Like the compression utilities discussed earlier, the tar utility accepts options to determine the location of the archive and the action to perform on the archive; any arguments specified to the tar command list the file(s) to place in the archive. Table 12-5 depicts a list of common options used with the tar command.

Table 12-5 Common options used with the tar utility

Option	Description
-A --catenate --concatenate	Appends whole archives to another archive
-c --create	Creates a new archive
--exclude *FILENAME*	Excludes *FILENAME* when creating an archive
-f *FILENAME* --file *FILENAME*	Specifies the location of the archive (*FILENAME*); it can be a file on a filesystem or a device file
-h --dereference	Prevents tar from backing up symbolic links; instead tar backs up the target files of symbolic links
-j --bzip	Compresses/decompresses the archive using the bzip2 utility

Table 12-5 Common options used with the tar utility (Continued)

Option	Description
-P --absolute-paths	Stores filenames in an archive using absolute pathnames
-r --append	Appends files to an existing archive
--remove-files	Removes files after adding them to an archive
-t --list	Lists the filename contents (table of contents) of an existing archive
-u --update	Appends files to an existing archive only if they are newer than the same filename inside the archive
-v --verbose	Displays verbose output (file and directory information) when manipulating archives
-w --interactive --confirmation	Prompts the user for confirmation of each action
-W --verify	Verifies the contents of each archive after creation
-x --extract --get	Extracts the contents of an archive
-z --gzip --ungzip	Compresses/decompresses the archive using the gzip utility
-Z --compress --uncompress	Compresses/decompresses the archive using the compress utility

NOTE

Because `tar` is a widely used utility, the options shown in Table 12-5 are often used in other similar utilities. One example is the `jar` utility, which archives reusable class files used by the Java programming language.

To create an archive called /backup.tar that contains the contents of the current directory and view the results, you can use the following commands:

```
[root@server1 root]# tar -cvf /backup.tar *
Desktop/
Desktop/starthere.desktop
samplefile
samplefile2
[root@server1 root]# ls -l /backup.tar
-rw-r--r--    1 root      root       40960 Jul 27 10:49 /backup.tar [root@server1 root]# _
```

Note from the preceding command that the -f option is followed by the pathname of the archive and that the * metacharacter indicates that all files in the current directory will be added to this archive. Also note that files are backed up recursively by default and stored using relative pathnames; to force the use of absolute pathnames when creating archives, simply use the -P option to the tar command.

NOTE

The filename used for an archive need not have an extension; however, it is good practice to name archive files with an extension to identify their contents, as with /backup.tar in the preceding example.

The tar utility cannot back up device files or files with filenames longer than 255 characters.

You can view the detailed contents of an archive after creation by specifying the -t (table of contents) option to the tar command and the archive to view. For example, to view the detailed contents of the /backup.tar archive created earlier, you can issue the following command:

```
[root@server1 root]# tar -tvf /backup.tar
drwx------ root/root          0 2005-07-21 08:15:09 Desktop/
-rw-r--r-- root/root       3595 2005-06-21 20:32:48 Desktop/starthere.desktop
-rw-r--r-- root/root      20239 2005-07-21 08:15:35 samplefile
-rw-rw-r-- root/root        574 2005-07-21 08:18:08 samplefile2
[root@server1 root]# _
```

The -x option can be used with the tar command to extract a specified archive. To extract the contents of the /backup.tar file to a new directory called /tartest and view the results, you can issue the following commands:

```
[root@server1 root]# mkdir /tartest
[root@server1 root]# cd /tartest
[root@server1 tartest]# tar -xvf /backup.tar
Desktop/
Desktop/starthere.desktop
samplefile
samplefile2
[root@server1 tartest]# ls -F
Desktop/  samplefile  samplefile2
[root@server1 tartest]# _
```

After an archive has been created in a file on a filesystem, that file can be sent to other computers across a network such as the Internet. Unfortunately, the tar utility does not compress files inside the archive; thus, the time needed to transfer the archive across a network is high. To reduce transfer times, you can compress the archive using a compression utility before transmission. Because this is a common task, the tar command accepts options that allow you to compress an archive immediately after creation using the compress, gzip, or bzip2 utilities.

To create a gzip-compressed archive called /backup.tar.gz that contains the contents of the current directory and view the results, you can use the following commands:

```
[root@server1 root]# tar -zcvf /backup.tar.gz  *
Desktop/
Desktop/starthere.desktop
samplefile
samplefile2
[root@server1 root]# ls -l /backup.tar*
-rw-r--r--  1 root    root       40960 Jul 27 10:49 /backup.tar
-rw-r--r--  1 root    root       12207 Jul 27 11:18 /backup.tar.gz
[root@server1 root]# _
```

Note from the preceding output, that the -z option indicated compression using the gzip utility, and that we chose to end the filename with the .tar.gz extension. In addition, the size of the /backup.tar.gz file is much less than the /backup.tar file created earlier.

NOTE

Filenames that end with the .tar.gz or .tgz extensions are commonly called **tarballs** and represent gzip-compressed tar archives.

To view the contents of a gzip-compressed archive, you must use the -z option in addition to the -t option followed by the archive to view. The detailed contents of the /backup.tar.gz file can be viewed using the following command:

```
[root@server1 root]# tar -ztvf /backup.tar.gz
drwx------ root/root          0 2005-07-21 08:15:09 Desktop/
-rw-r--r-- root/root       3595 2005-06-21 20:32:48 Desktop/starthere.desktop
-rw-r--r-- root/root      20239 2005-07-21 08:15:35 samplefile
-rw-rw-r-- root/root        574 2005-07-21 08:18:08 samplefile2
[root@server1 root]# _
```

Similarly, when extracting a gzip-compressed archive, you must supply the -z option to the tar command. To extract the contents of the /backup.tar.gz file to a new directory called /tartest2 and view the results, you can issue the following commands:

```
[root@server1 root]# mkdir /tartest2
[root@server1 root]# cd /tartest2
[root@server1 tartest2]# tar -zxvf /backup.tar.gz
Desktop/
Desktop/starthere.desktop
samplefile
samplefile2
[root@server1 tartest2]# ls -F
Desktop/  samplefile  samplefile2
[root@server1 tartest2]# _
```

Backing up files to a compressed archive on a filesystem is useful when transferring data across a network, but is ill suited to backing up large amounts of data for system recovery. Devices such as tapes are better suited for this task. To back up files to a device, you can use the -f option to the tar command to specify the pathname to the appropriate device file. Files are then transferred directly to the device, overwriting any other data or filesystems that might be present.

For example, to create an archive on the first rewinding SCSI tape device containing the contents of the current directory, you can use the following command:

```
[root@server1 root]# tar -cvf /dev/st0 *
Desktop/
Desktop/starthere.desktop
samplefile
samplefile2
[root@server1 root]#
```

You can then view the contents of the archive on the tape device used in the preceding example using the command tar -tvf /dev/st0 or extract the contents of the archive on the tape device using the command tar -xvf /dev/st0 in a similar fashion to the examples shown earlier.

Because tape devices can hold large amounts of information, you might want to add to a tar archive that already exists on the tape device. To do this, simply replace the -c option with the -r option when using the tar utility. For example, to append a file called samplefile3 to the archive created in the previous output and view the results, you can use the following commands:

```
[root@server1 root]# tar -rvf /dev/st0 samplefile3
samplefile3
[root@server1 root]# tar -tvf /dev/st0
drwx------ root/root          0 2005-07-21 08:15:09 Desktop/
-rw-r--r-- root/root       3595 2005-06-21 20:32:48 Desktop/starthere.desktop
-rw-r--r-- root/root      20239 2005-07-21 08:15:35 samplefile
-rw-rw-r-- root/root        574 2005-07-21 08:18:08 samplefile2
-rw-r--r-- root/root        147 2005-07-27 16:15:18 samplefile3
[root@server1 root]# _
```

The cpio Utility

Another common back-up utility is **copy in/out (cpio)**. Although this utility uses options similar to the tar utility, cpio has some added features, including long filenames and the ability to back up device files.

Because its primary use is to back up files in case of system failure, cpio uses absolute pathnames by default when archiving. In addition, cpio normally takes a list of files to archive from Standard Input and sends the files "out" to an archive specified by the -O option. Conversely, when extracting an archive, the -I option must be specified to indicate the archive from which to read "in" files.

Table 12-6 provides a list of commonly used options to the cpio command and their descriptions.

Table 12-6 Common options used with the cpio utility

Option	Description
-A, --append	Appends files to an existing archive
-B	Changes the default block size from 512 bytes to 5 Kilobytes, thus speeding up the transfer of information
-c	Uses a storage format (SVR4) that is widely recognized by different versions of cpio for UNIX and Linux
-d, --make-directories	Creates directories as needed during extraction
-i, --extract	Reads files from an archive

Table 12-6 Common options used with the cpio utility (Continued)

Option	Description
-I *FILENAME*	Represents the input archive; it is the file or device file of the archive used when viewing or extracting files
-L, --dereference	Prevents cpio from backing up symbolic links; instead cpio backs up the target files of symbolic links
--no-absolute-filenames	Stores filenames in an archive using relative pathnames
-o, --create	Creates a new archive
-O *FILENAME*	Represents the output archive; it is the file or device file of the target archive when backing up files
-t, --list	Lists the filename contents (table of contents) of an existing archive
-u, --unconditional	Overwrites existing files during extraction without prompting for user confirmation
-v, --verbose	Displays verbose output (file and directory information) when manipulating archives

To create an archive using cpio, a list of filenames must first be generated; this can be accomplished using the find command. To list all filenames underneath the /root/sample directory, you can use the following command:

```
[root@server1 root]# find /root/sample
/root/sample
/root/sample/samplefile
/root/sample/samplefile2
[root@server1 root]# _
```

Now, you can send this list via Standard Input to the cpio command. For example, to verbosely back up all files in /root/sample to the first SCSI tape device using a block size of 5 Kilobytes and a common format, you can use the following command:

```
[root@server1 root]# find /root/sample | cpio -vocB -O /dev/st0
/root/sample
/root/sample/samplefile
/root/sample/samplefile2
5 blocks
[root@server1 root]# _
```

To view the verbose table of contents of this archive, you can use the following command:

```
[root@server1 root]# cpio -vitB -I /dev/st0
drwxr-xr-x  2 root    root            0 Jul 27 13:40 /root/sample
-rw-r--r--  1 root    root        20239 Jul 21 08:15 /root/sample/samplefile
-rw-rw-r--  1 root    root          574 Jul 21 08:18 /root/sample/samplefile2
5 blocks
[root@server1 root]# _
```

Following this, you can extract the archive on /dev/st0, creating directories and overwriting files as needed by using the following command:

```
[root@server1 root]# cpio -vicduB -I /dev/st0
/root/sample
/root/sample/samplefile
/root/sample/samplefile2
5 blocks
[root@server1 root]# _
```

Like tar, the cpio command can be used to create an archive on a file on the filesystem; to do this, simply specify the filename after the -O option. To create an archive called /root/sample.cpio that contains the files from the directory /root/sample, using a block size of 5 Kilobytes as well as a common header, and view the results, you can issue the following commands:

```
[root@server1 root]# find /root/sample | cpio -vocB -O /root/sample.cpio
/root/sample
/root/sample/samplefile
/root/sample/samplefile2
5 blocks
[root@server1 root]# ls -l sample.cpio
-rw-rw-rw-  1 root    root        25600 Jul 27 13:45 sample.cpio [root@server1 root]# _
```

As with the tar utility, cpio archive filenames need not have an extension to identify their contents. However, it is good practice to use extensions, as shown with /root/sample.cpio in the preceding example.

The dump/restore Utility

Like the tar and gzip utilities, the **dump/restore** utility can be used to back up files and directories to a device or to a file on the filesystem. However, the dump/restore utility can only work with files on ext2 and ext3 filesystems.

Although the dump/restore utility can be used to back up only certain files and directories, it was designed to back up entire filesystems to an archive and keep track of these filesystems in a file called **/etc/dumpdates**. Because archiving all data on a filesystem (known as a **full backup**) might take a long time, you can choose to perform a full backup only on weekends and incremental backups each evening during the week. An **incremental backup** only backs up the data that has been changed since the last backup. In the case of a system failure, you can restore the information from the full backup and then restore the information from all subsequent incremental backups in sequential order. You can perform up to nine different incremental backups using the dump/restore utility; number 0 represents a full backup, whereas numbers 1 through 9 represent incremental backups.

Suppose, for example, that you perform a full backup of the /dev/hda3 filesystem on Sunday, perform incremental backups from Monday to Wednesday, and on Thursday the /dev/hda3 filesystem becomes corrupted, as depicted in Figure 12-1.

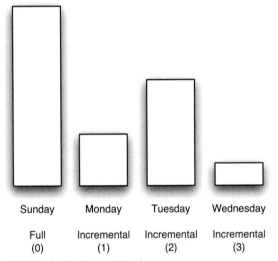

FIGURE 12-1 *A sample back-up strategy*

After the filesystem has been re-created, you should restore the full backup (0) followed by the first incremental backup (1), the second incremental backup (2), and the third incremental backup (3) to ensure that data has been properly recovered.

The dump/restore utility has many options available to it, as do the tar and cpio utilities. Table 12-7 provides a list of these options.

Table 12-7 Common options used with the dump /restore utility

Option	Description
-#	Specifies the type of backup when used with the dump command; if # is 0, a full backup is performed. If # is 1 through 9, the appropriate incremental backup is performed.
-b NUM	Specifies a certain block size to use in Kilobytes; the default block size is 10 Kilobytes.

Table 12-7 Common options used with the dump /restore utility (Continued)

Option	Description
-f *FILENAME*	Specifies the pathname to the archive; the *FILENAME* can be a file on a filesystem or a device file.
-u	Specifies to update the /etc/dumpdates file after a successful backup.
-n	Notifies the user if any errors occur and when the backup has completed.
-r	Extracts an entire archive when used with the restore command.
-x *FILENAME*	Extracts a certain file or files represented by *FILENAME* when used with the restore command.
-i	Restores files interactively, prompting the user for confirmation for all actions, when used with the restore command.
-t	Lists the filename contents (table of contents) of an existing archive when used with the restore command.
-v	Displays verbose output (file and directory information) when manipulating archives.

Take, for example, the output from the following df command:

```
[root@server1 root]# df
Filesystem          1K-blocks      Used Available Use% Mounted on
/dev/hda3           4032124     2840560    986736  75% /
/dev/hda2            101107       10550     85336  12% /boot
none                 192232           0    192232   0% /dev/shm
[root@server1 root]# _
```

To perform a full backup of the /boot partition (/dev/hda2) to the first rewinding SCSI tape device and update the /etc/dumpdates file when completed, you can issue the following command:

```
[root@server1 root]# dump -0uf /dev/st0 /dev/hda2
  DUMP: Date of this level 0 dump: Sat Jul 23 16:43:09 2005
  DUMP: Dumping /dev/hda2 (/boot) to /dev/st0
  DUMP: Exclude ext3 journal inode 8
  DUMP: Label: /boot
  DUMP: mapping (Pass I) [regular files]
  DUMP: mapping (Pass II) [directories]
  DUMP: estimated 6485 tape blocks.
  DUMP: Volume 1 started with block 1 at: Sat Jul 23 16:43:10 2005
  DUMP: dumping (Pass III) [directories]
  DUMP: dumping (Pass IV) [regular files]
```

```
DUMP: Closing /dev/st0
DUMP: Volume 1 completed at: Sat Jul 23 16:43:11 2005
DUMP: Volume 1 6470 tape blocks (6.32MB)
DUMP: Volume 1 took 0:00:01
DUMP: Volume 1 transfer rate: 6470 kB/s
DUMP: 6470 tape blocks (6.32MB) on 1 volume(s)
DUMP: finished in 1 seconds, throughput 6470 kBytes/sec
DUMP: Date of this level 0 dump: Sat Jul 23 16:43:09 2005
DUMP: Date this dump completed:  Sat Jul 23 16:43:11 2005
DUMP: Average transfer rate: 6470 kB/s
DUMP: DUMP IS DONE
[root@server1 root]# _
```

> **NOTE**
>
> Alternatively, you can specify the filesystem mount point when using the dump command; the command dump -0uf /dev/st0 /boot is equivalent to the one used in the preceding example.

The contents of the /etc/dumpdates file now indicates that a full backup has taken place:

```
[root@server1 root]# cat /etc/dumpdates
/dev/hda2 0 Sat Jul 23 16:43:09 2005
[root@server1 root]# _
```

To perform the first incremental backup and view the contents of the /etc/dumpdates file, you can place a new tape into the SCSI tape drive and issue the following commands:

```
[root@server1 root]# dump -1uf /dev/st0 /dev/hda2
  DUMP: Date of this level 1 dump: Sat Jul 23 16:50:57 2005
  DUMP: Date of last level 0 dump: Sat Jul 23 16:43:09 2005
  DUMP: Dumping /dev/hda2 (/boot) to /dev/st0
  DUMP: Exclude ext3 journal inode 8
  DUMP: Label: /boot
  DUMP: mapping (Pass I) [regular files]
  DUMP: mapping (Pass II) [directories]
  DUMP: estimated 21 tape blocks.
  DUMP: Volume 1 started with block 1 at: Sat Jul 23 16:50:58 2005
  DUMP: dumping (Pass III) [directories]
  DUMP: dumping (Pass IV) [regular files]
  DUMP: Closing /dev/st0
  DUMP: Volume 1 completed at: Sat Jul 23 16:50:58 2005
  DUMP: Volume 1 20 tape blocks (0.02MB)
```

```
DUMP: 20 tape blocks (0.02MB) on 1 volume(s)
DUMP: finished in less than a second
DUMP: Date of this level 1 dump: Sat Jul 23 16:50:57 2005
DUMP: Date this dump completed:  Sat Jul 23 16:50:58 2005
DUMP: Average transfer rate: 0 kB/s
DUMP: DUMP IS DONE
[root@server1 root]# cat /etc/dumpdates
/dev/hda2 0 Sat Jul 23 16:43:09 2005
/dev/hda2 1 Sat Jul 23 16:50:57 2005
[root@server1 root]# _
```

To view the contents of an archive, you can specify the -t option to the restore command followed by the archive information. To view the contents of the full backup performed earlier,
you can place the appropriate tape into the tape drive and execute the following command:

```
[root@server1 root]# restore -tf /dev/st0
Dump   date: Sat Jul 23 16:43:09 2005
Dumped from: the epoch
Level 0 dump of /boot on localhost.localdomain:/dev/hda2
Label: /boot
        2      .
       11      ./lost+found
     4033      ./grub
     4035      ./grub/grub.conf
     4034      ./grub/splash.xpm.gz
     4036      ./grub/menu.lst
     4037      ./grub/device.map
     4038      ./grub/stage1
     4039      ./grub/stage2
     4040      ./grub/e2fs_stage1_5
     4041      ./grub/fat_stage1_5
     4042      ./grub/ffs_stage1_5
     4043      ./grub/reiserfs_stage1_5
     4044      ./grub/vstafs_stage1_5
     4045      ./grub/xfs_stage1_5
       12      ./boot.b
       13      ./chain.b
       14      ./config-2.6.5-1.358
       15      ./initrd-2.6.5-1.358.img
       17      ./memtest86+-1.11
       19      ./os2_d.b
       22      ./System.map-2.6.5-1.358
       20      ./vmlinuz-2.6.5-1.358
[root@server1 root]# _
```

To extract the full backup shown in the preceding output, you can specify the -r option to the restore command followed by the archive information. In addition, you can specify the -v option to list the filenames restored, as shown in the following example:

```
[root@server1 root]# restore -vrf /dev/st0
Verify tape and initialize maps
Input is from file/pipe
Input block size is 32
Dump   date: Sat Jul 23 16:43:09 2005
Dumped from: the epoch
Level 0 dump of /boot on localhost.localdomain:/dev/hda2
Label: /boot
Begin level 0 restore
Initialize symbol table.
Extract directories from tape
Calculate extraction list.
restore: ./lost+found: File exists
restore: ./grub: File exists
Extract new leaves.
Check pointing the restore
extract file ./boot.b
extract file ./chain.b
extract file ./config-2.6.5-1.358
extract file ./initrd-2.6.5-1.358.img
extract file ./memtest86+-1.11
extract file ./os2_d.b
extract file ./System.map-2.6.5-1.358
extract file ./vmlinuz-2.6.5-1.358
extract file ./grub/grub.conf
extract file ./grub/splash.xpm.gz
extract file ./grub/menu.lst
extract file ./grub/device.map
extract file ./grub/stage1
extract file ./grub/stage2
extract file ./grub/e2fs_stage1_5
extract file ./grub/fat_stage1_5
extract file ./grub/ffs_stage1_5
extract file ./grub/reiserfs_stage1_5
extract file ./grub/vstafs_stage1_5
extract file ./grub/xfs_stage1_5
Add links
Set directory mode, owner, and times.
Check the symbol table.
Check pointing the restore
[root@server1 root]# _
```

Burning Software

The `tar`, `cpio`, and `dump` utilities copy data to a back-up medium in a character-by-character or block-by-block format. As a result, they are typically used to create back-up copies of files on tape, floppy, and hard disk media because those media accept data in that format. To write files to CD-RW and DVD-RW media, you must use a program that allows you to select the data to copy, organize that data, build a CD or DVD filesystem, and write the entire filesystem (including the data) to the CD-RW or DVD-RW. Programs that can be used to do this are collectively called **burning software**.

Although some CD-RW and DVD-RW drives are SCSI-based, most are usually ATAPI compliant and connect to the IDE controller of your computer; as such, they are configured much like hard drives. Unfortunately, CD-RW and DVD-RW drives do not write data like hard drives, and because they are still relatively new, there is no standard driver implementation for them in the Linux kernel. As a result, you must ensure that your burning software supports the specific brand and model of your CD-RW or DVD-RW.

Many different burning software packages are available for Linux. Red Hat Fedora Core 2 comes with the **X-CD-Roast** burning software, as shown in Figure 12-2. To start X-CD-Roast, simply navigate to the Red Hat button, System Tools, CD Writer from within a desktop environment. X-CD-Roast attempts to determine the model of your CD-RW or DVD-RW drive upon system startup; if it is unsuccessful, you can manually choose the model using the Setup button shown in Figure 12-2.

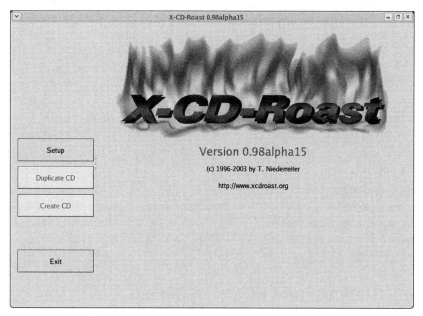

FIGURE 12-2 *The X-CD-Roast program*

Software Installation

Primary responsibilities of most Linux administrators typically include the installation and maintenance of software packages. Software for Linux can consist of binary files that have been precompiled to run on certain hardware architectures such as 32-bit Intel (i386), or as source code, which must be compiled on the local architecture before use. The largest advantage to obtaining and compiling source code is that the source code is not created for a particular hardware architecture. After being compiled, the program executes on the architecture from which it was compiled.

> **NOTE**
>
> The most common method for obtaining software for Linux is via the Internet. Appendix C, "Finding Linux Resources on the Internet," lists some common Web sites that host Linux Open Source Software for download.

> **TIP**
>
> When downloading software files from the Internet, many Internet sites list a **checksum** value for the file, which was calculated from the exact file contents. Nearly all checksum values are calculated using a Message Digest 5 (MD5) algorithm. To ensure that the file was received in its entirety after you download it, you should use the **sum command** to verify that the MD5 checksum value is still the same. Simply run the `sum filename` command, where *filename* is the name of the file downloaded.

Program source code is typically distributed in tarball format; the tarball can then be uncompressed and the source code extracted so that it can be compiled. Precompiled binary programs can also be distributed in tarball format, but are typically distributed in a format for use with a package manager.

Recall from Chapter 1, "Introduction to Linux," that a **package manager** provides a standard format for distributing programs as well as a central database to store information about software packages installed on the system; this allows software packages to be queried and easily uninstalled. The most common package manager used by Linux systems today is the **Red Hat Package Manager (RPM)**.

Compiling Source Code into Programs

The procedure for compiling source code into binary programs is standardized today among most Open Source Software developers. Because most source code comes in tarball format, you must uncompress and extract the files. This creates a subdirectory under the current directory containing the source code. In addition, this directory typically contains a README file with information about the program and an INSTALL file with instructions for installation.

While inside the source code directory, the first step to installation is to run the `configure` program. This performs a preliminary check for system requirements and creates a list of what to compile inside a file called Makefile in the current directory.

Next, you can type the `make` command, which looks for the Makefile and uses the information within to compile the source code into binary programs using the **GNU C Compiler (gcc)** for the local hardware architecture. After this has completed, the binary files the program comprises are still stored in the source code directory. To copy the files to the appropriate location on the filesystem, such as a directory listed in the PATH variable, you must type `make install`.

> ### NOTE
>
> Most Linux programs are installed to a subdirectory of the /usr/local directory.

After the program has been compiled and copied to the correct location on the filesystem, the source code directory and its contents can be removed from the system.

Suppose, for example, that you download the source code for rdesktop (Remote Desktop Protocol client) version 1.3.1 from the Internet at *http://www.sourceforge.net*:

```
[root@server1 root]# ls -F
Desktop/    rdesktop-1.3.1.tar.gz
[root@server1 root]# _
```

The first step to installing this program is to uncompress and extract the tarball, as shown in the following output. This creates a directory called rdesktop-1.3.1 containing the source code and supporting files.

```
[root@server1 root]# tar -zxvf rdesktop-1.3.1.tar.gz
rdesktop-1.3.1/COPYING
rdesktop-1.3.1/README
rdesktop-1.3.1/configure
rdesktop-1.3.1/Makefile
rdesktop-1.3.1/rdesktop.spec
rdesktop-1.3.1/bitmap.c
rdesktop-1.3.1/cache.c
rdesktop-1.3.1/channels.c
rdesktop-1.3.1/cliprdr.c
rdesktop-1.3.1/ewmhints.c
rdesktop-1.3.1/iso.c
rdesktop-1.3.1/licence.c
```

```
rdesktop-1.3.1/mcs.c
rdesktop-1.3.1/orders.c
rdesktop-1.3.1/printer.c
rdesktop-1.3.1/rdesktop.c
rdesktop-1.3.1/rdp.c
rdesktop-1.3.1/rdp5.c
rdesktop-1.3.1/rdpdr.c
rdesktop-1.3.1/rdpsnd.c
rdesktop-1.3.1/rdpsnd_oss.c
rdesktop-1.3.1/rdpsnd_sun.c
rdesktop-1.3.1/secure.c
rdesktop-1.3.1/serial.c
rdesktop-1.3.1/tcp.c
rdesktop-1.3.1/xclip.c
rdesktop-1.3.1/xkeymap.c
rdesktop-1.3.1/xwin.c
rdesktop-1.3.1/constants.h
rdesktop-1.3.1/orders.h
rdesktop-1.3.1/parse.h
rdesktop-1.3.1/proto.h
rdesktop-1.3.1/rdesktop.h
rdesktop-1.3.1/scancodes.h
rdesktop-1.3.1/types.h
rdesktop-1.3.1/xproto.h
rdesktop-1.3.1/crypto/README
rdesktop-1.3.1/crypto/md32_common.h
rdesktop-1.3.1/crypto/md5.h
rdesktop-1.3.1/crypto/md5_locl.h
rdesktop-1.3.1/crypto/rc4.h
rdesktop-1.3.1/crypto/sha.h
rdesktop-1.3.1/crypto/sha_locl.h
rdesktop-1.3.1/keymaps/common
rdesktop-1.3.1/keymaps/modifiers
rdesktop-1.3.1/keymaps/convert-map
rdesktop-1.3.1/doc/HACKING
rdesktop-1.3.1/doc/AUTHORS
rdesktop-1.3.1/doc/TODO
rdesktop-1.3.1/doc/ChangeLog
rdesktop-1.3.1/doc/keymapping.txt
rdesktop-1.3.1/doc/keymap-names.txt
rdesktop-1.3.1/doc/ipv6.txt
rdesktop-1.3.1/doc/rdesktop.1
[root@server1 root]# _
```

Next, you can move to this directory and view the file contents, as shown in the following output:

```
[root@server1 root]# cd rdesktop-1.3.1
[root@server1 rdesktop-1.3.1]# ls -F
bitmap.c      crypto/      mcs.c        rdesktop.h      rdpsnd_sun.c  xclip.c
cache.c       doc/         orders.c     rdesktop.spec   README        xkeymap.c
channels.c    ewmhints.c   orders.h     rdp5.c          scancodes.h   xproto.h
cliprdr.c     iso.c        parse.h      rdp.c           secure.c      xwin.c
configure*    keymaps/     printer.c    rdpdr.c         serial.c
constants.h   licence.c    proto.h      rdpsnd.c        tcp.c
COPYING       Makefile     rdesktop.c   rdpsnd_oss.c    types.h
[root@server1 rdesktop-1.3.1]# _
```

Notice from the preceding output that a README and configure file exist and that the configure file is executable. To execute this file without using the PATH variable, you can enter the following command:

```
[root@server1 rdesktop-1.3.1]# ./configure
rdesktop build configuration script


X Window System:
  includes  /usr/X11R6/include
  libraries /usr/X11R6/lib


OpenSSL:
  includes  /usr/include
  libraries /usr/lib


Sound support enabled: Open Sound System


configure complete - now run make
[root@server1 rdesktop-1.3.1]# _
```

After the configure script has run, a Makefile exists in the current directory, as shown in the following output:

```
[root@server1 rdesktop-1.3.1]# cat Makefile
# rdesktop: A Remote Desktop Protocol client
# Makefile
# Copyright (C) Matthew Chapman 1999-2004
# Configuration defaults
prefix      = /usr/local
exec_prefix = $(prefix)
bindir      = $(exec_prefix)/bin
mandir      = $(prefix)/man
datadir     = $(prefix)/share/rdesktop
```

```
VERSION     = 1.3.1
KEYMAP_PATH = $(datadir)/keymaps/
RDPOBJ   = tcp.o iso.o mcs.o secure.o licence.o rdp.o orders.o bitmap.o cache.o rdp5.o
channels.o rdpdr.o serial.o printer.o
X11OBJ   = rdesktop.o xwin.o xkeymap.o ewmhints.o xclip.o cliprdr.o
VNCOBJ   = vnc/rdp2vnc.o vnc/vnc.o vnc/xkeymap.o vnc/x11stubs.o
CRYPTOBJ = crypto/rc4_enc.o crypto/rc4_skey.o crypto/md5_dgst.o crypto/sha1dgst.o
crypto/bn_exp.o crypto/bn_mul.o crypto/bn_div.o
crypto/bn_sqr.o crypto/bn_add.o crypto/bn_shift.o crypto/bn_asm.o
crypto/bn_ctx.o crypto/bn_lib.o

include Makeconf  # configure-generated

all: $(TARGETS)

rdesktop: $(X11OBJ) $(SOUNDOBJ) $(RDPOBJ) $(CRYPTOBJ)
$(CC) $(CFLAGS) -o rdesktop $(X11OBJ) $(SOUNDOBJ) $(RDPOBJ)
$(CRYPTOBJ) $(LDFLAGS) -lX11

rdp2vnc: $(VNCOBJ) $(SOUNDOBJ) $(RDPOBJ) $(CRYPTOBJ)
$(CCLD) $(CFLAGS) -o rdp2vnc $(VNCOBJ) $(SOUNDOBJ) $(RDPOBJ) $(CRYPTOBJ)
$(LDFLAGS) $(LDVNC)

vnc/rdp2vnc.o: rdesktop.c
$(CC) $(CFLAGS) $(VNCINC) -DRDP2VNC -o vnc/rdp2vnc.o -c rdesktop.c

vnc/vnc.o: vnc/vnc.c
$(CC) $(CFLAGS) $(VNCINC) -DRDP2VNC -o vnc/vnc.o -c vnc/vnc.c

vnc/xkeymap.o: xkeymap.c
$(CC) $(CFLAGS) $(VNCINC) -DRDP2VNC -o vnc/xkeymap.o -c xkeymap.c

vnc/x11stubs.o: vnc/x11stubs.c
$(CC) $(CFLAGS) $(VNCINC) -o vnc/x11stubs.o -c vnc/x11stubs.c

Makeconf:
        ./configure

install: installbin installkeymaps installman

installbin: rdesktop
        mkdir -p $(DESTDIR)/$(bindir)
        $(INSTALL) rdesktop $(DESTDIR)/$(bindir)
        strip $(DESTDIR)/$(bindir)/rdesktop
        chmod 755 $(DESTDIR)/$(bindir)/rdesktop
```

```
installman: doc/rdesktop.1
        mkdir -p $(DESTDIR)/$(mandir)/man1
        cp doc/rdesktop.1 $(DESTDIR)/$(mandir)/man1
        chmod 644 $(DESTDIR)/$(mandir)/man1/rdesktop.1


installkeymaps:
        mkdir -p $(DESTDIR)/$(KEYMAP_PATH)
# Prevent copying the CVS directory
        cp keymaps/?? keymaps/??-?? $(DESTDIR)/$(KEYMAP_PATH)
        cp keymaps/common $(DESTDIR)/$(KEYMAP_PATH)
        cp keymaps/modifiers $(DESTDIR)/$(KEYMAP_PATH)
        chmod 644 $(DESTDIR)/$(KEYMAP_PATH)/*


proto:
        cproto -DMAKE_PROTO -DWITH_OPENSSL -o proto.h *.c


clean:
        rm -f *.o crypto/*.o *~ vnc/*.o vnc/*~ rdesktop rdp2vnc


dist:
        mkdir -p /tmp/rdesktop-make-dist-dir
        ln -sf `pwd` /tmp/rdesktop-make-dist-dir/rdesktop-$(VERSION)
        (cd /tmp/rdesktop-make-dist-dir; \
        tar zcvf /tmp/rdesktop-$(VERSION).tar.gz \
        rdesktop-$(VERSION)/COPYING \
        rdesktop-$(VERSION)/README \
        rdesktop-$(VERSION)/configure \
        rdesktop-$(VERSION)/Makefile \
        rdesktop-$(VERSION)/rdesktop.spec \
        rdesktop-$(VERSION)/*.c \
        rdesktop-$(VERSION)/*.h \
        rdesktop-$(VERSION)/crypto/README \
        rdesktop-$(VERSION)/crypto/*.c \
        rdesktop-$(VERSION)/crypto/*.h \
        rdesktop-$(VERSION)/keymaps/?? \
        rdesktop-$(VERSION)/keymaps/??-?? \
        rdesktop-$(VERSION)/keymaps/common \
        rdesktop-$(VERSION)/keymaps/modifiers \
        rdesktop-$(VERSION)/keymaps/convert-map \
        rdesktop-$(VERSION)/doc/HACKING \
        rdesktop-$(VERSION)/doc/AUTHORS \
        rdesktop-$(VERSION)/doc/TODO \
        rdesktop-$(VERSION)/doc/ChangeLog \
        rdesktop-$(VERSION)/doc/keymapping.txt \
```

```
            rdesktop-$(VERSION)/doc/keymap-names.txt \
            rdesktop-$(VERSION)/doc/ipv6.txt \
            rdesktop-$(VERSION)/doc/rdesktop.1 )
            rm -rf /tmp/rdesktop-make-dist-dir


.SUFFIXES:
.SUFFIXES: .c .o


.c.o:
$(CC) $(CFLAGS) -o $@ -c $<


[root@server1 rdesktop-1.3.1]# _
```

This Makefile contains most of the information and commands necessary to compile the program. Some program source code that you download might contain commented lines that should be uncommented to enable certain features of the program or to allow the program to compile on your computer architecture. Instructions for these commented areas are documented in the Makefile itself; thus, it is good form to read the Makefile after you run the configure script. You can also edit the Makefile if you want to change the location to which the program is installed. For rdesktop, simply change the line prefix=/usr/local shown in the preceding output to reflect the new directory.

Next, you must compile the program according to the settings stored in the Makefile by typing the make command while in the source code directory. This uses the gcc program to compile the source code files, as shown in the following output:

```
[root@server1 rdesktop-1.3.1]# make
gcc -DKEYMAP_PATH=\"/usr/local/share/rdesktop/keymaps/\" -Wall -O2 -I/usr/X11R6/include -
DWITH_OPENSSL -DWITH_RDPSND -o rdesktop.o -c rdesktop.c
gcc -DKEYMAP_PATH=\"/usr/local/share/rdesktop/keymaps/\" -Wall -O2 -I/usr/X11R6/include -
DWITH_OPENSSL -DWITH_RDPSND -o xwin.o -c xwin.c
gcc -DKEYMAP_PATH=\"/usr/local/share/rdesktop/keymaps/\" -Wall -O2 -I/usr/X11R6/include -
DWITH_OPENSSL -DWITH_RDPSND -o xkeymap.o -c xkeymap.c
gcc -DKEYMAP_PATH=\"/usr/local/share/rdesktop/keymaps/\" -Wall -O2 -I/usr/X11R6/include -
DWITH_OPENSSL -DWITH_RDPSND -o ewmhints.o -c ewmhints.c
gcc -DKEYMAP_PATH=\"/usr/local/share/rdesktop/keymaps/\" -Wall -O2 -I/usr/X11R6/include -
DWITH_OPENSSL -DWITH_RDPSND -o xclip.o -c xclip.c
gcc -DKEYMAP_PATH=\"/usr/local/share/rdesktop/keymaps/\" -Wall -O2 -I/usr/X11R6/include -
DWITH_OPENSSL -DWITH_RDPSND -o cliprdr.o -c cliprdr.c
gcc -DKEYMAP_PATH=\"/usr/local/share/rdesktop/keymaps/\" -Wall -O2 -I/usr/X11R6/include -
DWITH_OPENSSL -DWITH_RDPSND -o rdpsnd.o -c rdpsnd.c
gcc -DKEYMAP_PATH=\"/usr/local/share/rdesktop/keymaps/\" -Wall -O2 -I/usr/X11R6/include -
DWITH_OPENSSL -DWITH_RDPSND -o rdpsnd_oss.o -c rdpsnd_oss.c
gcc -DKEYMAP_PATH=\"/usr/local/share/rdesktop/keymaps/\" -Wall -O2 -I/usr/X11R6/include -
DWITH_OPENSSL -DWITH_RDPSND -o tcp.o -c tcp.c
```

```
gcc -DKEYMAP_PATH=\"/usr/local/share/rdesktop/keymaps/\" -Wall -O2 -I/usr/X11R6/include -
DWITH_OPENSSL -DWITH_RDPSND -o iso.o -c iso.c
gcc -DKEYMAP_PATH=\"/usr/local/share/rdesktop/keymaps/\" -Wall -O2 -I/usr/X11R6/include -
DWITH_OPENSSL -DWITH_RDPSND -o mcs.o -c mcs.c
gcc -DKEYMAP_PATH=\"/usr/local/share/rdesktop/keymaps/\" -Wall -O2 -I/usr/X11R6/include -
DWITH_OPENSSL -DWITH_RDPSND -o secure.o -c secure.c
gcc -DKEYMAP_PATH=\"/usr/local/share/rdesktop/keymaps/\" -Wall -O2 -I/usr/X11R6/include -
DWITH_OPENSSL -DWITH_RDPSND -o licence.o -c licence.c
gcc -DKEYMAP_PATH=\"/usr/local/share/rdesktop/keymaps/\" -Wall -O2 -I/usr/X11R6/include -
DWITH_OPENSSL -DWITH_RDPSND -o rdp.o -c rdp.c
gcc -DKEYMAP_PATH=\"/usr/local/share/rdesktop/keymaps/\" -Wall -O2 -I/usr/X11R6/include -
DWITH_OPENSSL -DWITH_RDPSND -o orders.o -c orders.c
gcc -DKEYMAP_PATH=\"/usr/local/share/rdesktop/keymaps/\" -Wall -O2 -I/usr/X11R6/include -
DWITH_OPENSSL -DWITH_RDPSND -o bitmap.o -c bitmap.c
gcc -DKEYMAP_PATH=\"/usr/local/share/rdesktop/keymaps/\" -Wall -O2 -I/usr/X11R6/include -
DWITH_OPENSSL -DWITH_RDPSND -o cache.o -c cache.c
gcc -DKEYMAP_PATH=\"/usr/local/share/rdesktop/keymaps/\" -Wall -O2 -I/usr/X11R6/include -
DWITH_OPENSSL -DWITH_RDPSND -o rdp5.o -c rdp5.c
gcc -DKEYMAP_PATH=\"/usr/local/share/rdesktop/keymaps/\" -Wall -O2 -I/usr/X11R6/include -
DWITH_OPENSSL -DWITH_RDPSND -o channels.o -c channels.c
gcc -DKEYMAP_PATH=\"/usr/local/share/rdesktop/keymaps/\" -Wall -O2 -I/usr/X11R6/include -
DWITH_OPENSSL -DWITH_RDPSND -o rdpdr.o -c rdpdr.c
gcc -DKEYMAP_PATH=\"/usr/local/share/rdesktop/keymaps/\" -Wall -O2 -I/usr/X11R6/include -
DWITH_OPENSSL -DWITH_RDPSND -o serial.o -c serial.c
gcc -DKEYMAP_PATH=\"/usr/local/share/rdesktop/keymaps/\" -Wall -O2 -I/usr/X11R6/include -
DWITH_OPENSSL -DWITH_RDPSND -o printer.o -c printer.c
gcc -DKEYMAP_PATH=\"/usr/local/share/rdesktop/keymaps/\" -Wall -O2 -I/usr/X11R6/include -
DWITH_OPENSSL -DWITH_RDPSND -o rdesktop rdesktop.o xwin.o xkeymap.o ewmhints.o xclip.o
cliprdr.o rdpsnd.o rdpsnd_oss.o tcp.o iso.o mcs.o secure.o licence.o rdp.o orders.o
bitmap.o cache.o rdp5.o channels.o rdpdr.o serial.o printer.o  -L/usr/X11R6/lib -lcrypto
-lX11
[root@server1 rdesktop-1.3.1]# _
```

After being compiled, these binary programs can then be copied to the correct location on the filesystem by typing the following command:

```
[root@server1 rdesktop-1.3.1]# make install
mkdir -p //usr/local/bin
install rdesktop //usr/local/bin
strip //usr/local/bin/rdesktop
chmod 755 //usr/local/bin/rdesktop
mkdir -p //usr/local/share/rdesktop/keymaps/
cp keymaps/?? keymaps/??-?? //usr/local/share/rdesktop/keymaps/
cp keymaps/common //usr/local/share/rdesktop/keymaps/
cp keymaps/modifiers //usr/local/share/rdesktop/keymaps/
```

```
chmod 644 //usr/local/share/rdesktop/keymaps//*
mkdir -p //usr/local/man/man1
cp doc/rdesktop.1 //usr/local/man/man1
chmod 644 //usr/local/man/man1/rdesktop.1
[root@server1 rdesktop-1.3.1]# _
```

After being compiled and copied to the appropriate directory (the README file typically contains the location of the program), you can remove the source code and tarball and locate the main binary file for the program, as shown in the following example:

```
[root@server1 rdesktop-1.3.1]# cd ..
[root@server1 root]# rm -rf rdesktop-1.3.1
[root@server1 root]# rm -f rdesktop-1.3.1.tar.gz
[root@server1 root]# which rdesktop
/usr/local/bin/rdesktop
[root@server1 root]# _
```

Following this, you can view the rdesktop manual page, then switch to a desktop environment and run the command rdesktop remote_server_name to connect to a remote Windows server that runs the Remote Desktop Protocol, as shown in Figure 12-3.

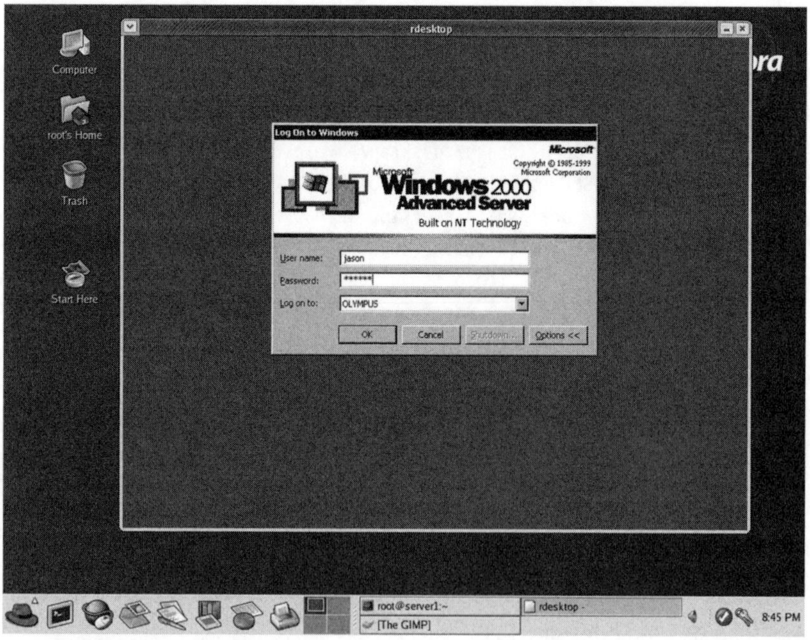

FIGURE 12-3 *The rdesktop program*

Installing Programs Using RPM

The Red Hat Package Manager format is the most widely used format for Linux software distributed via the Internet. Packages in this format have filenames that indicate the hardware architecture for which the software was compiled and end with the .rpm extension. The following output indicates that the bluefish RPM package (a Web page editor) version 0.13-1.1 was compiled for Fedora Core 2 (fc2) on the Intel i386 platform:

```
[root@server1 root]# ls -F
Desktop/    bluefish-0.13-1.1.fc2.i386.rpm
[root@server1 root]# _
```

To install an RPM package, you can use the -i option to the **rpm command**. In addition, you can use the -v and -h options to print the verbose information and hash marks, respectively during installation. The following command installs the bluefish RPM package using these options:

```
[root@server1 root]# rpm -ivh bluefish-0.13-1.1.fc2.i386.rpm
Preparing... ########################################### [100%]
   1:bluefish           ########################################### [100%]
[root@server1 root]# _
```

> **NOTE**
>
> Some RPM packages require that other RPM packages be installed on your system first; these are called **package dependencies**. If you attempt to install an RPM package that has package dependencies, you receive an error message that indicates the RPM packages that need to be installed first. After installing these prerequisite packages, you can successfully install your desired RPM package.

After being installed, the RPM database (stored within files in the /var/lib/rpm directory) contains information about the package and the files contained within. To query the full package name after installation, you can use the -q (query) option to the rpm command followed by the common name of the package:

```
[root@server1 root]# rpm -q bluefish
bluefish-0.13-1.1.fc2
[root@server1 root]# _
```

In addition, you can add the -i (info) option to the preceding command to display the detailed package information for the bluefish package:

```
[root@server1 root]# rpm -qi bluefish
Name        : bluefish              Relocations: (not relocatable)
Version     : 0.13                  Vendor: http://dag.wieers.com/apt/
```

```
Release      : 1.1.fc2.dag            Build Date: 15 May 2004 07:57:46 AM
Install Date: 01 Aug 2005 08:56:44 PM  Build Host: localhost
Group        : Development/Tools       Source RPM: bluefish-0.13-1.1.fc2.dag.src.rpm
Size         : 5883879                 License: GPL
Signature    : DSA/SHA1, 15 May 2004 08:13:04 AM, Key ID a20e52146b8d79e6
Packager     : Dag Wieers <dag@wieers.com>
URL          : http://bluefish.openoffice.nl/
Summary      : Graphical Web development application for experienced users
Description :
Bluefish is a GTK+ HTML editor for the experienced Web designer or
programmer. It is not finished yet, but already a very powerful site-
creating environment. Bluefish has extended support for programming
dynamic and interactive Web sites. There is, for example, a lot of PHP
support.
[root@server1 root]# _
```

Because the Red Hat Package Manager keeps track of all installed files, you can find the executable file for the bluefish program by using the -q and -l (list) options followed by the package name to list all files contained within the package:

```
[root@server1 root]# rpm -ql bluefish
/usr/bin/bluefish
/usr/share/application-registry/bluefish.applications
/usr/share/applications/bluefish.desktop
/usr/share/bluefish
/usr/share/bluefish/bluefish_splash.png
/usr/share/bluefish/custom_menu.default
/usr/share/bluefish/encodings.default
/usr/share/bluefish/filetypes.default
/usr/share/bluefish/funcref_css.xml
/usr/share/bluefish/funcref_html.xml
/usr/share/bluefish/funcref_php.xml
/usr/share/bluefish/funcref_python.xml
/usr/share/bluefish/highlighting.default
/usr/share/bluefish/icon_c.png
/usr/share/bluefish/icon_cfml.png
/usr/share/bluefish/icon_dir.png
/usr/share/bluefish/icon_html.png
/usr/share/bluefish/icon_image.png
/usr/share/bluefish/icon_java.png
/usr/share/bluefish/icon_pascal.png
/usr/share/bluefish/icon_php.png
/usr/share/bluefish/icon_python.png
/usr/share/bluefish/icon_r.png
/usr/share/bluefish/icon_unknown.png
```

```
/usr/share/bluefish/icon_xml.png
/usr/share/doc/bluefish-0.13
/usr/share/doc/bluefish-0.13/AUTHORS
/usr/share/doc/bluefish-0.13/COPYING
/usr/share/doc/bluefish-0.13/README
/usr/share/doc/bluefish-0.13/TODO
/usr/share/locale/bg/LC_MESSAGES/bluefish.mo
/usr/share/locale/cs/LC_MESSAGES/bluefish.mo
/usr/share/locale/da/LC_MESSAGES/bluefish.mo
/usr/share/locale/de/LC_MESSAGES/bluefish.mo
/usr/share/locale/el/LC_MESSAGES/bluefish.mo
/usr/share/locale/es/LC_MESSAGES/bluefish.mo
/usr/share/locale/fi/LC_MESSAGES/bluefish.mo
/usr/share/locale/fr/LC_MESSAGES/bluefish.mo
/usr/share/locale/hu/LC_MESSAGES/bluefish.mo
/usr/share/locale/it/LC_MESSAGES/bluefish.mo
/usr/share/locale/ja/LC_MESSAGES/bluefish.mo
/usr/share/locale/nl/LC_MESSAGES/bluefish.mo
/usr/share/locale/no/LC_MESSAGES/bluefish.mo
/usr/share/locale/pl/LC_MESSAGES/bluefish.mo
/usr/share/locale/pt/LC_MESSAGES/bluefish.mo
/usr/share/locale/pt_BR/LC_MESSAGES/bluefish.mo
/usr/share/locale/ro/LC_MESSAGES/bluefish.mo
/usr/share/locale/ru/LC_MESSAGES/bluefish.mo
/usr/share/locale/sr/LC_MESSAGES/bluefish.mo
/usr/share/locale/sv/LC_MESSAGES/bluefish.mo
/usr/share/locale/ta/LC_MESSAGES/bluefish.mo
/usr/share/locale/zh_CN/LC_MESSAGES/bluefish.mo
/usr/share/mime-info/bluefish.keys
/usr/share/mime-info/bluefish.mime
/usr/share/pixmaps/bluefish-icon.png
/usr/share/pixmaps/gnome-application-bluefish.png
[root@server1 root]# _
```

From the preceding output, you can see that the pathname to the executable file is /usr/bin/bluefish, which resides in a directory that is in our PATH variable. Upon execution in a desktop environment, you see the screen depicted in Figure 12-4.

Conversely, you can find out which package a certain file belongs to by using the -q and -f (file) options with the rpm command, followed by the filename:

```
[root@server1 root]# rpm -qf /usr/bin/bluefish
bluefish-0.13-1.1.fc2
[root@server1 root]# _
```

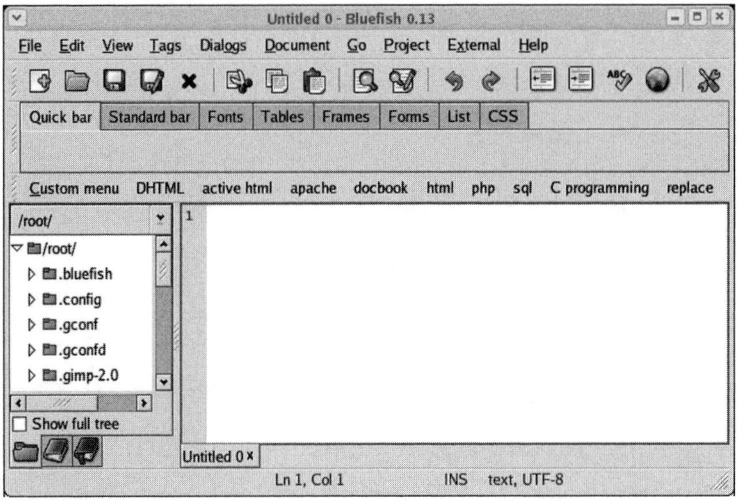

FIGURE 12-4 *The bluefish program*

To remove a package from the system, you can use the -e option to the rpm command; all files that belong to the package will be removed as well. To remove the bluefish package and verify its deletion, you can use the following commands:

```
[root@server1 root]# rpm -e bluefish
[root@server1 root]# rpm -q bluefish
package bluefish is not installed
[root@server1 root]# _
```

Table 12-8 displays a list of common options used with the rpm utility.

Table 12-8 Common options used with the rpm utility

Option	Description
-a, --all	Displays all package names installed on the system (when used with the –q option)
-e, --erase	Removes a specified package from the system
-F, --freshen	Upgrades a specified package only if an older version exists on the system
-f, --file	Displays the package to which the specified file belongs (when used with the –q option)
-h, --hash	Prints hash marks on the screen to indicate installation progress (when used with the –i option)
-i, --install	Installs a specified package (provided the –q option is not used)

Table 12-8 Common options used with the rpm utility (Continued)

Option	Description
-i, --info	Displays full information about the specified package (when used with the −q option)
-l, --list	Lists the filenames the specified package comprises (when used with the −q option)
-q, --query	Queries information about packages on the system
--test	Performs a test installation only (when used with the −i option)
-U, --upgrade	Upgrades a specified package; the package is installed even if no older version exists on the system
-V, --verify	Verifies the location of all files that belong to the specified package
-v	Prints verbose information when installing or manipulating packages

Most Linux distributions install packages during Linux installation from RPM files on the installation media. If you forgot to install a certain RPM that is available with the Fedora Core 2 Linux distribution during installation, or want to remove some packages that were loaded during installation, you can run the **system-config-packages command**, as shown in Figure 12-5. You can open this dialog box by clicking the Red Hat icon, System Settings, Add/Remove Applications.

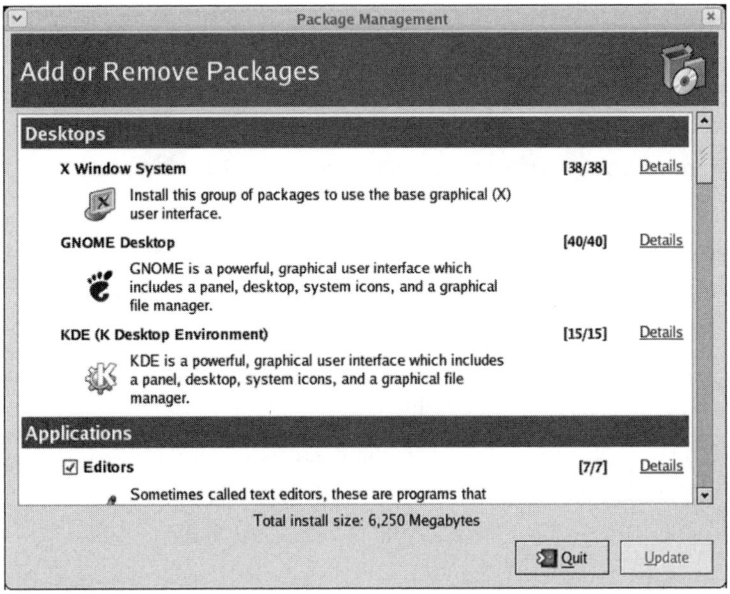

FIGURE 12-5 *Configuring Fedora core software packages after installation*

Chapter Summary

- ◆ Many compression utilities are available for Linux systems; each of them uses a different compression algorithm and produces a different compression ratio.
- ◆ Files can be backed up to an archive using a back-up utility. Tape devices are the most common medium used for archives.
- ◆ To back up files to CD-RW or DVD-RW, you must use burning software instead of a back-up utility.
- ◆ The tar utility is the most common back-up utility used today; it is typically used to create compressed archives called tarballs.
- ◆ The source code for Linux software can be obtained and compiled afterward using the GNU C Compiler; most source code is available in tarball format via the Internet.
- ◆ Package Managers install and manage compiled software of the same format.
- ◆ The Red Hat Package Manager is the most common package manager available for Linux systems today.

Key Terms

/etc/dumpdates — The file used to store information about incremental and full backups for use by the dump/restore utility.

archive — The location (file or device) that contains a copy of files; it is typically created by a back-up utility.

bunzip2 command — The command used to decompress files compressed by the bzip2 command.

burning software — The software that can write files to CD and DVD.

bzcat command — A command used to view the contents of an archive created with bzip2 to Standard Output.

bzless command — A command used to view the contents of an archive created with bzip2 to Standard Output in a page-by-page fashion.

bzmore command — A command used to view the contents of an archive created with bzip2 to Standard Output in a page-by-page fashion.

bzip2 command — The command used to compress files using a Burrows-Wheeler Block Sorting Huffman Coding compression algorithm.

checksum — A calculated value that is unique to a file's size and contents.

compress command — The command used to compress files using a Lempel-Ziv compression algorithm.

compression — The process in which files are reduced in size by a compression algorithm.

compression algorithm — The set of instructions used to reduce the contents of a file systematically.

compression ratio — The amount of compression that occurred during compression.

copy in/out (cpio) command — A common back-up utility.

dump command — A utility used to create full and incremental backups.

full backup — An archive of an entire filesystem.

GNU C Compiler (gcc) command — The command used to compile source code into binary programs.

GNU zip (gzip) command — A command used to compress files using a Lempel-Ziv compression algorithm.

gunzip command — The command used to decompress files compressed by the gzip command.

incremental backup — An archive of a filesystem that contains only files that were modified since the last archive was created.

magnetic tape (mt) command — A command used to control tape devices.

package dependencies — A list of packages that are prerequisite to the current package being installed on the system.

package manager — A system that defines a standard package format and can be used to install, query, and remove packages.

Red Hat Package Manager (RPM) — The most commonly used package manager for Linux.

restore command — The command used to extract archives created with the dump command.

rpm command — The command used to install, query, and remove RPM packages.

sum command — A command that can generate an MD5 checksum from file contents.

system backup — The process whereby files are copied to an archive.

system-config-packages command — A utility that can be used to install or remove RPMs from the Red Hat Fedora core installation media.

tape archive (tar) command — The most common utility used to create archives.

tarball — A gzip-compressed tar archive.

uncompress command — The command used to decompress files compressed by the compress command.

X-CD-Roast — A common burning software used in Linux.

zcat command — A command used to view the contents of an archive created with compress or gzip to Standard Output.

zless command — A command used to view the contents of an archive created with compress or gzip to Standard Output in a page-by-page fashion.

zmore command — A command used to view the contents of an archive created with compress or gzip to Standard Output in a page-by-page fashion.

Review Questions

1. Which of the following is one of the oldest compression utilities common to most UNIX and Linux systems?

   a. bzip2

   b. lzip

   c. gzip

   d. compress

2. Which option of the `tar` command prevents `tar` from backing up symbolic links; instead tar backs up the target files of symbolic links?

   a. -A

   b. -c

   c. -h

   d. -u

3. The _____ option of the cpio utility changes the default block size from 512 bytes to 5 Kilobytes, thus speeding up the transfer of information.

   a. -A

   b. -B

   c. -c

   d. -d

4. When downloading files from the Internet, administrators can use the _____ command to verify the checksum for the file.

   a. sum

   b. check

   c. checksum

   d. verify

5. The _____ format is the most widely used format for Linux software distributed via the Internet.

   a. Red Hat Software Distributor

   b. Red Hat Package Manager

   c. Bluefish

   d. Gnu Package Manager

6. True or false? To decompress files that have been compressed with the `compress` utility, use the `decompress` command followed by the names of the files to be decompressed.

7. True or false? One of the largest advantages that the gzip utility has over the compress utility is its ability to control the level of compression via a numeric option.

8. True or false? A typical Linux system can have hundreds of thousands of files on it, and all of these files need be included in an archive.

9. True or false? Primary responsibilities of most Linux administrators typically include the installation and maintenance of software packages.

10. True or false? The procedure for compiling source code into binary programs is not at all standardized among most Open Source Software developers.

11. The rate of compression for a file is known as a compression _____.

12. The filename extension given to files compressed with bzip2 is _____.

13. Filenames that end with the .tar.gz or .tgz extensions are commonly called _____ and represent gzip-compressed tar archives.

14. A(n) _____ backup only backs up the data that has been changed since the last backup.

15. You can compile programs according to the settings stored in a Makefile by typing the _____ command while in the source code directory.

Chapter 13

Troubleshooting and Performance

After completing this chapter, you will be able to:

◆ Describe and outline common troubleshooting procedures

◆ Identify good troubleshooting practices

◆ Effectively troubleshoot common hardware-related problems

◆ Effectively troubleshoot common software-related problems

◆ Monitor system performance using command-line and graphical utilities

◆ Identify and fix common performance problems

◆ Understand the purpose and usage of kernel modules

◆ Recompile and patch the Linux kernel

Throughout this textbook, you have examined various areas of a Linux system. In this chapter, you focus on fixing common problems that affect these areas. First, you explore system maintenance and troubleshooting procedures. Next, you learn about common hardware-related and software-related problems and their solutions, followed by a discussion of performance-related problems and utilities that can be used to monitor performance. Finally, you learn how to provide support for hardware and kernel features using modules, as well as how to compile this support directly into a new kernel.

Troubleshooting Methodology

After you have successfully installed Linux, configured services on the system, and documented settings, you must maintain the system's integrity over time. This includes monitoring, proactive maintenance, and reactive maintenance, as illustrated in Figure 13-1.

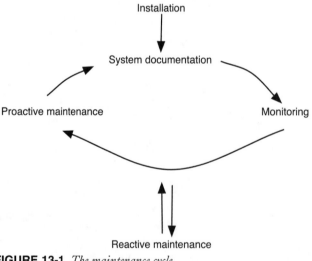

FIGURE 13-1 *The maintenance cycle*

Monitoring is the activity on which Linux administrators spend the most time; it involves examining log files and running performance utilities periodically to identify problems and their causes. **Proactive maintenance** involves taking the necessary steps required to minimize the chance of future problems as well as their impact. Performing regular system backups and identifying potential problem areas are examples of proactive maintenance. All proactive maintenance tasks should be documented for future reference; this information, along with any data backups, is vital to the reconstruction of your system, should it suffer catastrophic failure.

Reactive maintenance is used to correct problems when they arise during monitoring. When a problem is solved, it needs to be documented and the system adjusted proactively to reduce the likelihood that the same problem will occur in the future. Furthermore, documenting the solution to problems creates a template for action, allowing subsequent or similar problems to be remedied faster.

> **NOTE**
>
> Any system **documentation** should be printed and kept in a log book, because this information might be lost during a system failure if kept on the Linux system itself.

Reactive maintenance is further composed of many procedures known as **troubleshooting procedures**, which can be used to efficiently solve a problem in a systematic manner.

When a problem occurs, you need to gather as much information about the problem as possible; this might include examining system log files and viewing the contents of the /proc filesystem, as well as running information utilities, such as `ps` or `mount`. In addition, you might research the symptoms of the problem on the Internet; Web sites and newsgroups often list log files and commands that can be used to check for certain problems.

> **NOTE**
>
> The `tail -f name_of_log_file` command opens a log file for continuous viewing; this allows you to see entries as they are added, which is useful when gathering information about system problems.

Following this, you need to try to isolate the problem by examining the information gathered. Determine whether the problem is persistent or intermittent, and whether it affects all users or just one.

Given this information, you might then generate a list of possible causes and solutions organized by placing the most probable solution at the top of the list and the least probable solution at the bottom of the list. Using the Internet at this stage is beneficial because solutions for many Linux problems are posted on Web sites or newsgroups. In addition, posing the problem at a local Linux Users Group will likely generate many possible solutions.

Next, you need to implement and test each possible solution for results until the problem is resolved. When implementing possible solutions, it is very important that you only apply one change at a time. If you make multiple modifications, it will be unclear as to what worked and why.

After the problem has been solved, document the solution for future reference and proceed to take proactive maintenance measures to reduce the chance of the same problem recurring in the future. These troubleshooting procedures are outlined in Figure 13-2.

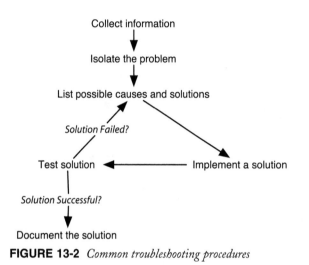

FIGURE 13-2 *Common troubleshooting procedures*

The troubleshooting procedures listed in Figure 13-2 serve as a guideline only; they might need to be adjusted for certain problems because troubleshooting is an art on which you will improve over time. There are, however, two golden rules that should guide you during any troubleshooting process:

◆ *Prioritize problems*—If there are multiple problems to be solved, prioritize the problems according to severity and spend a reasonable amount of time on each problem given its priority. Becoming fixated on a small problem and ignoring larger issues results in much lower productivity. If a problem is too difficult to solve in a given period of time, it is good practice to ask for help.

◆ *Try to solve the root of the problem*—Some solutions might appear successful in the short term, yet problems recur because there might be an underlying cause to the problem. Effective troubleshooting also relies a great deal on instinct, which comes from a solid knowledge of the system hardware and configuration. To avoid missing the underlying cause of any problem, try to justify why a certain solution was successful. If it is unclear why a certain solution was successful, there is likely an underlying cause to the problem that might need to be remedied in the future to prevent the same problem from recurring.

Resolving Common System Problems

Many possible problems can occur on different types of Linux systems. These problems are too numerous to mention here; however, some problems are common to many Linux systems that are examined throughout this section. All Linux problems can be divided into two categories: hardware-related and software-related.

Hardware-Related Problems

Although hardware problems might be the result of damaged hardware, many hardware-related problems involve improper hardware or software configuration. This is most likely the case if the hardware problem presents itself immediately after Linux installation.

As discussed in earlier chapters, ensuring that all SCSI drives are properly terminated, that the video card and monitor settings have been configured properly, and that all hardware is on the Hardware Compatibility List minimizes problems later. In addition, if the POST does not complete or alerts the user with two or more beeps at system startup, there is likely a peripheral card, cable, or memory stick that is loose or connected improperly inside the computer.

Some hardware-related problems prevent the use of hardware with the Linux operating system. This can be caused if an IRQ or I/O address is used by two different devices; in this case, neither device will work properly. Error messages indicating these IRQ and I/O address conflicts are typically written to log files during boot time and when applications try to access the device afterward. Viewing the output of the `dmesg` command or the contents of the /var/log/boot.log and /var/log/messages log files can isolate the devices with conflicting parameters.

> ### TIP
>
> As discussed in Chapter 7, "Advanced Installation," it is good form to verify each hardware device in your computer and the detected resources that they use (IRQs, I/O addresses, DMA channels) from the appropriate files in the /proc directory. This information also helps narrow down resource conflicts as well as other hardware-related problems.

After an IRQ or I/O address conflict has been identified, you can take the necessary steps to resolve it. Many conflicts are the result of PnP selecting parameters for a device when another non-PnP device has already configured itself the same parameters; to prevent this, reserve all parameters that are used by non-PnP devices in the computer BIOS. Alternatively, you can change the parameters on the non-PnP device manually because many devices come with a configuration program that allows them to change their IRQ and I/O address parameters on a CMOS chip stored on the peripheral card itself.

The absence of a device driver also prevents the operating system from using the associated hardware device. Normally, the **kudzu program** runs at each boot time, detects new hardware devices, and configures the device driver for them automatically. For example, if you add an Ethernet NIC card to the system, simply boot the computer, and the screen depicted in Figure 13-3 is displayed. Pressing Enter at this screen allows you to configure the new hardware, as shown in Figure 13-4.

If a hardware device is not detected by kudzu, the device driver for it must be configured manually. Device drivers can be inserted into the kernel as modules or can be compiled directly into the kernel. These topics are discussed later in this chapter.

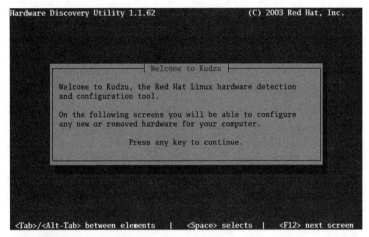

FIGURE 13-3 *The kudzu welcome screen*

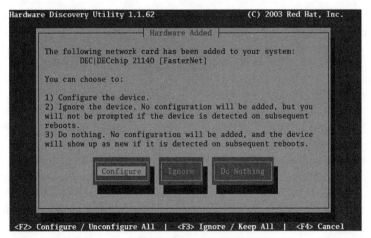

FIGURE 13-4 *Configuring new hardware using kudzu*

Although less common than other hardware problems, hardware failure can also render a device unusable. In this case, you must replace the hardware and allow `kudzu` to detect it, or configure the device driver for it manually. Because hard disks are used frequently and consist of moving parts, they are the most common hardware component to fail on Linux systems. If the Linux system uses hardware RAID level 1 or 5, the data on the hard disk can be regenerated using the configuration utility for the RAID controller. Most SCSI RAID controllers allow you to enter this utility by pressing a key combination such as `Ctrl+a` when prompted during system startup.

If, however, the Linux system does not use hardware RAID and the hard disk that failed contained partitions that were mounted on noncritical directories, such as /home or /var, then you can perform the following steps:

1. Power down the computer and replace the failed hard disk.
2. Boot the Linux system.
3. Use fdisk to create partitions on the replaced hard disk.
4. Use mkfs to create filesystems on those partitions.
5. Restore the original data using a back-up utility.
6. Ensure that /etc/fstab has the appropriate entries to mount the filesystems at system startup.

Alternatively, if the hard disk that contains the / filesystem fails, you can perform the following steps:

1. Power down the computer and replace the failed hard disk.
2. Reinstall Linux on the new hard disk (you can choose to leave partitions on other hard disks intact and mount them to the appropriate directory).
3. Restore the original configuration and data files using a back-up utility.

Software-Related Problems

Software-related problems are typically more difficult to identify and resolve than hardware-related problems. As a result, you should identify whether the software-related problem is related to application software or operating system software.

Application-Related Problems

Applications can fail during execution for a number of reasons, including missing program libraries and files, process restrictions, or conflicting applications.

As discussed in Chapter 12, "Compression, System Backup, and Software Installation," when software is installed using the Red Hat Package Manager, it does a preliminary check to ensure that all shared program libraries and prerequisite packages (package dependencies) required for the application to work properly have been installed. If these are missing, the Red

Hat Package Manager prints an error message to the screen and quits the installation. Similarly, uninstalling software using the Red Hat Package Manager fails if the software being uninstalled is a package dependency for another package. Also, when compiling source code, the configure script checks for the presence of any required shared program libraries and programs and fails to create the Makefile if they are absent. Thus, you must download and install the necessary shared libraries and/or packages before installing most software packages.

Some programs, however, might fail to check for dependencies during installation, or files that belong to a package dependency might be accidentally removed from the system over time. If this is the case, certain programs fail to execute properly.

To identify any missing files in a package or package dependency, recall that you can use the -V option to the rpm command, followed by the name of the package. The following output indicates that there are two missing files in the bash package:

```
[root@server1 root]# rpm -V bash
missing    /usr/share/doc/bash-2.05b/NEWS
missing    /usr/share/doc/bash-2.05b/NOTES
[root@server1 root]# _
```

To identify which shared libraries are required by a certain program, you can use the **ldd command**. For example, the following output displays the shared libraries required by the /bin/bash program:

```
[root@server1 root]# ldd /bin/bash
        linux-gate.so.1 =>  (0x004c8000)
        libtermcap.so.2 => /lib/libtermcap.so.2 (0x00c23000)
        libdl.so.2 => /lib/libdl.so.2 (0x00a07000)
        libc.so.6 => /lib/tls/libc.so.6 (0x008c5000)
        /lib/ld-linux.so.2 => /lib/ld-linux.so.2 (0x008a8000)
[root@server1 root]# _
```

If any shared libraries listed by the ldd command are missing, you can download the appropriate library from the Internet and install it to the correct location, which is typically underneath the /lib or /usr/lib directories. After downloading and installing any shared libraries, it is good practice to run the **ldconfig command** to ensure that the list of shared library directories (**/etc/ld.so.conf**) and the list of shared libraries (**/etc/ld.so.cache**) are updated.

Recently, multimedia applications that play sound and video have been popular on the Linux platform. Many different formats are used to store and retrieve multimedia information; thus, multimedia programs often work with several different types of multimedia data. In addition, because multimedia data is usually large in size, it is often compressed using a format such as MP3 or DivX. For a multimedia program to decompress multimedia files, it requires the appropriate **compressor/decompressor (codec)**, which is typically a shared library file. Codecs for most multimedia programs are available in tarball format from the Internet. After download, most codecs contain the shared library files as well as a script (install.sh) that, when executed, copies the shared libraries to the appropriate directory and runs the ldconfig command to update the /etc/ld.so.conf and /etc/ld.so.cache files. If no script is available, you must manually copy the shared library files to the appropriate location and update the /etc/ld.so.conf and /etc/ld.so.cache files.

Processes are restricted by a number of constraints that can also prevent them from executing properly. Recall that all processes require a PID from the system process table. Too many processes running on the system can use all available PIDs in the process table; this is typically the result of a large number of zombie processes. Killing the parent process of the zombie processes then frees several entries in the process table.

In addition, processes can initiate numerous connections to files on the filesystem in addition to Standard Input, Standard Output, and Standard Error. These connections are called **filehandles**. The shell restricts the number of filehandles that programs can open to 1024 by default; to increase the maximum number of filehandles to 5000, you can run the command ulimit -n 5000. The **ulimit command** can also be used to increase the number of processes that users can start in a shell; this might be required for programs that start a great deal of child processes. For example, to increase the maximum number of user processes to 8000, you can use the command ulimit -u 8000.

To isolate application problems that are not related to missing dependencies or restrictions, you should first check the log file produced by the application. Most application log files are stored in the **/var/log** directory or subdirectories of the /var/log directory named for the application. For example, to view the errors for the Apache Web Server daemon, you can view the file /var/log/httpd/error_log.

Applications might run into difficulties gaining resources during execution and stop functioning. Often, restarting the process using a SIGHUP solves this problem. This condition might also be caused by another process on the system that attempts to use the same resources. To determine this, attempt to start the application when fewer processes are loaded, such as in Single User Mode. If resource conflict seems to be the cause of the problem, check the Internet for a newer version of the application or an application fix.

Operating System-Related Problems

Many software-related problems are related to the operating system itself. These typically include problems with boot loaders, filesystems, and serial devices.

As discussed in Chapter 9, "System Initialization and X Windows," boot loaders can encounter problems while attempting to load the operating system kernel. For the LILO boot loader, placing the word "linear" and removing the word "compact" from the /etc/lilo.conf file usually remedies the problem. For the GRUB boot loader, errors are typically the result of a missing file in the /boot directory. Also, ensuring that the Linux kernel resides before the 1024th cylinder of the hard disk and that 32-bit large block addressing (lba32) is specified in the boot loader configuration file eliminates BIOS problems with large hard disks.

It is safe practice to create a boot disk after installation; if the boot loader fails to load the kernel, you can then use the bootloader and kernel on the boot disk to mount the root filesystem and continue the boot process. The **mkbootdisk command** can be used to create a boot disk after installation; to create a boot disk with the 2.6.5-1.358 kernel on it, you can use the command `mkbootdisk 2.6.5-1.358` at the command prompt and insert a blank floppy disk when prompted. This boot disk can then be used to boot into a system such that the boot loader can be repaired.

Because the operating system transfers data to and from the hard disk frequently, the filesystem can become corrupted over time; a corrupted filesystem can be identified by very slow write requests, errors printed to the console, or failure to mount. If the filesystem on a partition mounted to a noncritical directory, such as /home or /var, becomes corrupted, you should perform the following troubleshooting steps:

1. Unmount the filesystem if mounted.

2. Run the `fsck` command with the `-f` (full) option on the filesystem device.

3. If the `fsck` command cannot repair the filesystem, use the `mkfs` command to re-create the filesystem.

4. Restore the original data for the filesystem using a back-up utility.

> **NOTE**
>
> Do not restore data onto a damaged filesystem; ensure that the filesystem has been re-created first.

If the / filesystem becomes corrupted, the system is unstable and must be turned off. Following this, you can use a copy of Linux on the installation media to remedy the problem using the following troubleshooting steps:

1. Place the first Red Hat Fedora installation CD-ROM in the CD-ROM drive and turn on the computer.

2. At the welcome screen shown in Figure 13-5, type `linux rescue` and press Enter. When prompted for language and keyboard layout, choose English and U.S (us), respectively. When prompted to start the network, choose No.

3. At the screen depicted in Figure 13-6, choose Skip to enter a shell for the Linux system on the CD-ROM, as shown in Figure 13-7. This system contains utilities in the /usr/bin and /usr/sbin directories that can restore the filesystem on the hard disk.

4. Use the `mkfs` command on the CD-ROM Linux system to create a new / filesystem on the appropriate partition on the hard disk.

5. Use a back-up utility on the CD-ROM Linux system (`tar`, `dump`, or `cpio`) to restore the original data to the re-created / filesystem.

6. Type `exit` at the shell prompt to reboot the system.

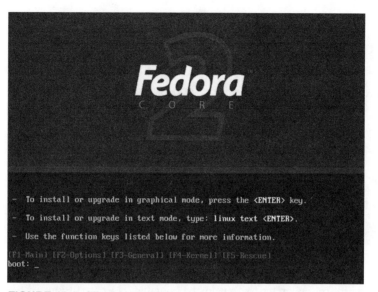

FIGURE 13-5 *The Red Hat Fedora Linux installation welcome screen*

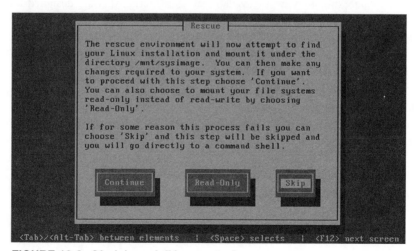

FIGURE 13-6 *Obtaining a shell in rescue mode*

FIGURE 13-7 *The command-line shell used in rescue mode*

Some Linux administrators prefer to download a bootable CD-based Linux distribution that contains more filesystem repair utilities than the first Red Hat Fedora installation CD-ROM. Many small Linux distributions are available on the Internet that are designed for this purpose; two examples are **Knoppix Linux** (*http://www.knoppix.org*) and **BBC Linux** (*http://www.lnx-bbc.org*). Simply download the ISO image for the Linux distribution and burn the image to a CD-ROM using burning software. Following this, you can boot the computer using this CD-based Linux distribution and use the utilities on it to repair your / filesystem and restore the files from backup.

Another common problem encountered on Linux systems is improper serial port configuration. Modem devices are identified as serial devices to the system; however, many modems use the same IRQ and I/O address settings as a serial port that is connected to the mainboard of the computer, which results in parameter conflicts. In addition, some serial devices such as serial printers and terminal stations require communication at a set speed, rather than the default speed of 115 KB/s for most serial ports. To remedy these problems, you can use keyword arguments to the **setserial command** to set the IRQ, I/O address, and speed of a specified serial device. For example, to set the IRQ of the first serial port (/dev/ttyS0) to 11 and the I/O address to 0x03f8, and view the results, you can use the following commands:

```
[root@server1 root]# setserial /dev/ttyS0 irq 11 port 0x03f8
[root@server1 root]# setserial /dev/ttyS0
/dev/ttyS0, UART: 16550A, Port: 0x03f8, IRQ: 11
[root@server1 root]# _
```

Table 13-1 lists other keywords that can be used with the setserial command.

Table 13-1   Common keywords used with the setserial utility

Option	Description
port n	Sets the I/O address to n for a serial device
irq n	Sets the IRQ to n for a serial device
auto_irq	Attempts to automatically detect the IRQ setting for a serial device
spd_hi	Sets the speed of a serial port to 56KB/s
spd_vhi	Sets the speed of a serial port to 115KB/s
spd_normal	Sets the speed of a serial port to 38.4KB/s

Performance Monitoring

Some problems that you will encounter on a Linux system are not as noticeable as those discussed in the previous section; such problems affect the overall performance of the Linux system. Like the problems discussed earlier, performance problems can be caused by software or hardware or a combination of the two.

Hardware that is improperly configured might still work, but at a slower speed. In addition, when hardware ages, it might start to malfunction and send large amounts of information to the CPU when not in use; this process is known as **jabbering** and can slow down a CPU and, hence, the rest of the Linux system. To avoid this hardware malfunction, most companies retire computer equipment after two to three years of use.

Software can also affect the overall performance of a system; software that requires too many system resources monopolizes the CPU, memory, and peripheral devices. Poor performance can also be the result of too many processes running on a computer, processes that make a great deal of read/write requests to the hard disk (such as databases), or rogue processes. To remedy most software performance issues, you can remove software from the system to free up system resources; if this software is needed for business activity, you can instead choose to move the software to another Linux system that has more free system resources.

Software performance problems can also sometimes be remedied by altering the hardware. Upgrading or adding another CPU allows the Linux system to execute processes faster and reduce the number of processes running concurrently on the CPU. Alternatively, some peripheral devices can perform a great deal of processing that is normally performed by the CPU; this is known as **bus mastering**. Using bus mastering peripheral components reduces the amount of processing the CPU must perform and, hence, increases system speed.

Adding RAM to the computer also increases system speed as processes will have more working space in memory and the system will swap much less information to and from the hard disk. Because the operating system, peripheral components, and all processes use RAM constantly, adding RAM to any system often has a profound impact on system performance.

In addition, replacing slower hard disk drives with faster ones or using Disk Striping RAID improves the performance of programs that require frequent access to filesystems. Recall from earlier that SCSI hard disks typically have faster access speeds than their IDE counterparts; many Linux servers use SCSI hard disks for this reason. In addition, CD-ROMs have a slower access speed than hard disks; thus, keeping CD-ROM drives and hard disk drives on separate controllers also improves hard disk performance.

The size of the Linux kernel itself has an impact on system performance; a smaller kernel can execute faster on the CPU than a larger one. Thus, recompiling the kernel (discussed later in this chapter) to remove unnecessary components and reduce its size improves overall system performance.

To ease the identification of performance problems, you should run performance utilities on a healthy Linux system on a regular basis during normal business hours and record the results in a system log book. The average results of these performance utilities are known as **baseline** values because they represent normal system activity. When performance issues arise, you can compare the output of performance utilities to the baseline values found in the system log book; values that have changed dramatically from the baseline can indicate the source of the performance problem.

Although many performance utilities are available to Linux administrators, the most common of these belong to the sysstat package.

Monitoring Performance with sysstat Utilities

The **System Statistics (sysstat) package** contains a wide range of utilities that monitor the system using information from the /proc directory and system devices.

To monitor CPU performance, you can use the **Multiple Processor Statistics (mpstat) utility**. Without arguments, the mpstat utility gives average CPU statistics for all processors on the system since the most previous system boot, as shown in the following output:

```
[root@server1 root]# mpstat
Linux 2.6.5-1.358 (server1)     07/14/2005

02:35:10 PM  CPU  %user %nice %system %iowait %irq %soft %idle  intr/s
02:35:10 PM  all  17.53  1.48    6.21   11.73 0.19  0.00 62.85 1042.90
[root@server1 root]# _
```

> **NOTE**
>
> If your system has multiple CPUs, you can measure the performance of a single CPU by specifying the -P # option to the mpstat command, where # represents the number of the processor starting from zero. Thus, the command mpstat -P 0 displays statistics for the first processor on the system.

The %user value shown in the preceding output indicates the amount of time the processor spent executing user programs and daemons, whereas the %nice value indicates the amount of time the processor spent executing user programs and daemons that had nondefault nice values. These numbers combined should be greater than the value of %system, which indicates the amount of time the system spent maintaining itself such that it can execute user programs and daemons.

A system that has a high %system compared to %user and %nice is likely executing too many resource-intensive programs.

The %iowait value indicates the percentage of time the CPU was idle when there was an outstanding disk I/O request. The %irq and %soft values indicate the percentage of time the CPU is using to respond to normal interrupts and interrupts that span multiple CPUs, respectively. If these three values rapidly increase over time, the CPU cannot keep up with the number of requests it receives from software.

The %idle value indicates the percentage of time the CPU did not spend executing tasks. Although it might be zero for short periods of time, %idle should be greater than 25% over a long period of time.

A system that has a %idle less than 25% over a long period of time might require faster or additional CPUs.

The intr/s is the number of interrupts or requests that a CPU receives from peripheral devices on average per second; a very high value compared to the average baseline value might be the result of a jabbering peripheral device.

Although the average values given by the mpstat command are very useful in determining the CPU health of a Linux system, you might choose to take current measurements using mpstat. To do this, simply specify the interval in seconds and number of measurements as arguments to the mpstat command; for example, the following command takes five current measurements, one per second:

```
[root@server1 root]# mpstat 1 5
Linux 2.6.5-1.358 (server1)       07/14/2005

02:46:10 PM  CPU  %user %nice %system %iowait %irq %soft %idle  intr/s
02:46:11 PM  all   8.91  1.98    0.00    0.00 0.99  0.00 88.12 1013.86
02:46:12 PM  all   7.07  2.02    0.00    0.00 0.00  0.00 90.91 1011.11
02:46:13 PM  all   7.92  1.98    0.99    0.00 0.00  0.00 89.11 1011.88
02:46:14 PM  all   7.07  2.02    0.00    0.00 0.00  0.00 90.91 1013.13
02:46:15 PM  all   6.93  2.97    0.99    0.00 0.00  0.00 89.11 1011.88
Average:     all   7.58  2.20    0.40    0.00 0.20  0.00 89.62 1012.38
[root@server1 root]# _
```

The preceding output must be used with caution because it was taken over a short period of time; if, for example, the %idle values are under 25% on average, they are not necessarily abnormal because the system might be performing a CPU-intensive task during the short time the statistics were taken.

Another utility in the sysstat package is **Input/Output Statistics (iostat)**; this utility measures the flow of information to and from disk devices. Without any arguments, the iostat command displays CPU statistics similar to mpstat, followed by statistics for each disk device on the system. If your Linux system has one IDE hard disk drive (/dev/hda), the iostat command produces output similar to the following:

```
[root@server1 root]# iostat
Linux 2.6.5-1.358 (server1)     07/14/2005

avg-cpu:  %user   %nice    %sys  %iowait  %idle
          6.98    1.78    2.05     3.26  85.92

Device:          tps  Blk_read/s  Blk_wrtn/s  Blk_read  Blk_wrtn
hda             8.34      248.19       43.43    536458     93864
[root@server1 root]# _
```

The output from iostat displays the number of transfers per second (tps) as well as the number of blocks read per second (Blk_read/s) and written per second (Blk_wrtn/s), followed by the total number of blocks read (Blk_read) and written (Blk_wrtn) for the device since the last boot. An increase over time in these values indicates an increase in disk usage by processes. If this increase results in slow performance, the hard disks should be replaced with faster ones or a RAID Disk Stripe. Like mpstat, the iostat command can take current measurements of the system. Simply specify the interval in seconds followed by the number of measurements as arguments to the iostat command.

Although iostat and mpstat can be used to get quick information about system status, they are limited in their abilities. The **System Activity Reporter (sar) command** that is contained in the sysstat package can be used to display far more information than iostat and mpstat; as such, it is the most widely used performance monitoring tool on UNIX and Linux systems.

By default, sar commands are scheduled using the cron daemon to run every 10 minutes in Red Hat Fedora Linux; all performance information obtained is logged to a file in the /var/log/sa directory called sa#, where # represents the day of the month. If today were the 14th day of the month, the output from the sar command that is run every 10 minutes would be logged to the file /var/log/sa/sa14. Next month, this file will be overwritten on the 14th day; thus, only one month of records is kept at any one time in the /var/log/sa directory.

NOTE

You can change the sar logging interval by editing the cron table /etc/cron.d/sysstat.

Without arguments, the sar command displays the CPU statistics taken every 10 minutes for the current day, as shown in the following output:

```
[root@server1 root]# sar
Linux 2.6.5-1.358 (server1)     07/14/2005

09:00:00 AM     CPU     %user   %nice   %system %iowait %idle
09:10:00 PM     all     13.95   0.04    1.78    0.33    83.90
09:20:00 PM     all     5.67    0.64    1.51    1.44    90.74
09:30:00 PM     all     6.73    0.03    1.18    0.44    91.61
09:40:00 PM     all     17.73   0.04    3.34    5.33    73.55
09:50:00 PM     all     1.32    0.03    0.15    1.87    96.63
10:00:01 PM     all     1.33    0.03    0.14    0.04    98.46
10:10:00 PM     all     14.56   0.04    2.01    5.82    77.57
10:20:00 PM     all     1.30    0.03    0.15    0.04    98.48

10:20:00 PM     CPU     %user   %nice   %system %iowait %idle
10:30:01 PM     all     1.32    0.03    0.16    0.05    98.44
10:40:00 PM     all     1.33    0.03    0.17    0.05    98.43
10:50:00 PM     all     1.29    0.03    0.15    0.04    98.49
11:00:01 PM     all     1.31    0.03    0.15    0.05    98.46
11:10:00 PM     all     1.37    0.03    0.17    0.04    98.39
11:20:00 PM     all     1.32    0.03    0.16    0.04    98.45
11:30:00 PM     all     1.30    0.03    0.15    0.04    98.47
11:40:01 PM     all     1.32    0.03    0.16    0.04    98.45
11:50:00 PM     all     1.29    0.03    0.17    0.04    98.46
Average:        all     5.94    0.15    0.97    1.20    91.73
[root@server1 root]# _
```

Note from the preceding output that a new set of column headers is printed each time the computer is rebooted.

To view the CPU statistics for the 10th of the month, you can specify the pathname to the file using the -f option to the sar command:

```
[root@server1 root]# sar -f /var/log/sa/sa10
Linux 2.6.5-1.358 (server1)     07/10/2005

07:40:01 PM     CPU     %user   %nice   %system %iowait %idle
07:50:00 PM     all     1.44    0.00    0.11    0.01    98.43
08:00:00 PM     all     1.47    0.00    0.12    0.01    98.40
08:10:01 PM     all     1.51    0.00    0.14    0.04    98.31
08:20:00 PM     all     1.47    0.00    0.11    0.02    98.41
08:30:01 PM     all     1.47    0.00    0.11    0.01    98.40
08:40:00 PM     all     2.23    12.97   3.94    22.86   58.00
08:50:00 PM     all     1.52    2.56    4.38    29.00   62.54
```

```
09:00:01 PM    all    1.40    0.00    0.11    0.02    98.47
09:10:00 PM    all    1.32    0.00    0.12    0.04    98.52
Average:       all    1.54    1.72    1.02    5.78    89.94
[root@server1 root]# _
```

You must use the the -f option to the sar command to view files in the /var/log/sa directory with the aforementioned filenames because they contain binary information.

As with the iostat and mpstat command, the sar command can be used to take current system measurements. To take four CPU statistics every two seconds, you can use the following command:

```
[root@server1 root]# sar 2 4
Linux 2.6.5-1.358 (server1)    07/14/2005

12:29:40 PM    CPU    %user    %nice    %system    %iowait    %idle
12:29:42 PM    all    10.05    2.51     3.52       0.00       83.92
12:29:44 PM    all    6.50     2.00     1.00       0.00       90.50
12:29:46 PM    all    5.45     2.48     0.99       0.50       90.59
12:29:48 PM    all    5.00     2.00     1.00       0.00       92.00
Average:       all    6.74     2.25     1.62       0.12       89.26
[root@server1 root]# _
```

Although the sar command displays CPU statistics by default, you can display different statistics by specifying options to the sar command. Table 13-2 lists common options used with the sar command.

Table 13-2 Common options to the sar command

Option	Description
-A	Displays the most information; this option is equivalent to all options
-b	Displays I/O statistics
-B	Displays swap statistics
-c	Displays the number of processes created per second
-d	Displays Input/Output statistics for each block device on the system
-f *FILENAME*	Displays information from the specified file; these files typically reside in the /var/log/sa directory
-n FULL	Reports full network statistics; network monitoring is discussed in Chapter 14
-o *FILENAME*	Saves the output to a file in binary format

Table 13-2 Common options to the sar command (Continued)

Option	Description
-q	Displays statistics for the processor queue
-r	Displays memory and swap statistics
-R	Displays memory statistics
-u	Displays CPU statistics; this is the default action when no options are specified
-v	Displays kernel-related filesystem statistics
-W	Displays swapping statistics

From Table 13-2, you can see that the -b and -d options to the sar command display information similar to the output of the iostat command. In addition, the -u option displays CPU statistics equivalent to the output of the mpstat command.

Another important option to the sar command is -q, which shows processor queue statistics. Recall that a queue, also known as a cache, is used to store information temporarily for a certain device; the queues that surround the CPU are known as L1, L2, and L3 cache. To view processor queue statistics every five seconds, you can execute the following command:

```
[root@server1 root]# sar -q 1 5
Linux 2.6.5-1.358 (server1)     07/14/2005

12:31:10 PM   runq-sz  plist-sz   ldavg-1   ldavg-5   ldavg-15
12:31:11 PM        0        82      0.45      0.36       0.21
12:31:12 PM        0        82      0.45      0.36       0.21
12:31:13 PM        0        82      0.45      0.36       0.21
12:31:14 PM        0        82      0.41      0.35       0.21
12:31:15 PM        0        82      0.41      0.35       0.21
Average:           0        82      0.43      0.36       0.21
[root@server1 root]# _
```

The runq-sz (run queue size) indicates the number of processes that are waiting for execution on the processor run queue; for most Intel architectures, this number is typically two or less on average.

NOTE

A runq-sz much greater than two for long periods of time indicates that the CPU is too slow to respond to system requests.

The plist-sz (process list size) value indicates the number of processes currently running in memory and the ldavg-1 (load average – 1 minute), ldavg-5 (load average – 5 minutes), and ldavg-15 (load average – 15 minutes) values represent an average CPU load for the last 1 minute, 5 minutes, and 15 minutes, respectively. These four statistics display an overall picture of processor activity. A rapid increase in these values is typically caused by software that is running on the system.

Recall that all Linux systems use a swap partition to store information that cannot fit into physical memory; this information is sent to and from the swap partition in units called pages. The number of pages that are sent to the swap partition (pswpin/s) and the pages that are taken from the swap partition (pswpout/s) can be viewed using the -W option to the sar command, as shown in the following output:

```
[root@server1 root]# sar -W 1 5
Linux 2.6.5-1.358 (server1)     07/14/2005

12:32:06 PM  pswpin/s pswpout/s
12:32:07 PM     0.00      0.54
12:32:08 PM     1.32      1.93
12:32:09 PM     0.38      0.00
12:32:10 PM     0.00      0.00
12:32:11 PM     0.00      0.00
Average:        0.00      0.00
[root@server1 root]# _
```

If there is a large number of pages being sent to and taken from the swap partition, the system will suffer from slower performance. To remedy this, you can add more physical memory (RAM) to the system.

Other Performance Monitoring Utilities

The sysstat package utilities are not the only performance monitoring utilities available in Red Hat Fedora Linux. The top utility discussed in Chapter 10, "Managing Linux Processes," also displays CPU statistics, memory usage, swap usage, and average CPU load at the top of the screen, as shown next:

```
top - 12:33:49 up  1:00,  2 users,  load average: 0.04, 0.22, 0.17
Tasks:  77 total,   2 running,  75 sleeping,   0 stopped,   0 zombie
Cpu(s): 23.5% us,  5.0% sy,  2.6% ni, 68.2% id,  0.0% wa,  0.7% hi,  0.0% si
Mem:    387172k total,   377176k used,     9996k free,    38896k buffers
Swap:   614368k total,        0k used,   614368k free,   200636k cached

  PID USER      PR  NI  VIRT  RES  SHR S %CPU %MEM    TIME+  COMMAND
 2929 root      15   0 20992  14m 9.8m S 14.8  3.8  1:44.77 X
 3488 root      15   0 26156  12m  20m S 12.8  3.2  0:17.30 gnome-terminal
 3424 root      25  10 33244  18m  22m R  3.0  5.0  1:16.75 rhn-applet-gui
```

```
3643 root      17   0  3400  900 1620 R  1.0  0.2   0:00.10 top
3208 root      15   0 14412 7020  11m S  0.3  1.8   0:04.47 metacity
3453 root      16   0 19204 8216  16m S  0.3  2.1   0:01.51 clock-applet
   1 root      16   0  2540  460 1316 S  0.0  0.1   0:04.89 init
   2 root      34  19     0    0    0 S  0.0  0.0   0:00.00 ksoftirqd/0
   3 root       5 -10     0    0    0 S  0.0  0.0   0:00.03 events/0
   4 root       5 -10     0    0    0 S  0.0  0.0   0:00.00 kblockd/0
   7 root       5 -10     0    0    0 S  0.0  0.0   0:00.03 khelper
   5 root      15   0     0    0    0 S  0.0  0.0   0:00.11 khubd
   6 root      15   0     0    0    0 S  0.0  0.0   0:00.00 kapmd
   8 root      15   0     0    0    0 S  0.0  0.0   0:00.00 pdflush
   9 root      15   0     0    0    0 S  0.0  0.0   0:00.10 pdflush
  11 root      14 -10     0    0    0 S  0.0  0.0   0:00.00 aio/0
  10 root      15   0     0    0    0 S  0.0  0.0   0:00.05 kswapd0
```

Furthermore, the **free command** can be used to display the total amounts of physical and swap memory in Kilobytes and their utilizations, as shown in the following output:

```
[root@server1 root]# free
                total       used       free     shared    buffers     cached
Mem:           387172     376432      10740          0      39092     198140
-/+ buffers/cache:        139200     247972
Swap:          614368          0     614368
[root@server1 root]# _
```

The Linux kernel reserves some memory for its own use (cached) to hold requests from hardware devices (buffers); the total memory in the preceding output is calculated with and without these values to indicate how much memory the system has reserved. The output from the preceding free command indicates that there is sufficient memory in the system because no swap is used and a great deal of free physical memory is available.

Like the free utility, the vmstat utility can be used to indicate whether more physical memory is required by measuring swap performance:

```
[root@server1 root]# vmstat
procs -----------memory---------- ---swap-- -----io---- --system-- ----cpu----
 r  b   swpd   free   buff  cache   si   so    bi    bo   in    cs us sy id wa
 2  0      0  10756  39128 198160   ~0    0    73    18 1030   186 10  2 87  2
[root@server1 root]# _
```

The **vmstat command** shown previously indicates more information than the free command used earlier, including the following:

- The number of processes waiting to be run (r)
- The number of sleeping processes (b)
- The amount of swap memory used in Kilobytes (swpd)

- The amount of free physical memory (free)
- The amount of memory used by buffers in Kilobytes (buff)
- The amount of memory used as cache (cache)
- The amount of memory in Kilobytes per second swapped in to the disk (si)
- The amount of memory in Kilobytes per second swapped out to the disk (so)
- The number of blocks per second sent to block devices (bi)
- The number of blocks per second received from block devices (bo)
- The number of interrupts sent to the CPU per second (in)
- The number of context changes sent to the CPU per second (cs)
- The CPU user time (us)
- The CPU system time (sy)
- The CPU idle time (id)
- The time spent waiting for I/O (wa)

Thus, the output from vmstat shown previously indicates that no swap memory is being used because swpd, si, and so are all zero; however, it also indicates that the reason for this is that the system is not running many processes at the current time (r=2, id=87).

Customizing the Kernel

Because the Linux kernel interfaces with the computer hardware, you can provide additional hardware support or change existing hardware support by altering the way in which the kernel works. This can be done by inserting a module into the kernel or recompiling the kernel to incorporate different features. Alternatively, it might be necessary to download and compile a new kernel to obtain certain hardware support that is not available in the current version. In addition, the Linux kernel also affects performance; recompiling the kernel to remove unnecessary kernel features reduces its size and increases its speed.

Kernel Modules

Many device drivers and kernel features are compiled into the kernel; however, these can also be inserted into the kernel as modules to reduce the size of the kernel. It is good form to compile standard device support into the kernel and leave support for other devices and features as modules. Because a wide variety of sound card and NIC manufacturers exist, drivers for these components are typically represented by modules that can be inserted into the kernel as compared to IDE hard disk support, which is typically compiled into the kernel because it is so often needed.

Some kernel features are available as modules; these modules must be manually inserted into the kernel. In addition, if kudzu does not detect new hardware properly, you need to load the appropriate module into the kernel to provide the necessary hardware support.

Modules are typically stored in subdirectories of the /lib/modules/<kernel-version> directory. For example, to see a partial list of NIC driver modules for the 2.6.5-1.358 kernel, you can list the contents of the /lib/modules/2.6.5-1.358/kernel/drivers/net directory:

```
[root@server1 root]# ls -F /lib/modules/2.6.5-1.358/kernel/drivers/net/
3c501.ko*    b44.ko*        forcedeth.ko*    ppp_async.ko*    starfire.ko*
3c503.ko*    bonding/       hamachi.ko*      ppp_deflate.ko*  sundance.ko*
3c505.ko*    cs89x0.ko*     hp100.ko*        ppp_generic.ko*  sungem.ko*
3c507.ko*    de600.ko*      irda/            pppoe.ko*        sungem_phy.ko*
3c509.ko*    de620.ko*      ixgb/            pppox.ko*        sunhme.ko*
3c515.ko*    depca.ko*      lance.ko*        ppp_synctty.ko*  tg3.ko*
3c59x.ko*    dgrs.ko*       mii.ko*          r8169.ko*        tlan.ko*
8139cp.ko*   dl2k.ko*       natsemi.ko*      rcpci.ko*        tulip/
8139too.ko*  dummy.ko*      ne2k-pci.ko*     s2io.ko*         tun.ko*
82596.ko*    e1000/         netconsole.ko*   sb1000.ko*       typhoon.ko*
8390.ko*     e100.ko*       ni52.ko*         sis900.ko*       via-rhine.ko*
ac3200.ko*   eepro100.ko*   ni65.ko*         sk98lin/         wd.ko*
acenic.ko*   epic100.ko*    ns83820.ko*      skfp/            wireless/
amd8111e.ko* eql.ko*        pcmcia/          slhc.ko*         yellowfin.ko*
appletalk/   ethertap.ko*   pcnet32.ko*      smc9194.ko*
atp.ko*      fealnx.ko*     plip.ko*         smc-ultra.ko*
[root@server1 root]# _
```

Most files shown in the preceding output have the .ko extension which indicates that they are compiled and ready to be inserted into the kernel.

> **NOTE**
>
> Modules in older kernels, such as the 2.4 kernel, use the .o extension.

If you have a PCI NE2000 NIC in your computer, you can use the insmod ne2k-pci command to insert the module into the kernel. The **insmod command** does not require the full path to the module underneath the /lib/modules/<kernel-version> directory because it searches there by default and locates the ne2k-pci.ko file, as shown in the preceding output.

Alternatively, you can use the modprobe ne2k-pci command to insert the module into the kernel. The **modprobe command** checks to ensure that any prerequisite modules have been loaded first and loads them if needed before loading the specified module.

Some modules might require extra parameters when inserted into the kernel. For example, a non-PnP ISA NIC requires the IRQ and I/O address be specified alongside its module name; to insert this module into the kernel for a NIC that uses IRQ 10 and an I/O address range of 0x300-31F, you can use the command insmod module_name irq=10 io=0x300.

> **NOTE**
>
> Both the `insmod` and `modprobe` commands fail to insert a driver module if the associated device is not present.

To see a list of modules that have been inserted into the Linux kernel, you can use the **lsmod command**:

```
[root@server1 root]# lsmod
Module                 Size  Used by
nls_utf8               1536  0
nls_cp437              5376  0
vfat                  10496  0
fat                   33472  1 vfat
snd_mixer_oss         13824  0
snd                   38372  1 snd_mixer_oss
soundcore              6112  1 snd
parport_pc            19392  1
lp                     8236  0
parport               29640  2 parport_pc,lp
autofs4               10624  0
rfcomm                27164  0
l2cap                 16004  5 rfcomm
bluetooth             33636  4 rfcomm,l2cap
sunrpc               101064  1
tulip                 36256  0
floppy                47440  0
sg                    27552  0
scsi_mod              91344  1 sg
microcode              4768  0
dm_mod                33184  0
cpia_usb               5892  0
cpia                  36356  1 cpia_usb
videodev               6656  1 cpia
uhci_hcd              23708  0
ipv6                 184288  8
ext3                 102376  1
jbd                   40216  1 ext3
[root@server1 root]# _
```

The `lsmod` command can also be used to show module dependencies; from the preceding output, the snd_mixer_oss module requires the snd module because the snd module is used by snd_mixer_oss.

To remove a module from the kernel, you can use the **rmmod command**. To remove the snd_mixer_oss module shown in the preceding output, you can use the command rmmod snd_mixer_oss at the command prompt.

Normally, modules are inserted into the kernel automatically at boot time using the modprobe command from entries in the **/etc/modprobe.conf file**; an example of this file is shown in the following output:

```
[root@server1 root]# cat /etc/modprobe.conf
alias eth0 tulip
alias usb-controller usb-uhci
[root@server1 root]# _
```

NOTE

Older Linux distributions typically load modules at boot time from entries in the /etc/modules.conf or /etc/conf.modules files.

The preceding output loads the tulip module at boot time for a PnP Macronix NIC and gives it an alias of eth0. If the NIC is not PnP, you also need to specify the IRQ and I/O address options, as shown in the following output:

```
[root@server1 root]# cat /etc/modprobe.conf
alias eth0 tulip
options tulip irq=10 io=0x300
alias usb-controller usb-uhci
[root@server1 root]# _
```

You can edit the /etc/modules.conf file and add a line to load a particular module on system startup if hardware is not detected properly or certain kernel features are required. Alternatively, you can place the appropriate insmod or modprobe command in the /etc/rc.d/rc.local file, which is executed at the end of system startup, as discussed in Chapter 9.

Compiling a New Linux Kernel

To gain certain hardware or kernel support, it might be necessary to recompile the current kernel with different features or download the source code for a newer kernel and compile it.

Kernel source code is stored under the /usr/src/<kernel-version> directory. The source code for the current kernel version is present underneath this directory. You can instead choose to download source code in tarball format for a newer kernel and place the tarball in the /usr/src directory. Upon extraction, the appropriate <kernel-version> directory is created underneath /usr/src.

Regardless of whether you are recompiling the current kernel version or a new one, the remaining steps are identical. The next step is to create a symbolic link called **/usr/src/linux** to the correct kernel version directory /usr/src/<kernel-version>. Next change to this directory and execute one of many make commands.

If the source code has been compiled previously, you can optionally use the make mrproper command to remove any files created by previous kernel compilations; this speeds up compiling the new kernel. In addition, if you are compiling the same kernel version that is used, you can use the make oldconfig command to record the current kernel features and settings that can then be used as a starting point for further configuration.

Next, you must choose the certain features required for the kernel; this can be done using one of four commands:

◆ make config—Provides a text-based interface that prompts the user for information regarding kernel configuration in a question-by-question format, as shown in the following output:

```
root@server1 linux]# make config
  HOSTCC   scripts/basic/fixdep
  HOSTCC   scripts/basic/split-include
  HOSTCC   scripts/basic/docproc
  SHIPPED scripts/kconfig/zconf.tab.h
  SHIPPED scripts/kconfig/zconf.tab.c
  SHIPPED scripts/kconfig/lex.zconf.c
  HOSTCC   -fPIC scripts/kconfig/zconf.tab.o
  HOSTLLD -shared scripts/kconfig/libkconfig.so
  HOSTCC   scripts/kconfig/conf.o
  HOSTCC   scripts/kconfig/mconf.o
  HOSTLD   scripts/kconfig/conf
scripts/kconfig/conf arch/i386/Kconfig
#
# using defaults found in /boot/config-2.6.5-1.358
#
*
* Linux Kernel Configuration
*
*
* Code maturity level options
*
Prompt for development and/or incomplete code/drivers
(EXPERIMENTAL) [Y/n/?]
```

◆ make menuconfig—Provides a text-based menu that allows easy navigation of kernel features for configuration, as shown in Figure 13-8.

◆ make xconfig or make gconfig—Allows the easiest navigation of kernel features via a graphical interface, as shown with make gconfig in Figure 13-9. make xconfig must be run in a KDE (Qt-based) GUI environment, and make gconfig must be run in a GNOME (GTK-based) GUI environment.

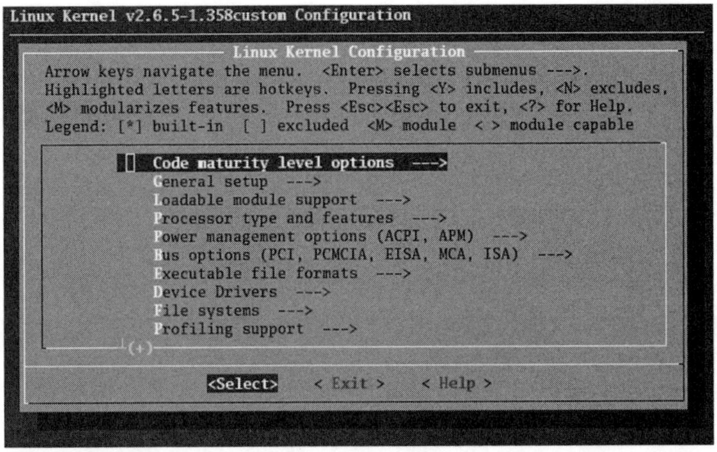

FIGURE 13-8 *The make menuconfig interface*

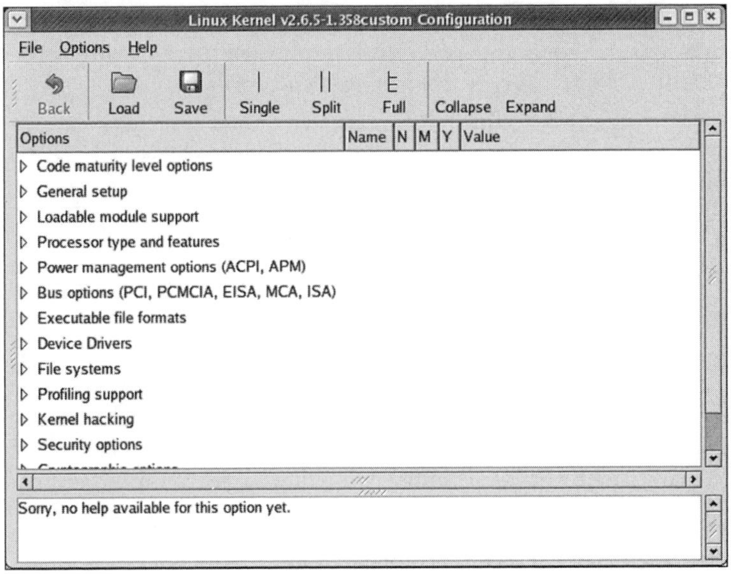

FIGURE 13-9 *The make gconfig interface*

If you expand Power management options (ACPI, APM) in Figure 13-9, you can configure your kernel with ACPI support, as shown in Figure 13-10.

Note from Figure 13-10 that the Software Suspend feature is Experimental; if you are building a production server, it is good practice to avoid setting any experimental options. In addition, a Y in the Y column beside the option indicates that the support will be compiled into the kernel, whereas an M in the M column indicates that the support will be compiled into a module that can be inserted into the Linux kernel. An N in the N column disables support for a certain kernel feature.

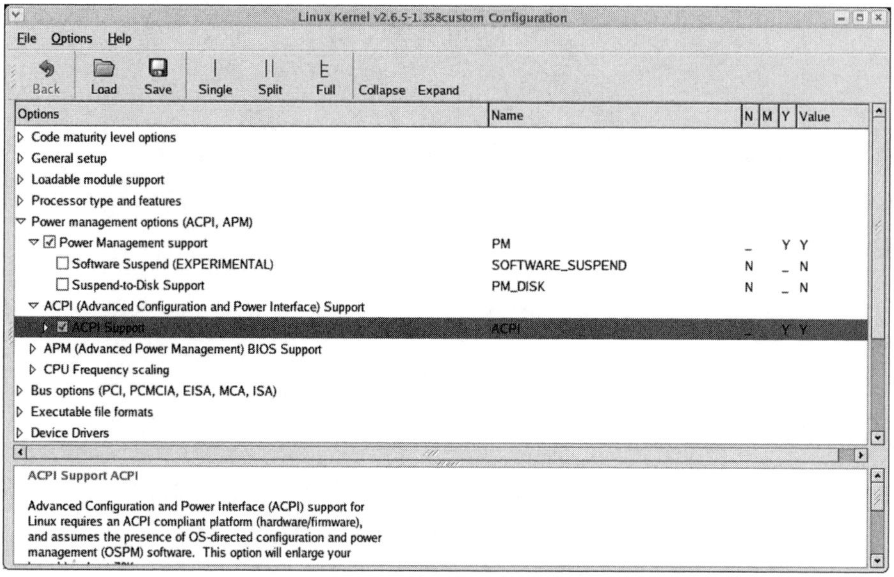

FIGURE 13-10 *Configuring power options in the Linux kernel*

NOTE

All three choices (Y, M, N) might not be available for some features.

You should disable support for unused kernel features to reduce the size of the Linux kernel and increase its speed. For the same reason, you should compile rarely used features as modules.

After you have configured the options you desire for your kernel, you can choose the Save button shown in Figure 13-10, exit the program, and return to the command prompt.

After the kernel features have been selected, you should run the make clean command to remove any files that are not required for compiling the kernel; this speeds up the time it takes to compile the kernel.

Next, you can compile the kernel by typing make bzImage (or just make). After this has completed, you have a bzip2-compressed kernel called /usr/src/linux/arch/i386/boot/bzImage, which can then be copied to the /boot directory and renamed vmlinuz-<kernel version>. Following this, you should also copy the /usr/src/linux/System.map file to the /boot directory.

Afterward, to compile the necessary modules and copy them to the appropriate location under /lib/modules, you can type make modules_install at a command prompt.

> **NOTE**
>
> Compiling a 2.6 Linux kernel and the associated modules typically takes anywhere from two to six hours depending on the options selected and the hardware of the computer. This is in addition to the time taken to research and select the appropriate options for the kernel.

Because many kernel features and device support are required by the Linux kernel while it is being loaded at boot time, you should create a kernel ramdisk image. To do this, simply use the command `mkinitrd -v /boot/initrd-<kernel version>.img  <kernel version>`.

Finally, you can configure the boot loader to boot the new kernel by adding the appropriate lines for the kernel and ramdisk image to /etc/lilo.conf (if LILO is your boot loader) or /boot/grub/grub.conf (if GRUB is your boot loader), as described in Chapter 9.

Patching the Linux Kernel

To install a more current Linux kernel version, you normally download the source code for that kernel and place it in a directory that will be referenced by /usr/src/linux. If the /usr/src/linux directory already contains the source code for the current kernel, you can instead choose to download and apply patch files to this source code to change it into the desired version. Patches are not cumulative; to patch the Linux kernel version 2.6.7 to 2.6.9, you must apply the Linux kernel patches 2.6.8 and 2.6.9.

Patches are typically distributed in compressed form; to apply a patch, simply download and uncompress the patch file into the /usr/src/linux directory and execute the **patch command**. To execute a kernel patch, you can type `patch < patchfile`. When all patches have been applied, you can compile the kernel, as described in the previous section.

Chapter Summary

◆ After installation, Linux administrators monitor the system, perform proactive and reactive maintenance, and document important system information.

◆ Common troubleshooting procedures involve collecting data to isolate and determine the cause of system problems, as well as implementing and testing solutions that can be documented for future use.

◆ System problems can be categorized as hardware- or software-related.

◆ IRQ conflicts, invalid hardware settings, absence of kernel support, and hard disk failure are common hardware-related problems on Linux systems.

◆ Software-related problems can be further categorized as application-related or operating system-related.

◆ Absence of program dependencies or shared libraries, program limits, and resource conflicts are common application-related problems, whereas boot failure, filesystem corruption, and the misconfiguration of serial devices are common operating system-related problems.

◆ System performance is affected by a variety of hardware and software factors, including the amount of RAM, CPU speed, kernel size, and process load.

◆ Using performance monitoring utilities to create a baseline is helpful when diagnosing performance problems in the future. The sysstat package contains many useful performance monitoring commands.

◆ System features and hardware support can be compiled into the Linux kernel or provided by a kernel module.

◆ You can compile a Linux kernel with only the necessary features and support to increase system performance.

Key Terms

/etc/ld.so.cache file — The file that contains the location of shared library files.

/etc/ld.so.conf file — The file that contains a list of directories that contain shared libraries.

/etc/modprobe.conf file — The file used to load and alias modules at system initialization.

/usr/src/linux directory — The directory that typically contains source code for the Linux kernel during compilation.

/var/log directory — The directory that contains most system log files.

baseline — A measure of normal system activity.

BBC Linux — A CD-based Linux distribution.

bus mastering — The process by which peripheral components perform tasks normally executed by the CPU.

compressor/decompressor (codec) — A file that contains the rules to compress or decompress multimedia information.

documentation — The system information that is stored in a log book for future reference.

filehandles — The connections that a program makes to files on a filesystem.

free command — A command used to display memory and swap statistics.

Input/Output Statistics (iostat) command — A command that displays Input/Output statistics for block devices.

insmod command — A command used to insert a module into the Linux kernel.

jabbering — The process by which failing hardware components send large amounts of information to the CPU.

Knoppix Linux — A CD-based Linux distribution.

kudzu program — A program used to detect and install support for new hardware.

ldconfig command — The command that updates the /etc/ld.so.conf and /etc/ld.so.cache files.

ldd command — The command used to display the shared libraries used by a certain program.

lsmod command — A command that lists modules currently used by the Linux kernel.

mkbootdisk command — A command used to create a boot floppy disk.

modprobe command — A command used to insert a module and all necessary prerequisite modules into the Linux kernel.

monitoring — The process by which system areas are observed for problems or irregularities.

Multiple Processor Statistics (mpstat) command — A command that displays CPU statistics.

patch command — The command used to apply a patch to the Linux kernel source code.

proactive maintenance — The measures taken to reduce future system problems.

reactive maintenance — The measures taken when system problems arise.

rmmod command — The command that removes a module from the Linux kernel.

setserial command — The command used to set the parameters of serial device.

System Activity Reporter (sar) command — The command that displays various system statistics.

System Statistics (sysstat) package — A software package that contains common performance monitoring utilities, such as mpstat, iostat, sar, and isag.

troubleshooting procedures — The tasks performed when solving system problems.

ulimit command — The command used to modify process limit parameters in the current shell.

vmstat command — The command used to display memory, CPU, and swap statistics.

Review Questions

1. It is good form to verify each hardware device in your computer and the detected resources that they use (IRQs, I/O addresses, DMA channels) from the appropriate files in the /_____ directory.

   a. dev

   b. proc

   c. device

   d. irq

2. To identify any missing files in a package or package dependency, you can use the _____ option to the rpm command followed by the name of the package.

   a. -A

   b. -m

   c. -p

   d. −V

3. The shell restricts the number of filehandles that programs can open to _____ by default.

   a. 100

   b. 512

   c. 1024

   d. 5000

4. To monitor CPU performance, you can use the _____ utility.

   a. mpstat

   b. psstat

   c. cpuhealth

   d. iostat

5. Compiling a 2.6 Linux kernel and the associated modules typically takes anywhere from _____ depending on the options selected and the hardware of the computer.

   a. ten to thirty minutes

   b. one to two hours

   c. two to six hours

   d. one to two days

6. True or false? Proactive maintenance involves taking the necessary steps required to minimize the chance of future problems as well as their impact.

7. True or false? The most common hardware problem is when a device becomes unstable.

8. True or false? Software-related problems are typically more difficult to identify and resolve than hardware-related problems.

9. True or false? IDE hard disks typically have faster access speeds than their SCSI counterparts.

10. True or false? The sysstat package utilities are the only performance monitoring utilities available in Red Hat Fedora Linux.

11. _____ is the largest activity that Linux administrators do; it involves examining log files and running performance utilities periodically to identify problems and their causes.

12. The _____ program runs at each boot time, detects new hardware devices, and configures the device driver for them automatically.

13. When hardware ages, it might start to malfunction and send large amounts of information to the CPU when not in use; this process is known as _____ and can slow down a CPU and, hence, the rest of the Linux system.

14. The _____ command can be used to display the total amounts of physical and swap memory in Kilobytes and their utilizations.

15. To see a list of modules that have been inserted into the Linux kernel, you can use the _____ command.

Chapter 14

Network Configuration

After completing this chapter, you will be able to:

◆ Describe the purpose and types of networks, protocols, and media access methods

◆ Understand the basic configuration of TCP/IP

◆ Configure a NIC interface to use TCP/IP

◆ Configure a modem, ISDN, and DSL interface to use PPP and TCP/IP

◆ Understand the purpose of host names and how they are resolved to IP addresses

◆ Use common network utilities to interact with network services

Throughout this book, you have examined the installation and administration of local Linux services; this chapter focuses on configuring Linux to participate on a network. First, you become acquainted with some common network terminology, and then learn about TCP/IP and the procedure for configuring a network interface. Next, you learn about the Domain Name Space and the processes by which host names are resolved to IP addresses. Finally, you learn about the various network utilities that can be used on a Linux system.

Networks and TCP/IP

Most functions that computers perform today involve the sharing of information betwe\en computers. Information is usually transmitted from computer to computer via media such as fiber optic, telephone, coaxial, or unshielded twisted pair (UTP) cable, but can also be transmitted via wireless media such as radio, micro, or infrared waves. This media typically attaches to a peripheral card on the computer such as a network interface card (NIC) or modem device.

Two or more computers that are connected with media that can exchange information are called a **network**. Networks that connect computers within close proximity are called **local area networks (LANs)**, whereas networks that connect computers separated by large distances are called **wide area networks (WANs)**.

Many companies use LANs to allow employees to connect to databases and other shared resources such as printers. Home users can also use LANs to connect several home computers together. Alternatively, home users can use a WAN to connect home computers to an **Internet service provider (ISP)** to gain access to resources such as Web sites on the worldwide public network called the Internet.

> ### NOTE
>
> The Internet (Internetwork) is merely several public networks that are interconnected; both home and company networks can be part of the Internet. Special computers called **routers** transfer information from one network to another.

Computers that are connected via network media still require a method for sending and receiving information to and from other computers on the network. This is achieved by using a network **protocol** that formats information into packages of information called **packets**, as well as a **media access method** that can send these packets onto the media itself.

You can configure many different network protocols in Linux, including but not limited to the following list:

◆ TCP/IP (Transmission Control Protocol/Internet Protocol)

◆ UDP/IP (User Datagram Protocol/Internet Protocol)

◆ IPX/SPX (Internetwork Packet Exchange/Sequenced Packet Exchange)

◆ AppleTalk

◆ DLC (Data Link Control)

◆ DECnet (Digital Equipment Corporation network)

NOTE

The most common LAN protocol used today is TCP/IP. It is the standard protocol used to transmit information across the Internet and the one discussed in this chapter.

When transmitting information across a WAN, you might also use a WAN protocol in addition to a specific LAN protocol to format packets for safer transmission. The two most common WAN protocols are Serial Line Internet Protocol (SLIP) and Point-to-Point Protocol (PPP).

Although many media access methods are available, the most common one used to send TCP/IP packets onto network media is called **Ethernet**. It ensures that any TCP/IP packets are retransmitted onto the network if a network error occurs. Another popular media access method is called **Token Ring**, which gives the computer that has a special token the ability to transmit information on a network; the token is passed from computer to computer to allow multiple computers to communicate. The media access method is usually contained within the hardware on the NIC or modem.

The TCP/IP Protocol

To participate on a TCP/IP network, your computer must have a valid **Internet Protocol (IP) address** and **subnet mask**. Optionally, you can configure a **default gateway** to participate on larger networks such as the Internet.

IP Addresses

An IP address is a unique number assigned to the computer that identifies itself on the network, similar to a unique postal address that identifies your location in the world. If any two computers have the same IP address, it is impossible for information to be correctly delivered to them. Directed communication from one computer to another single computer using TCP/IP is referred to as a **unicast**.

The most common format for IP addresses is four numbers called **octets** that are separated by periods. Each octet represents an 8-bit binary number (0–255). An example of an IP address in this notation is 192.168.5.69.

You can convert between decimal and binary by recognizing that an 8-bit binary number represents the decimal binary powers of two in the following order:

128 64 32 16 8 4 2 1

Thus, the number 255 is 11111111 (128+64+32+16+8+4+2+1) in binary and the number 69 is 01000101 (64+4+1) in binary. When the computer looks at an IP address, the numbers are converted to binary.

All IP addresses are composed of two parts: the network ID and the host ID. The **network ID** represents the network on which the computer is located, whereas the **host ID** represents a single computer on that network. No two computers on the same network can have the same host ID; however, two computers on different networks can have the same host ID.

You can compare the network ID and the host ID to a postal mailing address. A postal mailing address is composed of two portions: the street name and the house number. The street name is similar to a network ID. No two streets can have the same name, just as no two networks can have the same network ID. The host ID is like the house number. Two houses can have the same house number as long as they are on different streets, just as two computers can have the same host ID as long as they are on different networks.

Only computers with the same network ID can communicate among each other without the use of a router. This allows administrators to logically separate computers on a network; computers in the Accounting Department could use one network ID, whereas computers in the Sales Department could use a different network number. If the two departments are connected by a router, computers in the Accounting Department can communicate with computers in the Sales Department and vice versa.

NOTE

If your TCP/IP network is not connected to the Internet, the choice of IP address is entirely up to you. However, if your network is connected to the Internet, you might need to use preselected IP addresses for the computers on your network. IP addresses that can be used on the Internet are assigned by your Internet service provider.

The IP address 127.0.0.1 is called the loopback IP address; it always refers to the local computer.

Subnet Masks

Each computer that has an IP address must also be configured with a subnet mask to define which part of its IP address is the network ID and which part is the host ID. Subnet masks are composed of four octets just like an IP address. The simplest subnet masks use only the two values of 0 and 255. Wherever there is a 255 in the subnet mask, that octet is part of the network ID. Wherever there is a 0 in the subnet mask, that octet is part of the host ID. Your computer uses the **ANDing** binary process to find the network ID. This is a mathematical operation that compares two binary digits and gives a result of 1 or 0. If both binary digits being compared have a value of 1, the result is 1. If one digit is 0 and the other is 1, or if both digits are zero, the result is 0.

When an IP address is ANDed with a subnet mask, the result is the network ID. Figure 14-1 shows an example of how the network ID and host ID of an IP address can be calculated using the subnet mask.

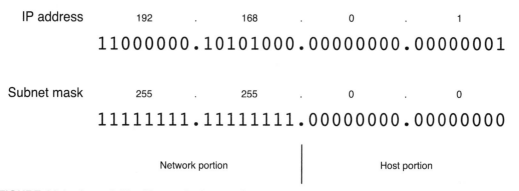

| IP address | 192 | . | 168 | . | 0 | . | 1 |

11000000.10101000.00000000.00000001

| Subnet mask | 255 | . | 255 | . | 0 | . | 0 |

11111111.11111111.00000000.00000000

Network portion   Host portion

FIGURE 14-1 *A sample IP address and subnet mask*

Thus, the IP address shown in Figure 14-1 identifies the first computer (host portion 0.1) on the 192.168 network (network portion 192.168).

> ### NOTE
>
> IP addresses and their subnet masks are often written using the **classless interdomain routing (CIDR) notation**. For example, the notation 172.11.4.66/16 refers to the IP address 172.11.4.66 with a 16-bit subnet mask (255.255.0.0).

The IP addresses 0.0.0.0 and 255.255.255.255 are not allowed to be assigned to a host computer because they refer to all networks and all computers on all networks, respectively. Similarly, using the number 255 (all 1s in binary format) in an IP address can specify many hosts. For example, the IP address 192.168.255.255 refers to all hosts on the 192.168.0.0 network; this IP address is also called the **broadcast** address for the 192.168 network.

> **NOTE**
>
> A computer uses its IP address and subnet mask to determine what network it is on. If two computers are on the same network, they can deliver packets directly to each other. If two computers are on different networks, they must use a router to communicate.

Default Gateway

Typically, all computers on a LAN are configured with the same network ID and different host IDs. A LAN can connect to another LAN by means of a router, which has IP addresses for both LANs and can forward packets to and from each network. Each computer on a LAN can specify the IP address of a router in their TCP/IP configuration; any packets that are not destined for the local LAN are then sent to the router, which can then forward the packet to the appropriate network or to another router. The IP address of the network interface on the router to which you send packets is called the default gateway.

A router is often a dedicated hardware device from a vendor such as Cisco, D-Link, or Linksys. Other times, a router is actually a computer with multiple network cards. The one consistent feature of routers, regardless of the manufacturer, is that they can distinguish between different networks and move (or route) packets between them. A router has an IP address on every network to which it is attached. When a computer sends a packet to the default gateway for further delivery, the address of the router must be on the same network as the computer, as computers can send packets directly to devices only on their own network.

TCP/IP Classes and Subnetting

IP addresses are divided into classes for management. The class of an IP address defines the default subnet mask of the device using that address. All of the IP address classes can be identified by the first octet of the address, as shown in Table 14-1.

Table 14-1 IP address classes

Class	Subnet Mask	First Octet	Maximum Number of Networks	Maximum Number of Hosts	Example IP Address
A	255.0.0.0	1–127	127	16,777,214	3.4.1.99
B	255.255.0.0	128–191	16,384	65,534	144.129.188.1
C	255.255.255.0	192–223	2,097,152	254	192.168.1.1
D	N/A	224–239	N/A	N/A	224.0.2.1
E	N/A	240–254	N/A	N/A	N/A

Class A addresses use 8 bits for the network ID and 24 bits for the host ID. You can identify this from the subnet mask of 255.0.0.0. The value of the first octet will always be in a range from 1 to 127. This means there are only 127 potential Class A networks available for the entire Internet. Class A networks are only assigned to very large companies and Internet providers.

Class B addresses use 16 bits for the network ID and 16 bits for the host ID. The subnet mask of 255.255.0.0 defines this. The value of the first octet ranges from 128 to 191. There are 16,384 class B networks with 65,534 hosts on each network. Class B networks are assigned to many larger organizations, such as governments, universities, and companies with several thousand users.

Class C addresses use 24 bits for the network ID and 8 bits for the host ID. This is defined by the subnet mask 255.255.255.0. The value of the first octet ranges from 192 to 223. There are 2,097,152 class C networks with 254 hosts on each network. Although there are very many class C networks, they have a relatively small number of hosts, and, thus, are suited only to smaller organizations.

Class D addresses are not divided into networks and they cannot be assigned to computers as IP addresses; instead, Class D addresses are used for multicasting. **Multicast** addresses are used by groups of computers. A packet addressed to a multicast address is delivered to each computer in the multicast group. This is better than a broadcast message because routers can be configured to allow multicast traffic to move from one network to another. In addition, all computers on the network process broadcasts, while only computers that are part of that multicast group process multicasts. Streaming media and network conferencing software often use multicasting to communicate to several computers at once.

Like Class D addresses, Class E addresses are not typically assigned to a computer. Class E addresses are considered experimental and are reserved for future use.

Notice from Table 14-1 that Class A and B networks can have many thousands or millions of hosts on a single network. Because this is not practically manageable, Class A and B networks are typically subnetted. **Subnetting** is the process in which a single large network is subdivided into several smaller networks to control traffic flow and improve manageability. After a network has been subnetted, a router is required to move packets from one subnet to another.

> ### NOTE
>
> You can subnet any Class A, B, or C network.

To subnet a network, you take some bits from the host ID and give them to the network ID. Suppose, for example, that you want to divide the 3.0.0.0/8 network into 17 subnets. The binary representation of this network is:

```
3.0.0.0   =     00000011.00000000.00000000.00000000
255.0.0.0 =     11111111.00000000.00000000.00000000
```

You then borrow some bits from the host portion of the subnet mask. Because the number of combinations of binary numbers can be represented in binary powers of two, and valid subnet masks do not contain all 0s or 1s, you can use the equation $2^n - 2$ to represent the minimum number of subnets required, where n is the number of binary bits that are borrowed from the host portion of the subnet mask. For our example, this is represented as:

```
2ⁿ - 2 ≥ 15
2ⁿ ≥ 17
```

Thus, n = 5 (because $2^4 = 16$ is less than 17, but $2^5 = 32$ is greater than 17). Following this, our subnet mask borrows five bits from the default Class A subnet mask:

```
255.248.0.0 =      11111111.11111000.00000000.00000000
```

Similarly, because there are 19 zeros in the preceding subnet mask, you can use the $2^n - 2$ equation referred to previously to identify the number of hosts per subnet:

```
2¹⁹ - 2   = number of hosts per subnet
          = 524,286 hosts per subnet
```

You can then work out the IP address ranges for each of the network ranges. Because three bits in the second octet were not borrowed during subnetting, the ranges of IP addresses that can be given to each subnet must be in ranges of $2^3 = 8$. Thus, the first five ranges that can be given to different subnets on the 3.0.0.0/8 network that use the subnet mask 255.248.0.0 are as follows:

```
3.0.0.1-3.7.255.254
3.8.0.1-3.15.255.254
3.16.0.1-3.23.255.254
3.24.0.1-3.31.255.254
3.32.0.1-3.39.255.254
```

From the preceding ranges, a computer with the IP address 3.34.0.6/13 cannot communicate with the computer 3.31.0.99/13 because they are on different subnets. To communicate, there must be a router between them.

NOTE

When subnetting a Class C network, ensure that you discard the first and last IP address in each range to account for the broadcast and network address for the subnet.

Configuring a NIC Interface

Linux computers in a business environment typically connect to the company network via a NIC. At home, more and more people are connecting to the Internet by means of a NIC, using technologies such as Digital Subscriber Line (DSL) and Broadband Cable Networks (BCNs).

If the NIC was detected during installation, Red Hat Fedora Linux automatically configures the appropriate driver module and prompts the user for the TCP/IP configuration required for the business or home network during installation, as seen earlier in Chapter 3, "Linux Installation and Usage." However, some NICs are not detected upon installation; these NICs are either detected and configured by kudzu after installation or configured manually.

NIC drivers are usually contained within modules that can be inserted into the Linux kernel; you can use their computer manual, the Internet, or other sources of information to find which Linux module underneath the /lib/modules directory to use for a particular NIC. If there is no module for that NIC underneath /lib/modules, you might need to download a module from the Internet. After the module has been identified or downloaded, this module can be inserted into the kernel using the insmod or modprobe commands discussed in the previous chapter. To load this module at boot time, you should edit the /etc/modprobe.conf file.

The /etc/modprobe.conf file also assigns an alias to the module that can be used when referencing the module in a configuration command because modules do not have a corresponding file in the /dev directory. The first Ethernet NIC is given the alias eth0, the second Ethernet NIC is given the alias eth1, and so on. Thus, to load the driver module for the first PCI NE2000 NIC, you could place the following line in /etc/moprobe.conf:

```
alias eth0 ne2k-pci
```

Along the same line, to load the driver module for the second NIC of type DEC Tulip, you could place the following line in /etc/modules.conf:

```
alias eth1 tulip
```

After the driver module for the NIC has been loaded into the Linux kernel, you can configure it to use TCP/IP. The **ifconfig command** can be used to assign a TCP/IP configuration to a NIC as well as view the configuration of all network interfaces in the computer. To assign eth0 the IP address of 3.4.5.6 with a subnet mask of 255.0.0.0 and broadcast address of 3.255.255.255, you can use the following command at a command prompt:

```
ifconfig eth0 3.4.5.6 netmask 255.0.0.0 broadcast 3.255.255.255
```

Alternatively, you can receive TCP/IP configuration from a Dynamic Host Configuration Protocol (DHCP) or Boot Protocol (BOOTP) server on the network. To obtain and configure TCP/IP information from a server on the network for the first Ethernet adapter, you can use the command dhclient eth0 at the command prompt.

To view the configuration of all interfaces, you can use the ifconfig command without any arguments, as shown in the following output:

```
[root@server1 root]# ifconfig
eth0      Link encap:Ethernet  HWaddr 00:80:C6:F9:1B:8C
          inet addr:3.4.5.6  Bcast:3.255.255.255  Mask:255.0.0.0
          inet6 addr: fe80::280:c6ff:fef9:1b8c/64 Scope:Link
          UP BROADCAST RUNNING MULTICAST  MTU:1500  Metric:1
          RX packets:47 errors:0 dropped:0 overruns:0 frame:0
          TX packets:13 errors:5 dropped:0 overruns:0 carrier:5
          collisions:0 txqueuelen:1000
          RX bytes:5560 (5.4 Kb)  TX bytes:770 (770.0 b)
          Interrupt:10 Base address:0x8000

lo        Link encap:Local Loopback
          inet6 addr: ::1/128 Scope:Host
          UP LOOPBACK RUNNING  MTU:16436  Metric:1
          RX packets:3142 errors:0 dropped:0 overruns:0 frame:0
          TX packets:3142 errors:0 dropped:0 overruns:0 carrier:0
          collisions:0 txqueuelen:0
          RX bytes:3443414 (3.2 Mb)  TX bytes:3443414 (3.2 Mb)

[root@server1 root]# _
```

The output of the ifconfig command also shows interface statistics and the special loopback adapter (lo) with the IP address 127.0.0.1; this IP address represents the local computer and is required on all computers that use TCP/IP.

> **NOTE**
>
> The netstat -i command can also be used to show interface statistics.

If you restart the computer, the TCP/IP information configured for eth0 will be lost. To allow the system to activate and configure the TCP/IP information for an interface at each boot time, simply place entries in the /etc/sysconfig/network-scripts/ifcfg-*interface* file, where *interface* is the name of the network interface. An example of the configuration file for the first Ethernet interface (eth0) is shown in the following output:

```
[root@server1 root]# cat /etc/sysconfig/network-scripts/ifcfg-eth0
DEVICE=eth0
BOOTPROTO=none
HWADDR=00:80:C6:F9:1B:8C
IPADDR=3.4.5.6
```

```
NETMASK=255.0.0.0
GATEWAY=3.0.0.1
ONBOOT=yes
IPV6INIT=no
[root@server1 root]# _
```

The entries in the preceding output indicate that the TCP/IP configuration for the first Ethernet adapter (eth0) will be activated at boot time (ONBOOT=yes). The NIC does not obtain information from a DHCP or BOOTP server (BOOTPROTO=none); it is instead configured using the IP address 3.4.5.6, a subnet mask of 255.0.0.0, and a default gateway of 3.0.0.1. The broadcast need not be included in this file because it can be easily calculated by the system given the subnet mask. Also, you can change the BOOTPROTO=none line to BOOTPROTO=dhcp or BOOTPROTO=bootp to gain all TCP/IP configuration information from a DHCP or BOOTP server on the network, respectively.

> **NOTE**
>
> The /etc/sysconfig/network-scripts/ifcfg-eth0 can also contain information regarding the configuration of other network protocols such as IPX/SPX.

After editing the /etc/sysconfig/network-scripts/ifcfg-eth0 file, you do not need to reboot your system to have the new TCP/IP configuration take effect; simply run the command ifdown eth0 to unconfigure the eth0 interface, followed by ifup eth0 to configure the eth0 interface using the settings in the /etc/sysconfig/network-scripts/ifcfg-eth0 file.

After a NIC has been configured to use TCP/IP, you should test the configuration by using the **Packet Internet Groper (ping) command**. The ping command sends a small TCP/IP packet to another IP address and awaits a response. By default, the ping command sends packets continuously every second until the Ctrl+c key combination is pressed; to send only five ping requests to the loopback interface, simply use the -c option to the ping command, as shown in the following example:

```
[root@server1 root]# ping -c 5 127.0.0.1
PING 127.0.0.1 (127.0.0.1) 56(84) bytes of data.
64 bytes from 127.0.0.1: icmp_seq=0 ttl=64 time=0.154 ms
64 bytes from 127.0.0.1: icmp_seq=1 ttl=64 time=0.109 ms
64 bytes from 127.0.0.1: icmp_seq=2 ttl=64 time=0.110 ms
64 bytes from 127.0.0.1: icmp_seq=3 ttl=64 time=0.119 ms
64 bytes from 127.0.0.1: icmp_seq=4 ttl=64 time=0.111 ms

--- 127.0.0.1 ping statistics ---
5 packets transmitted, 5 received, 0% packet loss, time 3999ms
rtt min/avg/max/mdev = 0.109/0.120/0.154/0.020 ms, pipe 2
[root@server1 root]# _
```

> **NOTE**
>
> If the `ping` command fails to receive any responses from the loopback interface, there
> is a problem with TCP/IP itself.

In addition, to send five ping requests to the IP address configured earlier, you can use the following command:

```
[root@server1 root]# ping -c 5 3.4.5.6
PING 3.4.5.6 (3.4.5.6) 56(84) bytes of data.
64 bytes from 3.4.5.6: icmp_seq=0 ttl=64 time=0.157 ms
64 bytes from 3.4.5.6: icmp_seq=1 ttl=64 time=0.113 ms
64 bytes from 3.4.5.6: icmp_seq=2 ttl=64 time=0.106 ms
64 bytes from 3.4.5.6: icmp_seq=3 ttl=64 time=0.107 ms
64 bytes from 3.4.5.6: icmp_seq=4 ttl=64 time=0.115 ms

--- 3.4.5.6 ping statistics ---
5 packets transmitted, 5 received, 0% packet loss, time 4000ms
rtt min/avg/max/mdev = 0.106/0.119/0.157/0.022 ms, pipe 2
[root@server1 root]# _
```

> **NOTE**
>
> If the `ping` command fails to receive any responses from the newly configured IP
> address, there is a problem with the TCP/IP configuration for the NIC.

Next, you need to test whether the Linux computer can ping other computers on the same
network; the following command can be used to send five ping requests to the computer that
has the IP address 3.0.0.2 configured:

```
[root@server1 root]# ping -c 5 3.0.0.2
PING 3.0.0.2 (3.0.0.2) 56(84) bytes of data.
64 bytes from 3.0.0.2: icmp_seq=0 ttl=128 time=0.448 ms
64 bytes from 3.0.0.2: icmp_seq=1 ttl=128 time=0.401 ms
64 bytes from 3.0.0.2: icmp_seq=2 ttl=128 time=0.403 ms
64 bytes from 3.0.0.2: icmp_seq=3 ttl=128 time=0.419 ms
64 bytes from 3.0.0.2: icmp_seq=4 ttl=128 time=0.439 ms

--- 3.0.0.2 ping statistics ---
5 packets transmitted, 5 received, 0% packet loss, time 4001ms
rtt min/avg/max/mdev = 0.401/0.422/0.448/0.018 ms, pipe 2
[root@server1 root]# _
```

> **NOTE**
>
> If the `ping` command fails to receive any responses from other computers on the network, there is a problem with the network media.

Configuring a NIC interface can also be done from a desktop environment, as shown in Figure 14-2. Simply navigate to the Red Hat button, System Settings, Network.

If you highlight your network interface and click the Edit button shown in Figure 14-2, you are prompted to supply the appropriate IP configuration and click OK, as shown in Figure 14-3.

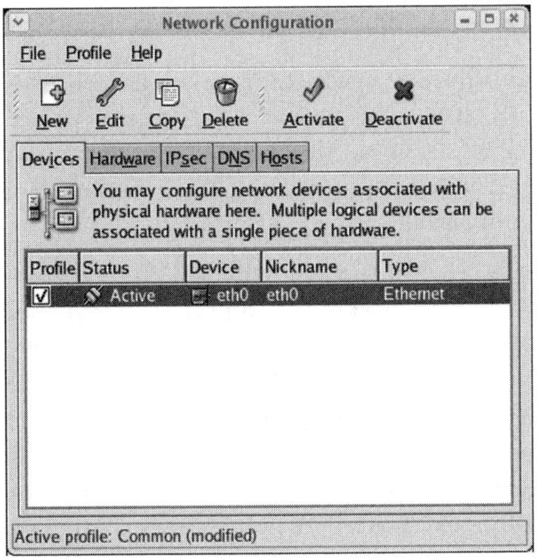

FIGURE 14-2 *Configuring network interfaces*

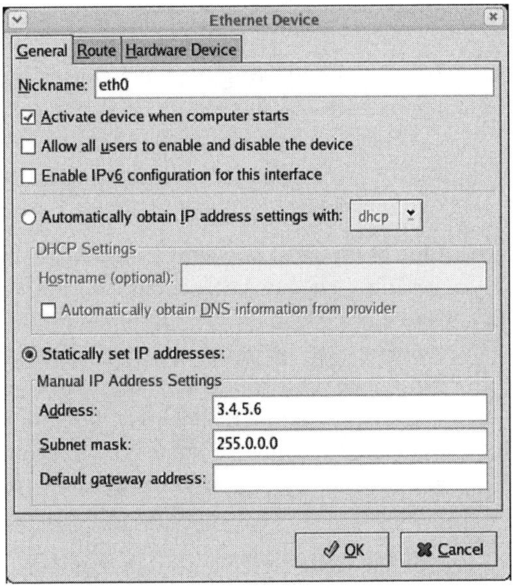

FIGURE 14-3 *Configuring TCP/IP information for a network interface*

After you have edited your IP configuration, be certain to click Save from the File menu to save your changes to the appropriate file in the /etc/sysconfig/network-scripts directory. Next, to activate your changes without rebooting, you need to click the Activate button.

Configuring a PPP Interface

Instead of configuring TCP/IP to run on a NIC to gain network access, you can instead run TCP/IP over serial lines using a WAN protocol, such as SLIP or PPP. PPP is a newer technology than SLIP and incorporates all of SLIP's features; thus, PPP is the standard protocol used today to connect to remote networks over serial lines.

Three common technologies use PPP today to connect computers to a network such as the Internet:

◆ Modems
◆ ISDN
◆ DSL

Modem (modulator-demodulator) devices use PPP to send TCP/IP information across normal telephone lines; they were the most common method for home users to gain Internet access in the last decade. Modem connections are considered slow today compared to most other technologies; most modems can only transmit data at 56KB/s. Modems are typically detected and configured during installation or by the kudzu program afterward. Because modems transmit information on a serial port, the system typically makes a symbolic link called /dev/modem that points to the correct serial port device, such as /dev/ttyS0 for COM1.

Integrated Services Digital Network (ISDN) was originally intended to replace normal telephone lines and allows data to be transferred at 128KB/s. ISDN uses an ISDN modem device to connect to a different type of media than regular phone lines. Although ISDN is popular in Europe, it does not have a large presence in North America. Like modems, ISDN modems are typically detected and configured by kudzu or during installation.

One of the most popular connection technologies in North America is DSL. DSL has many variants such as Asynchronous DSL (ADSL), which is the most common DSL used in homes across North America, and High-bit-rate DSL (HDSL), which is common in business environments; for simplification, all variants of DSL are referred to as xDSL. You use an Ethernet NIC to connect to a DSL modem using TCP/IP and PPP; the DSL modem then transmits information across normal telephone lines at speeds that can exceed 8MB/s. Because DSL modems are connected to a NIC via some type of media, they are not normally configured automatically during installation or by the kudzu program; instead, they are usually configured manually.

Configuring a PPP connection requires support for PPP compiled into the kernel or available as a module, the PPP daemon (pppd), and a series of supporting utilities such as the chat program, which is used to communicate with a modem. PPP configuration in the past was tedious at best; you needed to create a chat script that contained the necessary information to establish a PPP connection (user name, password, and so on), a connection script that contained device parameters used by the PPP daemon, as well as use a program such as minicom to initiate network communication. Because the TCP/IP configuration is typically assigned by the Internet service provider to which you connect, it rarely needs to be configured during the process.

Today, a wide variety of graphical programs can configure the necessary files and start the necessary utilities to allow PPP network communication. In Red Hat Fedora Linux, you simply navigate to the Red Hat button, System Settings, Network, as shown earlier in Figure 14-2, and click the New button and specify which type of device to add, as shown in Figure 14-4.

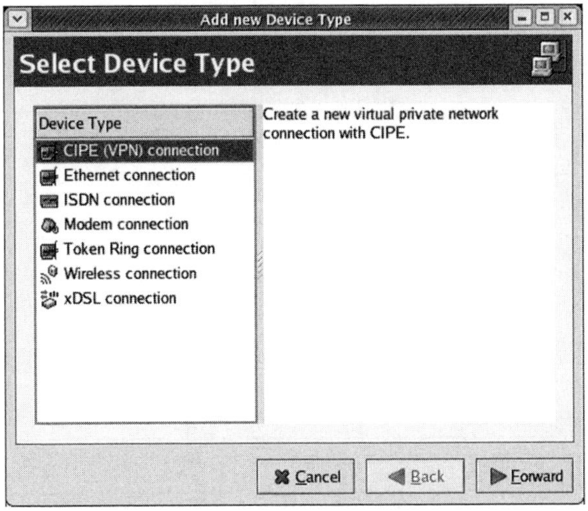

FIGURE 14-4 *Adding a network interface*

If you choose to configure a Modem connection or ISDN connection from Figure 14-4, you are first prompted for the device information shown in Figure 14-5 and Figure 14-6, respectively.

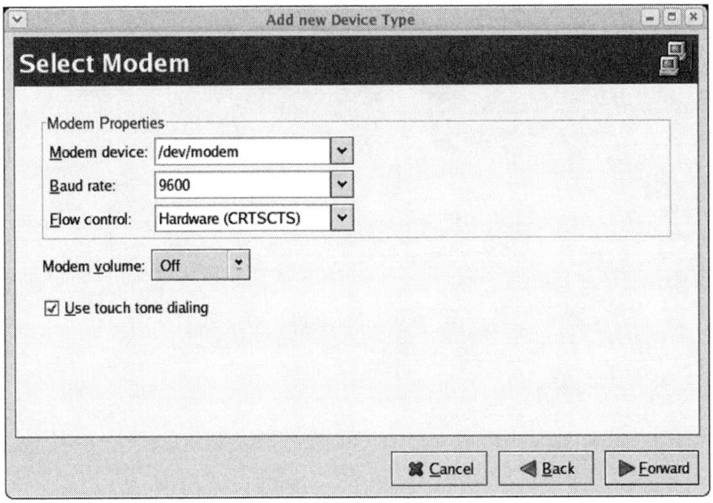

FIGURE 14-5 *Selecting modem hardware*

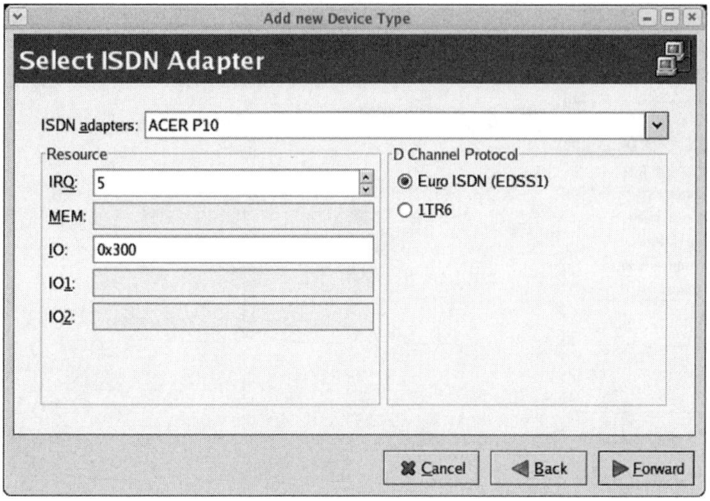

FIGURE 14-6 *Selecting ISDN hardware*

Regardless of whether you configure the hardware for a modem or ISDN connection, you are then prompted for the ISP and TCP/IP information, as shown in Figure 14-7 and Figure 14-8.

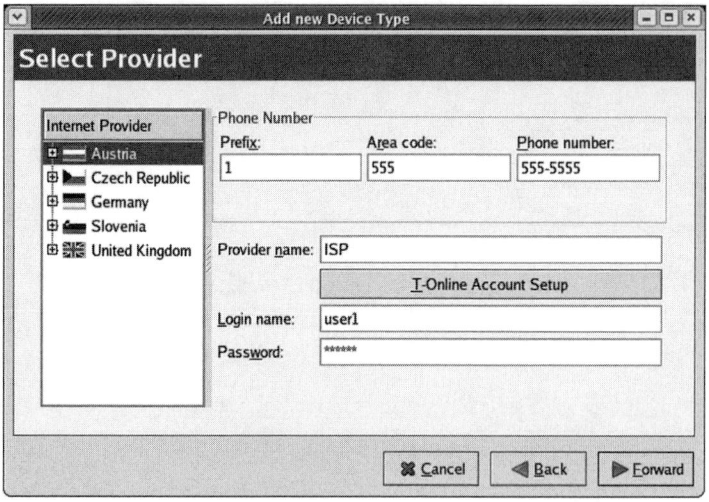

FIGURE 14-7 *Specifying ISP settings*

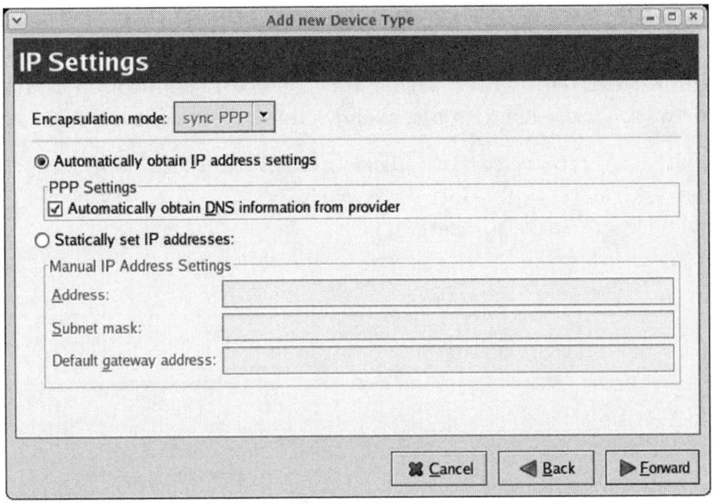

FIGURE 14-8 *Specifying TCP/IP settings*

Alternatively, if you chose to set up an xDSL connection from Figure 14-4, you are prompted to choose the Ethernet interface that is connected to the DSL modem as well as the ISP information, as depicted in Figure 14-9.

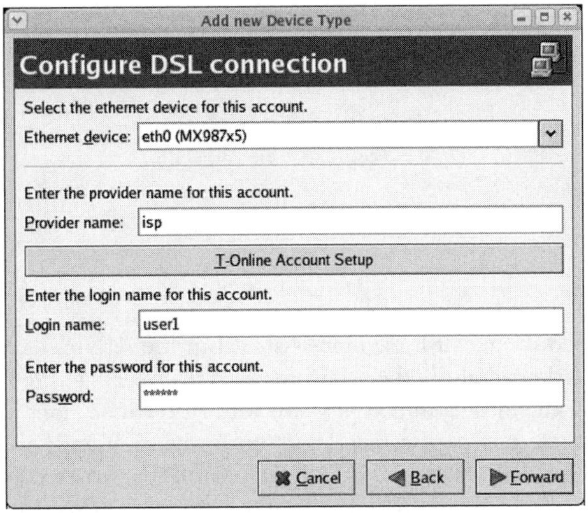

FIGURE 14-9 *Configuring an xDSL connection*

Like configuring a NIC, information about each PPP device in stored in files named ifcfg-*InternetServiceProviderName* underneath the /etc/sysconfig/network-scripts directory. For example, the information configured earlier for the xDSL connection is stored in the /etc/sysconfig/network-scripts/ifcfg-isp file, as shown in the following output:

```
[root@server1 root]# cat /etc/sysconfig/network-scripts/ifcfg-isp
# Please read /usr/share/doc/initscripts-*/sysconfig.txt
# for the documentation of these parameters.
IPV6INIT=no
ONBOOT=no
USERCTL=yes
PEERDNS=yes
TYPE=xDSL
DEVICE=ppp0
BOOTPROTO=dialup
PIDFILE=/var/run/pppoe-adsl.pid
FIREWALL=NONE
PING=.
PPPOE_TIMEOUT=80
LCP_FAILURE=3
LCP_INTERVAL=20
CLAMPMSS=1412
CONNECT_POLL=6
CONNECT_TIMEOUT=60
PERSIST=no
SYNCHRONOUS=no
DEFROUTE=yes
USER=user1
ETH=eth0
PROVIDER=isp
DEMAND=no
[root@server1 root]# _
```

Other configurations are used by the PPP daemon is stored in the /etc/ppp and /etc/isdn directories. It is good form to double-check the passwords used to connect to the ISP because incorrect passwords represent the most common problem with PPP connections. These passwords are stored in two files: /etc/ppp/pap-secrets (Password Authentication Protocol secrets) and /etc/ppp/chap-secrets (Challenge Handshake Authentication Protocol secrets). If the ISP accepts passwords sent across the network in text form, the /etc/ppp/pap-secrets file is consulted for the correct password; however, if the ISP requires a more secure method for validating the identity of a user, the passwords in the /etc/ppp/chap-secrets file are used. When you configure a PPP connection, this information is automatically added to both files, as shown in the following output:

```
[root@server1 root]# cat /etc/ppp/pap-secrets
# Secrets for authentication using PAP
# client          server  secret                  IP addresses
###### redhat-config-network will overwrite this part!!! (begin) ####
"user1"         "isp"   "secret"
###### redhat-config-network will overwrite this part!!! (end) ######
[root@server1 root]# cat /etc/ppp/chap-secrets
# Secrets for authentication using CHAP
# client          server  secret                  IP addresses
###### redhat-config-network will overwrite this part!!! (begin) ####
"user1"         "isp"   "secret"
###### redhat-config-network will overwrite this part!!! (end) ######
[root@server1 root]# _
```

After a PPP device has been configured, that device must be activated by connecting (or by dialing) the ISP. You can do this by using the command ifup InternetServiceProviderName at a command prompt, or by navigating to the Red Hat button, System Settings, Network and clicking the Activate button for the appropriate line for your PPP connection, as shown in Figure 14-10.

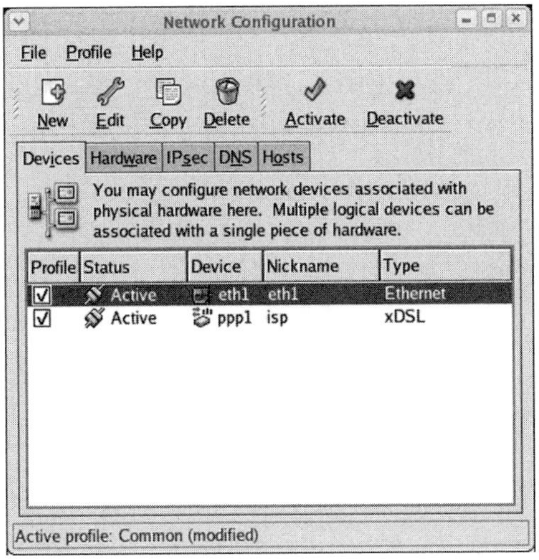

FIGURE 14-10 *Activating a PPP connection*

After being activated, the ifconfig command indicates the interface using the appropriate names such as ppp0 (for the first modem or xDSL device) or ippp0 (for the first ISDN device) as well as the IP configuration obtained from the ISP. The following output depicts the output of the `ifconfig` command when the xDSL interface is activated:

```
[root@server1 root]# ifconfig
eth0      Link encap:Ethernet  HWaddr 00:80:C6:F9:1B:8C
          inet addr:3.4.5.6  Bcast:3.255.255.255  Mask:255.0.0.0
          inet6 addr: fe80::280:c6ff:fef9:1b8c/64 Scope:Link
          UP BROADCAST RUNNING MULTICAST  MTU:1500  Metric:1
          RX packets:47 errors:0 dropped:0 overruns:0 frame:0
          TX packets:13 errors:5 dropped:0 overruns:0 carrier:5
          collisions:0 txqueuelen:1000
          RX bytes:5560 (5.4 Kb)  TX bytes:770 (770.0 b)
          Interrupt:10 Base address:0x8000

lo        Link encap:Local Loopback
          inet addr:127.0.0.1  Mask:255.0.0.0
          inet6 addr: ::1/128 Scope:Host
          UP LOOPBACK RUNNING  MTU:16436  Metric:1
          RX packets:3457 errors:0 dropped:0 overruns:0 frame:0
          TX packets:3457 errors:0 dropped:0 overruns:0 carrier:0
          collisions:0 txqueuelen:0
          RX bytes:3528110 (3.3 Mb)  TX bytes:3528110 (3.3 Mb)

ppp0      Link encap:Point-to-Point Protocol
          inet addr:65.95.13.217  P-t-P:65.95.13.1 Mask:255.255.255.255
          UP POINTOPOINT RUNNING NOARP MULTICAST  MTU:1492  Metric:1
          RX packets:15 errors:0 dropped:0 overruns:0 frame:0
          TX packets:31 errors:0 dropped:0 overruns:0 carrier:0
          collisions:0 txqueuelen:3
          RX bytes:1448 (1.4 Kb)  TX bytes:3088 (3.0 Kb)
[root@server1 root]# _
```

Name Resolution

Computers that communicate on a TCP/IP network identify themselves using unique IP addresses; however, this identification scheme is impractical for human use because it is difficult to remember IP addresses. As a result, computers are identified by a name; because each computer on a network is commonly called a host, computer names are called **host names**.

For computers that participate on the Internet, simple host names are rarely used; instead, they are given a host name called a **fully qualified domain name (FQDN)** according to a hierarchical naming scheme called **Domain Name Space (DNS)**. The Domain Name Space consists of an imaginary root with several top-level domain names that identify the type of organization that runs the network your computer is on. Several second-level domains exist underneath each top-level domain name to identify the name of the organization, and simple host names are listed underneath the second-level domains, as depicted in Figure 14-11.

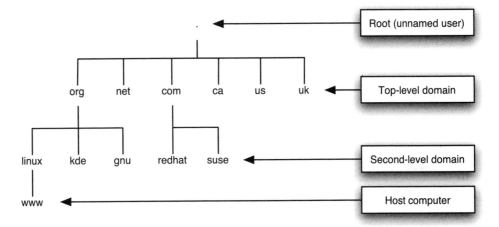

FIGURE 14-11 *The Domain Name Space*

Thus, the host computer shown in Figure 14-11 has an FQDN of *www.linux.org.*

You can view or set the host name for a Linux computer using the **hostname command**, as shown in the following output:

```
[root@server1 root]# hostname
server1
[root@server1 root]# hostname computer1.sampledomain.com
[root@server1 root]# hostname
computer1.sampledomain.com
[root@server1 root]# _
```

To configure the host name shown in the preceding output at every boot time, simply modify the HOSTNAME line in the /etc/sysconfig/network file, as shown in the following example:

```
[root@server1 root]# cat /etc/sysconfig/network
NETWORKING=yes
HOSTNAME=server1
[root@server1 root]# _
```

NOTE

Planning an appropriate host name prior to installation is good practice because many applications record this host name in their configuration files during installation. You might need to change these files if you change the host name after installation.

Although host names are easier to use when specifying computers on the network, TCP/IP cannot use them to identify computers. Thus, you must map host names to their associated IP addresses such that applications that contact other computers across the network can find the appropriate IP address for a host name.

The simplest method for mapping host names to IP addresses is by placing entries into the /etc/hosts file, as shown in the following example:

```
[root@server1 root]# cat /etc/hosts
# Do not remove the following line, or various programs
# that require network functionality will fail.
127.0.0.1     server1 localhost.localdomain  localhost
3.0.0.2       ftp.sampledomain.com  fileserver
192.168.0.1   alpha
[root@server1 root]# _
```

The entries in the preceding output identify the local computer, 127.0.0.1, by the host names server1, localhost.localdomain, and localhost. Similarly, you can use the host name ftp.sampledomain.com or fileserver to refer to the computer with the IP address of 3.0.0.2. Also, the computer with the IP address of 192.168.0.1 is mapped to the host name alpha.

> **NOTE**
>
> You can use the Network Information Service (NIS) to share the /etc/hosts configuration file among several Linux computers on the network. NIS is discussed in Chapter 15, "Configuring Network Services and Security."

Because it would be cumbersome to list names for all hosts on the Internet in the /etc/hosts file, ISPs can list FQDNs in DNS servers on the Internet. Applications can then ask DNS servers for the IP address associated with a certain FQDN. To configure your system to resolve names to IP addresses by contacting a DNS server, simply specify the IP address of the DNS server in the /etc/resolv.conf file. This file can contain up to three DNS servers; if the first DNS server is unavailable, the system attempts to contact the second DNS server followed by the third DNS server listed in the file. An example /etc/resolv.conf file is shown in the following output:

```
[root@server1 root]# cat /etc/resolv.conf
nameserver 209.121.197.2
nameserver 192.139.188.144
nameserver 6.0.4.211
[root@server1 root]# _
```

NOTE

To test the DNS configuration by resolving a name to an IP address, you can type
`nslookup name`, `dig name`, or `host name` at a command prompt, where *name* is the
host name or FQDN of a remote host.

When you specify a host name while using a certain application, that application must then resolve that host name to the appropriate IP address by searching either the local /etc/hosts file, a DNS server, or an NIS server. The method that applications use to resolve host names is determined by the "hosts" line in the /etc/nsswitch.conf file; an example of this file is shown in the following output:

```
[root@server1 root]# grep hosts /etc/nsswitch.conf
hosts:      files dns nis
[root@server1 root]# _
```

The preceding output indicates that applications first try to resolve host names using the /etc/hosts file (files). If unsuccessful, applications contact the DNS servers listed in /etc/resolv.conf (dns) followed by a NIS server (nis) if one is configured.

On older Linux computers, the /etc/host.conf file was used instead of /etc/nsswitch.conf; the /etc/host.conf file still exists today to support older application programs and should contain the same name resolution order as /etc/nsswitch.conf. An example /etc/host.conf file that tells applications to search the /etc/hosts file followed by DNS servers (bind) and NIS servers is shown in the following output:

```
[root@server1 root]# cat /etc/host.conf
order hosts,bind,nis
[root@server1 root]# _
```

Connecting to Network Resources

After an interface to the network has been configured, a Linux computer can use resources on the network, such as shared printers, applications, and files. To use a network resource, you must first have the appropriate network utility that can connect to that resource. Some network utilities are easy to use, such as a Web browser to access Web pages from a Web server on the network, whereas other network utilities such as FTP require that you learn specific commands before use.

This section examines the most common network utilities used to perform various network tasks on the system.

Downloading Files Using FTP

The most common method for transferring files across the Internet is by using the File Transfer Protocol, as discussed in Chapter 1, "Introduction to Linux." Most Web browsers have a built-in FTP utility that allows you to enter a FQDN in the form of *ftp://ftp.sampledomain.com* and view publicly available files and directories on a remote computer using the Web browser screen, as depicted in Figure 14-12.

> ### NOTE
>
> You can also use *ftp://IP_address* to connect to a public FTP server without using name resolution.

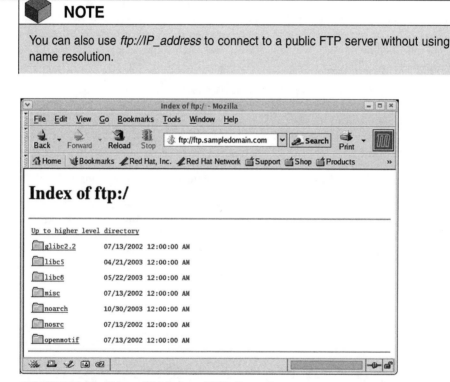

FIGURE 14-12 *Using a Web browser FTP client*

Using the mouse to click a file displayed in Figure 14-12 results in a dialog box that allows you to save the file to the appropriate location on a local filesystem.

Alternatively, you can specify the host name or IP address of a computer running the FTP service as an argument to the **ftp utility** to open a connection that allows the transfer of files to and from that computer. Following this, you can then log in as a valid user on that computer and be placed in your home directory on that computer, or log in as the user "anonymous" and be placed in a publicly available FTP directory (usually /var/ftp). After you are logged in, you receive an `ftp>` prompt that accepts FTP commands; a list of common FTP commands is depicted in Table 14-2.

> **NOTE**
>
> Most FTP servers require that the user enter a password when logging in as the anonymous user; this password is typically your e-mail address.

Table 14-2 Common FTP commands

Command	Description
help	Displays a list of commands
pwd	Displays the current directory on the remote computer
dir, ls	Displays a directory listing from the remote computer
cd *directory*	Changes the current directory to *directory* on the remote computer
lcd *directory*	Changes the current directory to *directory* on the local computer
get *filename*	Downloads the *filename* to the current directory on the local computer
ascii	Specifies text file downloads (default)
binary	Specifies binary file downloads
mget *filename*	Downloads the *filename* to the current directory on the local computer; it also allows the use of wildcard metacharacters to specify the *filename*
put *filename*	Uploads the *filename* from the current directory on the local computer to the current directory on the remote computer
mput *filename*	Uploads the *filename* from the current directory on the local computer to the current directory on the remote computer; it also allows the use of wildcard metacharacters to specify the *filename*
!	Runs a shell on the local computer
close	Closes the FTP connection to the remote computer
open *hostname* or *IP*	Opens an FTP connection to the *hostname* or *IP* address specified
bye, quit	Quits the FTP utility

The exact output that is displayed during an FTP session varies slightly depending on the version of the FTP software used on the FTP server. The following output is an example of using the ftp utility to connect to an FTP server named ftp.sampledomain.com as the root user:

```
[root@server1 root]# ftp ftp.sampledomain.com
Connected to ftp.sampledomain.com.
220 www.sampledomain.com FTP server (Version wu-2.6.1-18) ready.
530 Please login with USER and PASS.
530 Please login with USER and PASS.
KERBEROS_V4 rejected as an authentication type
Name (ftp.sampledomain.com:root): root
331 Password required for root.
Password:
230 User root logged in.
Remote system type is UNIX.
Using binary mode to transfer files.
ftp>
```

The current directory on the remote computer is the home directory for the root user in the preceding output. To verify this and see a list of files to download, you can use the following commands at the ftp> prompt:

```
ftp> pwd
257 "/root" is current directory.
ftp> ls
227 Entering Passive Mode (192,168,0,1,56,88)
150 Opening ASCII mode data connection for directory listing.
total 2064
-rw-r--r--   1 root     root         1756 Aug 14 08:48 file1
-rw-r--r--   1 root     root          160 Aug 14 08:48 file2
-rw-r--r--   1 root     root      1039996 Aug 14 08:39 file3
drwxr-xr-x   2 root     root         4096 Aug 14 08:50 stuff
226 Transfer complete.
ftp>
```

The preceding output shows three files and one subdirectory. To download file3 to the current directory on the local computer, you can use the following command:

```
ftp> get file3
local: file3 remote: file3
227 Entering Passive Mode (192,168,0,1,137,37)
150 Opening BINARY mode data connection for file3 (1039996 bytes).
226 Transfer complete.
ftp>
```

> **NOTE**
>
> If your Internet connection is slow, you can instead use the `get file3.gz` command. The FTP service automatically compresses file3 with the gzip utility before transmission.

Similarly, to change the current directory on the remote computer to /root/stuff and upload a copy of file4 from the current directory on the local computer to it, as well as view the results and then exit the `ftp` utility, you can use the following commands at the `ftp>` prompt:

```
ftp> cd stuff
250 CWD command successful.
ftp> pwd
257 "/root/stuff" is current directory.
ftp> mput file4
mput file4? y
227 Entering Passive Mode (192,168,0,1,70,109)
150 Opening BINARY mode data connection for file4.
226 Transfer complete.
929 bytes sent in 0.00019 seconds (4.8e+03 Kbytes/s)
ftp> ls
227 Entering Passive Mode (192,168,0,1,235,35)
150 Opening ASCII mode data connection for directory listing.
total 8
-rw-r--r--   1 root     root          929 Aug 14 09:26 file4
226 Transfer complete.
ftp> bye
[root@server1 root]# _
```

Accessing Files with NFS

Although not as common as FTP, the Network File System (NFS) is another common method for transferring files among UNIX and Linux computers. To access files using NFS, you simply mount a directory from a remote computer on the network that has the NFS daemons started to a local directory. Simply specify the nfs filesystem type, server name or IP address, remote directory, and local directory as arguments to the `mount` command. For example, to mount the /var directory on the remote computer named nfs.sampledomain.com (IP address 192.168.0.1) to the /mnt directory on the local computer using NFS and view the results, you can use the following commands:

```
[root@server1 root]# mount -t nfs nfs.sampledomain.com:/var /mnt
[root@server1 root]# mount
/dev/hda1 on / type ext3 (rw)
none on /proc type proc (rw)
```

```
none on /sys type sysfs (rw)
usbdevfs on /proc/bus/usb type usbdevfs (rw)
none on /dev/pts type devpts (rw,gid=5,mode=620)
none on /dev/shm type tmpfs (rw)
sunrpc on /var/lib/nfs/rpc_pipefs (rw)
nfsd on /proc/fs/nfsd type nfsd (rw)
192.168.0.1:/var on /mnt type nfs (rw,addr=192.168.0.1)
[root@server1 root]# ls /mnt
arpwatch  ftp     kerberos  lock  mailman  nis       run    tux
cache     gdm     lib       log   mars_nwe opt       spool  www
db        iptraf  local     mail  named    preserve  tmp    yp [root@server1 root]# _
```

Now, you can use the /mnt directory as any other local directory; all file operations are performed in the /var directory on the remote computer. The NFS filesystem can then be dismounted normally using the umount command.

Accessing Windows Files

NFS is a common method for transferring information to and from Linux and UNIX computers; however, it is difficult to find NFS software for the Microsoft Windows operating system. To transfer information to and from a shared Windows directory, you can mount that directory to a local Linux directory much like NFS; however, the filesystem type must be smbfs.

> **NOTE**
>
> SMB stands for Server Message Block. It defines the format that Microsoft computers use for information transfer across networks.

For example, to mount the shared directory called accounting on the Windows computer named windowsxp to the /mnt directory and view the results, you can use the following commands:

```
[root@server1 root]# mount -t smbfs //windowsxp/accounting /mnt
[root@server1 root]# mount
/dev/hda1 on / type ext3 (rw)
none on /proc type proc (rw)
none on /sys type sysfs (rw)
usbdevfs on /proc/bus/usb type usbdevfs (rw)
none on /dev/pts type devpts (rw,gid=5,mode=620)
none on /dev/shm type tmpfs (rw)
sunrpc on /var/lib/nfs/rpc_pipefs (rw)
//windowsxp/accounting on /mnt type smbfs (0)
```

```
[root@server1 root]# ls /mnt
Final Exam.doc            Part 0.DOC  Part 2.doc Part 4.doc  Part 6.doc
homework questions.doc    Part 1.DOC  Part 3.DOC Part 5.DOC  TOC.doc [root@server1 root]# _
```

> **NOTE**
>
> The **smbmount command** can also be used to mount a Windows shared directory.
> The command smbmount //windowsxp/accounting /mnt is equivalent to the com-
> mand used to mount the accounting directory in the preceding output.

Like NFS, the umount command can be used to dismount the Windows shared directory from the local /mnt directory.

Another useful utility when sharing files between Linux and Windows computers is the **smb-client utility**. To see information about the windowsxp computer used earlier, you can use the following command:

```
[root@server1 root]# smbclient -L windowsxp
added interface ip=192.168.0.1 bcast=192.168.255.255 nmask=255.255.0.0
Got a positive name query response from 192.168.0.1 ( 192.168.0.1 65.95.13.77 )
Password:
Domain=[HOME] OS=[Windows 5.1] Server=[Windows 2000 LAN Manager]

        Sharename     Type      Comment
        ---------     ----      -------
        IPC$          IPC       Remote IPC
        print$        Disk      Printer Drivers
        movies        Disk
        My Jams       Disk
        HPLaserJ      Printer   HP LaserJet 6P/6MP PostScript
        accounting    Disk
        ADMIN$        Disk      Remote Admin
        C$            Disk      Default share


        Server                Comment
        ---------             -------
        WINDOWSXP


        Workgroup             Master
        ---------             -------
        HOME                  WINDOWSXP
[root@server1 root]# _
```

The smbclient utility also offers an FTP-like interface for transferring files to and from shared directories on Windows computers, as shown in the following output when connecting to the accounting shared directory seen earlier:

```
[root@server1 root]# smbclient //windowsxp/accounting
Password:
Domain=[HOME] OS=[Windows 5.1] Server=[Windows 2000 LAN Manager]
smb: \> dir
  .                          D        0  Wed Aug 14 22:28:12 2005
  ..                         D        0  Wed Aug 14 22:28:12 2005
  Final Exam.doc             A    26624  Tue Aug  6 23:17:30 2005
  homework questions.doc     A    46080  Tue Aug  6 23:33:03 2005
  Part 0.DOC                 A    13312  Tue Aug  6 23:27:51 2005
  Part 1.DOC                 A    35328  Tue Aug  6 23:24:44 2005
  Part 2.doc                 A    70656  Tue Aug  6 23:25:28 2005
  Part 3.DOC                 A    38912  Tue Aug  6 23:26:07 2005
  Part 4.doc                 A    75776  Tue Aug  6 23:26:57 2005
  Part 5.DOC                 A    26624  Tue Aug  6 23:27:23 2005
  Part 6.doc                 A    59904  Tue Aug  6 23:05:32 2005
  TOC.doc                    A    58880  Tue Aug  6 23:09:16 2005
              39032 blocks of size 262144. 14180 blocks available

smb: \> help
?            altname     archive      blocksize    cancel
cd           chmod       chown        del          dir
du           exit        get          hardlink     help
history      lcd         link         lowercase    ls
mask         md          mget         mkdir        more
mput         newer       open         print        printmode
prompt       put         pwd          q            queue
quit         rd          recurse      reget        rename
reput        rm          rmdir        setmode      symlink
tar          tarmode     translate    vuid         logon
!
smb: \> get TOC.doc
smb: \> exit
[root@server1 root]# _
```

Running Remote Applications

On large Linux systems, users typically gain access to a BASH shell by using a utility that connects to the server across the network. The traditional utility used to obtain a BASH shell from a remote Linux computer on the network is **telnet**; nearly all operating systems today, such as Windows, Macintosh, and UNIX, come with a telnet utility. Simply specify the host name or IP address of the target computer to the `telnet` command and log in as the appropriate user and password. A shell obtained during a telnet session runs on a pseudoterminal rather than a local terminal and works much the same way a normal shell does; you can execute commands and use the `exit` command to kill the BASH shell and end the session. A sample telnet session is shown in the following output using a computer with a host name of appserver:

```
[root@server1 root]# telnet appserver
Trying 192.168.0.1...
Connected to appserver (192.168.0.1).
Escape character is '^]'.
Fedora Core release 2 (Tettnang)
Kernel 2.6.5-1.358 on an i686
login: root
Password:
Last login: Tue Aug 10 14:14:27 from server1
You have new mail.
[root@server1 root]# who
root     :0           Aug 10 14:13
root     pts/8        Aug 10 14:14 (:0.0)
root     pts/10       Aug 10 14:17 (server1)
[root@server1 root]# exit
Connection closed by foreign host.
[root@server1 root]# _
```

Although telnet is a common utility, it does not encrypt the communication that passes from your computer to the telnet server. As a result, organizations typically use the **Secure Shell (ssh)** utility instead of telnet. A sample `ssh` session is shown in the following output:

```
[root@server1 root]# ssh appserver
root@appserver's password:
Last login: Tue Aug 10 14:13:22 2005
[root@server1 root]# who
root     :0           Aug 10 14:13
root     pts/8        Aug 10 14:14 (:0.0)
root     pts/9        Aug 10 14:14 (server1)
[root@server1 root]# exit
Connection to appserver closed.
[root@server1 root]# _
```

Notice from the preceding output that you were prompted for the root user's password on the appserver computer because you were logged in locally as the root user on your own computer. If you need to log in using a different user name on the remote appserver computer, you can instead use the `ssh -l username appserver` command.

> ### 🗔 NOTE
>
> Both `telnet` and `ssh` are commonly used by network administrators to remotely administer and monitor servers within a company.
>
> Most hardware-based network devices, such as Cisco routers, can be connected to and administered or monitored using the `telnet` and `ssh` utilities. For monitoring, however, many organizations use utilities that typically monitor these devices using the Simple Network Management Protocol (SNMP) or Remote Monitoring (RMON) protocol. Several different commercial and open source SNMP and RMON packages are available for Linux.

Another utility that can be used to obtain a shell from a remote computer on the network is `rlogin`. This utility is one of several "r" utilities that can allow a user access to remote systems on the network without specifying a password; the `rcp` utility can be used to copy files between computers and the `rsh` utility can be used to execute a command on a remote computer.

The "r" utilities allow access to remote computers without a password, provided the remote computer has **trusted access** set up. One method of setting up trusted access is to add the host names of computers to the /etc/hosts.equiv file on the remote computer; the following /etc/hosts.equiv file allows users who have logged in to the computers *www.sampledomain.com* and *www.sampledomain2.com* the ability to use the `rlogin`, `rcp`, and `rsh` utilities to connect to the computer as the same user without specifying a password:

```
[root@server1 root]# cat /etc/hosts.equiv
www.sampledomain.com
www.sampledomain2.com
[root@server1 root]# _
```

Thus, if the user "mary" logs in to the computer *www.sampledomain.com* and uses an "r" utility to connect to the local computer, she is automatically logged in to the system using the local "mary" account without having to specify a password. The only user that cannot be trusted using the /etc/hosts.equiv file is the root user. Trusted access is common in companies that have several Linux servers that have the same user accounts; setting up trusted access allows users who log in to one Linux computer the ability to access other computers without having to reenter their password.

Another method for setting trusted access is to create an .rhosts file in the home directory of each user who wants to connect using trusted access. Consider the following /home/mary/.rhosts file:

```
[root@server1 root]# cat /home/mary/.rhosts
www.sampledomain.com
www.sampledomain2.com
[root@server1 root]# _
```

This allows the user "mary" on the computers *www.sampledomain.com* and *www.sampledo-main2.com* the ability to use the "r" utilities to connect to the local Linux computer as the user "mary" without specifying a password. In addition, the /root/.rhosts file can be used to allow the "root" user on other trusted computers the ability to use "r" utilities to connect to the local computer without specifying a password.

> **NOTE**
>
> Newer versions of the "r" utilities attempt to validate trusted users using the Kerberos protocol, which prevents other network users from viewing the traffic generated by the "r" utility. To use Kerberos with "r" utilities, you must have a .k5login file in your home directory or an /etc/krb.equiv file that lists the users and Kerberos realms that are allowed. If these files do not exist, the /etc/hosts.equiv and ~/.rhosts files are examined, as discussed earlier.

Suppose that a remote computer called remoteserver has trusted access set up; you can use the following command to obtain a shell:

```
[root@server1 root]# rlogin remoteserver
Last login: Thu Aug 15 13:16:51 from 100.6.6.0
You have new mail.
[root@server1 root]# _
```

Similarly, you can copy the /etc/hosts file from the computer remoteserver to the /root directory of the local computer by using the following command:

```
[root@server1 root]# rcp remoteserver:/etc/hosts localhost:/root
[root@server1 root]# ls -F /root
Desktop/  hosts
[root@server1 root]# _
```

In addition, to run the who command on the computer remoteserver and display the results to the local terminal, you can use the following command:

```
[root@server1 root]# rsh remoteserver who
root      tty2     Aug 15 12:26
root      pts/0    Aug 15 13:16 (100.6.6.0)
[root@server1 root]# _
```

Accessing E-mail

Recall from Chapter 1 that you can use a variety of mail user agent (MUA) programs to obtain e-mail from an e-mail server. E-mail is typically downloaded from an e-mail server via a protocol called Post Office Protocol (POP) or Internet Message Access Protocol (IMAP). POP usually downloads e-mail messages from the e-mail server to the client computer, whereas

IMAP typically stores e-mail messages on the e-mail server and views them across the network. Regardless of the method used to send e-mail from the e-mail server to the mail user agent, mail is sent from the mail user agent to the e-mail server via Simple Mail Transfer Protocol (SMTP). The address of the necessary POP, IMAP, and SMTP servers should be configured to the appropriate values in the mail user agent program.

The most common mail user agent used in Red Hat Fedora Linux is Mozilla, which can also function as a Web browser, FTP client, and newsgroup reader. Simply navigate to the Red Hat button, Internet, Mozilla Mail. When you open this utility for the first time, you can create a mail account, as shown in Figure 14-13, that contains the POP/IMAP server name or IP address, the SMTP server name or IP address, and the account information. After the server and account information have been configured, Mozilla allows you to send and view e-mails, as shown in Figure 14-14.

Mozilla is well suited for public e-mail accounts because it has a great deal of user-oriented features. However, Linux systems typically use an internal mail system that is designed for administration; most daemons e-mail the root user when important events or problems occur. For these e-mails, it is more efficient to use a command-line mail user agent that can be viewed remotely using telnet or ssh. The basic e-mail reader that is available on most Linux distributions is mail. If you invoke the **mail utility**, you will see the contents of your mail queue (/var/spool/mail/username), as shown in the following output:

```
[root@server1 root]# mail
Mail version 8.1 6/6/93. Type ? for help.
"/var/spool/mail/root": 27 messages 27 unread
>U  1 root@localhost.local  Sat Jul 24 00:24  22/850    "Anacron job 'cron.dai"
 U  2 root@localhost.local  Sat Jul 24 04:02  108/3362  "LogWatch for server1"
 U  3 root@localhost.local  Sat Jul 24 04:08  26/977    "Cron <root@server1> r"
 U  4 root@localhost.local  Wed Jul 28 20:43  22/850    "Anacron job 'cron.dai"
 U  5 root@localhost.local  Thu Jul 29 13:59  63/1795   "LogWatch for server1"
 U  6 root@localhost.local  Thu Jul 29 14:06  22/850    "Anacron job 'cron.dai"
 U  7 root@localhost.local  Fri Jul 30 19:17  113/3686  "LogWatch for server1"
 U  8 root@localhost.local  Fri Jul 30 19:25  22/850    "Anacron job 'cron.dai"
 U  9 root@localhost.local  Sat Jul 31 10:28  121/3509  "LogWatch for server1"
 U 10 root@localhost.local  Sat Jul 31 10:35  22/850    "Anacron job 'cron.dai"
 U 11 root@localhost.local  Sun Aug  1 08:17  138/4319  "LogWatch for server1"
 U 12 root@localhost.local  Sun Aug  1 08:25  22/847    "Anacron job 'cron.dai"
 U 13 root@localhost.local  Mon Aug  2 04:02  105/2949  "LogWatch for server1"
 U 14 root@localhost.local  Mon Aug  2 04:08  26/974    "Cron <root@server1> r"
 U 15 root@localhost.local  Mon Aug  2 11:07  499/36033 "server1 08/02/04:11.0"
 U 16 root@localhost.local  Tue Aug  3 12:40  111/3310  "LogWatch for server1"
 U 17 root@localhost.local  Tue Aug  3 12:48  22/847    "Anacron job 'cron.dai"
 U 18 root@localhost.local  Mon Aug  9 13:17  21/793    "Low disk space warnin"
 U 19 root@localhost.local  Mon Aug  9 14:01  21/793    "Low disk space warnin"
 U 20 root@localhost.local  Mon Aug  9 14:33  22/847    "Anacron job 'cron.dai"
&
```

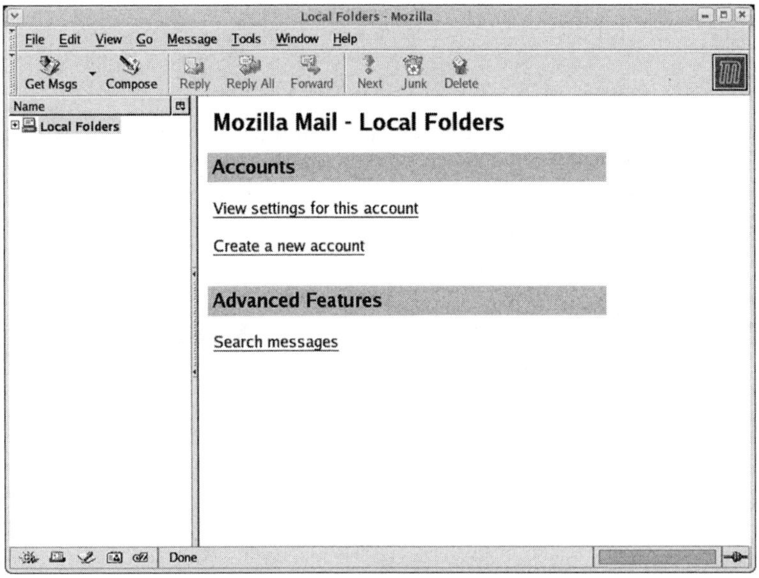

FIGURE 14-13 *Configuring a mail account in Mozilla Mail*

FIGURE 14-14 *Using Mozilla Mail*

Following this, you can read messages by typing the appropriate number at the & prompt. Similarly, you can delete a message by using the d command followed by the message number or quit the mail utility by typing the q command at the & prompt.

Another popular mail user agent that can be run in a terminal is mutt, which displays a list of common functions along the top of the screen and allows you to use the cursor keys on your keyboard to display e-mail messages. An example of the **mutt utility** is shown in Figure 14-15.

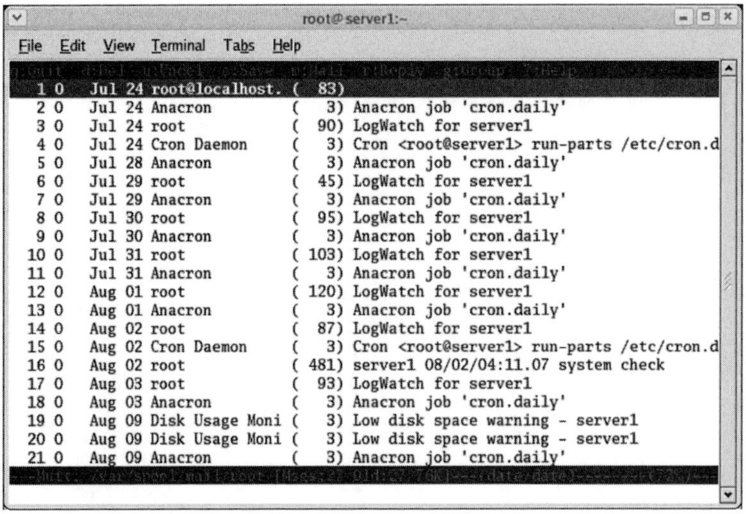

FIGURE 14-15 *The mutt mail user agent*

Chapter Summary

- ◆ A network is a collection of computers that are connected together and share information.

- ◆ Protocols define the format of information that is transmitted across a network. The protocol used by the Internet and most networks is TCP/IP.

- ◆ Each computer on a TCP/IP network must have a valid IP address and subnet mask.

- ◆ The /etc/sysconfig/network-scripts directory contains the configuration for NIC and PPP interfaces.

- ◆ The TCP/IP configuration of a network interface can be specified manually or obtained automatically from a DHCP or BOOTP server.

- ◆ Host names are used to easily identify computers on a network; host names that follow the Domain Name Space are called fully qualified domain names.

◆ Host names must be resolved to an IP address before network communication can take place.

◆ Files, applications, and e-mail can be accessed across the network with the appropriate network utility.

Key Terms

ANDing — The process by which binary bits are compared to calculate the network and host IDs from an IP address and subnet mask.

broadcast — The TCP/IP communication destined for all computers on a network.

classless interdomain routing (CIDR) notation — A notation that is often used to represent an IP address and its subnet mask.

default gateway — The IP address of the router on the network used to send packets to remote networks.

Domain Name Space (DNS) — A hierarchical namespace used for host names.

Ethernet — The most common media access method used in networks today.

fully qualified domain name (FQDN) — A host name that follows DNS convention.

ftp utility — A utility that can be used to download files from an FTP server.

host ID — The portion of an IP address that denotes the host.

host name — A user-friendly name assigned to a computer.

hostname command — A command used to display and change the host name of a computer.

ifconfig command — A command used to display and modify the TCP/IP configuration information for a network interface.

Internet Protocol (IP) address — A series of four 8-bit numbers that represent a computer on a network.

Internet service provider (ISP) — A company that provides Internet access.

local area networks (LANs) — The networks in which the computers are all in close physical proximity.

mail utility — A common Linux mail user agent.

media access method — A system that defines how computers on a network share access to the physical medium.

multicast — The TCP/IP communication destined for a certain group of computers.

mutt utility — A common Linux mail user agent.

network — Two or more computers joined together via network media and able to exchange information.

network ID — The portion of an IP address that denotes the network.

octet — A portion of an IP address that represents eight binary bits.

Packet Internet Groper (ping) command — A command used to check TCP/IP connectivity on a network.

packets — The packages of data formatted by a network protocol.

protocol — A set of rules of communication used between computers on a network.

routers — The devices capable of transferring packets from one network to another.

Secure Shell (ssh) — A utility that can be used to run remote applications on a Linux computer; it encrypts all client-server traffic.

smbclient utility — A utility used to connect to shares on a Windows system.

smbmount command — A command used to mount directories from Windows computers to mount points on Linux computers.

subnet mask — A series of four 8-bit numbers that determine the network and host portions of an IP address.

subnetting — The process in which a single large network is subdivided into several smaller networks to control traffic flow.

telnet — A utility that can be used to run remote applications on a Linux computer.

Token Ring — A popular media access method.

trusted access — A configuration in which computers are allowed to access a given computer without having to provide a password first.

unicast — The TCP/IP communication destined for a single computer.

wide area networks (WANs) — The networks in which computers are separated geographically by large distances.

Review Questions

1. What is the most common LAN protocol used today?
    a. DLC
    b. AppleTalk
    c. IPX/SPX
    d. TCP/IP

2. What is the subnet mask for a Class C IP address?
    a. 0.0.0.0
    b. 255.0.0.0
    c. 255.255.0.0
    d. 255.255.255.0

3. Which of the following is a popular, high-speed connection technology used in North America?
    a. modems
    b. DSL
    c. ISDN
    d. PPP

4. Which ftp command is used to change the directory on the remote computer?
    a. lcd
    b. rcd
    c. cd
    d. remcd

5. The most common mail user agent used in Red Hat Fedora Linux is _____.
    a. Mozilla
    b. Exchange
    c. POP
    d. Simple Mail Transfer Protocol

6. True or false? ANDing is a mathematical operation that compares two binary digits and gives a result of 1 or 0.

7. True or false? The IP address 255.255.255.255 refers to all networks.

8. True or false? All routers are dedicated hardware devices.

9. True or false? All NIC cards are detected during Linux installation.

10. True or false? PPP is the standard protocol used today to connect to remote networks over serial lines.

11. Two or more computers that are connected with media that can exchange information are called a(n) _____.

12. To participate on a TCP/IP network, your computer must have a valid Internet Protocol (IP) address and _____ mask.

13. The _____ command sends a small TCP/IP packet to another IP address and awaits a response.

14. The simplest method for mapping host names to IP addresses is by placing entries into the _____ file.

15. The traditional utility used to obtain a BASH shell from a remote Linux computer on the network is _____.

Chapter 15

Configuring Network Services and Security

After completing this chapter, you will be able to:

◆ Identify and configure common network services

◆ Configure routing and firewalls

◆ Describe the different facets of Linux security

◆ Increase the security of a Linux computer

◆ Outline measures that can be used to detect a Linux security breach

In the previous chapter, you examined the configuration of a network interface and the usage of network utilities to interact with network services on the network. In this chapter, you examine the configuration of common network services, routing, and firewalls. Following this, you examine local and network security concepts, good security practices, and the utilities that you can use to secure your Linux computer and detect intruders.

Network Services

Recall from Chapter 1, "Introduction to Linux," that Linux provides a wide variety of services that are available to users across a network. Before you are able to organize the appropriate network services to meet your organization's needs, you must first identify the types and features of network services. Following this, you can configure these network services as required, as well as configure additional network-related services, such as routing and firewalls.

Identifying Network Services

Network services are processes that run on your computer and provide some type of valuable service for client computers on the network. They are often represented by a series of daemon processes that listen for certain requests on the network. Daemons identify to which packets they should respond by listening only for packets that have a certain number. This number is called a **port** and uniquely identifies a particular service. A port number is like an apartment number for the delivery of mail. The network ID of the IP address ensures that the packet is delivered to the correct street (network); the host ID ensures that the packet is delivered to the correct building (host); and the transport layer protocol and port number ensure that the packet is delivered to the proper apartment (service).

Ports and their associated protocol are defined in the /etc/services file. To see to which port the telnet daemon listens, you can use the following command:

```
[root@server1 root]# grep telnet /etc/services
telnet          23/tcp
telnet          23/udp
rtelnet         107/tcp                       # Remote Telnet
rtelnet         107/udp
telnets         992/tcp
telnets         992/udp
[root@server1 root]# _
```

The preceding output indicates that the telnet daemon listens on port 23 using both TCP/IP and UDP/IP.

Ports range in number from 0 to 65534. The ports 0–1023 are called **well-known ports** because they represent commonly used services. Table 15-1 provides a list of common well-known ports.

> ### ◆ NOTE
>
> The **User Datagram Protocol/Internet Protocol (UDP/IP)** is a faster and consequently less-reliable version of TCP/IP.

Table 15-1 Common well-known ports

Service	Port
FTP	TCP 20, 21
Telnet	TCP 23
SMTP	TCP 25
HTTP	TCP 80
DNS	TCP 53, UDP 53
Trivial FTP (TFTP)	UDP 69
POP3	TCP 110
NNTP	TCP 119
IMAP	TCP 143
Secure HTTP	TCP 443

In addition, network utilities, such as those seen in the previous chapter, can connect to daemons that provide network services directly, or they can connect to network daemons via the **Internet Super Daemon (xinetd)**, as shown in Figure 15-1.

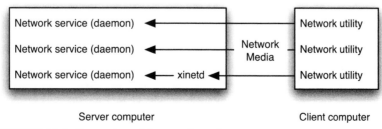

FIGURE 15-1 *Interacting with network services*

The Internet Super Daemon is typically used to start and manage connections for smaller network daemons such as the telnet, rlogin, and FTP daemons. It is started automatically at boot time and uses the configuration file /etc/xinetd.conf. Normally, this file incorporates all of the files in the /etc/xinetd.d directory as well. Most daemons that are managed by the Internet Super Daemon are configured by files in the /etc/xinetd.d directory named after the daemons. For example, the telnet daemon is configured by the Internet Super Daemon via the /etc/xinetd.d/telnet file, as shown in the following output:

```
[root@server1 root]# cat /etc/xinetd.d/telnet
# default: on
# description: The telnet server serves telnet sessions; it uses \
#       unencrypted username/password pairs for authentication.
service telnet
{
        flags           = REUSE
        socket_type     = stream
        wait            = no
        user            = root
        server          = /usr/sbin/in.telnetd
        log_on_failure  += USERID
        disable         = yes
}
[root@server1 root]# _
```

The preceding output displays the full path to the telnet daemon (/usr/sbin/in.telnetd). In addition, the disable = yes line in the /etc/xinetd.d/telnet file indicates that the telnet daemon is currently disabled.

> **NOTE**
>
> After a Red Hat Fedora Core 2 Linux installation, most files in the /etc/xinetd.d directory have the line disable = yes in them to prevent them from being used.
>
> Older Linux systems use a version of the Internet Super Daemon called inetd, which uses the configuration file /etc/inetd.conf.

Large network daemons are rarely started by the Internet Super Daemon and are hence called **stand-alone daemons**. Stand-alone daemons are typically started at boot time from files in the /etc/rc.d/rc*.d directories; the ntsysv utility discussed in Chapter 9, "System Initialization and X Windows," can be used to configure most stand-alone daemons to start in various runlevels. In addition, most stand-alone daemons can be started manually from files in the /etc/init.d or /etc/rc.d/init.d directories.

Many stand-alone and xinetd managed daemons also have configuration files that control how they operate and indicate the pathname to other important files used by the daemon. For simplicity, many of these daemons store all information in only one configuration file that contains comments which indicate the syntax and purpose of each line. As a result, these configuration files can be very large; the configuration file used by the Apache Web Server is over 1000 lines long. In addition to this, most stand-alone network daemons do not use the syslog daemon to log information related to their operation. Instead, they log this information themselves to subdirectories of the same name underneath the /var/log directory. For example, log files for the Samba daemon are located in the /var/log/samba directory.

NOTE

The location of configuration and log files for network daemons can vary between different Linux distributions; the locations discussed in this chapter are for Red Hat Fedora Core 2 only.

Configuring Common Network Services

To configure most network services on a Linux system, you must first identify the features of the network service, including it purpose, configuration files, port number(s), and whether the service is a stand-alone service or managed by the Internet Super Daemon. Table 15-2 lists the names and features of network services that are commonly found on Linux computers that participate in a network environment.

Table 15-2 Common network services

Network Service	Type	Port	Description
Apache Web Server (httpd)	Standalone	80 443	Serves Web pages using HTTP to other computers on the network that have a Web browser. Configuration file: /etc/httpd/conf/httpd.conf
BIND / DNS Server (named)	Standalone	53	Resolves fully qualified domain names to IP addresses for a certain namespace on the Internet. Configuration file: /etc/named.conf
DHCP Server (dhcpd)	Standalone	NA	Provides IP configuration for computers on a network.

Table 15-2 Common network services (Continued)

Network Service	Type	Port	Description
FTP Server (in.ftpd)	xinetd	20 21	Transfers files to and accepts files from other computers on the network with an FTP utility. Configuration file: /etc/ftpaccess Hosts denied FTP access: /etc/ftphosts Users denied FTP access: /etc/ftpusers FTP data compression: /etc/ftpconversions
IMAP Server (imapd)	xinetd or standalone	143	Allows users with an e-mail reader (mail user agent) to obtain e-mail from the server using the Intenet Message Access Protocol.
Internetwork News Server (innd)	Standalone	119	Accepts and manages newsgroup postings and transfers them to other news servers. Configuration file: /etc/news/inn.conf
NFS Server (rpc.nfsd)	Standalone	2049	Shares files to other computers on the network that have an NFS client utility. Configuration file: /etc/exports
NIS Server (ypserv & ypbind)	Standalone	111	Shares configuration information to NIS clients that are members of an NIS domain. Configuration file: /etc/ypserv.conf
POP3 Server (ipop3d)	xinetd or standalone	110	Allows users with an e-mail reader (mail user agent) to obtain e-mail from the server using the Post Office Protocol version 3.
rlogin Daemon (in.rlogind)	xinetd	513	Allows users who use the rlogin and rcp utilities the ability to copy files and obtain shells on other computers on the network using trusted access.
rsh Daemon (in.rshd)	xinetd	514	Allows users who use the rsh utility the ability to run commands on other computers on the network using trusted access.
Samba Server (smbd & nmbd)	Standalone	137 138 139	Allows Windows users to view shared files and printers on a Linux server. Configuration file: /etc/samba/smb.conf

Table 15-2 Common network services (Continued)

Network Service	Type	Port	Description
Secure Shell Daemon (sshd)	Standalone	22	Provides a secure alternative to the telnet, rlogin, and rsh utilities by using encrypted communication. Configuration File: /etc/ssh/sshd_config
Sendmail Email Server (sendmail)	Standalone	25	Accepts and sends e-mail to users or other e-mail servers on the Internet using the Simple Mail Transfer Protocol (SMTP). Configuration file: /etc/sendmail.cf
Squid Proxy Server (squid)	Standalone	3128	Allows computers on a network the ability to share one connection to the Internet. It is also known as a proxy server. Configuration file: /etc/squid/squid.conf
telnet Daemon (in.telnetd)	xinetd	23	Allows users who have a telnet utility the ability to log in to the system from across the network and obtain a shell.
Very Secure FTP Server (vsftpd)	Standalone	20 21	Transfers files to and accepts files from other computers on the network with an FTP utility. Configuration file: /etc/vsftpd/vsftpd.conf Users denied FTP access: /etc/vsftpd.ftpusers and /etc/vsftpd.user_list
X Server	Stand-alone	0	Generates graphics that will be displayed on a computer on the network that has an X client using the DISPLAY variable on the X server.

> ### ◆ NOTE
>
> By default, you are prevented from logging in and obtaining a shell as the root user to certain network services such as telnet due to entries in the /etc/securetty file. This file lists terminals that the root user is allowed to access. Removing or renaming this file allows the root user to log in and receive a shell across the network.

Some of the network services in Table 15-2 have become a vital component of many networks today; these include DNS, DHCP, Apache, Samba, NFS, FTP, NIS, and the Secure Shell Daemon.

Configuring DNS

Recall that DNS is a hierarchical namespace used to identify computers on large TCP/IP networks such as the Internet. Each part of this namespace is called a **zone** and DNS servers contain all host name information for a zone. DNS servers typically resolve FQDNs to IP addresses (called a **forward lookup**), but can also resolve IP addresses to FQDNs (called a **reverse lookup**).

When you contact a Web server on the Internet using a Web browser, the Web browser performs a forward lookup of the FQDN such that it can contact the IP address of the Web server. This forward lookup can be performed by a DNS server, or series of DNS servers. The whole process used to resolve the FQDN *www.linux.org* is illustrated in Figure 15-2.

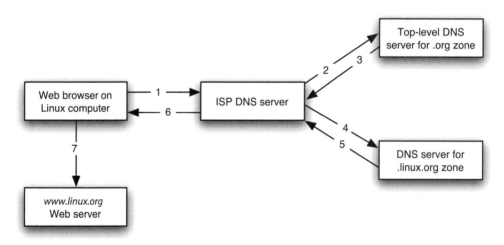

FIGURE 15-2 *The DNS lookup process*

In the first step from Figure 15-2, the Linux computer sends a forward lookup request for *www.linux.org* to the DNS server that is configured in /etc/resolv.conf; this is typically the DNS server at your ISP. If the ISP DNS server has recently resolved the FQDN and placed the result in its local DNS cache, you receive the response immediately (called an **iterative query**). If it has not, the ISP DNS server normally contacts the DNS server for the .org top-level zone (Step 2) and repeats the forward lookup request for *www.linux.org* (called a **recursive query**). The .org DNS server will not contain the IP address for the *www.linux.org* computer in its zone, but will reply with the IP address of the DNS server for the linux.org zone (Step 3).

📦 NOTE

All DNS servers contain a **DNS cache file** that contains the IP addresses of DNS servers that hold top-level DNS zones.

Your ISP DNS server then contacts the DNS server for the linux.org zone (Step 4) and repeats the forward lookup request for *www.linux.org* (another recursive query). The DNS server for the linux.org domain contains a record that lists the IP address for the *www.linux.org* computer, and returns this IP address to the ISP DNS server (Step 5). The local DNS server then returns the result to the client Web browser (Step 6), which then uses the IP address to connect to the Web server (Step 7).

> ### NOTE
>
> Each zone typically has more than one DNS server to ensure that names can be resolved if one server is unavailable. The first DNS server in a zone is called the **master** or **primary DNS server** and all additional DNS servers are called **slave** or **secondary DNS servers**. New zone information is added to the master DNS server; slave DNS servers periodically copy the new records from the master DNS server in a process known as a **zone transfer**.

To configure your Linux computer as a DNS server, you must configure the name daemon (named) for a specific zone and add resource records that list FQDNs for computers in that zone as well as their associated IP addresses. Table 15-3 lists the files that can be used to configure this zone information.

Table 15-3 Common zone configuration files

File	Description
/etc/named.conf	Contains the list of DNS zones and their type (master/slave) that the name daemon will manage.
/var/named/*zonename*.zone	Contains resource records used to perform forward lookups for a particular *zonename*. Lines in this file have a type that determines the type of resource record: ◆ A (add host) records map FQDNs to IP addresses. ◆ CNAME (canonical name) records provide additional aliases for A records. ◆ NS (name server) records provide the names of DNS servers for the zone. ◆ MX (mail exchange) records provide the IP address for the e-mail server for a zone.

Table 15-3 Common zone configuration files (Continued)

File	Description
/var/named/*.in-addr.arpa	Contains resource records of type PTR (pointer), which list names used for reverse lookups for a particular network. The network is incorporated into the filename itself; for example, the filename that contains PTR records for the 192.168.1.0 network would be called 1.168.192.in-addr.arpa.
/var/named/named.local	Contains a PTR record used to identify the loopback adapter (127.0.0.1).
/var/named/named.ca	Contains the IP addresses of top-level DNS servers; commonly called the DNS cache file.

After the files that contain the zone information have been created, you can simply start the name daemon to provide DNS services on the network using the command /etc/rc.d/init.d/named start. If you modify any files associated with the name daemon, for example, to add additional resource records, you must restart the name daemon for those changes to take effect. To do this, you can simply use the command /etc/rc.d/init.d/named restart.

Configuring DHCP

Recall from the previous chapter that your network interface can be configured manually or automatically using DHCP. If your network interface is configured using DHCP, it sends a DHCP broadcast on the network requesting IP configuration information. If there is a DHCP server on the network that has a range of IP addresses, it leases an IP address to the client computer for a certain period of time; after this lease has expired, the client computer must send another DHCP request. Because DHCP servers keep track of the IP addresses that they lease to client computers, they can ensure that no two computers receive the same IP address. If two computers are accidentally configured manually with the same IP address, neither would be able to communicate using the IP protocol.

In addition, DHCP servers can also send other IP configuration information to client computers, such as the default gateway and DNS server that should be used on the network.

To configure your Linux computer as a DHCP server, simply create a /etc/dhcpd.conf file that lists the appropriate IP address range for your network, as well as lease information and other IP configuration options. An example /etc/dhcpd.conf file that leases IP addresses on the 192.168.1.0/24 network is shown in the following output:

```
[root@server1 root]# cat /etc/dhcpd.conf
default-lease-time 36000;
ddns-update-style ad-hoc;
```

```
option routers 192.168.1.254;
option domain-name-servers 192.168.1.200;
subnet 192.168.1.0 netmask 255.255.255.0 {
   range 192.168.1.1 192.168.1.100
}
[root@server1 root]# _
```

Note from the preceding output that the DHCP server leases clients an IP address between 192.168.1.1 and 192.168.1.100 for 36,000 seconds. In addition, the DHCP server configures the client with a default gateway of 192.168.1.254 and a DNS server of 192.168.1.200.

After the /etc/dhcpd.conf file has been configured with the appropriate information, you can start the DHCP daemon using the command /etc/rc.d/init.d/dhcpd start and view current DHCP leases by examining the /var/lib/dhcp/dhcpd.leases file. Like the name daemon, if you change the /etc/dhcpd.conf configuration file, you must restart the DHCP daemon.

Configuring Apache

Apache is the world's most common Web server. Recall that Web servers hand out HTML files and other Web content using the Hyper Text Transfer Protocol (HTTP) from a specific directory in the directory tree. This directory is called the **document root** directory and contains the default Web site that is used on the server. The default document root directory on Red Hat Fedora Core 2 is /var/www/html, and the default document that is handed out from this directory is index.html. Nearly all configuration options for Apache are set in a single large configuration file; by default, this configuration file is /etc/httpd/conf/httpd.conf. Each line in the httpd.conf file is called a **directive**. Table 15-4 lists some common directives.

Table 15-4 Common httpd.conf directives

Directive	Description
Listen 80	Specifies that the Apache daemon will listen for HTTP requests on port 80
ServerName server1.class.com	Specifies that the name of the local server is server1.class.com
DocumentRoot "/var/www/html"	Specifies that the document root directory is /var/www/html on the local computer
DirectoryIndex index.html	Specifies that the index.html file in the document root directory will be sent to clients who request an HTML document
ErrorLog /var/log/httpd/error_log	Specifies that all Apache daemon messages will be written to the /var/log/httpd/error_log file
MaxClients 150	Sets the maximum number of simultaneous requests to 150

Table 15-4 Common httpd.conf directives (Continued)

Directive	Description
User apache	Specifies that the Apache daemon will run as the "apache" local user account
Group apache	Specifies that the Apache daemon will run as the "apache" local group account

<Directory /var/www/html>
   Order allow,deny
   Allow from all
   Deny from 192.168.1.51
</Directory>
	Specifies that all hosts are allowed to access HTML files and other Web content from the /var/www/html directory except for the computer with the IP address 192.168.1.51

The default settings in the httpd.conf file are sufficient for most simple Web servers; thus, you simply need to copy the appropriate HTML files to the /var/www/html directory, including the index.html file and start the Apache Web Server daemon (/etc/rc.d/init.d/httpd start) to host Web content on your network. If you change the HTML content inside the document root directory, you do not need to restart the Apache daemon. However, if you change the contents of httpd.conf, you need to restart the Apache daemon to activate those changes.

Configuring Samba

The most common client computer operating system that exists on networks today is Windows. Recall from the previous chapter that Windows computers format TCP/IP data using Server Message Blocks (SMB). Thus, to share information to Windows client computers, you can use the SaMBa daemon, which emulates the SMB protocol. In addition, Windows computers advertise their computer names using the NetBIOS protocol; thus, you can use the NetBIOS name daemon to create and advertise a NetBIOS name that Windows computers can use to connect to your Linux server.

When a Windows client computer accesses a shared directory using SMB, the Windows user name and password are transmitted alongside the request in case the shared directory allows access to certain users only. As a result, you should create local Linux user accounts for each Windows user and create a Samba password for them using the **smbpasswd command** that matches the password that they use on their Windows computer, as shown in the following output:

```
[root@server1 root]# useradd mary
[root@server1 root]# passwd mary
Changing password for user mary.
New UNIX password: *******
Retype new UNIX password: *******
passwd: all authentication tokens updated successfully.
```

```
[root@server1 root]# smbpasswd -a mary
New SMB password: *******
Retype new SMB password: *******
Added user mary.
[root@server1 root]# _
```

Following this, you can edit the main configuration file for Samba; on Red Hat Fedora Core 2, this file is /etc/samba/smb.conf by default. Like the httpd.conf file for Apache, the smb.conf contains directives that can be used to set your NetBIOS name, server settings, shared directories, and shared printers. By default, the smb.conf file shares all printers and home directories (for recognized Windows users); however, you need to add a line under the [global] section of this file to set your NetBIOS name. For example, to set your NetBIOS name to server1, you could add the directive netbios name = server1 to the smb.conf file.

Finally, you can start the Samba and NetBIOS name daemons using the command /etc/rc.d/init.d/smb start. As with Apache, if you change the smb.conf file, you must restart the Samba and NetBIOS name daemons.

NOTE

Many tools have been developed that modify the smb.conf file and ease the sharing of resources using Samba. For example, in Red Hat Fedora Core 2, you can use the **system-config-samba command** from within a desktop environment.

Configuring NFS

Network File System (NFS) allows UNIX and Linux computers the capability to share files transparently. In NFS, one computer shares a certain directory in the directory tree (a process called exporting) by placing the name of that directory in the /etc/exports file, and the other computer can access that directory across the network by using the mount command to mount the remote directory on the local computer, as discussed in Chapter 14, "Network Configuration." To configure the NFS server, you can perform the following steps:

1. Create a directory that contains the information that is to be shared to client computers. Although you can use an existing directory, try to avoid doing so because you might accidentally allow client computers the ability to view or modify existing system files.

2. Next edit the /etc/exports file and add a line that lists the directory to be shared and the appropriate options. For example, the following lines in the /etc/exports file share the /source directory to the computer server1, allowing users to read and write data, and ensuring that the root user is treated as an anonymous user on the NFS server, as well as share the /admin directory to all users, allowing users to read and write data:

   ```
   /source   server1(rw,root_squash)
   /admin    (rw)
   ```

   Save your changes to the file and return to the command prompt.

3. Run the command `exportfs -a` to update the list of exported filesystems in memory from the /etc/exports file.

4. Restart the NFS processes by typing the following commands at the command prompt and pressing Enter:

    ```
    /etc/rc.d/init.d/nfs restart
    /etc/rc.d/init.d/nfslock restart
    ```

Configuring FTP

The most common protocol used to transfer files on public networks today is the File Transfer Protocol (FTP). Most operating systems come with an FTP client program, which can connect to an FTP server that hosts directories of files for users to download to their computers, as discussed in Chapter 14. FTP hosts files differently than NFS. A special directory can be made available to any user who wants to connect (called anonymous access) or users can be connected to their home directory on the FTP server, provided they enter a valid user name and password in the FTP client program. The most common FTP server program is the Washington University FTP daemon (wu-ftpd). To configure wu-ftpd to host files for other computers to download provided they log in as the user "user1" with a valid password, you can perform the following steps:

1. Create a directory underneath user1's home directory to host the files and ensure that user1 owns this directory.

2. Next edit the /etc/xinetd.d/wu-ftpd file and change the line:

    disable   =   yes

    Such that it reads:

    disable   =   no

    Save your changes to the file and return to the command prompt.

3. At the command prompt, run the command `/etc/init.d/xinetd restart` to restart the Internet Super Daemon.

Next, you can run the ftp client utility to log in to the FTP server as user1 and be placed in the /home/user1 directory. By default, you are prevented from logging in as the root user to wu-ftpd. To change this, simply remove the line root from the /etc/ftpusers file and remove the lines deny-uid %-99 %65534- and deny-gid %-99 %65534- from the /etc/ftpaccess file; this allows users with a name of root and users with a UID less than 99 to log in via FTP.

Anonymous FTP access is granted by default; any users who log in as the user "anonymous" using the ftp client utility are placed in the /var/ftp directory. Simply perform Steps 2 and 3 shown previously to ensure that the FTP daemon is started.

Unfortunately, you must download the wu-ftpd package from the Internet because Red Hat Fedora Core 2 does not ship with it. Instead, the Very Secure FTP daemon (vsftpd) is available in Fedora Core 2; it is a stand-alone daemon that is much easier to configure than wu-ftpd. To configure vsftpd to host files for other computers to download, provided they log in as the user "user1" with a valid password, you can perform the following steps:

1. Create a directory underneath user1's home directory to host the files and ensure that user1 owns this directory.

2. At the command prompt, run the command `/etc/rc.d/init.d/vsftpd start` to start the vsftpd daemon.

Like wu-ftpd, anonymous FTP access is granted by default when the `vsftpd` daemon is started, and anonymous ftp clients are placed in the /var/ftp directory. In addition, to log in as the root user to vsftpd, you can remove the line `root` from the /etc/vsftpd.ftpusers and /etc/vsftpd.user_list files.

Configuring NIS

Network Information Service (NIS) can be used to coordinate common configuration files, such as /etc/passwd and /etc/hosts, across several Linux computers within an organization. Each computer that participates in NIS belongs to an NIS domain and uses an NIS map for accessing certain information rather than use the local configuration file. Furthermore, you can configure a master NIS server to send all NIS map configuration to NIS slave servers, which then hand out these NIS maps to all other Linux computers, known as NIS clients.

The most common configuration files that companies use NIS to coordinate are password databases (/etc/passwd and /etc/shadow) such that users can log in to several different Linux servers using the same user name and password. The steps required to set up an NIS server and NIS client for this purpose are shown in the following list:

1. Define the NIS domain name by typing the command `domainname NIS_domain_name` at a command prompt.

2. Add the following line to /etc/sysconfig/network to configure the NIS domain from Step 1 at every boot time:

   `NISDOMAIN="NIS_domain"`

3. Edit the file /var/yp/Makefile, navigate to the line that starts with all:, and edit the list of files to be made into maps. If you have no slave servers, also ensure that NOPUSH=true is in this file. If you have slave servers, they must be listed in the /var/yp/ypservers file.

4. Add the names or IP addresses of allowed clients to the /var/yp/securenets file.

5. Allow the clients from Step 4 access to the appropriate maps in the /etc/ypserv.conf file.

6. Start the NIS server daemon by typing `/usr/sbin/ypserv` at the command prompt.

7. Start the NIS password server daemon by typing `/etc/init.d/yppasswdd` at the command prompt.

8. Generate the configuration file maps by typing `/usr/lib/yp/ypinit -m` at a command prompt.

9. Allow clients to connect by typing `ypbind` at a command prompt.

Setting up the NIS Client:

1. Define the NIS domain name by typing the command `domainname NIS_domain_name` at a command prompt.

2. Add the following line to /etc/sysconfig/network to configure the NIS domain from Step 1 at every boot time:

   `NISDOMAIN="NIS_domain"`

3. Edit the /etc/yp.conf file and add the following line to query a specific NIS server:

   `domain NIS_domain server NIS_server`

Alternatively, you can add the following line to listen for NIS broadcasts on the network:

   `domain NIS_domain broadcast`

1. Start the NIS client program by typing `ypbind` at a command prompt.

2. Locate the NIS server by typing the command `ypwhich` at a command prompt.

3. Add the following line to /etc/passwd to redirect all requests to the NIS server:

   `+:*:0:0:::`

After the NIS server and client have been set up, ensure that all users on NIS clients use the `yppasswd` command to change their NIS password; using the `passwd` command only modifies the local password database.

> **NOTE**
>
> NIS was originally called Yellow Pages; as a result, many configuration commands and files are prefixed with the letters yp.

Configuring the Secure Shell Daemon

The Secure Shell daemon (sshd) allows you the ability to use the `ssh` utility to log in to a server across the network in a secure manner and receive a BASH shell that can be used to run applications or monitor the server. The configuration file that specifies the options used by the ssh daemon is called /etc/ssh/sshd_config. Most of this file is commented, and should only be edited to change the default settings that the ssh daemon uses when servicing ssh clients. The most common options that are changed in this file are those that deal with authentication and encryption.

By default, sshd uses a secure challenge-response authentication method that ensures that the password is not transmitted on the network, but this can be changed to Kerberos authentication or authentication that allows uses based on the ~/.rhosts or /etc/hosts.equiv files.

Organizations use many types of encryption to secure communication on the network. Each type of encryption differs in its method of encryption and the cryptography key length used to encrypt data; the longer the key length, the more difficult it is for malicious users to decode the data. The main types of encryption supported by sshd are as follows:

◆ Triple Data Encryption Standard (3DES), which encrypts blocks of data in three stages using a 168-bit key length

◆ Advanced Encryption Standard (AES), which is an improvement on 3DES encryption and is available in 128-, 192-, and 256-bit key lengths

◆ Blowfish, which is an encryption algorithm that is much faster than 3DES and can use keys up to 448 bits in length

◆ Carlisle Adams Stafford Tavares (CAST), which is a general-purpose encryption similar to 3DES and is commonly available using a 128-bit key length

◆ ARCfour, which is a fast encryption algorithm that operates on streams of data instead of blocks of data and uses variable-length keys up to 2048 bits in length

In addition, all of the aforementioned types of encryption except ARCfour typically use Cipher Block Chaining (CBC), which can be used to encrypt larger amounts of data.

> **NOTE**
>
> Client computers can use a /etc/ssh/ssh_config or $HOME/ssh/ssh_config file to set ssh options for use with their ssh client utility. The authentication and encryption settings on the client computer must match those in the server configuration file (/etc/ssh/sshd_config) for a connection to be successful.

Routing and Firewall Services

Some network services are not provided entirely by network daemons; instead, these services are provided by the Linux kernel and do not listen to a particular port. The two most common of these types of services are routing and firewall services.

Routing

Every computer on a network maintains a list of TCP/IP networks so that packets are sent to the appropriate location; this `list` is called a **route table** and is stored in system memory. To see the route table, you can simply use the **route command**, as shown in the following output:

```
[root@server1 root]# route
Kernel IP routing table
Destination    Gateway        Genmask        Flags Metric Ref   Use Iface
192.168.0.0    *              255.255.0.0    U     0      0     0   eth0
127.0.0.0      *              255.0.0.0      U     0      0     0   lo
default        192.168.0.1    0.0.0.0        UG    0      0     0   eth0
[root@server1 root]# _
```

NOTE

The `netstat -r` command is equivalent to the `route` command.

The route table shown in the preceding output indicates that all packets destined for the 192.168.0.0 network will be sent to the device eth0. Similarly, all packets destined for the 127.0.0.0 network will be sent to the loopback adapter (lo). Packets that must be sent to any other network will be sent to the default gateway; the final line in the preceding output indicates that the default gateway is a computer with the IP address 192.168.0.1, which is on the same network as the eth0 device.

If your computer has more than one network interface configured, the route table will have more entries that define the available TCP/IP networks; computers that have more than one network interface are called **multihomed hosts**. Multihomed hosts can be configured to forward packets from one interface to another to aid a packet in reaching its destination; this process is commonly called **routing** or **IP forwarding**. To enable routing on your Linux computer, simply place the number 1 in the file /proc/sys/net/ipv4/ip_forward, as shown in the following output:

```
[root@server1 root]# cat /proc/sys/net/ipv4/ip_forward
0
[root@server1 root]# echo 1 > /proc/sys/net/ipv4/ip_forward
[root@server1 root]# cat /proc/sys/net/ipv4/ip_forward
1
[root@server1 root]# _
```

To enable routing at every boot, ensure that the line net.ipv4.ip_forward = 1 exists in the /etc/sysctl.conf file.

If your computer has more than one network interface and routing is enabled, your computer will route packets only to networks for which it has a network interface. On larger networks, however, you can have several routers; packets might need to be sent through several routers to reach their destination. Because routers only know the networks to which they are directly connected, you might need to add entries to the route table on a router such that it knows where to send packets that are destined for a remote network. Suppose, for example, your organization has three TCP/IP networks (1.0.0.0/8, 2.0.0.0/8, and 3.0.0.0/8) divided by two routers, as shown in Figure 15-3.

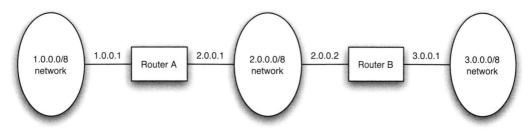

FIGURE 15-3 *A sample routed network*

RouterA has an entry in its route table that says it is connected to the 1.0.0.0/8 network via the network interface that has the IP address 1.0.0.1 and connected to the 2.0.0.0/8 network via the network interface that has the IP address 2.0.0.1. These two routes are automatically made when TCP/IP is configured. If RouterA receives a packet that is destined for the 3.0.0.0/8 network, it does not know where to forward it because it does not have a route for the 3.0.0.0/8 network in its routing table. To add the appropriate route to the 3.0.0.0/8 network on RouterA, you can run the following command on RouterA:

```
[root@server1 root]# route add net 3.0.0.0 mask 255.0.0.0 2.0.0.2
[root@server1 root]# _
```

Now, RouterA sends any packets destined for the 3.0.0.0/8 network to the computer 2.0.0.2 (RouterB). RouterB then forwards the packets to the 3.0.0.0/8 network because it has a route in its route table that says it is connected to the 3.0.0.0/8 network via the network interface that has the IP address 3.0.0.1.

Similarly, for RouterB to forward packets it receives destined for the 1.0.0.0/8 network, it must have a route that sends those packets to RouterA via the interface 2.0.0.1:

```
[root@server1 root]# route add net 1.0.0.0 mask 255.0.0.0 2.0.0.1
[root@server1 root]# _
```

Because the list of all routes on large networks such as the Internet is too large to be stored in a route table on a router, most routers are configured with a default gateway. Any packets that are addressed to a destination that is not listed in the route table are sent to the default gateway, which is a router that can forward the packet to the appropriate network or to its default gateway and so on until the packets reach their destination.

> **NOTE**
>
> You can use the `route del <route>` command to remove entries from the route table.
>
> The **ip command** can also be used to manipulate the route table. The command `ip route add 1.0.0.0/8 via 2.0.0.1` can be used to add the same route to the route table, as shown in the previous output.
>
> The contents of the route table are lost when the computer is powered off; to load routes to remote networks to the route table at every boot time, simply place the appropriate `route` or `ip` command in the /etc/rc.d/rc.local file.
>
> You can also use a routing protocol on routers within your network to automate the addition of routes to the routing table. Two common routing protocols are Routing Information Protocol (RIP) and Open Shortest Path First (OSPF).

If computers on your network are unable to connect to other computers on a remote network, the problem is likely routing-related. A common utility used to troubleshoot routing is the **traceroute command**; it displays all routers between the current computer and a remote computer. To trace the path from the local computer to the computer with the IP address 3.4.5.6, you can use the following command:

```
[root@server1 root]# traceroute 3.4.5.6
traceroute to 3.4.5.6 (3.4.5.6), 30 hops max, 38 byte packets
 1  server1 (192.168.0.1)  2.048 ms  0.560 ms  0.489 ms
 2  apban.pso.com (7.43.111.2)  2.560 ms  0.660 ms  0.429 ms
 3  tfs.ihtfcid.net (3.0.0.1)  3.521 ms  0.513 ms  0.499 ms
 4  sr1.lala.com (3.4.5.6)  5.028 ms  0.710 ms  0.554 ms
[root@server1 root]# _
```

Firewall Services

Another network service that is not provided directly by daemons is netfilter/iptables, which can be used to create a firewall on your Linux computer. Recall from Chapter 1 that firewalls can be used in your organization to block unwanted network traffic; as a result, firewalls are typically enabled on router interfaces.

Netfilter/ipchains discards certain network packets according to **chains** of **rules** that are stored in your computer's memory. By default, you can specify certain rules for three types of chains:

◆ INPUT chain, for network packets destined for your computer

◆ FORWARD chain, for network packets that must pass through your computer (if you are a router)

◆ OUTPUT chain, for network packets that originate from your computer

By default, no rules exist for the INPUT, FORWARD, or OUTPUT chains after a Red Hat Fedora Core 2 installation. To create rules that are used for each chain, you must use the **iptables command**. Rules can be based on the source IP address, destination IP address, protocol used (TCP, UDP, ICMP), or packet status. For example, to flush all previous rules from memory, specify that forwarded packets are dropped by default, and only packets are to be forwarded if they originate from the 192.168.1.0 network, you can use the following commands:

```
[root@server1 root]# iptables -F
[root@server1 root]# iptables -P FORWARD DROP
[root@server1 root]# iptables -A FORWARD -s 192.168.1.0/24 -j ACCEPT
[root@server1 root]# _
```

You can then verify the list of rules for each chain in memory by using the following command:

```
[root@server1 root]# iptables -L
Chain INPUT (policy ACCEPT)
target     prot opt source           destination


Chain INPUT (policy DROP)
target     prot opt source           destination
ACCEPT     all  --  192.168.1.0/24   anywhere


Chain INPUT (policy ACCEPT)
target     prot opt source           destination
[root@server1 root]# _
```

> **NOTE**
>
> Because chains and rules are stored in memory, they are lost when your computer is shut down; to ensure that they are loaded on each boot, simply place the appropriate iptables commands in the /etc/rc.d/rc.local file. Alternatively, you can add entries to the /etc/sysconfig/iptables file.

Table 15-5 provides a list of common options to the iptables command.

> **NOTE**
>
> Older Linux kernels used the ipchains utility to provide firewall services; support for this utility is not supported by the Linux kernel in Red Hat Fedora Core 2 by default.

Table 15-5 Common iptables options

Option	Description
-s address	Specifies the source address of packets for a rule.
-d address	Specifies the destination address of packets for a rule.
-p protocol	Specifies the protocol type for a rule.
-j action	Specifies the action that is taken for a rule.
-L chain	Lists rules for a certain chain. If no chain is given, all chains are listed.
-P chain policy	Specifies the default policy for a certain chain type.
-D number	Deletes a rule for a chain specified by additional arguments. Rules start at number 1.
-R number	Replaces a rule for a chain specified by additional arguments. Rules start at number 1.
-F chain	Removes all rules for a certain chain. If no chain is specified, it removes all rules for all chains.

Security

In the past decade, hundreds of new services have been made available to Linux systems and the number of Linux users has risen to millions. In addition, Linux systems today are typically made available across networks such as the Internet. As a result, Linux is more prone today to security loopholes and attacks both locally and from across networks. To protect your Linux computer, you should take steps to improve local and network security as well as understand how to detect intruders who manage to breach your Linux system.

Securing the Local Computer

One of the most important security-related practices is to limit access to the physical Linux computer itself. If a malicious user has access to the Linux computer, that user could boot the computer using a floppy disk, USB flash memory drive, or CD-ROM that contains a small operating system and use it to access files on the partitions on the hard disk of the Linux computer without having to log in to the operating system installed on the hard disk. To prevent this, you should lock important computers, such as Linux servers, in a specific room to which only Linux administrators or trusted users have key access; this room is commonly called a **server closet**. Unfortunately, some Linux computers, such as Linux workstations, must be located in public areas. For these computers, you should remove the floppy and CD-ROM devices from the computer. In addition, you should ensure that the boot order listed in the computer BIOS prevents booting from the USB ports, as well as ensure that a system BIOS password is set to prevent other users from changing the boot order.

Along these same lines, anyone who has access to the physical Linux computer could boot the computer and interact with the LILO or GRUB boot loader. This could allow a user to specify options that would boot the system in Single User Mode and gain root access to the system without specifying a password. To prevent this, simply ensure that you set a boot loader password in the LILO or GRUB configuration files, as discussed in Chapter 9.

Another important security consideration for Linux computers is to limit access to graphical desktops and shells. If you leave your workstation for a few minutes and leave yourself logged in to the system, another user can use your computer while you are away. As a result, it is good security practice to lock your desktop environment or exit your command-line shell before leaving the computer. To lock the GNOME or KDE desktop, simply navigate to the Red Hat button and choose Lock Screen; you will need to enter your password to use your desktop again. Exiting a command-line shell also ends any background processes because the parent of those processes is your shell. If you run background processes that take a long time to complete, simply run them using the **nohup command**; this allows you to exit your command-line shell without ending any background processes. For example, to run the updatedb command and exit your system afterward such that you can leave your workstation, simply perform the following commands:

```
[root@server1 root]# nohup updatedb &
[1] 3773
nohup: appending output to 'nohup.out'
[root@server1 root]# exit

Fedora Core release 2 (Tettnang)
Kernel 2.6.5-1.358 on an i686

server1 login:
```

If you have root access to a Linux system, it is important to minimize the time that you are logged in as the root user to reduce the chance that another user can access your terminal if you accidentally leave your system without locking your desktop or exiting your shell. It is best practice to create a regular user account that you can use to check e-mails and perform other day-to-day tasks. You can then use the **su (switch user) command** to obtain root access only when you need to perform an administrative task. When you are finished, you can use the exit command to return to your previous shell where you are logged in as a regular user account, as shown in the following output:

```
[user1@server1 user1]$ su - root
Password: *****
[root@server1 root]# _
[root@server1 root]# rm -f /etc/securetty
[root@server1 root]# exit
[user1@server1 user1]$ _
```

The − option to the su command shown in the preceding output loads the root user's environment variables. Also, you can omit the root user's name in the preceding output; if a name is not specified as an argument to the su command, the root user is assumed by default.

If you only intend to run one command as the root user, you can instead choose to use the -c option to the su command; this returns you to your current shell automatically. The following demonstrates how to run the root command shown in the previous output using the -c option to the su command:

```
[user1@server1 user1]$ su -c "rm -f /etc/securetty" root
Password: *****
[user1@server1 user1]$ _
```

Still, some users, such as software developers, need to run certain commands as the root user in certain situations. Instead of giving them the root password, it is best to give them the ability to run certain commands as the root user via the **sudo command**. The sudo command checks the /etc/sudoers file to see if you have rights to run a certain command as a different user. The following /etc/sudoers file allows the software developers, mary and bob, the ability to run the kill and killall commands as the root user on the computers server1 and server2:

```
[root@server1 root]# cat /etc/sudoers
User_Alias SD = mary, bob
Cmnd_Alias KILL = /bin/kill, /usr/bin/killall
Host_Alias SERVERS = server1, server2


SD      SERVERS = (root) KILL
[root@server1 root]# _
```

Now, if mary needs to kill the cron daemon on server1 (which was started as the root user) to test a program that she wrote, she needs to use the sudo command, as shown in the following output, and supply her own password:

```
[mary@server1 mary]$ ps -ef |grep crond
root      2281     1  0 21:20 ?        00:00:00 crond
[mary@server1 mary]$ kill -9 2281
-bash: kill: (2281) - Operation not permitted
[mary@server1 mary]$ sudo kill -9 2281

We trust that you have received the usual lecture from the local System
Administrator. It usually boils down to these two things:

        #1) Respect the privacy of others.
        #2) Think before you type.


Password: ******
[mary@server1 mary]$ _
```

Protecting Against Network Attacks

Recall from earlier in this chapter that network services listen for network traffic on a certain port number and interact with that traffic. As long as network services exist on a computer, there is always the possibility that crackers can manipulate the network service by interacting with it in unusual ways. One example of this type of network attack is a **buffer overrun,** which can replace program information used by the network service in memory with new program information, consequently altering how the network service operates.

The first step to securing your computer against network attacks such as buffer overruns is to minimize the number of network services running. If you run only the minimum number of network services necessary for your organization, you greatly reduce the chance of network attacks. To see what network services are running on your network, you can run the **nmap (network mapper) command.** The following output demonstrates how nmap can be used to determine the number of services running on the server1 computer:

```
[root@server1 root]# nmap -sT server1

Starting nmap3.50(http://www.insecure.org/nmap/) at 2005-09-05 9:29EDT
Interesting ports on server1 (127.0.0.1):
(The 1648 ports scanned but not shown below are in state: closed)
PORT      STATE SERVICE
22/tcp    open  ssh
25/tcp    open  smtp
80/tcp    open  http
111/tcp   open  rpcbind
139/tcp   open  netbios-ssn
443/tcp   open  https
445/tcp   open  microsoft-ds
631/tcp   open  ipp
783/tcp   open  hp-alarm-mgr
32770/tcp open  sometimes-rpc3
32771/tcp open  sometimes-rpc5

Nmap run completed -- 1 IP address (1 host up) scanned in 0.928 seconds
[root@server1 root]# _
```

From the preceding output, you can determine which services are running on your computer by searching the descriptions for the port numbers in the /etc/services file or on the Internet. For services that are not needed, ensure that they are not started automatically by the Internet Super Daemon from entries in the /etc/rc.d/rc*.d directories or via lines in other startup scripts such as /etc/rc.d/rc.local.

For services that must be used because they are essential to your organization, you can take certain steps to ensure that they are as secure as possible. For example, you could enable encryption for network services that support encrypted communication (for example, sshd), and use netfilter/iptables INPUT chain rules to allow only desired network traffic to reach your network services. It is also important to ensure that network service daemons are not run as the root user on the system when possible. If a cracker gains access to your system via a network service daemon run as the root user, the cracker has root access as well. Many network daemons, such as Apache, set the user account by which they execute in their configuration files.

In addition, because network attacks are reported in the open source community, new versions of network services usually include fixes for known network attacks. As such, these new versions are more resilient to network attacks. Because of this, it is good form to periodically check for new versions of network services, install them, and check the associated documentation for new security-related parameters that can be set in the configuration file.

If you use network services that are started by the Internet Super Daemon, you can use TCP wrappers to provide extra security. A **TCP wrapper** is a program (/usr/sbin/tcpd) that can start a network daemon. To enable TCP wrappers, you must modify the appropriate file in the /etc/xinetd.d directory and start the network daemon as an argument to the TCP wrapper. For the telnet daemon, you modify the /etc/xinetd.d/telnet file, as shown in the following example:

```
[root@server1 root]# cat /etc/xinetd.d/telnet
# default: on
# description: The telnet server serves telnet sessions; it uses \
#       unencrypted username/password pairs for authentication.
service telnet
{
        flags           = REUSE
        socket_type     = stream
        wait            = no
        user            = root
        server          = /usr/sbin/tcpd
        server_args     = /usr/sbin/in.telnetd
        log_on_failure  += USERID
        disable         = yes
}
[root@server1 root]# _
```

Now, the telnet daemon (/usr/sbin/in.telnetd) will be started by the TCP wrapper (/usr/sbin/tcpd). Before a TCP wrapper starts a network daemon, it first checks the /etc/hosts.allow and /etc/hosts.deny files. This allows you to restrict the network service such that it can only be accessed by certain hosts within your organization. The following /etc/hosts.allow and /etc/hosts.deny files only allow the computers client1 and client2 the ability to use the telnet utility to connect to your telnet server.

```
[root@server1 root]# cat /etc/hosts.deny
in.telnetd:  ALL
[root@server1 root]# _
```

```
[root@server1 root]# cat /etc/hosts.allow
in.telnetd:  client1, client2
[root@server1 root]# _
```

Another important component of network security involves local file permissions. If everyone had read permission on the /etc/shadow file, any user could read the encrypted passwords for all user accounts, including the root user, and possibly decrypt the password using a decryption program. Fortunately, the default permissions on /etc/shadow read for the root user only, and enabling MD5 password encryption during installation minimizes this possibility. However, similar permission problems exist with many other important files, and crackers typically exploit these files as a result. Thus, you need to carefully examine the permissions on files and directories associated with system and network services.

Take, for example, the Apache Web Server discussed earlier in this chapter. Apache daemons are run as the user apache and the group apache by default. These daemons read HTML files from the document root directory such that they can give the information to client Web browsers. The following directory listing from a sample document root directory shows that the Apache daemons also have write permission because they own the index.html file:

```
[root@server1 root]# ls -l /var/www/html
total 64
-rw-r--r--  1 apache apache  61156  Sep  5 08:36 index.html
[root@server1 root]# _
```

Thus, if a cracker was able to manipulate an Apache daemon, the cracker would have write access to the index.html file and would be able to modify it. It is secure practice to ensure that the index.html is owned by the Webmaster, webma (who needs to modify the file), and that the Apache daemons are given read access only through membership in the other category, as shown in the following example:

```
[root@server1 root]# chown webma:webma /var/www/html/index.html
[root@server1 root]# ls -l /var/www/html
total 64
-rw-r--r--  1 webma webma    61156  Sep  5 08:36 index.html
[root@server1 root]# _
```

Detecting Intrusion

Although you can take many security precautions on your Linux computers, there is always the chance that someone will gain access to your system either locally or from across a network. Quite often, log files contain information or irregularities that indicate an intrusion has taken place. As a result, it is best to regularly analyze the log files in the /var/log directory associated with the network services that are run on your computer. In addition, you should also review system log files associated with authentication to detect whether unauthorized users have logged in to the system. Network applications that authenticate users typically do so via **Pluggable Authentication Modules (PAM)**. PAM logs information to the /var/log/secure file and its variants; thus, you should regularly check this file for PAM errors and alerts. You should also check the /var/log/wtmp log file, which lists users who logged in to the system and received a BASH shell. Because this file is in binary format, you must use the who /var/log/wtmp command to view it, as shown in the following output:

```
[root@server1 root]# who /var/log/wtmp
root     pts/2     Sep  4 15:35
root     tty2      Sep  4 18:22
bob      tty3      Sep  4 21:14
root     tty2      Sep  4 22:00
root     :0        Sep  5 08:35
root     pts/1     Sep  5 09:24 (:0.0)
root     pts/2     Sep  5 09:29 (:0.0)
root     :0        Sep  5 11:02
root     pts/1     Sep  5 15:31 (:0.0)
mary     pts/2     Sep  5 15:35 (192.168.1.66)
[root@server1 root]# _
```

If a cracker has gained access to your system, he has likely changed certain files on the hard disk to gain more access, modify sensitive data, or vandalize services. To detect whether a cracker has modified files on your system, you can use a program that checks the integrity of important files and directories. Recall from Chapter 12, "Compression, System Backup, and Software Installation," that the sum command can be used to generate a checksum to determine whether a file's contents have been changed; however, it is too difficult to manually use the sum command to generate and record checksums for each important file on the filesystem. Instead, most administrators use a program such as **Tripwire** to track file and directory modifications.

To configure tripwire to check for altered files and directories, you can perform the following steps:

1. Download and install the latest tripwire RPM or source code tarball.

2. Edit the /etc/tripwire/twpol.txt file and change the line HOSTNAME=localhost; to HOSTNAME=yourhostname;.

3. Run the program /etc/tripwire/twinstall.sh and enter a passphrase when prompted. This passphrase is a password used to administer tripwire later on and will be required when running any tripwire-related program. The /etc/tripwire/tw.cfg binary file will be created with default tripwire settings for monitoring your system. The same settings exist in the /etc/tripwire/twcfg.txt text file; you can optionally modify those settings and use the twadmin program to save those settings to the /etc/tripwire/tw.cfg file.

4. Run the tripwire --init command to create a tripwire database with settings from the files and directories specified in /etc/tripwire/tw.cfg.

5. Run the tripwire --check command periodically in the future to analyze the files and directories in the /etc/tripwire/tw.cfg file against the settings in the tripwire database to see if any files were modified.

Because tripwire can be used to detect intruders on a Linux system, it is referred to as an **Intrusion Detection System (IDS)**. Several IDS programs are available for Linux that can be used to detect crackers who are trying to gain access to your system or have done so already. Table 15-6 lists some common IDS programs.

Table 15-6 Common Linux Intrusion Detection Systems

Name	Description
Advanced Intrusion Detection Environment (AIDE)	An alternative to tripwire that has added functionality for checking the integrity of files and directories.
Integrity Checking Utility (ICU)	A PERL-based program that is designed to work with AIDE to check the integrity of Linux computers remotely across a network.
PortSentry	An IDS that monitors traffic on ports and allows you to detect whether crackers are probing your ports using port scanning utilities such as nmap.
Snort	A complex IDS that can be used to capture and monitor network packets. It can be used to detect a wide range of network attacks and port probing.
Linux Intrusion Detection System (LIDS)	An IDS that involves modifying the Linux kernel to increase process and file security as well as detect security breaches.
Simple WATCHer (SWATCH)	An IDS that monitors log files and alerts administrators when an intrusion is detected.

Chapter Summary

- Most network services are either started by the Internet Super Daemon or as a stand-alone daemon and listen for requests on a certain port.
- Commonly configured network services include NIS, DNS, DHCP, Samba, Apache, NFS, FTP, and Secure Shell.
- Routing and firewall services are provided by the Linux kernel and are used to provide connectivity between networks and network security, respectively.
- Securing a Linux computer involves improving local and network security as well as monitoring to detect intruders.
- By restricting access to your Linux computer and using the root account only when required via the su and sudo commands, you greatly improve local Linux security.

◆ Reducing the number of network services, implementing firewalls, preventing services from running as the root user, restricting permissions on key files, and using TCP wrappers can greatly reduce the chance of network attacks.

◆ Log files as well as IDS applications such as tripwire can be used to detect intruders on a Linux network.

Key Terms

buffer overrun — An attack in which a network service is altered in memory.

chains — The components of a firewall that specify the general type of network traffic to which rules apply.

directive — A line within a configuration file.

DNS cache file — A file that contains the IP addresses of top-level DNS servers.

document root — The directory that stores default HTML content for a Web server.

forward lookup — A DNS name resolution request whereby a FQDN is resolved to an IP address.

Internet Super Daemon (xinetd) — The daemon responsible for initializing and configuring many networking services on a Linux computer.

Intrusion Detection System (IDS) — A program that can be used to detect unauthorized access to a Linux system.

ip command — A command that can be used to manipulate the route table.

IP forwarding — The act of forwarding TCP/IP packets from one network to another. *See also* Routing.

iptables command — The command used to configure a firewall in Red Hat Fedora.

iterative query — A DNS resolution request that was resolved without the use of top-level DNS servers.

master DNS server — The DNS server that contains a read/write copy of the zone. *See also* Primary DNS server.

multihomed hosts — The computers that have more than one network interface.

nmap (network mapper) command — A command that can be used to scan ports on network computers.

nohup command — A command that prevents other commands from exiting when the parent process is killed.

Pluggable Authentication Modules (PAM) — The component that handles authentication requests by daemons on a Linux system.

port — A number that uniquely identifies a network service

primary DNS server — The DNS server that contains a read/write copy of the zone.

recursive query — A DNS resolution request that was resolved with the use of top-level DNS servers.

reverse lookup — A DNS name resolution request whereby an IP address is resolved to a FQDN.

route command — A command that can be used to manipulate the route table.

route table — A table of information used to indicate which networks are connected to network interfaces.

routing — The act of forwarding data packets from one network to another.

rules — The components of a firewall that match specific network traffic that is to be allowed or dropped.

secondary DNS server — A DNS server that contains a read-only copy of the zone. *See also* Slave DNS server.

server closet — A secured room that stores servers within an organization.

slave DNS server — A DNS server that contains a read-only copy of the zone.

smbpasswd command — A command used to generate a Samba password for a user.

stand-alone daemons — The daemons that configure themselves at boot time without assistance from the Internet Super Daemon.

su (switch user) command — A command that can be used to switch your current user account to another.

sudo command — A command that is used to perform commands as another user via entries in the /etc/sudoers file.

system-config-samba command — A utility that can be used to simplify the editing of the /etc/samba/smb.conf file.

TCP wrapper — A program that can be used to run a network daemon with additional security via the /etc/hosts.allow and /etc/hosts.deny files.

traceroute command — A command used to trace the path a packet takes through routers to a destination host.

tripwire — A common IDS for Linux that monitors files and directories.

User Datagram Protocol/Internet Protocol (UDP/IP) — A faster but unreliable version of TCP/IP.

well-known ports — Of the 65,535 possible ports, the ports from 0 to 1024 used by common networking services.

zone — A portion of the Domain Name Space that is administered by one or more DNS servers.

zone transfer — The process of copying resource records for a zone from a master to a slave DNS server.

Review Questions

1. What is the most common LAN protocol used today?

   a. DLC

   b. AppleTalk

   c. IPX/SPX

   d. TCP/IP

2. What is the subnet mask for a Class C IP address?

   a. 0.0.0.0

   b. 255.0.0.0

   c. 255.255.0.0

   d. 255.255.255.0

3. Which of the following is a popular, high-speed connection technology used in North America?

   a. modems

   b. DSL

   c. ISDN

   d. PPP

4. Which ftp command is used to change the directory on the remote computer?

   a. lcd

   b. rcd

   c. cd

   d. remcd

5. The most common mail user agent used in Red Hat Fedora Linux is _____.

    a. Mozilla

    b. Exchange

    c. POP

    d. Simple Mail Transfer Protocol

6. True or false? ANDing is a mathematical operation that compares two binary digits and gives a result of 1 or 0.

7. True or false? The IP address 255.255.255.255 refers to all networks.

8. True or false? All routers are hardware devices.

9. True or false? All NIC cards are detected during Linux installation.

10. True or false? PPP is the standard protocol used today to connect to remote networks over serial lines.

11. Two or more computers that are connected with media that can exchange information are called a(n) _____.

12. To participate on a TCP/IP network, your computer must have a valid Internet Protocol (IP) address and _____ mask.

13. The _____ command sends a small TCP/IP packet to another IP address and awaits a response.

14. The simplest method for mapping host names to IP addresses is by placing entries into the _____ file.

15. The traditional utility used to obtain a BASH shell from a remote Linux computer on the network is _____.

Appendix A

Certification

As technology advances, so does the need for educated people to manage technology. One of the principal risks that companies take is the hiring of qualified people to administer, use, or develop programs for Linux. To lower this risk, companies seek people who have demonstrated proficiency in certain technical areas. Although this proficiency can be demonstrated in the form of practical experience, practical experience alone is often not enough for companies when hiring for certain technical positions. Certification tests have become a standard benchmark of technical ability and are sought after by many companies. Certification tests can vary based on the technical certification, but usually involve a multiple-choice computer test administered by an approved testing center. Hundreds of thousands of computer-related certification tests are written worldwide each year, and the certification process is likely to increase in importance in the future as technology advances.

TIP

It is important to recognize that certification does not replace ability, but demonstrates it. An employer might get 30 qualified applicants and part of the hiring process will likely be a demonstration of ability. It is unlikely the employer will incur the cost and time it takes to test all 30. Rather, it is more likely the employer will look for benchmark certifications, which indicate a base ability, and then test this subgroup.

Furthermore, certifications are an internationally administered and recognized standard. Although an employer might not be familiar with the criteria involved in achieving a computer science degree from a particular university in Canada or a certain college in Texas, certification exam criteria is well published on Web sites and is, hence, well known. In addition, it does not matter in which country the certification exam is taken because the tests are standardized and administered by the same authenticating authority using common rules.

Certifications come in two broad categories, vendor-specific and vendor-neutral. Vendor-specific certifications are ones in which the vendor of a particular operating system or program sets the standards to be met and creates the exams. Obtaining one of these certifications demonstrates knowledge of, or on, a particular product or operating system. Microsoft, Novell, and Oracle, for example, all have vendor-specific certifications for their products. Vendor-neutral exams, such as those offered by CompTIA, demonstrate knowledge in a particular area, but not on any specific product or brand of product. In either case, the organizations that create the certification exams and set the standards strive to ensure they are of the highest quality and integrity to be used as a true benchmark worldwide. One globally recognized and vendor-neutral Linux certification used by the industry is CompTIA's Linux+ certification.

Linux+ Certification

Linux is a general category of operating system software that shares a common operating system kernel and utilities. What differentiates one Linux distribution from another are the various accompanying software applications, which modify the look and feel of the operating system. Vendor-neutral certification suits Linux particularly well because there is no one specific vendor; Linux distributions can have different brands attached to them, but essentially work in the same fashion. To certify on one particular distribution might well indicate the ability to port to and work well on another distribution, but with the varied number of distributions, it is probably best to show proficiency on the most common features of Linux that the majority of distributions share. The CompTIA Linux+ certification exam achieves this well and tests a wide body of knowledge on the various ways Linux is distributed and installed, as well as common commands, procedures, and user interfaces. The exam can be taken at any participating VUE or Sylvan Prometric testing center worldwide and involves 95 questions to be answered within a two-hour timeframe.

> **NOTE**
>
> To find out more about the Linux+ certification exam and how to book one, visit the CompTIA Web site at *http://www.comptia.org/certification/linux/*.

Linux+ Certification Objectives

The following tables identify where these topics are covered in this book. Each table represents a separate domain, or skill set, measured by the exam.

Domain 1: Installation 19%

Objective		Chapter
1.1	Identify all system hardware required and check compatibility with Linux distribution	2
1.2	Determine appropriate method of installation based on environment	7
1.3	Install multimedia options	13
1.4	Identify purpose of Linux machine based on predetermined customer requirements	1
1.5	Determine what software and services should be installed	1, 2
1.6	Partition according to preinstallation plan using fdisk	3, 6

Domain 1: Installation (Continued)

Objective		Chapter
1.7	Configure filesystems	6
1.8	Configure a boot manager	9
1.9	Manage packages after installing the operating systems	12
1.10	Select appropriate networking configuration and protocols	14, 15
1.11	Select appropriate parameters for Linux installation	2, 3
1.12	Configure peripherals as necessary	2, 11

Domain 2: Management 26%

Objective		Chapter
2.1	Manage local storage devices and filesystems using CLI commands	6
2.2	Mount and unmount varied filesystems using CLI commands	6, 14
2.3	Create files and directories and modify files using CLI commands	4, 5
2.4	Execute content and directory searches using find and grep	4, 5
2.5	Create linked files using CLI commands	5
2.6	Modify file and directory permissions and ownership using CLI commands	5
2.7	Identify and modify default permissions for files and directories using CLI commands	5
2.8	Perform and verify backups and restores (tar, cpio)	12
2.9	Access and write data to recordable media	7, 12
2.10	Manage runlevels and system initialization from the CLI and configuration files	9
2.11	Identify, execute, manage, and kill processes	10
2.12	Differentiate core processes from noncritical services	10
2.13	Repair packages and scripts	12
2.14	Monitor and troubleshoot network activity	14, 15
2.15	Perform text manipulation	4, 8

Domain 2: Management (Continued)

Objective		Chapter
2.16	Manage print jobs and print queues	11
2.17	Perform remote management	14, 15
2.18	Perform NIS-related domain management	15
2.19	Create, modify, and use basic shell scripts	8
2.20	Create, modify, and delete user and group accounts using CLI utilities	6, 11
2.21	Manage mail queues using CLI utilities	14, 15
2.22	Schedule jobs to execute in the future using "at" and "cron" daemons	10
2.23	Redirect output	8

Domain 3: Configuration 20%

Objective		Chapter
3.1	Configure client network services and settings	14
3.2	Configure basic server network services	15
3.3	Implement basic routing and subnetting	14, 15
3.4	Configure the system and perform basic makefile changes to support compiling applications and drivers	12, 13
3.5	Configure files that are used to mount drives or partitions	6, 14
3.6	Implement DNS and describe how it works	14, 15
3.7	Configure a Network Interface Card (NIC) from a command line	14
3.8	Configure Linux printing	11, 15
3.9	Apply basic printer permissions	11
3.10	Configure log files	11
3.11	Configure the X Window system	8, 9
3.12	Set up environmental variables	8

Domain 4: Security 21%

Objective		Chapter
4.1	Configure security environment files	14, 15
4.2	Delete accounts while maintaining data stored in that user's home directory	11
4.3	Given security requirements, implement appropriate encryption configuration	15
4.4	Detect symptoms that indicate a machine's security has been compromised	11, 15
4.5	Use appropriate access level for login	15
4.6	Set process and special permissions	5
4.7	Identify different Linux Intrusion Detection Systems (IDS)	15
4.8	Given security requirements, implement basic IP tables/chains	15
4.9	Implement security auditing for files and authentication	15
4.10	Identify whether a package or file has been corrupted/altered	12, 15
4.11	Given a set of security requirements, set password policies to match (complexity/aging/shadowed passwords)	11
4.12	Identify security vulnerabilities within Linux services	15
4.13	Set up user-level security	11, 13

Domain 5: Documentation 6%

Objective		Chapter
5.1	Establish and monitor system performance baseline	13
5.2	Create written procedures for installation, configuration, security, and management	1–15
5.3	Document installed configuration	2, 3, 12, 13, 15
5.4	Troubleshoot errors using systems logs	4, 7, 11, 13
5.5	Troubleshoot application errors using application logs	4, 11, 13
5.6	Access system documentation and help files	1, 3

Domain 6: Hardware 8%

Objective	Chapter
6.1 Describe common hardware components and resources	2, 7
6.2 Diagnose hardware issues using Linux tools	7, 13, 14
6.3 Identify and configure removable system hardware	2
6.4 Configure advanced power management and Advanced Configuration and Power Interface (ACPI)	7
6.5 Identify and configure mass storage devices and RAID	2, 6, 7, 12

Appendix B

A copy of the GNU Public License referred to in Chapter 1 is shown here in Figure B-1. It can also be found on the Internet at *http://www.gnu.org*.

```
GNU GENERAL PUBLIC LICENSE
          Version 2, June 1991

Copyright (C) 1989, 1991 Free Software Foundation, Inc.
59 Temple Place, Suite 330, Boston, MA  02111-1307  USA
Everyone is permitted to copy and distribute verbatim copies
of this license document, but changing it is not allowed.


          Preamble

  The licenses for most software are designed to take away your
freedom to share and change it.  By contrast, the GNU General Public
License is intended to guarantee your freedom to share and change free
software--to make sure the software is free for all its users.  This
General Public License applies to most of the Free Software
Foundation's software and to any other program whose authors commit to
using it.  (Some other Free Software Foundation software is covered by
the GNU Library General Public License instead.)  You can apply it to
your programs, too.

  When we speak of free software, we are referring to freedom, not
price.  Our General Public Licenses are designed to make sure that you
have the freedom to distribute copies of free software (and charge for
this service if you wish), that you receive source code or can get it
if you want it, that you can change the software or use pieces of it
in new free programs; and that you know you can do these things.

  To protect your rights, we need to make restrictions that forbid
anyone to deny you these rights or to ask you to surrender the rights.
These restrictions translate to certain responsibilities for you if you
distribute copies of the software, or if you modify it.

  For example, if you distribute copies of such a program, whether
gratis or for a fee, you must give the recipients all the rights that
you have.  You must make sure that they, too, receive or can get the
source code.  And you must show them these terms so they know their
rights.
```

We protect your rights with two steps: (1) copyright the software, and
(2) offer you this license which gives you legal permission to copy,
distribute and/or modify the software.

Also, for each author's protection and ours, we want to make certain
that everyone understands that there is no warranty for this free
software. If the software is modified by someone else and passed on, we
want its recipients to know that what they have is not the original, so
that any problems introduced by others will not reflect on the original
authors' reputations.

Finally, any free program is threatened constantly by software
patents. We wish to avoid the danger that redistributors of a free
program will individually obtain patent licenses, in effect making the
program proprietary. To prevent this, we have made it clear that any
patent must be licensed for everyone's free use or not licensed at all.

The precise terms and conditions for copying, distribution and
modification follow.

GNU GENERAL PUBLIC LICENSE
TERMS AND CONDITIONS FOR COPYING, DISTRIBUTION AND MODIFICATION

0. This License applies to any program or other work which contains
a notice placed by the copyright holder saying it may be distributed
under the terms of this General Public License. The "Program", below,
refers to any such program or work, and a "work based on the Program"
means either the Program or any derivative work under copyright law:
that is to say, a work containing the Program or a portion of it,
either verbatim or with modifications and/or translated into another
language. (Hereinafter, translation is included without limitation in
the term "modification".) Each licensee is addressed as "you".

Activities other than copying, distribution and modification are not
covered by this License; they are outside its scope. The act of
running the Program is not restricted, and the output from the Program
is covered only if its contents constitute a work based on the
Program (independent of having been made by running the Program).
Whether that is true depends on what the Program does.

1. You may copy and distribute verbatim copies of the Program's
source code as you receive it, in any medium, provided that you
conspicuously and appropriately publish on each copy an appropriate
copyright notice and disclaimer of warranty; keep intact all the

notices that refer to this License and to the absence of any warranty; and give any other recipients of the Program a copy of this License along with the Program.

You may charge a fee for the physical act of transferring a copy, and you may at your option offer warranty protection in exchange for a fee.

  2. You may modify your copy or copies of the Program or any portion of it, thus forming a work based on the Program, and copy and distribute such modifications or work under the terms of Section 1 above, provided that you also meet all of these conditions:

  a) You must cause the modified files to carry prominent notices stating that you changed the files and the date of any change.

  b) You must cause any work that you distribute or publish, that in whole or in part contains or is derived from the Program or any part thereof, to be licensed as a whole at no charge to all third parties under the terms of this License.

  c) If the modified program normally reads commands interactively when run, you must cause it, when started running for such interactive use in the most ordinary way, to print or display an announcement including an appropriate copyright notice and a notice that there is no warranty (or else, saying that you provide a warranty) and that users may redistribute the program under these conditions, and telling the user how to view a copy of this License. (Exception: if the Program itself is interactive but does not normally print such an announcement, your work based on the Program is not required to print an announcement.)

These requirements apply to the modified work as a whole. If identifiable sections of that work are not derived from the Program, and can be reasonably considered independent and separate works in themselves, then this License, and its terms, do not apply to those sections when you distribute them as separate works. But when you distribute the same sections as part of a whole which is a work based on the Program, the distribution of the whole must be on the terms of this License, whose permissions for other licensees extend to the entire whole, and thus to each and every part regardless of who wrote it.

Thus, it is not the intent of this section to claim rights or contest your rights to work written entirely by you; rather, the intent is to exercise the right to control the distribution of derivative or collective works based on the Program.

In addition, mere aggregation of another work not based on the Program with the Program (or with a work based on the Program) on a volume of a storage or distribution medium does not bring the other work under the scope of this License.

   3. You may copy and distribute the Program (or a work based on it, under Section 2) in object code or executable form under the terms of Sections 1 and 2 above provided that you also do one of the following:

   a) Accompany it with the complete corresponding machine-readable source code, which must be distributed under the terms of Sections 1 and 2 above on a medium customarily used for software interchange; or,

   b) Accompany it with a written offer, valid for at least three years, to give any third party, for a charge no more than your cost of physically performing source distribution, a complete machine-readable copy of the corresponding source code, to be distributed under the terms of Sections 1 and 2 above on a medium customarily used for software interchange; or,

   c) Accompany it with the information you received as to the offer to distribute corresponding source code. (This alternative is allowed only for noncommercial distribution and only if you received the program in object code or executable form with such an offer, in accord with Subsection b above.)

The source code for a work means the preferred form of the work for making modifications to it. For an executable work, complete source code means all the source code for all modules it contains, plus any associated interface definition files, plus the scripts used to control compilation and installation of the executable. However, as a special exception, the source code distributed need not include anything that is normally distributed (in either source or binary form) with the major components (compiler, kernel, and so on) of the operating system on which the executable runs, unless that component itself accompanies the executable.

If distribution of executable or object code is made by offering access to copy from a designated place, then offering equivalent access to copy the source code from the same place counts as distribution of the source code, even though third parties are not compelled to copy the source along with the object code.

4. You may not copy, modify, sublicense, or distribute the Program except as expressly provided under this License. Any attempt otherwise to copy, modify, sublicense or distribute the Program is void, and will automatically terminate your rights under this License. However, parties who have received copies, or rights, from you under this License will not have their licenses terminated so long as such parties remain in full compliance.

5. You are not required to accept this License, since you have not signed it. However, nothing else grants you permission to modify or distribute the Program or its derivative works. These actions are prohibited by law if you do not accept this License. Therefore, by modifying or distributing the Program (or any work based on the Program), you indicate your acceptance of this License to do so, and all its terms and conditions for copying, distributing or modifying the Program or works based on it.

6. Each time you redistribute the Program (or any work based on the Program), the recipient automatically receives a license from the original licensor to copy, distribute or modify the Program subject to these terms and conditions. You may not impose any further restrictions on the recipients' exercise of the rights granted herein. You are not responsible for enforcing compliance by third parties to this License.

7. If, as a consequence of a court judgment or allegation of patent infringement or for any other reason (not limited to patent issues), conditions are imposed on you (whether by court order, agreement or otherwise) that contradict the conditions of this License, they do not excuse you from the conditions of this License. If you cannot distribute so as to satisfy simultaneously your obligations under this License and any other pertinent obligations, then as a consequence you may not distribute the Program at all. For example, if a patent license would not permit royalty-free redistribution of the Program by all those who receive copies directly or indirectly through you, then the only way you could satisfy both it and this License would be to refrain entirely from distribution of the Program.

If any portion of this section is held invalid or unenforceable under any particular circumstance, the balance of the section is intended to apply and the section as a whole is intended to apply in other circumstances.

It is not the purpose of this section to induce you to infringe any patents or other property right claims or to contest validity of any such claims; this section has the sole purpose of protecting the integrity of the free software distribution system, which is implemented by public license practices. Many people have made generous contributions to the wide range of software distributed through that system in reliance on consistent application of that system; it is up to the author/donor to decide if he or she is willing to distribute software through any other system and a licensee cannot impose that choice.

This section is intended to make thoroughly clear what is believed to be a consequence of the rest of this License.

8. If the distribution and/or use of the Program is restricted in certain countries either by patents or by copyrighted interfaces, the original copyright holder who places the Program under this License may add an explicit geographical distribution limitation excluding those countries, so that distribution is permitted only in or among countries not thus excluded. In such case, this License incorporates the limitation as if written in the body of this License.

9. The Free Software Foundation may publish revised and/or new versions of the General Public License from time to time. Such new versions will be similar in spirit to the present version, but may differ in detail to address new problems or concerns.

Each version is given a distinguishing version number. If the Program specifies a version number of this License which applies to it and "any later version", you have the option of following the terms and conditions either of that version or of any later version published by the Free Software Foundation. If the Program does not specify a version number of this License, you may choose any version ever published by the Free Software Foundation.

10. If you wish to incorporate parts of the Program into other free programs whose distribution conditions are different, write to the author to ask for permission. For software which is copyrighted by the Free Software Foundation, write to the Free Software Foundation; we sometimes make exceptions for this. Our decision will be guided by the two goals of preserving the free status of all derivatives of our free software and of promoting the sharing and reuse of software generally.

NO WARRANTY

11. BECAUSE THE PROGRAM IS LICENSED FREE OF CHARGE, THERE IS NO WARRANTY
FOR THE PROGRAM, TO THE EXTENT PERMITTED BY APPLICABLE LAW. EXCEPT WHEN
OTHERWISE STATED IN WRITING THE COPYRIGHT HOLDERS AND/OR OTHER PARTIES
PROVIDE THE PROGRAM "AS IS" WITHOUT WARRANTY OF ANY KIND, EITHER EXPRESSED
OR IMPLIED, INCLUDING, BUT NOT LIMITED TO, THE IMPLIED WARRANTIES OF
MERCHANTABILITY AND FITNESS FOR A PARTICULAR PURPOSE. THE ENTIRE RISK AS
TO THE QUALITY AND PERFORMANCE OF THE PROGRAM IS WITH YOU. SHOULD THE
PROGRAM PROVE DEFECTIVE, YOU ASSUME THE COST OF ALL NECESSARY SERVICING,
REPAIR OR CORRECTION.

12. IN NO EVENT UNLESS REQUIRED BY APPLICABLE LAW OR AGREED TO IN WRITING
WILL ANY COPYRIGHT HOLDER, OR ANY OTHER PARTY WHO MAY MODIFY AND/OR
REDISTRIBUTE THE PROGRAM AS PERMITTED ABOVE, BE LIABLE TO YOU FOR DAMAGES,
INCLUDING ANY GENERAL, SPECIAL, INCIDENTAL OR CONSEQUENTIAL DAMAGES ARISING
OUT OF THE USE OR INABILITY TO USE THE PROGRAM (INCLUDING BUT NOT LIMITED
TO LOSS OF DATA OR DATA BEING RENDERED INACCURATE OR LOSSES SUSTAINED BY
YOU OR THIRD PARTIES OR A FAILURE OF THE PROGRAM TO OPERATE WITH ANY OTHER
PROGRAMS), EVEN IF SUCH HOLDER OR OTHER PARTY HAS BEEN ADVISED OF THE
POSSIBILITY OF SUCH DAMAGES.

END OF TERMS AND CONDITIONS

How to Apply These Terms to Your New Programs

If you develop a new program, and you want it to be of the greatest
possible use to the public, the best way to achieve this is to make it
free software which everyone can redistribute and change under these terms.

To do so, attach the following notices to the program. It is safest
to attach them to the start of each source file to most effectively
convey the exclusion of warranty; and each file should have at least
the "copyright" line and a pointer to where the full notice is found.

, 1 April 1989
Ty Coon, President of Vice

This General Public License does not permit incorporating your program into
proprietary programs. If your program is a subroutine library, you may
consider it more useful to permit linking proprietary applications with the
library. If this is what you want to do, use the GNU Library General
Public License instead of this License.

Appendix C

Open source development has made Linux a powerful and versatile operating system; however, this development has also increased the complexity of Linux and Linux resources available on the Internet. Newcomers to Linux might find this bounty of resources intimidating, but there are some simple rules that make finding particular types of Linux resources easier. Understanding how to navigate the Internet to find these resources is a valuable skill to develop.

By far, the easiest way to locate resources on any topic is by using a search engine such as *http://www.google.com* in which you can simply enter a phrase representing what you are searching for and receive a list of Web sites containing relevant material. However, because a plethora of Linux-related Web sites are available on the Internet, a search of the word "Linux" yields thousands of results. You might need to be more specific in your request to a search engine to obtain a list of Web sites that likely contain the information you desire. Thus, it is very important to approach Linux documentation by topic; otherwise, you might search for hours through several Web sites to find the resources you need.

Many Web sites describe the features of Linux and Open Source Software. Many of these Web sites contain links to other Linux resources organized by topic, and, hence, are a good place for people to start if they are new to Linux and desire some background or terminology. Unfortunately, many of the sites do not follow a common naming scheme. Table C-1 is a partial list of some valuable Web sites offering general Linux information.

Table C-1 General Linux and open source Web sites

Description	Web Site
Linux Online	*http://www.linux.org*
Linux International	*http://www.li.org*
Linux Jargon File (Terminology)	*http://catb.org/~esr/jargon/html/*
The Cathedral and the Bazaar (History of Open Source)	*http://www.catb.org/~esr/writings/cathedral-bazaar/*
The Free Software Foundation	*http://www.gnu.org*

Other important sources of information, for inexperienced and expert Linux users alike, are Linux news sites. Some of these Web sites are hosted by organizations that publish trade magazines, and, as a result, share the same name as the magazine with a .com suffix, making the

Web site easier to find. One example is the Linux Journal, which can be found at *http://www.linuxjournal.com*. Often, these sites contain more than just Linux news; they also contain tutorials, FAQs (frequently asked questions), and links to other Linux resources. Table C-2 lists some common Linux news Web sites.

Table C-2 Common Linux news Web sites

Description	Web Site
Linux Journal (magazine)	*http://www.linuxjournal.com*
Linux Today (magazine)	*http://www.linuxtoday.com*
Slashdot	*http://www.slashdot.org*
Linux Weekly News	*http://www.lwn.net*
Linux News	*http://www.linuxnews.com*
Linux Gazette (magazine)	*http://www.linuxgazette.com*
Linux Focus	*http://www.linuxfocus.org*
Linux Magazine (magazine)	*http://www.linux-mag.com*
SysAdmin Magazine (magazine)	*http://www.samag.com*

Although many Web sites offer general information and news regarding Linux and Open Source Software, the most important resources the Internet offers are help files and product documentation. These resources take many forms, including instructions for completing tasks (HOWTO documents), frequently asked questions (FAQs), supporting documentation (text files and HTML files), and newsgroup postings (Usenet). Almost every Web site containing Linux information of some type provides at least one of these resources; however, many centralized Web sites make finding this information easier. Table C-3 lists some common Web sites that make locating documentation and help files easier.

Table C-3 Common Linux documentation and help resources

Description	Web Site
Linux Documentation Project (HOWTOs)	*http://www.tldp.org*
Linux Help Network	*http://www.linuxhelp.net*
Google Newsgroups (formerly Deja News)	*http://groups.google.com*

In many cases, you can find help on a particular Open Source Software component for Linux by visiting its development Web site. Most large Open Source Software projects, such as the KDE project, have their own Web site where information and news regarding the software is available and the latest release can be downloaded. These Web sites usually follow the naming convention http://www.*projectname*.org, where "*projectname*" is the name of the project, and, thus, are easy to locate without the use of a search engine. Table C-4 is a partial list of common Open Source Software project Web sites available on the Internet.

Table C-4 Open Source Software project Web sites

Description	Web Site
The Apache Web Server	*http://www.apache.org*
The KDE Desktop	*http://www.kde.org*
The GNOME Desktop	*http://www.gnome.org*
The Xfree86 Project (X Windows)	*http://www.xfree86.org*
The X.org Project (X Windows)	*http://www.x.org*
The Linux Kernel	*http://www.kernel.org*

Smaller Open Source Software packages and projects rarely have Web sites hosting the development. Instead, they are listed on Open Source Software repository Web sites, also known as Open Source Software archives, which contain thousands of software packages available for download. Often, these Web sites offer several different distributions of Linux as well, conveniently saving a visit to a distribution Web site in order to obtain one. There are many repository Web sites, a sampling of which is listed in Table C-5.

Table C-5 Common Open Source Software archives

Description	Web Site
Freshmeat	*http://www.freshmeat.net*
SourceForge	*http://www.sourceforge.net*
Tucows	*http://linux.tucows.com*
Linux Online	*http://www.linux.org/apps/*
Ibiblio	*http://www.ibiblio.org/pub/Linux/*

Appendix D

Answers to Chapter Review Questions

Chapter 1

1. b
2. a
3. c
4. c
5. a
6. True
7. False
8. False
9. False
10. True
11. programming language
12. artistic
13. package manager
14. workstation
15. Beowulf

Chapter 2

1. d
2. a
3. c
4. c
5. d
6. False
7. True
8. True
9. True
10. False
11. Level 2 (L2)
12. articulated
13. partitions
14. Plug-and-Play (PnP)
15. 12

Chapter 3

1. c
2. a
3. c
4. b
5. a
6. True
7. False
8. False
9. True
10. False
11. Framebuffers
12. server
13. Dual
14. shell
15. manual

Chapter 4

1. b	**9.** False
2. a	**10.** True
3. a	**11.** tab-completion
4. c	**12.** Linked
5. d	**13.** ls –l
6. True	**14.** head
7. True	**15.** grep
8. False	

Chapter 5

1. d	**9.** False
2. c	**10.** True
3. a	**11.** mv
4. c	**12.** hard
5. d	**13.** primary
6. False	**14.** mode
7. True	**15.** umask
8. True	

Chapter 6

1. b	**9.** False
2. d	**10.** True
3. a	**11.** device
4. d	**12.** root
5. b	**13.** SCSI
6. True	**14.** fdisk
7. False	**15.** syncing
8. False	

Chapter 7

1. a
2. c
3. c
4. d
5. c
6. False
7. True
8. True
9. False
10. False
11. Interrupt Request (IRQ)
12. mirroring
13. Server Message Block (SMB)
14. CMOS
15. install.log.syslog

Chapter 8

1. c
2. a
3. b
4. d
5. b
6. True
7. False
8. True
9. False
10. False
11. descriptors
12. nl
13. $PWD
14. subshell
15. env

Chapter 9

1. b
2. c
3. d
4. a
5. c
6. False
7. True
8. True
9. False
10. False
11. U
12. NTLOADER
13. runlevel
14. Window
15. mouseconfig

Chapter 10

1.	b	**9.**	True
2.	c	**10.**	True
3.	a	**11.**	child
4.	d	**12.**	S
5.	b	**13.**	rogue
6.	True	**14.**	forking
7.	False	**15.**	slice
8.	False		

Chapter 11

1.	d	**9.**	True
2.	a	**10.**	False
3.	c	**11.**	Common Unix
4.	d	**12.**	cancel
5.	a	**13.**	auth (security)
6.	True	**14.**	authentication
7.	False	**15.**	groups
8.	False		

Chapter 12

1.	d	**9.**	True
2.	c	**10.**	False
3.	b	**11.**	ratio
4.	a	**12.**	bz2
5.	b	**13.**	tarballs
6.	False	**14.**	incremental
7.	True	**15.**	make
8.	False		

Chapter 13

1. b
2. d
3. c
4. a
5. c
6. True
7. False
8. True

9. False
10. False
11. Monitoring
12. kudzu
13. jabbering
14. free
15. lsmod

Chapter 14

1. d
2. d
3. b
4. c
5. a
6. True
7. False
8. False

9. False
10. True
11. network
12. subnet
13. ping
14. /etc/hosts
15. telnet

Chapter 15

1. c
2. b
3. d
4. b
5. a
6. True
7. False
8. True

9. False
10. True
11. port
12. reverse
13. Apache
14. Network Information Service (NIS)
15. su (switch user)

Glossary

<—A shell metacharacter used to obtain Standard Input from a file.

>—A shell metacharacter used to redirect Standard Output and Standard Error to a file.

|—A shell metacharacter used to pipe Standard Output from one command to the Standard Input of another command.

~ metacharacter—A metacharacter used to represent a user's home directory.

/bin directory—The directory that contains binary commands for use by all users.

/boot—The directory that contains the kernel and boot-related files.

/boot directory—The directory that contains the Linux kernel and files used by the boot loader data block.

/boot/grub/grub.conf—The GRUB configuration file.

/dev directory—The directory off the root where device files are typically stored.

/dev/MAKEDEV—The command used to recreate a device file if one or more of the following pieces of device information is unknown: major number, minor number, or type (character or block).

/etc directory—The directory that contains system-specific configuration files.

/etc/at.allow—A file listing all users who can use the at command.

/etc/at.deny—A file listing all users who cannot access the at command.

/etc/cron.allow—A file listing all users who can use the cron command.

/etc/cron.d—A directory that contains additional system cron tables.

/etc/cron.deny—A file listing all users who cannot access the cron command.

/etc/crontab—The default system cron table.

/etc/cups/cupsd.conf—A file that holds daemon configuration for the cups daemon.

/etc/cups/printers.conf—A file that holds printer configuration for the cups daemon.

/etc/default/useradd—A file that contains default values for user creation.

/etc/dumpdates—The file used to store information about incremental and full backups for use by the dump/restore utility.

/etc/fstab—A file used to specify which filesystems to mount automatically at boot time and queried by the mount command if an insufficient number of arguments are specified.

/etc/group—The file that contains group definitions and memberships.

/etc/inittab—The configuration file for the init daemon.

/etc/ld.so.cache file—The file that contains the location of shared library files.

/etc/ld.so.conf file—The file that contains a list of directories that contain shared libraries.

/etc/lilo.conf—The LILO configuration file.

/etc/login.defs—A file that contains default values for user creation.

/etc/logrotate.conf—The file used by the logrotate utility to specify rotation parameters for log files.

/etc/modprobe.conf file—The file used to load and alias modules at system initialization.

/etc/mtab—A file that stores a list of currently mounted filesystems.

/etc/passwd—The file that contains user account information.

/etc/rc.d/init.d—The directory in which most daemons are located.

/etc/rc.d/rc*.d—The directories used to start and kill daemons in each runlevel.

/etc/rc.d/rc.local—The final script executed during system startup.

/etc/rc.d/rc.sysinit—The first script executed during system startup.

/etc/shadow—The file that contains the encrypted password as well as password and account expiry parameters for each user account.

/etc/skel—A directory that contains files that are copied to all new users' home directories upon creation.

/etc/syslog.conf—The file that specifies the events that the System Log Daemon listens for and the log files to which it saves the events.

/etc/X11/XF86Config—The configuration file used by the XFree86 implementation of X Windows.

/etc/X11/xorg.conf—The configuration file used by the X.org implementation of X Windows.

/home directory—The default location for user home directories.

/lib directory—The directory that contains shared program libraries (used by the commands in /bin and /sbin) as well as kernel modules.

/mnt directory—An empty directory used for accessing (mounting) disks, such as floppy disks and CD-ROMs.

/opt directory—The directory that stores additional software programs.

/proc directory—The directory that contains process and kernel information.

/proc/cpuinfo—The directory that contains information on current CPU setup on the system.

/proc/devices—A file that contains currently used device information.

/proc/dma—The directory that contains information on current direct memory access assignments on the system.

/proc/interrupts—The directory that contains information on current Interrupt Request assignments on the system.

/proc/ioports—The directory that contains information on current Input/Output address assignments on the system.

/proc/meminfo—The directory that contains information on the current memory usage situation, both physical and virtual, on the system.

/proc/modules—The directory that contains information on what modules are currently incorporated into the kernel.

/root directory—The root user's home directory.

/sbin directory—The directory that contains system binary commands (used for administration).

/tmp directory—The directory that holds temporary files created by programs.

/usr directory—The directory that contains most system commands and utilities.

/usr/local directory—The location for most additional programs.

/usr/src/linux directory—The directory that typically contains source code for the Linux kernel during compilation.

/var directory—The directory that contains log files and spools.

/var/log—A directory that contains most log files on a Linux system.

/var/log directory—The directory that contains most system log files.

/var/spool/at—A directory that stores the information used to schedule commands using the at daemon.

/var/spool/cron—A directory that stores user cron tables.

absolute pathname—The full pathname to a certain file or directory starting from the root directory.

Accelerated Graphics Port (AGP)—A motherboard connection slot designed for video card peripherals allowing data transfer speeds of over 66MHz.

accepting printer—A printer that accepts print jobs into the print queue.

active partition—The partition searched for an operating system after the MBR.

Advanced Configuration and Power Interface (ACPI)—A standard that allows an operating system the ability to control when power is supplied to peripheral components.

Advanced Power Management (APM)—A BIOS feature that shuts off power to peripheral devices that are not being used to save electricity; commonly used on laptop computers.

Advanced Technology Attachment (ATA)—*See also* Integrated Drive Electronics.

AIX—A version of UNIX developed by IBM.

alias command—A command used to create special variables that are shortcuts to longer command strings.

ANDing—The process by which binary bits are compared to calculate the network and host IDs from an IP address and subnet mask.

application—The software that runs on an operating system and provides the user with specific functionality (such as word processing or financial calculation).

architecture—The design and layout of a CPU; also called a computer platform.

archive—The location (file or device) that contains a copy of files; it is typically created by a back-up utility.

arguments—The text that appears after a command name, does not start with a dash "-" character, and specifies information the command requires to work properly.

Arithmetic Logic Unit (ALU)—The section of the CPU in which all the mathematical calculations and logic-based operations are executed.

artistic license—An open source license that allows source code to be distributed freely, but changed at the discretion of the original author.

asymmetric multiprocessing—A system containing more than one processor in which each processor is given a certain role or set of tasks to complete independently of the other processors.

at command—The command used to schedule commands and tasks to run at a preset time in the future.

at daemon (atd)—The system daemon that executes tasks at a future time; it is configured with the at command.

authentication—The act of verifying a user's identity by comparing a user name and password to a system database (/etc/passwd and /etc/shadow).

awk command—A filter command used to search for and display text.

background (bg) command—The command used to run a foreground process in the background.

background process—A process that does not require the BASH shell to wait for its termination; upon execution, the user receives the BASH shell prompt immediately.

bad blocks—The areas of a storage medium unable to store data properly.

baseline—A measure of normal system activity.

BASH shell—The Bourne Again Shell; it is the default command-line interface in Linux.

BBC Linux—A CD-based Linux distribution.

Beowulf clustering—A popular and widespread method of clustering computers together to perform useful tasks using Linux.

binary data file—A file that contains machine language (binary 1s and 0s) and stores information (such as common functions and graphics) used by binary compiled programs.

BIOS (Basic Input/Output System) ROM—The computer chips on a computer mainboard that contain the programs used to initialize hardware components at boot time.

bit—The smallest unit of information that a computer can compute.

block—The unit of data commonly used by filesystem commands; a block can contain several sectors.

block devices—The storage devices that transfer data to and from the system in chunks of many data bits by caching the information in RAM; they are represented by block device files.

boot loader—A small program started by BIOS ROM, which executes the Linux kernel in memory.

boot.ini—The file used to configure NTLOADER.

broadcast—The TCP/IP communication destined for all computers on a network.

BSD (Berkeley Software Distribution)—A version of UNIX developed out of the original UNIX source code and given free to the University of California at Berkeley by AT&T.

buffer overrun—An attack in which a network service is altered in memory.

bunzip2 command—The command used to decompress files compressed by the bzip2 command.

burning—The process of writing information to a CD-R, CD-RW, DVD-R, or DVD-RW.

burning software—The software that can write files to CD and DVD.

bus—A term that represents the pathway information takes from one hardware device to another via a mainboard.

bus mastering—The process by which peripheral components perform tasks normally executed by the CPU.

bzcat command—A command used to view the contents of an archive created with bzip2 to Standard Output.

bzip2 command—The command used to compress files using a Burrows-Wheeler Block Sorting Huffman Coding compression algorithm.

bzless command—A command used to view the contents of an archive created with bzip2 to Standard Output in a page-by-page fashion.

bzmore command—A command used to view the contents of an archive created with bzip2 to Standard Output in a page-by-page fashion.

cache—A temporary store of information used by the processor.

cancel command—The command used to remove print jobs from the print queue in the CUPS print system.

cat command—A Linux command used to display (or concatenate) the entire contents of a text file to the screen.

cd (change directory) command—A Linux command used to change the current directory in the directory tree.

central processing unit (CPU)—An integrated circuit board used to perform the majority of all calculations on a computer system; also known as a processor or microprocessor.

chage command—The command used to modify password expiry information for user accounts.

chains—The components of a firewall that specify the general type of network traffic to which rules apply.

character devices—The storage devices that transfer data to and from the system one data bit at a time; they are represented by character device files.

checksum—A calculated value that is unique to a file's size and contents.

chgrp (change group) command—The command used to change the group owner of a file or directory.

child process—A process that was started by another process (parent process).

chipset—The common set of computer chips on a peripheral component such as a video adapter card.

chmod (change mode) command—The command used to change the mode (permissions) of a file or directory.

chown (change owner) command—The command used to change the owner and group owner of a file or directory.

chsh command—The command used to change a valid shell to an invalid shell.

classless interdomain routing (CIDR) notation—A notation that is often used to represent an IP address and its subnet mask.

clock speed—The speed at which a processor (or any other hardware device) can execute commands related to an internal time cycle.

closed source software—The software whose source code is not freely available from the original author; Windows 98, for example.

cluster—A grouping of several smaller computers that function as one large supercomputer.

clustering—The act of making a cluster; *see also* Cluster.

color depth—The total set of colors that can be displayed on a computer video screen.

COM ports—The rectangular, nine-pin connectors that can be used to connect a variety of different peripherals to the mainboard, including mice, serial printers, scanners, and digital cameras; also called serial ports.

command—A program that exists on the hard drive and is executed when typed on the command line.

command mode—One of the two input modes in vi; it allows a user to perform any available text editing task that is not related to inserting text into the document.

Common Unix Printing System (CUPS)—The printing system commonly used on Linux computers today.

compact disc-read only memory (CD-ROM)—The physically durable, removable storage media, which is resistant to data corruption and used in CD-ROM drives and CD-RW drives.

complementary metal-oxide semiconductor (CMOS)—A memory store on the mainboard used to store configuration information for use during the boot process; not a true ROM chip, it requires a low level flow of electricity from an onboard battery to maintain the memory store.

Complex Instruction Set Computers (CISC)—The processors that execute complex instructions on each time cycle.

compress command—The command used to compress files using a Lempel-Ziv compression algorithm.

compression—The process in which files are reduced in size by a compression algorithm.

compression algorithm—The set of instructions used to reduce the contents of a file systematically.

compression ratio—The amount of compression that occurred during compression.

compressor/decompressor (codec)—A file that contains the rules to compres or decompress multimedia information.

concatenation—The joining of text together to make one larger whole. In Linux, words and strings of text are joined together to form a displayed file.

Control Unit (CU)—The area in a processor where instruction code or commands are loaded and carried out.

copy in/out (cpio) command—A common back-up utility.

cp (copy) command—The command used to create copies of files and directories.

cracker—A person who uses computer software maliciously for personal profit.

cron daemon (crond)—The system daemon that executes tasks repetitively in the future—it is configured using cron tables.

cron table—A file specifying tasks to be run by the cron daemon; there are user cron tables and system cron tables.

crontab command—The command used to view and edit user cron tables.

cups daemon (cupsd)—The daemon responsible for printing in the CUPS printing system.

cylinder—A series of tracks on a hard disk that are written to simultaneously by the magnetic heads in a hard disk drive.

daemon—A Linux system process that provides a certain service.

daemon process—A system process that is not associated with a terminal.

data blocks—A filesystem allocation unit in which the data that makes up the contents of the file as well as the filename are stored.

database—An organized set of data.

Database Management System (DBMS)—The software that manages databases.

decision construct—A special construct used in a shell script to alter the flow of the program based on the outcome of a command or contents of a variable—common decision constructs include if, case, &&, and ||.

default gateway—The IP address of the router on the network used to send packets to remote networks.

desktop environment—The software that works with a Window Manager to provide a standard GUI environment that uses standard programs and development tools.

Desktop Switching Tool—A graphical tool that allows Red Hat Linux users to set the default desktop environment or Window Manager.

developmental kernel—A Linux kernel whose minor number is odd and has been recently developed, yet not thoroughly tested.

device driver—A piece of software, which contains instructions that the kernel of an operating system uses to control and interact with a specific type of computer hardware.

device file—A file used by Linux commands that represents a specific device on the system; these files do not have a data section and use major and minor numbers to reference the proper driver and specific device on the system, respectively.

df (disk free space) command—A command that displays disk free space by filesystem.

direct memory access (DMA)—A capability provided by some bus architectures that allows peripheral devices the ability to bypass the CPU and talk directly with other peripheral components to enhance performance.

directive—A line within a configuration file.

directory—A special file on the filesystem used to organize other files into a logical tree structure.

disabled printer—A printer that does not send print jobs from the print queue to a printer.

disk drive—A device that contains either a hard disk, floppy disk, CD-ROM, CD-RW, or Zip disk.

Disk Druid—An easy-to-use graphic program used to partition or modify the partitions on an HDD.

disk imaging software—The software that is used to make identical copies of hard drives or hard drive partitions.

disk mirroring—A RAID configuration, also known as RAID 1, that consists of two identical hard disks, which are written to in parallel with the same information to ensure fault tolerance.

disk striping—A RAID configuration, a type of RAID 0, which is used to write separate information to different hard disks to speed up access time.

disk striping with parity—A RAID configuration, also known as RAID 5, that is used to write separate information to hard disks to speed up access time, and also contains parity information to ensure fault tolerance.

distribution—A complete set of operating system software, including the Linux kernel, supporting function libraries, and a variety of OSS packages that can be downloaded from the Internet free of charge. These OSS packages are what differentiate the various distributions of Linux.

DNS cache file—A file that contains the IP addresses of top-level DNS servers.

DNS servers—The servers that resolve fully qualified domain names (FQDNs) such as *www.linux.org* to IP addresses so that users can connect to them across the Internet.

document root—The directory that stores default HTML content for a Web server.

documentation—The system information that is stored in a log book for future reference.

Domain Name Space (DNS)—A hierarchical namespace used for host names.

Double Data Rate Synchronous Dynamic Random Access Memory (DDR SDRAM)—A form of SDRAM that can transfer information at higher speeds than traditional SDRAM.

du (directory usage) command—A command that displays directory usage.

dual boot—A configuration in which two or more operating systems exist on the hard disk of a computer; a boot loader allows the user to choose which operating system to load at boot time.

dual inline memory modules (DIMM)—A newer connection slot having connectors (pins) along both edges, allowing the array of integrated circuits comprising a stick of RAM to connect to the motherboard.

dump command—A utility used to create full and incremental backups.

Dynamic Host Configuration Protocol (DHCP) server—A server on the network that hands out Internet Protocol (IP) configuration to computers that request it.

dynamic RAM (DRAM)—A type of RAM that needs to refresh its store of information thousands of times per second and is available as a SIMM or DIMM stick.

echo command—A command used to display or echo output to the terminal screen—it might utilize escape sequences.

edquota command—A command used to specify quota limits for users and groups.

egrep command—A variant of the grep command used to search files for patterns using extended regular expressions.

electronically erasable programmable read-only memory (EEPROM)—A type of ROM whose information store can not only be erased and rewritten as a whole, but can also be modified singly, leaving other portions intact.

ELILO—A boot loader used with computers that support Intel Extensible Firmware Interface (EFI) technology.

Emacs (Editor MACroS) editor—A popular and widespread text editor more conducive to word processing than vi; developed by Richard Stallman.

enabled printer—A printer that sends print jobs from the print queue to a printer.

env command—A command used to display a list of exported variables present in the current shell except special variables.

environment files—The files used immediately after login to execute commands; they are typically used to load variables into memory.

environment variables—The variables that store information commonly accessed by the system or programs executing on the system—together these variables form the user environment.

erasable programmable read-only memory (EPROM)—A type of ROM whose information store can be erased and rewritten, but only as a whole.

escape sequences—The character sequences that have special meaning inside the echo command—they are prefixed by the \ character.

Ethernet—The most common media access method used in networks today.

executable program—A file that can be executed by the Linux operating system to run in memory as a process and perform a useful function.

Explicitly Parallel Instruction Computing (EPIC)—The RISC architecture used to describe the Itanium processor.

export command—A command used to send variables to subshells.

ext2—A nonjournaling Linux filesystem.

ext3—A journaling Linux filesystem.

Extended Multiuser Mode—Also called run-level 3; the mode that provides most daemons and a full set of networking daemons.

extended partition—A partition on a HDD that can be further subdivided into components called logical drives.

facility—The area of the system from which information is gathered when logging system events.

fault tolerant—A device that exhibits a minimum of downtime in the event of a failure.

fdisk command—A command used to create, delete, and manipulate partitions on hard disks.

fgrep command—A variant of the grep command that does not allow the use of regular expressions.

file command—A Linux command that displays the file type of a specified filename.

file descriptors—The numeric labels used to define command input and command output.

File Transfer Protocol (FTP)—The most common protocol used to transfer files across the Internet.

filehandles—The connections that a program makes to files on a filesystem.

filename—The user-friendly identifier given to a file.

filename extension—A series of identifiers following a dot (.) at the end of a filename used to denote the type of the file; the filename extention .txt denotes a text file.

filesystem—The organization imposed on a physical storage medium that is used to manage the storage and retrieval of data.

filesystem corruption—The errors in a filesystem structure that prevent the retrieval of stored data.

Filesystem Hierarchy Standard (FHS)—A standard outlining the location of set files and directories on a Linux system.

filter command—A command that can take from Standard Input and send to Standard Output—in other words, a filter is a command that can exist in the middle of a pipe.

find command—The command used to find files on the filesystem using various criteria.

FireWire (IEEE 1394)—A mainboard connection technology that was developed by Apple Computer Inc. in 1995 and supports data transfer speeds of up to 800MB per second.

First nondestructive Interactive Partition Splitter (FIPS)—A program used to create a new partition out of the free space on an existing FAT16 or FAT32 partition.

firstboot wizard—A configuration utility that is run at system startup immediately following a Red Hat Fedora Linux installation.

flash memory drive—A storage medium that uses EEPROM chips to store data.

floppy disks—A removable storage media consisting of a flexible medium coated with a ferrous material that are read by floppy disk drives.

foreground (fg) command—The command used to run a background process in the foreground.

foreground process—A process for which the BASH shell that executed it must wait for its termination.

forking—The act of creating a new BASH shell child process from a parent BASH shell process.

formatting—The process in which a filesystem is placed on a disk device.

forward lookup—A DNS name resolution request whereby a FQDN is resolved to an IP address.

framebuffer—An abstract representation of video hardware used by programs such that they do not need to communicate directly with the video hardware.

free command—A command used to display memory and swap statistics.

Free Software Foundation (FSF)—An organization started by Richard Stallman, which promotes and encourages the collaboration of software developers worldwide to allow the free sharing of source code and software programs.

freeware—The computer software programs distributed and made available at no cost to the user by the developer.

frequently asked questions (FAQs)—An area on a Web site where answers to commonly posed questions can be found.

fsck (filesystem check) command—A command used to check the integrity of a filesystem and repair damaged files.

ftp utility—A utility that can be used to download files from an FTP server.

full backup—An archive of an entire filesystem.

fully qualified domain names (FQDN)—The user-friendly names used to identify machines on networks and on the Internet.

fuser command—A command used to identify any users or processes using a particular file or directory.

gateway—Also known as default gateway or gateway of last resort, the address of a computer that accepts information from the local computer and sends it to other computers if the local computer cannot.

gedit editor—A text editor for the GNOME desktop.

General Electric Comprehensive Operating System (GECOS)—The field in the /etc/passwd file that contains a description of the user account.

GNOME Display Manager (gdm)—A graphical login program that provides a graphical login screen.

GNU—An acronym, which stands for "GNU's Not Unix."

GNU C Compiler (gcc) command—The command used to compile source code into binary programs.

GNU Image Manipulation Program (GIMP)—An open source graphics manipulation program that uses the GTK+ toolkit.

GNU Network Object Model Environment (GNOME)—One of the two competing graphical user interface (GUI) environments for Linux.

GNU Object Model Environment (GNOME)—The default desktop environment in Red Hat Fedora Linux; it was created in 1997.

GNU Project—A free operating system project started by Richard Stallman.

GNU Public License (GPL)—A software license, ensuring that the source code for any Open Source Software will remain freely available to anyone who wants to examine, build on, or improve upon it.

GNU zip (gzip) command—A command used to compress files using a Lempel-Ziv compression algorithm.

Grand Unified Bootloader (GRUB)—A program used to boot the Linux operating system.

graphical user interface (GUI)—The component of an operating system that provides a user-friendly interface comprising graphics or icons to represent desired tasks. Users can point and click to execute a command rather than having to know and use proper command-line syntax.

grep (Global Regular Expression Print) command—A Linux command that searches files for patterns of characters using regular expression metacharacters.

group—When used in the mode of a certain file or directory, the collection of users who have ownership of that file or directory.

Group Identifier (GID)—A unique number given to each group.

groupadd command—The command used to add a group to the system.

groupdel command—The command used to delete a group from the system.

groupmod command—The command used to modify the name or GID of a group on the system.

GRUB root partition—The partition containing the second stage of the GRUB boot loader and the /boot/grub/grub.conf file.

grub-install command—The command used to install the GRUB boot loader.

grub-md5-crypt command—The command used to generate an encrypted password for use in the /etc/grub/grub.conf file.

GTK+ toolkit—A development toolkit for C programming; it is used in the GNOME desktop and the GNU Image Manipulation Program (GIMP).

GUI environment—A GUI core component such as X Windows, combined with a Window Manager and desktop environment that provides the look and feel of the GUI. Although functionality might be similar among GUI environments, users might prefer one environment to another due to its ease of use.

gunzip command—The command used to decompress files compressed by the gzip command.

hacker—A person who explores computer science to gain knowledge. Not to be confused with cracker.

hard disk drive (HDD)—A device used to write and read data to and from a hard disk.

hard disk quotas—The limits on the number of files, or total storage space on a hard disk drive, available to a user.

hard disks—Nonremovable media consisting of a rigid disk coated with a ferrous material and used in hard disk drives (HDD).

hard limit—A limit imposed that cannot be exceeded.

hard link—A file joined to other files on the same filesystem that shares the same inode.

hardware—The tangible parts of a computer, such as the network boards, video card, hard disk drives, printers, and keyboards.

Hardware Compatibility List (HCL)—A list of hardware components that have been tested and deemed compatible with a given operating system.

hardware platform—A particular configuration and grouping of computer hardware, normally centered on and determined by processor type and architecture.

hashpling—The first line in a shell script, which defines the shell that will be used to interpret the commands in the script file.

head command—A Linux command that displays the first set of lines of a text file; by default, the head command displays the first 10 lines.

home directory—A directory on the filesystem set aside for users to store personal files and information.

host ID—The portion of an IP address that denotes the host.

host name—A user-friendly name used to uniquely identify a computer on a network. This name is usually a FQDN.

hostname command—A command used to display and change the host name of a computer.

hot fix—A solution for a software bug made by a closed source vendor.

hot-swappable—The ability to add or remove hardware to or from a computer while the computer and operating system are functional.

HOWTO—A task-specific instruction guide to performing any of a wide variety of tasks; freely available from the Linux Documentation Project at *http://www.linuxdoc.org*.

HP-UX—A version of UNIX developed by Hewlett-Packard.

HSync (horizontal refresh)—The rate at which horizontal elements of the video screen image are refreshed, allowing for changes or animation on the screen; HSync is measured in Hertz (Hz).

Hypertext Transfer Protocol (HTTP)—The underlying protocol used to transfer information over the Internet.

I/O (Input/Output) address—The small working area of RAM where the CPU can pass information to and receive information from a device.

ifconfig command—A command used to display and modify the TCP/IP configuration information for a network interface.

incremental backup—An archive of a filesystem that contains only files that were modified since the last archive was created.

Industry Standard Architecture (ISA)—An older motherboard connection slot designed to allow peripheral components an interconnect, and which transfers information at a speed of 8MHz.

info pages—A set of local, easy-to-read command syntax documentation available by typing the info command-line utility.

init command—The command used to change the operating system from one runlevel to another.

initialize (init) daemon—The first process started by the Linux kernel; it is responsible for starting and stopping other daemons.

initstate—*See also* Runlevel.

inode—The portion of a file that stores information on the file's attributes, access permissions, location, ownership, and file type.

inode table—The collection of inodes for all files and directories on a filesystem.

Input/Output (I/O) address—An address in physical memory that is used by a particular hardware device.

Input/Output Statistics (iostat) command—A command that displays Input/Output statistics for block devices.

insert mode—One of the two input modes in vi; it allows the user the ability to insert text into the document but does not allow any other functionality.

insmod command—A command used to insert a module into the Linux kernel.

installation log files—The files created at installation to record actions that occurred or failed during the installation process.

Integrated Drive Electronics (IDE)—Also known as ATA, it consists of controllers that control the flow of information to and from up to four hard disks connected to the mainboard via a ribbon cable.

interactive mode—The mode that file management commands use when a file can be overwritten; the system interacts with a user asking for the user to confirm the action.

International Standards Organization (ISO) images—The large, single files that are exact copies of the information contained on a CD-ROM or DVD.

Internet—A large network of interconnected networks connecting company networks, home computers, and institutional networks together so that they can communicate with each other.

Internet Protocol (IP) address—A unique string of a series of four 8-bit numbers that represent a computer on a network.

Internet service provider (ISP)—A company that provides Internet access.

Internet Super Daemon (xinetd)—The daemon responsible for initializing and configuring many networking services on a Linux computer.

Interrupt Request (IRQ)—A method of sharing processor time used by the processor to prioritize simultaneous requests for service from peripheral devices.

Intrusion Detection System (IDS)—A program that can be used to detect unauthorized access to a Linux system.

ip command—A command that can be used to manipulate the route table.

IP forwarding—The act of forwarding TCP/IP packets from one network to another. *See also* Routing.

iptables command—The command used to configure a firewall in Red Hat Fedora.

iterative query—A DNS resolution request that was resolved without the use of top-level DNS servers.

jabbering—The process by which failing hardware components send large amounts of information to the CPU.

jobs command—The command used to see the list of background processes running in the current shell.

journaling—A filesystem function that keeps track of the information that needs to be written to the hard drive in a journal; common Linux journaling filesystems include ext3 and REISER.

K Desktop Environment (KDE)—A desktop environment created by Matthias Ettrich in 1996.

K Window Manager (kwin)—The Window Manager that works under the KDE Desktop Environment.

KDE Display Manager (kdm)—A graphical login screen for users that resembles the KDE desktop.

kedit editor—A text editor for the KDE desktop.

kernel—The central, core program of the operating system. The shared commonality of the kernel is what defines Linux; the differing OSS applications that can interact with the common kernel are what differentiates Linux distributions.

kernel parameters—The specific pieces of information that can be passed to the Linux kernel to alter how it works.

Kickstart Configurator—A graphical utility that can be used to create a kickstart file.

kickstart file—A file that can be specified at the beginning of a Red Hat Fedora Linux installation to automate the installation process.

kill command—The command used to kill or terminate a process.

kill signal—The type of signal sent to a process by the kill command; different kill signals affect processes in different ways.

killall command—The command that kills all instances of a process by command name.

Knoppix Linux—A CD-based Linux distribution.

Kommon Desktop Environment (KDE)—One of the two competing graphical user interfaces (GUI) available for Linux.

kudzu program—A program used to detect and install support for new hardware.

large block addressing 32-bit (LBA32)—A parameter that can be specified that enables large block addressing in a boot loader; it is required only if a large hard disk that is not fully supported by the system BIOS is used.

ldconfig command—The command that updates the /etc/ld.so.conf and /etc/ld.so. cache files.

ldd command—The command used to display the shared libraries used by a certain program.

less command—A Linux command used to display a text file page-by-page on the terminal screen; users can then use the cursor keys to navigate the file.

Level 1 (L1) cache—The cache memory stored in the processor itself.

Level 2 (L2) cache—The cache memory stored in a computer chip on the motherboard for use by the processor or within the processor itself.

Level 3 (L3) cache—The cache memory stored in a computer chip on the motherboard for use by the processor.

lilo command—The command used to reinstall the LILO boot loader based on the configuration information in /etc/lilo.conf.

Line Printer Daemon (LPD)—A printing system typically used on legacy Linux computers.

linked file—The files that represent the same data as other files.

Linus Torvalds—A Finnish graduate student who coded and created the first version of Linux and subsequently distributed it under the GNU Public License.

Linux—A software operating system originated by Linus Torvalds. The common core, or kernel, continues to evolve and be revised. Differing Open Source Software bundled with the Linux kernel is what defines the wide variety of distributions now available.

Linux Documentation Project (LDP)—A large collection of Linux resources, information, and help files, supplied free of charge and maintained by the Linux community.

LInux LOader (LILO)—A program used to boot the Linux operating system.

Linux User Group (LUG)—The open forums of Linux users who discuss and assist each other in using and modifying the Linux operating system and the Open Source Software run on it. There are LUGs worldwide.

ll command—An alias for the ls -l command; it gives a long file listing.

ln (link) command—The command used to create hard and symbolic links.

local area networks (LANs)—The networks in which the computers are all in close physical proximity.

locate command—The command used to locate files from a file database.

locking an account—The act of making an account temporarily unusable by altering the password information for it stored on the system.

log file—A file containing information about the Linux system. **log file**—A file that contains past system events.

logical drives—The smaller partitions contained within an extended partition on a HDD.

Logical Unit Number (LUN)—A unique identifier for each device attached to any given node in a SCSI chain.

logrotate command—The command used to rotate log files; typically uses the configuration information stored in /etc/logrotate.conf.

lp command—The command used to create print jobs in the print queue in the CUPS printing system.

lpadmin command—The command used to perform printer administration in the CUPS printing system.

lpc command—The command used to view the status of and control printers in the LPD printing system.

lpq command—The command used to view the contents of print queues in the LPD printing system.

lpr command—The command used to create print jobs in the print queue in the LPD printing system.

lprm command—The command used to remove print jobs from the print queue in the LPD printing system.

lpstat command—The command used to view the contents of print queues and printer information in the CUPS printing system.

LPT port—A rectangular, 25-pin connection to the mainboard used to connect peripheral devices such as printers; also called parallel ports.

ls command—A Linux command used to list the files in a given directory.

lsmod command—A command that lists modules currently used by the Linux kernel.

magnetic tape (mt) command—A command used to control tape devices.

Mail Delivery Agent (MDA)—The service that downloads e-mail from a mail transfer agent.

Mail Transfer Agent (MTA)—An e-mail server.

Mail User Agent (MUA)—A program that allows e-mail to be read by a user.

mail utility—A common Linux mail user agent.

mainboard—A circuit board that connects all other hardware components together via slots or ports on the circuit board; also called a motherboard.

major number—The number used by the kernel to identify which device driver to call to interact properly with a given category of hardware; hard disk drives, CD-ROMs, and video cards are all categories of hardware; similar devices share a common major number.

Mandrake—A popular distribution of Linux in North America, distributed and supported by MandrakeSoft.

manual pages—The most common set of local command syntax documentation, available by typing the man command-line utility. Also known as man pages.

Master Boot Record (MBR)—A small area normally located on the first sector of the first hard disk drive used to define partitions and a boot loader.

master DNS server—The DNS server that contains a read/write copy of the zone. *See also* Primary DNS server.

maximum resolution—The best clarity of an image displayed to the screen; it is determined by the number of pixels making up the image (for example, 640_480 pixels).

mcedit editor (Midnight Commander Editor)—A user-friendly terminal text editor that supports regular expressions and the computer mouse.

media access method—A system that defines how computers on a network share access to the physical medium.

metacharacters—The key combinations that have special meaning in the Linux operating system.

Metacity Window Manager—The default Window Manager for the GNOME Desktop Environment in Red Hat Fedora Core 2.

mingetty—A program used to display a login prompt on a character-based terminal.

MINIX—Mini-UNIX created by Andrew Tannenbaum. Instructions on how to code the kernel for this version of the UNIX operating system were publicly available. Using this as a starting point, Linus Torvalds improved this version of UNIX for the Intel platform and created the first version of Linux.

minor number—The number following the first dot in the number used to identify a Linux kernel version denoting a minor modification. If odd, it is a version under development and not yet fully tested. *See also* major number, developmental kernel, and production kernel.

mkbootdisk command—A command used to create a boot floppy disk.

mkdir (make directory) command—The command used to create directories.

mkfs (make filesystem) command—A command used to format or create filesystems.

mknod command—A command used to re-create a device file, provided the major number, minor number, and type (character or bock) are known.

mode—The part of the inode that stores information on access permissions.

modprobe command—A command used to insert a module and all necessary prerequisite modules into the Linux kernel.

monitoring—The process by which system areas are observed for problems or irregularities.

more command—A Linux command used to display a text file page-by-page and line-by-line on the terminal screen.

motherboard—*See also* mainboard.

mount command—A command used to mount filesystems on devices to mount point directories.

mount point—The directory in a file structure to which something is mounted.

mounting—A process used to associate a device with a directory in the logical directory tree such that users can store data on that device.

mouseconfig—A command used to configure a mouse for use by X Windows.

multicast—The TCP/IP communication destined for a certain group of computers.

multihomed hosts—The computers that have more than one network interface.

Multiple Processor Statistics (mpstat) command—A command that displays CPU statistics.

Multiplexed Information and Computing Service (MULTICS)—A prototype timesharing operating system that was developed in the late 1960s by AT&T Bell Laboratories.

multitasking—A type of operating system that has the capability to manage multiple tasks simultaneously.

multiuser—A type of operating system that has the capability to provide access to multiple users simultaneously.

Multiuser Mode—Also called runlevel 2; the mode that provides most daemons and a partial set of networking daemons.

mutt utility—A common Linux mail user agent.

mv (move) command—The command used to move/rename files and directories.

named pipe file—A temporary connection that sends information from one command or process in memory to another; it can also be represented by a file on the filesystem.

nedit editor—A commonly used graphical text editor available in most Linux distributions.

netmask—Also known as the network mask or subnet mask, it specifies which portion of the IP address identifies the logical network the computer is on.

network—Two or more computers joined together via network media and able to exchange information.

Network File System (NFS)—A distributed filesystem developed by Sun Microsystems that allows computers of differing types to access files shared on the network.

network ID—The portion of an IP address that denotes the network.

network interface card (NIC)—A hardware device used to connect a computer to a network of other computers and communicate or exchange information on it.

newgrp command—The command used to change temporarily the primary group of a user.

newsgroup—An Internet protocol service accessed via an application program called a newsreader. This service allows access to postings (e-mails in a central place accessible by all newsgroup users) normally organized along specific themes. Users with questions on specific topics can post messages, which can be answered by other users.

nice command—The command used to change the priority of a process as it is started.

nice value—The value that indirectly represents the priority of a process; the higher the value, the lower the priority.

nmap (network mapper) command—A command that can be used to scan ports on network computers.

nohup command—A command that prevents other commands from exiting when the parent process is killed.

NTLOADER—The boot loader used to boot Windows NT, Windows 2000, and Windows XP operating system kernels.

ntsysv—A utility that can be used to alter the daemons that are started in each runlevel.

octet—A portion of an IP address that represents eight binary bits.

od command—A Linux command used to display the contents of a file in octal format.

Open Source Software (OSS)—The programs distributed and licensed so that the source code making up the program is freely available to anyone who wants to examine, utilize, or improve upon it.

operating system (OS)—The software used to control and directly interact with the computer hardware components.

options—The specific letters that start with a dash "-" or two and appear after the command name to alter the way the command works.

other—When used in the mode of a certain file or directory, it refers to all users on the Linux system.

overclocked—A CPU that runs at a higher clock speed than it has been rated for.

owner—The user whose name appears in a long listing of a file or directory and who has the ability to change permissions on that file or directory.

package dependencies—A list of packages that are prerequisite to the current package being installed on the system.

package manager—The software used to install, maintain, and remove other software programs by storing all relevant software information in a central software database on the computer.

Packet Internet Groper (ping) command—A command used to check TCP/IP connectivity on a network.

packets—The packages of data formatted by a network protocol.

parallel port—*See also* LPT port.

parent process—A process that has started other processes (child processes).

parent process ID (PPID)—The PID of the parent process that created the current process.

partition—A small section of an entire hard drive created to make the hard drive easier to use. Partitions can be primary or extended.

passwd command—The command used to modify the password associated with a user account.

patch command—The command used to apply a patch to the Linux kernel source code.

PATH variable—A variable that stores a list of directories that will be searched in order when commands are executed without an absolute or relative pathname.

peripheral component—The components that attach to the mainboard of a computer and provide a specific function, such as a video card, mouse, or keyboard.

Peripheral Component Interconnect (PCI)—The most common motherboard connection slot found in computers today, which can transfer information at a speed of 33MHz and use DMA.

permissions—A list that identifies who can access a file or folder, and their level of access.

Personal Computer Memory Card International Association (PCMCIA)—A mainboard connection technology that allows a small card to be inserted with the electronics necessary to provide a certain function.

physical memory—A storage area for information that is directly wired through circuit boards to the processor.

pipe—A string of commands connected by | metacharacters.

Plug-and-Play (PnP)—A technology that allows peripheral devices to automatically receive the correct IRQ, I/O address, and DMA settings without any user intervention.

Pluggable Authentication Modules (PAM)—The component that handles authentication requests by daemons on a Linux system.

polling—The act of querying devices to see if they have services that need to be run.

port—A number that uniquely identifies a network service

Power On Self Test (POST)—An initial series of tests run when a computer is powered on to ensure that hardware components are functional.

primary DNS server—The DNS server that contains a read/write copy of the zone.

primary group—The group that is specified for a user in the /etc/passwd file and that is specified as group owner for all files created by a user.

primary partitions—The separate divisions into which a HDD can be divided (up to four are allowed per HDD).

print job—The information sent to a printer for printing.

print job ID—A unique numeric identifier used to mark and distinguish each print job.

print queue—A directory on the filesystem that holds print jobs that are waiting to be printed.

Printer Configuration tool—A graphical utility used to configure printers on the system.

printing—The process by which print jobs are sent from a print queue to a printer.

priority—The importance of system information when logging system events.

proactive maintenance—The measures taken to reduce future system problems.

process—A program loaded into memory and running on the processor performing a specific task.

process ID (PID)—A unique identifier assigned to every process as it begins.

process priority—A number assigned to a process, used to determine how many time slices on the processor it will receive; the higher the number, the lower the priority.

process state—The current state of the process on the processor; most processes are in the sleeping or running state.

production kernel—A Linux kernel whose minor number (the number after the dot in the version number) is even and deemed stable for use through widespread testing.

program—The sets of instructions that know how to interact with the operating system and computer hardware to perform specific tasks; stored as a file on some media (for example, a hard disk drive).

programmable read-only memory (PROM)—A blank ROM computer chip that can be written to once and never rewritten again.

programming language—The syntax used for developing a program. Different programming languages use different syntax.

protocol—A set of rules of communication used between computers on a network.

ps command—The command used to obtain information about processes currently running on the system.

PS/2 ports—The small, round mainboard connectors developed by IBM with six pins that typically connect keyboards and mice to the computer.

pwconv command—The command used to enable the use of the /etc/shadow file.

pwd (print working directory) command—A Linux command used to display the current directory in the directory tree.

pwunconv command—The command used to disable the use of the /etc/shadow file.

Qt toolkit—The software toolkit used with the K Desktop Environment.

queuing—*See also* Spooling.

quota command—A command used to view disk quotas imposed on a user.

quotaoff command—A command used to deactivate disk quotas.

quotaon command—A command used to activate disk quotas.

quotas—The limits that can be imposed on users and groups for filesystem usage.

Rambus Dynamic Random Access Memory (RDRAM)—A proprietary type of RAM developed by the Rambus Corporation.

random access memory (RAM)—A computer chip able to store information that is then lost when there is no power to the system.

reactive maintenance—The measures taken when system problems arise.

read command—A command used to read Standard Input from a user into a variable.

read-only memory (ROM)—A computer chip able to store information in a static, permanent manner, even when there is no power to the system.

recursive—A term referring to itself and its own contents; a recursive search includes all subdirectories in a directory and their contents.

recursive query—A DNS resolution request that was resolved with the use of top-level DNS servers.

Red Hat—One of the most popular and prevalent distributions of Linux in North America, distributed and supported by Red Hat Inc.

Red Hat Package Manager (RPM)—The most commonly used package manager for Linux.

redirection—The process of changing the default locations of Standard Input, Standard Output, and Standard Error.

Reduced Instruction Set Computers (RISC) processors—The relatively fast processors that understand small instruction sets.

Redundant Array of Independent Disks (RAID)—The process of combining the storage space of several hard disk drives into one larger, logical storage unit.

refresh rate—The rate at which information displayed on a video screen is refreshed; it is measured in Hertz (Hz).

regular expressions (regexp)—The special metacharacters used to match patterns of text within text files; they are commonly used by many text tool commands such as grep.

REISER—A journaling filesystem used in Linux.

rejecting printer—A printer that does not accept print jobs into the print queue.

relative pathname—The pathname of a target directory relative to your current directory in the tree.

removable media—The information storage media that can be removed from a computer, allowing transfer of data between machines.

renice command—The command used to alter the nice value of a process currently running on the system.

repquota command—A command used to produce a report on quotas for a particular filesystem.

resolution—The total number of pixels that can be displayed horizontally and vertically on a computer video screen.

restore command—The command used to extract archives created with the dump command.

reverse lookup—A DNS name resolution request whereby an IP address is resolved to a FQDN.

revision number—The number after the second dot in the version number of a Linux kernel that identifies the certain release number of a kernel.

rm (remove) command—The command used to remove files and directories.

rmdir (remove directory) command—The command used to remove empty directories.

rmmod command—The command that removes a module from the Linux kernel.

rogue process—A process that has become faulty in some way and continues to consume far more system resources than it should.

root filesystem—The filesystem that contains most files that make up the operating system; it should have enough free space to prevent errors and slow performance.

route command—A command that can be used to manipulate the route table.

route table—A table of information used to indicate which networks are connected to network interfaces.

router—A computer running routing software, or a special function hardware device, providing interconnection between networks; it contains information regarding the structure of the networks and sends information from one component network to another.

routers—The devices capable of transferring packets from one network to another.

routing—The act of forwarding data packets from one network to another.

rpm command—The command used to install, query, and remove RPM packages.

rules—The components of a firewall that match specific network traffic that is to be allowed or dropped.

runlevel—A term that defines a certain type and number of daemons on a Linux system.

runlevel command—The command used to display the current and most recent previous runlevel.

scalability—The capability of computers to increase workload as the number of processors increases.

SCSI ID—A number that uniquely identifies and prioritizes devices attached to a SCSI controller.

search engine—An Internet Web site such as *http://www.google.com* where you simply enter a phrase representing your search item, and you receive a list of Web sites that contain relevant material.

secondary DNS server—A DNS server that contains a read-only copy of the zone. *See also* Slave DNS server.

sector—The smallest unit of data storage on a hard disk; sectors are arranged into concentric circles called tracks and can be grouped into blocks for use by the system.

Secure Shell (ssh)—A utility that can be used to run remote applications on a Linux computer; it encrypts all client-server traffic.

sed command—A filter command used to search for and manipulate text.

serial port—*See also* COM port.

server—A computer configured to allow other computers to connect to it from across a network.

server closet—A secured room that stores servers within an organization.

server services—The services that are made available for other computers across a network.

set command—A command used to view all variables in the shell except special variables.

setserial command—The command used to set the parameters of serial device.

shareware—The programs developed and provided at minimal cost to the end user. These programs are initially free but require payment after a period of time or usage.

shell—A user interface that accepts input from the user and passes the input to the kernel for processing.

shell scripts—The text files that contain a list of commands or constructs for the shell to execute in order.

single inline memory modules (SIMM)—An older type of memory stick that connects to the mainboard using connectors along only one edge.

Single User Mode—Also called runlevel 1; the mode that provides a single terminal and a limited set of services.

skeleton directory—A directory that contains files that are copied to all new users' home directories upon creation; the default skeleton directory on Linux systems is /etc/skel.

slave DNS server—A DNS server that contains a read-only copy of the zone.

Small Computer Systems Interface (SCSI)—A technology that consists of controllers that can connect several SCSI HDDs to the mainboard and control the flow of data to and from the SCSI HDDs.

small outline dual inline memory modules (SODIMM)—A DIMM module that is physically smaller than traditional DIMM modules and used in notebook and Macintosh computers.

smbclient utility—A utility used to connect to shares on a Windows system.

smbmount command—A command used to mount directories from Windows computers to mount points on Linux computers.

smbpasswd command—A command used to generate a Samba password for a user.

socket file—A named pipe connecting processes on two different computers; it can also be represented by a file on the filesystem.

soft limit—A limit imposed that can be exceeded for a certain period of time.

software—The programs stored on a storage device in a computer, that provide a certain function when executed.

Solaris—A version of UNIX developed by Sun Microsystems from AT&T source code.

sort command—A command used to sort lines in a file.

source code—The sets of organized instructions on how to function and perform tasks that define or constitute a program.

source file/directory—The portion of a command that refers to the file or directory from which information is taken.

spanning—A type of RAID level 0 that allows two or more devices to be represented as a single large volume.

special device file—A file used to identify hardware devices such as hard disks and serial ports.

spooling—The process of accepting a print job into a print queue.

stand-alone daemons—The daemons that configure themselves at boot time without assistance from the Internet Super Daemon.

Standard Error (stderr)—A file descriptor that represents any error messages generated by a command.

Standard Input (stdin)—A file descriptor that represents information inputted to a command during execution.

Standard Output (stdout)—A file descriptor that represents the desired output from a command.

static RAM (SRAM)—An expensive type of RAM commonly used in computer chips on the mainboard and which has a fast access speed.

strings command—A Linux command used to search for and display text characters in a binary file.

su (switch user) command—A command that can be used to switch your current user account to another.

subdirectory—A directory that resides within another directory in the directory tree.

subnet mask—A series of four 8-bit numbers that determine the network and host portions of an IP address.

subnetting—The process in which a single large network is subdivided into several smaller networks to control traffic flow.

subshell—A shell started by the current shell.

sudo command—A command that is used to perform commands as another user via entries in the /etc/sudoers file.

sum command—A command that can generate an MD5 checksum from file contents.

superblock—The portion of a filesystem that stores critical information, such as the inode table and block size.

superscalar—The ability for a computer processor to complete more than one command in a single cycle.

SuSE—One of the most popular and prevalent distributions of Linux in Europe.

swap memory—*See also* Virtual memory.

symbolic link—A pointer to another file on the same or another filesystem; commonly referred to as a shortcut.

symmetric multiprocessing (SMP)—A system containing more than one processor in which each processor shares tasks and memory space.

Synchronous Dynamic Random Access Memory (SDRAM)—A form of RAM that uses the standard DIMM connector and transfers data at a very fast rate.

syncing—The process of writing data to the hard disk drive that was stored in RAM.

System Activity Reporter (sar) command—The command that displays various system statistics.

system backup—The process whereby files are copied to an archive.

System Log Daemon (syslogd)—The daemon that logs system events to various log files via information stored in /etc/syslog.conf.

system service—The additional functionality provided by a program that has been incorporated into and started as part of the operating system.

System Statistics (sysstat) package—A software package that contains common performance monitoring utilities, such as mpstat, iostat, sar, and isag.

system-config-display—A command used to configure a video adapter card and monitor for use by X Windows.

system-config-keyboard—A command used to configure a keyboard for use by X Windows.

system-config-mouse—*See also* Mouseconfig.

system-config-packages command—A utility that can be used to install or remove RPMs from the Red Hat Fedora core installation media.

system-config-samba command—A utility that can be used to simplify the editing of the /etc/samba/smb.conf file.

Tab Window Manager (twm)—One of the oldest Window Managers used on Linux systems.

Tab-completion feature—A feature of the BASH shell that fills in the remaining characters of a unique filename or directory name when the user presses the Tab key.

tac command—A Linux command that displays a file to the screen beginning with the last line of the file and ending with the first line of the file.

tail command—A Linux command used to display the last set number of lines of text in a file; by default, the tail command displays the last 10 lines of the file.

tape archive (tar) command—The most common utility used to create archives.

tarball—A compressed archive of files that contains scripts that install Linux software to the correct locations on a computer system.

target file/directory—The portion of a command that refers to the file or directory to which information is directed.

target ID—*See also* SCSI ID.

TCP wrapper—A program that can be used to run a network daemon with additional security via the /etc/hosts.allow and /etc/hosts.deny files.

tee command—A command used to take from Standard Input and send to both Standard Output and a specified file.

telinit command—An alias to the init command.

telnet—A utility that can be used to run remote applications on a Linux computer.

terminal—The channel that allows a certain user to log in and communicate with the kernel via a user interface.

terminator—A device used to terminate an electrical conduction medium to absorb the transmitted signal and prevent signal bounce.

test statement—A statement used to test a certain condition and generate a True/False value.

text file—A file that stores information in a readable text format.

text tools—The programs that allow for the creation, modification, and searching of text files.

time slice—The amount of time a process is given on a CPU in a multiprocessing operating system.

Token Ring—A popular media access method.

top command—The command used to give real-time information about the most active processes on the system; it can also be used to renice or kill processes.

total cost of ownership (TCO)—The full sum of all accumulated costs, over and above the simple purchase price of utilizing a product. It includes such sundries as training, maintenance, additional hardware, and downtime.

touch command—The command used to create new files. It was originally used to update the time stamp on a file.

tr command—A command used to transform or change characters received from Standard Input.

traceroute command—A command used to trace the path a packet takes through routers to a destination host.

track—The area on a hard disk that forms a concentric circle of sectors.

trapping—The process of ignoring a kill signal.

tripwire—A common IDS for Linux that monitors files and directories.

troubleshooting procedures—The tasks performed when solving system problems.

trusted access—A configuration in which computers are allowed to access a given computer without having to provide a password first.

tune2fs command—A command used to modify ext2 and ext3 filesystem parameters.

ulimit command—The command used to modify process limit parameters in the current shell.

umask—A special variable used to alter the permissions on all new files and directories by taking away select default file and directory permissions.

umask command—The command used to view and change the umask variable.

umount command—A command used to break the association between a device and a directory in the logical directory tree.

uncompress command—The command used to decompress files compressed by the compress command.

unicast—The TCP/IP communication destined for a single computer.

universal serial bus (USB)—A mainboard connection technology that allows data transfer speeds of up to 480MB per second and is used for many peripheral components, such as mice, printers, and scanners.

UNIX—The first true multitasking, multiuser operating system developed by Ken Thompson and Dennis Ritchie, and from which Linux was originated.

user—When used in the mode of a certain file or directory, the owner of that file or directory.

user account—The information regarding a user that is stored in a system database (/etc/passwd and /etc/shadow), which can be used to log in to the system and gain access to system resources.

User Datagram Protocol/Internet Protocol (UDP/IP)—A faster but unreliable version of TCP/IP.

User Identifier (UID)—A unique number assigned to each user account.

user interface—The interface the user sees and uses to interact with the operating system and application programs.

user process—A process begun by a user that runs on a terminal.

user-defined variables—The variables that are created by the user and are not used by the sys-tem—these variables are typically exported to subshells.

useradd command—The command used to add a user account to the system.

userdel command—The command used to remove a user account from the system.

usermod command—The command used to modify the properties of a user account on the system.

variable—An area of memory used to store information—variables are created from entries in environment files when the shell is first created after login and are destroyed when the shell is destroyed upon logout.

variable identifier—The name of a variable.

VFAT (Virtual File Allocation Table)—A nonjournaling filesystem that might be used in Linux.

vi editor—A powerful command-line text editor available on most UNIX and Linux systems.

video adapter card—A peripheral component used to display graphical images to a computer monitor.

virtual memory—An area on a hard disk (swap partition) that can be used to store information that normally resides in physical memory (RAM), if the physical memory is being used excessively.

vmlinuz-<kernel version>—The Linux kernel file.

vmstat command—The command used to display memory, CPU, and swap statistics.

volatile—A term used to describe information storage devices that store information only when there is electrical flow. Conversely, nonvolatile information storage devices store information even when there is no electrical flow.

VSync (vertical refresh)—The rate at which vertical elements of the video screen image are refreshed measured in Hertz (Hz).

well-known ports—Of the 65,535 possible ports, the ports from 0 to 1024 used by common networking services.

which command—The command used to locate files that exist within directories listed in the PATH variable.

wide area networks (WANs)—The networks in which computers are separated geographically by large distances.

wildcard metacharacters—The metacharacters used to match certain characters in a file or directory name; they are often used to specify multiple files.

Window Manager—The GUI component that is responsible for determining the appearance of the windows drawn on the screen by X Windows.

workstation—A computer used to connect to services on a server.

workstation services—The services that are used to access shared resources on a network server.

X client—The component of X Windows that requests graphics to be drawn from the X server and displays them on the terminal screen.

X Display Manager (xdm)—A graphical login screen.

X server—The component of X Windows that draws graphics to windows on the terminal screen.

X Windows—The component of the Linux GUI that displays graphics to windows on the terminal screen.

X-CD-Roast—A common burning software used in Linux.

X.org—A common implementation of X Windows used in Linux distributions.

xemacs editor—A graphical version of the Emacs text editor.

Xfce desktop environment—A desktop environment that is commonly used by Linux systems.

XFree86—A common implementation of X Windows used in Linux distributions.

xvidtune—A program used to fine-tune the vsync and hsync video card settings for use in X Windows.

zcat command—A command used to view the contents of an archive created with compress or gzip to Standard Output.

Zip disk—A removable information storage unit similar to a floppy disk that can store much more information than floppy disks and which is used in Zip drives.

zless command—A command used to view the contents of an archive created with compress or gzip to Standard Output in a page-by-page fashion.

zmore command—A command used to view the contents of an archive created with compress or gzip to Standard Output in a page-by-page fashion.

zombie process—A process that has finished executing, but whose parent has not yet released its PID; it still retains a spot in the kernel's process table.

zone—A portion of the Domain Name Space that is administered by one or more DNS servers.

zone transfer—The process of copying resource records for a zone from a master to a slave DNS server.

Index

Numerics and Symbols

A